William Woodruff was born in 1916 into a family of Lancashire cotton workers. Leaving school at thirteen, he became a delivery boy in a grocer's shop. In 1933, with bleak prospects in the north of England, he decided to try his luck in London. In 1936, with the aid of a London County Council Scholarship he went to Oxford University. During the Second World War he fought with the British Army in North Africa and the Mediterranean region. In 1946 Woodruff renewed his academic career. He was a world historian whose work has been widely translated. Woodruff had seven children.

William Woodruff died in 2008.

For more information, visit www.williamwoodruff.com

A Concise History
of the Modern World

1500 TO THE PRESENT
A GUIDE TO WORLD AFFAIRS

William Woodruff

ABACUS

First published in Great Britain in 1991 by Palgrave Macmillan
Revised editions published in 1993, 1998 and 2001
This revised paperback edition first published in 2005 by Abacus

9 11 13 15 14 12 10

A CIP catalogue record for this book
is available from the British Library.

ISBN 978-0-349-11837-6

New maps and revisions to maps by John Gilkes

Typeset in Caslon by Palimpsest Book Production Limited,
Grangemouth, Stirlingshire
Printed and bound in Great Britain by
Clays Ltd, St Ives plc

Papers used by Abacus are from well-managed forests
and other responsible sources.

Abacus
An imprint of
Little, Brown Book Group
100 Victoria Embankment
London EC4Y 0DY

An Hachette UK Company
www.hachette.co.uk

www.littlebrown.co.uk

In memory of
Hedwig and Richard
Anne and William

Contents

List of Maps

Preface to the Fifth Edition

This overview of world history since AD 1500, with its underlying theme of shifting global power, tells in short compass how the modern world has come to be what it is.

In emphasizing the study of humanity as a whole, I share the thoughts of the English poet John Donne: 'No man is an island entire of itself, every man is part of the main.' In seeking to understand the totality, complexity and diversity of the past, I shifted my focus from the parts to the whole: from the nation to the world. While not denying the uniqueness of national or regional history, or the sub-specialisms that have proliferated these past fifty years, I felt that the growing communality and interdependence of nations justified my taking the wider, more pluralistic view.

It has not been easy to provide insights into five hundred years of world history and put them into compact form. No matter how much one tries to avoid it, some items will invariably be given more – and others less – attention than they deserve; the tendency will be to present the past as much more unidirectional and continuous than events in the real world confirm. In sifting the wheat from the chaff, I have followed the maxim of Voltaire: 'Les détails qui ne mènent à rien sont dans l'histoire ce que sont les bagages dans une armée, *impedimenta*; il faut voir les choses en grand' (Meaningless details in history are like the baggage of an army, *impedimenta*; one must take the wider view). Details are not ends in themselves.

Ultimately, it is the wider view that must gain our attention. In geopolitics there has been a tilt in the direction of an Asian-dominated world. China, with its own world outlook, is undergoing rapid change that must eventually affect both East and West. States that until recently were part of the old Soviet Union have transferred their loyalties to the expanded European Union. With the return of transcendentalism, the Middle East and the rest of the Islamic world are playing greater roles in geopolitics; nothing is of greater concern to the Muslim world than the Israeli–Palestinian conflict. Because of the ongoing quest for oil, the Muslim countries of Central Asia have gained new importance. There is a growing rivalry between the powers to control world oil resources. The world economy requires stability and order, yet we are threatened by world-wide terrorism, which might suddenly take a dramatic turn. Meanwhile, the United States has undertaken to liberate the world, whatever that may entail. As a result of a troubled Western conscience, Africa is being rediscovered. AIDS has grown to crisis proportions in parts of that continent. A resurgent South America is looking beyond the USA and Western Europe to Asia. Thinking globally has become a necessity.

Only by using the past to cast light on the present[1] can we hope to know how the world has come to be what it is and where it might be headed. We are the only species that can learn from the past; we are threatened with extinction if we fail to do so.

The greatest hazard confronting any historian lies not in the breadth of the subject, or in its complexity, but in the point of view from which he tells his tale. I know of no historical writing of lasting value that does not reveal the man behind the pen. Of necessity, my views are personal, temporal and locational.

I have been helped by scholars in many parts of the world. My debt to others in knowledge and inspiration (as the acknowledgements in the first edition and the footnotes and bibliography of this book make abundantly clear) is considerable.

My debt to Helga, as always, is immeasurable.

William Woodruff

1

Introduction

The perpetual aggressiveness of both individuals and states underlies all history. It is the theme of the Greek historian Thucydides (471–*c.* 400 BC), who wrote about the Peloponnesian Wars, as it is of Herodotus (484–425 BC), who dealt with the Greek–Persian Wars. National power underlies the emergence of the modern state in the seventeenth century. The nineteenth-century German historian Leopold von Ranke (1795–1886) in his *Weltgeschichte*[1] viewed the past as the history of power. Power is essentially what Charles Darwin (1809–82) and Karl Marx (1818–83) talked about – one in biology, the other in economics. Darwin, who placed the whole of Christian history and Christian theology in peril, spoke of the 'struggle for existence', Marx of 'class conflict'. The German philologist and philosopher Friedrich W. Nietzsche (1844–1900) expressed the individual's will to power in *Der Wille zur Macht*.

For those who believe in Realpolitik the struggle for power dictates the course taken by any political institution. Every age has known the dangers of power politics. 'The lust for power,' wrote the Roman historian Tacitus (AD 55–*c.* 118), 'is the most flagrant of all the passions.' It is the only appetite that cannot be appeased. It is not love, or morality, or international law that determines the outcome of world affairs, but the changing distribution of organized force. While love and trust make our personal worlds go round, we delude ourselves in thinking that the same is true of the relations between states, or groups of armed fanatics operating outside a state's control. A cynical doctrine, but one that has all too often directed the course of world events. 'Justice is the advantage of the stronger,' says Thrasymachus in Plato's *Republic*. Weak states invite aggression.

Such was the view of the Florentine courtier and political theorist Niccolò Machiavelli (1469–1527), who had hoped to serve the sixteenth-century Florentine financiers – the Medici – but was racked by them instead. His principal work, *Il Principe* (*The Prince*), was published in 1513. Morally blind, as were most princes of the time, with limited belief in conscience or right and wrong, the book tells how a prince (chiefly Cesare Borgia – 1476–1507) must seek the one crucial element of statecraft – power. Not righteousness, but expediency must be his guide. To bring down one's rival is the purpose of political life.

The idea that power has primacy over justice has sat ill with many European thinkers, including the influential French political philosopher Jean Bodin (1530–96), the Spanish Franciscan monk Francisco de Vitoria (1492–1546), who some call the father of international law, Francisco Suárez (1548–1617), the Spanish philosopher and theologian, the Italian Alberico Gentili (1552–1608), Oxford professor of civil law, and the Dutch jurist Hugo Grotius (1583–1645), all of whom insisted that morality, not force, must direct human action. The English historian Lord Acton (1834–1902) also condemned the primacy of power, which 'tends to corrupt', while 'absolute power corrupts absolutely'. The American historian and philosopher Henry Adams (1838–1918) said that power is poison – which is borne out by the lives of Mussolini, Hitler, Lenin, Stalin, Mao, Pol Pot and all the other dictators of recent times.

However condemned, power remains as important in political life today as it ever did. Power is to politics what energy is to the physical world. No society, national or international, is possible when power and compulsion are absent. Without authority, anarchy reigns. 'Covenants without swords are but words,' wrote the Englishman Thomas Hobbes (1588–1678) in *Leviathan*. In his day, a new idea of the legitimacy of power was needed, and Hobbes provided it with 'That Mortal God – our peace and defense [: the state].' In seventeenth-century Europe, feudalism and absolute monarchies were about to give way to the secular, sovereign state. From the Peace of Westphalia in 1648, which concluded the Thirty Years War, there emerged the nation state[2] and the beginning of a new world order.

There is no period of the past when the realities of power were not in play. This is true of the Holy League, founded in 1495 by Pope Alexander VI (*c.* 1431–1503), of the Holy Alliance, founded by the Tsar of Russia in 1815, of the League of Nations, established after the First World War, and of the United Nations, established after the Second. International forums organized for rational discussion and cooperation have inevitably given way to a struggle for power. Until a code of international law is enforced against those who prefer violence to dialogue, power politics will continue to determine our lot. It was not a universal moral imperative but nuclear deterrence (a euphemism for mutual assured destruction – MAD) that spared the world during the Cold War.

Obviously, the struggle for power is not the only key to the course of world affairs – the past is also a story of the struggle for justice and mutual aid – yet power, however it is defined, remains the master key. In the international sphere, material might continues to triumph over moral right. While the United Nations and the Hague Court[3] proclaim what is right and wrong – as they did about the 'ethnic cleansing' that took place in the 1990s in the Balkans, central Africa, and more recently in the Darfur region of the Sudan – the nations continue to enforce their will.

The greatest difficulty in explaining the role of power in helping to shape the modern world is the illusive nature of power itself. There is no clear-cut line that enables us to separate the power of the sword from the power of the purse, or those powers from the more intangible power of the word. On the evidence of the past, it is chiefly military force that has prevailed. 'War', said Heraclitus five hundred years before Christ, 'is the father of all and king of all.' In contrast, the early Christians looked upon war as expressing 'the fallen condition of man'. Others have regarded it as an indispensable instrument of policy in statecraft – witness the present Iraq War. Certainly, war has been the midwife of the modern age. The destructiveness of modern weapons now threatens life on earth.

One of the greatest and unchanging realities of power is money. Throughout history, military power has depended on economic power. 'Money to get power, power to guard money' was the motto of the sixteenth-century Medici family. Hear Nathan Rothschild (whose family was the nineteenth-century equivalent of the Medici) writing to the Prussian government in May 1818: 'The cabal there can do nothing against N. M. Rothschild, he has the strength, the money and the power.'[4] Crucial to the prolonged European wars of the seventeenth and eighteenth centuries was the creditworthiness of the combatants; the ability to raise funds is one of the reasons why the British and the Dutch were able to fight for as long as they did. Today, international terrorists obtain a good deal of their power by controlling the sale of 'conflict' diamonds in Liberia, Sierra Leone, Guinea, Angola and the Congo.[5] The international drug trade and international crime and corruption are other sources of economic power.[6] The Arab oil embargo of 1973 disrupted the world economy, as did the economic sanctions imposed by the United Nations against Vietnam, Rhodesia, South Africa, Libya, Cuba, North Korea and Iraq. The hostage crisis with Iran during the Carter administration was solved only when the US government returned $9 billion of Iranian assets that it had seized. In geopolitics, money counts.

Yet the power of the word has often proved stronger than finance. 'In the beginning was the Word,' says the Gospel of St John. Rome first conquered Europe with the sword, but more thoroughly with the Christian Word. Christ, Mohammed, Luther and Marx led no armies, owned no banks, yet their ideas changed history. The 'soul force' of non-violence practised by Mohandas Karamchand Gandhi (1869–1948) against British rule in South Africa, and later in India,[7] and the role played by Pope John Paul II (1920–2005) against Soviet power in Poland are classic examples of the power of the spirit.

No matter which aspect of power we consider – whether it is weapons, or money, or the spiritual word – in this day and age one must take a world view. 'Nur das Ganze spricht' (Only the whole has meaning) said the Swiss historian Jacob Burckhardt (1818–97). Alas, the words of Burckhardt are lost on the wind. Far from thinking globally, mankind continues to think in tribal or national terms. 'We are global citizens with tribal souls,' said the Danish poet Piet Hein

(1905–96). There is, in fact, no important problem that we face today that is not of world dimension.[8] Because of the spread of international terrorism[9] and the danger of nuclear, biological and chemical weapons falling into the hands of fanatics, we are now faced by terrorist threats that are beyond the control and vision of any state. The problems of war and peace, nuclear arms, the militarization of space, population, migration, disease, human rights, commerce, economic fluctuations, corruption, entertainment, sport, drug trafficking, ecology, pollution, climate change and communications cannot be confined to the nation-state. Despite the achievements of the nineteenth-century antislavery movement, the trafficking of human beings continues.[10] The market for money has become worldwide – no one country controls it. The effect of the destruction of the rain forests reaches far beyond Brazil, the Congo or the countries of Southeast Asia. Indeed, in the global age in which we live, some nations can no longer control their own physical or economic destinies; they are swayed by world forces.

Equally important is the need to take a historical view. Life demands a sense of continuity. It is only in historical terms that we can hope to understand the metamorphosis of the modern world. We cannot see the present except through the past. The past *is* the present. 'The past is never dead,' wrote William Faulkner (1897–1963), 'it's not even past.' People not only have a history; they *are* history. Without some knowledge of the past the present is unintelligible, and much more hazardous than it need be. It is not only language that divides the human race but history. The alternative to experience and accumulated knowledge – which we call history – is a sickness called amnesia. We can no more shed the past than we can shed our shadows (except by blundering about in the dark). To wander out of history, as the Americans and the British appear to have done in invading Iraq in 2003, is to wander out of reality. In assessing the present war, no one mentions that this is Britain's third invasion of Iraq, and that Iraq is the only part of Asia still fought over by the West. Terrorism is steeped in history.

Truly, those who ignore history will be forced to relive it. Not that history is the source of ready answers; nor is it a science; historians usually find what they are looking for. An isolated historical fact explains nothing; it has to be selected and interpreted. The role of chance, the way in which history is overtaken by events and the difficulty of predicting human action all invalidate any scientific claim. There is no way that we can anticipate the outcome of human behaviour; no way to tell precisely what lies ahead – especially in times of war. The French astronomer and mathematician Pierre Simon Laplace (1749–1827), the father of present-day futurists, thought otherwise: 'Give me full knowledge and I will predict the future precisely,' he said. In the end he could not even predict the circumstances of his own death. To see the past 'wie es eigentlich war' (as it actually was), as the German historian Leopold von Ranke advocated, will never be completely possible. Unlike an experiment in science, which can be repeated, in human affairs nothing is constant; all is flux. There are no ascertainable, inflexible laws that determine our destiny. As the collapse of communist power in Eastern Europe and the reunification of Germany in 1990 confirm, history is both evolutionary and cataclysmic. We never know the past; we know only someone's story of the past. Meaning is always shaped by writer and context. Even with abundant facts, there will always be different interpretations of the same historical data.

The difficulties of understanding history are compounded when it is realized that – in contrast to the Western idea of linear progress – history is oblique. 'God writes straight, with crooked lines,' says a Portuguese proverb. Crooked or straight, in providing us with an imaginative understanding of the origins and consequences of what we are doing, history provides us with perspective, with balance, with wisdom – not for the moment, or the day, but for the totality of our lives and the society in which we live.

Having stressed the role of power politics in world affairs, and the need to take both a world and a historical view, it remains to explain why I chose to begin this inquiry in AD 1500. I did so because it was about then that the West proceeded to effect changes on a world scale greater than those made by any previous civilization. It was about then that the European Middle Ages ended and the increasingly secular modern age began. A certain interrelatedness of continents had already existed, but after 1500 the scope, significance and speed of change became much greater and much more far-reaching.

The fifteenth-century defeat of the Arabs by the Portuguese and the Spaniards in the Iberian peninsula – the Reconquista – became a Christian crusade which carried the West into the world, giving a tremendous impetus to discovery and colonization. The Iberians sincerely felt the biblical injunction to convert mankind to Christianity before the onset of the Apocalypse and the end of the world. There was an urgency about it.

Two years after Christopher Columbus (1451–1506) set out in search of Asia, Pope Alexander VI (under the Treaty of Tordesillas, 1494) divided the Americas between Spain and Portugal (see Map I).[11] In 1498 the Portuguese navigator Vasco da Gama (*c.* 1460–1524), directed by an Arab pilot, reached the Malabar coast of India. The capture by the Portuguese of Goa (1510) and the Strait of Ormuz (1515) made their control of the Indian Ocean possible. In 1519–22 the Spaniard Juan Sebastián del Cano, who had taken command after Ferdinand Magellan's (*c.* 1480–1521) death in the Philippines, made the first European circumnavigation of the globe. By the early 1600s English, Dutch, French and Danish trading companies had all reached India, eager to exploit the riches of Asia. Impelled by the desire to profit, to explore and to Christianize, the scales of fortune began to tip in Europe's favour.

The sixteenth century also witnessed the beginning of nationalism in the West. National consciousness, based on ethnic identity, customs, culture, language and territory, rather than crude force, had scarcely existed in Europe's Middle Ages, which knew feudal particularism, the divine right of kings and Christian universalism. People had loyalty to their immediate lord; beyond that they were conscious of membership of the universal Christian Church. In time, feudalism was undermined by nationalism, war and a growing money economy.

If the power of nationalism grew rapidly in the West, it was because the newly emerging nations of Britain, France and Spain put an end to both feudalism and Christian universalism. The Congress of Mantua (1459–60) was the last European gathering presided over by the pope. By the time Henry VIII (reigned

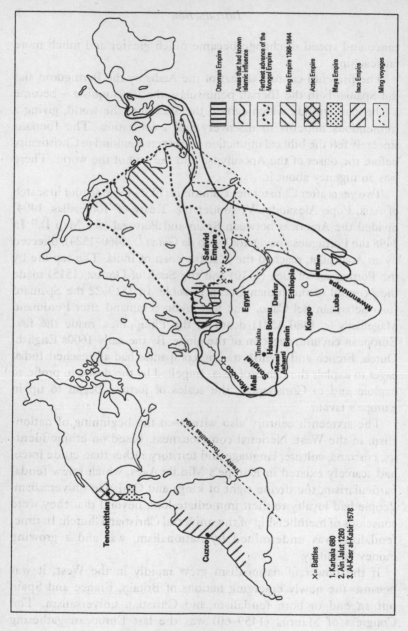

Map 1 The World before 1500

1509–47) declared himself 'supreme head' of the Church of England in 1534, the prestige of papal authority had been shattered by the Protestant Reformation. By 1700 the European secular states had come to overshadow Christendom.[12] What mattered henceforth was not the feudal lord or the universal Church but the nation. The foundation of the modern state system helped to give the Europeans the vigour, the purpose, the resources, the organization and the administration to go out and conquer the world.

Finally, this study begins in 1500 because the sixteenth century was an age of great scientific and technological achievement in the West. Although the idea of scientific progress is taken for granted today, against the backcloth of time it was an innovation of first importance. Before the sixteenth century, Europe had depended upon Asia for many of the important developments in science and technology. Now Asia became reliant upon the more dynamic Europe. Western science and technology came to be used not as they had always been – to ensure stability in society – but to stimulate change.

Of course, in 1500 no one foresaw these things. No one predicted that Europe would eventually control most of the world. In the sixteenth century, all the major empires in Eurasia were Asian, so it is to Asia that we must first turn.

2

Origin of our Times:
An Asian-Dominated World

As early as the eighth century AD the Arabic Saracen Empire stretched from Mecca and Medina in Arabia westward via Egypt, Libya and the Mediterranean Sea to the Atlantic, and eastward to the China Sea. For a period, the mental vigour of their civilization grew. By the ninth century they were in charge of the trade from Europe to Persia, India and China, binding together the Eurasian world. It was the Arabs who laid the groundwork of the world economy that Europe would later transform.

The rapid expansion of Muslim Arabs from the eighth to the eleventh century was fostered by the power of prophecy, by the fire of the Islamic faith,[1] by the call to brotherhood, as well as by a prowess in arms. Not least, the Arabs were able to expand because many of those whom they conquered were overwhelmingly weak. In AD 711 the Muslim general Tarik ibn Ziyad, having crossed from Ceuta in Morocco to Gibraltar, began a Muslim occupation of Spain that would last almost eight hundred years. In AD 732 an army led by Abd al-Rahman crossed the Pyrenees and captured Bordeaux.

Wherever they spread, the Arabs stamped the unity and culture of Islamic life upon the areas they conquered. Almost all the languages of the Muslim world have borrowed heavily from Arabic, which (as Greek had done earlier and Latin would do later) provided a bridge between Asia and Europe. Under Muslim rule, cities such as Baghdad in Iraq (immortalized in *The Thousand and One Nights*), Damascus in Syria, Córdoba in Spain and Cairo in Egypt experienced extraordinary bursts of creative activity and became centres of scientific, artistic and philosophical learning. The Arab philosophers Ibn Hazm (994–1064) and Ibn Rushd (known as Averroës, 1126–98), and the leading Jewish scholar of the Middle Ages, Maimonides (1135–1204), who wrote in Arabic, were all sons of Córdoba. Averroës helped to liberate scientific research from Christian and Islamic theological dogmatism. Ibn Sina (980–1037 – known as Avicenna) earned the title the 'prince of physicians'. The Muslim mathematician, astronomer and geographer Muhammad ibn-Musa al-Khwarizmi (*c.* 780–*c.* 850), perhaps the greatest mathematician of the Middle Ages, originated the zero and the decimal system (although this claim is disputed by Indian mathematicians) and laid the foundations of algebra.

Córdoba, boasting 500 mosques with their richly ornamented minarets and cupolas, 300 public baths, 70 libraries and lamp-lit streets, became one of the great cultural centres of Europe. While the Muslims in Spain were creating buildings of breathtaking beauty and establishing famous libraries, the leaders of Christian Europe were only just learning to write their names.

The Arab world provided a conduit through which passed the ideas of East and West. It was through an Arab window that Europe first saw Asia. In translating and diffusing the learning of the Greeks, the Romans, the Jews, the Persians and the Hindus, the Arabs made available to the West the heritage of antiquity. Arabic contributions to the sciences (in geometry, trigonometry, physics and optics, chemistry and medicine) and the arts (including business and finance) were crucial to later Western developments. Before 1500 many of the classical Greek and Arab scientific works had been translated by them into Latin, increasingly the language of Christendom. Not least, the Arabic empire helped to transfer superior Asian technology to the West. The Arabs were skilled in the working of metals, textiles, glass, pottery, leather, farming and horticulture, and in the distillation of alcohol (an Arabic word). Through them, the all-important discovery of making paper reached the West.

The Christian victory over the Marinids (Muslim Berbers from Fez in Morocco) at Salado in Spain in 1340 brought to an end the long history of the Arab-Berber invasion of the Iberian peninsula. The Reconquista was completed in 1492 when the last Muslim outpost was crushed in Granada by the armies of Ferdinand of Aragon and Isabella of Castile (united in 1469), and Arabs (and Jews) were expelled from Spain. Henceforth, faced by the dual threats of Christian Europe and the Ottoman Turks, the Arab light dimmed.

Descended from Central Asian nomadic, pastoral tribes, the Turks had founded an empire in the late thirteenth century. Overrunning Persia, they continued westward, conquering Arabic-speaking lands. Under the tribal leader Osman (b. 1259; emir 1299–1326) they reached the northwest corner of Anatolia. Following his death they founded the Ottoman Empire, in which Turkish became the dominant language. In 1352 they crossed from Asia into Europe. From the Gallipoli peninsula they infiltrated the Balkans, conquering Bulgaria as they went. In blocking the land and sea routes to the East, they caused the Iberians to explore the Atlantic, where they discovered the Canary Islands, Madeira and the Azores. Hoping to reach India by going around the Turkish empire, European ships increasingly began to appear off Africa's western coast.

A century later, in 1453, under Sultan Mehmet II (1451–81), the Turks captured Constantinople (Istanbul), the capital of the Greek Orthodox Byzantine Empire, which had been founded as a second Rome by Constantine the Great a thousand years before. The fall of Constantinople sent a chill throughout Christian Europe. In 1459 Mehmet II conquered Serbia and by 1460 the Morea (the Peloponnese). In 1461 the Turkish army stood on the banks of the Euphrates. In 1516 they overran Syria and Egypt, and in 1517 Arabia. At sea they fought the Iberians in the Mediterranean and in the Indian Ocean. In the 1520s, under the Turkish leader Suleiman the Magnificent (b. 1495; reigned 1520–66), most of the Balkan peninsula and Hungary were overrun. In 1521 Belgrade was taken. To the growing fear of Western Europe, the Turks defeated a European army at the Battle of Mohács in Hungary in 1526, and threatened Vienna in 1529 (see Map II). More concerned with plunder and taxes, the Turks (unlike the Arabs before them) showed little interest in changing the religion or the ethnic groupings of those they conquered.

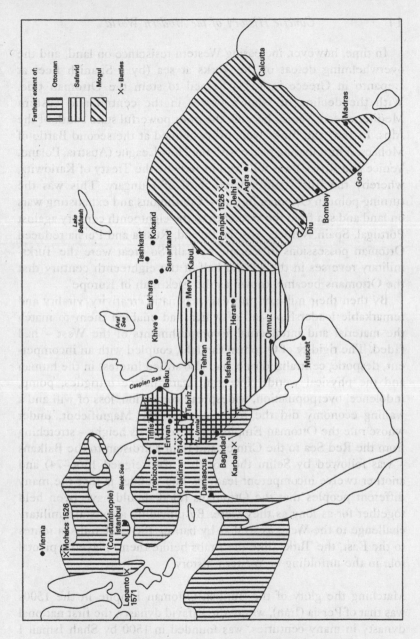

Map II The Ottoman, Safavid and Mogul Empires

Farthest extent of:
Ottoman
Safavid
Mogul
X = Battles

Calcutta
Madras
Panipat 1526 X
Agra
Delhi
Diu
Bombay
Goa
Tashkent
Kokand
Semarkand
Kabul
Merv
Bukhara
Herat
Lake Balkhash
Khiva
Ormuz
Aral Sea
Tehran
Muscat
Isfahan
Caspian Sea
Baku
Tabriz
Tiflis
Erivan
L. Urmia
Trebizond
Chaldiran 1514 X
Baghdad
Karbala X
Black Sea
Damascus
Vienna
X Mohács 1526
(Constantinople)
Istanbul
Lepanto 1571 X

In time, however, increasing Western resistance on land, and the overwhelming defeat of the Turks at sea (by a Spanish fleet at Lepanto in Greece in 1571) helped to stem the Ottoman tide. With the decline of Islam's power in the central and eastern Mediterranean, Venice became the most powerful state south of the Alps. In 1687 the Turks were overwhelmed at the second Battle of Mohács. A humiliating peace with the Holy League (Austria, Poland, Venice and Russia) was followed in 1699 by the Treaty of Karlowitz, whereby the Turks surrendered most of Hungary. This was the turning point in Ottoman fortunes. Continuous and exhausting wars on land and sea from the sixteenth to the eighteenth century against Portugal, Spain, Venice, Austria, Poland, Russia and Persia reduced Ottoman possessions in Europe by half. So great were the Turks' military reverses in the second half of the eighteenth century that the Ottomans became known as the 'sick man of Europe'.

By then their military prowess, pragmatic creativity, vitality and remarkable leadership – all of which had enabled them to match the material and intellectual accomplishments of the West – had faded. The rigidity of Ottoman thought, coupled with an incompetent, despotic, centralized rule, had also stifled interest in the human and the physical worlds. Incessant wars, palace intrigues, pomp, indolence, overpopulation, widespread corruption, loss of will and a waning economy did the rest. Suleiman the Magnificent, under whose rule the Ottoman Empire had reached its height – stretching from the Red Sea to the Crimea and from Kurdistan to the Balkans – was followed by Selim the Sot (b. 1524; reigned 1566–74) and another twelve incompetent leaders. The wonder is that the many different peoples that the Ottomans ruled should have been held together for as long as they were. By providing a constant military challenge to the West, as well as by barring the land and sea routes to the East, the Turks (like the Arabs before them) played a pivotal role in the unfolding of Western history.

Matching the glory of the Turkish Ottoman Empire in the 1500s was that of Persia (Iran), where the Safavid dynasty, the first national dynasty in many centuries, was founded in 1500 by Shah Ismail I (1487–1524). Descended from a long line of militant Shi'ites, Ismail declared Shi'ite Islam to be the religion of the state.[2] Previously, as a result of the Arab invasions of the seventh century, Persia had adhered to the Sunni sect. The adoption of Shi'ism so intensified the discord between Persia and its Sunni neighbours that warfare between them was common throughout the sixteenth century. In 1514 Shah Ismail was defeated by the Turks at Chaldiran, but he managed to hold on to the greater part of Persia, as did his successor Shah Tahmasp I (b. 1513; reigned 1524–76; see Map II).

Persia's fortunes improved under the strong leadership of Shah Abbas I (b. 1571; reigned 1587–1629). Between 1603 and 1612 he recovered Tabriz from the Ottomans, recaptured all of northwest Persia, took Erivan and won a decisive victory against the Turks near Lake Urmia. To strengthen his rule, he encouraged the English and Dutch East India trading companies to establish branches in Persia. In 1622 the English assisted Abbas to seize the island of Ormuz from the Portuguese, thus gaining trading privileges there. Abbas's conquest of Azerbaijan and Kurdistan was followed in 1623 by his seizure of Baghdad. With great splendour, a new Persian capital was established at Isfahan.

Alas, the reign of Abbas the Great was followed by that of Shah Safi, the Weak (reigned 1629–42), who, having been raised in the harem, lacked political and military experience. Helped by Safi's ineptitude, the aggressive Ottoman Turks returned to reconquer large parts of Persian territory; Azerbaijan fell to them in 1635. The final blow to the Safavids, however, came not from the Turks but from the Ghilzai Afghans in the East. In 1722 the Afghan ruler Mir Mahmud invaded Persia, defeated its army and took Isfahan. Under invasion by Turk and Afghan, the Safavid empire of Persia collapsed in 1723; the last of the Safavids was deposed in 1736.

Mir Mahmud's taking of Isfahan was the signal for the Russians and the Turks to seize whatever Persian territory they could. They were prevented from dismembering Persia altogether only by the appearance of a powerful new leader, Nadir Shah (b. 1688; reigned 1736–47), a Sunni Turk from Afghanistan. In a series of battles he routed the Afghans, the Turks and the Russians. In 1739 he carried his wars of conquest across Afghanistan into Mogul India, where he sacked and looted Delhi. His brutal efforts to suppress Shi'ism and make Sunnism the leading sect in Persia ended with his assassination in 1747. His death was followed by political divisions and civil war. Only in 1750, with the establishment of the Zand dynasty, was some stability restored. But in 1794 Persia was again thrown into disruption by an internal struggle for power. As a result, for much of the nineteenth century a weakened Persia was a pawn of Russian-British rivalry in Central and Eastern Asia.

Another great Muslim empire – the Mogul[3] of India – was founded in 1526 by Babar (1483–1530), who had invaded India from Afghanistan. Babar's victory over the much more powerful Sultan of Delhi at the Battle of Panipat in 1526 was to the eastern wing of Muslim power what the victory at Mohács on the Danube (also in 1526) was to the Ottomans in the west. With these victories Islam extended from Morocco in the west and Austria in the north, through the Safavids of Persia, to the centre of India.

Babar laid the foundations of a Muslim dynasty that lasted over three centuries. Within four years he had conquered the greater part of Hindustan. Thenceforth, his followers extended their power and their religion across most of the subcontinent. The reign of his grandson Akbar the Great (b. 1542; reigned 1556–1605), who renewed and consolidated Mogul and Muslim rule, is considered a golden age in India's history. There had not been – so it was said – an Indian empire of its like for two thousand years. A benevolent despot, Akbar is remembered for the synthesis and unity between Hindu and Islamic cultures he achieved throughout the subcontinent. His religious tolerance was matched by his fairness in assessing taxes and his astuteness in establishing a centralized government. Following the death of his successor Jahangir (b. 1569; reigned 1605–27), who had neglected his duties for a self-indulgent life at court, further extensions of Mogul rule were made by Shah Jahan (reigned 1627–58). Like his predecessors, he encouraged the arts and the building of palaces and mosques; the Taj Mahal at Agra was built as a mausoleum for his wife.

The turning point in Islam's fortunes in India came with the accession to power of Aurangzeb (b. 1618; reigned 1658–1707), whose attempts to consolidate power – very difficult to achieve at any time in India – were undone by rebellions, political infighting and wars. His efforts to convert Hindus forcibly to Islam aroused widespread hostility, and following his death in 1707, the Mogul Empire began to disintegrate. Thenceforth, harried by Marathas, Sikhs and Persians, as well as by Europeans (Portuguese, Dutch, Danes, British and French) who had made their way around the Ottoman Empire by way of the Atlantic and Indian oceans, there was a steady decline in Mogul power, which was accelerated by internal weaknesses and the rigid and unchanging outlook of the Mogul elite.

With the collapse of the Mogul Empire, Europeans in India were drawn into the country's political conflicts and intrigues. By defeating the Nawab of Bengal and the French at Plassey in 1757, the Dutch at Chinsura in 1759 and the titular Mogul emperor at Buxar in 1764, Britain established her supremacy in Bengal, and later – with the defeat of the Marathas in 1818 – the whole of India fell under British control (see Maps III and IV). In 1786 the first British governor-general of India was appointed to administer an area many times greater than Britain itself. Neighbouring Ceylon (Sri Lanka) was seized by British forces in 1796.

Britain's conquest of India led to war between Burma and British India. By the Treaty of Yandabo (1826) Burma was forced to concede border areas to British India. In 1830 a revolt by Burmese peasants was crushed; six years later Britain tried to appease the Burmese by recognizing Burma as a crown colony. Burma's answer was to demand full independence. Two further wars (1852 and 1885) followed to give the British complete control of Burma. Under British rule, Burma's natural resources were developed, a railway network was built and the export of metals increased. Exploitation of oil deposits in central Burma began in 1871. It was not until the 1930s that Burma was separated from British India and a modicum of self-rule granted.

The most populous and powerful empire in Asia in the 1500s was the Ming (1368–1644) of China,[4] which in 1368 had overthrown the Yuan (Mongol) dynasty (1260–1368).[5] Coming from Central Asia in the early years of the thirteenth century, the Mongol armies under

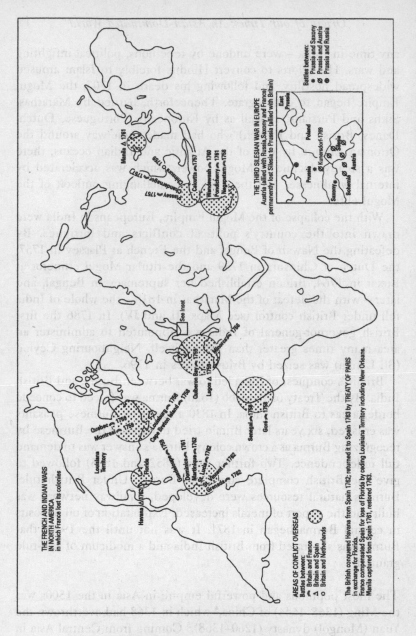

THE THIRD SILESIAN WAR IN EUROPE
Austria (allied with Russia, Saxony and France)
permanently lost Silesia to Prussia (allied with Britain)

Battles between:
✳ Prussia and Saxony
⊘ Prussia and Austria
◉ Prussia and Russia

East
Prussia

Poland

Prussia

Silesia
Kunersdorf 1759

Saxony

Bohemia

Austria

See inset

Manila △ 1761

Chinsura ○ 1759
Calcutta △ 1757
Wandewash ~ 1760
Pondicherry ~ 1761
Negapatam ~ 1758
Plassey △ 1757
Plandsanabor 1759

Quebec ~ 1759
Montreal ~ 1760
Louisburg ~ 1758
Cape Breton Island ~ 1758
Quiberon Bay △ 1759
Minorca ~ 1756
Lagos △ 1759
Senegal ~ 1758
Goré △ 1758

Louisiana
Territory

Florida
Havana △1762
Louisiana ~ 1762
Guadeloupe ~ 1759
Dominica ~ 1761
Martinique ~ 1762
St. Lucia ~ 1762
St. Vincent ~ 1762
Grenada 1762

THE FRENCH AND INDIAN WARS
IN NORTH AMERICA
in which France lost its colonies

AREAS OF CONFLICT OVERSEAS
Battles between:
△ Britain and France
▲ Britain and Spain
○ Britain and Netherlands

The British conquered Havana from Spain 1762; returned it to Spain 1763 by TREATY OF PARIS
in exchange for Florida.
France compensated Spain for loss of Florida by ceding Louisiana Territory including New Orleans.
Manila captured from Spain 1761, restored 1763.

Map III   Battles of the Seven Years War, 1756–63

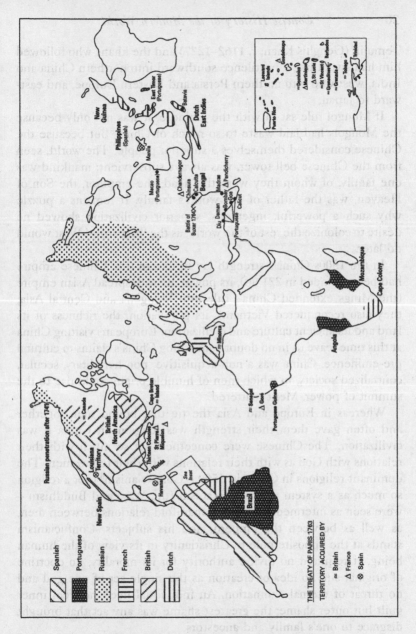

THE TREATY OF PARIS 1763
TERRITORY ACQUIRED BY
△ France
⊗ Spain

Spanish
Portuguese
Russian
French
British
Dutch

New Guinea

East Timor
(Portuguese)

Philippines
(Spanish)

Manila

Batavia

Dutch
East Indies

Macao △Chandernagore
Portuguese ○Chinsura
△Calicutta
Bengal
△Pondicherry
Madras
Diu Daman ○Bombay △Goa
Portuguese Goa
Calicut

Battle of
Buxar 1760

Mozambique

Cape Colony

Angola

Minorca

Portuguese Guinea
⊗ Goree
△ Senegal

Canada

British
North America

Cape Breton
Island

Russian penetration after 1741

Louisiana
Territory

Thirteen Colonies
St Pierre
Miquelon

New Spain

⊗ Havana

Florida

Sea
Inset

Brazil

Guadeloupe

Dominica △
Martinique △
St Lucia △
St Vincent △
Grenadines △
Grenada △

Barbados

Tobago △

Leeward Islands

Porto Rico

Trinidad

Map IV European Empires after 1763

Temujin (Genghis Khan; *c.* 1162–1227) and the khans who followed him had swept like a pestilence southward into northern China and India, westward into northern Persia and Eastern Europe, and eastward to Japan.

If Mongol rule sat ill with the Chinese, it was not only because the Mongols had laid waste to so much of China, but because the Chinese considered themselves a superior people. The world, seen from the Chinese bell tower, was always subservient; mankind was one family, of whom they were the head; the emperor, the Son of Heaven, was the father of the world's family. It remains a puzzle why such a powerful, ingenious, superior civilization showed no desire to colonize the rest of the world, as the 'barbarous' West would do later.

In the 1500s China's strength lay in its age (the Chinese empire had been founded in 221 BC), its power, its widespread Asian empire (the Mings extended China's rule into Mongolia and Central Asia; they also reconquered Vietnam), its population, the richness of its land and its ancient culture and civilization. Europeans visiting China at this time leave us in no doubt concerning China's claims to cultural pre-eminence. China was a non-acquisitive, non-hereditary, secular, centralized society, in which men of humble origin could rise to the summit of power. Merit mattered.

Whereas in Europe and Asia the tie that bound men together and often gave them their strength was religion, in China it was civilization. The Chinese were concerned not so much with their relations with God as with their relations with their fellow men. The dominant religions in China in 1500 – Confucianism[6] (not a religion so much as a system of order), Taoism (the Way) and Buddhism – were seen as intermediaries in the manifold relations between men, as well as between the emperor and his subjects. Confucianism stands at the opposite pole to Christianity in its view of the human being. It required no divine authority for its morality, no doctrine of original sin, no idea of creation as the single act of one god and no threat of eternal damnation. An individual need not feel inner guilt but outer shame; the greatest shame was any act that brought disgrace to one's family and ancestors.

Confucianism (proclaimed China's state doctrine in 136 BC) was particularly successful among the Chinese because it provided them with a viable perception of order for the individual, the family, society and the world. With Taoism, Confucianism provided the foundation from which Chinese culture is spiritually derived. The cornerstone of Confucian teaching is the sanctity of the family. Respect for family and for the past is what respect for the individual came to mean in the West. The Chinese aspired to harmony, stability and continuity. What was just or unjust equated to what was socially harmonious or discordant.

Since the visit of the Venetian traveller Marco Polo in the thirteenth century, China's wealth and power had impressed Europeans as much as its culture. Yet, until very recently China did not seek to become a commercial civilization. The Chinese mandarinate system and the agrarian self-sufficiency of the Chinese people inhibited the rise of a merchant class, which for most of Chinese history was regarded as parasitical. Although the merchant's lot improved during the Sung dynasty (AD 960–1279), and there was probably much more internal and foreign trade and commercialism than scholars have allowed, markets and money (even though the Chinese invented paper money) have not played the pivotal roles in Chinese history that they came to play in the West and the Islamic Middle East. Except during the Yuan dynasty, founded by the Mongol Kublai Khan (1257–94), trade – foreign and domestic – was not allowed to change the empire's economic, cultural and intellectual institutions. Agriculture was the right and proper source of wealth. The goal of Confucian harmony, based as it was on the land, the family and the scholar-gentry, remained the ideal.

However, China's official attitude towards the merchant class does not seem to have hindered its technological development. In the first fourteen centuries of Christian Europe many Chinese inventions were adopted by the Europeans without knowing where they originated. These inventions included gunpowder, silk, porcelain, paper money and the use of coal and gas for heating. The West probably had little to teach China in agrarian or industrial techniques before the eighteenth century. Until the nineteenth century China's agrarian standards were unmatched.

Furthermore, the Chinese excelled in shipbuilding technology.

In the fifteenth century they possessed the world's greatest sea-going fleet – large enough, had they willed it, to have blocked European expansion into Asian waters. The Chinese passed to the Arabs (who subsequently brought the ideas to Europe) such essentials as watertight bulkheads, stern-post rudders and the maritime compass. Unlike the European single-masted vessels, which could sail only downwind, their multiple-masted vessels – which were also adopted in the West – could sail into the wind, making long voyages feasible.

Between 1405 and 1433, in order to establish diplomatic relations, exchange gifts and impress distant lands with Chinese technology and civilization, do some trade and collect tribute and exotica (including a giraffe), seven great naval expeditions were sent by the Ming emperors into the Indian Ocean. They reached Arabia, Africa and beyond (see Map I). The first voyage began with more than 60 vessels (the largest were 440 feet long and 186 feet wide with a crew of about 28,000 men). Contrast this with Columbus's three much smaller ships and crew of ninety. Columbus's flagship, the *Santa Maria*, was just 117 feet long.[7] Apart from establishing trading stations such as Malacca, the Chinese expeditions sought no conquest. In 1423, roughly seventy years before da Gama rounded the Cape of South Africa, the Chinese returned home to resume their traditional policy of isolation. After the death of the Ming Emperor Yong Le (1360; reigned 1403–24), his successor ordered the voyages stopped, the charts and logs of the expeditions destroyed. After Yong Le's grandson came to power, one last expedition was launched in 1431, but after 1435 imperial edicts forbade foreign trade and travel on pain of death. The Chinese became concerned with enemies in the interior of Asia and political rivalries at court. China remained closed until it was forced open by the West in the nineteenth century.

The decision of the Ming dynasty – having routed the Mongols in 1368 – to revert to a defensive strategy did not save it from attacks. In the sixteenth century Japanese pirates raided the Chinese coast with impunity; in 1550 the Mongols invaded the northern part of the country again. In 1592, when the Japanese invaded Korea, the Chinese crossed the Yalu River and successfully intervened. In the seventeenth century, by which time the Mings were in decline, they were beset by the Manchus from neighbouring Manchuria. Because of weak rulers, growing famine, sickness and want, rebellions swept through much of China from the 1620s onwards. The fall of Beijing to a rebel force in 1644 provided the Manchus with the ideal conditions for invasion. Like the Mongols, the Manchus were an expansive society.

Having seized Beijing and crushed all resistance to their new Ch'ing dynasty (1644–1912), the Manchus extended their rule to the entire region (see Map V). The country was pacified; the worst ills redressed. As a sign of submission, the native Chinese were required to adopt Manchu dress and wear their hair in a queue or pigtail. Sharing power with the conquered, Manchu rule proved strong and judicious. The Manchus also followed a policy of expansion in inner Asia, including the Amur Valley, Mongolia and Tibet, which became the home of Buddhist monasticism. Their invasions of Burma in the 1760s, like their later eighteenth-century invasions of Nepal and Vietnam, proved abortive. Meanwhile, a new threat to China had appeared from the West.

In 1514 a party of Portuguese traders and buccaneers reached the southern Chinese coast. Arab, Persian and Indian sea-traders had long preceded them. By 1557 the Portuguese had established a coastal trading station at Macao. Eight years later the Spaniards reached China from the Philippines, bringing with them a new religion, superior weapons and produce from the recently discovered New World (including maize, sweet potatoes, tobacco and silver). With these intrusions the colonization of China by the West began.

Convinced of their superior civilization, the Chinese sought to keep the foreign 'barbarians' at bay; they had no desire to know what the inferior West was doing, so they largely ignored the industrial and scientific changes in Europe. Except for gold and silver specie, eyeglasses, astrological and musical instruments, clocks and novelties such as mechanical toys, the West had little that they desired. Nor did they encourage trade relations. Since China's self-imposed seclusion, beginning in 1433, they had kept their trade by sea and land (along the Silk Road) to a minimum. The potential benefits of world trade never seemed to have occurred to them.

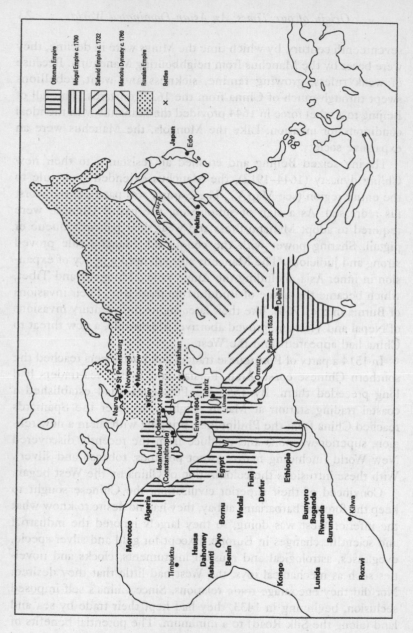

Map V Asian and African Empires before 1763

Ottoman Empire
Mogul Empire c. 1700
Safavid Empire c. 1732
Manchu Dynasty c. 1760
Russian Empire
Battles

Japan
Edo
Amur R.
Peking
Delhi
Panipat 1526
Ormuz
Narva
St Petersburg
Novgorod
Moscow
Kiev
Poltava 1709
Astrakhan
Tabriz
Erivan 1604
Odessa
Istanbul (Constantinople)
Lake Urmia
Egypt
Algeria
Morocco
Bornu
Wadai
Darfur
Funj
Ethiopia
Hausa
Timbuktu
Dahomey
Oyo
Ashanti
Benin
Kongo
Lunda
Bunyoro
Buganda
Rwanda
Burundi
Kilwa
Rozwi

It was not until 1601 that several Jesuit priests,[8] led by Matteo Ricci (1552–1610), who had spent seven years proselytizing on the coast, were allowed to visit Beijing. Prompting the Chinese decision to allow foreigners to reside in the capital was a new-found interest in the scientific knowledge that the Jesuits brought with them. In due course, Ricci and his companions translated several important Western scientific works, such as those of Euclid and Copernicus, into Chinese. In helping to reform the Chinese dynastic calendar (primarily the work of Johann Schall von Bell; 1591–1666), which was crucial in regulating every aspect of the emperor's life, the Jesuits altered the whole outlook of Chinese astronomy.

In turn, the Jesuits were so impressed by the civilized conduct and bearing of the Mandarin class that they extolled the Chinese as superior among Orientals. In particular they noted the contrast between China's tolerance towards other religious beliefs and the horrors of seventeenth-century European religious strife. This was noted by Ricci in his diary:

> To begin with, it seems to be quite remarkable . . . that in a kingdom of almost limitless expanse and innumerable population, and abounding in copious supplies of every description, though they have a well-equipped army and navy that could easily conquer the neighboring nations, neither the King nor his people ever think of waging a war of aggression. They are quite content with what they have and are not ambitious of conquest. In this respect they are much different from the people of Europe, who are frequently discontent with their own governments and covetous of what others enjoy . . .
>
> Another remarkable difference . . . is that the entire kingdom is administered by the Order of the Learned, commonly known as the Philosophers . . . The army, both officers and soldiers, hold them in high respect . . . Policies of war are formulated and military questions are decided by the Philosophers only . . . From the beginning and foundation of this empire the study of letters was always more acceptable to the people than the profession of arms, as being more suitable to a people who had little or no interests in the extension of the empire.[9]

In Ricci's view the Chinese were justified in calling their country the 'Middle Kingdom' – the centre of the earth. He and other foreigners even began to dress like them. European leaders of the Enlightenment, such as Voltaire (François Marie Arouet; 1694–1778), François Quesnay (1694–1774) and Gottfried Wilhelm Leibniz (1646–1716), looked upon China as a model that Europe should imitate. The fact that the Confucian social code stressed conformity, and hence was less stimulating to the development of scientific thought, was glossed over. A passion for things Chinese swept through the elite of eighteenth-century Europe: superior Chinese porcelain became the vogue; with the help of the Jesuits, the Chinese examination system was adopted first by France and then by the other European powers.

It took time before the Jesuits began to notice aspects of Chinese life that they were less willing to praise. Some Jesuits thought ancestor worship idolatrous. They also questioned the emperor's spiritual authority in relation to that of the pope. Western priests in the emperor's employment faced the problem of serving two masters. In 1715 the pope appeared to insult the emperor by telling him how the word 'God' should be translated into Chinese. Worse, the rival Christian orders began to squabble: the Spanish Dominicans accused the Portuguese Jesuits of compromising themselves with respect to Confucianism. All of this caused the Emperor K'ang-hsi (reigned 1661–1722) to tire of the Western presence. His successor, Yung Cheng (reigned 1722–35), put an end to Western intrusion by suppressing Christianity and banishing the Europeans. As the Europeans were in no position, militarily or psychologically, to challenge Yung Cheng's decision, the theological quarrel among the Christians (rather than a political threat to the Chinese throne) eventually put an end to more than a hundred years of almost unbroken European presence at the Chinese court.[10] By then, hundreds of court officials and thousands of ordinary Chinese had been converted to the Western faith.

Thenceforth, for more than a century, Manchu China remained largely closed to Western influence. The Chinese themselves were forbidden to travel abroad, and foreign trade was proscribed or severely restricted. Chinese shipping was confined to coastal waters. When, in 1793, the British King George III sent Lord Macartney, his 'ambassador extraordinary', to negotiate improved foreign trading conditions (by then the British had replaced the Portuguese as the most important traders in the East), the emperor, seeing no reason why Britain or any other European nation should be granted rights other than those of a tributary state, politely turned him away. In 1816 another British mission suffered the same fate. The Manchu dynasty was probably at the peak of its power at this point and had little to fear from the British. There was simply nothing that China needed from the West; the idea of increasing the exchange of commodities with Europeans was quite unnecessary, if not inconceivable. But this was an attitude that the trading, colonizing West rejected out of hand.

Instead of fostering its links with the Europeans, China directed its energies to extending and maintaining its relations with surrounding areas, including the Amur Valley, Nepal, Tibet, Siam, Burma, Korea, Vietnam and Mongolia. The frontier between Russia and Mongolia (then part of China) was drawn in 1727. Under the Treaty of Kiakhta of that year, Russia alone was given the right to trade regularly with China, but only annually and overland. In return, Chinese rule was confirmed by Russia over all of Mongolia. The only link with the West – a tenuous one – was that maintained by a handful of European traders at Canton (Guangzhou), where ever-increasing quantities of tea, silk, fine cottons, highly valued porcelain and lacquerware were traded for Western wool, tin, copper, honey, salt, opium and specie. Much of the silver came via the Philippines from the Spanish silver mines in America. Britain profited immensely from the sale of opium from British India. Even this limited trade with foreigners was considered a privilege, which was only grudgingly granted. Not until the British forced China to accept Western commerce through the Opium Wars (1839–42) was China's policy of isolation ended.

European intrusion into Japan began in 1543 when a group of Portuguese traders on board a Chinese ship arrived at Tanegashima harbour. Portuguese guns fascinated the Japanese, who studied them and quickly began to reproduce them. By the mid-sixteenth century (the Chinese government having forbidden its subjects to trade directly with Japan) the Portuguese at Macao controlled the carrying trade between them. The most important item was Chinese silk, which was exchanged for Japanese silver.

The Japanese greeted the first Portuguese ships with similar fear as the Chinese had done, but also with great curiosity. Unlike the Chinese, they were fascinated by the newcomers' dress and the items they brought with them. They showed a similar eagerness to learn from the Europeans as they had shown earlier in learning from the Chinese.

The port of Nagasaki, opened to Western commerce in 1570, became the meeting place of an ever-growing throng of Portuguese, Spanish, Dutch and British merchants. Firearms from Europe were shipped to Japan in exchange for Japanese silver and copper. In the sixteenth century the Japanese put the Portuguese musket to use in the incessant feudal wars that devastated the land.

Helping to shape Japanese reactions to Western intrusion was the Shinto religion, which appealed to the Japanese sense of national identity and uniqueness as a divinely begotten race. Shinto demanded reverence for ancestors, for the emperor and for the past. Although overshadowed by Buddhism in earlier centuries, it always managed to coexist with it. Shinto was a national religion long before it was proclaimed as such in 1871.

Equally important was bushido, the Japanese warrior code of moral principles, which stressed filial piety, benevolence, loyalty to one's lord unto death, personal courage, conscious choice of where one's duty lay, self-discipline, endurance, kindness and honesty. Its martial spirit emphasized duties rather than rights. Unlike in China, family loyalties came after those of lord and vassal. Bushido placed the warrior ruler first, followed by the peasant, the artisan and then the merchant. Perhaps the stress on military prowess explains why in the nineteenth century Japan was able to make a much more realistic appraisal of the Western military threat than China did.

The Japanese displayed the same interest in Western religion as they did in other aspects of Western intrusion. Christianity (first introduced into Japan by the Jesuit missionary St Francis Xavier (1506–52) in 1549) received the protection and the apparent encouragement of two of Japan's military leaders: Oda Nobunaga (1534–82) and Toyotomi Hideyoshi (1537–98). These men were of paramount importance in unifying the country and deciding Japan's relations with the West. With their tolerance, and sometimes their help, in less than fifty years the Christian missionaries had made 300,000 conversions. Japan came to be regarded as the most promising field of Christian evangelism.[11]

Ironically, the very success of the Europeans in Japan proved to be their undoing. The growing Christian presence began to alarm Japanese leaders (especially Hideyoshi), who came to suspect the Church as an agent of Western imperialism. The Jesuits and the Dominicans came to be viewed as secret agents of Portugal and Spain. Loyalty and authority were at stake. To the quarrel between the Iberian Christians that had tired the Chinese emperor was added an acrimonious dispute between the Jesuits and the Buddhists.

Increasingly fearful that the Europeans might try to seize power in Japan as they had done in the Philippines (1565–71) and Formosa (Taiwan; 1624), the Japanese proceeded to reverse their attitude towards Western commerce and beliefs. In 1587 Christianity was denounced by Hideyoshi as a threat to the state. In 1612 Tokugawa Ieyasu (1543–1616), the most powerful military leader, decreed that all missionaries must leave forthwith; Japanese converts were called upon to renounce the Christian faith. In 1636 a seclusion edict was proclaimed.[12] The following year the Japanese stamped out a peasant insurrection at Shimabara (close to Nagasaki) in which the Christians had played a leading role. (Dutch cannons were eventually used to put down the uprising.) Everything was done to exterminate opposition, either from Christians or disabused Japanese. By the mid-seventeenth century European traders had also been banished from the mainland.

Thenceforth, the only Europeans allowed to stay in Japan were a few Protestant Dutch traders in virtual imprisonment on the islet of Deshima in Nagasaki harbour. To prove that they were not true Christians, and therefore not agents of Western imperialism, they were required annually to trample on either the Christian cross or an image of Christ. A few Chinese ships, and two supply vessels each year from Holland, became Japan's only link with the outside world. The Japanese themselves were forbidden to travel abroad. Any Japanese returning from overseas was put to death. This isolation endured for two relatively peaceful and progressive centuries.

3

The Rise of the West

Europe's rise from relative obscurity to greatness began with the Renaissance,[1] which changed the course of European art, music, literature, architecture, politics, religion, education, commerce and science and technology. It was one of those widespread, deep cultural changes that take place every now and again (such as the spread of Christianity and Islam in earlier times, or the imposition of communist rule and its eventual unravelling in the twentieth century) concerning the world and humanity. The focus of that change – whether we are dealing with the art of Leonardo da Vinci (1452–1519) and Michelangelo (1475–1564), the writings of Niccolò Machiavelli and Desiderius Erasmus, or the literature of William Shakespeare (1564–1616) and François Rabelais (1494–1553) – was on the human and the secular.

With the Renaissance – in contrast to the static nature of medieval society – the air became charged with the excitement of experimentation. A new stress was placed on the dynamic; on merit rather than on birth; on the individual rather than the group. It was the West which first elevated man to a dominating position in nature. It is not surprising that the Protestant Reformation, with its triumph of conscience over dogma, and its emphasis on the direct contact of the individual soul with God, followed in the early sixteenth century. In placing a new stress on individual judgement the Reformation, like the Renaissance, provided a tremendous spur to action and change.

It is equally understandable why the Pole Nicolaus Copernicus (1473–1543), the Dane Tycho Brahe (1546–1601), the Italian Galileo Galilei (1564–1642) and the German Johannes Kepler (1571–1630), all of whom studied astronomy, should have clashed with church doctrine when they did. Their challenge was worldly; yet their purpose was not to undermine scripture but to confirm it by revealing God's divine will and purpose in nature. Increasingly, nature, which had been the shadow, became reality; the soul, which had been reality, became the shadow. Luther's challenge – 'Only faith can gain salvation' – was spiritual.

Thus were sown the seeds of modern science (later called the Scientific Revolution), whose origins can be traced to the shift in emphasis during the Renaissance from authoritative truth – the truth God had revealed in holy scripture concerning mankind's origin and destiny – to factual, objective truth regarding the processes and laws governing the natural world. Interest shifted progressively from the next world to this, from concern with something effecting redemption or eternal damnation to the actual manner of causation in the objective world. A new consciousness, a new humanism, was brought to bear on the relations existing between man and the universe. By the late sixteenth century, pragmatic, creative scientists coming from all over Europe had turned the Italian cities of Padua, Ferrara, Florence and Bologna – heirs to the much earlier Greek heritage of rational thought – into the foremost centres of science and technology.[2] All these cities were free of the constricting feudalism of other parts of Europe; Bologna was also free of papal influence.

From the scientific ferment of the fourteenth and fifteenth centuries there emerged a new rational spirit based on mathematics and logic, which sought reasoned truth in contrast to revealed truth: 'I believe because I know' rather than 'I know because I believe'. Without this belief there would have been no modern science, no capitalist spirit of enterprise, no Industrial Revolution and no Western idea of progress.[3] The idea that man could independently improve his lot, that he (not God or the hidden forces of nature) was the originator and the measure of all things (something which many Westerners never stop to question), was perhaps the most profound revolution that Western thought has undergone. Increasingly, the concern in the West became not for man to *adjust* himself to the inherently incalculable vicissitudes of life, but to *control* life. There was a gradual shift from the perfection of the spirit to the perfection of matter.

The new stress placed upon man, rather than God, the new questioning of religion and spiritual authority, the new emphasis placed upon the individual, rather than the family, tribe or state, the new insistence placed upon the growing freedom to make individual choices and individual decisions, the new power of money, the new desire to change for change's sake, the new disregard of the traditional sanctity of nature – all these things helped to release a veritable torrent of vital energy upon the West and the world.

The importance placed by the West upon the role of the individual (especially in the post-Protestant period of European history) cannot be exaggerated. While the Orient is conscious of individualism, it tends to stress the idea of a common collective destiny, of harmony and of a central authority. One of the great problems of the early Christian missionaries was to establish individual guilt: family or tribal shame was understood, but not individual guilt. To this day, one of the questions asked of a traveller in China is 'To which group do you belong?'

Even the texture of time was changed in the West: the 'timeless, perpetual present', as portrayed in the work of fifteenth-century artists like Fra Angelico (*c.* 1387–1455), gave way to linear, goal-oriented progress. Like his contemporaries, Fra Angelico was primarily concerned with redemption, which was not linked to time, and for which goal-oriented 'time', as we know it, had no meaning. For him, all time was uniform: 'Watch therefore: for ye know not what hour your Lord doth come' (Matthew: XXIV, 42). Thenceforth, especially after the Reformation, emphasis was placed not on timeless redemption but on progressive, worldly, tempestuous, volcanic, demoniac action. Time, purposive time, came to play a new role in the West: with the growth of a money economy, time became money; the market became supreme. Gradually the medieval concepts of a 'living wage' and a 'just price', which had begun with an edict of the Emperor Diocletian in the fourth century, fell into disuse. Increasingly, nothing was permanent, fixed, stable or immutable.

Accompanying these changes was the explosive force of capitalism under which a country's economy was privately owned and directed by individuals rather than by feudal customs and privileges of the rich or the state. Nothing hastened more the end of feudalism and monarchism, nothing proved to be a greater world force, than Western capitalism.

This shift in emphasis during the Renaissance towards the secular, towards science, towards action, towards constant change, towards the quest expresses the genius of European civilization. Whereas one of the most powerful instincts that man possesses is the instinct to resist change, Europe's uniqueness lay in its willingness to accept change. 'Im Anfang war die Tat' (In the beginning was action), says Johann Wolfgang von Goethe (1749–1832) in *Faust*, explaining the genius of Western civilization. (In contrast, the Greeks were diverted from action to the study of action.) More than any other civilization, the West made change part of a common process of thought. In the acceptance of change the West excelled. The maxims 'What is not can be' and 'Resources are not, they become' are purely Western. Compare these with the maxim of Chinese Taoism:[4] 'Do nothing so that it might be done.' European man's desire to mould the world to his will was in contrast to the Buddhist's desire to escape from worldly strivings, the Hindu's sense of illusion when speaking of the actual world and of individual man, and the stress placed by Confucius on the need for harmony and stability. The emphasis in the Orient in earlier centuries, if not today, was upon age-old tradition, conformity, letting matters take their course. Fatalism predominated; change was feared. The Chinese vision of life encompassed a perfect, changeless world. In contrast to the idea of a Western quest – to the idea of reaching out purposefully for some distant goal – the East, even allowing for the stress Confucius placed on self-cultivation, was relatively static. The Asian empires that preceded the rise of the West were probably more glorious than anything that Europe subsequently achieved. China in the thirteenth century was undoubtedly the most technically advanced and economically powerful state of all. Yet, being more despotic, these states provided less scope for individual action, and hence were less dynamic. China and India have never felt compelled to change the world in their image.

The growing role of secularism in the Renaissance, as well as the ever-growing competitiveness among Europeans in commerce, technology and arms, should not lead us to underestimate the significance of the spiritual factor in the rise and expansion of Europe. In post-Reformation Europe it is often difficult to separate politics from religion. Not until the end of the Thirty Years War in 1648 does national rivalry take precedence over religious disputes. Christianity did in fact combine a material with a spiritual role; it is concerned with the resurrection of the spirit as well as the body. Portugal's Henry the Navigator was not only a man of worldly activity he was also a religious ascetic. Leonhard Euler (1707–83) was not only the leading mathematician of eighteenth-century Europe and a pioneer of calculus; he was also the leader for the revival of piety in the Lutheran Church. Christianity's spiritual dynamism invaded the temporal sphere and helped to provide the foundation for the rise of the West.

It was Christianity's certainty, righteousness and messianic outlook, coupled with its domination complex, which compelled it to go out into the world in search of souls. This took the form of a crusade, which began with the defeat of the Moors at Granada in 1492. With that, the Christian defeat by the Turks at Constantinople in 1453 had been avenged. Christianity, like Buddhism (but unlike Hinduism and Judaism), was a universal religion. It was founded not on birth but on faith. Unlike Taoism, Confucianism, Hinduism and Judaism, Christianity was also a missionary religion. Without the messianic and evangelizing aspects of its beliefs (not to mention its bold self-confidence, aggressiveness and, thanks to St Paul, intolerance of other religions), it is doubtful if Christian Europe could have gone out into the world and done as it did.

Europe's rise to greatness is also explained by its supremacy in weapons. Portuguese power in the Indian Ocean in the sixteenth century rested upon its superior naval artillery. The Muslim fleets, though greater in number, were no match for them.[5] Underpinning all European efforts from the seventeenth century onwards was

Europe's overwhelming military and naval power. 'They have found out Artillery,' wrote the English poet John Donne in 1621, 'by which warres come to quicker ends than heretofore, and the great expense of bloud is avoyded.' Donne, of course, was proved wrong. In the development of superior weapons on land and sea, these improvements in artillery (some of which the West had gleaned from the East) were only the beginning.[6] The improvement of arms since the sixteenth century is a field of activity in which the West excelled – not least because developments were too widespread, and too competitive, for any one European country to be able to establish a monopoly (as the government did in China) or a lasting superiority in armaments manufacture. The exceptional progress made by Europeans in the science and technology of navigation, weapons and military organization ensured their superiority. However regrettable, war was all.

Geography also favoured the maritime nations of Europe. The control by the Italians and the Arabs of trade in the Levant was broken by Vasco da Gama, who returned to Portugal in 1499 with pepper, cinnamon and cloves. He had sailed in a single, unbroken voyage from southern India to Lisbon, bypassing Venice, the *entrepôt* for the European spice trade. Like Columbus, he expressed the great breaking out of European energy and adventure. It took about twenty years for the Muslim merchants who controlled the shorter route to Europe through the Red Sea partly to reassert their control of the Eastern trade. Eventually, there would be a shift in the centre of gravity of world trade from the Mediterranean to the Atlantic seaboard of Western Europe.

Worldwide commerce became the source of much of Europe's strength, which it mobilized and deployed with great skill. Development of mercantilist regulations in agriculture, industry and trade to ensure favourable balances of trade with other countries grew during the 1500s and 1600s. Subsidies, the protection of industries and high tariffs were all used to increase the power of the Western states in the world economy. Free trade as a concept did not exist. Success to the mercantilist states depended upon the accumulation of gold and silver.

The Western merchant and capitalist had far more freedom of

action than his Chinese counterpart to seek the profits of foreign trade. In the nineteenth century Western merchants and manufacturers established almost complete control of Ottoman markets and manufactures. Superior business organizations, such as the joint stock company, were devised to exploit growing world trade. Shares could be bought and sold on the newly founded stock exchange of Amsterdam. Marine, life and fire insurance reduced the risks of trade. Double-entry bookkeeping, of the highest importance in the development of capitalism, became widespread in the West. Private property rights were protected under the rule of law. (Capitalism has always succeeded best where property rights are protected.) The medieval restrictions on usury were revoked. Western capital became free of religious authority. The Western Europeans also enjoyed a degree of personal security which sprang not only from important legal documents – such as the Magna Carta (1215), which curbed the power of the monarch – and the gradual acceptance of the rule of law, but from the fact that the West was now safe from the incursions of Mongols and Turks. Had the Byzantines (before the fall of Constantinople in 1453), the Poles and the Russians not provided a bulwark which kept the Mongols and later the Turks at bay, Western Europe might never have experienced the Renaissance or its scientific and industrial revolutions. In 1238 the Russian city of Vladimir was razed by the Mongols. Today, the city commemorates its heroic forebears who 'by their self-sacrifice . . . saved Western Europe from suffering the same fate, and saved European civilization from extinction'. All in all, Europe faced less despoliation and fewer hindrances than Asia. Europeans were never beset to the same extent as, say, India or China by natural calamities. They never depended upon the coming of the monsoon, as did India, or on the vagaries of the Yellow and the Yangtze rivers, known as 'China's sorrows'.[7] There also was a better relation in the West between human and material resources. While Europe displayed demographic vigour, no European country was as overwhelmed with numbers as China. Population pressure there could lead to the collapse of a dynasty. One can understand why the very idea of progress originated in the West rather than in the more convulsive East.

Perhaps the explanations of Europe's rise were human qualities and human toil, coupled with Europe's resources. It was a matter of success breeding success. Not least important was the self-transformation that Europe underwent as a result of the discovery and colonization of the New World, and the discovery of new sea routes to Asia. Europe could not embrace the whole world without being profoundly affected by it. However we explain the rise of the West[8] – and we cannot account for it if we ignore the fortuitous conjunction of circumstances of the time, such as the relative decline of Asian empires and the narrow margin by which the Christian armies triumphed over their Muslim opponents before Vienna in 1529 – we do know that Europe's success bred a sense of superiority and illusions of grandeur, from which stemmed its megalomania and the will to power.

Finally, it was the West that developed and adhered to the rule of law. Legalism in China is as old as China's first emperor, Ch'in (third century BC), but too often Chinese law has been used by its rulers as an instrument of convenience. Mao Zedong (1893–1976) himself explicitly admitted this.

Whereas the stress in the Occident came to be placed upon action, tension and change, upon increased social mobility, upon reason, logic and linear progress, the emphasis in the Orient remained upon the collective, upon harmony, stability and continuity. The Orient has never separated itself from the past; it does not make such fine distinctions as the West between past, present and future. Its world view was the antithesis of Western logic and rationality upon which the rise of the West was based.

4

Europe: 1500–1914

In contrast to the dominant continent it would became, Europe in the first millennium AD was the scene of an unending fight for survival. In the seventh and eighth centuries it was attacked by Arab Muslim invaders who struck through Spain and later through the Balkans. In the ninth and tenth centuries Asiatic nomad Magyar horsemen raided deep into Europe. From the eighth to the eleventh century Europe was threatened by the pagan Vikings, whose dragon-prowed ships penetrated its waterways, and whose plundering and murdering spread terror throughout Christendom. Later, in the thirteenth century, Europe was battered by the nomadic Mongols, who with astonishing speed and organization swept from the heartland of Asia through Eastern Europe to the shores of the Adriatic.

Indeed, an observer in 1500 might have concluded that the settled life of European Christendom was about to die, and that the great nomadic invasions of the Mongols and the Turks, who already ruled in China, India, Persia, Egypt, North Africa, the Balkans and Russia, were going to overrun Western Europe, too. Europe's future seemed to lie not with Christ, but with Mohammed. But then, in 1529, Christian Europe halted the Ottoman Turks at the gates of Vienna. However, it was only with the crumbling of the Ottoman Empire in the eighteenth century that the Turks finally ceased to threaten Europe and its unifying faith. By then the papacy and the Holy Roman Empire[1] had long since passed the peak of their spiritual and temporal power; the unity of the Church had given way to the unity of the nation.[2]

The deadliest threat to the unity of Christendom came not from foreign invasion but from within Christianity itself. In the fourteenth and fifteenth centuries the spiritual and temporal authority of both pope and emperor was increasingly challenged. In a growing urban, capitalistic economy, merchants were eager to free themselves of the Church's medieval moral restraint regarding usury, 'the just price' and 'the living wage'. When Pope Boniface VIII (reigned 1294–1303) tried to meet the growing criticism of the Church by declaring in a papal bull ('Unum Sanctam', 1302) that 'subjection to the Roman pontiff is absolutely necessary to salvation', the French king, Philip IV (reigned 1285–1314), openly defied him. When a French archbishop succeeded Boniface as Pope Clement V (1305–16) he moved his papal residence from Rome to Avignon in France, and from 1305 to 1377 the papacy remained under French influence. Two popes, one at Avignon and the other in Rome, indulged in a papal squabble that ended with each excommunicating the other. Even after 1409, when both pontiffs were deposed and a third was elected in their place, the Great Schism (1378–1418) in the Church remained. In fact, the disintegration of papal power was exacerbated, for there were now three popes to satisfy, all of whom claimed divine authority.

The decline of feudalism[3] between 1300 and 1450 had also stimulated the rise of Europe's dynastic states, whose interests were often contrary to that of the papacy and the Holy Roman Empire. The wars of the fourteenth and fifteenth centuries between France and England, as well as the political unification of Portugal and Spain, had fostered the growth of a nationalist spirit. As a result, relations between European monarchs and the pope deteriorated.

In 1414, in an attempt to re-establish Christian unity, the Holy Roman Emperor Sigismund summoned the leaders of the Church to a council at Constance in Switzerland. For the first time, members of the council voted not according to their position in the Church but as members of a nation, each nation having one vote. This was the last occasion on which the hierarchy of Latin Christendom met as a single commonwealth.

While the Council of Constance helped to heal the schism in the Church, it did not halt the decline of church authority. Nor did it silence the clash of doctrines about (among other things) the precise meaning of the Eucharist and the role of the Virgin Mary. Leading critics of church abuse and doctrine were: John Wycliffe (*c*. 1320–84), Master of Balliol College, Oxford; Jan Huss (*c*. 1369–1415), Rector of Prague University; and Girolamo Savonarola (1452–98), a Dominican priest in Florence. Wycliffe called for the establishment of a national church, for salvation as an individual matter and for the abandonment of the doctrine of transubstantiation. He refused to believe that any priest could convert bread and wine into the body and blood of the Saviour, and condemned the veneration of church relics as idolatrous. In his protests against church abuse, Huss was greatly influenced by Wycliffe. Unlike Wycliffe, he accepted the Church's doctrine on transubstantiation – which did not save him from being burned as a heretic in 1415. In 1419 there was an insurrection of Hussites in Bohemia; the war that followed was to be the precursor of many dreadful religious wars. Savonarola's aim was to reform the Church of its inequities under the Borgia Pope Alexander VI. Seen as a threat to the Church, he suffered the same fate as Huss. In 1511, in *Encomium moriae* (Praise of Folly), the leading Christian humanist Desiderius Erasmus (*c*. 1466–1536)[4] added his voice to those criticizing the Church, but he never suggested the overthrow of its authority.

Accompanying the revolt against the Church in the fourteenth and fifteenth centuries were widespread rebellions against serfdom and feudalism, which were cruelly suppressed.

By the time the German Augustinian friar Martin Luther (1483–1546)[5] nailed his 'ninety-five theses' to the door of the ducal chapel at Wittenberg (31 October 1517), it was too late for the Church to stem the tide of doubt and distrust; the Protestant Reformation was under way. 'Hier stehe ich, ich kann nicht anders' (Here I stand, I can do no other). In emphasizing that each man was his own priest, in placing scripture-based faith above priestly and papal authority, in rejecting the doctrine of transubstantiation, in denouncing the sale of indulgences for the remission of sins[6] and in rebuking the Church for its wealth, worldly power and corruption, Luther's criticisms had much in common with those of Wycliffe and Huss: conscience was at stake. Like Wycliffe, Luther translated the New Testament into the vernacular, so all men could now hear the Word in their own language. In his tract *An den christlichen Adel deutscher Nation* (*Appeal to the Christian Nobility of the German Nation*, 1520) he called upon the German princes to establish a national German church. In northern Germany no message could have been more politically appealing. In 1521 Luther was excommunicated; one year later he was tried and condemned as a heretic. Without the protection of the Elector of Saxony, who sheltered him, Luther would have died at the stake. Others had weakened Christian unity; unwittingly, Luther destroyed it. One hundred and fifty years later, the northern half of Europe, including Scandinavia, was Protestant.

When the Christian monarchs of France, Francis I (b. 1494; reigned 1515–47), and England, Henry VIII (b. 1491; reigned 1509–1547), had their spectacular meeting on the Field of the Cloth of Gold in 1520 at Calais, the concept of a Europe unified in a *res publica Christiana* was as good as dead. By then the countries of Christian Europe were all going their separate ways (see Map VI). Loyalty to the Christian ideal, to lord and king, would remain; loyalty to the pope and the Holy Roman Empire would diminish. In 1534 Henry VIII – whom the pope had called 'Defender of the Faith' – having failed to bend the Church to his will, denounced the papacy and, asserting national authority, declared himself 'Supreme Head of the Church of England'. For the first time a king was superior to the pope. Under the Tudors,[7] England became a truly national state, with Christendom replaced by a Machiavellian monarchy. Henry profited greatly from looting church property, but he was not the only European monarch to do so – the vast wealth of the Church was tempting bait.

The fires of dissent were fanned in 1541 when a new wave of Protestantism was launched from Geneva by the Frenchman John Calvin (1509–64).[8] His doctrine of predestination – God's elect were predestined for salvation – appealed strongly to middle-class interests. Following Luther, he believed that biblical authority took precedence over priestly mediation. His disciple John Knox (1505–72) launched the Reformation in Scotland, then ruled by

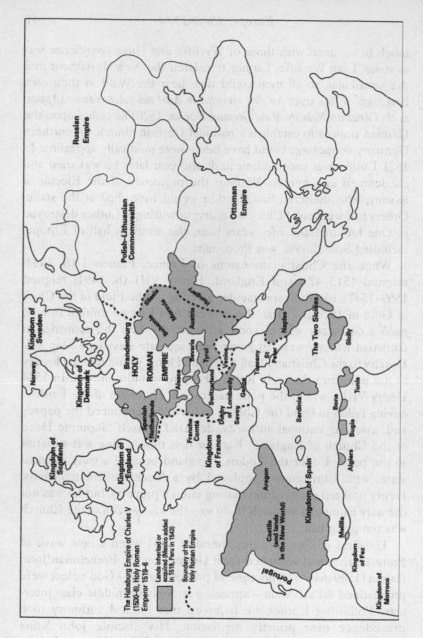

Map VI Europe in the Sixteenth Century

The Habsburg Empire of Charles V (1500–8), Holy Roman Emperor 1519–6

Lands inherited or acquired (Mexico added in 1519, Peru in 1543)

Boundary of the Holy Roman Empire

Russian Empire

Ottoman Empire

Polish–Lithuanian Commonwealth

Kingdom of Sweden

Norway

Kingdom of Denmark

Kingdom of Scotland

Kingdom of England

Brandenburg

Silesia

Lusatia

Moravia

Hungary

Bohemia

HOLY ROMAN EMPIRE

Austria

Bavaria

Tyrol

Alsace

Switzerland

Venice

Duchy of Lombardy

Franche Comté

Savoy

Genoa

St Peter

Tuscany

Naples

The Two Sicilies

Sicily

Sardinia

Kingdom of France

Spanish Netherlands

Aragon

Castile (and lands in the New World)

Kingdom of Spain

Portugal

Kingdom of Fez

Kingdom of Morocco

Melilla

Bone

Bugia

Tunis

Algiers

Catholic Mary Stuart (b. 1542; reigned 1561–7; d. 1587), Queen of Scots.[9] In 1560 the Scottish Parliament severed its relations with Rome in favour of Knox's Scottish Presbyterian Church.

Five years earlier, at the Peace of Augsburg, the Holy Roman Emperor Charles V (1500–58; reigned 1519–56),[10] desperate to put an end to the incessant wars between Christian factions, had allowed each member state to follow the religion of its choice: 'Cuius regio, eius religio' (The rulers determine the religion). This decision ratified the idea of individual state supremacy: one state should not interfere in the affairs of another. The pope's authority over the moral lives of nations, even within the Christian commonwealth, was irreparably harmed. Thenceforth, nations would be their own moral arbiters; *raison d'état* and expediency, not moral principles, would direct the conduct of governments and nations. Charles V's hope of reuniting Christendom in a *res publica Christiana* was now lost. He abdicated, and with nearly 150 attendants sought seclusion in a monastery for the rest of his days. Weary of the intrigues of princes, he turned his attention to making his peace with God. There was also time to consider his gout, his diet and his many illnesses. In 1558 he died, and the Holy Roman Empire would continue as a ghost of its former self until Napoleon Bonaparte wrote *finis* to it in 1806.

Fortunately for the Roman Catholic Church, the Reformation did not deal a lethal blow to the papacy. In fact, it stirred the papacy to its most successful period of expansion outside Europe, where its moral authority increased.[11] The establishment of monastic orders was encouraged. Unique among them was the Society of Jesus, founded in 1534 (recognized by a papal bull in 1540) by the Spanish nobleman Ignatius de Loyola (1491–1556). Loyola's 'Soldiers of Christ', professing absolute obedience to the papacy, were soon to be found throughout Europe and in every corner of the globe. Through them, missionary energy returned to the Church. Their influence in theology, diplomacy, education, exploration, agriculture, the sciences and the arts is legendary. Within a century the Jesuits had become the most influential group of Catholic clerics.[12]

In 1535, in an attempt to meet the challenges being made to the unity of Christendom, Pope Paul III (reigned 1534–49) began an investigation into the need for reform. The report in 1537 led eventually to the establishment of the Council of Trent. The council, which met intermittently between 1545 and 1563, was the Church's response to the attacks made upon it by the Reformation. The council rejected compromise with the Protestants and upheld and strengthened the authority of the pope. (Only in the mid-twentieth century would the idea of a reunified Christendom be reborn.) The basic tenets of Catholic faith were redefined: salvation required not only faith but also good works; the source of doctrine was not only scripture but also 'unwritten traditions', some of which had been received by the apostles from Christ Himself; the seven sacraments were reaffirmed, with special emphasis on transubstantiation; the usefulness of indulgences, the veneration of relics and the cult of the Virgin were approved. In addition, the Inquisition was founded to restore discipline among Christians.

The eventual breakdown of Christian unity plunged Europe into a long and bloody religious struggle in which Catholics and Protestants tried to destroy each other. The German states split into two hostile camps, most of the north becoming followers of Luther, with the south remaining Catholic. In the German principalities, religious wars became endemic. Central Europe, where the armies met, was wasted by fanatically waged religious wars[13] in which every kind of outrage was perpetrated. Extremism thrived; madness prevailed. Luther was so shocked at the excesses committed in God's name that he shifted from loyalty to the people to support of the princes. His chief concern became not greater freedom but greater order.

Between 1562 and 1598, under Henry IV, King of France (b. 1553; reigned 1589–1610), religiously inspired civil wars dominated his country. Peace was achieved only with the acknowledgement of Catholicism as the official religion of France. The Edict of Nantes (1598) guaranteed French Protestants (the Huguenots) religious, civil and political rights.

Spain fought almost constant wars of religion, first against the Moors, then against France, Holland and Protestant England. Philip II (reigned 1556–98), Spain's 'most Catholic king', seemed blind to everything except the need to defend the Catholic faith. His father,

Charles V, had hoped to link Spain, Holland and England in one grand Christian maritime union by marrying Philip to the Catholic Mary Tudor of England in 1554. But Mary died, and (the English having taken care to ensure that Philip would not succeed Mary) the Protestant Elizabeth I (reigned 1558–1603) ascended the throne. England was lost to the Spanish Catholic cause.

The religious wars of 1618–48 (the Thirty Years War) were also a continuous dynastic struggle between the Spanish and Austrian Habsburgs and the French Bourbons. Only after these conflicts ended, with about two million battlefield deaths, were the religious and political frontiers in Europe given some permanence; only then did European politics become relatively free of religious passion; only then did the Peace of Augsburg of 1555, with its stress on nationalism, become a reality.

The outcome of the disunity within the universal Christian Church was the decline of the power of the pope and the holy Roman emperor. In their place appeared a variety of national states, all of them concerned with national territory, power, prestige, wealth, security and independence; each of them at dagger's point with the others; all of them prepared to switch sides for the slightest political gain; all of them unsettled, ambitious, creative and dynamic. For three hundred years – with weaponry, tactics and strategy developing continuously – the struggles of these territorial states, both in Europe and in the rest of the world, were incessant. Spain led in the seventeenth century, France in the eighteenth and early nineteenth, and Britain from then until the First World War. In these struggles, moral and religious scruples were discarded. France on two occasions even allied itself with the Turkish infidel.

Monarchical and national rivalries were also responsible for the European wars of the sixteenth, seventeenth and eighteenth centuries. In the War of the Spanish Succession (1701–14) the Austrians, the Dutch and the English intervened to prevent France from seizing Spain's empire. In the Great Northern War (1700–21), caused by the general opposition of Russia, Poland and Denmark to Swedish supremacy in the Baltic region, Russia wrested the provinces of Livonia and Estonia from Swedish control. In 1709 at

Poltava, Peter the Great defeated the Swedes. The outcome was a further reduction in Swedish power, which had been in decline since the 1650s. In the War of the Austrian Succession (1740–8), Friedrich II of Prussia forced the Austrians under Maria Theresa (b. 1717; reigned 1740–80) to relinquish all claims to Silesia. In the Seven Years War (1756–63) Prussia was enlarged at the expense of Austria (though the coffers of both countries were emptied). This war also allowed England to surpass French power in North America, India and the Caribbean.

Since the beginning of the sixteenth century, Europe's internal struggles were accompanied by struggles of world dimension. The first European monarch to demonstrate his nation's might on a world scale was Portugal's Manoel I (reigned 1495–1521), 'Lord of the Conquest, Navigation and Commerce of India, Ethiopia, Arabia and Persia'. By 1511 the Portuguese had taken the strategic Strait of Malacca – a key position in their control of the spice trade of the East. In 1519 Magellan, a Portuguese in the employment of Spain, attempted to sail around the world in a heroic voyage of eighty-nine days. Where Portugal led, Spain followed. Beginning with the voyage of Columbus, the Spaniards eventually made their way around the globe. The only limits to Iberian expansion were those set by the other European powers – Britain, France and the Netherlands. Of these, Britain became Spain's nemesis.

From hoping at one time to rule England, Philip II came to fear it. Elizabeth I and her Protestant adventurers were determined to break the grip of the Catholic Iberians around the world. English 'pirates' preyed on Spanish possessions and Spanish treasure fleets interminably. In 1562 John Hawkins (1532–95) challenged the Spanish monopoly in the transatlantic slave trade. In 1577 Francis Drake (*c.* 1540–96) sacked Spain's American colonies and seized a Spanish treasure ship in the mid-Pacific. The booty he brought back in the *Golden Hind* is said to have been 'the fountain and origin of British foreign investment'. In 1585 England sent an army of six thousand men to fight with the Dutch against Spain in the Netherlands. Two years later Drake and other English sea captains destroyed the Spanish fleet at Cadiz. Any hopes that Philip II may have entertained to remove Elizabeth in favour of her Catholic cousin, Mary Stuart, Queen of Scots, ended with Mary's execution in 1587. In desperation, the next year Philip launched his 'Invincible Armada' against England.

While Spain's vast empire in Europe, the Americas, North Africa and Asia had passed the height of its power by 1600, its navy was still the equal of the English and the Dutch combined. Yet the loss of the Armada undoubtedly undermined its leading position at sea and provided a serious challenge to its global power. Spain's spurning of commerce and capitalism meant that much of the wealth of its majestic empire ended up in British and Dutch hands. In the sixteenth and seventeenth centuries it was the Dutch fleet that carried Spain's colonial products from the Iberian peninsula to Northern Europe. Much of the profit of Spain's colonial trade went to British North American merchants who spent their gains in England. Smugglers and buccaneers also waxed fat off Spain's wealth. Spain became so weak that in 1640 the Portuguese were able to reassert their independence from it.

After the Treaty of Utrecht in 1713 – the first treaty specifically to consider the need for a 'balance of power'; the last to refer to Europe as *res publica Christiana* – Britain openly penetrated Spain's American colonies from the West Indies. Thereafter, for more than a century, Spain had to defend its empire in the New World from those who would bring it down. Because of Spain's constant wars in Europe and the New World, between 1492 and 1700 its population had fallen from nine to six million. The campaigns of Charles V, the Thirty Years War and the wars of the Austrian and Spanish Successions had all drained Spanish resources. By the time of the War of Jenkins' Ear (1739–40) – a conflict that sprang from the harsh treatment by Spain of English smugglers at sea – Spain was unable to assert its will. In 1744 England's Admiral Hanson, ignoring Spanish protests, entered the Pacific. Three years later the last Spanish bullion convoy set sail for Spain from Vera Cruz, Mexico.

In many ways Spain's history is unique. Sheltered from the rest of Europe by the Pyrenees, the Spaniards never accepted the secularism of the Renaissance, the pluralism of the Reformation or the general demand for change. The great commercial, scientific and industrial revolutions taking root in sixteenth-century Europe also left Spain largely undisturbed. The Spaniards took little part in the expansion of commerce from the seventeenth century onwards. Money and the values of the market place – however stimulating to the development of the nation state – were never allowed to play the dominant roles that they did elsewhere. Unlike their commercial rivals, Britain and the Netherlands, Spain did not develop a middle class. In contrast, wealth to the British and Dutch Protestants, instead of being shunned, was a sign of God's providence as well as a reward for their own industry.

Heeding the warning of the Spanish philosopher Lucius Annaeus Seneca (*c.* 4 BC–AD 65), 'From the time money came to be regarded with honour, the real value of things was forgotten,'[14] the Spaniards seem to have disregarded the loss of money as they disregarded the loss of blood. Like Don Quixote, they pointed and fought in all directions at once. Between 1500 and 1659 they fought in every dynastic and religious struggle they could find. With brief interludes, they fought France for fifty years and the Dutch for eighty. Always, they fought the Turks. Peace with England when it came was always forced. They remained deaf to the warnings of contemporaries that war – with its staggering costs and its consequent runaway inflation – would undo them. For a hundred years, in a great and prolonged drama, Spain also fought those who were trying to tear apart its empire. Well might Philip II's motto be *Nec Pluribus Impar* (A Match for Many).

Fortunately for Spain, while it showed no enthusiasm for the patient, organized work that modern science, industry and the capitalist system demanded, it was able to obtain wealth elsewhere. In addition to windfall gains in precious metals from South America, Spain drew upon the income obtained from Castile taxes, and the growing mercantile wealth of Italy and the Lowlands. Before the inroads made by the British and the Dutch, Spain also had a virtual monopoly of the slave, spice (mainly pepper, cinnamon, cloves and nutmeg) and sugar trades. Thus did a relatively poor, unimportant nation rise to power and prominence. Astonishingly, though wallowing in wealth, Spain went bankrupt regularly. Charles V, whose revenues were consumed by interest payments on past debts, had insufficient funds to bury his mother, Joan the Mad. In 1556 Philip

II inherited an empty treasury. Three times in his reign (1556–98), and five times between 1557 and 1627, Spain was bankrupt. When Philip died, the official debt of 20 million ducats, which he had inherited, had risen to 100 million.[15] Said Spain's Don Francisco de Quevedo y Villegas (1580–1645): 'As poor men we conquered the riches of others; as rich men these same riches are conquering us.'

After the defeat of the Armada, Spain, its crusading spirit spent, its earlier vigour and vitality lost, preferred to withdraw from the centre of the European stage and sleep. In the material realm – though not in the religious sphere, where Spain was influenced by the mystics St Teresa of Avila and St John of the Cross – the country passed from 'wanting to be too much, to too much wanting not to be'.

In terms of territorial aggrandizement, Spain achieved what it did not only because of the material and spiritual elements of Christianity but because it exercised the power of a nation.[16] European expansion and the system of national states were born at the same time. The rise of nations such as Spain and their continual struggle for power heightened Western energies and provided an immeasurable impetus to Western expansion. For a period – perhaps until 1914 – European national states and European nationalism were the engines of change in the world. The so-called 'discoveries' – which were preceded by long rivalries between Spain and Portugal in the Atlantic – stemmed directly from the growth of central government in these newly founded rival nations.

France proved a powerful successor to Spain. In the mid-fifteenth century it had driven the English from continental Europe. On and off, from the 1290s until the 1450s, England, with whatever support it could raise on the continent, had fought France for control of Northern Europe, including Flanders, at that time the continent's industrial centre. But for Joan of Arc's triumph over the English at the Battle of Orleans in 1429, France might have become a vassal of England.

In the 1490s the French under Charles VIII (b. 1470; reigned 1483–98) extended their power to Italy. Because Italy was too weak and too divided to resist invasion, it was fought over by France and

Spain. Without a common rule or government, its separate states –
Naples, Sicily, Venice, Genoa, Lucca, Milan, Florence and Piedmont
– were menaced by all; only Venice managed to keep its would-be
conquerors at bay.

In the seventeenth and eighteenth centuries France fought
Britain around the world. With the sole exception of the War of
American Independence (1775–83), Britain emerged triumphant.
Nothing served it as well as the English Channel, which had deterred
one French king after another. After 1066, Britain never again fought
a battle on its own soil against a European enemy. In contrast, France
suffered from its continental vulnerability. In the Seven Years War
(1756–63) it failed to stop the British from controlling the Atlantic
and isolating French forces in North America (see Map III). France,
like Spain, was both a land and a sea power. The wars it fought
between 1688 and 1815 were always double wars – a war in Europe
and a war abroad. During the Seven Years War it fought the British
overseas and the Germans in Europe simultaneously.

England had the advantage over France not only in terms of location and insularity; its very compactness had encouraged national
unity, centralized government and the rule of law. By 1500 the first
of the English Tudors, Henry VII (b. 1457; reigned 1485–1509), had
become firmly established on the English throne. In Elizabeth I,
Tudor England found the strongest queen it had ever had. Crowned
at twenty-five, for forty years she outwitted and outfought all
England's enemies. It was during her reign that the foundations of
Britain's future maritime predominance – to say nothing of its growing
strength in finance and trade – were laid. Gradually, Britain concentrated its efforts on controlling the sea lanes of the world. By the
eighteenth century sea power had become the basis of all British
strategy. 'Rule Britannia, Britannia rules the waves' was first sung in
1740. By then, English parliamentarianism and constitutionalism had
triumphed over monarchical absolutism, such as that enjoyed by
Louis XIV (b. 1638; reigned 1643–1715) in France. In the struggle
between Parliament and the Crown, England could fall back on the
Magna Carta (the Great Charter) forced from King John (b. 1167;
reigned 1199–1216) in 1215, which limited royal power. In 1628
Parliament's Petition of Right, which dealt with the limitation of the

powers of the king, cited the Great Charter again. Charles I's (b. 1600; reigned 1625–49) dismissal of Parliament cost him his life on the scaffold. The trial and execution of a king sent a chill through the courts of Europe. The people under God, not the king, had asserted themselves.

The fight against the divine right of kings was played out in the English Civil War (1642–8), out of which the military dictator Oliver Cromwell (1599–1658) emerged as the victor and Charles I as the victim. Parliamentarianism was furthered by the 'Glorious Revolution' against James II in 1688. In deposing this Catholic king in favour of Protestant William of Orange – ruler of the Dutch – Parliament determined the conditions under which an English sovereign could rule. In 1707 the union between England and Scotland was sealed. In 1714, for its own reasons, Parliament appointed the Protestant Elector of Hanover as King George I (reigned 1714–27). The common people were not consulted. He was followed by George II (reigned 1727–60) and George III (b. 1738; reigned 1760–1820).

The French were eventually undone by the British on both sea and land. France's dream of supremacy at sea – much desired by Louis XIV and his chief finance minister, Jean Baptiste Colbert (1619–83) – died in May 1692 at the Battle of Cap de La Hogue. With this defeat, Louis's intention of restoring the Catholic James II to the English throne was also abandoned. Despite Louis's extraordinary capacity for bribery, which he thought more sensible than war, France's dream of supremacy on land ended with its defeat at the Battle of Blenheim in 1704. In that battle, John Churchill, 1st Duke of Marlborough, allied with Eugene of Savoy, inflicted the greatest defeat that France had suffered in fifty years. This preserved the alliance of England, Austria and the United Provinces of the Netherlands against France, and eliminated Bavaria from the War of the Spanish Succession. It only remained for French arms to be defeated in India (1747) and North America (1759). Thereafter, Britain's concern was how best to maintain the balance of power in Europe.

In 1763 – at the time of the Treaty of Paris – France emerged from the century-long struggle with Britain with a ruined foreign trade, a depleted treasury and a hurt pride. (Its pride would be somewhat restored when it helped the American colonists to defeat Britain at Yorktown in 1781.) Its ruinous war-making, coupled with rampant inflation, helped to sow the seeds of the social discord that culminated in the French Revolution of 1789.

Among the other European powers who were to exercise great influence on European and world affairs after 1500 were the Spanish Netherlands (see Map VI). In the mid-sixteenth century this was one of the richest areas in Europe. Its population of about 2 million was small compared with that of Spain (approximately 8 million), France (approximately 20 million) and Britain (6 million), but what the Dutch lacked in numbers they made up for with their financial acumen, their fighting qualities, their skill as shipbuilders and their knowledge and command of the seas. Once the Dutch revolt against Spain had started in the 1560s, they fought the Spanish oppressors with one hand and founded a great colonial empire with the other. Holland became effectually independent in 1609.

Even more to their credit, in the seventeenth century the Dutch also experienced a remarkable flowering in the humanities. The Netherlands became a haven for some of the outstanding thinkers of the time. Seventeenth-century Holland was one of the few places in the Western world where a man could speculate freely without losing his head. One of the dissenter sects to take refuge there – the Pilgrims – chose to leave their Dutch hosts for an unexplored wilderness in America partly because of a fear that their children were being corrupted by such a religiously tolerant and materialistic society.

At the time of the truce with Spain in 1609, the Dutch felt sufficiently confident to found the Dutch Republic. In 1639 they placed the seal on their liberty by decisively defeating Spanish sea power before Dover in the Battle of the Downs. Spain never again attempted to conquer the northern half of the old Spanish Netherlands. The Peace of Westphalia in 1648, which largely determined the shape of Europe until the French Revolution, fully recognized the existence of the Dutch Republic.

Behind all Dutch triumphs was the sea – the focus of their energies. In the sixteenth century they had wrested control of the lucrative trade of Seville from Genoa. In their golden seventeenth century they built up an enormously profitable carrying trade in Europe and abroad.[17] While the Thirty Years War engulfed much of Europe, the Dutch fought to establish their rule on the major sea lanes of the world. It was they who first challenged the right of other powers to claim exclusive sovereignty over the oceans. Hugo Grotius, who declared the doctrine of the freedom of the seas – that every nation has equal rights on the ocean – was a Dutchman. Dutch intrusions into the Eastern seas, as well as into the Gulf of Mexico, had put the older doctrine of *mare clausum* to the test.

The harsh experience of Spanish occupation had made supreme political realists of the Dutch. In appealing to England for help against Spain they emphasized English interests. They realized that when England attacked Spanish troops in the Netherlands – as Elizabeth I did openly in 1587 – it would not be striking a blow for its fellow Protestant 'rebels' but for England. Elizabeth came to their aid because she reasoned – as English leaders have reasoned ever since – that wars are better fought on foreign soil.

The Dutch were as realistic about trade as they were about politics. The sole purpose of the Dutch East Indies Company (founded in 1602, and which soon became the largest trading company in Europe) was not to explore the world, or save it for Christianity (as Portugal and Spain had tried to do), but to increase its share of the newly found Eastern commerce. Strategic bases rather than territory were their aim. In 1641 they took Malacca from the Portuguese; and challenged Portuguese trade in China and Japan. On the one occasion they mixed Calvinism with commerce – in their West Indies Company – they did poorly. Nor did they have any disinclination towards money-making, as some of the Iberians had had. On the contrary, like Florence and Venice before them, emphasizing the necessary unity of business and politics, the voice of the merchant was heard wherever policy was made. Because they were commercially oriented, they were quick to use the financial talents possessed by the Portuguese Jews who had fled the Spanish Inquisition. In the last quarter of the seventeenth century money was so plentiful in the Netherlands that the interest rate in Amsterdam was below that in London.

While the Dutch were excelling in navigation, commerce and

politics, they were also making outstanding contributions in other fields. Dutch artisans, shipbuilders, canal lock builders, merchants, architects and engineers were employed throughout Europe. They were the forerunners of the nineteenth- and twentieth-century Western highly skilled workers overseas.

However, for the Dutch, as for the other Europeans, there was to be no profit without war. The end of the long expansion of the Baltic grain trade in 1651 resulted in a trade war being fought by them against the English and the French. In 1652 they began the first of three naval wars with their chief rival at sea and in world trade – the English. The struggle arose directly out of their desire to exploit the highly profitable trade of Malacca, India, the Malay Archipelago and Macao, and to fight against the introduction of trade restrictions brought about by the English Navigation Laws of 1650 and 1651. Thenceforth, economic warfare would become an acceptable instrument of power to be exploited by all states. In the second Anglo-Dutch War (1665–7), when the Dutch sailed up the Thames and burned an English fleet, the stakes were still the same and the outcome equally indecisive, except that the Netherlands abandoned claims to New Amsterdam (New York) in exchange for the return of Suriname. In the third Anglo-Dutch War (1672–4) France again joined Britain against the Dutch. Later, France fought both England and the Netherlands. By the beginning of the eighteenth century, England had come to fear the French more than the Dutch and expediently had thrown in its lot with the Netherlands.

The drain on Dutch resources was not limited to the cost of the wars against the English and the French. In an age that accepted war as a form of diplomacy, the Dutch intervened in the Swedish-Danish War (1657–61) to prevent Sweden closing the Baltic to the Dutch grain trade. Also in the 1650s they fought Portugal over Brazil. In the East Indies they were forever suppressing native insurrections. Year after year, the Netherlands could never shake itself free of war. Eventually, the rapidly rising costs of making endless war outran Dutch ability to make money.

The turning point in Dutch fortunes in the seventeenth and eighteenth centuries is difficult to discern. Perhaps the War of the Spanish Succession marked the decline of Dutch power in India and the East

– though for another seventy years after 1713 the volume of Dutch world trade remained about the same. Eventually, however, they lost their lead at sea. There was also a problem of shallow harbours, a growing inability to compete as shipbuilders and middlemen, a neglect of manufacturing and fishery, stagnation in their population and the migration of Dutch capital and labour. Yet it was not so much a matter of the Dutch falling short of their own past efforts as their inability to match England's superior performance.

Dutch decline was matched by Prussia's rise. By the mid-seventeenth century, Prussia had become one of the many separate provinces into which the Holy Roman Empire of the German nation had been divided. In the thirteenth century the empire had consisted of the territory ruled by successive German kings. The Peace of Westphalia, which in 1648 ended the Thirty Years War, ratified the existence of more than three hundred such sovereign German principalities or petty states, divorced from the higher authority of pope and emperor. This plethora of German states retarded the evolution of a mature German nationalism. France and Britain were nations in the 1400s. The United States was a nation in the 1700s. Germany did not become a unified nation until the second half of the nineteenth century.

Not until the reigns of Friedrich I (1657–1713), who was crowned Prussia's first monarch in 1701, Friedrich Wilhelm I (b. 1688; reigned 1713–40) and his son Friedrich II, the Great (b. 1712; reigned 1740–86), did Prussia's power begin to grow. Indeed, until the beginning of the eighteenth century, Brandenburg-Prussia was outstripped in wealth and numbers by Bavaria. By the time of the War of the Austrian Succession (1739–48), in which between 300,000 and 400,000 men were killed, things had changed. Prussia had become 'not a state with an army, but an army with a state'. For Prussia, nothing succeeded like military success. In the Silesian Wars (1740–2, 1744–5 and 1756–63) Friedrich II eventually forced the Austrians to surrender all claims to Silesia (see Map VI). Although he had written a book[18] against the unprincipled Realpolitik of Machiavelli, he had no scruples in doing what was best for Prussia. 'The question of right', he said to his foreign secretary when Prussia was about to take Silesia, 'is for you to elaborate . . . the orders for the army have already been issued.' Through warfare, Friedrich II increased the area of Prussia by more than one-third, and made the Hohenzollern kingdom a European power strong enough to resist Austro-Russian attempts to recover Silesia during the Seven Years War, not least because in Silesia Friedrich II had at his disposal Germany's first heavy industries and weaponry.[19]

Prussia's rise might have ended with its crushing defeat by the Russians at Kunersdorf in 1759, but then Russia withdrew, and Britain triumphed over France. The subsequent stalemate peace of Hubertusburg in 1763 (by which time approximately one million men had died on the various battlefields) allowed Prussia to survive as a great power; in doing so it set the stage for the later struggle between Austria and Prussia for the mastery first of Germany and then of the whole of Europe.

Whereas in the eighteenth century the Europeans fought each other for strategic points and for mastery of the high seas of the world, from 1800 to 1918, on and off, they fought each other at home.[20] The event that was to cause the longest of these wars was the revolution that broke out in France in 1789;[21] it was to bring changes to every corner of the continent. As an elite and middle-class rather than a working-class revolt, the French Revolution opposed absolute monarchy and the existing state control of the economy. In this it had been preceded by the English Civil War and the American War of Independence. The Declaration of the Rights of Man was made in America in 1789. The French Revolution also strengthened the movement for individual rights, written constitutions, equality against privilege (secular and spiritual) and the assertion of national independence. As a result of the developments in France, a number of small republics sprang up in Europe.[22] The role played by Europe's changing attitude towards government was paramount. The theory of government expounded by John Locke (1623–1704) in 1688 ('government with the consent of the governed'), which was meant to justify the English seventeenth-century revolution and the end of absolute monarchy, underlay a good deal of contemporary French philosophical thought. Along with liberalism and self-government, the idea of nationalism – of loyalty to a nation rather than to an absolute monarch – was perhaps the most influential. Out of this intellectual ferment came the decree of the French Convention on 19 November 1792, which offered fraternity and assistance to all peoples wishing to recover their liberty. Instead of ensuring liberty, however, the revolution resulted in a 'reign of terror' and a deplorable cheapening of human life. The despotism of a score of men who led the revolution, including Georges Jacques Danton (1759–94), Maximilien Robespierre (1758–94) and Louis Saint-Just (1767–94), was unprecedented. They coerced a nation of twenty-seven million, arrested hundreds of thousands and put thousands to death. Not liberty but the guillotine became the symbol of France.

The French Revolution also spawned the concept of total war. The idea expressed in the Convention's decree of 23 August 1793 that 'all Frenchmen are permanently required for service in the armies' marked the beginning of a nation in arms. King and God had been replaced by the People and the State. As in the religious wars of the sixteenth and seventeenth centuries, a note of fanaticism and unparalleled zeal entered international relations. Under the French *tricolore*, all wrongs would be righted; a new world order was afoot in which there would be freedom for all.

In addition to changing the purpose of war, the scale of combat was also altered: millions of men were mobilized. In the mid-eighteenth century France, with a population of more than 20 million, had an army of only 200,000. Austria had half that number. When the Duke of Marlborough (1650–1722) fought the Battle of Blenheim in 1704, the British army boasted about 70,000 men; in the 1780s its total strength of soldiers and sailors did not exceed the number of men in the Prussian army – about 200,000. The French Revolution changed all this: it brought about the conscription of the masses.

Although Prussia and Austria began the struggle against revolutionary France in 1792 (the French queen Marie Antoinette (1755–93), who faced execution, was an Austrian Habsburg), it was Britain, led by William Pitt the Younger (1759–1806), that wore down France and eventually stripped it of its power. Britain was the only country that the French were never able to conquer. In the coalitions formed against France from 1792 to 1815, Britain, from the security of its island, played the leading role. The first of these coalitions, which endured from 1792 to 1797, was formed when France declared war on Austria, Prussia and Savoy. The issue was whether dynastic monarchy or French revolutionary nationalism should govern Europe. The execution of Louis XVI and his queen and many of the French nobility, coupled with a counter-attack made by France against Prussia and Austria, caused Britain, the Netherlands, Spain and Sardinia to join the Prussians and Austrians.

Without British gold, there might never have been a coalition.[23] Not even this united front, however, could stem the French tide. In 1792–3 the French defeated the allies in the Netherlands. Two years later the Netherlands, Prussia, several German principalities and Spain were forced to come to terms. In 1796 the French invaded northern Italy and southern Germany. Venice (the dominant maritime power of the Middle Ages) was overwhelmed. The extraordinary fervour of the French army shattered whatever stood in its way. Distinguishing himself in the Italian campaign was a young general, Napoleon Bonaparte (1769–1821),[24] who later, as the Emperor of France, would see war not as the failure of diplomacy but as the core of foreign policy. In 1797 Austria, the last of Britain's continental allies, was forced to sue for peace.

Britain was able to hang on when all others had succumbed because of its strength at sea. Defeated by the French at Yorktown in 1781, by 1796 the British navy had reasserted itself in the West Indies at the Battle of the Saints, where it had shown itself the master of the French navy and mercantile marine. In 1797 at the Battle of Cape St Vincent (Portugal), it triumphed over the combined French–Spanish fleet. Never throughout this period did Britain lose its grip on the Atlantic, the North Sea or the sea routes to the East.

The second coalition was formed in 1798 when Britain found a new continental ally in Russia, which also feared French expansion. Austria, Naples (including Sicily and the Vatican), Portugal and the Ottoman Empire, whose interests were also imperilled, soon joined them. At the Battle of the Nile (1798), Admiral Horatio Nelson (1758–1805) thwarted Napoleon's attempt to sever Britain's sea route to the East. At one stroke, he restored the Mediterranean to British control.

Undeterred, Napoleon returned to France (he was then only thirty years of age), where he promptly seized power from an impotent and corrupt government. Within a year, through a series of brilliant victories, he restored French pride. Every major power had been removed from the field save Britain and Austria. With the French victory over the Austrian army at Marengo in Italy in 1800, Britain stood alone.

The third coalition against France was formed by Britain in 1805 and comprised Britain, Austria, Russia and Sweden. Spain on this occasion had switched sides and had allied itself with France. This coalition, however, fared no better than the first or the second. In 1805, abandoning his plans for an invasion of England, Napoleon proceeded to destroy Britain's allies once more. Before Christmas of that year, after an unprecedented march from the English Channel, he defeated the Austrians at Ulm and the combined Austrians and the Russians at Austerlitz. The Austrians sued for terms; the Russians retreated. In the following year Napoleon destroyed the Prussian army at Jena and Auerstädt in Saxony. Overcome by the Prussian army's defeat, the German philosopher Hegel concluded that history had come to an end. In 1807, following Russian defeats at Eylau and Friedland, Russia abandoned the fight. Napoleon was master of the continent of Europe.

Realizing that not even his brilliant victories could undermine Britain's superior industrial and commercial strength, Napoleon decided to deny Britain access to continental markets and thus weaken it economically. Without command of the seas, however, France was unable to seal off the continent from Britain. British attacks on Copenhagen (1801) and British naval power in the Baltic neutralized French efforts. Nelson's victory over the French at Trafalgar (Spain) in 1805 gave Britain and the Royal Navy control of the oceans of the world for another century.

Following his greatest victories, Napoleon made his greatest mistakes. In 1808, in support of his brother Joseph, who ruled Spain between 1808 and 1813, he sent a quarter of a million men over the Pyrenees, whereupon the British entered the fray. Although defeated, Britain was able to evacuate its army from Corunna in northwest Spain in 1809. With command of the sea, it was able to send and maintain another army under Lord Arthur Wellesley (1769–1852; later the 1st Duke of Wellington) for a further four years. Eventually, Britain's decisive victory at Vittoria on 21 June 1813 ended French rule in Spain.

Napoleon's second and greatest error was his decision in 1812 to invade Russia. This prompted Britain to form a fourth coalition against him. In June he set out from France with about 600,000 men, probably the largest European army assembled until then. Its flanks were guarded by Austrians and Prussians who also feared the Russians. On 14 September, a week after his costly victory at Borodino (about 70 miles west of Moscow), where seventy thousand soldiers died in one day, Napoleon entered Moscow. Five weeks later, the Russians having refused either to come to terms or to make battle, the emperor began his famous retreat from the burnt-out city. Exposure, famine, illness (especially typhus) and Russian attacks took a horrific toll on his army, of whom hundreds of thousands died. Perhaps one French soldier in ten eventually made his way back to France.

In the following year Napoleon was defeated at Leipzig with the loss of another thirty thousand men. Unable to defend Paris, he surrendered, abdicated the throne unconditionally and was exiled in April 1814 to Elba in the Mediterranean. After his escape from the island in March 1815, he was finally defeated by the combined armies of Belgium, Britain, the Netherlands and Prussia one hundred days later at Waterloo – where another eighty thousand men died. Exiled this time to St Helena in the South Atlantic (under much more penurious conditions), he died there in 1821. Far from establishing a united Europe under French command, he accelerated the growth of nationalism, which would eventually lead to the First World War.

Though ultimately defeated, Napoleon has remained a giant on the world stage. His genius extended far beyond the battlefield. He was responsible for changing the administrative and judicial systems of France, and for leaving behind him the enduring Code Napoléon, promulgated between 1804 and 1810, which he considered his most significant contribution. Its influence would be felt in legal reform as far afield as South America and Japan. He also fostered higher education and scientific enquiry, and was always keen to have 'men of talent' around him. His decision to bring the Jews out of the French ghetto was regarded as one of his more humane acts. The Concordat made with the Vatican in 1801 would last until 1905.

After Napoleon's defeat before Paris in 1814, the four major victors – Britain, Russia, Prussia and Austria; now called 'the great powers' rather than 'the grand monarchies' – proceeded to settle the terms of peace at Vienna. Even Napoleon's dramatic escape from Elba and his attempt to regain power caused only a temporary lull in the negotiations. The first peace treaty of 30 May 1814 – in which the French and British statesmen Charles de Talleyrand (1754–1838) and Robert Stewart Castlereagh (1769–1822) played leading roles – was marked by aristocratic restraint.[25] Considering the havoc that Napoleon had wreaked in Europe, the allies were magnanimous. To shield the Channel ports from any future French attack, the Congress of Vienna created the Kingdom of the Netherlands, comprising the former Dutch Republic and Belgium. In addition, it created a German Confederation of thirty-nine states which replaced the Holy Roman Empire (dissolved by Napoleon in 1806). Austria gained territory from Poland, Italy, France and Bavaria. Prussia expanded into former Polish, Swedish and other German territories.

Sweden, which in 1809 had ceded Finland to Russia, obtained Norway from Denmark. Independent from Denmark since 1397, Sweden had become the dominant power in the Baltic under King Gustavus II Adolphus (reigned 1611–32) – a talented statesman and military innovator.[26] By invading its neighbours, Sweden had won most of the Baltic sea coast in the seventeenth century. Defeated by Russia in 1700–21, its power declined. The Napoleonic Wars marked the end of its aggressiveness. Since 1814, Sweden has remained neutral.[27] Norway was appeased by being granted a separate constitution (it became completely independent in 1905). Denmark's loss was offset by obtaining German Lauenburg. Of all the countries, Poland (whose power at one time stretched from the Baltic to the Black Sea) fared worst. The prey of Russia, Prussia and Austria, by 1795 it ceased to exist as a nation. Not until the First World War and the Treaty of Versailles (1919) did it regain its independence.

The second peace treaty at Vienna on 20 November 1815 – after Napoleon's defeat at Waterloo – was also lenient.[28] The terms might

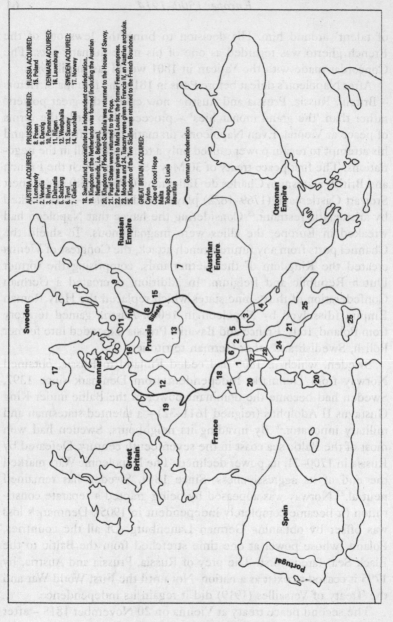

ACQUIRED:

AUSTRIA ACQUIRED:
1. Lombardy
2. Venetia
3. Illyria
4. Dalmatia
5. Salzburg
6. Tyrol
7. Galicia

PRUSSIA ACQUIRED:
8. Posen
9. Danzig
10. Pomerania
11. Rügen
12. Westphalia
13. Saxony
14. Neuchatel

RUSSIA ACQUIRED:
15. Poland

DENMARK ACQUIRED:
16. Lauenburg

SWEDEN ACQUIRED:
17. Norway

18. Switzerland reconstituted as independent confederation.
19. Kingdom of the Netherlands was formed (including the Austrian Netherlands, i.e. Belgium).
20. Kingdom of Piedmont-Sardinia was returned to the House of Savoy.
21. Papal States were returned to the Pope.
22. Parma was given to Maria Louisa, the former French empress.
23. Modena and 24. Tuscany were given to Francis IV, an Austrian archduke.
25. Kingdom of the Two Sicilies was returned to the French Bourbons.

GREAT BRITAIN ACQUIRED:
Ceylon
Cape of Good Hope
Malta
Tobago, St Lucia
Mauritius

— — — German Confederation

Map VII Europe after the Napoleonic Wars, 1815

have been harsher if the great powers had not feared Russia, which stood at the peak of its strength under the tsarist regime. The more France came to be seen as the balance between Britain and Austria on the one side and Russia and Prussia on the other, the greater was the leniency shown it. In 1818 France was readmitted into the society of the great powers. Its expanded 1792 borders were confirmed, as were Britain's conquests in South Africa, Ceylon and Mauritius. Contrary to the Peace of Westphalia (1648), the powers undertook to intervene in the affairs of a sovereign state where chaos threatened.

The business of the Congress completed, Napoleon was bundled off unceremoniously to St Helena, 'as an enemy and disturber of the tranquillity of the world'. With the return of his body to France in 1840 – by which time the age of great monarchs had ended and the age of the great powers was well established – his legend began to grow.

Peace reigned in Europe until the Crimean War (1854–6) between Britain, France, Piedmont and Turkey, on one side, and Russia, on the other. The main threat to stability came from the internal disturbances within states, whose people – exploring their ethnic, linguistic and cultural roots – sought to replace the divine right of kings with the power of nationhood.

Traditionalism and the European monarchies, which had been re-established in 1815, came under attack from all sides.[29] A revolution in France in 1830 brought Louis Philippe (1773–1850) to the throne, but in 1848 the monarchy was overthrown and a second republic installed. In the 1830s Greece and Belgium won their national independence. The revolts that broke out in Poland, Denmark, Germany, Italy, Hungary, the Balkans and Romania in the 1830s and 1840s all ultimately failed. Yet while the old guard held on to power and privilege, the impulse to rebel remained. The revolt in Austria in 1848 led to French intervention and to the dual monarchy of Austria-Hungary in 1867. Barely, and only with the essential introduction of the Reform Bill of 1830, which greatly extended the franchise, was social peace maintained in Britain.

In meeting these internal challenges the divergent attitudes of the great powers became apparent. When in 1820 the tsar called upon the Quadruple Alliance of 1814 to suppress the new radical government in Spain,[30] Britain demurred. 'Things are getting back to a wholesome state again,' said Britain's foreign secretary, George Canning, in the 1820s, as the alliance of the European powers dissolved: 'Every nation for itself and God for us all.' The Quadruple Alliance of 1814 was followed by the Quintuple Alliance of 1818, which readmitted France into the society of the great powers.

Out of the mid-nineteenth-century revolts in Italy there emerged a modern state. Italy had been in revolt since Austria's reconquest of northern Italy in the 1840s. In 1859 the Austrians, having invaded Piedmont to put down a rising engineered by the premier of Sardinia-Piedmont, Count Camillo Benso di Cavour (b. 1810; premier 1851–61), were defeated by French troops under Napoleon III (b. 1808; reigned 1852–70; d. 1873). The French troops arrived at the front in six days by rail instead of the two months required by road. Thanks to Cavour, who was largely responsible for uniting Italy under the House of Savoy, Piedmont gained its independence, and France obtained Nice and Savoy. The next year Giuseppe Garibaldi (1807–82) and his guerrilla army of Red Shirts, having defeated a Neapolitan army in Sicily, took Naples. On his triumphal march to Rome Garibaldi met Victor Emmanuel II (1820–78),[31] King of Sardinia-Piedmont, whom he greeted as the King of Italy. Victor Emmanuel would not become king, however, until his kingdom was proclaimed by the first Italian parliament in March 1861. With the withdrawal of French troops from Rome in 1870, and the annexation of Rome as the kingdom's capital, Italy became truly free and united. The papacy's temporal power, which had been crucial at the Vienna peace conferences in 1815, ended.

While the years 1871–1914 are regarded as the longest peace between the European powers since Roman times, the uprisings in Russia (1905), Spain (1909), Portugal (1910) and Italy (1913) indicate that civil war was still in the air. Peace during these years was obtained because the greatest power – Britain – was peacefully inclined. Abandoning its earlier policy of crude force, it had become the executor of international law. The idea of such a law had been gathering force in the West since the appearance of sovereign states in the seventeenth century. Primarily, Britain's view was that of a satiated great power wanting only to enjoy its ever-growing domestic and foreign wealth undisturbed. Backed by the greatest navy on the seas, it was content to occupy its rightful place at the top. Provided the other powers conceded British supremacy, and the balance of world power remained in its favour, peace would be maintained. Britain saw no reason why it should join either with France and Russia, on the one hand, or Germany, Austria and Italy, on the other. Britain's role in the second half of the nineteenth century was to stand by uncommitted and keep the peace.

Of the four other European contestants for power (France, Russia, Prussia and Austria), Prussia offered the greatest challenge to British supremacy. Overwhelming Denmark in 1864, Austria in 1866 (which made Prussia the leader of all German states) and France in 1870–1, the Prussians had come to look upon themselves as invincible. When France declared war on them in 1870, most rulers expected French troops to be in Berlin within a few weeks. Instead, France was thoroughly beaten. There followed an uprising in Paris – the Commune – which was brutally suppressed. Because of their skill in mobilizing troops and moving them by rail, the Prussians were able to throw against the French twice the number of troops Napoleon had deployed against Russia. It was Prussia's victory over France in 1871 that caused other European states, especially Austria, to ally themselves with the Prussians. The myth of German-Austrian dualism died, and the idea of a Greater Germany was born. On 18 January 1871 at Versailles, Wilhelm I (1797–1888) was declared Emperor of All the Germans; the balance of power within Europe had been changed.

In Germany's struggle for European and world leadership, no one played a greater role than Count Otto von Bismarck (1815–98).[32] Holding the reins of power first as Minister President of Prussia (1862), and then as Chancellor of the German Empire from 1871 to 1890, he employed his policy of 'blood and iron' to ensure that Germany would become pre-eminent. He was convinced that France would one day try to regain Alsace-Lorraine, which had been claimed by Prussia after the war of 1870–1. France's recovery from that war was indeed much swifter than anyone had anticipated:

it paid its war indemnity of five million gold franks in two rather than four years. In 1873, in the hope of avoiding confrontation with the other European powers, as well as attempting to isolate France, Bismarck helped to form the League of the Three Emperors (Prussia, Austria-Hungary and Russia). Six years later, Germany forged an alliance with Austria-Hungary. This alliance, in so far as it ran counter to Russia's Balkan interests, was contrary to Bismarck's usual policy. Hence, the subsequent secret treaty made with Russia behind Austria's back.

Yet it was Russia, rather than France or Britain, that Germany feared most. Germany proceeded to strengthen its hand against Russia by encouraging France to annex Tunisia from an Ottoman Empire, by now in growing disarray. It also made a secret defence alliance in 1882 with Austria and a disenchanted Italy (which itself had hoped to seize Tunisia). Enjoying great-power status more by the courtesy of the other powers than through its martial skills ('Italy has such poor teeth and such a large appetite,' said Bismarck), Italy would remain disenchanted. Too shrewd to challenge the British Empire, throughout the 1870s and 1880s Bismarck worked to isolate or neutralize British actions. On a world front, Germany gained confidence from its intervention, along with Russia and France, in the Sino-Japanese War of 1894–5. On this occasion it was Germany, not Britain, that played the role of arbiter.

Supporting Germany's belief in its destiny as a great power and its right to come up in the world was its extraordinary development in every field in the second half of the nineteenth century. Germany's rise was fostered by the energy, discipline and unity of its people, by its resources and by its talent in science and technology – all of which would be put to the test in the war of 1914–18.

5

The Expansion of the Russian Empire

Russia's first settlers were Slavic tribes migrating from the west in the fifth century AD. In the ninth century the Slavs were themselves invaded by the Varangians, Scandinavian Vikings, who followed the Russian rivers to trade with Constantinople, capital of the Byzantine Empire. One group of Norsemen, called the Rus, established trading posts at Kiev and Novgorod in Slav territory. Kiev was the seed out of which the first Russian kingdom grew. In AD 989–90, soon after the Grand Prince of Kiev, Vladimir the Great (980–1015), embraced the Byzantine Orthodox Christian faith, the Kievian pagan state was forcibly converted to Christianity. From Kiev, the Eastern Orthodox faith spread to the other Russian principalities. Thenceforth, until the sacking of Russia by the Tatars[1] (the Mongols and their Turkic-speaking allies) in the thirteenth century, the infant Russian state – which was little more than a scattering of principalities – continued to extend its power and foster its relations with Byzantium.

Central to the story of Russia's past is the influence of war, want, struggle and suffering. Stalin once remarked:

> Old Russia . . . was ceaselessly beaten for her backwardness. She was beaten by the Mongol khans. She was beaten by the Turkish beys. She was beaten by the Swedish feudal lords. She was beaten

by the Polish-Lithuanian gentry. She was beaten by Anglo-French capitalists. She was beaten by the Japanese barons.[2]

But not all Russia's suffering has come from other hands as the Russian poet Yevgeny Yevtushenko (b. 1933) testifies:

> She was christened in childhood with a lash,
>> torn to pieces,
>>> scorched.
> Her soul was trampled by the feet,
>> inflicting blow upon blow,
>>> of Pechenegs,
>>>> Varangians,
>>>>> Tatars,
>> and our own people –
>>> much more terrible than the Tatars.

From these roots stem Russia's melancholia, paranoia, passivity, xenophobia and national self-pity.

Between the thirteenth and the fifteenth centuries, the Russians made war against the Tatar invaders. The Mongol yoke was a catastrophe of such proportions that Russians have never forgotten it. Only by submissively paying tribute and fighting for the Mongol Golden Horde were they tolerated. A Russian victory over a Mongol army at Kulikovo on the Don in 1380 – the first time that the Russians had beaten the Tatars – is a hallowed day in Russian history.[3] Kulikovo signalled the eventual waning of Mongol power and the waxing of the Russian state. Yet it was not until 1480, when Ivan III, the Great (b. 1440; Grand Duke of Moscow 1462–1505), refused to kiss the stirrup of the khan that Russia broke the vice-like grip of Mongol rule. It is thought that by then the Mongols had killed at least one-tenth of Russia's population and had deported many thousands into slavery.

When, in 1453, Constantinople perished at the hands of the Ottoman Turks, it was taken for granted that Moscow, the largest of the Russian principalities, would become the centre of Eastern Orthodox Christianity and Russian authority. (Kiev had been destroyed by the Mongols in 1240.) When Ivan III came to the Russian throne in 1462 – by which time Russians had successfully repulsed invasions by Lithuanians, Poles, Germans and Swedes – he emphasized Russia's connection with Byzantium by declaring himself the successor of the last of the Greek Byzantine emperors. He adopted as his insignia the Byzantine double-headed eagle. In 1471 the rival principalities of Novgorod and Kiev were subdued by Moscow; in 1485 Tver suffered the same fate; the fall of Pskov, Ryazan, Yaroslavl and Rostov followed. Underpinning Ivan III's autocratic rule was the expansion of the gentry cavalry, which became the corps of his army and reduced his dependence on the feudal lords. He also introduced the practice of recruiting infantry from the towns. His need of weapons was met by the English via Archangel on the White Sea.

In 1492 Ivan began Russia's westward expansion by invading Lithuania, reaching the coveted harbours of the Baltic Sea. The push to the sea – a traditional Russian goal – had begun in earnest. Before his death in 1505, by conquest or diplomacy, the unification of modern Russia had taken place. By the time his son Vasily III died in 1533 a nation had been born.

In 1547 the Kievian tradition of a confederation of equal sovereign princes gave way to the absolute rule of Ivan IV, the Terrible (b. 1530; Grand Duke of Moscow 1533–84), who was crowned Russia's first tsar in 1547. In 1560, on the death of his wife Anastasia Romanov, who he thought had been poisoned, he became increasingly mad. Suspecting conspiracies everywhere, he tolerated no one who questioned his authority. He wiped out individuals and whole communities who opposed him; in 1570 the citizens of Novgorod, suspected of sympathizing with the Poles and Lithuanians (who, regardless of the invasions of the Mongols and the Russians, had remained Roman Catholic and users of the Roman alphabet), were tortured to death. Ivan is said to have also killed his eldest son and heir in a fit of rage. Political opponents were exiled to the recently conquered territory (1581–3) of Siberia. As his reign progressed, he took all power from the assembly of boyars, the elite nobles who had advised him, and ruled single-handedly and dictatorially.

In the protracted and exhausting Livonian War of 1557–82, against Lithuanians, Poles and Swedes, Ivan seized the ports of Narva and

Dorpat in the eastern Baltic. In 1578, in the ongoing struggle with Sweden and Poland for the Baltic territories, Russia was defeated. The peace treaties that followed forced the tsar to renounce his territorial gains and cede additional territory to Sweden.

Ivan's son Feodor I inherited the throne, but power was seized by the regent Boris Godunov, who had been a close confidant of Ivan IV. Upon Feodor's death in 1598, Boris became tsar. During his reign peace was obtained with Poland and Sweden, while the colonization of the southern steppes continued. After Boris's sudden death in 1604, Russia was beset by a 'Time of Troubles'. In a state of utmost confusion the crown was fought over by rival claimants. Two of the pretenders claimed to be Ivan's murdered son Dmitri; several would-be tsars were murdered, deposed or died mysteriously. One of the Polish pretenders, supported by Poland and Lithuania, received widespread support and in 1605 was crowned tsar, but in 1610 Moscow was attacked by a rival Swedish force, which had its own candidate for tsar. In 1612 a national militia rid the city of the Poles and their candidate for the crown. In 1613 an urgently formed national assembly offered the throne to Prince Mikhail Romanov, grand-nephew of Ivan IV. The Romanovs stabilized the government and fought off the foreign invaders. They would remain the ruling dynasty until 1917.

Russian expansion was not limited to the west. In the sixteenth and seventeenth centuries it also fought its way eastward against the Mongols and the Turks (see Map VIII). In 1552 Ivan IV had seized Kazan, a Muslim Tatar stronghold on the middle Volga. (St Basil's Cathedral was built in Red Square to celebrate this victory.) With the fall of Kazan, the way was opened to cross the Urals into Siberia, an area rich in furs and minerals. A leading figure in the conquest of Siberia was the Cossack Yermak (d. 1584?). By 1700, Europeans were the majority there. Ivan's triumph also led to increased trade with Persia. Astrakhan on the Caspian Sea was taken in 1556. Yet Russian expansion eastward had constantly to be defended from the rear. In 1571 Moscow was once more sacked by an invading force of Crimean Tatars. For the remainder of the sixteenth and the whole of the seventeenth century, Russia colonized the valleys of the Dnieper, the Don and the Volga. With control

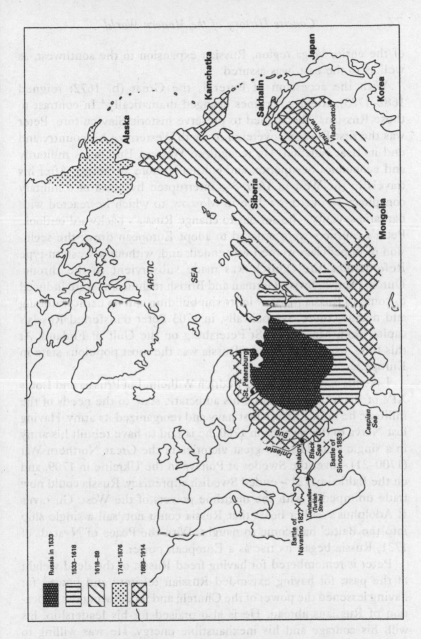

Map VIII Expansion of the Russian Empire, 1533–1914

Russia in 1533
1533–1618
1618–89
1741–1876
1689–1914

Alaska
Kamchatka
Sakhalin
Japan
Korea
Siberia
Mongolia
ARCTIC SEA
St. Petersburg
Bug
Dniester
Ochakov
Black Sea
Dardanelles (Turkish Straits)
Battle of Navarino 1827
Battle of Sinope 1853
Caspian Sea
Amur River
Vladivostok

of the entire Volga region, Russian expansion to the southwest, as well as to the east, was assured.

With the accession of Peter I, the Great (b. 1672; reigned 1682–1725), Russian fortunes changed dramatically.[4] In contrast to those Russians who wished to preserve historic Slav culture, Peter was the first Russian sovereign to try to Westernize his country and end its near isolation. He recognized Western Europe as militarily and economically superior, and culturally more advanced. After his travels in the West in 1697–8 – interrupted by news of a military conspiracy to overthrow him in Moscow, to which he reacted with barbaric severity – he set out to change Russia's backward outlook. Peter's courtiers were ordered to adopt European dress; the seclusion of upper-class women was ended; and, without a Western-type Reformation, the Church was made subservient to the throne. Dutch, Danish, Swiss, German and British technicians were induced to come to Russia to assist in its shipbuilding and its earliest mining and manufactures. Symbolically, in 1703 Peter transferred Russia's capital from Moscow to St Petersburg on the Gulf of Finland. At this time, except for France, Russia was the most populous state in Europe.[5]

Like his contemporaries Friedrich Wilhelm I of Prussia and Louis XIV of France, Peter geared his autocratic state to the needs of the military: he built Russia's first navy and reorganized its army. Having lost Narva to the Swedes in 1700, he is said to have rebuilt his army in a single year. His two great victories in the Great Northern War (1700–21) – over the Swedes at Poltava in the Ukraine in 1709, and on the Baltic in 1721 – ended Swedish supremacy. Russia could now trade unimpeded with the maritime powers of the West. Gustavus II Adolphus's earlier boast that Russia could not 'sail a single ship into the Baltic' had come to naught. With the Peace of Nystadt of 1721, Russia began its rise as a European power.

Peter is remembered for having freed Russia of the dead weight of the past; for having expanded Russian territory and power; for having lessened the power of the Church; and for allowing the education of Russians abroad. He is also praised for his leadership, his will, his courage and his inexhaustible energy. He was willing to learn from both East and West. Less favourable memories stem from his disregard of Russia's national traditions; for his introduction of Western manners and ways; for his subjection of the Orthodox Church to the state; and, finally, for his tyranny and brutality.[6]

Peter's objective – expansion at the expense of Sweden, Turkey and Poland – was furthered by Catherine the Great (b. 1729; reigned 1762–96), a German princess who came to the throne (after the murder of her husband, Peter III) with the support of British gold. Having helped to terminate the Seven Years War (1756–63), in which Russia had joined Austria and France against Prussia and Britain, Catherine was able to turn to other foreign challenges. Under her rule, Russia came to be feared by the Turks on the Black Sea as well as by the Swedes on the Baltic. Catherine's wars against the Turks (1768–74 and 1787–92) eventually brought the northern shores of the Black Sea under Russian control and strengthened her position in the Caucasus. The Crimea was annexed in 1783; Odessa was founded in 1794 as a southern outlet for Russian trade. In 1772, 1793 and 1795, the Polish–Lithuanian Commonwealth was divided between Russia, Austria and Prussia. Meanwhile, in 1780, Catherine, determined to play a leading international role, had offended both Britain and Spain with her Declaration of Armed Neutrality, which supported the efforts of the neutral countries to protect their merchant shipping from British and French seizures. In October 1799 a second League of Armed Neutrality was formed between Russia and Sweden.

The longer Catherine reigned, the more autocratic she became. Beginning as a progressive and benevolent ruler, she reversed her liberal policies after a peasant revolt in 1773. Thereafter, any challenge to her authority was crushed. The French Revolution, with its reign of terror and the execution of Louis XVI, ended her fascination with Reformation and Enlightenment ideas and those who espoused them.

After Catherine, Russia continued to play a leading role in European power politics. It joined the other European powers in their efforts to impede French expansion, which threatened Russian interests in the Balkans, the Dardanelles and Poland. In 1798 it successfully intervened against France in the eastern Mediterranean. Austrian–Russian forces fought the French in Italy. Between 1805 and

1807, under Tsar Alexander I (b. 1777; reigned 1801–25), Russia fought Napoleon in Central Europe; at the same time it fought the Turks (1806–12) and the Persians (1804–13). In 1807 it made a truce with Napoleon that divided Europe into Russian and French spheres of influence. In the same year in a war with Sweden, it annexed Finland as a grand duchy within the Russian Empire. In 1812 it repelled a French invasion in the 'First Fatherland War',[7] which was fought to decide who would be supreme on the continent: France or Russia. The defeat of the French left a vacuum of power in Western Europe, which Russia proceeded to fill decisively. It played a leading role in the Congress of Vienna, which, building on the Peace of Westphalia (1648) and the Treaty of Utrecht (1713), established an order that averted a general conflict in Europe for a hundred years (see Map VII). Russia's further westward expansion, however, was impeded by Prussia and Austria.

In 1826 Russia went to war with Persia over Armenia. The following year it helped to destroy the Ottoman fleet at Navarino Bay, which brought to a head Russian–Ottoman conflicts in the Balkans, the Caucasus and the Black Sea, and led to war in 1828–9. By mid-century Russia was at war again in the Crimea (1853–6). Earlier, in 1851, on the pretext that it was exercising its supposed rights as the guardian of the Orthodox Church, Russia had occupied Ottoman-controlled territory on the Danube. France had intervened as guardian of Western Roman Catholic rights. The British, unimpressed by the 'quarrel of monks', but equally alarmed at Russia's invasion of European Turkey and its growing power in the Black Sea, supported France. In October 1853, encouraged by Britain and France, Ottoman Turkey declared war on Russia. A month later Russian armoured vessels, using new shell guns, annihilated a Turkish squadron of wooden battleships off Sinope in the Black Sea (see Map VIII). Although it was the Turks who had started the Crimean War, the 'massacre' of Sinope did much to enrage public opinion in Paris and London: the cry went up to rid Europe of Russian tyranny. To prevent Russia from subduing Turkey and seizing the Dardanelles, which gave it access to the Mediterranean, and which had been closed to Russian warships since the international Straits Convention of 1841, British and French warships were sent into the Black Sea, where they ordered the Russian fleet back to port. The Russians became increasingly convinced that Britain and France intended to close the straits against them. By March 1854, seemingly in a willy-nilly way, Britain and France had committed themselves to battle on the side of the ailing Ottoman Empire; landings were made by them in the Crimea. Under the added threat of Austrian intervention,[8] Russia, having lost almost half a million men (more by sickness than by combat), was eventually forced to evacuate European Turkey and in 1856 (under the Treaty of Paris) to agree to the neutralization of the Black Sea. It was also forced to give up the mouth of the Danube and part of Bessarabia; its right to be the protector of Christians in Turkey was rescinded. Britain, France and Austria declared that any future threat by Russia to Turkish independence would be met by them with war. Although, by now, it was almost defunct, the Ottoman Empire was reinstated as a buffer against Russian expansion, and was admitted to the European concert of powers. Russia's humiliating defeat in the Crimean War exposed its military and industrial weaknesses and helped to discredit the tsarist regime.

A decade later, Russia's attention was drawn to events in the Balkans, where its western ambitions clashed with Germany's eastern ambitions. The long-term hope of the pan-Slavic movement in Russia was hegemony over the Slavic states of Eastern Europe. In July 1875 Orthodox Serbs in the province of Bosnia-Herzegovina – secretly armed by Russia – revolted against their Ottoman masters, who had ruled the area since 1463. The Turks responded fiercely. In 1876, to prevent Serbia's destruction, Russia issued an ultimatum to the Turks. Using Turkey's supposed brutal repression of Bulgarian insurrectionists as an excuse, the next year Russia penetrated Turkish territory as far as Adrianople (Edirne). The Turkish army was overrun and Constantinople threatened.

The harsh peace terms imposed by Russia in 1878 in the Treaty of San Stefano caused Britain, Germany, France, Italy and Austria to call a second peace conference at Berlin, convened by Germany's chancellor, Otto von Bismarck. (In London there was talk of war with Russia.) At this conference Russian terms were softened, and in the new treaty the powers insisted upon the independence of

Romania, Serbia and Montenegro; Austria was given the right to occupy – but not annex – Bosnia-Herzegovina; half of Bulgaria became a self-governing Turkish province named East Rumelia. To strengthen its hand further, several weeks before the congress took place in Berlin, Turkey had secretly formed a defensive alliance with Britain. As a result of this alliance, Turkey ceded Cyprus – which it had taken from the Venetians in 1571 – to Britain, which had no earthly reason to want it. Russian attempts to reach the Mediterranean at Turkey's expense had again been denied. 'Peace with honour,' said Disraeli, the British Prime Minister, on returning from the Berlin Congress. Britain and France were implacably opposed to Russia's presence in both the Balkans and the Mediterranean.

While all this was taking place, Russia had never ceased its eastward march. In less than a century, by the late 1630s, it had crossed the whole of Northern Asia and had reached the Sea of Okhotsk. The Russians then swept southward to the banks of the Amur River, where for the next two centuries their expansion was held in check by the Manchus, who had established their rule in China in 1644. The Treaty of Nerchinsk (overseen by the Jesuits and concluded in 1689), which demarcated the Chinese–Russian border, was the first treaty between East and West. In 1707 the Kamchatka peninsula was annexed. By 1741 Russian traders had crossed the Bering Straits to Alaska, which Catherine the Great later claimed in Russia's name. Only in 1812, by which time the Russians had reached the vicinity of present-day San Francisco, did their eastern march finally end. With the sale of Alaska to the United States in 1867, the Russians withdrew from North America.

By 1900 Britain and Japan had good reason to be concerned about the extension of Russian power in Eastern Asia. Britain had commercial interests in the Yangtze Valley; Japan had similar interests in Manchuria and Korea. The unequal treaties of Aigun (1858) and Beijing (1860), forced upon China, brought the Russian frontier to the Amur River, and to positions south of Vladivostok (founded by Russia in 1860). Under the Treaty of Aigun, all the territory north of the Amur passed into Russian control. Territories that the Treaty of

Nerchinsk had assigned to China became Russian. China's attempts to dispute this treaty in 1859 resulted in Russia occupying parts of Manchuria. The sea coast north of Korea (territory that Russia still holds) was also annexed.

Despite the warnings of Britain and Japan, in the 1890s Russia continued to penetrate Manchuria, as well as China and Korea. The Trans-Siberian Railway to the Pacific,[9] which gave Russia control of northern Manchuria and made it a great power in the East, was begun in 1891 and completed in 1903. It spurred industrialization, facilitated eastward migration and consolidated Russia's hold on eastern Siberia. Built with French money, it was also meant to woo Russia into an alliance against Germany. In 1898 Russia leased Port Arthur (Lushun) on the southern half of the Liaotung peninsula from the Chinese. Five days later the British occupied the neighbouring port of Weihaiwei (see Map IX). In 1902, with insufficient strength to meet both a German threat of war in the West and Russian advances in the East, the British made a formal naval agreement with Japan, which was emboldened to request Russia to evacuate Manchuria – a request that was treated with contempt. In 1904 Japan struck at Russia's fleet in Port Arthur and against Russian ground forces in Manchuria without warning. The following year Russia was defeated by Japan on land and sea. Japan's victory signalled the beginning of the end of Western hegemony in the Orient.

Russia's defeat in East Asia was so humiliating that it gave rise to the Russian Revolution of 1905. Sparked by the massacre of peaceful demonstrators in St Petersburg on 9 January (Bloody Sunday), unprecedented violence swept through the country. Many aristocratic estates were seized and sacked by the peasantry. Although the revolution failed to overthrow the tsarist regime, it provided Vladimir Ilyich Ulyanov (Lenin; 1870–1924), Leib Davydovich Bronstein (Leon Trotsky; 1879–1940) and other revolutionary leaders with valuable lessons and enhanced their reputations within the Communist Party. It also resulted in political concessions from the tsarist regime, the most important of which was the establishment in 1905 of the Duma, a largely ineffective parliament.

Under the subsequent Treaty of Portsmouth (1905) between Russia and Japan, Russia left southern Manchuria and returned southern

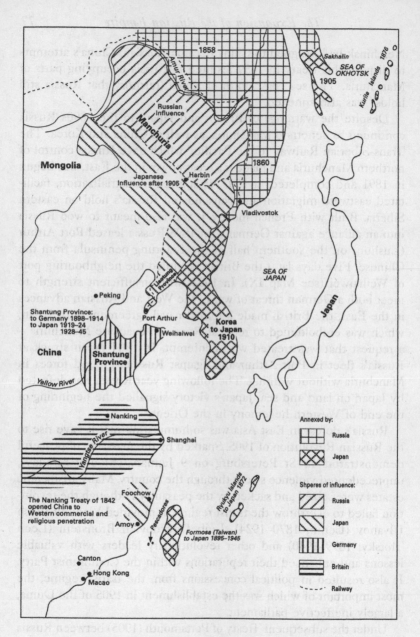

1858

Sakhalin

SEA OF
OKHOTSK

Kurile Islands 1876

1905

Amur River

Russian
Influence

Manchuria

Mongolia

Japanese
Influence after 1905 ✕ Harbin

1860

Vladivostok

*Liaotung
Province*

SEA OF
JAPAN

Peking

Shantung Province:
to Germany 1898–1914
to Japan 1919–24
1928–45

Port Arthur

Weihaiwei

Korea
to Japan
1910

Japan

China

Shantung
Province

Yellow River

Nanking

Annexed by:

Russia

Japan

Shanghai

Spheres of influence:

Russia

Japan

Germany

Britain

Railway

The Nanking Treaty of 1842
opened China to
Western commercial and
religious penetration

Foochow

*Ruikyu Islands
to Japan 1872*

Amoy

Pescadores

*Formosa (Taiwan)
to Japan 1895–1945*

Canton

Hong Kong
Macao

Map IX Colonization of East Asia, 1858–1945

Sakhalin to Japan. To the satisfaction of Britain as well as Japan, further Russian ambitions in the East were terminated. Yet Russia still retained control of northern Manchuria (including the Chinese Eastern Railway), parts of Mongolia and the Chinese maritime provinces (which the Chinese alleged had been seized illegally). Thenceforth, with France and Britain, Russia focused its attention on the growing threat of imperial Germany in Europe.

Even prior to being halted in the East, Russian expansion had accelerated in Central Asia. Russia's encroachment into Turkistan in the mid-nineteenth century, encouraged by military ambition and its presumed civilizing mission, had been regarded by Britain as a threat to India. Britain's response was to use Persia and Afghanistan as buffer states. By the 1860s, with its control of the Caucasus complete, Russia extended its influence to still wider areas of Central Asia. In 1868 it took Samarkand and subdued Bukhara in Uzbekistan; in 1873 Khiva fell. Bukhara was occupied in 1874, Kokand in 1876. With the occupation of the Merv Oasis in southern Turkestan in 1884, Russia approached the frontiers of Persia and Afghanistan. By 1885 the Russian Trans-Caspian Railway reached Ashkabad. From there, it was extended through Merv to Chardzhou on the Oxus in 1886. Only mountains now separated Russia from Persia, Afghanistan, India and China. When the Russians defeated an Afghan army at Penjdeh in March 1885, Britain prepared for war. War was avoided because the Germans sided with Russia, and also because Russia became preoccupied in Bulgaria. Russia and Britain reached a diplomatic compromise.

Thenceforth, Russian interests were played out in Persia, which, like Afghanistan, the British regarded as a buffer state to India. In 1907, prompted by the revolution in Persia and the growing German threat in Southwest Asia (the Germans had undertaken to build a railway from Berlin to Baghdad), the Russians, eager to reach the Persian Gulf, secretly divided Persia with Britain. Without consulting the Persians, the British agreed to exercise tutelage over the southeast, which was chiefly desert, while the Russians settled for the entire northern half of the country, which contained three-quarters of Persia's population. The southwestern part remained neutral. Britain, the leading sea power, retained control of the Gulf and, for the most part, the Turkish Middle East. The agreement with Russia also recognized Britain's predominant position in Afghanistan. Ignoring Persian protests, the Russian–British secret agreement was implemented when war came in 1914.

In October 1908 Russia had come close to war with Austria concerning the Serbian-claimed territory of Bosnia-Herzegovina. In support of Serbia, and as mother of the Slavs, Russia called upon Austria to withdraw; Austria refused. Instead, Emperor Franz Joseph (b. 1830; reigned 1848–1916) of Austria appealed to Emperor Wilhelm II (b. 1859; reigned 1888–1918; d. 1941) of Germany. France, with whom Russia had closed ranks against the Germans since the 1890s, showed little interest in becoming involved; Britain watched the growing crisis with studied unconcern. Under threat of war from Germany, Russia capitulated, but the problem would re-emerge in August 1914.

If Russia's traditions appear less humane than those of other European countries, it is because for a thousand years it has had to fight for the right to exist. Besieged from east, west, north and south, Russia has had every reason to be nervous about the territorial ambitions of others; hence, an expansive, imperial Russian state able to protect its frontiers has always been acceptable to the Russian psyche. Its historical preoccupation with security explains why the Russian state has always dominated every aspect of political, social, economic and religious life. Without a heritage of common law or of public political debate to support the individual against the state, the state became the end, the individual the means. Security and order are to Russia what freedom and individualism have been to the West.

Not only was Russia unfamiliar with Roman law, it was equally unacquainted with the Age of Chivalry, the Renaissance, the Reformation (with its challenge to authority), the Counter-Reformation and the Enlightenment. Nor did it experience the challenge to political authority that the French Revolution presented to other parts of Europe. While Peter the Great introduced some Western ideas and Catherine the Great flirted with Western liberalization, the Oriental traits in the Russian soul (in spite of the European inheritance of the Russian Orthodox Church) have remained.

In the nineteenth century, despite palace revolts, military coups, dynastic chaos, revolutionary agitation, government corruption, conspiracy and upheaval, the exercise of absolute monarchy and absolute bureaucracy continued. Ironically, the only tsar seriously to attempt reform, Alexander II, the Tsar Liberator (b. 1818; reigned 1855–81), was assassinated. There followed the repressive rule and absolute monarchy of Alexander III (b. 1845; reigned 1881–94) and Nicholas II (b. 1868; reigned 1894–17), the last of the Romanovs. Alas, Nicholas's claim to divine right was coupled with extraordinary incompetence. When he came to the throne, a fatal clash in Russia between the desire for modernity and absolute monarchy was only a matter of time.

From the fifteenth to the nineteenth century most Russians – overwhelmingly rural and agrarian – were isolated, bound and hobbled by a rigid serfdom enforced by the state. Initially the Russian serf enjoyed freedom from his master for only two weeks each year, but from 1593 onwards even this right was revoked. After 1648 a runaway serf had no rights whatsoever. Those who did not conform were regarded as a threat to society and punished; dissidence was feared.

The emancipation of the serfs in 1861 by Tsar Alexander II did little to improve their lot.[10] The emancipation edict, coupled with rural overpopulation (between 1861 and 1910 there was a remarkable growth in Russian numbers), exacerbated rather than alleviated the problem of finding land for the freed serfs. In order to repay the cost of their emancipation, the ex-serfs were required to ransom their own persons to the state (in effect, the village), which left them in economic if not legal bondage. The vested interests of the aristocracy and the other landowners, added to the general inertia and incompetence of the bureaucracy, ensured that nothing would be done to reduce the suffering of the peasantry. Genuine emancipation arrived only with the Stolypin reforms of the early 1900s. Although some relief was obtained by migration to Siberia and to the growing urban centres, rural unrest, culminating in violent uprisings, was endemic in the half-century after 1861. Until the twentieth century, personal freedom and individual ownership of land remained a mirage for Russia's lower classes.

In 1914 Russia was still a great imperial state. It had the necessary territory, resources and population for such a role. Yet it lacked the industrial power needed to become supreme. Although there had been a state-promoted industrial boom in the closing decades of the nineteenth century, in 1914 85 per cent of its people still worked on the land. In industrial development Russia lagged behind the more dynamic Western powers (especially Germany), as well as Japan. Politically, socially, industrially and economically, it was ill equipped to enter the Great War.

6

Africa: 1500–1914

Long before 1500 indigenous forces had swept aside several great sub-Saharan West African empires and kingdoms, such as Ghana (eighth–eleventh century) and Mali (twelfth–fourteenth century). Songhai, the greatest of them all, flourished from the fourteenth to the fifteenth century. Between the fifteenth and eighteenth centuries there arose the West African states of Mossi, Ashanti, Benin, Dahomey, Oyo and Funj. At this time, Ethiopia (the ancient Christian kingdom of 'Prester John') was under siege by Islamic and pagan groups alike. Native forces were also responsible for the rise of kingdoms such as Bunyoro and Buganda (south of Ethiopia), and Burundi on Lake Tanganyika. Between Lake Tanganyika and the Atlantic lay the dominions of Luba, Lunda and the Congo. Kilwa lay east of Lake Malawi opposite Madagascar. Where Zimbabwe is today were the kingdoms of Mwenemutapa and later Rozwi (see Map I).

The only outside groups to have affected Africa deeply prior to the eighteenth century were Arabs, Ottoman Turks and Christian missionaries. North Africa had been conquered by the Arabs in the eighth century. Coming from Arabia, they had crossed the Sahara in search of gold, wax, ivory, skins, pepper, timber, palm oil and slaves, in exchange for salt, cloth, iron, brass and copper goods. The Arabs had also penetrated the Sudan via the Nile and the Red Sea. The Star and Crescent came to prevail from the Senegal River in the west to the upper Nile in the east, to Zimbabwe in the south. Except in those areas where the tsetse fly kept the Arabs' horses and camels out, their language and faith (Islam) made far greater inroads in Africa than Christianity would do a thousand years later. Prior to the coming of the Europeans, commerce in the Indian Ocean and along the east coast of Africa to Mozambique and Madagascar was chiefly under Muslim control. In the sixteenth and seventeenth centuries the Ottomans were the strongest colonial power in Africa. In 1517 they triumphed over the Egyptian Mameluks and extended their control as far as Algiers. Christian Europe began to play a part in Africa's history from the fifteenth century onwards. The Iberians first attempted to conquer Islamic-held North Africa,[1] but in 1578 the Portuguese suffered a shattering defeat at Al-Qasr-al-Kabir in Morocco.

Islam and Christianity have had incalculable effects on African life. Islam accepted all men, regardless of colour, as brothers. In drought-stricken Africa the promise of a 'wet Paradise', with its imagery of fountains and running water, was particularly attractive; also inviting to some converts was Islam's acceptance of polygamy. Scattered bands of Christians had found their way to East Africa several centuries after the birth of Christ. Christianity was practised by a group of Ethiopian 'Copts' before the fifth century. In time there developed in Europe rumours of this kingdom of 'Prester John'. The Portuguese went in search of it when they attempted to outflank the Muslims of North Africa and the Mediterranean by sea. Improvements that had been made in naval technology in the mid-1400s enabled the Portuguese to plot their positions on the high seas, and to forge their way up and down the West African coast. A Portuguese diplomat, Pero da Covilhã, reached Ethiopia in 1487. Concerned to profit from the trade of the Orient, Bartolomeu Dias rounded the Cape of Good Hope in that year. In 1498 Vasco da Gama, with the aid of an Arab pilot, crossed the Indian Ocean.

In making their way down the West African coast to the Cape of Good Hope and beyond, the Spaniards, Dutch, French and British, all following the Portuguese, developed a vigorous trade rivalry among themselves. The Gold, Slave and Ivory coasts began to appear on European maps. Because of the difficulties of African commerce, only the most lucrative items were traded. Although the first Portuguese traders reached the ancient state of Congo, as well as the Bantu-speaking states of Luba, Lunda and Angola, at the end of the fifteenth century, it was not until much later that their influence was felt there. One hundred years had to pass before the Europeans established permanent outposts on Africa's shores. French and British trading stations first began to appear on the west coast. By 1652 the Dutch, who had occupied Portuguese Angolan Luanda between 1641 and 1648, had established themselves at the Cape of Good Hope. They became known as Boers (farmers), and spoke a Dutch dialect called Afrikaans. From there, Dutch fleets sought out the rich spice trade of the East Indies. By this time they had replaced the Portuguese as the dominant traders in the Indian Ocean.

In the sixteenth century the horrendous enslaving of Africans by the Christian West began to take its incalculable toll.[2] The expansion of slavery by Europeans, Arabs and Africans (some of whom enslaved their own people) was of epochal importance to Africa and the world. The Europeans did not introduce slavery; what they did was to vastly increase its scope, which led to serious demographic changes. By 1700 the slave trade, which was now largely controlled by the British, Dutch and French, exceeded the export trade in gold, ivory and other African products. Estimates of the number of slaves shipped from the West African coast to the Americas (at first to provide labour on the plantations of Brazil and the Caribbean) between the sixteenth and the nineteenth century range from ten to fifteen million. The eighteenth century was probably the peak, when the traffic was six to seven million. About two million are thought to have died en route. Despite all the rhetoric about Christian love and salvation, the Europeans treated slaves shipped to the Americas like cattle. By the end of the eighteenth century slaves were also traded by Arabs and Africans from East African ports to Zanzibar and North Africa, as well as to countries around the Red Sea and the Persian Gulf.

About 40 per cent of slave shipments went to the Caribbean (together with hundreds of thousands of East Indians), 38 per cent to Brazil, the rest (about 500,000) to the thirteen colonies (later the United States) and Canada. The first black slaves to arrive in

North America were landed at Jamestown in Virginia in 1619 – one hundred years after their forebears had been transported to Latin America. British traders took the lead: British ships delivered textiles, spirits, iron bars, pots and pans, trinkets, glass beads, fish, cutlery and muskets to West African ports in exchange for slaves, ivory and gold. Once in the Americas, the slaves were traded for sugar, rum, rice, indigo, ginger, tobacco and cotton, which were then shipped back to England. The sale of Africans for labour in the New World became an intrinsic part of the triangular trade between the Americas, Europe and Africa. The eighteenth-century world economy was inconceivable without slavery. Yet it was the Muslims who dominated the *internal* slave trade of Africa until it was abolished in the nineteenth century.

Slavery provided the European settlers of the New World with the labour they badly needed. Slaves turned Caribbean sugar into the 'white gold' that helped to finance Britain's Industrial Revolution. Their labour resulted in the export of new foods and plants to the rest of the world. In North America African slaves culti-vated the cotton without which the British textile industry – with its worldwide ramifications – could never have been started. In the southern United States the slave-based plantation industry created a society so incompatible with that of the North that it led to the Civil War.

The African slave trade undoubtedly created a different kind of world. For the blacks it added to their suffering; inevitably, it increased their powers of endurance and courage. In Africa European weapons, drink and human and cattle diseases did great harm. The sale of muskets changed the political balance, leading to the emergence of the coastal Guinea states and the decline of the Sudan states. Armed with European weapons, Benin, Dahomey, Ashanti and Oyo rose to predominance. The introduction of European knick-knacks caused tribal arts and crafts to deteriorate. European intrusions on the west and east coasts also undermined the ancient trans-Saharan trade based on Timbuktu, and wreaked havoc among the coastal towns and trading ports of the Indian Ocean. As a result, in the eighteenth and nine-teenth centuries a westward shift of African population, trade and shipping took place from the Indian Ocean to the Atlantic.

Nevertheless, before the mid-eighteenth century, except for the ravages of the slave trade, the West's overall influence upon Africa was slight. In 1800 European interests were still concentrated in a number of tiny outposts on the West African coast.[3] However, except for Christian missionaries (who often preceded colonization) and European explorers (who defined the source and course of Africa's great river systems[4]), European intrusion hardly went beyond the periphery of the continent. Climate, disease – especially malaria and yellow fever – and geography debarred it. When the Christian missionary David Livingstone reached Africa in 1841, with his call for 'Christianity, commerce and civilization', Europe still knew little about Africa beyond the lower course of the Nile, and the mouths of the Niger, the Congo and the Zambezi. With the exception of North Africa – where by 1800 the power of the Ottomans had declined – and the Cape of Good Hope, for the Europeans the map of the 'Dark Continent' was almost blank. Until the late nineteenth century the continent remained largely tribal, remote and oriented (where it was oriented to the outside world at all) towards the west coast, where the slave trade had cut deeply, the Mediterranean and the Indian Ocean.

Responding to public outcry in the West, slavery was abolished by the Dutch in 1795, the Danes in 1803 and the British in 1807. It was not abolished in the British West Indies until 1833. Although about two million slaves were bought and sold after this, by the 1880s all the major countries of the world had outlawed it. The last African slave market, at Zanzibar, was finally closed in 1873. Despite slavery being outlawed more than a hundred years ago, it still exists in Niger and other African states today.

Because of the growing rivalry of the European powers, and improvements in transport and communications (such as steam railways and improved river boats), European incursions increased dramatically in the closing decades of the nineteenth century. In an attempt to bring some kind of order to the ever-increasing 'scramble for Africa',[5] and to work towards the abolition of slavery and the slave trade, the European powers (and a representative from the United States) met at the Berlin Conference on African Affairs in 1884–5.[6] No Africans were present; none were consulted. Africa was regarded by the

Europeans as a continent that they could divide as they wished, and change for the better. Unable to match the West's weapons, Africans were in no position to meet the European challenge. In agriculture and mining all colonial economies were greatly exploitive. By 1914 only Liberia, Abyssinia (Ethiopia) and parts of Morocco were unoccupied by a European power (see Map X). Great Britain claimed 5 million of Africa's 11.7 million square miles. Fifty years earlier, in the 1860s, European control of African territory had extended to no more than one-tenth of the continent.

The inroads made by the Europeans into Africa brought many changes to African life. Across the continent a network of political boundaries was drawn (called 'straight-line diplomacy') that had little relation to ethnic or economic reality. But it did serve the Europeans' strategy of divide and rule. Those boundaries still exist and are the cause of wars being fought in several parts of Africa today. To make matters worse, the colonizers would sometimes strengthen one tribe against another. Great market-oriented agricultural export industries were established to meet Western demands; modern, large-scale mining (and the railways to accompany it) was developed to meet Western needs. Africa became dependent upon markets thousands of miles away. Western economic ideas affecting the use of money, taxation (head tax and hut tax) and labour were imposed. Except for those who went to spread the Christian gospel and certain dedicated government officials, the objects of Western invasion were profit and imperialism. However enlightened, the general intention was to serve Western ends. Altruism and imperialism in any age are contradictory.

Christianity, commerce and civilization may have brought great benefits to Africa, not least in education (a number of Africa's leaders were educated in Christian mission schools), medicine and law, but they also brought with them the bastardization of native cultures, dispossession of land, growing instability and an astonishing population decline. Africa is the only continent whose population fell in the nineteenth century.

The wonder about the colonization of Africa is that it was achieved with so little friction between the European powers. In the division of African territory between the Europeans at Berlin (where

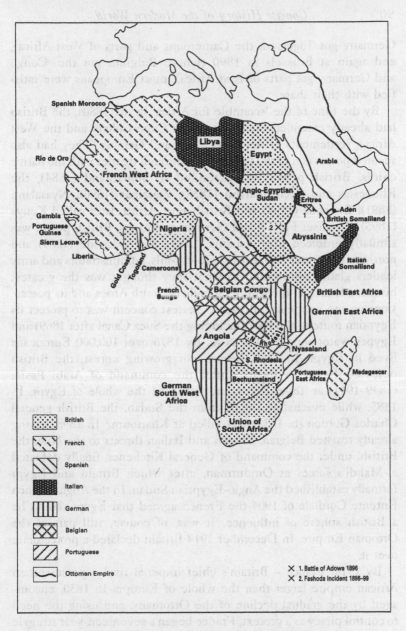

Map X European Colonies in Africa in 1914

Germany got Togoland, the Cameroons and parts of West Africa), and again at Brussels in 1890 (where Belgium got the Congo and Germany got parts of East Africa), most Europeans were satisfied with their share.

By the time of the 'scramble for Africa' in the 1880s, the British had already extended their rule to the Cape Colony and the West African settlements of the Gold Coast and Gambia. They had also secured possession of the Lagos coast through treaties with the native chiefs. British power was extended to Somaliland (1884), the Rhodesias and Bechuanaland (1885), Zanzibar (1890), Nyasaland (1891), Buganda (1894) and British East Africa, later called Kenya (1895). To offset French and German ambitions, British power was similarly enforced over Ashanti (1886), Sierra Leone (1889) and northern Nigeria (1900). British pro-consuls, administrators and army leaders gladly contributed to what they thought was the greatest human advance in the world. Outside of South Africa and its possessions on the west coast, Britain's greatest concern was to protect its Egyptian route to the East (including the Suez Canal after 1869) and Egypt's water supply – the Nile. By 1876 over 100,000 Europeans lived in Egypt. In 1882, because of growing unrest, the British defeated Egyptian forces under the command of Arabi Pasha (1839–1911) at Tel-el-Kebir, and occupied the whole of Egypt. In 1885, while evacuating troops from the Sudan, the British general Charles Gordon (b. 1833) was killed at Khartoum.[7] In 1898, having already resisted Belgian, French and Italian threats to the Nile, the British, under the command of General Kitchener, finally defeated al-Mahdi's forces at Omdurman, after which Britain and Egypt formally established the Anglo-Egyptian Sudan. In the Anglo-French Entente Cordiale of 1904 the French agreed that Egypt should be a British sphere of influence. It was, of course, still part of the Ottoman Empire. In December 1914 Britain declared a protectorate over it.

By 1914, France – Britain's chief imperial rival – possessed an African empire larger than the whole of Europe. In 1830, encouraged by the gradual decline of the Ottomans, and using the need to control piracy as a pretext, France began a seventeen-year struggle to conquer Algeria. From 1879 the French also moved inland from

Senegal; they then added Guinea and the protectorates of the Ivory Coast (1889) and Dahomey (1890). The colonies of the Ivory Coast and French Guinea were formally established in 1893, that of Dahomey in 1894. Excluded from the east coast by Portuguese, British, Danish and German interests, the French in 1890 declared a protectorate over Madagascar, which became a colony in 1906. By then they were challenging the British on the Guinea coast, the lower Niger and the upper Nile. In 1898 British troops forced a French withdrawal from Fashoda on the Nile. The next year, in return for what then appeared to be worthless British territory in the Sahara, the French renounced all territorial claims to the Nile area.

In 1881, having been offered a free hand in Tunisia by Britain, France used tribal raids as an excuse to declare a protectorate over the whole country. In doing so it forestalled the Italians, whose rivalry with France in the region was growing. The Ottomans, part of whose empire it still was – an Ottoman army had taken Tunis in 1574 – protested, as did Britain and Italy, but by then France had exchanged British for German support, and Tunisia, like Algeria, remained under its control. North Africa was no longer an Ottoman domain. In 1884, in an attempt to curtail Italian ambitions on the Red Sea, France and Britain declared a protectorate over Somaliland. In its drive from West to East Africa, France inevitably became involved in a struggle to control Central Africa. French power also spread in Morocco from 1906 onwards. A French protectorate was established in the southern zone in 1912. France, having clashed with Germany over Morocco, used German threats in 1911 to test its alliance (the Entente Cordiale of 1904) with Britain.

Germany's participation in the division of Africa may be dated from the Berlin Conference. Having acquired Southwest Africa, Togoland and the Cameroons in 1884, in 1886 it shared parts of East Africa with the British. In return for a German promise to keep out of Uganda, and Germany's recognition of a British protectorate over Zanzibar, the British surrendered the island of Heligoland in the North Sea, which they had obtained from Denmark in 1815.

Italy, like Germany, was a latecomer in the division of Africa. In 1885 the Italians established a colony at Massawa on the Red Sea.

In 1889 they took possession of part of Somalia. In 1890 Italy's previously held Eritrean possessions were organized as the colony of Eritrea. In trying to extend their control to Abyssinia (Ethiopia), which was still free of European and Ottoman control, they suffered one of the rare Western defeats at the Battle of Adowa in 1896. In 1900 the Italians gave France a free hand in Morocco in return for freedom of action in Ottoman-controlled Libya. In 1911, while Germany and France were squabbling over Agadir, Morocco, Italy – brushing aside Ottoman claims to Libya – seized the provinces of Tripoli and Cyrenaica – the Ottomans' last North African possessions. In the Turko-Italian War of 1912 the Italians successfully retained their recent North African conquest. The outbreak of the First World War in 1914 and the subsequent revolt of the Arabs caused the Italians to be driven back to Tripoli and Homs on the coast. Twenty-one years of intermittent fighting against the Italians had decimated the native population by one-third.

In the division of Africa in the nineteenth century the Portuguese and the Spaniards, once foremost in colonizing, took little part. The Portuguese contented themselves by enlarging their earlier trading posts into the protectorates of Angola and Mozambique (the last great rebellion in Africa took place there in 1917). The Spaniards continued to hold, but not enlarge, their small Guinea protectorate in Equatorial Africa, their possessions on the northwest coast of Morocco (Rio de Oro) and the northern zone of Morocco opposite Gibraltar. In 1921 at the Battle of Anual a Spanish army of about 200,000 troops suffered an overwhelming defeat by the Moroccans. Not until 1926, when a Franco-Spanish army overcame the ongoing revolt of Abd-el Krim (1882–1963), was Spanish power restored.

The Belgians, who had been active in the Congo since the 1870s, established the Congo Free State in 1885 as a neutral concession of Belgium's King Leopold II under international sanction. The British supported Belgium's claim in order to thwart the ambitions of the French. Because of outrages against native labour, in 1908 the Congo Free State was transferred from the ailing king to the Belgian state and renamed the Belgian Congo.

US influence on African colonization in the nineteenth century was limited to helping freed American slaves establish themselves at Liberia on the west coast in 1822. Becoming the Free and Independent Republic of Liberia, it was recognized by Britain and other states almost immediately, but not by America itself until 1862. In 1909, however, the Americans gave direct support to Liberia in quelling native insurrections (the resistance of tribes who had occupied Liberia before the freed American slaves arrived). So great was America's subsequent economic penetration of Liberia that it came to be regarded as an American colony.

Several times the Europeans came close to blows – at Fashoda on the Nile in 1898 and at Morocco in 1905 – but they always resolved their differences peacefully. The economic stakes in trade and investment were just not big enough to tempt the powers to go to war. European foreign investments did not necessarily follow the flag: between 1865 and 1914 only a quarter of British foreign investments went to its much-enlarged empire. Trade and investment in the Americas, China and even Russia proved more attractive. Prestige and fear of not getting one's rightful share of African territory weighed more heavily.

The exception was the Boer War of 1899–1902,[8] which brought to a head a long rivalry between the British and the Dutch. In the 1830s the Dutch Boers, in an attempt to escape from English rule at the Cape,[9] had begun to penetrate the interior. By the 1850s they had founded the republics of Natal (1839), the Orange Free State (1848) and the Transvaal (1849). After the British had annexed the Transvaal in 1877, the Boers fought a successful war in 1880–1 to regain it, but the discovery of gold in the Witwatersrand in 1886 made a second Boer War inevitable. As the leading sea power, Britain was able to transport the necessary men and materials to the battle front, and to block German contraband. The Germans, who sided with the Boers, were not prepared to challenge the Royal Navy in African waters. Fear of Germany in Europe had caused France and Russia to stay out of the fight.

The guerrilla tactics of the Boers turned what should have been a short, sharp campaign into two and a half years of bitter fighting (the British had an army of 500,000 – including contingents from Canada, Australia and New Zealand – against the Boers' 60,000). The herding of Boer women and children into concentration camps, where twenty thousand died, stripped Britain of its hitherto assumed role as the moral arbiter of the Western world. The war Britain won in May 1902 cost it dearly in lives, morale and money (£222 million). Britain never recovered the moral stature it had had before the war – not even after it had granted South Africa dominion status in 1908. In 1910 the Cape, Natal, the Transvaal and the Orange Free State became the Union of South Africa. Yet, when war came in 1914, the majority of white South Africans opted to support Britain. Swiftly, contingents of white and black South Africans captured and occupied German East and Southwest Africa (territory of the only power that had shown sympathy to the Boers in their earlier struggle against the British).

Clashes between the Europeans and native Africans were piecemeal until resistance stiffened towards the end of the nineteenth century. France had to contend with continuing resistance to its rule in North and West Africa, as well as in Madagascar; Britain faced unrest in Egypt, the Sudan, Somaliland, Uganda and other parts of East, West and South Africa. In Nyasaland in the 1880s it also encountered Arab resistance. The Ndebele of Southern Rhodesia launched a revolt in 1896, which resulted in the besieging of Bulawayo. The Ashanti revolted in the same year; it took months for the British to suppress the revolt. The Germans had to put down the Maji-Maji uprising of 1900–6 in East Africa (in which a third of the population died), as well as the Herero Revolt (1904–7) in West and Southwest Africa. A census in 1911 showed about 15,000 Herero survivors from an earlier population of 80,000. Anti-Portuguese risings broke out in Angola and Mozambique, territories that dwarfed Portugal itself in size. Disturbances took place after the Italians took possession of Somaliland in 1905 and Libya in 1911. There was organized resistance against the Belgians, who had an insatiable demand for forced labour in the Congo Free State. The attempts made by the mystic Muhammad Ahmad al-Mahdi and his followers to establish an Islamic fundamentalist state in Egypt and the Sudan in 1881–98 had religious origins. The Matabele and Mashona revolts that broke out in Rhodesia in 1896, and the Zulu Revolt in South Africa in 1905, were fought over territory. In Tunisia nationalists fought the French. It is to the credit of the Christian missionaries

(Roman Catholic and Protestant alike) that they protested at the brutal way in which some of these insurrections were suppressed.

The overwhelming superiority of arms almost always ensured European victories over native resistance movements. Such was true of the struggles between the Ashanti and the British (1824–96), the Anglo-Zulu War of 1879, Abd al-Qadir's (1808–83) rebellion against the French in Algeria in the 1880s and the Battle of Omdurman against Sudanese Dervishes in 1898. However uneven the contest, the fire of native resistance against the European occupying powers never died.

Europe's intrusion into Africa (naked exploitation to some; economic development, as well as political and religious enlightenment to others) continued until the First World War. In undermining European prestige, the war gave new life to the African resistance movements that had already been fighting European intrusion for fifty years. The first Pan-African Nationalist Conference met in 1919. The First World War – and the Russian Revolution – fructified the seed of nationalism that the Europeans themselves had sown. In time, African nationalism would lead to the death of European colonialism.

7

The Expansion of the American Empires

Although Columbus's discovery of America in 1492 is a landmark in the history of the human race, he went to his grave convinced that what he had found were islands off the landmass of Asia.[1] Not until 1513, when Vasco Núñez de Balboa (1475–1519) set eyes on the Pacific (the whole of which he claimed for the King of Spain), did the Europeans realize their error. By then, the continent had been named not after Columbus but after another Italian, Amerigo Vespucci (1451–1512), who had sailed as far as present-day Argentina. A hundred years later the focus of European attention was still on Asia. It took a long time before Europe fully conceded the existence of a continent that would radically change its own history and that of the world.

One year after Columbus's first landfall, Pope Alexander VI, in a papal bull of demarcation, divided the New World between Spain and Portugal. In 1494 the division was formalized in the Treaty of Tordesillas, under which the Spaniards obtained most of the southern half of the American continent (see Map I). Later they would also claim sovereignty over land further north, from Mexico to Oregon and east to the Carolinas. The Portuguese, who under Henry the Navigator (1394–1460) had done the pioneering work in the exploration of the Atlantic, had been granted Brazil by the 1550s.

Beginning with the settlement of Hispaniola in 1493, the

Spaniards went on to establish a base at Panama in 1519. From there they continued to seek a route to Cathay (China), which, as Columbus had done, they thought was near by. In the same year Hernando Cortés arrived with 11 ships, 600 men, 17 horses and 14 guns in Aztec Mexico. Having reached the Aztec capital, Tenochtitlán (Mexico City), he was defeated and fled to the coast. But three years later he returned and overwhelmed the Aztec Empire. In 1531 Francisco Pizarro (1470–1541), with 180 men and 27 horses, sailed from the Isthmus of Panama to Inca Peru (which included modern Peru, Ecuador, northern Chile, western Bolivia and northern Argentina). Five years later – devastating European diseases having preceded him – the once great Inca Empire was overthrown. Because Mexico and Peru were the chief centres of the Amerindian population,[2] and because they were the areas in which immensely productive silver mines were discovered – Potosí in upper Peru (now Bolivia) and Zacatecas in Mexico – they became the focus of Spanish conquest. An ever-growing stream of gold and silver made its way back to Spain. While the conquest of the Mayan Yucatán peninsula dragged on through the sixteenth and seventeenth centuries, the fate of Guatemala was settled between 1523 and 1542. Ecuador, Colombia and Venezuela (1536–9) and central Chile (1540–58) also fell to Spanish arms. Each has its own story of conquest and loot. By 1659 the Spaniards had taken possession of an area reaching roughly from northern Mexico to south of the Rio de la Plata in Argentina.

Although the Mayas had long since passed the peak of their civilization by the time Pedro de Alvarado (*c.* 1485–1541) reached Guatemala and Francisco de Montejo (1473–1553) reached Yucatán in the 1520s, they had achieved the most highly developed society of pre-Columbian America. The Mayan calculation of the solar year (in use before AD 1000) was a remarkably accurate system of reckoning time. In mathematics the Mayas had developed the idea of place value and the concept of zero. Their hieroglyphic system of writing was one of the most complex ever devised: it had both alphabetic and pictographic characters. Their art styles were brilliant, their architecture unparalleled. Although they did not possess precious metals on the scale of Mexico or Peru, they had enough agricultural resources, especially maize, to guarantee their independence. Religion pervaded their culture. Contrary to their earlier reputation as peaceful agriculturalists, their history is a story of unending warfare. Mayan rulers possessed near-absolute powers in government, religion, war and commerce. Partly for reasons of climate, disease and warfare, the Mayas had been in decline from the ninth century onwards (they numbered about half a million at the time of Western intrusion). Why their empire collapsed, and the jungle reclaimed its ruins, is still unknown. Some writers put it down to natural disasters.

In contrast to the Mayas, the Aztecs were probably at their peak in 1519. They had migrated to the central valley of Mexico in the fourteenth century; estimates of their number range from ten to twenty million. When Cortés arrived in Mexico, Tenochtitlán (which had a population to rival any European capital of the time) was the wonder of the Spaniards. While the use of iron and steel, the plough, draught animals, the rotary quern and the wheel were unknown to the Aztecs, they had all that was necessary to live well and extend their empire. Everything they did was motivated by religion. It was to obtain victims to sacrifice to the sun god (by taking their heart out) that compelled them to wage war constantly. They believed that, without sacrifice, the sun would not rise and the world would perish. As war was the guarantor of the survival of the universe, a long peace spelled disaster. Solidarity with the universe was more important than human life.

The richest, most integrated and dynamic pre-Columbian state in the 1500s was that of the Incas. From north to south it stretched for 2600 miles and had a population of between eight and ten million. A successful totalitarian state, it used its resources productively and with concern for the common good. When Pizarro appeared in 1531, the Incas' military skills, transport (though they did not make use of the wheel) and communications, engineering, stone- and metal-working, architecture, medicine and surgery, textiles and ceramics were all highly developed – as were their economics, politics and art. Their lack of a system of writing did not prevent them from having an efficient imperial administration. In the *quipu* (long ropes made of knotted cords) they possessed an effective system of calculation.

Governing through an absolute theocracy, the Incas imposed their rule upon all whom they conquered. From their capital, Cuzco in Peru, they united the different peoples of their far-flung realm by the use of a common tongue; they recognized one language, one nobility, one emperor.

The overwhelming defeat of the pre-Columbian empires by the Spaniards must be ascribed to the devastating sicknesses (such as smallpox) introduced by the Europeans, to superior weaponry, as well as to the audacity, fanaticism and treachery of the invaders. The Spaniards were propelled by their thirst for adventure, by the vibrancy and energy of their Mediterranean origins, by their Christian zeal (in 1492 they had ended Arab and Berber rule in Spain), by their desire to serve their king, by their unmatchable, warlike pride and by their lust for plunder. 'We want', said Bernal Díaz del Castillo, one of Cortés's soldiers in the conquest of Mexico, 'to give light to those in darkness and to get rich.'[3] Acutely aware of their desperate situation, the Spaniards fought ferociously, taking advantage of the natives' ritualistic and ceremonial way of making war. Aiding them were dissident tribes, the low morale of the native warriors and their utter dependence on their chiefs, who were the pillars of the state: when the Aztec leader Montezuma and the Inca leader Atahualpa fell, their states fell. Prophecy and omens also played a part. The Aztecs were filled with dread when a comet appeared above Tenochtitlán and split into three; a tongue of fire burned in the sky; the waters of the lake boiled. Mayas, Aztecs and Incas had a legend of a white god who would return one day: the conquistadors embodied the white god. Unable to meet the European challenge, the pre-Columbian civilizations were conquered, enslaved, baptized and slaughtered – despite the protests made by the Dominican Order and later by the Franciscans and the Jesuits, which led to the banning of all expeditions in the Americas between 1549 and 1560. Crucial to the ongoing conquest was the later collapse of the natives' birthrate.

Not until after the Peace of the Pyrenees in 1659, which caused a shift in world power from Spain to France, and a shift from the Mediterranean to the Atlantic, did the other European powers feel able to dispute Spain's hold on the New World. England and the Netherlands began to challenge Spanish power by raiding its American possessions and harrying it at sea; France disputed the military primacy of Spain in Europe. In the sugar-rich West Indies, initially claimed by Spain, the other powers succeeded in breaking Spain's grip. Barbados, Jamaica and Bermuda became British colonies; Saint Dominique, Martinique and Guadeloupe became French. European-colonized Caribbean islands would eventually yield high profits from sugar, tobacco, coffee, cotton, indigo and timber.

Despite these inroads by its rivals, Spain continued to rule what was still a great empire with outstanding administrative skill. As late as the eighteenth century, it was still expanding into Texas (1718–20) and California (1770s), while founding the future sea ports of San Diego (1769), Monterey (1770), San Francisco (1776) and Los Angeles (1781). At the end of the eighteenth century there were four major divisions in Spanish America: the vice-royalties of New Spain (founded at Mexico City in 1535), Peru (Lima, 1542), New Granada (Bogotá, 1739) and Rio de la Plata (Buenos Aires, 1776). If Britain, the Netherlands and France failed to bring down Spanish power in the New World, it was because they were more focused on trade in Asia, the Ottoman threat at sea, and Russian expansion into Central Asia and China.

The policy followed by Portugal in the colonization of Brazil discovered by Pedro Cabral (*c.* 1467–*c.* 1519) in 1500, and defended 150 years later by the Portuguese against Dutch intrusion) differed from that of Spain. Possessed in 1549 by the Portuguese, Brazil's colonization was directed by the Crown, and remained a tightly controlled colony. There were no Portuguese conquistadors. Brazil was the world's first great plantation economy – hence its use of Amerindian and African slaves. No country received more slaves from Africa than Brazil: by 1800 there were 150,000 of them – many employed in the sugar plantations – accounting for half Brazil's population. New racial mixtures of Europeans, Asians, Africans and indigenous Americans were the consequence. Showing more interest than the Spaniards in developing their colony's agriculture than in searching for gold and silver, the Portuguese extended the frontiers of Brazil beyond the line established at Tordesillas.

The conquest by Western Europeans of pre-Columbian America is a story of gain and loss.[4] The loss was the destruction of indigenous cultures and the extension of war, sickness and slavery – whence sprang the tumultuous, unstable Latin America of today. The gain was the widening of the world economy and the transformation of world agriculture. Imports of maize, manioc and other crops from the New World cannot compensate for the dual scourges of looting and slavery, but slavery-supported plantation industries in both the north and south of the continent provided Africans, Europeans and Asians with more to eat. The Western conquest also provided a bonanza of precious metals, which gave a stimulus to the North Atlantic region at a critical moment in its economic development.[5] The history of capitalism, which led to the world economy of today, began at this time. All other considerations aside, in purely material terms, the ultimate outcome was to enrich and unify the world economy.

In the early nineteenth century, encouraged by the American and French revolutions, as well as by Napoleon's invasion of the Iberian peninsula in 1808, the Iberian colonists of the New World won their independence. Whereas revolution by the English colonists of North America had been an affirmation of existing middle-class rights, the Spanish American revolutions, led by priests, landed gentry and the military, possessed the abruptness of the French Revolution. In 1804 a revolt against French control had made Haiti the first independent state in Latin America. In 1810 Mariano García Moreno (1778–1811) headed a revolutionary *junta* that replaced the Spanish administration in Argentina. Three years later José Maria Morelos (b. 1765), a Mexican priest and revolutionary, declared Mexican independence. In 1815 he was captured by the Spaniards and shot. Regardless, by 1838 the Spanish Empire in South and Central America had broken up into fifteen independent states. In the Western Hemisphere only Cuba and Puerto Rico remained tied to Spain, and even these would be lost later. Since 1850, with the exception of Cuba and Panama (both of which gained independence with the help of the USA), the map of Latin America has remained virtually unchanged.

While the history of Brazil during the early nineteenth century is not free of armed insurrection, the independence movement there followed a much less violent course than in Spanish America. As a result of Napoleon's invasion of Portugal (Britain's ally in the Napoleonic Wars) the Portuguese prince regent, Dom João, had taken refuge in Brazil (with the help of the British fleet). Having become the centre of Portuguese government, Brazil developed a will of its own. After Portugal's revolution of 1820 had caused the return of Dom João to Lisbon as King João VI of Portugal, Brazil declared its independence in 1822 under Dom Pedro, his eldest son. It was then that President James Monroe of the United States announced the Monroe Doctrine, which was a clear warning to Latin Europe not to try to recover their American empires. Behind Monroe's warning was the British fleet. Dom Pedro, having resigned as emperor in 1831, was succeeded by his son Pedro II in 1840. Brazil finally became a republic in 1889.

Of all the powers, Britain and the USA stood to gain most commercially and financially from Latin American independence. It was Britain, with the connivance of the USA, which interfered most in Spanish and Portuguese imperial affairs. Although willing to restore royalty in Europe after the Napoleonic Wars, Britain resolutely opposed the restoration of the Iberian empires in the New World. In the early 1800s, Britain financed the radical Francisco de Miranda (1750–1816) to make trouble in Spanish America. They also openly supported the republican Simón Bolívar (1783–1830), who fought for independence in Venezuela, and José de San Martín (1778–1850), who liberated Argentina, Chile and Peru. By the 1820s Peru, Uruguay, Paraguay, Colombia, Venezuela, Argentina and Bolivia had all freed themselves of Iberian rule. The strong naval force sent by Spain in 1815 to restore Spanish rule was unable to match the revolutionary privateers and the crucial military support provided by Britain and the USA.

The unity that Bolivar and San Martín sought among the newly freed colonies of Latin America was never realized. With no tradition of self-government, such as the much more pragmatic North American colonists had had, and weary of the centralization that Portugal and Spain had imposed, the semi-feudal aristocracies of Latin America chose political freedom rather than unified control.

Even where union was a possibility, disputes over boundaries and poor transport and communications impeded common action. 'Those who have made the revolution with me', said Bolivar, 'have ploughed the sea.' His Greater Colombia – comprising Venezuela, Colombia and Ecuador – was formed, only to break up again. A similar fate befell the move to join Mexico with the rest of Central America.

The struggle for power among the people of Latin America continued long after they had gained their independence from Spain and Portugal. Between the 1820s and the 1850s, Latin America was plagued by political, economic and social disorder bordering on anarchy. With the military, the rural aristocracy, the Church and the burcaucratic elite retaining control, the necessary social and political changes were evaded. If anything, property, especially land with all the power that it entailed, became concentrated in fewer hands after the wars of independence than it had been before. The poverty of the masses remained unchanged. Spawned by the turbulent conditions of the time, by the contradictions of an economic organization that ranged from slavery through feudalism to an emerging industrial capitalism, the *caudillos* – the military dictators or warlords – became the final arbiters. Some of them, having freed Latin America from Iberian oppression, became oppressors themselves. Usually they added nothing positive before being swept aside by a more powerful opponent. Of all the republics, only Chile was able to avoid the worst excesses of despotic *caudillism*. Elsewhere (especially in Brazil, Argentina, Mexico, Colombia, Bolivia, Peru, Ecuador and Uruguay) *caudillism* ruled. In Mexico the *caudillo* Antonio López de Santa Anna ruled from 1829 to 1855. In Argentina the more popular Juan Manuel de Rosas ruled from 1829 to 1852. In Guatemala Rafael Carrera ruled from 1839 to 1865. Between 1835 and 1845 the unity of Brazil was almost lost in the struggle for power by such lawless adventurers.

While most unrest in Latin America after independence was internal, several countries were also threatened from outside. Mexico, having elected Agustín de Itúrbide (1783–1824) as emperor in 1821, had to meet the challenge of the Spaniards in 1829, the Texans in 1836 and US troops in 1848. Later the Amerindian leader Benito Pablo Juárez (1806–72) had to defend Mexican territory again, this time from the French. In 1863, as a result of French intrigue, Maximilian I (b. 1832; reigned 1864–7), younger brother of the Austrian Emperor Franz Josef, became the Emperor of Mexico. With the departure of French troops in 1867 – the alternative was war with the USA – Maximilian was overthrown by Mexican republicans and executed.

Other Latin American countries affected by outside pressure included Argentina, which fought a British blockade of the Rio de la Plata (1845–7), and whose government was eventually overthrown by a coalition of Brazilian, Uruguayan and Argentinian insurgents. Between 1865 and 1870 Paraguay's population was halved in a devastating war over the territorial claims made on it by Argentina, Brazil and Uruguay. In the Pacific War of 1879–84 Chile took from Bolivia territory bordering the Pacific. In the 1890s there was a dispute over Venezuelan boundary rights between Britain and the USA.

In war and peace the countries of Latin America remained subservient to the economic hegemony exercised by Europeans and North Americans, who in exchange for manufactured goods took the bulk of Latin American raw materials and foodstuffs – chiefly grain, tobacco, fibres, coffee, sugar and hides. By 1900 Spanish and Portuguese commercial interests had been supplanted by those of Britain, the USA and France. In trade and investment Britain led; in immigration the Latins of Europe remained supreme: in the closing decades of the nineteenth century millions of immigrants arrived – chiefly Portuguese in Brazil, and Italians and Spaniards in Argentina.

With southern sea routes to Asia and the riches of the Orient controlled by the Spaniards and the Portuguese, the exploration of the northern half of the continent by the English, French and Dutch began with the search for a 'northwest passage' to the riches of the Orient. In 1497 the British sent the Italian John Cabot (1425–*c.* 1499) on a voyage in which he sighted the coast of Newfoundland. Cabot's second voyage to North America the following year was used to support England's claim to Canada, as well as to the territory of the thirteen colonies. In 1523 the French sent Giovanni da Verrazzano (*c.* 1485–*c.* 1528) on a voyage

in which he sailed as far as Newfoundland. Like Cabot, he failed to
find a passage to Asia. In 1576 the Elizabethan sea dog Martin
Frobisher (c. 1539–94) entered Arctic waters. The English naviga-
tors John Davis (c. 1550–1605) and William Baffin (c. 1584–1622)
would continue the search. In 1583 Newfoundland became Britain's
first overseas possession. Earlier, in 1534, the French navigator
Jacques Cartier (1491–1557) had entered the Gulf of St Lawrence
hoping that it would lead him to China. He claimed the St Lawrence
area as New France. Arriving there in 1603, Samuel de Champlain
(c. 1567–1635) founded the first French colony at Quebec in 1608;
Montreal was founded in 1642. In 1663 New France became a royal
colony in the French Empire. In 1673 Louis Jolliet (1645–1700) and
Père Jacques Marquette (1637–75) followed the Mississippi as far
as Arkansas. In 1682 René de La Salle (1643–87) explored the
Mississippi to the Gulf of Mexico. The territory from Quebec to
the Gulf he called Louisiana in honour of Louis XIV. After La Salle
the search for a new passage to Asia was abandoned, the development and settlement of New France was earnestly begun. By then,
New France (with a much smaller population than the English
colonies) stretched crescent-like from the mouth of the St Lawrence
to the mouth of the Mississippi.

While the first successful English colony was planted at Jamestown
in Virginia in 1607, England's search for a northwest passage to Asia
would continue until the 1630s. With the arrival of the Puritans at
Cape Cod in 1620, an English colony took root in New England. By
1642, twenty thousand Puritans – a description covering many kinds
of religious dissent – had settled on the New England coast. Maryland
became a refuge for English Catholics, the Carolinas a refuge for French
Protestants, as well as for English, German and Swiss settlers. In addition, New Jersey (1664), Pennsylvania (1681) and Delaware (1704)
were founded. Georgia (1733) was meant to be a buffer state between
the southern colonies and Spanish Florida. Instead of being faced
with an immediate life-and-death struggle with native civilizations[6]
(such as Spain had met in the southern half of the continent), the
English were able to encroach piecemeal on scattered native Indian
domains. Unable to halt the incursions of the Europeans, the Indians
found temporary relief by escaping to the plains.

Dutch interests in North America began in 1609 with Henry Hudson's search for a northwest passage. It ended later in the seventeenth century with the founding of trading colonies on Manhattan Island (1624), in Connecticut, New Jersey, Delaware and Pennsylvania.

Of the European contestants for power in North America, the strongest became Britain and France. Compared with the French or the Dutch (who possessed a valuable gateway to the interior in the Hudson River), the claims of the small, isolated pockets of Englishmen on the Atlantic seaboard to inherit the continent were improbable; especially after the English had been cut off from the interior by a line of French forts stretching from the St Lawrence via the Mississippi to New Orleans.

The clash between British and French interests in the world was not decided in America but in Europe, in the War of the Spanish Succession. In 1713, by the Treaty of Utrecht, the British obtained Acadia (which was renamed Nova Scotia), Newfoundland and the Hudson's Bay Territory. Under William Pitt 'the Elder' (1708–78), British power was extended in Canada. In 1759 a decisive battle was fought between the British and the French on the Heights of Abraham above Quebec City, in which Britain's General James Wolfe (b. 1727) triumphed over France's General Louis de Montcalm (b. 1712). Both died in the battle. In 1762 a defeated France ceded to Spain its lands west of the Mississippi (the Louisiana Territory), including the island of New Orleans.

Under the subsequent Treaty of Paris of 1763, which ended the near-global Seven Years War between the two leading powers, France ceded to Britain the whole of New France, which included the lands east of the Mississippi. In effect, France, Spain and Portugal recognized Britain as a leading world power for the first time. Through a superior maritime strategy and a superior fleet, the century-old contest between Britain and France had ended in Britain's favour (see Map IV).

The Treaty of Paris illustrates the limited nature of eighteenth-century wars among the Europeans. It was not Britain's purpose to annihilate France but to secure a balance of power among Europeans so that Britain's will would prevail. France was allowed to keep certain fishing rights on the Newfoundland banks, as well as the islands of St Pierre and Miquelon; it was also allowed to retain the valuable West Indian sugar islands of Martinique, Guadeloupe and St Lucia, and have restored to it the French settlements in India at Chandernagor and Pondicherry, as well as Gorée on the West African coast. Pitt might have talked about 'finishing off the French once and for all', but by and large it was sufficient for Britain to achieve dominance. Indeed, having won the whole of Canada, the British then played with the idea of giving it back to the French in exchange for the rich Caribbean sugar island of Guadeloupe. Britain was similarly prepared to reconcile itself to Catholic Spain's existence. Having surrendered Florida to Britain and returned the Mediterranean island of Minorca, Spain was handed back Havana and the Philippines.

In the fight to possess and exploit the New World millions perished: countless Amerindians in North and South America died in battle; others from the epidemic diseases introduced by the Europeans to which the natives were terrifyingly vulnerable.[7] It has been estimated that within 130 years 85 per cent of the native population of central Mexico had died.[8] Estimates of those killed in the Americas within a century of Columbus's landfall range from 50 to 90 per cent of the native populations. The populations of some West Indian islands, such as Haiti, were also decimated. The solution to the labour shortage in the European plantations of the New World was to substitute African slaves, but they died too, as did the Europeans who owned them. Without still more black slaves, the southern part of the Americas could not have been colonized at all.

The discovery and exploitation of the New World also altered Europe's relations with Asia. The enormous quantity of precious metals that reached Europe from Peru, Mexico and Colombia – one of the greatest windfalls in history – could now be used to buy the luxuries of the East. As a result, the first true world economy was established. The arrival of so much gold and silver in Europe, however, caused great inflation – prices in Spain increased fourfold in less than a century. A business boom followed, influencing the course of European economic development. In 1795 the German political theorist and statesman Friedrich von Gentz wrote: 'The discovery of America and a new route to the East Indies opened the greatest market, the greatest inducement to human industry, that had ever existed since the human race emerged from barbarism.'[9]

In 1763, when France ceded to England all claims to New France, there were about 65,000 Europeans there, most of them French and Catholic. There were many more native Indians, but these were poorly armed and powerless in the struggle to prevail. Far from obstructing the Europeans' intrusion, some Indian tribes helped the settlers to colonize the land. By the 1750s, with Indian help, enterprising Scots and perdurable Frenchmen in search of furs had already reached the Canadian Rockies; on their heels followed the gold-diggers, and after them the farmers.

Britain's hope that the French Canadians would eventually succumb to British culture was never realized. French Canadians resisted Anglicization. With the Quebec Act of 1774, French Canadians were guaranteed the right to their own language, religion and civil law. By 1852, when the Canadian population stood at 2.5 million, British immigrants in Upper Canada centred on Toronto, exceeded the much longer-established French population centred on Quebec.

Ironically, the destruction of French power in New France ensured the end of British power in the thirteen American colonies. With the French threat removed, British power could now be challenged. The enforcing of half-forgotten mercantile regulations that threatened the profits of American commerce, as well as the introduction of new measures (including restrictions on western settlement, interference with the profitable American West Indian sugar trade and the obnoxious Stamp Act of 1765), only served to make the need for a break by the North American colonists with the mother country all the more urgent. American grievances against Britain were first discussed at the Continental Congress, which met at Philadelphia in 1774.

With the battles of Lexington and Concord, Massachusetts, on 19 April 1775, the hope of compromise with the British died. On 15 June George Washington (1732–99) was appointed commander of the continental forces. At the Second Continental Congress on 4 July 1776 the colonists declared their intention to substitute home rule for foreign rule. They challenged the authority of the British Parliament to legislate for them 'in all cases whatsoever'. Not a vestige of monarchy remained; liberty and equality were at stake. 'All men are by nature equally free and independent,' stated the Virginia Declaration of Rights (12 June 1776). Those who led the revolt were not revolutionaries but a group of aristocrats steeped in European eighteenth-century Enlightenment ideas. Their aim was to enlarge individual freedom: 'life, liberty and the pursuit of happiness'. It is the voice of John Locke – as well as that of Thomas Paine (1737–1809), with his call for freedom of speech – that resounds in the American Declaration of Independence.

Thenceforth, the thirteen colonies fought for self-rule. The war itself, except for terrain and distance, was not a large-scale affair. Washington never commanded a force greater than twenty thousand in any single battle. While he may have been one of the least spectacular of history's great generals, he nevertheless held together a ragtag army for six almost impossible years without once committing any serious tactical error. With the indispensable help of a French army and a French fleet under Admiral de Grasse, the Americans achieved victory over British troops commanded by Charles Earl Cornwallis (1738–1805) at Yorktown on 19 October 1781. 'Humanity has won its battle,' said the French Marquis de Lafayette (1757–1834). 'Liberty now has a country.'

This, the only major war Britain fought without an ally, it lost – not least because it had already lost command of the sea to France.[10] 'United Empire Loyalists', or 'Tories', fled to Nova Scotia, the St Lawrence area and territory north of the Great Lakes. For the French, the Spaniards, the Dutch and even the Russians, who had formed a League of Armed Neutrality, the outcome at Yorktown meant the settling of long-standing grievances against the British in Europe and the rest of the world.

The main concern of those who met to draft a new constitution at Philadelphia in 1787 was not so much how to extend freedom as how to limit the power of the majority. The result was a compromise between the equalizing conditions of a frontier society and the aristocratic traditions of the Europeans. The word 'democracy' was not used. A Bill of Rights was added in 1789. The provision for slavery and provincial autonomy would become crucial in setting the stage for civil war in the 1860s.

Whatever credence is given to the American Revolution as a revolution – the Americans were just as middle class, Protestant and capitalistic at the end of it as they had been at the beginning – its influence would be felt around the world. It inspired the leaders of the French Revolution, as it did those who drafted the constitutions of Switzerland, Norway, Belgium and Canada. It was used as a precept by the Boers of South Africa on their historic trek into the interior in the 1830s, as it was by Chinese nationalists in 1911. The American Revolution stimulated nationalist revolutions in the West, as Japan's victory over Russia in 1905 would stimulate them in the East. From the point of view of world politics, it meant that a great new Anglo-Saxon power had appeared on the American continent, and that the Europeans would be forced to turn to Asia and Africa for further expansion.

Under the peace settlement of 1783 between the United States and Great Britain, all the land between Canada and Florida east of the Mississippi was assigned to the Americans. Florida was ceded to Spain. The Louisiana Territory was returned from Spain to France. American territory had more than doubled overnight from 400,000 to 895,415 square miles. At that time only about 25,000 white settlers were strung out in the new area from the Appalachians to the Mississippi.

The next great acquisition of territory by the Americans was the Louisiana Purchase of 1803, which President Thomas Jefferson (b. 1743; president 1801–9; d. 1826) obtained from the French for $11.3 million (raised chiefly in London). The territory comprised 909,380 square miles and stretched from the Mississippi to the Rocky Mountains (see Map XI). The price paid by the Americans was under three cents per acre. Any rights that native Indians had to the land were ignored. Without bloodshed, the United States had again doubled its territory. In 1804 Jefferson sent Meriwether Lewis (1774–1809) and William Clark (1770–1838) to find out what he had bought. They were also charged with the search for a water route from the Missouri to the Pacific coast.

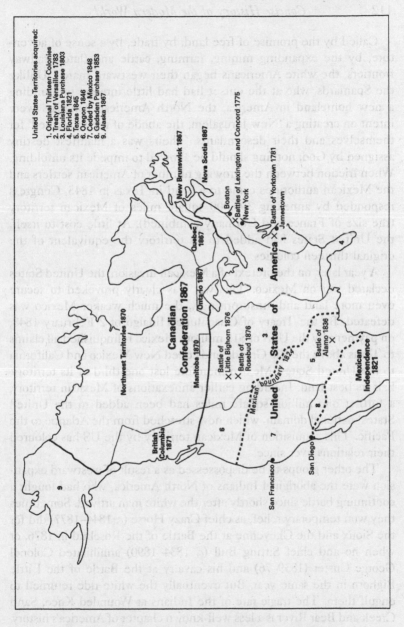

Map XI North American Expansion, 1776–1867

United States Territories acquired:
1. Original Thirteen Colonies
2. Treaty of Versailles 1783
3. Louisiana Purchase 1803
4. Florida 1821
5. Texas 1845
6. Oregon 1846
7. Ceded by Mexico 1848
8. Gadsden Purchase 1853
9. Alaska 1867

New Brunswick 1867

Nova Scotia 1867

Boston
Battles of Lexington and Concord 1775
New York
Battle of Yorktown 1781
Jamestown

Quebec
1867

Canadian
Confederation 1867

Ontario 1867

Battle of
Little Bighorn 1876
Battle of
Rosebud 1876

Manitoba 1870

Northwest Territories 1870

British Columbia 1871

San Francisco

San Diego

America

United States of

Mexican boundary

1824

Battle of
Alamo 1836

Mexican
Independence
1821

Called by the promise of free land, by trade, by a sense of adventure, by the expanding mining, farming, cattle and (later) railway frontiers, the white Americans began their westward march. Unlike the Spaniards, who at the outset had had little interest in founding a new homeland in America, the North American colonists were intent on creating a 'New Jerusalem, the abode of the redeemed' for themselves and their descendants. Theirs was a manifest destiny assigned by God; nothing should be allowed to impede its unfolding. When friction between the growing number of American settlers and the Mexican authorities came to a head in Texas in 1845, Congress responded by annexing 390,000 square miles of Mexican territory (the size of France and Germany combined). At little cost to itself, the United States had added to its territory the equivalent of the original thirteen colonies.

A year later, on the pretext of a Mexican invasion, the United States declared war on Mexico. This war was clearly provoked to secure even more land and, unsurprisingly, the much weaker Mexico was defeated. By the Treaty of Guadalupe Hidalgo of 2 February 1848, on payment by the USA of $15 million, Mexico relinquished all claims to Texas above the Rio Grande and ceded New Mexico and California to the United States. Mexico therefore lost one-third of its territory, half its best land. Including earlier annexations of Mexican territory, a further one million square miles had been added to the United States' national domain, which now stretched from the Atlantic to the Pacific. This acquisition of Mexican territory by the US has coloured their relations ever since.

The other groups to be dispossessed as a result of westward expansion were the aboriginal Indians of North America, who had fought a continuing battle since shortly after the white man arrived. Sometimes they won temporary relief, as chief Crazy Horse (*c.* 1844–1877) did for the Sioux and the Cheyenne at the Battle of the Rosebud in 1876, or when he and chief Sitting Bull (*c.* 1834–1890) annihilated Colonel George Custer (1839–76) and his cavalry at the Battle of the Little Bighorn in the same year. But eventually the white tide returned to engulf them. The tragic fate of the Indians at Wounded Knee, Sand Creek and Bear River is a less well-known chapter of America's history.

Propelled as they were by overwhelming numbers, by an extraordinary aggressiveness, by superior arms, by a righteous belief in their race, their cause and their destiny, nothing could hold back the white settlers. In contrast to the profound respect that the Indians had for nature, the white man was determined to subdue it and anyone who stood in his way.[11] The attitude that man must master nature and exploit it was alien to the natives' traditions. Their land was sacred; it could not be bought and sold. There was no escape, no compromise that the native Americans could make, no terms they could accept other than death or exile. 'Hear me, my chiefs,' said Chief Joseph (*c.* 1840–1904), a great Indian warrior and leader of the Nez Percé Indians in 1877, 'I am tired . . . my heart is sick and sad. From where the sun now stands, I will fight no more for ever.' By the 1890s Indian resistance had ended. Most Indian chiefs were dead, their people decimated, torn apart, scattered to the winds. Judged by deeds rather than words, the ultimate arbiter in the disposition of North America was naked force.

Meanwhile, America's territory had been rounded out by a compromise with the British in 1846 over the Oregon Territory, which added a further 286,541 square miles to the United States. In 1853, under the Gadsden Purchase, the USA bought what is now southern Arizona and New Mexico (29,670 square miles) from a bankrupt Mexican government at a cost of $10 million. In 1867 it also purchased Alaska's 570,374 square miles from Russia – 'a waste of snow and ice' some US senators called it – for $7.2 million (about two cents an acre). The Russians needed the money, and Siberia, Mongolia, Manchuria and Korea offered better spoils for them.

By 1868, eighty-five years after the peace treaty with Britain, US territory had grown from 393,152 to 3,608,787 square miles, a more than ninefold increase. Never was so much territory obtained so quickly and at so low a price. By the 1890s, the continental expansion of the USA was complete. It now occupied an area equivalent to the whole of Europe (including European Russia). States such as Texas and California were larger than the largest European countries. Increasingly, Americans felt that their manifest destiny called them not only across the continent but across the seas.

The more one ponders the expansion of the white man's empire across North America, the more one is struck by how relatively easy it was. Except for the colonization of Australia, there is no other example in world history of any group coming into possession of such a vast, rich area so swiftly and at so little human cost. While each death represents a tragedy that cannot be expressed with statistical detachment, American casualties in the period of its most rapid expansion were minimal. At Yorktown the Continental Army and its French allies lost 262 men. The War of 1812 with Canada, the Mexican War of the 1840s and the Spanish–American War of the 1890s were all minor clashes. The battles of the Alamo (187 dead) and the Little Bighorn (246 dead) are chiefly of symbolic importance. America was also fortunate in having only two neighbours, Canada (unified in 1867) and Mexico, both of whom were weak and (if left alone) peaceful. The relative ease with which the white American obtained what he considered to be his true inheritance must surely help to explain the Americans' sense of innocence, righteousness, confidence and optimism, especially the belief in a happy ending. Little wonder that Americans saw themselves as a distinct civilization, separate and superior to the people of the southern half of the continent.

Not only were America's wars low in casualties, they also conferred considerable benefits. The war of 1776–83 (4435 combat deaths) brought independence; the War of 1812 (2260 combat deaths) extended that independence to the high seas as well as to the Mississippi valley; the wars against Mexico in the 1840s[12] (1733 combat deaths) brought great territorial gains; even the Civil War of the 1860s (184,594 combat deaths and about 400,000 from sickness and wounds), scourge though it was – in the loss of blood and treasure it was the worst the Americans have ever fought, safeguarded the unity of the nation, abolished slavery[13] and stimulated development; the Spanish–American War of the 1890s (385 combat deaths) made the USA a world power.

In contrast to the settling of Russia (or of Europe generally), which is a story of fortified villages and towns, the settling of America in the nineteenth century entailed the clearing of the forests and the dividing of the plains. The speed with which territory was won has no better example than the whirlwind occupation of Oklahoma in 1889:

At the sound of a gun . . . a flood of 50,000 white settlers poured like an avalanche into the last great Indian reservation. By nightfall, under conditions of utter pandemonium, almost 2,000,000 acres of land had been claimed, most of it to be sold again. Within half a day, Guthrie and Oklahoma City, each with an instant population of 10,000, had come into being.[14]

The conquest of North America had repercussions around the world. Politically, it resulted in the appearance of a new, great, industrialized power. The USA not only became a great political and industrial power, through the crucible of the Civil War (with its tragic losses at Gettysburg, Antietam, the Wilderness, Fredericksburg, Petersburg, Cold Harbour and Vicksburg), which more than any other historical event defined the American character,[15] it became a unified power. Had President Abraham Lincoln (b. 1809; president 1861–5) not insisted on unity, the history of the Western world would have been very different. A dis-United States could not have intervened as decisively as it did in the two world wars. Having fought the Civil War – the first modern war – the Americans, according to the London *Spectator* of 17 February 1866, had become 'a power of the first class, a nation which is very dangerous to offend, and almost impossible to attack'. With the victory of the Union, the USA emerged as the largest naval and military force the world had ever seen. Thenceforth, America's viewpoint was taken seriously. It says a great deal for the growth in the actual and the potential power of the nation that the Americans were able to bundle Napoleon III's imperialistic-minded French troops out of Mexico (French intervention lasted from 1862 to 1867) once the Civil War was over.

The economic consequences stemming from the colonization of the North American continent were as significant as the political. Not least, it released a torrent of cheap food upon the world. By the late 1860s a US bushel of wheat cost about half as much as a European bushel. From 1852 to roughly the end of the century, the average annual American exports of wheat and wheat flour grew from 19 to 197 million bushels; in the same five decades exports of corn and corn meal rose from 7 to over 200 million bushels. The export of chilled and refrigerated meat of all kinds to Europe became a veritable flood. By 1900, American farm produce made up three-quarters of the country's total exports. By 1914, the USA (although still a net debtor nation) had vast trade surpluses with Europe. Cheaper food led to falling European death rates and a growth in population. Thanks to America's riches, famine in the Western world became a thing of the past. The flood of food from the New World, however, proved disastrous for some sectors of European agriculture; Western Europe experienced a marked fall in agricultural prices, land rents and land values.

Accompanying the avalanche of food to Europe were immense quantities of minerals, metals and raw materials, which provided a powerful stimulus to the growth of Western industrialism. The US production of crude petroleum rose from 3 million barrels in 1865 to more than 55 million in 1898. The availability of large quantities of Californian gold enabled the Western world to abandon a bimetallic standard of silver and gold in favour of a common gold standard,[16] which further facilitated the economic integration of the Old World and the New. The outcome was a reallocation of the world's resources and white hegemony around the globe.

By 1914, almost comet-like, the USA had become the agrarian, industrial and financial colossus of the world. Blessed by its resources, its abundant supplies of capital and labour, its political stability, its work ethic, its skills, its mystique of the 'American Dream' and its aggressive entrepreneurial spirit, its per capita income of $377 in 1914 soared above all the rest.[17] No other country had set aside the basic law of political economy – the law of diminishing returns – as America did. No other country had such economic potential. By moving labour and capital from Europe (where they were relatively plentiful) to the USA (where they were relatively scarce), the world – especially the white world – was economically better off.

Long before 1914, America's manifest destiny had carried it far beyond its own shores: the USA had no intention of standing aside while the Europeans were occupying the world. In 1867 it annexed

Midway Island; in 1878 it established a semi-protectorate over Tutuila in Samoa; it annexed Hawaii in 1893 (which foreshadowed its clash with Japan at Pearl Harbor in 1941) and Wake Island and Guam in 1898. Then, led by President William McKinley (b. 1843; president 1897–1901), following the sinking of the US battleship *Maine* in the port of Havana, it conquered Spanish Cuba, Puerto Rico, the Philippines (1898)[18] and whatever else was left of Spain's empire, other than Morocco. The Philippines were regarded by the USA as a suitable jumping-off point for China, and a possible redoubt against future Japanese aggression, but Filipino insurgents bitterly contested the US presence in a brutal and costly six-year war. In the first three years of occupation 4234 Americans were killed in guerrilla attacks; between 1898 and 1900 more than 200,000 Filipinos – most of them civilians – died in the fighting. President Theodore Roosevelt (b. 1858; president 1901–9; d. 1919)[19] thought it 'the most glorious war in our nation's history'.

At the turn of the century, unsuccessful efforts were made to lease Samsah Bay from China. Americans began to talk about Manchuria becoming America's 'new West' (which is partly why, in 1907 and 1910, Russia and Japan divided it between themselves). The US Secretary of State, John Hay, proclaimed his 'open door' policy, whereby economic opportunities in China should be available to the Americans on equal terms with the Europeans. American Christian missionaries were sent there.[20]

As a 'corollary' to the Monroe Doctrine (1823), Theodore Roosevelt announced the right of the USA to intervene in Latin America to prevent 'chronic wrongdoing' and European interference. Thus the door was opened to subsequent military intervention (thirty instances in all between 1898 and 1928) in Nicaragua, Cuba, the Dominican Republic, Haiti, Panama, Mexico and Grenada. In 1902 Cuba became a US protectorate. The next year Colombian territory was seized by American-backed Panamanians. This allowed the eventual construction of the Panama Canal, which was completed in 1914. In 1907, to demonstrate how powerful the USA had become, Roosevelt sent his Great White Fleet (the world's third most powerful) around the globe.

Encouraging the Americans' expansive urge was the belief in

their role as God's chosen people: the American way was the right way, the normal way, the only way to save the world. Americans took it for granted that it was all part of God's plan. That is why America was called 'God's country'. 'Almighty God', said Senator Beveridge in 1900, 'has marked us as His chosen people, henceforth to lead in the regeneration of the world.' In his book *Our Country* (1885) Josiah Strong wrote:

> This race . . . having developed peculiarly aggressive traits calculated to impress its institutions upon mankind, will spread itself over the earth . . . this powerful race will move down upon Mexico, down upon Central and South America, out upon the islands of the sea, over upon Africa and beyond.

The expansion of America and American commercial and financial interests, so it was thought, would usher in a worldwide golden age of justice, democracy and economic well-being. All of which was contrary to the outlook of the Founding Fathers, who had been concerned to safeguard the nation's interests at home: 'The United States', warned President John Quincy Adams (b. 1767; president 1825–9; d. 1848), 'should never go abroad in search of monsters to destroy. [If she should do so,] she might become the dictatress of the world; [but] she would no longer be ruler of her own spirit.'

This idea of a manifest destiny was not peculiarly American. Most nineteenth-century Europeans felt the same. The British spoke of a 'white man's burden' to Christianize and raise up the rest of the world; the French stressed their *'mission civilisatrice'*; the Germans the Russians and the Belgians also thought that they possessed a superior civilization and that they had a right and a duty to tell the world what to do.

On the eve of war in 1914, most Americans would have agreed with the sentiments expressed by Senator Beveridge and Josiah Strong. No mention was made at the time that America's gains had been won at a high cost to the Mexicans, the Filipinos, the Amerindians and the African blacks. That would, of course, have smacked of imperialism – which was not what American history was about. The truth is that while Americans have been more idealistic and moralistic in their outlook on the world, they have essentially been involved with the struggle for power that has affected all other expansionist nations. No matter how altruistic a nation might intend to be, if imperialism means taking other people's land by force, if it means imposing one's will on others, if it means plundering other people's wealth without moral scruples, if it means considering oneself superior, then Americans – the moralistic rhetoric of presidents Theodore Roosevelt, William Howard Taft (b. 1857; president 1909–13; d. 1930) and Thomas Woodrow Wilson (b. 1856, president 1913–21, d. 1924) notwithstanding – were imperialistic. They ascribed to themselves a purity of motive, and altruism towards others, that no expansionist nation could possibly possess.

Meanwhile, the seeds of a new nation – Canada – were being sown north of America's border. After the American War of Independence between 40,000 and 60,000 British loyalists had settled on the northern shores of the Great Lakes and the upper St Lawrence, causing friction with the French in Lower Canada. By 1791, the British in Upper Canada (Ontario) outnumbered the French of Lower Canada (Quebec).

The American attempt in 1812 to seize eastern Canada compelled the British and the French Canadians to close ranks, but disunity was not banished for long. In 1837–8, following rebellions for self-government in both Upper and Lower Canada, the British government appointed Lord Durham (1792–1840) to carry out an inquiry. The famous Durham Report appeared in 1839 and found 'two nations warring in the bosom of a single state'. Durham recommended that English-speaking Upper Canada and French-speaking Lower Canada should be united under one legislature. French and English differences, however, were not so easily settled. In 1864 the Quebec Conference was still discussing self-government for English- and French-speaking areas.

Pressure from the United States – in 1846 Canada lost more than 250,000 square miles to the USA under the Oregon Treaty – fostered Canadian unity. A compromise about the boundary was reached between Britain and the USA, whereby President James K. Polk's (b. 1795; president 1845–9) demand for the whole of the Oregon territory up to the boundary of Russian America ('Fifty-four forty or fight') was met at the 49th Parallel. After much bickering, Vancouver remained Canadian. In 1848 Canada won limited self-government from Britain.

New threats to Canadian territory came in the 1860s at the time of the American Civil War. Fearful of US intrusion (the Canadians were accused of having harboured Confederate guerrillas) and expansion (America purchased Alaska), in 1867 the British North America Act established the Dominion of Canada, which included Ontario, Quebec, Nova Scotia and New Brunswick. The population was about 3.5 million, most of them living east of the Great Lakes. Canada's new constitution modestly called for 'peace, order and good government'. In 1870, following an Indian rebellion, Manitoba was created. British Columbia joined the confederation in 1871. In the same year, in the Treaty of Washington, a northwest boundary dispute was settled in favour of the USA.

While the completion of the Canadian Pacific Railway in 1885 (the unifying factor of Canadian history) and a growing prairie population (one million in 1881) strengthened Canada's hold on the western provinces, the Canadians still feared that the USA might try to wrest territory from them. In 1911 the US House Speaker Champ Clark declared that he hoped to see the day 'when the American flag will float over every square foot clear to the North Pole'. In the same year, by which time Canada had become the second-largest country in the world next to Russia, President Taft caused a storm by talking about annexation. Canada's population at that time was just 7 million, compared to the USA's 92 million.

Although successful in maintaining its political independence, Canada was unable to stem US commercial infiltration. By 1914, American interests controlled much of Canada's transport, banking, agriculture and manufacture. Canada had become America's greatest field of foreign investment. Nor was it able to prevent the departure to the USA of many of its nationals: throughout the second half of the nineteenth century more Canadians were migrating to the USA than there were Europeans entering Canada. In the period 1870–90 Canada received 1.5 million immigrants from Europe, but lost 2 million emigrants to the USA, most of them Canadian-born.

Only in the first two decades of the twentieth century was the process reversed. On 21 May 1913 the first Asian migrants appeared off Canada's western shores. The Japanese ship that entered Vancouver harbour with three hundred Hindu would-be migrants was turned away. But in little more than a year the Canadians would be fighting alongside Indians in defence of the British Empire.

The First World War was a major turning point in Canadian history. Although Canada had sent troops to fight alongside the British in the Boer War (1899–1902), the French Canadians had protested and the Canadian soldiers had to be brought back home. In 1914, with the fate of France as well as Britain at stake, Canada's response was un-equivocal: within weeks thirty thousand of Canada's best sons had voluntarily embarked for Europe to fight on the Western Front. While formal independence from Britain would have to wait until 1931, effec-tive independence for Canada (which by 1914 included nine provinces) was won by the valour shown by its troops in France and elsewhere. In consequence, in 1919 Canada was accorded a separate seat at Versailles.

8

The West in the World

The importance of Christopher Columbus is not that he 'discovered' America; America had been discovered long before 1492.[1] His importance lies in the fact that he began a process whereby Western man extended his influence by sea across the world. By the end of the eighteenth century – whether in the cause of God, greed or glory – most of the world's seas and coastlines had been explored by Europeans. The first stages of Western colonialism and global integration had been completed.

It was a process in which the claim of one European power was always being disputed by that of another. No sooner had Spain and Portugal divided the world between them (one claiming the West, the other the East) than their claims were contested by other European powers, as well as by the Arabs and the Turks. With the defeat of the Spanish Armada by the English in 1588, Spain forfeited its leading position at sea. In the seventeenth century English, Dutch and French East India companies were formed to wrest the monopoly of Eastern trade from the Portuguese, who – under the Portuguese empire-builder Afonso de Albuquerque (1453–1515) – had earlier wrested sea power from the Arabs and their allies. Each harrowing the other, British and French efforts were concentrated on India, while the Dutch attacked the Portuguese in Indonesia. France established its first colony in India in 1674. Unable to beat off the other Europeans, by 1700 all that was left of the Portuguese East Indian empire was Timor in Indonesia, the forts Goa, Daman and Diu in India, and Macao in China.

A similar threat to Spanish and Portuguese interests was made by the British, Dutch, French, Prussians and Scandinavians along the north and west coasts of Africa. In 1652 the Dutch began their colonization of the Cape Province in South Africa. Because it was more profitable to colonize North America and the Caribbean, and also because the British, French and Dutch were too busy fighting one another to concentrate their efforts on robbing the Iberians of their South American possessions, Spanish and Portuguese power in South America remained intact until it was broken by the indigenous revolutionary movements of the early nineteenth century.

By 1800, the worldwide struggle between the European powers had been settled in Britain's favour.[2] Robert Clive's victory over the French-supported forces of the Nawab of Bengal Siraj-ud-Daulah at Plassey in India in 1757,[3] and General James Wolfe's victory over the French at Quebec in 1759, had laid the foundations for an empire that would eventually comprise about a quarter of the globe (see Maps IX, X and XII), For Britain, there followed a glorious century of prosperity and peace.

The eighteenth-century victories over the French in India and North America set the stage for British exploration in the Southern Hemisphere. To enhance its naval power, Britain needed additional naval bases, as well as access to naval stores. In particular, Britain sought to confirm the existence of an island continent which since earliest times had appeared on European maps as Terra Australis Incognita.

Exploration by the British of Australia began with the three voyages of James Cook (1728–79), who in 1768–9 charted the coasts of New Zealand and sailed north along the east coast of Australia. Although he gave positive geographical identity to Australia and New Zealand, he at first claimed for Britain only eastern Australia and the adjacent islands in the Pacific. His later voyages (1772 and 1776) added greatly to Europe's knowledge of the region.

Not until after the arrival of the first British convicts, soldiers and government officials in 1788 did Britain consider claiming the entire continent of Australia. By the 1830s, almost without bloodshed, the

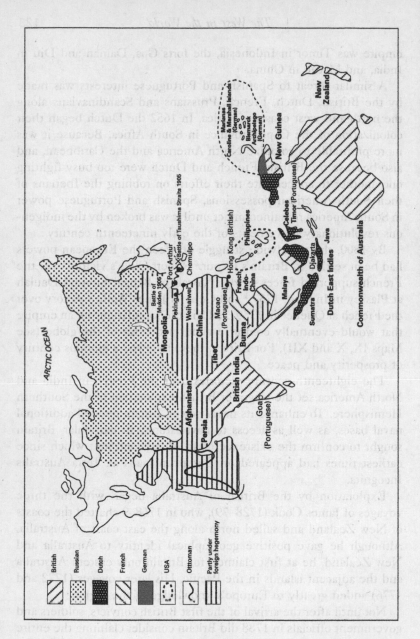

Map XII European Empires in Asia and Australasia in 1914

British

Russian

Dutch

French

German

USA

Ottoman

Partly under
foreign hegemony

ARCTIC OCEAN

New Zealand

New Guinea

Marianas
Caroline & Marshall Islands
(German)
Bismarck
Archipelago
(German)

Commonwealth of Australia

Celebes
Timor (Portuguese)
Java
Dutch East Indies
Djakarta
Sumatra
Malaya
French
Indo-China
Macao
(Portuguese)
Burma
Philippines
Hong Kong (British)
Chemulpo
Port Arthur
Battle of Tsushima Straits 1905
Weihaiwei
Peking
Battle of
Mukden 1905
China
Tibet
British India
Goa
(Portuguese)
Afghanistan
Persia
Mongolia

British had laid claim to an area almost equal in size to the continental United States. Tasmania became a British colony in 1803. New Zealand was claimed as British territory in 1814 and, to foil the French, as a British colony in 1840. By 1850, the British population of Australia had grown to 400,000. Stimulated by gold discoveries in 1851, the immigrant population had passed the million mark by 1860. The dominant stock was English, Scottish, Irish and Welsh.

With the improvement of sea transport, both Australia and New Zealand became sources of wool, sugar and wheat for Britain. The improvement of steamship communications in the 1870s, and the successful introduction of refrigeration in the 1880s, made possible the development of the great Australian and New Zealand meat and dairy industries for the British market. Culturally, politically, economically and militarily, Australia and New Zealand remained tied to Britain, twelve thousand miles away.

In 1901 the Commonwealth of Australia was formed – the only nation with a continent to itself. By then, the British population of Australia had grown to four million. To guard itself from being inundated by Asians (the implications of Japan's defeat of China in 1895 and of Russia in 1904–5 were not lost on Australia's leaders), in 1902 Australia introduced its immigration restriction (white Australia) policy.[4] By this time, the aboriginal population had undergone a dramatic decline; victims of acute cultural shock, and of European sicknesses, arms and alcohol, they were overwhelmed by the ever-growing, aggressive tide of white immigrants.

In the First World War Australian troops played a crucial role in defending the British Empire. It was from the crucible of war, especially out of the battle for Gallipoli in 1915, that Australia found its national identity.

The first Europeans to visit New Zealand were seal and whale hunters; the first permanent European settlements there were those of British missionaries. Pioneering British agricultural settlements were founded in the 1840s. The British fought two long wars (1843–8 and 1860–70) against the native Maoris, a race of Polynesian–Melanesian descent, without success. The discovery of gold in the 1860s caused an enormous influx of British immigrants; non-European migrants were kept out by restrictive policies. In 1907

New Zealand became a dominion within the British Empire. Seven years later, with a European population of approximately one million and a Maori population of about 50,000 (one-fifth their eighteenth-century numbers), New Zealand identified itself with the British cause in the First World War.

Meanwhile, throughout the eighteenth and nineteenth centuries, the rivalry of the European powers in the Pacific never ceased. In 1828 the Dutch annexed western New Guinea. Tahiti and the Marquesas became a French protectorate in 1842. In 1853 the French acquired New Caledonia; in 1864 they took the Loyalty Islands. To offset these French moves, in the 1870s the British claimed Fiji. In the 1870s and 1880s the United States and Britain squabbled over Samoa and New Guinea. In 1884 the British annexed the southeastern part of New Guinea, which was turned over to Australia in 1906 and given the old Portuguese name of Papua. The Germans had already annexed the northeastern part of the island, as well as those of the Bismarck Archipelago. In 1885 they also laid claim to the Marshall and Solomon islands. In 1887 Britain and France forestalled Germany by establishing their rule in the New Hebrides. The Cook Islands became a British protectorate the next year. In 1900, in exchange for German possessions in the Solomons, Britain relinquished its rights in Samoa. The United States retained Tutuila (Pago Pago became its naval base). The last extension of European rule in the Pacific before the outbreak of war in 1914 was Britain's action in 1900 in making the Friendly and Savage islands its protectorates. By then, the colonization of the world by European man had almost run its course. Because of their supremacy at sea, Western European empires comprised about half the landmass and half the population of the world. It was the greatest acquisition of land in world history (see Maps X and XII).

Much imperial action in the nineteenth century can be traced to the growth of an imperialist ideology, which eventually meant that unless a country obtained a share in the world's colonial possessions it could not rank as a great power. French action in Algeria in the 1830s, and German action in Southwest Africa in the 1880s, sprang more from national pride than from the economic inadequacies of

French and German capitalism. 'All great nations', the German historian Heinrich von Treitschke (1834–96) wrote in 1887, 'in the fullness of their strength have desired to set their mark upon barbarian lands ... Those who take no share in this great rivalry will play a pitiable part in time to come. The colonizing impulse has become a vital question for a great nation.'[5]

The growth of an imperialist ideology was closely linked with a European mission to civilize the world. From the fifteenth to the twentieth century the West felt a psychological necessity to impose the superiority of its civilization upon others.[6] The early European missionaries and the old-time colonial administrators felt that religious change, a Western liberal education and a general European culture were necessities for the native ruling classes of their colonial wards. Hear King Leopold II (b. 1835; reigned 1865–1909) of the Belgians opening a geographical conference at Brussels in September 1876: 'To open up to civilization the sole part of the globe [Africa] to which it has not yet penetrated, to pierce the darkness which still envelops whole populations, is, I venture to say, a crusade worthy of this century of progress.'[7] Was Leopold speaking the truth, or was he, like the other imperialists of the time, trying to justify colonialism?

The prevailing European belief in the superiority of the white race also carried with it an obligation to the coloured peoples of the world. While the national ethos of each European country was projected overseas, to a greater or lesser degree all the European nations felt the same consciousness of destiny and duty to others. The degree of sympathy developed by the West for the whole of mankind undoubtedly influenced its African and Asian colonial developments. With the benefit of hindsight, it is not difficult to see that the ethics and the political ideology of the West would eventually be rejected by those they colonized; that in the things that mattered the non-European world already had traditions of civilization; and that in the last count the Christian gospel of love would be surpassed by the power of Mammon.

Ignoring the social and historical circumstances of the territory over which they came to rule, ignoring tradition and social customs, ignoring human rights, ignoring or suppressing native religions and social order, the Europeans imposed their political, economic, religious, philosophical and legal ideas on many parts of the non-European world. Land, labour and capital became factors of production to be bought and sold in a self-regulating world market. In the eighteenth and nineteenth centuries Western concepts concerning saving, investment and production were introduced to non-Western communities for the first time. Also introduced were new ideas concerning time, punctuality, discipline, personal responsibility, taxes, monetary rewards and punishments. Under European tutelage, change came to be looked upon as a virtue rather than a threat.

In divorcing economic motives from the social environment, in introducing an all-purpose money (in place of self-sufficiency and barter) which could buy and sell anything (including land, which hitherto had not been monetized), in emphasizing the role of the individual instead of that of the family or the tribe, in treating individual ownership as sacrosanct, in exaggerating the power of reason in the making of economic decisions, in creating a world economy dependent upon the West – in all these ways Western man transfigured the world. As a result, the economies of the other continents became linked to and interdependent with the interests of a politically and technically superior Europe. Under European aegis, a world system was born that would lead to the globalism of today. For many people – especially the Europeans – it created a richer world; yet it was a world that was much more complicated, much more sensitive to the booms and busts of the capitalist West. For Europeans and non-Europeans alike, it was a less stable world than that which had existed before.

European spiritual and secular ideas were part of the baggage carried by an unparalleled number of Europeans migrating to the rest of the world. Between 1830 and 1930 about sixty million Europeans left their homelands for overseas or for Siberia. It was the greatest migration of all time, leaving some countries with a much-reduced workforce. The vast majority migrated to the Americas, where there was an unlimited demand for labour and higher wages. In the 1850s the largest groups of migrants were British and Irish. They were soon joined by Germans and Scandinavians, and from the 1880s onwards by Italians, Spaniards, Portuguese, Greeks, Austro-Hungarians, Turks (or, more accurately, minority groups living in Turkey), Poles and Russians (including many ethnic Jews). By the early twentieth century, the Latin and the Slavic migrants outnumbered the Anglo-Saxons. The peak of the movement was reached in the first decade of the twentieth century: between 1903 and 1914 the annual flow from Europe to America was never less than three-quarters of a million emigrants.

Prompting this movement was rapid population growth. Between about 1730 and about 1780, Britain and Prussia increased their numbers by 100 per cent, France by 50 per cent. Between 1750 and 1850, the European population rose by as much as 80 per cent. Between 1850 and 1910, the population rose from 270 to 460 million.[8] It was fortunate for Europe that at the time of its most rapid population growth a vast new world, whose native populations had been decimated, had become available for colonization. Between 1800 and 1900, the population of areas of European settlement (in Europe itself and the rest of the world) increased from 24 to 36 per cent of the total world population.

Until the First World War, European large-scale migration was essentially the transfer of agricultural workers from areas where land was scarce to areas where land was plentiful. By and large, the movement of Europeans was characterized by individual want, individual hope, individual decision, individual enterprise and individual suffering. Because of the potato blight, and the resultant famine and sicknesses, no nation lost as great a proportion of its people to emigration as Ireland, whose population between 1845 and 1851 declined from 9 to 6.5 million. The 'great starving' was a defining moment in Irish history; the blessing was that, in America, the Irish emigrants found an open door.

The outcome of all these migrations was the establishment, in the Americas, Siberia, Australasia and the temperate zones of Africa, of a new European world outside Europe. If Europe had not risen and expanded as it did, white Americans, Canadians, Latin Americans, Australians, New Zealanders, South Africans and many Russians would not be where they are today. Nor would non-white people, who throughout the nineteenth century – either because of individual wants or because of the need for labour by the Europeans – migrated throughout Southeast Asia and South America. While the European powers have lost their colonial empires, their descendants remain in possession of great parts of the world.

Europe's unprecedented migration was not achieved without inflicting much suffering upon the peoples of other continents. The African slave trade cannot be understood in any other way; nor can the transfer of coolie labour from China to the Americas. Western needs – sometimes expressed as Western *greed* – aided by superior weapons, alcohol and devastating sicknesses,[9] accelerated the decline of many native American, African, Australian and Asian societies. The number of indigenous peoples lost to Western-transmitted diseases is uncertain; yet it was of catastrophic proportions. The onslaught of European microbes was far more deadly than that of European weapons.

Europeans not only wrought change in the world through the migration of people. Assisted by the relative peace prevailing among the great powers during the nineteenth century, they eventually developed a network of world finance, upon which depended the growth of world transport, trade and migration. To do so required changes in the outlook of self-subsisting colonial societies. Where circumstances were favourable, as in the United States, the British dominions and certain Latin American countries – the areas which before 1914 received most financial assistance from Europe – the effect of Western investment was considerable.[10] In the economically less developed regions of the world, including China, India, most of Africa and Latin America, its visible impact was limited to those export sectors of the economy in which European interests and influence were greatest. The bulk of these investments in the century before 1914 went into critically important public utilities – especially transport and communications – which provided the economic foundations of a Eurocentric world.[11]

The diffusion by Europeans of new ideas and practices, as well as the redistribution in the world of existing plants and animals, transformed world agriculture. Vast areas in the temperate and tropical zones were opened up for primary production. Cereals such as maize,[12] wheat, rice, barley, rye and oats, fruits such as bananas, oranges, limes, peaches and grapes, fibres such as cotton, beverages such as tea and coffee, crops such as sugar cane, draught animals such as the horse, the mule and the ox, and animals for food such as fowl, hogs, sheep, goats and cattle (many of which Europe had itself inherited from Asia) were carried by Europeans to every part of the world. In particular, Europe's colonization of the New World allowed it to transfer to other continents many native American plants, including tobacco, coffee, sugar, corn, cacao, certain beans, yams, manioc, peanuts, pineapples, tomatoes and potatoes. After 1492 nobody ate the same food again.

From Peru came two important plants: cinchona, the source of quinine, and coca, the source of cocaine. South America was also the source of rubber-bearing plants, which became the basis of the rubber plantation industry of East Asia. Europeans also diffused scientific knowledge concerning the breeding of plants and animals, soil bacteriology, the use of artificial fertilizers and systems of cultivation. The most important single way in which European influence was felt in tropical agriculture was through the establishment overseas of botanical gardens, laboratories, experimental stations and departments of agriculture. Accompanying plants and animals were European agricultural techniques, tools and machinery. The extension of British and other European agricultural techniques and machinery allowed Canada, Australia and New Zealand and parts of Africa to win a place in the forefront of agricultural development.

The earliest industrial techniques diffused from Europe to the world were the simple basic manufactures (such as textiles) as well as those employed in food and raw-material processing and refining (such as food refrigeration and mining technology). These were followed by techniques needed for manufacturing capital equipment (for example, steel). Techniques in all these fields had, of course, existed before the European age began. Europe's contribution was to change the scale of industry: mass-production techniques and concentrated, steam-driven industry were the hallmarks of Britain's Industrial Revolution and its impact in the world. As the Western industrialized countries became rich and powerful, industrialization came to be regarded as the key to worldly success.

These industrial techniques could never have been developed had the Europeans not also provided the technology to exploit the great mining areas of the world. Although minerals have attracted the attention of mankind since the earliest times, it was not until the end of the eighteenth and the beginning of the nineteenth century (most mining activity has come into existence since then) that important advances in the science of mineralogy (especially in the improvement of certain mechanical and chemical processes) were made by Western man. The rapid growth of coal, copper, precious-metal (such as gold) and oil mining over the past two hundred years was made possible by these developments.

None of these changes had as dramatic an effect upon the world as the European and North American development of transport and communications. In the eighteenth century transport was essentially what it had been since the discovery of the sail, the wheel, the stirrup and the modern harness. Between 1815 and 1914, under Western auspices, a veritable revolution in transport and communications took place. In terms of economic opportunities a new world emerged. The steam locomotive (indispensable to the spread of industrialization), steamship (first used to cross the Atlantic in 1819), car, submarine, aeroplane, radio, cable (in 1866 the Old and the New worlds were connected by cable), telegraph and telephone were all invented before the First World War.

At the beginning of the nineteenth century Napoleon could travel no faster than Caesar had done two thousand years before. Half a century later – thanks to European and North American developments – the situation was transformed. In 1869 the Suez Canal – its principal architect was the Frenchman Ferdinand de Lesseps (1805–94) – was completed, reviving commerce in the eastern Mediterranean, and shortening the distance from London to Bombay from 10,700 to 6270 miles. Also in the second half of the nineteenth century improved steamships cut the time of their voyages by half or two-thirds. In 1901 Guglielmo Marconi (1874–1937) transmitted wireless signals across the Atlantic. The following year the first trans-Pacific cable was laid. In 1918 Alexander Graham Bell (1847–1922) made the first telephone call across America. The extraordinary progress made more recently in aviation, space exploration, nuclear science, television, weaponry, electronics and computer science, while making a greater degree of globalization inevitable, should not blind us to the significant changes that took place prior to the First World War, including the domestic comforts which we now take for granted, such as heat for the home, safe drinking water and gas and electric lighting.

While many techniques have originated in non-Western parts of the world (particularly Asia), and have sometimes spread without Western help, Western man's contribution to the raising of general technical levels and living standards in the world probably has no equal. The USA's pre-eminence in technology is one of the reasons why the twentieth century has been called the 'American century'. While we could never fully explain the changes the world has undergone this past half-millennium, we know enough to be able to conclude that the development and transfer of Western scientific and technological ideas and practices have changed the relations hitherto existing among mankind.

One of the outcomes of the worldwide diffusion of Western science and technology was a vast increase in international commerce. From the early decades of the nineteenth century, a world economy emerged focused upon Western Europe (in particular upon the leading trading nation of the time, Britain). The great traders of the modern age were Europeans. They developed international trade until it embraced not only the luxury items of commerce, but the indispensable things of daily life. Under Western direction the scale of international trade was transformed. The mercantile system of the seventeenth century, in which a state was concerned to amass wealth (gold and silver) by protecting its national monopolies in foreign and colonial trade, gave way to the movement for freer trade.[13] The essential benefits accruing from the growth of world commerce were the enlargement and concentration of production in the areas of the world most suitable for particular items of trade.

For some countries, trade with the West was the essential forerunner of their economic development. Consider the early dependency of European-settled parts of the world, such as the Americas and Australasia, upon the export to Europe of primary produce. For many countries, the commercial needs of the West became vital to their very existence. Witness the dependence of Mauritius on sugar, Colombia on coffee, Ghana on cocoa, Sri Lanka on tea, Liberia on rubber, Egypt on cotton, Bolivia on tin and Suriname on bauxite. More recently, many countries, including Kuwait, Saudi Arabia, Bahrain, Venezuela and Brunei, have become almost totally dependent on the sale of oil. Nor is the economic impact the end of the story. There could not be economic impact without cultural impact: accompanying Western trade were the principles and objectives of Western civilization.

While one should not exaggerate the influence of Western man in the creation of the modern world – the modern world is in fact the result of an extremely complicated, interrelated process in which it is often impossible to distinguish the impact of one civilization or era from that of another – the colonization of the world by Western man left behind it a legacy of dependency between Europe and the rest of the world that had not existed before. There had been 'world economies' before the sixteenth century, but they had always been transformed into empires. Only Europe embarked on the path of capitalistic development on a world scale. Without European expansion there would have been no international economy as we know it; certainly there would have been no global economy. However critical of Western expansion one may be, whatever disadvantages one may list against it, there can be no denying that it eventually brought within the grasp of mankind the hope of a better human lot.

In its immensity, in its worldwide ramifications, in its religious, social, cultural and economic effects, the impact of Western man is without historical parallel.[14] Yet it did not go unchallenged. Opposition to the Western powers in Asia was similar to that in Africa and South America. From the 1880s until 1914, French rule was resisted in Chinese Annam, Indo-China and Cambodia. The British experienced widespread mutiny in India (1857), large-scale warfare in Burma (1886–91) and terrorist campaigns in the western and eastern provinces of India (1905–9). Growing disturbances in China culminated in the Boxer

Uprising (1899–1900) and the Chinese Nationalist Revolution (1911–12). There was also Muslim hostility against the extension of Russian rule in Central Asia (which was to become a revolt in 1916), widespread rebellion against Dutch rule in the Dutch East Indies, especially between 1881 and 1908, and continuing warfare against the Americans in the Philippines from 1898 until 1913. Whatever the causes of these anti-Western revolts, they proved to be precursors of the independence movements that swept through the colonial world in the half-century after 1914.

Few Europeans recognized what their expansion in the world had entailed for others. It took men of the calibre of James Cook and Alexander von Humboldt (1769–1859) to appreciate the clash of cultures that was taking place. Cook tried to see the manners and the morals of the Polynesian people through their eyes, not through the eyes of a European. 'That thieves are hanged in England,' he wrote, 'I thought no reason why they should be shot in Otaheite. They had no such law among themselves, and it did not appear to me that we had any right to make such a law for them.' Humboldt, in his South American journeys, was sharply critical of the Christian missionaries. 'The colonized Indian', he wrote, 'is frequently no more a proper Christian than the independent heathen. Both are totally concerned with the needs of the moment – both are equally indifferent to Christian concepts.' It was because the West was largely blind to other people's cultures, and the destructive aspects of its own civilization, that its belief in the superiority of its own ways continued unimpaired.

Europe's imprint on the world remains, but its empires have vanished; most of the political ties which once bound the rest of the world to Europe have been broken. With the exception of the North and South Americans, Australasians and other groups of ex-Europeans abroad, Europe's rule was short-lived – especially so in Africa. Even with the Aztecs, the Incas and the Mayas, where Western intrusion had such dramatic results, elements of linguistic and cultural unity survived and are now growing. The West went on to carve up China into spheres of influence, but China never ceased to be China; nor India, India. Until the eighteenth century, changes in India came more from religious revival than from Mogul or Western invasion. Hindus, rooted securely in their own culture, treated Moguls and Europeans as what they were – aliens. It was only in the second half of the nineteenth century that Europe truly extended its dominion over the world; its control of the land area grew from about one-third in 1800 to three-quarters in the 1870s. In Africa, European political dominance disappeared in a couple of generations.

In 1914 Europe was still a world civilization; European history was still the most important part of world history. European science and technology, European systems of administration and bureaucratization (such as that imposed by Britain upon India) and even European finance continued to have an impact on the world. In 1914 much of the world was still dependent upon Europe. European ideas – not least the ideas of secular rationality, of progress, of self-determination, of nationalism and of revolutionary socialism – were also very much alive. Even so, the Eurocentric world of the nineteenth century was about to crumble. There were Europeans, of course, who still believed in Christianity as a world religion, in the Western idea of progress for the human race, in the inherent superiority of Europeans to other peoples and cultures, in their duty to colonize and lift up the people of the world, in individualism, in a liberal economic and political world order, in capitalism, rationalism and egalitarianism, but by then they were becoming a minority. Even those who clung to the idea of Europe's mission to the world no longer held that belief with the certainty, fervour and compulsion – least of all with the megalomania and will to power – of earlier times.

9

Europe's Scientific and Industrial Revolutions

Europe's ability to straddle and exploit the world depended upon its pre-eminence in science[1] and technology. Whereas between the third and the fifteenth centuries Arabic, Persian, Chinese and Indian science and technology had been more advanced than those of the West, from the sixteenth century onwards the balance shifted to Europe.

Of incalculable importance in the progress of the West's scientific revolution was the fifteenth-century introduction of printing,[2] which made available a vast store of new and accumulated knowledge, both secular and divine. Knowledge became fluid and mobile. Originating in China, the manufacture of paper was taken up by the Arab world and then – possibly through the capture of Muslim paper mills during the reconquest of Spain – by the Europeans.

The new spirit of rational enquiry in sixteenth-century Europe – the new mental vigour – owed a debt to the earlier path-breaking work of the Arab mathematician Abu Ali al-Hazen (*c*. 965–1038) in optics and the Florentine architect Filippo Brunelleschi (1377–1446) in perspective geometry. With the aid of the new perspective drawing, one could not only depict the precise image of the human body; more important, one could begin to depict and eventually measure the entire globe.[3] The fanciful maps of Marco Polo's day, which placed Jerusalem or Beijing at the centre, were replaced by less theological and picturesque but much more accurate maps of the earth. In providing, visually and philosophically, a new view of the world, the arts and the sciences could be pursued more realistically. In the West man and science, not God, became the measure of things.[4]

Although the birth of modern science – the dominant intellectual passion of our age – is thought to have begun with the work of the astronomers Copernicus and Galileo, their observations were dependent upon earlier Chinese, Arabic, Indian and Persian contributions.[5] Vital to the progress of scientific work in Europe was the translation and literary transmission of ancient Greek and Arabic scientific texts from Spain – including the works of Euclid, Archimedes, Hippocrates and Galen – which stimulated scientific enquiry and criticism. Although Western Europe had had access to Greek and Arabic science and logic since the twelfth century (the reconquest of Toledo in 1085 had yielded an astonishing number of such literary treasures), it was not until the middle of the sixteenth century that the rediscovery of ancient science by the Europeans reached its climax.

In shifting the focus from the earth to the sun, Western scientists overturned the older Hellenistic, geocentric view of the universe. Kepler, using data compiled by Brahe, eventually reduced the Copernican system to mathematical exactitude: mathematics became the key to understanding the universe. For saying that the earth was smaller than and orbited the sun, whereas church doctrine held that the earth was the very centre of God's creation, Galileo almost lost his life. In 1633 he was forced to recant. It is hardly surprising (given the influence of the Inquisition) that in the seventeenth century Italy lost its leading position in scientific innovation to France, England and the Netherlands.

The radical, new view of the universe helped to overthrow not only the intellectual traditions of the Middle Ages but those of the ancient world. In ignoring the authority of scripture and tradition, the moral component was removed from science. The Church could no longer defend its actions with theological arguments. If the Church's view of the universe, which was based on Aristotle (384–322 BC) and Ptolemy (AD 87–165), was wrong, what was right? It was not until 1616 (more than half a century after its publication) that the Catholic Church placed Galileo's book on the *Index of Prohibited*

Books. It was not used for teaching in most European universities for another two hundred years.[6]

The writings of Copernicus and Galileo released a force of critical enquiry based on scientific observation and mathematical calculation that would eventually remodel the whole of Western scientific thought. Long before either man, though, Leonardo da Vinci was filling his notebooks with scientific observations. The role of magic, which hitherto had been considered a vital force in intellectual enquiry,[7] was reduced; empirical observations and experiments became the systematic and logical way of seeking truth. All of which required precise measurements. Indeed, the progress of mankind was thought to be dependent upon taking careful measurements. This was the method adopted by the English statesman and essayist Francis Bacon (1561–1626). He had no training in science, yet in his *Novum Organum* (1620) he was bold enough to advocate a new scientific method based on inductive rather than deductive principles – pragmatic rather than abstract, experimental rather than theoretical or traditional. Everything should be verified or disproved by observation or experiment; investigation should take precedence over ancient dogma. Today he is considered the father of British pragmatism.[8]

The stress placed on counting and measuring was assisted by the introduction of decimals in 1585, logarithms in 1614, the slide rule in 1622 and the first adding machine in 1645. In addition, a close link was forged between scientists and instrument-makers. At the end of the sixteenth century and the beginning of the seventeenth, the telescope and the first crude microscope were invented by the Dutchman Anton van Leeuwenhoek (1632–1723). Thermometers were also devised. The watch and the pendulum clock brought accuracy to the measurement of time. The invention of the micrometer, the barometer and air and vacuum pumps (also in the seventeenth century) was followed by the eighteenth-century invention of navigational aids, such as the sextant (1730), the octant (1731), which replaced the astrolabe, and the chronometer (1735).[9]

The new spirit of enquiry also brought changes to medicine. The observations and experiments of Andreas Vesalius (1514–64), whose *On the Fabric of the Human Body* appeared in 1543, and William Harvey

(1578–1657), whose *On the Motion of the Heart and Blood* was published in 1628, corrected the much earlier assertions of Galen (AD 130–201), who until then had been the authority.

The Frenchman René Descartes (1596–1650), who lived for most of his life in the comparative security of Holland, made a major contribution to modern scientific thought with his *Discours de la méthode de bien conduire sa raison et chercher la vérité dans les sciences (Discourse on the Method of Properly Guiding the Reason in the Search for Truth in the Sciences)*, published in 1637. Only thought, he maintained, was real: 'Cogito ergo sum' (I think, therefore I am). The fact that one exists and that all else must be doubted until proved was the starting point of his contribution. With mathematics, geometry and human reason, order would be imposed on the seeming chaos of the universe. Reason, not the spiritual and intellectual authority of the past, was the only reliable guide to truth. Outside mathematical quantitative analysis and proof, nothing should be believed. For Descartes, the real world was a world of geometric symbols; counting was causation. Qualitative things, such as truth, virtue, courage, emotion, beauty, or love – things that could not be expressed in numbers – were largely ignored. With the aid of mathematics, universal, rational, invariant scientific laws could be formulated. All material phenomena would obey such laws. Reality was not beyond the grasp of logical analysis.

Descartes's analytical geometry, his logical progressions and his overwhelming reliance upon reason helped to undermine the religious and collective framework of medieval institutions. His *Discourse on Method*, which was placed on the papal *Index of Prohibited Books*, eventually provided the leaders of Western society with a uniquely mechanistic, humanistic attitude towards life and work. It is this mechanistic outlook which has separated Western man from other branches of the human race. Perhaps it is Descartes's separation of mind and matter, his assumption that mind must predominate over matter, which gave Western man his peculiar powers.

Another giant figure in the story of Western science was the Englishman Sir Isaac Newton (1642–1727), born in the year of Galileo's death. In his *Philosophiae Naturalis Principia Mathematica (Mathematical Principles of Natural Philosophy)*, published in 1687, he claimed to have established the universal, scientific laws concerning space, time and motion that his predecessors had sought. It was Newton who finally established absolute principles of motion and defined the forces of gravity. Like Galileo, he felt that the world of nature worked to strict mechanical laws: mechanistic, mathematical, linear and predictable. He was the first to present 'the universe as one great unity operating according to rational, calculable, unalterable principles'. Although Newton was a devout Christian who believed in faith and revelation, he also believed that once having been set in motion, the universal clock did not need the unseen hand of God to keep it going. The soul of rationality no longer needed the Almighty. Drawing upon the research and thinking of his predecessors, Newton was also the first to understand the composition of light; the first to build a reflecting telescope; and the first to develop calculus. To his British scientific contemporaries, he left little to be said that needed saying about physics, optics, mathematics and astronomy.

> Nature and nature's laws, lay hid in night:
> God said 'Let Newton be,' and all was light.[10]

Newton's 'light' continued to illuminate the British scientific world until the twentieth century, when Einstein revised the notions of space and time.

Although the Scientific Revolution affected only a very small part of Western society, and only much later and gradually affected other civilizations, the late seventeenth century was a high-water mark in Western scientific enquiry. New societies were formed in Italy, France and Britain to advance scientific research and knowledge. In 1662 the Royal Society of London was founded. Four years later, spurred by Louis XIV, the Académie Royale des Sciences was established in Paris. In 1675 the Royal Observatory was founded at Greenwich, primarily to resolve the problem of longitude and thus improve navigation – a pragmatic goal of which Bacon would have approved in an age of growing world trade and European expansion. Gradually, both abstract and practical science became respectable for the educated elite; it was needed by an increasingly commercial, industrial age and promised to be profitable.

This new, detached, mechanistic way of looking at the natural world also influenced alchemy. Chemical reactions could be explained not on a magical, but on a purely scientific basis. Robert Boyle (1627–91) led the way when in 1661 he published *The Sceptical Chymist*, in which he criticized Aristotle's theories about substances. Chemistry was founded as a separate science in the late eighteenth century when Antoine Lavoisier (1743–94) succeeded in measuring chemical reactions accurately. While the publication by Karl von Linné (known as Linnaeus; 1707–78) of *Philosophia Botanica* in 1751, which classified plants by genus and species, did something to restore the Almighty to His rightful place as the grand and perfect designer of nature, the secularization of Western life in general, and science in particular, continued.

The transition to a largely secular, rational and humanistic perspective has resulted in the eighteenth century being called the Age of Enlightenment; the Italians called it *illuminismo*, the Germans *Aufklärung*, the French *siècle des lumines*. Although contributions to the Enlightenment were made by scholars throughout the Western world, British and French writers (*les philosophes*) played the leading role. A varied group, their ideas ranged over a whole field of knowledge hitherto considered the province of the Church. The ultimate aim of all Enlightenment thinkers was to wrest from the Church the moral and intellectual leadership of Western civilization. With the Enlightenment, reason was enshrined – it was the key to truth; the door to positivism and human perfectibility was opened. According to the Enlightenment, human beings were naturally good and could be educated to be better. Evil was not innate, as the Church held, nor was hatred or racial or religious intolerance; such things sprang from ignorance and outmoded, irrational institutions. Education – knowledge not faith – was offered as the new dynamic, the panacea by means of which all political, social, economic and legal wrongs would be righted. Happiness was to be sought not in heaven but on earth.

Voltaire, who published his 'Traité sur la tolérance' (Treatise on Toleration) in 1763, was one of the leaders of the Enlightenment. A prolific writer, he won both fame and fortune. Reason and tolerance were his guidelines. Opposed to the intolerance and superstition of

Christianity, he espoused deism in which, following Newton's idea of a world machine operated by natural laws, God would have no direct influence upon the world He had created.

There were many other important Enlightenment figures. John Locke, in his *Essay Concerning Human Understanding* (1690), repudiated Descartes's belief that man is born with certain innate ideas. According to Locke, man arrives knowing nothing and is the product of his environment. The wrong environment is the cause of most troubles. Charles Louis de Secondat Montesquieu (1689–1755), in *De l'Esprit des lois* (*The Spirit of the Laws*; 1748), was the enemy of traditional religion, the champion of religious toleration and the supporter of reason. His work on government, especially the need for the separation of powers, was incorporated into the American Constitution. Denis Diderot (1713–84) published the *Encyclopédie*, an encyclopedia of thirty-four volumes, between 1751 and 1772. He reflected the growing secularism of his age; knowledge and happiness were synonymous. Charged with atheism, errors and impieties, the work was promptly placed on the Vatican's *Index of Prohibited Books*. Following the Church, the French government revoked the licence that allowed it to be printed. However, by a ruse, it was printed anyway, and played a leading role in spreading the ideas of the Enlightenment. During his life Diderot passed from Christianity to deism to atheism. Adam Smith (1723–90), who wrote *An Inquiry into the Nature and Causes of the Wealth of Nations* (1776), claimed (with the Frenchman François Quesnay) to have discovered the natural law of economic life, which the French called *laissez-faire* (leave alone). The natural law, to Smith, was the market economy and the exercise of individual economic self-interest. Marie Jean, Marquis de Condorcet (1743–94), who wrote *Esquisse d'un tableau historique des progrès de l'esprit humain* (*Sketch for a Historical Picture of the Progress of the Human Mind*; 1795), believed in the perfectibility of human nature, leading to enlightenment, virtue and happiness, and the equality of freedom and rights.

Immanuel Kant (1724–1804) was more cautious than his contemporaries. In his 'An Answer to the Question, what is Enlightening?' (published in *Essays and Treatises on Moral, Political and Various Philosophical Subjects* in 1798) he asserted that he lived in an enlightening but not yet an enlightened age. His statement 'Out of the crooked timber of humanity no straight thing was ever made' had nothing in common with the idea of human perfectibility. Suffering no illusions about the horrors and wastes of war, or the weakness of humankind, Kant was one of the first to promote the idea of a 'league of nations'. Like many who followed him, he thought that collective security was the only hope for mankind.

David Hume (1711–76), with *A Treatise on Human Nature: Being an Attempt to Introduce the Experimental Method of Reasoning into Moral Subjects* (1739–40), and Jean Jacques Rousseau (1712–78), in *Le Contrat Social* (*The Social Contract*; 1762), were the Enlightenment's most notable critics. Rousseau acclaimed the religion of feeling; his guide was emotion. In contrast to Smith, he believed that the individual should not be left to do as he pleased, but should be compelled to abide by the general will. Contrary to the spirit of the Enlightenment, he was prepared to use force to make men free. Thomas Malthus (1766–1834), whose *The Principle of Population* was published in 1798, held that as population always tends to outstrip food supply, and is limited only by war, famine, disease and abstinence from marriage, the perfectibility of society sought by the writers of the Enlightenment was both invalid and unattainable.

Meanwhile, for good or ill, the march of authentic, quantitative Western science continued unimpaired. The scientific discoveries of Luigi Galvani (1737–98), Alessandro Volta (1745–1827), Georg Simon Ohm (1787–1854), Hans Christian Oersted (1777–1851), André Marie Ampère (1775–1836), Michael Faraday (1791–1867) and others gave a tremendous stimulus to the use of electrical energy. The electric telegraph was introduced in 1835; the first undersea cable came into use in 1851.

In biology the Frenchman Louis Pasteur (1822–95) proposed the germ theory of disease. In chemistry the Russian Dmitri Mendeleev (1834–1907) and the German Lothar Meyer (1830–95) in the 1860s independently provided a systematic foundation for the periodic law. The experiments conducted by an obscure Austrian monk, Gregor Johann Mendel (1822–84), during the 1850s and 1860s led to the discovery of the basic principles of heredity and subsequently to the science of genetics. Because they were untimely, his published findings were ignored for many years.

Until the end of the nineteenth century, Western scientific thinking continued to be developed in the mechanical, atomistic framework outlined by Descartes and Newton. Theirs was a deterministic world of objective reality. Yet Newton's fixed and immutable world had already been challenged by his fellow Englishman Charles Darwin, who presented his theory of organic evolution in *On the Origin of Species by Means of Natural Selection* (1859). To Darwin, natural laws were as valid in the natural sciences as the laws of planetary motion and gravity were in the physical world. Humans were not unique in their relation to the cosmos; rules governing other species also governed them. Thus was born the Western idea of progress. Through the survival of the fittest, continuing growth and improvement among humankind were thought to be inevitable. The idea of human perfectibility was reflected in the nineteenth-century attempts to develop Utopian communities in Europe and America. Because of human weaknesses, almost all of them failed.

Albert Einstein (1879–1955), with his theory of relativity (1905),[11] based on perception and value judgements, as well as his new concepts of time, space, mass, motion and gravitation, was to shake the Newtonian world – which had assumed motion, gravity and time to be absolutes – to its foundations. Einstein maintained that the universe might have begun as a great thought; it certainly was not a great Newtonian machine. Scientists could no longer be considered as custodians of absolute truth, which could be found by atomizing knowledge in a mechanistic way. Truth did not reside in the realm of concepts linked with one another. It was much more relative and interdependent than either the Cartesian or the Newtonian approach had made it out to be. According to Einstein, there was no final, absolute truth; there was only flux. The real world allowed for probabilistic but not absolute statements. Once viewed as inherently orderly, nature came to be viewed by some scientists as disorderly. The supreme confidence of scientific rationalism gave way to the chaos theory.[12]

Einstein also added to the pioneering work of the German physicist Max Planck (1858–1947) in quantum physics ('Energy is emitted in minute, discrete quantities called quanta'). By treating matter and energy as exchangeable, which physicists had always regarded as inconvertible, Planck and Einstein helped to lay the basis for splitting the atom. Einstein was awarded the Nobel Prize in 1922 not for his theory of relativity, but for his work in quantum physics.

Werner Heisenberg (1901–76), in his 'uncertainty principle' ('the observer alters the observed by the act of observing') added further doubt to the absolute nature of science. Scientific truth, according to him, was the changing relation between subject and object. Heisenberg was awarded the Nobel Prize in 1932. For the first time since Copernicus, the fundamental faith of Western man in science and the scientific method, and especially scientific truth – the belief that the universe is not chaos but possesses an underlying order, a linear kind of certainty – was questioned.

Until recently, those who questioned Western rationalism were largely ignored; secularism and rationalism swept all before them. The more science was questioned, the more society sought absolute truth elsewhere. The late twentieth-century revival in religious fundamentalism throughout the world – the search for absolute truth – cannot be explained any other way. To the world's faithful, the major religions offer a greater degree of certainty than so-called 'scientific truths'; the absolute truths of religion are considered to be unchanging. Religion is not 'the opium of the people', as Marx held, but a necessary antidote to the uncertainties of life. Man may never know the absolute, may never find the true meaning of life, but he cannot help seeking it. Only religion tells us what we ought to do, rather than what we can do. Blaise Pascal (1623–62), scientist and mathematician, foresaw the division between science and religion: 'The heart', he said, 'has its reasons of which the reason knows nothing.'

The coming of the atom bomb and other weapons of mass destruction, in which the West first excelled, caused many people to have second thoughts about the role of science. Europe's scientific work on atomic particles and radioactivity[13] has placed the world in deadly peril. Hence the new stress placed upon religion and faith.

By the beginning of the nineteenth century, changes in Western technology[14] were taking place on such a wide front that writers used the term the 'Industrial Revolution' to describe them. Although the Industrial Revolution was long in forming, it is generally thought to describe the social and mechanical changes taking place in England between the years 1760 and 1830.[15] These changes sprang not so much from novelty in machines or power – there were factories before 1760 – as from new magnitudes in what was already known. From England, the revolution later spread to the rest of Western Europe[16] (to the coalfields of the German Ruhr and northeastern France) and to many other parts of the white-settled world.

The nub of the Industrial Revolution, through a series of improvements in technology, was an enormous increase in Western man's productive power. The outcome was the substitution of mechanized industry for agriculture and the traditional crafts, iron and coal for wood, steam for water and wind (as well as for animal and human muscle), the factory for the cottage and the urban for the rural scene.

The revolution in industry was much more than a revolution in technology. It also meant a vast increase in wage labour, new forms of economic and social organization, the concentration of capital, the growing power of the market and the seemingly limitless use of inanimate energy (steam, electricity, water, petroleum and diesel oil). The sum of these changes – though one can argue that none of them was essentially new or revolutionary – produced a civilization different in kind from that which had preceded it. Never before had wealth been obtained on this scale, except by seizing it from others. Unquestionably, the increased wealth enhanced the technical, economic and especially the military power of the West. Westerners were the first and have remained the principal arms salesmen in the world. It is not an accident that Europeans were the first to field the mobile artillery that helped to bring down feudalism and fortified city-states. They had also acquired a Chinese invention – gunpowder.

Prompted by these developments (which were certainly not as orderly as they appear), Western Europe's relative retardation in the industrial arts underwent marked change from the late eighteenth century onwards. For part of the eighteenth and nineteenth centuries, while the French led in science, the British led in technology. In the late nineteenth century and the early part of the twentieth the Germans excelled in both.

In the eighteenth century Britons became inventors and innovators

on a scale previously unequalled. The tinkering with machines that
went on in Britain in the eighteenth and nineteenth centuries was
called the 'mechanical revolution'. Human muscle was replaced by
machines. In agriculture, industry, metallurgy and later in mining the
machine proved cheaper than labour. It led to greater educational
opportunities for the common man. (From the 1830s onwards the standards of education were raised.) By inventing capital-intensive, labour-
saving devices, the British could compete with the great reservoirs of
cheap labour in Asia. Britain's supply of rich deposits of coal and iron,
the output of which seemingly multiplied overnight,[17] its improved
road, canal and railway systems, its growing supplies of credit and
money, its joint stock organization (one might add its mechanistic
system of double-entry bookkeeping, which it had inherited from the
East), its protection of property by law, its central government and
political stability, its class structure and social mobility, its expanding
labour and capital, its increasingly ambitious and talented middle class,
its Protestant ethic, its active dissenting religious minorities, its un-
rivalled navy, its contribution to maritime improvements in the
construction and operation of ships at sea, its natural harbours, its
rapidly growing numbers after 1830 and its ever-growing profitable
domestic and foreign trade – all these fostered its leading role as the
workshop of the world.[18]

By 1850 Britain led the world in steam power, industrial and manufacturing production, coal, iron, textiles, shipping and railways. It was
also the state where Adam Smith's philosophy of the free market in
land, labour and capital had taken root. In emphasizing the wealth of
nations rather than that of empires or city-states, Smith expressed a
new way of looking at economic life. For the time being, the social
abuses which his policy of laissez-faire implied were disregarded. The
Great Exhibition at the Crystal Palace in London in 1851 proclaimed
to the world the possibility of universal prosperity and progress. (A
few years earlier setbacks in harvests and the spread of cholera had
dimmed human hopes.)

Whatever the cause of Britain's advance, the technical changes
in the hundred years after 1760 were marked as much by their variety
as by their fundamental nature. In that century the ancient skills of
the craftsman gradually gave way to first a British and then a

European and world technology, dependent on metals, machines, fossil fuels and trained engineers.

The curious thing is that while some scientists were stimulated by the growing problems surrounding the rapid development of Western forms of production (the Royal Society in London had a committee to investigate technical advances; the French Académie gathered tools and machines), the majority of those who made Britain's Industrial Revolution were practical men, largely unaware of what was going on in the scientific world. The Industrial Revolution was as concrete as the Scientific Revolution was abstract; one was an intellectual phenomenon, the other was empirical; one was largely an achievement of the upper classes, the other of the common people. Such is true of John Kay (1704–c. 1764), a Lancashire textile machinist who, in 1733, patented the first of the great textile inventions, the flying shuttle; James Hargreaves (c. 1722–1778), who invented the spinning jenny in 1764, was a weaver; Richard Arkwright (1732–92), who invented the water frame in 1769, was the son of a barber and wigmaker; Samuel Crompton (1753–1827), who in 1779 devised what is essentially the spinning machine in use today, was a spinner; Edmund Cartwright (1743–1823), who in 1787 mechanized the weaving process,[19] was a country vicar.

This reliance upon practical rather than scientific men did not apply to textiles alone. Neither Thomas Newcomen (1663–1729), a mechanic, nor James Watt (1736–1819),[20] a builder of instruments at Glasgow University, whose names are linked with the development of steam and steam-driven machinery, was a scientist as such. Richard Trevithick (1771–1833) learned his skills in the mines, where the first steam engines pumped out water. Similarly self-taught were Abraham Darby (c. 1678–1717) and Henry Cort (1740–1800), who improved the smelting and refining of iron ore, John Wilkinson (1728–1808), one of the great ironmasters, and Henry Maudslay (1771–1831), who in 1794 invented one of the first lathes for cutting metal. James Nasmyth's (1808–90) steam hammer made larger, stronger forgings possible. By the 1860s, steel and iron were being melted, purified and cast on a hitherto unheard-of scale. Thomas Telford (1757–1834), who spanned the English landscape with iron bridges, was born a shepherd. James Brindley (1716–72), who laid

out a network of hundreds of miles of canals all over England, had
no scientific background.

Trevithick launched the first steam-powered locomotive in 1804.
In 1825 the first railway was opened between Stockton and Darlington
in England. George Stephenson (1781–1848) followed with his *Rocket*
in 1830. It ran at the unprecedented speed of 16 miles per hour. By
1850, 6000 miles of railway line covered Britain. In half a century the
speed of a locomotive increased more than tenfold. Pictures of iron
bridges and railways began to grace the drawing rooms of a new, prosperous urban middle class. The first steamboats had preceded the
first steam railways. There was a steamboat operating on the Forth
and Clyde Canal in 1802. In 1807 an American steamboat with British
engines appeared on the Hudson River.

In contrast to other societies and civilizations, the pioneers of
Britain's Industrial Revolution were prepared to work with their
hands. In all pre-modern societies the idea of an elite working with
their hands was unacceptable. To this day, the elites of Africa, Latin
America and Asia shun manual labour. In the East, the Buddhist
appears with his beggar's bowl. The early Western religious orders
– Franciscan, Dominican, Carmelite and Augustine – were all
required to live by alms, too, but this did not apply to the Benedictine
Order, whose chief principle of conduct was *laborare est orare* (to
work is to pray). In the West it was the Benedictine Order's stress
on the work ethic that prevailed. Whether we are dealing with
Richard Trevithick, Thomas Edison (1847–1931) or Henry Ford
(1863–1947), we are dealing with a peculiar breed of people who
were prepared to soil their hands tinkering with machines. The
Mandarin class of China, who cultivated long fingernails as a symbol
of their elitism, were no match for the pragmatists of the West.
These largely self-educated tinkerers coming from every class (most
of whom set out to solve a specific practical problem rather than
obtain immediate gain) set in motion a movement that was to change
the world. The contributions of head and hand – the Scientific and
Industrial revolutions – are really inseparable; yet it is interesting
that the practical men rather than the intellectuals should have had
the impact they did. The outcome of their joint efforts – especially
when steam shipping and steam railways linked the continents –

was the creation of an integrated economic unit of the major countries of the world. The shape of the world system was altered for good. Under Western command, the supply and demand of commodities was regulated primarily to serve Western interests. 'Free trade' simply meant freedom for the most powerful to inflict their rule on the rest. It still does. Another consequence of these developments in industry and trade[21] – especially with the rise of Germany and America – was a change in the balance of power not only between Asia and Europe but among the Western powers themselves. The outcome was the First World War.

The essential distinction between Western technology of today and that of the eighteenth and nineteenth centuries is the extent to which progress in technology has come to depend on progress in the sciences. From the second half of the nineteenth century onwards, empiricism gave way to exact science. Scientific developments have created many modern industries. In chemicals and electricity (as a source of energy to supplement steam), in the development of the internal combustion and the diesel engines[22] and in soil chemistry Germany played a leading role. It was the German Gabriel Fahrenheit (1686–1736) who introduced the Fahrenheit temperature scale. The French brothers Louis (1864–1948) and Auguste Lumière (1862–1954) gave the world the first motion picture in 1895. Major British contributions were synthetic dyes (with France), electrical energy (with Germany and France), the Bessemer steel converter, the Gilchrist–Thomas basic steel process and Parsons's steam turbine. Among many other inventions, the USA contributed the ring-spinning frame, the typewriter, the telephone, electric lighting, the first successful flight by Orville (1871–1948) and Wilbur Wright (1867–1912) in North Carolina in 1903,[23] the first mass-produced car, the first general-purpose computer, the first transistor and the first controlled nuclear chain reaction (Chicago, 1942). In the twentieth century America challenged Europe's pre-eminence in both science and technology.

Science and technology have become the social forces of our time, deciding whether a nation will be rich or poor. The technically advanced nations presently dominate the world. In the thirteenth century it seemed that all things were possible to faith; today, as a result of fundamental discoveries in physics and biology, all things are thought to be possible to science. In this age of antibiotics,[24] vaccines, antiseptics, X-rays (Wilhelm Conrad Roentgen; 1845–1923), molecular biology, virology, birth control, psychoanalysis, genetic engineering, nuclear fission, jets and rockets, lasers, space travel,[25] television, computers, the microchip and nanotechnology, we take it for granted that science can solve all problems, provide all answers. We refuse to acknowledge its limitations. Science's transient nature, its errors (as the history of science makes abundantly clear) and its inability to answer the ultimate questions concerning the meaning of man and the universe are disregarded. We think that all that is needed for us to increase our knowledge and our mastery of the world is to train more scientists; scientists to help us add to our material resources; scientists to help us shape our minds; scientists to cure our diseases. With the right science and technology the age-old curses of want, injustice, ignorance, ageing and evil will be banished. Tongue in cheek, Hilaire Belloc (1870–1953) said:

> When men of science find out something more,
> we shall all be happier than before

Contrast this with the words of Alfred Tennyson (1809–92):

> This truth within thy mind rehearse,
> That in a boundless universe
> Is boundless better, boundless worse

which echo both the cheer and the chill of the Scientific Age.

The rational, absolute universe, which was the object of the Scientific Revolution, is still a vision. Reality is that we live in an irrational world, where reason, objectivity and the mechanistic view of life are becoming suspect. (In June 1995 the New York Academy of Sciences organized a conference of more than two hundred scientists, physicians and humanists to consider 'The Flight from

Science and Reason'.) The power of faith, passion, mysticism, fundamentalism, intuition and instinct, which some scientists thought had been banished, are becoming centre-stage again. They are joined there by a growing gender, cultural and race ideology which accuses the founders of modern Western science – Copernicus, Galileo, Kepler, Brahe, Bacon, Newton and Descartes – of being 'eco-villains'.

Critics of objective science argue that most scientists see what the *Zeitgeist* (the spirit of the time) tells them to see. Science is not so much a value-free, objective search for the truth as a Baconian process of experimental testing. In his intellectual judgements the scientist, in saying what is important to science and what is not, is never free of the influence of faith and passion. His appreciation of scientific data depends ultimately on the belief that truth exists, which is an act of faith. The more original his work, the more likely that faith, passion and emotion will intervene. All the great steps in science have started with a vision.[26] 'The most beautiful thing we can experience', wrote Albert Einstein in *What I Believe*, published in 1930, 'is the mysterious. It is the source of all true art and science.' This is tantamount to saying that a spirit is manifest in the laws of the universe vastly superior to that of man or objective science; that man cannot live by science alone. While it is true that materialism by itself will not serve, how can those outside the scientific community decide what the spiritual, ethical and moral framework of science should be?

Perhaps some kind of holism, a new unity of subjective and objective knowledge, both mystical and rational, will emerge. The narrow, geometrizing Cartesian attitude towards life never did extend beyond a relatively small group of influential intellectuals in the West. Most people in the world still think of knowledge – objective and subjective – as integrated and interdependent.

Superficially at least, the Western impact in the world, in the Greco-Roman tradition, has been practical and material, mental and intellectual. In the past two hundred years the West has excelled in scientific knowledge and economically productive technology. It has excelled in these spheres because primarily they were the things it honoured.

Whether these changes were themselves dependent upon novel elements (not least the discovery of the New World) or upon universally applicable elements that other civilizations can follow is unclear. If the Western Scientific and Industrial revolutions – for good or ill – were facilitated by Western expansion and colonization (that is, not by ordinary and continuous events but by an extraordinary sporadic phase of history), then it behoves us not to use nineteenth-century Western economic growth and development as an example that twenty-first-century Africa, Asia and Latin America should follow.

The West became rich not because it industrialized; it industrialized because it was already relatively rich. Much of the high tide of human progress in the West over the past two centuries cannot be dissociated from the discovery of new sea routes to Asia, which brought wealth through trade, and the discovery of the New World, which made possible the cultivation of vast, new, fertile regions of the earth, the tapping of enormous mineral deposits, and the introduction of new forms of transport, communications and power. These things did not come about because of Western racial superiority or greater Western intelligence, but because the West developed different values and passed through a different historical experience than the people of other continents – an experience that gave full rein to curiosity, inventiveness and acquisitiveness.

No one can say with complete assurance that the circumstances which saw the rise of the West have not passed, and that an old, slower cycle of change might reassert itself. With the rise of religious fundamentalism in the twentieth century, no one can say that the trend towards secularization – which was stimulated by the Renaissance, the Enlightenment and the Industrial and Scientific revolutions – will continue. Surely, we know enough to realize that our confidence in science is rooted in the Western belief in progress, which is of only relatively recent origin. The question remains: will that 'Great Discontinuity of History' – the Industrial Revolution, if not the Scientific Revolution – prove to be one of the great mutations in history, an ongoing, universal process in which all civilizations will engage, or a 'great abnormality', a historical moment dependent on special circumstances?

10

'White Peril' in the East

Although Western traders and evangelists had been banished from Japan and China in the seventeenth century, the people of East Asia deceived themselves in believing that Western expansion in the East had been halted for good. In the eighteenth century Western traders continued to demand the right to trade where they wished and on equal terms – an idea inconceivable to the Chinese. China, they argued, should not be allowed to refuse Western trade, Western diplomacy and Western religion. Certainly, it should not be allowed to exclude Britain's manufactures or opium from British India. It was purposeless for the Chinese to point out that opium was outlawed in China, and that they needed nothing from the West except to be left alone. In the Opium Wars the British used cannons and gunpowder (Chinese inventions) to impose their will.[1]

What staggers the imagination about the British invasion of China is how a country of approximately twenty million people could try to dominate a much older civilization of enormous size and numbers. In 1840 China's population was thought to be in the region of 400 million – far more than the whole of Europe, including Russia. The British were able to triumph because they were technically super-ior, well armed, self-righteous, overwhelmingly aggressive and dominant at sea. The Chinese on the other hand were disunited, technologically weak, bound, ill-led and ill armed. Cannons made of bronze and bamboo were no match for British gunboats. The

Chinese might have been able to meet the military challenge of the Europeans in the fifteenth century, but not in the nineteenth, by which time their inventiveness had declined. The chaos caused by the importation of British opium, overpopulation, rebellions, corruption, incompetence and growing poverty made China too weak to resist; it had no choice but to come to terms with the more powerful West.

Britain chose to sell illegal opium because it was the only commodity that could produce a favourable balance of trade with a largely self-sufficient China. Raw cotton from India had been tried but had failed; opium proved to be unbelievably profitable. As ever-increasing opium imports exceeded China's exports of tea, silk, paper and porcelain, for which there was a great market in Europe, a net inflow of silver was converted into a net outflow.[2]

No sooner had the British obtained commercial and legal concessions under the humiliating Nanking (Nanjing) Treaty of 1842,[3] under which China also ceded Hong Kong to Britain, than the other Westerners, including Russians and Americans, hastened to obtain similar privileges. The Americans quickly took up the opium trade, bringing supplies from Turkey and the Levant. The first treaty between the USA and China in 1844 aimed not at expanding the American frontier overseas but at enlarging American commerce. The social cost of opium addiction to the Chinese was disregarded by the West. In contrast, Russia's interest lay in territory rather than trade. Taking advantage of growing Chinese disorder, in 1858, under the Treaty of Aigun, Russia laid claim to all the territory north of the Amur (see Map IX). The following year it seized the province of Manchuria. In 1860 Vladivostok was founded, and the Maritime Provinces north of Korea were annexed – territory which Russia still holds.

Under the Treaties of Tientsin (Tianjin) of 1858, between China and Britain, France, the United States and Russia, China was forced to open still more ports to Western traders. Under foreign pressure, the opium trade was legalized and expanded. Also forced upon China was the establishment of foreign legations at Beijing, and the unhindered activity of foreign traders. The establishment of foreign legations was particularly humiliating because it challenged the

Confucian tradition that held that the rulers of China were the divinely appointed rulers of the world. Restrictions on Christian evangelists were also removed. To ensure that the large war indemnities demanded would be paid, Britain took control of all customs duties levied on foreign goods. In retribution for Chinese intransigence, in 1860 British and French troops occupied Beijing and burned the Summer Palace. There followed even more humiliating concessions on the part of China. An added indignity was the recruiting of Chinese coolie labourers to work in European colonial territories. By the 1860s, 100,000 Chinese had been shipped to Peru in conditions not far removed from slavery; another 150,000 had gone to Cuba.

Although efforts were made by the Chinese from the 1870s to learn something about the basis of Western supremacy (by sending students abroad and by establishing overseas diplomatic missions), the Manchu elite never took such efforts seriously. Most of them scorned Western science and technology. How could the foreign barbarians teach a superior people anything? The first railway forced upon the Chinese was promptly dismantled and left to rust. Although the 'self-strengthening movement' of the 1860s and 1870s led to some improvements in Chinese railways, ports, metal and textile mills and weapons, the Chinese were never able to respond to the Western challenge as decisively as the Japanese had done. Anyone, including the emperor, who suggested adopting Western ways was either banished or imprisoned by the reactionary Dowager Empress Tzu Hsi (1835–1908). Failing to understand the Western threat, the Manchu court saw no reason to abandon its traditions.

And so, against a background of war (in 1883–5 France fought China over Indo-China), famine[4] and internal rebellions – the worst of which was the Taiping Rebellion (1850–64),[5] which aimed to free the Chinese from the grip of both the Manchus and the Europeans, and in which tens of millions of Chinese lost their lives – the exploiting of China by the West continued. Because of Western predation, civil war and famine, the population of China in 1900 was little more than it had been in the 1830s.

The final humiliation for China came not from the West but from the East. In 1894 a war broke out between the Chinese and the

Japanese over Korea. The Western-style Japanese army disastrously routed the Chinese. As a result, Japanese influence became paramount in Korea and Chinese Formosa (Taiwan), which was annexed.

By the end of the nineteenth century the Western nations had established claims in thirteen of China's eighteen provinces. Port Arthur was leased to Russia; the Germans seized Kiaochow (Jiaozhou) in Shantung Province; the British moved into the port of Weihaiwei. The US 'open door' policy on trade in China at the end of the century, despite its superior moral tone (it would, it was said, curb the worst effects of European imperial ambitions), ultimately served American business interests. The USA peacefully obtained from China all that the other powers had obtained by force. In 1900, during the Boxer Rebellion (1899–1900), which resulted in the murder of hundreds of Europeans and thousands of Chinese Christians, the Chinese laid siege to the foreign legations in Beijing. The foreign powers, including Britain, France, Germany, the United States, Japan and Russia (which seized the opportunity to occupy most of Manchuria) quickly put it down. Still more concessions and a huge indemnity were demanded of China.[6] Having failed to master Western technology, China was forced to succumb. A disunited China remained the prey of all. With reform denied by the conservative Manchus, who had ruled the country since 1644, with corruption at every level of government, the Chinese state could do nothing but collapse.

In October 1911 a revolution broke out under the leadership of Sun Yat-sen (1866–1925),[7] who aimed to establish a republic. In 1912 the Manchus were overthrown; the last Chinese emperor, the infant Pu Yi, was forced to abdicate.[8] But without the necessary military, political and financial backing, Sun Yat-sen's newly established republic soon foundered. He was obliged to surrender power of the Kuomintang (Guomindang) Party to the ambitious General Yuan Shi-kai (b. 1859), who concentrated power in his own hands. In 1913, after a failed attempt to overthrow Yuan, Sun Yat-sen and other radicals fled to Japan. On Yuan's death in 1916, political power was divided between provincial warlords. Not until Mao Zedong came to power in 1949 was China effectively united again under a single administration.

*   *   *

Japanese reaction to the renewed nineteenth-century Western incursions in East Asia differed markedly from that of the Chinese. Japan's martial samurai traditions, its intense nationalism, its strong sense of self-identity, its deeply ingrained 'work ethic', its remarkable homogeneity, its communal loyalty, its morale and its discipline, its good government, its insularity and its prosperity made it much more difficult to coerce. The Tokugawa shogunate's (1603–1868) ruthless exclusion of Western influence spared Japan the fate suffered by the Philippines, India, China and Formosa.

The turning point for Japan came in 1853 with the arrival of four American warships commanded by Matthew C. Perry (1794–1858). The next year Perry appeared again, this time with ten warships. Japan reluctantly agreed to open its ports to US trade, and to establish a consulate. In 1858 a more elaborate agreement was made, extending US commercial interests. Other Western nations eagerly pressed for similar concessions.

Japan met the signing of the shameful 'unequal treaties' forced upon it by America, the Netherlands and Britain in 1858 with a strategy of procrastination. Being the only nation on record to have given up using the gun,[9] it could hardly do otherwise. Baffled by the Japanese genius for forestalling, and in retaliation against acts of violence, in 1864 a squadron of British, French, Dutch and US warships bombarded the harbours of Kagoshima and Shimonoseki. Japan was forced to come to terms. This undermined the Tokugawa shogunate and in 1868 it was overthrown. The new political leaders had as their aim the restoration of imperial rule and the ending of centuries of isolation. The sixteen-year-old Emperor Mutsuhito became head of state. His reign, which lasted until 1912, became known as Meiji – enlightened government.[10]

Realizing that it could no longer be isolated from the world, the Meiji regime began an extraordinary process of Westernization. Japanese scholars and travellers were sent to the West in search of knowledge. At great expense to the state, foreign technicians and experts were brought to Japan. Countless Western books were imported and translated. Instead of shunning Western ways, as the Chinese had done, the Japanese eagerly studied the West's systems of government, industry and military and naval technology – the backbone of Western power. The new Japanese army was modelled on the French and later the Prussian military; the navy was built on British lines. In 1871 feudalism was abolished. The next year a national education system was introduced. In 1873 the samurai, the hereditary warrior class, were replaced by a regular, Western-type conscript army. With the aid of this army of commoners, the new government was able to quash the last of the samurai uprisings in 1877. Between the 1870s and the 1890s a modern legal system, based first on French and then on German models, was established. Western dress, first adopted by the military, spread to other parts of Japanese society. The beard, military uniform and medals worn by the Meiji emperor were copied from Western royalty. In 1890 Japan formulated a new constitution based upon the German Imperial Constitution of 1871. In 1897 it tied its currency to the European-devised gold standard. Increasingly, the cry became: 'Japanese spirit, Western talents.'

Japan was fortunate to be able to meet the Western threat when it did. Mutiny against the British in India in the 1850s, civil war in the United States in the 1860s and the struggle between France and Prussia in the 1870s, together with the wars fought by Britain in South Africa and the Sudan, and the Spanish-American War of 1898, all helped to deflect the attention of the West from Japan and preserve Japanese independence.

Emerging from 250 years of isolation, Japan faced an immense task in modernizing itself. Whereas Europe's Industrial Revolution had been a step-by-step organic process, growing naturally out of traditional crafts and the Scientific Revolution of the seventeenth century, Japan's ability to meet the West on its own terms depended on its taking giant strides. As Japan possessed the necessary human qualities – pride and a strong culture – as well as the required pre-industrial skills and technology, the Western challenge was met. It succeeded in developing an economy almost entirely independent of foreign money; even more remarkably, it transformed its society with less social and political disarray than had occurred in the West. The need and the desire for change was felt throughout Japanese society – even among the peasant class. In the mid-nineteenth century Japan was a medieval, feudal country; by the First World War, it had become one of the world's great powers.

In the closing decades of the nineteenth century Japan launched itself upon a course of territorial expansion. It could not become a great power in the world unless it did so. In the 1870s it attacked Formosa, annexed the Ryukyu Islands (including Okinawa), exchanged part of Sakhalin with Russia for the Kuriles and with subtle support from the British, who feared Russian more than Japanese expansion, began to contest China's interests in Korea (see Map IX). In 1894 it invaded Korea (as it had done unsuccessfully under Hideyoshi in the sixteenth century) and overwhelmed a much larger Chinese army and navy. Until then, the Chinese and the Koreans had looked on the Japanese as an inferior race, dependent for much of their culture upon their superior neighbours. Under the Treaty of Shimonoseki (1895), which ended the Sino-Japanese war in Korea, China was compelled to recognize the independence of Korea, open four more ports to international trade and pay an indemnity of $20 million (obtained from the British at 5 per cent interest). Japanese rule was extended over Korea, Formosa, the Pescadores Islands, the Liaotung peninsula (which the European powers later persuaded it to give up) and southern Manchuria.

Impressed by Japan's show of force, in 1899 the Western powers ceded their extra-territorial rights in Japan. In the Anglo-Japanese Alliance of 1902 Japan became an ally of the most powerful nation on earth. To offset growing Russian power in East Asia, Britain increased Japan's power. The move, in so far as it enabled Britain to bring home most of its Eastern Fleet to guard its own shores, strengthened Britain's hand against Germany.

In 1904 Japan decided to end the growing friction between itself and Russia over Korea and Manchuria by force.[11] Backed by Britain, it struck the Russian fleet stationed in the ports of Chemulpo (Inchon) in Korea and Port Arthur (Lushun) on the Liaotung peninsula without warning. Landings were made; the Russian army was pursued and eventually overwhelmed at Mukden in February 1905. The annihilation of Russia's Northern Battle Fleet at the Tsushima Straits off Japan in May 1905 (thirty-two Russian warships were sunk) completed the Russian disaster. This destruction of Russia's sea power in the East made it feasible for Britain to transfer still more of its Eastern Fleet to stations in the North Sea.

Japan's victory altered the balance of power in Asia, as well as in the Pacific. It was the first time that an Asian power had defeated a European power on land and sea simultaneously. With Russia's defeat, the myth of Western omnipotence exploded. Japan's success inspired nationalism in India, Persia, China and Turkey. The Russian Revolution of 1905 provided added impetus to the anti-colonial movements, especially in India. Like the turning of the tide, the return of Asia to the forefront of world affairs had begun.

Under the terms of the Treaty of Portsmouth of 1905, Russia acknowledged Japan's paramount interest in Korea. It also renewed Japan's lease of the Liaotung peninsula (including Port Arthur and the existing mining and railway privileges there), and ceded the southern half of Sakhalin. Manchuria was divided into spheres of Russian and Japanese influence. Not surprisingly, in 1905 Britain expressed its willingness to renew the Anglo-Japanese Alliance for another ten years. In 1910 Japan annexed Korea and called it Chosun. Despite uprisings there, which were brutally suppressed, the USA recognized the annexation in return for Japan's recognition of US authority in the Philippines.

The First World War brought further wealth and glory to Japan. With the USA, it was one of the war's principal victors. Quite apart from new trade opportunities, the war resulted in Japan's occupation of the Shantung (Shandong) Province of China, and of Germany's colonies in the Pacific. From the 'twenty-one demands' made by Japan of China in 1915 to the occupation of Shantung in 1919, China was treated by the Japanese as little more than a protectorate. Japan had become less the spearhead of Asia's freedom and more like a Western colonial power. Thus were sown the seeds of Asia's love–hate relationship with Japan. While few realized it, with Japanese expansion, a new and deadly threat to the United States and Australia had appeared on the horizon.

Korea's history goes back into a legendary past. Harassed from the earliest times by the Chinese, the Mongols, the Manchus and the Japanese, few nations have fought so hard and so long for independence. In 1392, following the Korean defeat of the Mongols, the Yi dynasty (which was to last until 1910) was established. During the first 150 years of its life, the dynasty flourished intellectually and culturally. In 1403, about fifty years before Johannes Gutenberg, the Koreans invented a moveable printing type. In 1420 a royal college of literature was established. In 1443 a phonetic alphabet was developed. Important advances were also made in medicine, astronomy, geology and agriculture. Buddhism (which was beginning to exercise political power) was replaced in the court and upper classes by the Confucian ethical system.

In 1592 Japan invaded Korea and occupied parts of it for seven years. In 1627 the Manchus invaded, withdrawing only after Korea acceded to Manchu suzerainty. When the Manchus seized power in China in 1644, Korea was still a vassal state. In the Confucian tradition, as the 'younger brother' Korea emulated China's policy of isolation. The first contact with the Western world occurred in 1653 when a Dutch ship was wrecked off its shores and the survivors were taken to Seoul. The narrative written by one of the survivors who escaped from Korea brought the country to the attention of the Western world, which until then had been almost totally ignorant of the 'Hermit Kingdom'.

Korea continued its policy of isolation until the intrusions of Europeans, Americans and Japanese in the second half of the nineteenth century.[12] In 1876 the Japanese forced the Koreans to grant them diplomatic recognition. In 1882 the United States (the first Western country to make incursions) pressured the Koreans to conclude a similar treaty. By the 1880s Korea had been compelled to establish diplomatic relations with the East and the West.

In 1884 a Japanese inspired revolt against the Korean court caused the Chinese to intervene on Korea's behalf. Under the Tientsin Agreement of the following year, China and Japan jointly agreed to remove their troops from Korea. The accord lasted until 1894, when Japan invaded Korea again and declared war on China.

Japan emerged from the short-lived Sino-Japanese War victorious. In October 1895 the Japanese forced upon Korea a pro-Japanese cabinet. In February 1896 the Korean king took refuge in the Russian legation, from where he continued a running fight with the Japanese invaders. From the turn of the century, Korea was a pawn in the much wider conflict of interest involving China, Russia, the United States, Britain and Japan. Russo-Japanese differences in Korea were settled by Japan's overwhelming victory over Russia in 1905. After that, Korea remained under Japanese control. Despite Korean appeals for help, the United States and Britain supported the Japanese. In 1907 the Korean emperor was replaced by his son. In that year Japan established a formal protectorate over the country. The annexation of Korea took place in 1910.

Until the defeat of Japan in 1945, the Koreans fought an unending battle for independence. Their desire to be a free country never died; scores of clashes took place between Korean insurgents and the Japanese authorities. Thousands of lives were lost.

Regardless of British pretensions that they had conquered India in a fit of absentmindedness, it took a century of sustained if cautious and measured effort to establish British rule. Only after the Mutiny (1857)[13] had been suppressed and the private East India Company had been taken over by the British government did they feel called to a new stewardship in the subcontinent: India would be saved through Christianity, the English language and Western science. In 1877 Queen Victoria became Empress of India.

Nothing that the British did in India was to have such widespread repercussions as the attempt to introduce a system of unified law – perhaps Britain's most enduring contribution. British law helped to banish slavery, female infanticide and suttee (the burning of a widow on her husband's funeral pyre) from many parts of India. Thuggee (organizations of assassins and cut-throats) were outlawed; some of the worst abuses of Indian land control and tenure were also removed through the efforts of British administrators. The Indian civil service, which Britain created, was a vital prerequisite of eventual Indian independence.

Equally important was Britain's economic contribution. In the second half of the nineteenth century widespread improvements were made in transport and communications, irrigation, agriculture and industry. Although India's railways and telegraph lines (begun

in 1853) were built in anticipation of the country's needs, and continuously extended through Indian taxes, they opened the interior of
India, connected the main ports with important agricultural regions,
stimulated foreign trade (which experienced a sevenfold increase
between 1869 and 1929), combated famine and helped to spread
the knowledge and application of engineering techniques. British
investments in India financed major developments.

In 1892, the father of Indian unrest – the radical nationalist Bal
Gangadhar Tilak (1856–1920) – while reluctantly conceding that
some benefits had been obtained under British rule, argued that
Britain had gained more. British loans to India had been spent on
importing British goods and developing British-owned industries.
British intrusion had not led to the development but to the distortion of the Indian economy. As India became a market for British
products and a source of raw materials, the productive strength of
India, which hitherto had met its own needs, was undermined. In
the 1850s India, having lost its world markets in fine textiles, was
forced to import cheap cloth from England. India's expanding trade
contributed substantially to Britain's balance of payments; it played
a vital role in helping to finance Britain's Industrial Revolution.

India also provided the east wing of Britain's imperial army.
Between 1858 and 1920, from Abyssinia to Hong Kong, this highly
trained and disciplined force was used to safeguard British interests
outside India nineteen times. After 1858, Europeans accounted for
about 50 per cent of the army; but India paid for the lot. Chiefly
fighting British battles, the army took almost half the total revenue
for almost a hundred years. In the First World War Indians fought
for the British on the Western Front. They fought again for the
British in the Middle East and Asia throughout the Second World
War. Before 1945, defence was the largest item in Indian government expenditure.

The unusual tolerance of Hinduism to other religions permitted
Western culture to make great inroads. While Indians grasped the
theoretical knowledge and the philosophy of the West, their spiritual orientation made it difficult for them to accept the Western
sense of progress and the need for improved technology. A faith in
education has not been at the heart of Indian culture. India's earliest

universities – Calcutta, Bombay, Madras, Allahabad – were established by the British in the 1850s. Allan Hume, an English civil servant, played an important role in the establishment of the Indian National Congress in 1885. Although it aspired to economic reforms and home rule, India remained linked to Britain until after the Second World War.

India did not assimilate Western culture so much as enrich it. Western pressure caused a reawakening of Hindu and Muslim traditions. In Ceylon there was a resurgence of Buddhism. Indian studies were taken up throughout the Western world, creating a romantic revival in nineteenth-century Britain and Germany.

While Persia was never colonized as India was, its location was too important for it to escape becoming a pawn of the leading European powers. It retained nominal independence because of the rivalry of British and Russian interests. French interests, except during the Napoleonic Wars (when Persia was thought of as a possible route to British India), were minimal before 1914. Germany's interests developed only in the 1890s.

Persia was especially important to Russia, as it not only blocked the path of Russian expansion in Central and East Asia but thwarted Russian ambitions to enter the world through the Persian Gulf. The annexation by Russia of two provinces of Persian Georgia in 1800 set the stage for the Russian–Persian War of 1804–13. Having been defeated, Persia was forced to yield the provinces of Daghestan and Shemakha. In 1826, while the Russians were preoccupied in the Balkans, the Persians, backed by the British, seized the opportunity to attack Russian positions in the Caucasus. Again, Persia was defeated, and in the Treaty of Turkmanchai (1828) was forced to cede more territory and give up claims to Georgia. The Russians obtained important commercial privileges, as well as the exclusive right to have a navy in the Caspian Sea.

In the 1830s it was Britain's turn to intervene. Pressed by the Russians in the north, the Persians decided to recoup their losses to Russia by regaining territories lost to Afghanistan. (As Persia's weaknesses had attracted the Russians, so Afghanistan's weaknesses attracted the Persians.) In 1837 they invaded as far as Herat, where they were defeated by a combined Afghan and British force. For the next two decades Herat remained the primary objective of Persian eastern expansion. Anticipating a Russian victory in the Crimean War of the mid-1850s, Persia invaded Afghanistan again. This time, Britain took strong measures: an expeditionary force was sent from India to the Persian Gulf. In early 1857 Persia conceded defeat. Under the terms of the treaty of that year, Persia undertook to evacuate Herat, recognize Afghanistan as an independent kingdom (although a kingdom since 1810, Afghanistan's boundaries were not defined until 1872) and grant to Britain the same commercial concessions given earlier to the Russians. By 1879, the British were supreme in Afghanistan.

During the reign of Muzaffar ud-Din (1896–1907), Anglo-Russian rivalry in Persia reached its most critical stage, each power trying to undermine the other's interests.[14] Britain did everything it could to block a Russian proposal to build a railway across Persia to the Gulf. On 15 May 1903 Britain's foreign secretary, Lord Lansdowne (1845–1927), said Britain would 'regard the establishment of a naval base or of a fortified port in the Persian Gulf by any other power as a very grave menace to British interests, and we should certainly resist it with all the means at our disposal'. The Russians did not feel the proposal was worth a war. In time, Persia's importance to the great powers would be transformed by its rich oil deposits, first discovered in 1899.

The events that caused Britain and Russia to take a common stand on Persian affairs were threefold: the Persian Revolution which broke out in 1905, the abortive revolution in Russia in the same year and German intrusion in Southwest Asia. Though politically free, Persia continued as a classic semi-colonial state, economically and diplomatically dependent upon the European powers. In 1909 revolution broke out again in Persia and the shah, Mohammed Ali, who had forcibly dissolved the parliament (first established in 1907), sought exile in Russia. Two years later the Russians made an unsuccessful attempt to reinstate Ali on the Persian throne. The gathering war clouds in the West, however, drew both Russia's and Britain's attention elsewhere.

With the outbreak of the First World War, Persia openly became

the spoil of British and Russian interests. On the pretext that the
new regime of Ahmad Shah was pro-German, Persia's declaration
of neutrality in 1914 was ignored. The Turks having violated
Persian territory in order to attack Russia, both Britain and Russia
forcibly occupied those parts of Persia agreed upon between them
in 1907.

Because the Ottomans were the immediate neighbours of the
Russians and constantly blocked Russian ambitions, war between
them from the end of the eighteenth century until the 1870s was
endemic. The Turks threatened Russian orthodoxy, denied Russia
access through the Black Sea to the Mediterranean and persecuted
Slavic minorities in the Balkans. In June 1788 the Russian Black Sea
Fleet overwhelmed a superior Turkish force, and in December of
that year captured the fortress town of Ochakov, on an estuary of
the Black Sea between the Bug and Dniester rivers. But the
encounter that unintentionally reduced the Turks to powerlessness
at sea was the naval battle of Navarino Bay (in the southern Greek
Peloponnese), fought in October 1827 (see Map VIII). Diplomatically,
Navarino was a success for the Russians and a disaster for the British,
whose main object had been neither to defeat the Turks nor liberate
the Greeks, but to check Russian power in the eastern Mediterranean.
The war between Russia and Turkey ended in 1829 with the Treaty
of Adrianople. Despite the loss of much of their fleet, the Ottomans
showed no sign of collapse. In 1833, with the help of Britain, Austria,
Prussia and Russia, they survived Egyptian attacks. In 1841 an international Straits Convention closed the Bosporus to Russian warships.
In 1853 Turkey committed France and Britain to the Crimean War,
the one major conflict since 1815. Russia honoured the policy of
maintaining the status quo in the Ottoman Empire – particularly in
the Balkans – until April 1877, when its army penetrated Turkish
territory as far as Adrianople.

In 1908 Russian (and Austrian) fears about Turkey were aroused
once more. The victory of the 'Young Turks' in that year – who
were concerned to revive their own traditions and resented Western
subjugation – had led to the restoration of the constitution of 1876
and widespread disorder in Turkey. The outcome was the forced

abdication of Sultan Abdul Hamid II. In 1908 Russia informally agreed that it would not oppose the formal annexation by Austria of Ottoman Bosnia-Herzegovina, despite the fact that the latter was also claimed by the Slavs of Serbia and Montenegro. In return, Austria agreed to work for the opening of the Dardanelles to Russian warships; Austria also conceded that Bulgaria should become a Russian sphere of influence, provided Austrian rights were extended in Macedonia and Serbia.

Accordingly, in October 1908, Austria proceeded to annex Bosnia-Herzegovina. To its surprise, the Russians then protested at Austria's action and came out as the champions of Serbia's claims. What the Russians had not foreseen was that Germany would now forcefully intervene on Austria's behalf. Eventually, the Russians were faced with the choice of either abandoning Serbia or going to war. On this occasion, they chose to abandon Serbia. The only satisfaction the Turks got was that they were paid compensation for the annexed provinces. Realizing how close to war they had been, in 1910 Russia and Austria both pledged their support of the status quo.

The Ottoman Empire survived as long as it did because Britain, France and Russia had more to lose from its collapse than from its survival. Divided, feudal in outlook, corrupt, decaying, beset by inter-clan warfare, rejected by other parts of Islam – especially by the Arab world – it was rarely free from racial strife and the demands of its many subject peoples for independence. Until 1914 the Ottoman Empire constantly threatened to disrupt the European balance of power. The First World War marked the final act of its dissolution.

At the time of Western incursion in Southeast Asia in the sixteenth century,[15] an enduring pattern of politics and culture under a series of kingdoms had begun to emerge. Buddhism superimposed on Hinduism dominated Burma, Siam (Thailand), Laos and Cambodia. Confucian–Tao values also prevailed. Diffused by Muslim traders from Malacca, the centre of a strong maritime commercial empire, Islam was adopted in Indonesia, the Spice Islands, North Borneo, the southern Philippines and the Malay peninsula. The Burmese migrating southward from the highlands of Tibet adopted chiefly Indian political institutions and culture. Their eastern neighbours, the more homogeneous Thais – who had migrated from China in the thirteenth century and with whom the Burmese fought incessantly – drew upon both the Chinese and the Indian cultures. In occupying Siam they destroyed the remnants of the Angkor kingdom.

The first Europeans to reach Siam were the Portuguese, who in 1516 (five years after their arrival) were granted trade concessions. In the sixteenth century similar concessions were granted to Dutch, Japanese and English trading companies. In the seventeenth century the Thais used the French to offset the more pressing demands of the Dutch. Wary of the growing Western intrusion, in the closing years of the seventeenth century they expelled the foreigners from their country and began a 150–year period of isolation from the West. In the nineteenth century they contested Vietnam's claims to part of Cambodia while laying claims of their own to territory in the Malay peninsula. In 1826 the British obtained trading concessions. Seven years later similar concessions were extended to the USA. Unable to resist the growing tide of Western intervention, more concessions followed. Eventually British and French interests predominated.

Cambodians were largely descendants of the great Khmer Empire, which in the eighth and ninth centuries had flourished at Angkor Wat. In the 1500s Laos was a group of petty princedoms fought over by their neighbours, the Thais, Cambodians and Vietnamese.

The only Southeast Asian nation uniquely subject to Chinese cultural and political domination was Vietnam, whose people had migrated from central China. By the 1470s they had subdued the rival state of Champa, and the Khmers of the Mekong Delta. Spending over a thousand years under Chinese rule (111 BC–AD 939), and much longer under its influence, as a Confucian state on the Chinese model, Vietnam was called the 'lesser dragon'. For much of its history, an amalgam of Confucianism and Buddhism prevailed. Acutely conscious of their own separate cultural identity, for thousands of years the Vietnamese have struggled to maintain their independence and integrity.

The first Europeans to reach Southeast Asia were the Portuguese. Using Indian ports and fortified trading posts, within a decade of da Gama's arrival at Calicut in 1498 they had won control of the trade routes of the Indian Ocean. In 1511, having challenged Islamic interests, they seized the all-important Straits of Malacca, and proceeded to occupy the spice-rich Molucca and Banda islands. Conquest did not come easily, though. In the sixteenth century Portugal's strategic base for eastern-bound trade – Malacca – was fought over with the Indonesians six times. In 1519 Spain sent Magellan to find a new route to the Moluccas; in 1565 it threatened Portugal's position in the spice trade by occupying the Philippines.

The conquest of Portugal by Spain in Europe in 1580 left the British, the Dutch and the French with no option but to trade with Spain, or find their own way to the East. Determined to obtain their share of the trade in pepper and spices, Indian cottons, Chinese silks, porcelain and tea, and Japanese silver, England (1600), Holland (1602) and France (1604) founded their own East India companies. Increasingly, the contest to colonize Southeast Asia was not between Western Christians and Eastern Muslims but between the Western powers themselves. The Dutch soon ousted the Portuguese and the British from Indonesia: in 1605 they defeated Portuguese forces at Amboina in the Moluccas; in 1613 they broke the British hold on part of Timor; in 1619 they took Jakarta, which they renamed Batavia; in 1641 they captured Malacca from the Portuguese; in 1666 they triumphed in the Celebes, and secured a trading post on the east coast of Sumatra. By 1750 they had secured the whole of Java. Because of these inroads made by the Dutch, by 1800 Portugal had lost almost all its Eastern empire.

For most of the nineteenth century Dutch imperial rule was largely confined to the islands of Sumatra and Java. From the 1820s to the 1880s native uprisings forced them to extend their control to the interior of both islands. In 1824 the British ceded the port of Bencoolen on Sumatra to the Dutch, who reciprocated by giving up Malacca. Not until the 1840s did they extend their rule to southern Borneo, Bali and the Celebes. In 1859 they divided Timor and the neighbouring islands with the Portuguese. In the early years of the twentieth century they finally subdued the outer islands of Indonesia; only then was the Indonesian archipelago united under one rule for the first time.

The British had first occupied Malacca and other Dutch settlements in 1795. In the Anglo-Dutch treaty of 1824, British influence, already extensive in China and India, was extended to Singapore as well as Malacca. To protect the eastern flank of India, in the same year the First Anglo-Burmese War broke out. The Second Anglo-Burmese War occurred in 1852. Also in the 1850s the British conquered Assam and lower Burma; Siam (Thailand) was opened. After much fighting (the Third Anglo-Burmese War began in 1885) upper Burma was annexed in the 1880s. Ruled as part of India and the British Empire, its centuries-old monarchy was ended. New boundaries were established and the rich natural resources of the country were developed with the help of large numbers of Indian and Chinese immigrants. Brunei[16] and Sarawak were claimed by the British in 1888.

Influential in determining French incursions into Southeast Asia were Catholic missionaries. It was due to them that a treaty was signed in 1787 between the King of Cochin China and Louis XVI of France. By the mid-nineteenth century the French and their missionaries had fallen out of favour with the Annamite court. Attacks upon them having caused the death of several missionaries, including the Spanish Bishop of Tonkin, the French responded with armed intervention. Touraine on the Vietnam coast was bombarded by them in 1858; Saigon was occupied the next year. In 1862, by the Treaty of Saigon, France obtained the three eastern provinces of Vietnam and greater freedom for French traders and missionaries. Gradually, by the use of 'gunboat diplomacy', a common tactic among Western powers at the time, France extended its control from Vietnam to Cambodia (1863), Annam and Tonkin. Fierce native resistance was put down. In 1885, by the Treaty of Tientsin, a defeated China was compelled to recognize French control of Tonkin. In 1887 the whole of this territory was administered as the Union Indochinoise. Six years later France acquired a protectorate over Laos.

By 1890, only Siam in Southeast Asia remained outside Western dominance. In 1893, encouraged by the British, it began forcibly to reject French claims. To avoid a rupture in British–French relations, in 1896 the two powers formally guaranteed the independence of

Siam. In 1907 Siamese territory to the east of the Nan River was placed under French control; that west of the river, closer to British Burma, was declared a sphere of British action. Siam therefore became a buffer state separating the Western powers' spheres of influence. In 1939 it changed its name to Thailand.

Although day-to-day life in mainland and island Southeast Asia had been little affected by the early Western presence, by 1914, because of the introduction by the West of a plantation economy, the independence of Southeast Asian states and their trade relations with the rest of the world had been changed dramatically.

11

The Great War: 1914–18

On 28 June 1914 a nineteen-year-old Serbian terrorist, Gavrilo Princip, assassinated the Archduke Franz Ferdinand of Austria and his wife Sophia at Sarajevo, the capital of Bosnia, by then under Austro-Hungarian rule. Convinced that the assassin had the secret backing of the kingdom of Serbia, on 28 July, regardless of Serbia's willingness to make concessions, Austria declared war. The death of Austria's crown prince provided it with the excuse it had sought to crush rebellious Serbia and to end Russia's meddling in the Balkans once and for all.

The next day Russia mobilized in support of the Serbs. As the so-called 'mother of the Slavs', Russia had no other choice, especially as it had given in to the Austrians over an earlier Balkan crisis in 1908–9.[1] On 1 August Germany, having already given its word to Austria that in the event of war it would come to Austria's aid, declared war on Russia. On 3 August Germany also declared war on Russia's ally, France. On 4 August, after German troops had invaded Belgium, Britain declared war on Germany as it had undertaken to do. The fact that Britain and Germany were parliamentary democracies was of no account. Almost immediately, Britain's dominions – Canada, Australia, New Zealand and South Africa – rallied to its support. German possessions in the Pacific – Samoa, New Guinea, the Bismarck Archipelago and the Solomons – were at once seized by troops from Australia and New Zealand. British, French and South

Africans (under the command of Jan Christiaan Smuts) conquered Germany's colonies in Africa (except for German East Africa, which held on until the war was over). German Southwest Africa (Namibia) was seized and later administered under a League of Nations mandate.

Like a Greek tragedy, no one was able to halt the rush to war. In a highly industrialized, mechanized Europe, the time sequence of war had changed: mobilizing and committing millions of men to battle depended on intricate movements of troops by road and rail, which could not be stopped and started once it was under way.[2] Enthusiasm to fight was unbounded: many of Europe's youths ran to meet their fate, convinced that their cause was just and true. At stake was their country's honour and the security of Europe and the world. 'The lamps are going out all over Europe,' said Sir Edward Grey, Britain's foreign secretary, 'we shall not see them lit again in our lifetime.' They might not have gone out had Sir Edward made the British position clear to the Germans earlier; many Germans felt that Britain would not intervene. *Pax Britannica*, established during the long reign of Queen Victoria (b. 1819; reigned 1837–1901), was about to end.

Although the war burst upon Europe out of a clear summer's sky (unusually peaceful decades had preceded it), for those with eyes to see, it had been long in forming. Far from being a 'ghastly accident', it was the culmination of all that was dangerous in Europe's excessive nationalism.[3] In the second half of the nineteenth century nationalism and patriotism had begun to play a new and vitally important role. Whereas Caesar and Christianity had brought unity to Europe, nationalism brought discord. Two nationalist wars, the Balkan Wars of 1912 and 1913 – involving Serbia, Greece, Bulgaria, Montenegro, Romania, Albania[4] and Turkey – had proceeded the Great War. Although the war of 1912 had largely rid Europe of the disintegrating Ottoman Empire, neither war had provided a permanent solution to the rivalry between Russia and Austria-Hungary in the Balkans. On the contrary, egged on by Russia, a landlocked Serbia (whose national territory had doubled as a result of the recent wars) had begun to exert even greater pressure on the already weakened Austro-Hungarian Empire. To prevent Serbia reaching the Adriatic, Austria-Hungary annexed

Bosnia and backed the independence of Albania. Britain, France and Germany were not directly involved in the 'Greater Serbia' question – the basis of Austria's antagonism to Serbia's and Russia's intrigues in the Balkans[5] – but their allies were.

The problem of Serbian national aspirations had become insoluble except by war. It required only the archduke's assassination to rekindle the flame. Monumental stupidity, ambiguity, cowardice, existing alliances, propaganda, miscalculations, impulsiveness, mobilizations and ultimata did the rest. If one adds the less visible but much more deadly forces of hysteria, honour, patriotism, nationalism, passion and glory, then war was certain.

With war declared, the military alliances agreed upon earlier between the powers came into effect (see Map XIII). Germany was committed to support Austria-Hungary and Italy (the Triple Alliance of 1882). France was committed to support Russia (the Franco-Russian Alliance of 1894). Britain was committed to assist France (the Anglo-French Entente of 1904), and to assist Russia and France (the Triple Entente of 1907). The Ottoman Empire joined the Central Powers (1914) because the Turks were the traditional enemies of the Russians; the Bulgarians joined in 1915 because they had lost territory to the Serbs in the Balkan War of 1913. Later, Italy (May 1915), Romania and Portugal (1916) and Greece and the United States (1917) would join the Allies. The Japanese entered the war against Germany because they were committed to do so under the Anglo-Japanese treaties of 1902 and 1905, and because they hoped to obtain the German-held Shantung Province of China and the German Mariana, Caroline, Marshall and Palau islands in the Pacific (which they did in 1914) (see Map XII). Hoping to secure future security against Japan, China entered the war on the side of the Allies in 1917; it provided 150,000 labourers for the Western Front.

Italy was actually committed under the Triple Alliance of 1882 to go to the aid of Germany and Austria.[6] However, Austria's action against Serbia, it argued, was an offensive action incompatible with the Triple Alliance, which it held had a defensive aim. Instead, in May 1915, after the Allies had made many secret promises, Italy switched sides (as it would do again in the Second World War) and threw in its lot with the British, French and Russians. By then, war

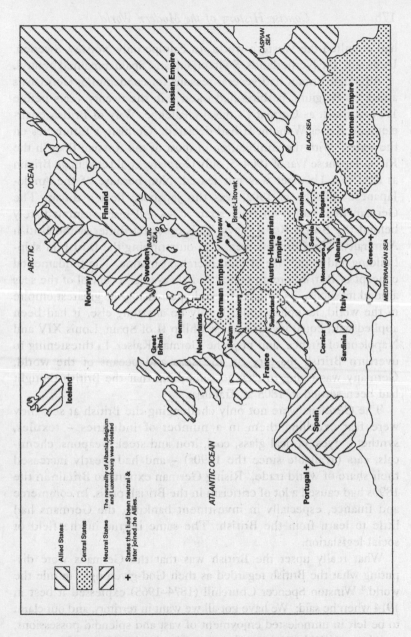

Map XIII European Alliances in the First World War

Allied States

Central States

Neutral States

+ States that had been neutral & later joined the Allies

The neutrality of Albania, Belgium and Luxembourg was violated

had engulfed the Western world. In Europe only Norway, Sweden, Denmark, the Netherlands, Switzerland and Spain remained neutral.

Although Britain had several reasons for condemning Germany's attack on Belgium, nothing had irked it in the twenty years before 1914 as much as Germany's naval challenge. Wary of British encirclement, Kaiser Wilhelm II had declared, 'Germany's future lies on the water.' With the annihilation of most of the Russian fleet in the Russo-Japanese War of 1904–5, only Germany could challenge Britain at sea. The US fleet was not feared. Nor, because of the Anglo-Japanese Alliance of 1902, was the Japanese fleet a threat. The German fleet had risen from sixth to second place – immediately behind the British Royal Navy. This caused a flutter at the British Admiralty. The Germans were also outstripping the British in shipbuilding and in the size of their merchant marine. The fundamental concept of British foreign policy had always been control of the seas around its shores. As an island people possessing the greatest empire in the world, its policy could hardly be anything else. It had been applied with equal vigour against Philip II of Spain, Louis XIV and Napoleon of France, and now the German Kaiser. In threatening to overturn British mastery on the seas and oceans of the world, Germany was trying to change something that the British thought had been settled in 1805 at Trafalgar.

The Germans were not only challenging the British at sea, they were fast excelling them in a number of industries – textiles, synthetic dyes, optical glass, coal, iron and steel, weapons, chemicals, cars (available since the 1890s) – and had greatly increased their share of world trade.[7] Rising German exports to Britain in the 1890s had caused a lot of criticism in the British press. In commerce and finance, especially in investment banking, the Germans had little to learn from the British. The same is true in the field of social legislation.

What really upset the British was that the Germans were disputing what the British regarded as their God-given right to rule the world.[8] Winston Spencer Churchill (1874–1965) expressed it best in 1914 when he said: 'We have got all we want in territory, and our claim to be left in unmolested enjoyment of vast and splendid possessions, mainly acquired by violence, largely maintained by force, often seems less reasonable to others than to us.'[9] Britain wanted nothing of Europe except peace, which meant upholding the existing balance of power. A change in the status quo has always been resisted by the leading power of the day.

Germany's outlook in 1914 was very different. Led by an active and aggressive ruler, Wilhelm II, the Germans saw no reason why Europe's or the world's destiny should be determined by Britain alone. For most of the nineteenth century Germany had been a federation of petty states which under Bismarck's leadership had united. Germany was not a 'Johnny-come-lately'.[10] The Germans, having defeated Denmark (1864), Austria (1866) and France (1870–1), had formed their Second Empire in 1871 (Napoleon had dissolved the first – the Holy Roman Empire – in 1806). In building a large fleet to defend its seaways and shores, in possessing unmatched military and industrial power, in claiming an ever-growing share of world trade, in demanding its 'place in the sun', in accepting war as an element of world order, the German Empire was doing only what the British Empire had done earlier. But what had been right for Britain was wrong for Germany.[11] Germany's proposal to build a railway from Berlin to Baghdad, as well as its cozying up to the Turks, merely added to Britain's fears. Britain, which was already losing ground in production and trade, was determined not to see its power reduced still further.

Looking back, it is evident that Britain bore its responsibilities as the world's superpower too lightly. Unlike France, and especially Prussia, it had scaled back its standing army dramatically after Waterloo (1815) and again after the Boer War (1899–1901). It made little effort to maintain a land army, and introduced conscription only in 1916. To be able 'to float downstream, occasionally putting out a diplomatic boat hook to avoid collisions' is how Lord Salisbury (1830–1903) described British foreign policy. While it may have been an enviable way of conducting foreign affairs, it does not say much for Britain's sense of responsibility as the world's leading power. When the crisis came in June 1914, Britain acted as a bystander rather than a leader. By the time Sir Edward Grey proposed a conference, Austria could not turn back without humiliation. Britain entered the fray because it feared that Germany would overwhelm

France and Belgium and reach the Channel ports. If Germany had reached the Channel, Britain itself would have been imperilled. Reluctant self-interest dictated British action. In Germany's violation of Belgian neutrality on 4 August 1914, Britain found the necessary moral pretext to make war. (The British royal family tactfully changed its name from the House of Saxe-Coburg-Gotha to the House of Windsor.)

France,[12] whose economic and military power in 1914 was far inferior to that of either Britain or Germany, and whose population was much smaller than that of Germany, had even more reason to fear war. It had never accepted its defeat by Prussia in 1871, which had destroyed the European balance of power established at Vienna in 1815. Nor was it prepared to lose for good the mineral-rich territories of Alsace and Lorraine, ceded to the newly established German Empire. Although Germany's military and industrial power exceeded that of France,[13] another struggle with the Germans was considered inevitable and feared. In preparation for such a struggle, in 1894 France compromised its principle of republicanism by allying itself with tsarist Russia. To foster better relations with the British, and add to its strength, it deliberately remained neutral (in word and deed) while Britain fought the Boer War, and accepted British power in Egypt (1904). As Britain was committed to France and Russia (in the Triple Entente of 1907), Germany became the common enemy. For France, alliances were its only hope of survival.

Some writers, such as the non-Marxist J. A. Hobson (whose *Imperialism: A Study* appeared in 1902) and the Marxist Vladimir Lenin[14] (whose *Imperialism: The Highest Stage of Capitalism* was published in 1917), saw the march to war before 1914 as springing more from economics than politics. They thought that the search for privileged spheres of foreign trade and investment in the decades preceding the First World War – the economic jostling and undercutting going on between the powers in Europe and the rest of the world – stemmed more from the changes taking place in the structure of the Western industrial economies than from politics. The scramble for parts of Africa and Asia after 1870 by the European powers was thought to be the logical and inevitable outcome in the development of Western capitalism trying to escape from its own inner dilemma; imperialism was an essential part of capitalism. The pre-war armaments race was simply a profitable substitute for more peaceful forms of manufacturing, such as railways, the demand for which had declined.

While the economic explanations of Hobson and Lenin have much to commend them, it is difficult to separate the economic from the political factors. It is evident that the great powers had more to lose than gain by going to war. In 1913, next to India, Germany was Britain's best customer. Britain also bought more from Germany than from any other country except the USA. Austria-Hungary's best markets were in the British Isles. As for the growing friction among the European powers in Africa and Asia, colonial trade and investments played only a minor role in world commerce and international investment. Trade and investment have not necessarily followed the flag. In the event, the strong commercial links that existed between the Europeans prior to 1914 did nothing to prevent war or alter the alignment of the belligerents.[15]

Europe's leaders seemed bent on war in the early years of the twentieth century with or without the aid of political or economic factors. Except in Britain, conscription had been introduced in most Western countries by 1914. France and Russia each had a standing army of more than a million men; Germany's figure was roughly twice that. Governments attempted to outdo each other in their preparations for war. Much of Europe's scientific and industrial talent was increasingly absorbed in the war industries. Since the invention in 1846 of pyroxylin by the German scientist Christian Friedrich Schönbein (1799–1868), the manufacture of explosives had been revolutionized. In 1846 nitroglycerine had been discovered by the Italian Ascanio Sobrero (1812–88), and (building on the work already done by Russian chemists and artillery officers) from 1862 was manufactured on a large scale by the Swede Alfred Bernhard Nobel (1833–96). Five years later Nobel invented dynamite. European civilization had come to be measured not by art, learning or religion, but by a country's ability to win a war. The people who would eventually be sacrificed were not consulted. It was taken for granted, as in all the wars of the nineteenth century, that there would be no shortage of men willing to fight.

In preparation for war every aspect of sea and land warfare was revolutionized. The destructiveness of weapons grew enormously. The use of steam and oil had raised the speed of warships from 6 knots in the 1870s to 27 knots in 1893. In due course oil, not 'blood and iron', would be the key to victory. Armour-plating, first introduced in the 1850s, had by 1905 reached a thickness of 24 inches. The Dreadnought class of battleship, which Britain first launched in 1906, with its 18,000 tons of steel, a speed of 21 knots and ten 12–inch guns with bored barrels (an eighteenth-century Swiss invention) mesmerized the world. World power in 1914 rested as never before or since on the capabilities of a nation's battle fleet.[16] Paradoxically, the submarine – the vessel that came closest to cutting Britain's lifeline – was the most neglected of all when the war began. Although a German submarine in September 1914 sank three British cruisers – *Aboukir*, *Hogue* and *Cressy* – in the English Channel with the loss of almost 1500 men, Germany did not have enough submarines to launch a major U-boat campaign against British shipping until 1917.

On land – as in sea warfare – by 1914 the Western powers had devised mechanized slaughter. The machine-gun, capable of firing six hundred bullets a minute, had made defence systems almost impregnable. The intensity, range and accuracy of side arms, shoulder arms and artillery had all undergone sweeping change. The earlier mercenary armies made up of pikemen and archers had long since been replaced by vast professional armies using long-range, rifled, fast-repeating firearms and guns. In the war against Austria in 1866 Prussia had used a breech-loading gun (in contrast to Austria's muzzle-loading gun) with deadly effect.[17] In addition there had been a veritable revolution in military transport and communications.

Despite the fact that both civil and military indices of power pointed to French weaknesses, the French plan called for an attack on the entire front with unprecedented speed. French bravery, dash and strategy would overwhelm the Germans. The danger of a German attack on the French exposed left flank (which eventually took place) was wished away. With a complete disregard for the evidence before them, the German General Staff (under the Schlieffen Plan) itself intended to end the conflict in six weeks. With the Russians at their back, a long, protracted war with modern weapons was out of the question. 'Paris for lunch, St Petersburg for dinner,' Kaiser Wilhelm boasted. Again, morale and dash would settle matters.

Contrary to those who predicted that the war would be swift and sure, Britain's Lord Kitchener upset the British public by saying that it would last for at least three years.

By 1914, with war clouds gathering, the Europeans (with the exception of Britain) had begun to assemble great armies for the coming fight.[18] If the worst came to the worst, war was still an acceptable way of settling a dispute. Increasingly, the question asked in the chancelleries of Europe was not 'Will there be war?' but 'When will there be war?' The preparations for war in Europe in the twenty years before 1914 did not go unchallenged. In 1910 the English writer Norman Angell published his influential book *The Great Illusion*. The economic and financial complexity of the modern world, he argued, made a major war between the powers obsolete; it was a message that growing numbers of Europeans found comforting. They agreed: war was unthinkable. Following the German navy's show of force at Agadir on the Atlantic coast of Morocco in 1911 (there had been disputes in that area between Germany and France in 1905), which heightened tensions between the European powers, the Socialist International (which by 1912 had nine million members) swore it would oppose a capitalist war with every means at its disposal.[19] The English pacifist Bertrand Russell (1872–1970) and the French socialist Jean Jaurès (1859–1914) were among the many influential voices raised against the growing danger. Oddly, the Catholic Church's voice was muted.

In an attempt to stem the mill-stream race to war, Tsar Nicholas II called the Hague Peace Conferences of 1899 and 1907 in Holland 'to discuss ways to make the world a peaceable kingdom';[20] the Olympic Games were resumed; Esperanto, a universal language, was introduced; students were exchanged; commerce and travel were encouraged. None of these efforts succeeded; nationalism and patriotism grew; the war clouds gathered. Oddest of all, when war came it was not treated as the scourge it proved to be but as the hope of European civilization. At the outset, the English poet Rupert Brooke (1887–1915) thanked God for having

> . . . matched us with His hour,
> And caught our youth, and wakened us from sleeping, . . .
> To turn, as swimmers into cleanness leaping,
> Glad from a world grown old and cold and weary . . .[21]

Thomas Mann (1875–1955), spokesman of German humanism, looked upon the war as 'a purification, a liberation, an enormous hope'. Older, wiser men, who knew these hopes were false, lacked the courage to warn those who were to be sacrificed; the young lacked the imagination to believe. The world would be saved not through force but through sacrifice. The only fear felt by many European males in 1914 was that they might reach the front after the war had ended.

Alas, the war did not end in six weeks, nor six months. This time there was to be no repetition of the swift, decisive military victories of the late nineteenth century. The concept of outflanking the enemy with a series of bold strokes failed. Instead, in September–October 1914, the Germans having been halted by Marshal Foch (1851–1929) at the Marne outside Paris, the war turned into a deadlock of trench warfare. For more than three years on the Western Front the battle line – stretching from the North Sea to Switzerland – hardly moved. In place of a swift fluid war there ensued a seemingly endless, exhausting, dogged struggle similar to some of the drawn-out European wars of the eighteenth century, and the American Civil War of the nineteenth century. The war of movement and manoeuvre, in which the military leaders had been trained, had become impracticable. Eventually, the numbers fighting on the Western and Eastern fronts exceeded any previous mobilization in history. The expenditure by governments of human, material and financial resources was on an unprecedented scale.[22] Government powers and propaganda grew as never before. Atrocities committed by the enemy in battle were exaggerated beyond belief to serve a country's purpose.

The men did not come home for Christmas; millions of them never saw their homes again. For four terrible years the war continued to consume the best that Europe had to offer. In one day, in August 1914, the French lost 27,000 men. One million men died on the Western Front in the first year. In 1916, for a few square miles of shell-torn ground on the Somme, 300,000 lives were sacrificed; on 1 July of that year the attacking British lost 19,000 men. Nothing of any consequence was gained. Yet the British commander in chief, Douglas Haig (1861–1928), like the other commanders (most of whom lived in splendid conditions in chateaux in the rear), continued a war of attrition. The three battles for Ypres between October 1914 and November 1917 resulted in almost one million killed and wounded. Ten months of struggle at Verdun in 1916 cost the French and the Germans 700,000 casualties. The Battle of Passchendaele (July–November 1917), fought in a sea of mud (the Allied preliminary bombardment had gone on unceasingly for nineteen days), in which 568,000 were killed or wounded, was not a tragedy so much as a crime. At Passchendaele, Ypres, the Somme, Verdun, Vimy Ridge and Cambrai the carnage was unforgivable. The 'red sweet wine of [Europe's] youth'[23] drenched the earth. Old men's errors were redeemed with young men's blood.

Western society was stunned. This was war of decimation. Marlborough, Washington, Napoleon and Wellington, who had shared the perils of battle with their troops, would never have permitted such endless, pointless killing. Only when widespread mutiny threatened, as it did in 1917, did the politicians order the staff to halt the slaughter. But this was a professional war; killing is what a professional army is supposed to do. The killing was soon renewed for month after ghastly month; attacks were met by bloody repulses with no visible effect on the outcome of the war. Whereas all the European wars since 1815 had been short and decisive, this war dragged on. One recalls de la Croix's words: 'Everything bears witness to the eternal and incorrigible barbarity of man.' Much of the Hague Court's efforts in 1899 and 1907 to make war less inhumane were undone.

Although the Eastern Front was much more fluid than the Western, the cost to Russia was equally great. Because of Russia's initial success against the Austrians in Galicia and Serbia, by the end of 1914 Austria had lost more than a million men, killed, wounded or missing. Quickly German troops were transferred from the West to fight the Russians.

Commanded by Paul von Hindenburg (1847–1934) and Erich von Ludendorff (1865–1937) they inflicted enormous losses upon the Russians. The Battle of Tannenberg in August 1914, in which Russia suffered 267,000 casualties, was the beginning of several dreadful setbacks. Another terrible defeat was inflicted upon them at the Masurian Lakes in September. The German victories over the Russians continued throughout 1915. In great disorder, the tsar's army was driven back into Russia. The wonder is that Russia (whose industrialization was half a century behind that of Western Europe) was able to fight as well as it did for three more years. Joined by Bulgaria in 1915, the Germans, Austrians and Hungarians recovered Galicia and eliminated Serbia. The cost was heavy on all sides. By the spring of 1915, the southern battles against the Serbs, when added to the battles in Russian Poland, had cost the ill-led Austro-Hungarian Empire two million men. By 1917 the Russian army had reached the point of collapse.

Almost nine million men died at the front in the First World War.[24] This far surpassed the total of those lost in *all* European wars since the outbreak of the French Revolution. Of the 65 million who were mobilized, 8.8 million were killed in battle, 21 million were wounded, many others were taken prisoner, or died from sickness and privation. The USA – although its help was decisive – had suffered just 53,513 combat deaths, a small percentage of the 1.2 million 'doughboys' (infantry) who saw action in France. The terrible suffering that the war inflicted upon civilians in the war zones defies calculation.

Everything was tried in an effort to break the stalemate. In 1915 – by which time women workers had flooded into armament and munitions industries – the Germans used poison gas (outlawed at the Hague Conferences); they also bombed from and fought in the air. The first German Zeppelin raids on Paris and London were condemned as barbaric.[25] The British soon stifled their sense of outrage and gassed and bombed back again.[26] The use of aircraft grew rapidly, and by 1916 they were armed for aerial combat. Greater use was made of the trench mortar and the grenade. In 1917, equally inconclusively, the British attacked at Cambrai with a new weapon

– the tank. The idea had been about for several years: a complete working model had been submitted to the British military in 1911 but was rejected because professional soldiers and cavalry opposed it.

In an attempt to knock Germany's ally Turkey out of the war (Turkish forces threatened Egypt across the Sinai), in April 1915 British, Australian and New Zealand troops made a desperate but disastrous attempt to reopen the Dardanelles at Gallipoli and seize the Turkish capital Constantinople. From the Allied side Gallipoli is a story of ill planning, incompetent leadership and heroic men. With 36,000 dead, and nothing gained, Allied troops were withdrawn at the end of the year. Also in 1915, under secret negotiations (the Treaty of London), the Allies persuaded Italy to attack its former ally Austria-Hungary, in return for which Italy was promised the Turkish Dodecanese Islands, as well as the southeastern and western coasts of Turkish Asia Minor, and territory in the Middle East. Greek claims to Smyrna and to parts of Turkey were also to be recognized. In June 1915 Italy attacked Austria-Hungary along the Isonzo River but was repulsed with enormous losses. It was decisively defeated at Caporetto in October 1917.

Under other secret agreements between the Allies – revealed by the Bolsheviks after the Russian Revolution – Russia had been promised Constantinople (Constantinople Agreement, April 1915) and parts of Turkish Asia Minor. The Sykes–Picot Agreement of May 1916 showed that while the Allies were promising the Arabs independence after the war, their true intentions were to enrich themselves at Arab expense. Arab hopes that their revolt against the Turks (which culminated in the liberation of Damascus in 1917) would result in a united Arab kingdom with the Sherif of Mecca at its head were sacrificed to Western interests. In 1917 Jerusalem fell to British troops commanded by General Edmund H. H. Allenby (1861–1936). The Arab world was subsequently divided between Britain and France on terms that suited the Western powers. A disillusioned Colonel T. E. Lawrence ('Lawrence of Arabia'; 1888–1935), who had joined the Arabs in their revolt against the Turks, resigned and sought obscurity with the British forces in India as 'Aircraftsman Shaw'.

In 1916, with the war widening and the casualties growing, Britain

introduced compulsory military service. On 30 May of that year the
Royal Navy fought an inconclusive battle with the German navy off
Jutland. The Germans sank fourteen British ships for the loss of
eleven of their own. Until then, the British Grand Fleet and the
German High Seas Fleet had studiously avoided each other. The
only sea battles were off Chile and the Falkland Islands in 1914.
The British coast was shelled by the Germans early in the war, but
these actions were inconsequential. Unlike in the eighteenth and
nineteenth centuries, when the clash of grand fleets decided the
outcomes of wars, the expected decisive dual between British and
German battleships never took place.

In February 1917, with the risk of bringing America into the war,
the Germans again resorted to unrestricted submarine warfare.[27] This
policy had been abandoned after the sinking of a British transatlantic
liner, the *Lusitania*,[28] in May 1915. By May 1917 the German U-
boats were destroying British ships faster than they could be built.
In the first three months of that year more than four hundred British
vessels were sunk, leaving the densely populated United Kingdom
desperately short of food and supplies. Fortunately for Britain, help
was on the way. In March 1917 the German sinking of a number of
American vessels on the high seas had aroused the anger of the US
government. A month later, following the German announcement
of unrestricted submarine warfare (which America claimed was a
violation of the rights of neutrals), the US decided to enter the war,
not as an ally but as an 'associate' on the side of the Allies.[29] The
totally pro-Allied sentiment pervading President Wilson's administration had at last openly declared itself; the world's third-greatest
navy had entered the fray; two million Americans volunteered. Soon
the Americans were building merchant vessels faster than the
Germans could sink them.

In March 1918 (Germany having forced an armistice upon Russia
at the Polish frontier town of Brest-Litovsk[30]), the German General
Staff staked everything on a spring offensive in the West. While
American troops crossed the Atlantic, German troops raced from
the Eastern Front. Although the Americans were not committed to
battle until the closing stages of the war, their presence in France
in such numbers (1.2 million by July 1918) was decisive. Despite

desperate efforts, and the loss of about a million Allied soldiers, the German spring offensive (March–July) was halted about 40 miles from Paris. With the Western Front collapsing, and unable to match Allied resources, Germany was forced to sue for terms. By then, the German navy had mutinied at Kiel (October); its ally Austria-Hungary was suing for peace; the threat of Russia's revolution was spreading, and uprisings were taking place in German cities (including Munich and Berlin). In conditions of growing disorder Kaiser Wilhelm II abdicated.

In November 1918, 'at the eleventh hour of the eleventh day of the eleventh month', while Europe waited in hushed silence, the guns fell silent. An armistice was signed. The most monstrous war, a war that might have been avoided, ended. Men being what they are, and history being tangential, Serbia and Belgium, where the war had started, had long since been forgotten (though before the war was over Serbia had absorbed Bosnia-Herzegovina). The dynastic and imperial rule of the Romanovs, the Hohenzollerns, the Habsburgs and the Ottomans had been swept away. Politically, little of the old Europe remained.

In December 1918 President Wilson reached France on board the *George Washington*. He was greeted by the common people of Europe as a saviour. Although a novice in world affairs – and despite the distractions of a Paris crammed with councillors, petitioners, visionaries, fanatics, charlatans and down-right rogues – he set about the task of ensuring perpetual peace. A new world order was about to begin. The reality is that instead of the 'just and lasting peace', a 'peace without victory', that he had promised,[31] Germany suffered total humiliation at the Peace Conference at Versailles in 1919. Delegates from twenty-seven Allied nations – not including Russia, which was in the throes of revolution – were represented. Germany was not invited except to sign a treaty that it had not negotiated. The 'big three' – Wilson (the idealist who intended to redeem the world), Georges Clemenceau (1841–1929; the 'Tiger', whose aims were simple: everything for France) and David Lloyd George (1863–1945; who was concerned to extend his own political life and to ensure that Britain remained Great) – dominated the negotiations. Italy (concerned to deny Yugoslavia an

Adriatic outlet at Fiume) and Japan (hungry to replace Germany in China and the Pacific islands) were the other great powers.

Germany was charged with sole guilt for the war – an accusation that Wilson thought improper and one that would later be refuted at length by the German government. In addition to having to disarm and pay enormous reparations,[32] Germany lost territory to France (Alsace and Lorraine), Belgium (Moresnet and Eupen-Malmédy), Lithuania (Memel), Czechoslovakia (parts of East Silesia) and Poland (parts of Upper Silesia and the Polish Corridor to the Baltic Sea, with German Danzig (Gdansk) declared a free city). The German military was disarmed to the point where it had only token forces – no tanks, no heavy artillery, no submarines, no aircraft. The fleet was to be handed over to the British. A plebiscite was planned in Schleswig-Holstein to settle the Danish–German frontier. German overseas possessions in Africa and East Asia were divided between the victors; the League was to supervise the seized territories, now called 'mandates'. The German Saar valley and the Rhineland (which was to be demilitarized) were to be occupied by the Allies for fifteen years. Six million Germans became expatriates (see Map XIV). The Germans refused to hand over their fleet to the British; on 21 June 1919, with the British navy looking on, the Germans scuttled their ships at Scapa Flow.

At Versailles, nationalism, vested interests, chicanery and hatred triumphed over Wilson's noble vision of a world governed by the rule of law.[33] War to Wilson was a condition of international disorder that should and could be remedied by international law. 'Hatred and revenge ran through the whole treaty,' said Herbert Hoover (1874–1964, a future president, 1929–33). Had Wilson been less rigid, less idealistic, less Calvinistic, he might have won the support of the others. 'If God could manage with Ten Commandments, why does Wilson want Fourteen?' Clemenceau asked. Frustrated by the implacable attitude of the British, French and Italian leaders to make the Germans solely culpable for the war, Wilson (in failing health) eventually retreated to his isolationist homeland, which refused (partly because of domestic politics) to ratify the treaty and to become a member of the newly founded League of Nations. Of Wilson's messianic vision of world redemption, only the League of Nations

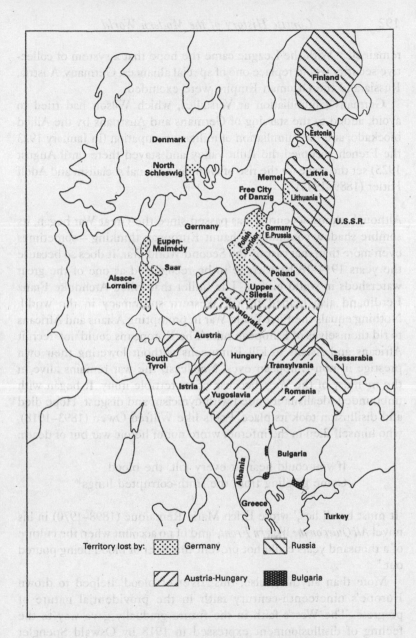

Map XIV Europe after the First World War

Territory lost by:

Germany

Russia

Austria-Hungary

Bulgaria

Finland

Denmark

North Schleswig

Estonia

Latvia

Memel

Free City of Danzig

Lithuania

Germany

Eupen-Malmédy

Saar

Alsace-Lorraine

Germany E.Prussia

Polish Corridor

U.S.S.R.

Poland

Upper Silesia

Czechoslovakia

Austria

South Tyrol

Hungary

Istria

Yugoslavia

Transylvania

Bessarabia

Romania

Albania

Bulgaria

Greece

Turkey

remained.[34] With the League came the hope that a system of collective security would replace one of special alliances; Germany, Austria, Russia and the Ottoman Empire were excluded.

Germany's humiliation at Versailles, which Wilson had tried to avoid, added to the starving of Germans and Austrians by the Allied blockade, and the humiliation of military occupation (in January 1923 the French occupied the Ruhr valley and stayed there until August 1925) set the stage for the rise of German national socialism and Adolf Hitler (1889–1945).[35]

Although almost a century has passed since the Great War began, its sombre shadow continues to haunt European thinking – sometimes even more than that cast by the Second World War. It does so because the years 1914–18 have come to be recognized as one of the great watersheds in world history. The bullet that killed Archduke Franz Ferdinand also helped to kill Western supremacy in the world. Nothing equals the First World War in prompting Asians and Africans to rid themselves of European rule. The Europeans could not recruit Africans and Asians to kill Europeans without lowering their own prestige in non-European eyes. Not least, the war remains alive in the memory of the West because of its terrible irony. It began with unbounded idealism; it ended with cynicism and disgust. Hope died and disillusion took its place. Poets like Wilfred Owen (1893–1918), who himself died in the inferno, wrote not of heroic war but of death:

> If you could hear, at every jolt, the blood
> Come gargling from the froth-corrupted lungs[36]

'It must be all lies,' wrote Erich Maria Remarque (1898–1970) in his novel *All Quiet on the Western Front*, 'and of no account when the culture of a thousand years could not prevent this river of blood being poured out.'

More than anything else, this 'river of blood' helped to drown Europe's nineteenth-century faith in the providential nature of progress. The West's faith in the future gradually gave way to the feeling of disillusionment expressed in 1918 by Oswald Spengler (1880–1936) in *Der Untergang des Abendlandes* (*The Decline of the West*).

Even Spengler's critics had to agree that much of what the Renaissance and the Age of Enlightenment had bequeathed to Europe – its belief in reason and social justice – had been lost for good in the mud of the Western Front. In 1918 the word 'progress' sounded like a cracked bell. Regardless of what happened at Versailles, Europe's belief in reason and the Christian belief in the reverence for life were never the same again.

Not only did the Great War prove to be ironic; for many Europeans it came to be identified with hypocrisy. The glowing promises made by the leaders of both sides were (in Remarque's words) 'downright lies'. Despite the sacrifices and all the fine words, the First World War did not prove to be 'the war to end all wars'; nor did it bring in 'a world ruled by law' – it was presumptive to think that it might. Wars went on. An even greater catastrophe befell the world just over twenty years later. By then, the Western world had become callous. Nor did the war 'make the world safe for democracy', a hope borne of nineteenth-century optimism. Instead, it fostered the rise of revolutionary communism in Russia, fascism in Italy and national socialism in Germany. There grew up a distrust of the older generation and the older modes of thought.

While the Treaty of Versailles, and the treaties with Austria, Hungary, Bulgaria and Turkey that followed, promised (and in some instances gave, at the expense of Germany, Russia, Austria-Hungary and Bulgaria) 'self-determination' to Czechs, Poles,[37] Serbs, Montenegrins, Croats, Slovenes,[38] Catalonians, Basques, Finns, Latvians, Lithuanians, Estonians and Romanians, it denied it to Asians, Africans and Latin Americans. At Versailles, when Wilson was arguing for national self-determination, he seemed oblivious of the fact that five Caribbean nations were then under US military occupation. Indians who had been fit enough to fight for Britain were not thought fit enough to govern themselves. Korea's efforts at the peace conferences to gain independence from Japan also failed. Against Chinese protests, Japan was awarded Shantung Province. Appeals for self-determination by Germans absorbed by Italy and Czechoslovakia, as well as by the Irish[39] (who had fought a running battle with the British for centuries) and the Egyptians, were given equally short shrift. Egypt, however, was not so easily shrugged off: in 1919 a revolt against the British there led to the creation of the anti-British Nationalist Party, the Wafd.

The earlier promises of independence made by Britain to the Arabs (the Hussein–McMahon correspondence of 1915),[40] together with the joint British–French declaration of 1918 to the people of Syria and Mesopotamia, 'promising national governments drawing their authority from the initiative and free choice of the native populations', were disregarded by the Allies once the war was over. The borders of modern Syria were redrawn. Britain's promise to 'stimulate national independence in the whole Arabic-speaking world' was conveniently forgotten. Except for parts of the Arabian peninsula, the Arab world was placed under European rule. Britain held on to Egypt, Iraq and Palestine (the latter two euphemistically called 'mandated territories'); France took Syria, which included Lebanon. The mandate for Palestine, approved by the League of Nations in 1920, incorporated the ambiguous Balfour Declaration,[41] which was Britain's wartime promise to the American Zionists that it would support the creation of a national home for the Jews in Palestine 'without prejudice to the civil and religious rights of the non-Jewish people'. For many Arabs of the Fertile Crescent there followed a struggle against Britain and France (and now against Israel and the USA) that has gone on from 1920 until the present day.

The economic promises of Europe's leaders proved to be just as hollow as the political. Far from providing 'homes for heroes', most European countries emerged from the war too impoverished to provide food or shelter. Hundreds of billions of dollars had been spent on the war, and most European treasuries were empty. Hundreds of thousands of Europeans were starving and homeless long after the peace had been made. In Italy and Germany there was a slide towards communism. Britain and France never regained their pre-eminent positions in the world; both nations experienced a relative erosion of their economic strength. By 1926, Britain was in the grip of a general strike. France's economic problems culminated in the repudiation of the French national debt. In 1934 Paris was beset by financial scandals of such magnitude that they resulted in the overthrow of the government. The international system of trade and investment upon which pre-war European economic greatness had been based was stricken. (Between 1928 and 1935 the value of European trade was more than halved from $58 billion to $20.8 billion.) Britain experienced a dramatic decline in the production of textiles, iron and steel, coal and shipbuilding. In 1931, its economy in a state of collapse, it was driven off the gold standard. Across the Atlantic, the US economy was also in desperate straits.

In contrast to the economic and political malaise that plagued the West, the war gave a tremendous stimulus to the industralization of India, China and Japan. The future of China and East Asia no longer rested with the Western European nations. Of considerable importance in the future struggle for world power was the transferring of the German Pacific possessions – the Mariana, Caroline, Palau and Marshall islands – to Japan, which enlarged the Japanese presence in the Pacific. Australian leaders looked upon this development with more alarm than did their British and American counterparts.

American attempts to replace Britain's economic leadership in the world also proved to be ill starred. No sooner had the USA provided a measure of economic stability in Europe through its Dawes Plan (1924), under which Germany would continue to pay reparations for an unlimited time, and the Young Plan (1929), under which Germany would pay $33 billion over 59 years,[42] than a speculative frenzy on the US stock market in October 1929 brought an economic slump – the Great Depression of 1929–33[43] – to the whole of the Western world. Banks, businesses and governments were threatened with bankruptcies. In May 1931 Vienna's leading bank collapsed; others quickly followed. In catastrophic proportions production plummeted while unemployment rose precipitously: Germany had 6 million, Britain 3 million and the USA 13 million unemployed; America's figure before the crash had been 2 million. President Franklin Delano Roosevelt's (b. 1882; president 1933–45) refusal to agree to the stabilization of currencies at the World Economic Conference in London in 1933 resulted in the further disintegration of the world economy.

The end of the Great War left Europe physically, emotionally, intellectually and morally exhausted.[44] National fears, national pride and national honour had led to international disaster. In place of the earlier romanticism and innocence, a vast fatigue dominated Europe. Perhaps this is one of the reasons why so many Europeans were carried off in the pandemic of the so-called 'Spanish influenza' (1918–19), which took at least twenty million lives – twice the number of those who had died in war. Other war-induced sicknesses, including typhus, typhoid, cholera and dysentery, are thought to have claimed another twenty million.[45] The one bright thing that did emerge was that women's suffrage[46] was widely extended.

While it took the devastating economic depression of the 1930s (which wiped out the savings of a generation) to bring the lesson home, politically and economically, Europe's period of overwhelming ascendancy was over. Protectionism soared; world trade shrank. Temporarily at least, economic and political might had passed to the United States. The war not only pushed America to the front of the world stage; it also made the Soviet Union a leading power – one whose example would inspire revolution everywhere. In addition, it stimulated the resurgence of Asia. The war had provided Japan with an excellent opportunity to develop its industries (especially textiles) and supplant European traders in the East. For those with eyes to see, the shape of world politics, self-evident at the close of the Second World War, were already visible in 1918.

At the instigation of the Allies, the Ottoman Empire was dismembered in 1920 by the Treaty of Sèvres. (Its dismemberment had been secretly agreed upon by Britain, France and Russia during the war.) Territorially, Greece was to be the treaty's chief benefactor. An independent Transcaucasian republic of Armenia was to be created. During a hundred years of persecution this had been the dream of the Armenian people. But in 1915, instead of obtaining independence from the Turks, between 500,000 and 1 million Armenians died on a Turkish-led forced march to Syria and Palestine. (The Turkish government denies that this act of genocide (ethnic cleansing) ever took place.[47]) There was another death march in 1915: after a four-month siege by Turkish forces (7 December 1915–29 April 1916) of British-held Kut on the River Tigris, ten thousand British and Indian prisoners were led by the Turks across the desert; two-thirds died on the way.

The Treaty of Sèvres, having been rejected by Turkish nationalists led by Mustapha Kemal Atatürk (1881–1938),[48] was replaced in 1923 by the Treaty of Lausanne, which recognized the new Turkish Republic as the sole and legitimate heir of the Ottoman Empire. Greece and its allies were driven out of Asia Minor. In 1923 Greece became a republic and its monarch, George II (1890–1947), whom Britain and the USA had helped to restore to the throne, was exiled. In 1924 the sultanate (the temporal leadership of the Ottoman Empire) and the caliphate (the spiritual leadership of Islam) were abolished by Atatürk. More poignantly, the Armenians, who had been offered freedom, remained subjects of their Turkish and Russian masters. In 1991 Armenia finally became independent from the Soviet Union.

While Britain and France seemed to have emerged from the war with greater political power, the initiative in world politics had passed to the capitalist United States and to revolutionary Russia. The Bolshevik Revolution of 1917 – which created the world's first revolutionary, socialist government – marked a new era in the world power struggle. From the start, it promised revolutionary support to colonial peoples everywhere.

12

1917: Communism – A New World Religion

In October 1917 the pent-up fury, misery and grievances of generations of Russians erupted in a bloody revolution. The uprising began innocently enough on 8 March 1917 with a peaceful women's march through Petrograd (St Petersburg) against bread rationing. The women were joined by other dissidents in an anti-government demonstration. On 10 March there were strikes in many parts of the city. Attempts to break these strikes by military force failed. On 11 March troops of the Petrograd garrison mutinied and joined the uprising. On 12 March, in a vast explosion of feeling, the people of Petrograd took to the streets. Panic seized the city. Russia's political, administrative and military situation had deteriorated beyond recall. Unplanned, unforeseen and uncoordinated, the revolution was under way.

This time, unlike the earlier uprising of 1905, which had followed Russia's defeat by Japan, nothing could hold it back. In an attempt to restore order the Duma[1] formed a Provisional Government. On 15 March Tsar Nicholas II, who in a desperate effort to turn the tide of war had assumed command of the army at the front, was forced to abdicate.[2] With his fall, the three-hundred-year-old Romanov dynasty died.

A month later, in April 1917, the revolutionary leader Vladimir Lenin, who had lived in exile in London and Geneva for most of the past seventeen years, reached Petrograd. The German High

Command, hoping that Lenin would undermine the provisional government and thus take Russia out of the war, had done everything (including providing a sealed train) to get him back to Russia. It is thought that secret German funds had been made available to the Bolsheviks.[3] Hastening to join Lenin were two other Bolsheviks: the Ukrainian Leon Trotsky,[4] from New York; and the Georgian Iosif Vissarionovich Dzhugashvili, alias Stalin (1879–1953),[5] from Siberia. Although Stalin alone of the trio was of working-class origin, the Bolsheviks intended to establish a 'dictatorship of the proletariat' along Marxist lines. Contrary to the Provisional Government's ill-conceived aim to continue the war against the Germans, the Bolsheviks called for 'peace, land and bread'; appeals to nationalism were conspicuously absent. In spite of their efforts Lenin and the rest failed to unseat the Provisional Government. By July, Lenin was in hiding in exile again; Trotsky was jailed on charges of treason; other leading Bolsheviks had gone to ground. Only Stalin remained free.[6]

For the moment it looked as if the head of the Provisional Government, Alexander Kerensky (1881–1970), a socialist, had succeeded in closing the floodgates of revolution. But then came the purported attempt by the ex-commander-in-chief of the Russian army, General Lavr Georgiyevich Kornilov (1870–1918), to overthrow the Provisional Government from the right. To help fight Kornilov, Kerensky appealed to the Bolsheviks for help. Trotsky and others were released from jail. Lenin, still in hiding in Finland, agreed to support Kerensky.

In turning to the Bolsheviks, Kerensky replaced Kornilov's challenge from the right with a much more dangerous threat from the left. By September, the Bolsheviks had won control of the Moscow and Petrograd soviets – councils of delegates from the land, factories and barracks. In October Lenin decided that the time had come to overthrow the Provisional Government, which Bolshevik doctrine held would ignite a revolution throughout Europe. Unless the revolution was taken up in other countries, it was thought the Bolsheviks themselves would fail. On the night of 23–4 October at a meeting of the Central Committee of the Bolshevik Party attended by Lenin, Trotsky, Stalin and nine others, the decision to seize power was made.

On the eve of 25 October 1917,[7] almost without bloodshed, the Bolsheviks seized the centres of government, transport, communications and energy in Petrograd. The Provisional Government, having neither the strength nor the will to defend itself (two of its members had been beaten to death), was forcibly disbanded; the Winter Palace, its last stronghold, was overrun. Kerensky fled the country, never to return; the Duma died. So far, Lenin had been proved right: all that was necessary in a country of age-old submissiveness was to seize power, and the rest of society would submit. On 15 December 1917 the Bolsheviks signed a humiliating armistice at Brest-Litovsk with Germany.

Seemingly overnight, the Soviet of the People's Commissars, with Lenin as Chairman, Trotsky as Foreign Minister and Stalin as Commissar for National Minorities, became Russia's only legitimate central government. All others, including the freely elected Constituent Assembly,[8] which met on 5 January 1918 and was forcibly dispersed by Lenin's militia, were treated as counter-revolutionary; Russia's first real experiment with democracy had been destroyed by the Bolsheviks at its birth. A resolute minority had obtained dictatorial powers over a submissive majority. Without any democratic experience, Russia had passed from feudalism to socialism; the absolute autocracy of the tsar was exchanged for the absolute autocracy of the people's commissars. Marxism was declared the official doctrine of the state. In place of Orthodox Christianity, atheistic communism was declared Russia's new secular religion. The Bolsheviks' answer to those who challenged their rule was widespread slaughter. The number of deaths from violence, malnutrition and disease grew enormously.

Marxist theory – not the sovereignty of the people – legitimized Bolshevik rule. The doctrine that made the 'will of the proletariat' (i.e., the will of a small group of resolute leaders) supreme also made coercion of the rest of society inevitable. Under Lenin, and later Stalin, terror was substituted for popular support. For those it crushed in the name of the new ideology, the revolution offered neither hope nor consolation.

Lenin's insistence on having peace at all costs so that the revolution might be sustained proved in vain. No sooner had hostilities against the Germans ceased than the Russians fell upon each other. In what came to be known as the Great Civil War (1918–21) Russia proceeded to tear itself to pieces. Untold numbers (perhaps twenty million) perished. The numerically inferior Bolshevik army (the Reds) was besieged by several anti-Bolshevik armies (the Whites). These were made up of a wide spectrum of Russian political opponents, including socialists, anarchists, monarchists, nationalists and conservatives; also fighting against the Reds were Balts, Ukrainians, Georgians and Poles. Finland, and the Baltic states of Latvia, Lithuania and Estonia, assisted by the occupying Germans, took advantage of the general chaos to declare their independence (which they kept until 1940). The Ukraine established an anti-Bolshevik government, as did Belorussia, parts of the Urals, the Don, western Siberia and the Caucasus.

Fearing that Petrograd was too exposed to invasion by sea, in 1918 the Bolshevik leaders fled to Moscow. Although the main threat to the Soviet regime first came from the east, by early 1919 the Bolshevik army was under attack from the north, south and west, too. In July 1918, while counter-revolutionary armies controlled three-quarters of the country from the Volga River to the Pacific Ocean, the assassination of the Romanov imperial family took place. On 30 August 1918, an attempt on Lenin's life unleashed a new reign of terror – far worse than that which had preceded it – during which many of those who opposed the communists were either systematically killed or banished by Lenin's secret police, the Cheka.[9] The idea that Lenin was unaware of slaughter on this scale is a Soviet myth. In eliminating opponents he was as ruthless and as paranoid as his successor Stalin.

In a vain attempt to restore a Russian front against Germany and strangle communism at its birth, Allied armies invaded Russia in 1918. Led by Britain, and including French, Italian, Serbian, Czech, Slovak, American and Japanese contingents, they entered Russia via the ports of Archangel in the north and Vladivostok in the east.[10] In mid-1919 an attacking White army coming from the Ukraine reached the outskirts of Moscow. There were occasions when it seemed that communist rule would be overthrown. The country was bankrupt; hyperinflation was putting an end to the use of paper money; in

1919 one egg cost 10,000 rubles. Yet, because of the ruthlessness, revolutionary fervour and single-mindedness of Lenin, Trotsky and Stalin, and because the anti-communist forces could never unite or gain widespread peasant support, by 1919 communism had triumphed. Its success made Lenin a demigod. Following Marxist doctrine, in 1919 the Third International (Comintern) was formed in Moscow with the aim of fomenting world revolution. Russia had become the centre for all socialist and anti-imperialist forces. By 1920, most of the invading armies had been driven from Russian soil. The last great task of the Red Army was to drive a Polish army – which in May 1920 had invaded the Ukraine as far as Kiev – back to Warsaw. In 1921, under the Treaty of Riga, the Polish state for which Josef Pilsudski (1867–1935) had fought for so long gained its independence.

By that time, although the communists had reasserted Russian rule in Georgia, Russian Armenia and Azerbaijan, the Civil War had brought the nation close to collapse. Between 1913 and 1921, production from industry and the land had fallen precipitously. Industrial production was about one-fifth of the 1913 figure. In 1921 drought and famine added to Russia's hardship; millions died and whole regions were depopulated. Faced with disaster, in March 1921 Lenin abandoned his 'war communism' in favour of a modified version of the economic system existing in Russia before the war. In agriculture and small businesses the market economy was reintroduced alongside the communist command economy. 'We have conjured up the devil of the market,' Trotsky warned. After Lenin's death in 1924, Stalin gradually assumed leadership. With the Civil War over, the economic conditions in Russia improved.

With the triumph of communism in Russia, a new experiment in living began. Supporting the experiment was the Marxist doctrine, which had first appeared in *The Communist Manifesto*, written by two German émigrés in England, Karl Marx[11] (1818–83) and Friedrich Engels (1820–95), and published in German in 1848. (The English translation did not appear until 1888.) Marx, the son of Jewish parents who had converted to Christianity, was a freelance writer, a born agitator and political revolutionary. Banished from Germany because of his political activities, driven from France, often beset by poverty, he eventually found asylum in London. Engels was the son of a well-to-do Manchester textile manufacturer. It was in London that Marx wrote his most important work, *Das Kapital* (1867).[12] This book was translated into Russian in 1872. (The Russian censor felt the work was so dull that he allowed it to appear.) Neither *The Communist Manifesto* nor *Das Kapital* attracted much attention. The latter remained almost unknown to the European labour movement until Marx's writings became the holy writ of the Bolshevik Revolution.

Adopted by Lenin as the new Russian ideology, *The Communist Manifesto* and *Das Kapital* became two of the most influential pieces of writing in world history. They not only recounted history; they *made* history. Their central message is clear: the whole of history (since the dissolution of primitive tribal societies) has been a history of class struggle, a contest between exploiters and exploited, between oppressor and oppressed. Marx argued that history is the story of the economic process; all is derived from the material conditions of life. To that extent, economic injustice is the sole cause of human conflict. To Marx, drawing upon the German philosopher Georg W. F. Hegel (1770–1831), the process of history is fundamentally a dialectic: a conflict of opposites – the rich versus the poor – producing progress. From the conflict between the feudal lord and the serf to the conflict between capital and labour, the eternal antagonism between classes develops its changing forms. Its last and most virulent form was precipitated by the capitalistically inspired Industrial Revolution of the nineteenth century. Because the capitalist system polarizes the enmity between capital and labour, as no other conflict has ever done, revolution – a violent climax – is inevitable. In the Marxist dialectic there is no place for compassion, accident or chance.

Marx provided a most convoluted explanation why this must be so. In a capitalist system, he held, the labourer must sell his labour in such a way that the difference between the value which the labourer creates and the bare cost of his own subsistence inevitably accrues to the capitalist in the form of surplus-value. It is a process in which, inexorably, the rich must get richer and the poor poorer.

Despite the productive power of the bourgeoisie,[13] for which Marx had great praise, the condition of the poor must worsen until they are forced to revolt. With the revolt, the injustices that had caused the conflict would be abolished. 'Workers of the world,' Marx cried, 'you have nothing to lose but your chains.' The right to rebel – nay, the *necessity* to rebel – was established as doctrine.

Marx thought that, with the decisive dictatorship of the proletariat, private property and the resultant class conflict would be abolished. The dialectic process – the conflict of opposites – would cease to exist. The state – hitherto the political implement of the bourgeoisie – would wither away. Darwin's 'law of organic nature' and Marx's 'law of economic motion', as well as the work in psychology of Ivan Pavlov (1849–1936) and Sigmund Freud (1856–1939), strengthened the growing deterministic trend in Western society.

Where Marx differed from earlier communalists or communists, such as Plato, St Luke, Thomas More and countless Benedictine monks, was that he sought a solution through violence. He also differed from them in his belief that the ultimate reality is economic – that God was dead. In promoting the notion of determinism (that social changes are determined by preceding causes), in arguing that social conditions rather than conscience determine existence, Marx stood the Western tradition (which emphasizes personal and collective responsibility) on its head. You cannot be personally responsible for something that is already predetermined. At least it is to his credit that, like the writers of the Enlightenment, he was concerned with the whole of mankind. In an age of growing nationalism, he was one of the first to appreciate that the spread of European capitalism and European systems of production were creating problems of a worldwide nature. 'Capitalism', he is said to have concluded, 'knows no flag.' Marx would have been fascinated with the manner in which international corporations operate today. Now, as then, capitalism has never been happy with national barriers that stand in the way of profit. According to Marx, the social problems of nineteenth-century Europe would eventually spread to the world: under capitalism, social injustice would grow and end in violence.

Marx was not alone at protesting the social conditions of the nineteenth century. Many others, including the German Catholic social pioneer Bishop Wilhelm von Ketteler (1811–77), the French sociologist Gustave le Bon (1841–1931) and a middle-class Manchester mill owner, Robert Owen (1771–1858), who is generally regarded as the founder of modern socialism, were also concerned with the growing social evils accompanying societies in transition from a rural to an industrial way of life. They too were appalled at the degrading working and living conditions that the Industrial Revolution had created in England, France and Germany. Like Marx, they deplored the regimentation of workers, the growing industrial unrest and the alarming injustice and instability associated with a capitalist economy. It did not require Marxist analysis for them to be able to recognize capitalist exploitation. While upholding the right to private property, they opposed capitalist wage slavery as much as they had opposed African slavery. In 1819, largely due to the efforts of Owen, the first Factory Act was passed in Britain: children under nine could no longer be exploited by heartless employers; the working day for all was reduced to twelve hours.

The two papal encyclicals on social conditions, 'Rerum Novarum' (1891) and 'Quadragesimo Anno' (1931), show that the Vatican was well aware of the momentous consequences of the economic and social changes taking place.[14] Where the Christian message differed from Marx was in its attempt to reduce class conflict through charity and understanding, rather than enlarge it through violence. The Church rejected Marxist atheism outright; the hope of the world lay not in class hatred – in godless malice – but in Christian love. In particular it rejected the Marxist tragic view of life, which must end in blood and fury. 'There is only one way', Marx wrote, 'to shorten and ease the convulsions of the old society and the bloody birth pangs of the new – revolutionary terror.'

While the study of Soviet communism must begin with Marx, the conclusions reached will depend as much on one's faith (or lack of it) in the Marxist system as on one's intellect. The true Marxist does not recognize bourgeois objectivity. He will defend the Marxist economic law of motion, which to him is gospel truth, with the same faith and fervour as are shown by a religious fundamentalist waging war for the literal interpretation of the Bible. The inevitability of Marx's perfect society must be believed; it cannot be proved.

Indeed, there is about Marxism the same dogmatic orthodoxy, the same apocalyptic vision, as that found in the Old Testament. One cannot help being struck by the fact that, for Marx, the eventual and inevitable destruction of the bourgeoisie by the proletariat was simply another way of restoring the chosen people (in this case the proletariat) in an earthly rather than a heavenly kingdom – a myth, of course, but no less powerful for that. In his dogmatism, in his condemnation of evil (capitalism), in his belief that right (communism) will prevail, in his grandeur of conception, in his vision and his messianism, in the blazing passages which from time to time light up his often turgid prose, in the white heat of his moral judgements (he denies moral motives but is passionately moral) – in all these things Marx is like an Old Testament prophet whose voice thunders across the world.[15] He realized, as the early Christians did before him, that we must not only have something to live for, but something to die for. He was a prophet among prophets, yet, unlike Jesus or Mohammed, he was a prophet without a god.

Marxism is ethical judgement rather than economic history. '*Das Kapital*', said the economic historian John Maynard Keynes (1883–1946), 'is an obsolete economics textbook which I know to be not only erroneous, but without interest or application for the modern world.' Economics alone – as Marx would have it – are not the cause of human conflict; human beings are. Ethnic, religious, linguistic and national differences, as well as territorial claims, are also sources of discord. Indeed, Max Weber (1864–1920)[16] maintained that an economy is derived from a society's underlying ideology and ethos, not the other way round. Even if Marxism had been deduced from history, which it was not, by the nature of things it could not provide the positive prescription (the ability to be clever for the next time) that Marx expected of it. Irrational, emotional nationalism or patriotism has often been a far more powerful force in history than rational, scientific socialism.

Moreover, as with all visionaries, some of the things Marx predicted never materialized. His prediction that the revolution would not come in Russia but in the advanced countries in the West (particularly Germany and Britain, which had undergone the Industrial Revolution) proved false. But then he always had a low opinion of the Russians: 'I do not trust any Russian,' he wrote to Engels. 'As soon as a Russian worms his way in, all hell breaks loose.' He was equally wrong in believing that the state would 'wither away' as an instrument of oppression. The Soviet state, in fact, became more oppressive than that of the tsars. He erred in stressing the primacy of economics at all times, in all situations. It was false for him to assume that change would come about primarily because of class conflict. History is much more than that. The First World War did not arise because of poor and rich nations, or for that matter because of poor and rich classes, but because of the struggle for power among Europe's leaders. Change is always the work of a small, resolute minority, regardless of class. Marx was equally wrong in expecting a communist revolution to result in worldwide worker solidarity. The workers of the world did not unite; the capitalists did. Nationalism proved a much more powerful force among the workers than socialist rhetoric. To think of a united world of tomorrow as a single community – as he did – shows a lack of knowledge of human psychology. Is it not unrealistic (and perhaps unappealing) to aspire towards a world state with homogenized values and homogenized institutions? A world without diversity would be a dead world. Finally, Marx was as wrong in ascribing selfishness and greed to the middle class rather than to incalculable human nature (selfishness and greed are universal attributes) as he was in placing so much stress upon the power of the intellect (his Marxist theory) and so little upon the power of passion and feeling. Marx not only misread history; he misread human nature as well. Marxism is too exact, too certain, to be true of life.

Regardless of whether one is a supporter or a critic of Marxist doctrine, the world would have been a very different place had Marx never lived. Without him, there would still have been a labour movement in Europe – perhaps a revolution in Russia – but it would have been a different labour movement, and a different revolution. Had Lenin never heard of Marx he would have lived and worked and perhaps made history, but it would not have been the history it came to be under the influence of Marxist doctrine. Lenin did for Marx what St Paul did for Christ. Without Lenin and the Russian Revolution, Marx might have remained unknown.

However heretical it may be to say so, the Great Socialist Revolution of 1917, far from being the outcome of the Marxist doctrine of historical and social determinism, was a straightforward coup. It depended more on a disastrous war, the desperation of the common people, mutiny at the front, the excesses of capitalism, the social and political decay of the Romanov dynasty, an enfeebled aristocracy, self-seeking politicians and a corrupt officialdom than it did on doctrinal exactitude. Communism grew because in *The Communist Manifesto* Marx provided a weapon with which the poor of the world could fight the rich; a psychological weapon which no other system had devised. For the underdeveloped, agrarian countries of Asia, Africa and Latin America, Marxism was a revolutionary call to arms – a clarion call for the overthrow of the Western capitalist world – a philosophy of action designed to change their world, not to interpret it.

After 1917 Marxism gave way to Leninism, Leninism to Stalinism, Stalinism to the policies of his successors. Doctrinally, the changes were slight. Lenin converted Marx's doctrine of dialectical, historical materialism into a practical instrument of revolution. In order to seize power it was permissible to transcend the economic situation – to leap across the historical stage. 'A Marxist', Lenin said, 'must take account of real life . . . and not hang on to the tails of the theories of yesterday.' It was the Communist Party's job to lead the proletariat in the revolutionary struggle. Lenin developed the theory that Western imperialism would prove to be the final stage of capitalism.[17] Stalin also made changes in communist doctrine concerning the paramount importance of class war. 'The right of self-determination' – he was referring to the states that had broken away from Russia during the Civil War – 'cannot and must not be an obstacle to the working class in the exercise of its dictatorship.'[18]

By 1928, contrary to Marxist doctrine of worldwide revolution, Stalin had settled for communism within Russia. His decision to change the course of the revolution – some said to *betray* the revolution – was challenged by those who supported the Marxist–Leninist ideal of ecumenical worldwide communism. The dispute led to Trotsky's exile in 1927, his founding of the Fourth International in 1938 and his assassination by a Stalinist agent in 1940 in Mexico City.

By 1938 Stalin had succeeded in removing – by death or exile – most of those who stood in his way. The record is staggering. Ten million Ukrainians died in 1930–1 from the famine Stalin imposed on them.[19] In the 1920s he had ruthlessly collectivized agriculture. His Great Terror in 1936–8 claimed many millions more. He is accused of having murdered more of his own countrymen (fourteen million) than the Germans killed in their invasion of Russia in the Second World War. The aristocracy and the middle class were destroyed. On the political front, few of the leaders of the October Revolution escaped him. The more senior they were, the more they had helped him to get where he was, the more certain their fall. His execution of political opponents culminated in the great purges of Communist Party leaders in Moscow in the late 1930s. Prior to the outbreak of the Second World War, he was especially harsh in ridding himself of army officers whom he suspected of disloyalty: he executed 3 of the Red Army's 5 field marshals, 14 of its 16 army commanders, all the navy's admirals and more than 20,000 other officers.

By the eve of war in 1939, Stalin's power was supreme. By then, Russia's agricultural and industrial bases were far stronger than when he had assumed power, as were the country's defences. Contrary to popular opinion, he was well aware of the nature of Germany's growing military might, and of Hitler's intention to colonize Russia. To buy time and avoid war, he signed a non-aggression pact with Hitler in August 1939. (Neville Chamberlain (1869–1940) had done the same at Munich a year earlier.) In anticipation of a German attack, in November 1939 Stalin made a pre-emptive strike against Finland, for which the Soviet Union was expelled from the League of Nations. (Russia had joined the League in 1934, a year after Germany and Japan had left it.)

Whether Stalin signed his pact with the Germans in the hope that it would enable Russia to stand aside while the capitalist world destroyed itself is a matter of conjecture. Certainly, Russia made no move to help the West in its moment of peril. On the contrary, the Russians did everything they could to placate the Germans. They dismissed envoys friendly to the Western powers from Moscow; they recognized a pro-German government in Iraq; and they continued to supply the German armed forces until, on 22 June 1941, they were attacked themselves. A few days earlier, the Soviet Tass News Agency had deemed absurd the possibility of a German attack. Stalin disregarded Churchill's eleventh-hour warning of the coming German assault on Russia because he thought that Churchill was plotting to involve Russia in a Western war; Germany's build-up of troops in the east was dismissed as provocation and scaremongering. He was proved wrong in believing that time was on his side.

13

Asia in the Inter-war Years

Whereas Japan had profited from the First World War – it emerged as a major power with new territories and a permanent seat on the Council of the League of Nations – the conflict left China in greater chaos than ever. In 1919, at the Treaty of Versailles (perhaps the first time that the Chinese willingly entered the corridors of world power), China lost its Shantung Province to Japan. In retaliation the Chinese ordered their delegates home, boycotted Western products and discarded Western democratic ideas. The grossly unfair terms of Versailles provoked a massive upsurge of nationalist feeling, expressed in the May Fourth movement. So divided had China become (not least as a result of foreign oppression[1]), so weak did it remain, that by 1923, eleven years after the republic had been established, whatever unity it possessed had been shattered by the competing claims of warlords, nationalists and communists. In the resulting confusion the Chinese provinces of Tibet and Outer Mongolia broke away.[2]

The collapse of order in China in the inter-war years caused the one-time liberal-minded leader Sun Yat-sen to advocate the adoption of Russian communism.[3] He conceded that the liberal and democratic ideals espoused in the Chinese October Revolution of 1911 had proved impracticable. Out of necessity, China would have to return to its traditional way of life based on the collective rather than the individual; the controlled rather than the free; the hierarchic principle rather than the egalitarian. The authoritarian ideology of the state implied in Confucian doctrine must be exchanged for the parallel authoritarian ideology of communism. In contrast, the Western historical pluralism upon which the West's liberal democracy depended, and upon which the Chinese experiment in republicanism had been based, was largely alien to Chinese thought. Western republicanism had nothing in common with Chinese traditions, hence its failure.

In 1923 Sun Yat-sen allied himself with the Chinese Communist Party, which had been founded two years earlier under the supervision of Russian agents. Soviet support was given to the rearming and training of Sun's Nationalist Party, the Kuomintang. The aim of both the nationalists and the communists was to undermine the warlords and bring about national reunification. In 1924, coincident with the calls for industrialization being made in Turkey, Persia and India, Sun advocated the industrialization of his country. Thanks partly to the impulse provided by the Russian Revolution of 1905, industrialization was thought to be the alchemy of the modern age.

In 1925 Sun died. Replacing him as head of the Kuomintang was his deputy, Moscow-trained Chiang Kai-shek (1887–1975).[4] The struggle for power in China now lay between the warlords, the Russian-led communists and the Chinese nationalists. After forming an alliance with the communists, Chiang carried out a successful expedition against the northern warlords. In 1927 he captured Beijing. Having done that, he turned around and slaughtered his communist allies; three hundred died in Shanghai alone. His Russian communist advisers fled to Moscow.

Having overcome his enemies, between 1928 and 1937 Chiang extended his rule to the whole of China. This was perhaps his greatest hour. His nationalist government was quickly recognized by all the great powers except the USSR. His abolishing of the hated extra-territorial rights of Westerners gained him support in his drive to create an independent, unified, progressive China. Foiling his efforts were widespread corruption[5] and Russian and Japanese intervention. The Russians invaded Manchuria in 1924 and directed communist insurrection within China itself. In an effort to prevent China becoming united under Chiang Kai-shek, the Japanese army annexed Manchuria in 1931 and established the puppet state of Manchukuo.

Thenceforth, China was divided between the nationalists led by Chiang (centred on Nanking), the communists led by Mao Zedong,[6] operating as guerrilla bands in the southern Kiangsi Province, and the Japanese. Born the son of a farmer, Mao had helped found the Chinese Communist Party in 1921; after 1935 he dominated it. Contrary to Marxist doctrine, he was the first communist leader to express the view that revolution must come from the peasantry rather than the urban proletariat. In 1933 Chiang launched another offensive against the communists. By October 1934, the communist army's position had become critical, and it was then that Mao, Chou En-lai (*c.* 1898–1976) and others led it on its incredible 'Long March' from Kiangsi Province in southeast China to Yenan in the far north-west. It was on this march that Mao established his leadership. Of the 100,000 men and 35 women who left Kiangsi, barely 30,000 reached Yenan a year later. With a price of $250,000 on his head, Mao stayed there for the next eleven years.

In 1937 Japan dropped all pretence and began a general war, occupying north and central China. Chiang and the nationalists fled to Chungking (Chongqing) in the upper Yangtze valley. They might have stood and fought had Chiang not squandered his forces fighting the communists earlier.

As the Second World War approached in the West, Russia's influence in the struggle for power in China declined. With Japan's attack upon the Western powers in December 1941, the Chinese nationalists and the communists made what proved to be largely unsuccessful efforts to form a common front to fight the Japanese. There matters rested until 1945, when (the Americans having forced the Japanese to surrender) the Chinese nationalists and communists began a fight to the death for supremacy.

Between 1918 and 1941, Japan's conduct towards the rest of the world oscillated between peaceful and warlike intentions. For most of the 1920s it gave the other powers little to grumble about. At the Washington Naval Conference[7] – called by the USA (November 1921–February 1922) to discuss political stability in East Asia and naval disarmament – Japan amicably accepted Britain's decision to terminate the Anglo-Japanese Alliance of 1902, an alliance never accepted by the United States, China or Australia. Americans saw the Pacific as a sphere of American influence. A Four Power Pacific Treaty was signed between the USA, the British Empire, France and Japan. Japan even became conciliatory towards China, handing back Shantung Province in 1922 (temporarily). Japan also cooperated with the USA and Britain by agreeing to scale down its naval armaments, and by accepting a ratio of major warships favourable to the Western powers. But this decision resulted in anti-American and anti-British feeling in Japan. An extraordinary spate of assassinations of political and industrial leaders followed; in four years three premiers were assassinated. Japan cooperated with the Western powers again on naval discussions at Geneva in 1927. With the London Naval Treaty of 1930, it extended to its heavy cruisers the three-to-five ratio it had accepted with the USA and Great Britain at the earlier conferences. With Britain and the USA, it pledged to maintain the status quo in the Pacific. The Americans and the British reciprocated by agreeing not to increase their bases at Pearl Harbor and Singapore – a decision all the Western powers, including Australia and New Zealand, would later regret.

Forces were at work, however, that would eventually undermine whatever goodwill was established between Japan and the West. Following the policies already introduced in the British dominions, the United States Immigration Quota Acts of 1921 and 1924 deliberately penalized Asian immigrants, including the Japanese.[8] The introduction of the measures was denounced in Japan as a 'day of shame'. Growing world autarchy resulted in the exclusion of Japanese products from American and other Western markets. The commercial and financial crash in the USA in 1929 led to the Smoot–Hawley Tariff Act of 1930, which caused the further decline of international trade, upon which Japan greatly depended. Between 1929 and 1931 the value of Japanese exports was halved. Protective measures taken by the Dutch in 1932 and by the British in 1933 further restricted the sale of Japanese goods. With vastly increased numbers (between 1873 and 1918 Japan's population rose from 35 to 65 million), and with its population growing by a million a year,

Japan needed to find – either through the expansion of world commerce or by territorial aggrandizement in Manchuria – a solution to its demographic and economic problems.

To the detriment of future world relations, the economic problems strengthened the hands of the Japanese militarists and ultra-nationalists. Condemned by the League of Nations for its invasion of Manchuria in 1931, Japan abandoned the League in March 1933. In 1931 China had called on the League and the USA (a signatory of the Kellogg–Briand Pact) for action against Japan without avail. Japan's subsequent invasion of China proper met with little resistance from Chiang Kai-shek. The flouting of the League Covenant by Japan seriously undermined the League's authority. In 1936 Japan withdrew from the London Naval Treaty; from being a friend of the British, Japan became a potential enemy.

In the same year Japan signed the Anti-Comintern Pact with Germany, there were more political assassinations and attempted coups in Tokyo. In 1937, taking advantage of the fact that Europe was preoccupied with the Spanish Civil War (1936–9), Japan began its long-prepared invasion of central and southern China. In December 1937 Japanese troops entered Nanking; an estimated 200,000 Chinese were massacred over the next two months; others died from Japan's use of biological weapons, such as plague. By now, the military were completely in charge of Japanese policy. In 1938 the League of Nations, prompted by the Americans, declared Japan an aggressor. The next year the USA rescinded its Treaty of Commerce and Navigation with Japan. As a warning, the American Pacific Fleet – now the world's greatest – was moved from its base in San Diego to Pearl Harbor, 2000 miles closer to the Japanese archipelago. In 1940 Japan signed a tripartite Pact of Mutual Assistance with Italy and Germany; it also signed a treaty of friendship with Thailand. President Roosevelt responded with economic sanctions, including the cutting off of scrap iron and steel supplies. In September 1940 Japan began its expansion in the Pacific by occupying northern French Indo-China. Roosevelt's answer was to ban oil shipments to Japan.

Denied vital oil supplies, Japan faced a stark choice: it either had to abandon its stake in China (which the Americans demanded and which Japan could not possibly concede) or seize the oil of Indonesia, then called the Dutch East Indies. Oil was the crucial issue. In 1941, though nominally still at peace with Japan, the USA banned virtually all normal trade and froze all Japanese assets. Japan found itself in a corner from which, outside of war or humiliation, it could not escape. The only thing it could do was try to neutralize the Soviet Union, which it did when it signed a non-aggression pact with Moscow in April 1941.

By then, the USA had come to be regarded by many Japanese as their country's chief enemy. The only crime Japan was committing in expanding on to the landmass of Asia was to upset the division of world territory already settled in the West's favour. It was doing nothing the West had not done. What was the difference, the Japanese asked, between US actions in Central America and the Caribbean and their own idea of a 'Co-prosperity Sphere' in Asia? Only the USA – sated with territory – prevented Japan from fulfilling its destiny as the leader of East Asia. In November 1941 (its last proposals having been rejected by the USA) Japan made the fateful decision to attack all the major Western powers in the Pacific.[9] According to the Japanese General Staff, the war would have to be won in four months. The longer the war, the less likely it was that Japan would win it; time was the crucial element. The Japanese military had no illusions about America's far greater productive capacity. Although severely under-utilized in the 1930s, US industrial might was still in a class of its own.

On 7 December 1941 the Japanese made their surprise attack against the US Pacific Fleet at Pearl Harbor and against installations in the Philippines.[10] The day after Pearl Harbor, Germany and Italy entered the war on Japan's side. The Japanese had reached the final stage of the great venture in aggression they had begun in Manchuria in 1931 – a venture which, if not beyond their motivation, proved beyond their means. More than two million Japanese perished in the Second World War.

The war ended with the atomic bombardments of Hiroshima and Nagasaki in August 1945. With the use of nuclear weapons, a new era in warfare had begun.

*   *   *

India's history in the inter-war years is one of growing antagonism between the Indians and the British. This antagonism dominated India's role in the world. The British clung to their rule over India; the Hindus and Muslims demanded independence. The impasse was broken by Gandhi, who more than any other won for India its freedom. He had returned to India from South Africa in 1915, and tolerated British rule until the First World War was over. Indian troops had fought for Britain with distinction on the Western Front and in the Middle East. Indian supplies sustained the Allies. Yet agitation for self-government in India during the war never ceased.

In an attempt to appease the Indians, in 1917 the British promised 'the gradual development of self-governing institutions'. The Montagu–Chelmsford Proposals of 1918 granted partial self-government to the provinces; the Government of India Act (1919) made further concessions – all of which were regarded by the Indian National Congress[11] (chiefly Hindu) and the All-India Muslim League as attempts to defer self-government. Subsequent uprisings, aggravated by severe crop failures and widespread famine, gave vent to the repressive British anti-sedition measures of 1919. These measures undid any good that might have resulted from the Montagu–Chelmsford Proposals, and brought Hindu, Muslim and Sikh discontent to a head.

It was at this point that Gandhi, shocked by the Amritsar massacre of 1919, in which 379 Indians were killed and over 1000 wounded by British troops, renewed the campaign of passive resistance he had practised in South Africa. Between 1922 and 1924, with other members of the Indian National Congress Party, he was imprisoned, on charges of sedition. The British had managed to make a martyr of him.

From 1924 until his dramatic protest march to the sea in March–April 1930, to protest a tax on salt, Gandhi travelled extensively through the villages of India, preaching his several gospels: the moral force of non-violence, the acceptance of the 'untouchables', the unity of Hindus and Muslims. In order to stem the corrupting influences of Western modernization and to boycott the imports of British textiles, he preached the adoption of *swadeshi* – the use of local, indigenous products, especially hand-spun and hand-woven cloth.

In the autumn of 1931, when Gandhi was representing the Indian Congress at the Second Round Table Conference in London, he became convinced that Britain was not serious about transferring power to the Indians. On his return to India in January 1932, he was again jailed for non-violent disobedience. It was then that he began his famous fasts.

Despite Gandhi's belief that the British would not yield until forced to do so, some gains were obtained. Positions in the armed forces and the civil service were thrown open to Indians. India was divided into eleven provinces, each with wide autonomy. By 1937, when the Government of India Act of 1935 took effect, the Congress Party had obtained control of nine of India's provincial governments. The principle of equality of all before the law was introduced – a revolutionary change for the inhabitants of a caste-ridden land. In the 1930s women were given the vote. The outbreak of the Second World War was a moment of truth for India. Against Gandhi's advice, India decided to fight with the British Commonwealth.

The war over, Britain's problem became not how to hang on to power in India, but how to transfer it. Long before political independence had been achieved in 1947, the Indians had extended their activities into industrial and business enterprises that had been the preserve of the British. It was only when the British gave a deadline for the peaceful transfer of power that the Indians gave serious thought to its use. Gandhi and his followers had wrongly assumed that there was an Indian nation to which power could be transferred effectively. 'You start with the theory of an Indian nation that does not exist,' wrote Mohammed Ali Jinnah (1876–1948)[12] to Gandhi in January 1940.

Western power was also challenged in other countries of Southeast Asia during the inter-war years. To obtain its independence, Burma had to free itself from both British and Japanese intrusion. Guerrilla resistance to British annexation had gone on in Burma since the 1820s. Immigrant Indians who had been brought in by the British controlled much of the land; immigrant Chinese much of the commerce. The outcome of this foreign influence was the growth of a nationalist movement whose origins were more religious than political. Although student strikes and a revolt by Burmese peasants in 1930 were crushed, by 1937, when Burma ceased to be a province of British India, the Burmese had managed to obtain a large measure of control over their internal affairs. The outbreak of war in late 1941 was the signal to Japan and Burmese patriots to overthrow British rule, which was never fully restored. Having rid Burma of British rule, the Japanese imposed their own. Following the Japanese defeat in 1945, and the initial efforts of the British to restore their power, in 1948 Burma declared itself an independent, democratic republic free of any ties with the British Commonwealth.

Malaya in 1914 was under British control. Its importance in world affairs in the inter-war years lay in its extraordinarily rich tin and rubber resources. In the inter-war years the number of Tamil Indians and Chinese introduced to work in the plantations and mines increased, until in 1939 the Chinese equalled the native Malay population; the Indians were 10 per cent of the total. Following the entry of Japan into the Second World War in December 1941, Malaya was easily overrun. Singapore, the greatest British naval base in Eastern waters, whose defence system had been strengthened piecemeal and only reluctantly by the British during the 1930s, was equally easily taken by the Japanese. Calls for independence during the inter-war years, from either the Malays or the Chinese in Singapore, were muted compared with those heard elsewhere. It was only after the war that Malaya's independence from the British was finally obtained.

Since 1914, the countries of Indo-China – Vietnam, Laos and Cambodia – had remained under French influence until the Japanese began their invasions in the autumn of 1940. Before then, the only challenge to French rule had come from the native independence movement founded by the Annamese peasant Ho Chi Minh (1890–1969).[13] With the collapse of the Japanese in 1945, Ho Chi Minh, who by now had become the unquestioned leader of Vietnamese resistance, declared Vietnamese independence. Fighting with the French was renewed at the end of 1946.

Thailand is unique in that it was the only Southeast Asian country to have escaped European colonial rule. It did so because its location precluded it from taking a leading role in world affairs, and also because the Thais have always proved adept at retaining their neutrality. In the inter-war years they continued to exploit the rivalry between the British and the French, while ensuring that neither country took command. Occupied by the Japanese in 1941, Thailand was pressured into declaring war on Britain and the USA. With the defeat of the Japanese in 1945, it again became an ally of the British and French.

Indonesian independence from the Dutch had been fought for bitterly since the end of the First World War. By the 1930s, the leading Indonesian nationalists and communists, who had grown in strength since the 1920s, were all in jail. It was Japanese intervention in 1942 and Japanese weapons that eventually allowed the Indonesians to break free of the Dutch.

Southwest Asia was also concerned to rid itself of Western tutelage once the First World War was over. For Turkey, the war had been a life-and-death struggle for its existence as a nation. Far from allowing the country to strengthen itself through a process of Westernization, the chief Allied powers – Britain, France and Russia – had connived during the war to dismember the Ottoman Empire. On 30 October 1918 the defeated Turks were forced to sign an armistice at Mudros. The Ottoman Empire was formally dissolved, and Allied troops began a four-year occupation of Constantinople – the city which tsarist Russia had always hoped to control, if not obtain. In 1920 a demoralized sultan had accepted the terms of the Treaty of Sèvres. Only Constantinople, a small part of Europe and Anatolia were now left to Turkey. Even Anatolia was to be divided into French and Italian spheres of influence. The Dardanelles were to be administered by an Allied commission. As a nation, Turkey had reached its nadir.

Following the Allied-backed Greek invasion of Anatolia in May 1919, in which British and American naval units took part, the Turks made a startling recovery. Allied aggression had provided Turkey with the will to live. After much bloodshed, by the summer of 1923, under the terms of the Treaty of Lausanne (24 July), the Allies were compelled to come to very different terms. By then, Turkey had won back whatever territory it had lost to Greece and the Allies. On 29 October 1923 the Turkish Republic, with Mustafa

Kemal as president, was proclaimed. The earlier departure from Constantinople of Sultan Mohammed VI (in November 1922) had ended five hundred years of Ottoman rule. In March 1924 the caliphate was abolished and the members of the House of Osman banished.

Having repulsed the Western powers, the Turks proceeded to imitate their ways; Westernization spread rapidly. The Islamic legal code – the sharia – was replaced by Western laws. Polygamy was abolished and divorce permitted; civil marriages were made compulsory; women were given the vote and allowed to become members of the National Assembly (1934); Sunday was decreed the day of rest, instead of Islam's traditional Friday. Dress was also Westernized: the use of the veil was made optional; the wearing of the fez was forbidden. Western-type family names were introduced in 1935 when Mustafa Kemal became Kemal Atatürk (Father of the Turks). Education was made compulsory for all; the metric system was introduced, and the Latin alphabet took the place of the Arabic and Persian; those under forty years of age were obliged to learn it. English replaced French as the principal foreign language. The shift in emphasis in education away from classical Persian and Ottoman poetry to European history, literature and science, which had begun in the nineteenth century, was accelerated. As a result of Kurdish opposition to the secularization of the state, all religious orders were suppressed. In the new wave of Turkish nationalism (Turkism), many aspects of Islamic life were abandoned.

While Turkey showed itself eager to adopt Western ways, it had no intention of sacrificing its exclusive character to Western liberalism. Turkish nationalism was depicted as unique. Historical and linguistic theories appeared that purported to show the Turks as the originators of civilization. It was not so much the restoration of Islam that was needed as the restoration of Turkism untainted by other nationalities. After 1934 all aliens were banned from professions and trades. In order to increase its power as a nation, also in 1934 Turkey undertook a five-year plan for the development of industry. Fear of foreign control, however, caused the government to discourage foreign investment and foreign ownership, particularly in those industries concerned with national defence. Turkey wanted to modernize, but on its own terms. One of the exceptions to this rule during the 1920s was the long-term credit negotiated with the Soviets for the acquisition of Russian cotton-spinning machinery. With the onset of the Great Depression of 1929–33 Turkey's development suffered a temporary halt, though agriculture, mining and transport continued to receive government aid.

In its foreign relations Turkey was forced to compromise. Following the Treaty of Lausanne, it made an alliance with Soviet Russia (1925), relinquished the district of Mosul to British-controlled Iraq (1926) signed a non-aggression pact with Italy (1928) and a treaty with Greece which settled outstanding Turkish-Greek problems. It also recognized the territorial status quo, and agreed to naval equality in the eastern Mediterranean (1930). In 1932 Turkey joined the League of Nations, and two years later concluded the Balkan Pact with Greece, Romania and Yugoslavia, which guaranteed the Balkan frontiers. Treaties of friendship were also signed with Iran, Afghanistan and Iraq.

By the eve of the Second World War, Turkey had come to be recognized as a crucial force in Eastern Europe and Southwest Asia. In May 1939 – following Italy's attack on Albania – it signed with Britain an agreement of mutual assistance in case of aggression or war in the Mediterranean area. In the following June it also signed a non-aggression pact with France. Turkey was now committed to the Western cause. No such agreements were made with the Russians. Despite the help that Bolshevik Russia had given Turkey in the 1920s, Atatürk's relations with the Russians had always been cool. His suppression of communist activities in Turkey in 1929 had given notice to the Soviet Union that he intended to be master in his own house.

Until his death in 1938, despite his despotic ways, Atatürk's popularity grew. Like Napoleon, he was a soldier rather than a statesman, a dictator rather than a democrat. The Turkish people will always remember him as the man who saved Turkey in its hour of greatest need. Without him, the power relations of Turkey and Southwest Asia with the rest of the world would have been very different from what they became.

*   *   *

With the outbreak of the First World War, Persia became the spoil of the Central Powers and the Allies. In conditions bordering on total anarchy, the Persians were in no position to argue. As a state with a will of its own, Persia had almost ceased to exist. Nor did the collapse of tsarist Russia in 1917, or of the Central Powers in 1918, bring any relief. The Persian delegation, which appealed to the Paris Peace Conference in 1919 for the restoration of its territory, by then in the hands of the Bolsheviks and the British, was turned away. Instead, the British drew up the Anglo-Persian Agreement (1919), which was meant to guarantee Persian integrity while ensuring British ascendancy. The agreement was never ratified. Instead, in 1920 Persia sought security as a member of the League of Nations.

British ambitions in Persia set the scene for the *coup d'état* of February 1921, as a result of which Zia ud-Din (*c.* 1888–1969), a writer and publisher, became prime minister, and a Russian-trained Cossack officer, Reza Khan (1877–1944), became minister of war and commander-in-chief. Almost at once, a treaty of non-intervention was concluded with the Bolsheviks, under which the Russians agreed to evacuate Persia, rescind any concessions and privileges, denounce past treaties, cancel all outstanding debts and hand over to the Persians without indemnity all Russian property in Persia. By the end of 1921, the Russians had withdrawn their troops from northern Persia as they had promised. Understandably, with the Russians being so generous, it was hardly possible for the British to be grasping. The proposed Anglo-Persian Agreement was dropped. Diplomatically, the Bolsheviks had scored a victory.

Thenceforth, Reza Khan sought to make himself the military dictator of Persia. Three months after the *coup d'état*, Zia ud-Din fled. In April 1926, having officially deposed the ineffectual Ahmad Shah in October 1925, Reza Khan ascended the peacock throne as the first of the Pahlavi line. The Qajar dynasty, which had ruled Persia since the 1790s, was ended.

Once in absolute control, the new monarch pressed on with reforms. His efforts were felt in education, law, religion, social relations and the arts. He was responsible for the introduction of civil marriage, compulsory primary education and the abolition of the veil for women. (For usurping some of the clergy's powers, he would pay dearly later.) He enlarged the armed forces, which he brought under the command of Persian rather than European officers. By 1928, he felt strong enough to revoke all restrictions and privileges held by foreigners in Persia (which the Bolsheviks had done voluntarily seven years earlier). After 1931 foreigners could no longer own agricultural land; foreign trade was more closely controlled; and the Persian sections of the Indo-European system of communications were nationalized. In 1931 Persia had put down a major rising of the Kurds on the Turkish frontier. Six years later Reza Khan increased Persia's cooperation with Turkey, Iraq and Afghanistan through the Saadabad Pact. Yet Persia was neither Westernized nor modernized on the same scale as Turkey. It never became a republic; Islam's power, though infringed, remained largely intact. Moreover, under Reza Khan's regime, legislation dealing with alcohol, drugs and corruption retained its own peculiarly Persian puritanical streak. In 1935 'Persia' was changed to the ancient name of 'Iran'.

On the financial side, Reza Khan was forced to compromise. The American financial advisers who had helped the country a decade earlier were allowed to return. While these officials had no control over army funds, between 1922 and 1927 they sorted out the chaotic conditions of the Persian treasury. On their heels came American oil company executives seeking concessions. In 1933 Persia obtained better terms with the Anglo-Persian Oil Company. Government-run enterprises were also started in the textile, sugar, glass, match and metals industries. One of Reza Khan's special projects was the Trans-Persian Railway, built between 1933 and 1939. Planned and built with the help of Scandinavian engineers, it was paid for out of taxes levied on the consumption of sugar, tea, opium and oil. Ironically, this railway, linking the Caspian Sea with the Gulf, became indispensable to the Allies in the Second World War. In 1941, under Western pressure, Reza Khan abdicated.

Although courted by the Turks (who had religious affinity) and the Germans, Afghanistan managed to remain neutral during the First World War. Subsidies from British India undoubtedly encouraged the country's amir to take a neutral stance. But Afghanistan's call for independence from British tutelage in 1919, and its sending of an emissary to Moscow, soon embroiled it in war with British India. In 1921, after an inconclusive struggle, the British granted full independence. From that time onwards Afghanistan's destiny rested with itself. Under King Amanullah (reigned 1919–29), relations with Russia were improved and attempts were made to modernize Afghanistan along European lines. But Amanullah proved unpopular with the military and the traditional element of Afghan society, who encouraged the brigand chief Bacha-i-Saquao (who later proclaimed himself Habibullah Ghazi) to attack him. Without allies, Amanullah was eventually driven into exile. With British connivance, the throne was then seized by his cousin, General Mohammed Nadir Khan, who executed Habibullah and his accomplices and turned Afghanistan once more in the direction of Western modernization. A constitution was introduced in 1930 providing for a bicameral legislature; education was encouraged, and Russian technical instructors were welcomed. Regardless of the constitution promulgated in 1931, power remained in the hands of the king. Islam remained supreme in religion and law.

In 1933 Nadir Khan was assassinated by those who opposed his reforms. His heir, Mohammed Zahir Shah, continued his father's work. Peace was maintained, and modernization – although slow – continued. The next year Afghanistan joined the League of Nations. In 1937, with Turkey, Iraq and Iran, it formed the Oriental Entente, designed to withstand pressure from the European powers. In the Second World War, as it had done in the First, Afghanistan remained neutral.

Prompted by the Manifesto of Arab Nationalism of 1914, Arab demands for independence grew throughout the First World War. Only by throwing off the Turkish yoke and asserting Arab nationalism throughout the Middle East could the Arabs and Islam be restored to their former power and glory.

The Western powers had other intentions. In dismembering the Ottoman Empire they had made no allowance for Arab independence. Allied treachery towards the Arabs, revealed by the Bolsheviks in 1918, had so aroused the Arab world that in 1919 Woodrow Wilson sent the King–Crane Commission of Inquiry to Syria and Palestine to investigate Arab aims and policies. The subsequent report, which was anti-Zionist, left no doubt about the Arabs' desire to govern themselves, and their opposition to Jewish immigration in Palestine, which 'should be definitely limited'. Considering the attention the report received, it might never have been prepared. Because it was almost entirely pro-Arab and anti-imperialist, it was not made public for another three years; by which time the important decisions regarding these countries had been made. France and Britain did not want America telling them what to do with their empires.

Meanwhile, at an Allied conference in Italy in 1920, the fate of the Arab states was decided in a manner contrary to what the King–Crane Commission had recommended: Iraq and all of Palestine were given to Britain; France obtained Syria. The only gesture made to Wilson's principle of national self-determination was to speak of the Arab countries not as colonies but as mandates. These mandates were approved by the League of Nations in 1922; the USA agreed to them in 1924. Earlier promises made by Britain to the Arabs were disregarded. Thus began a long trail of sorrow in the Arab world.

Syria was to be the site of the first test of strength between European imperial ambitions and the Arab nationalist movements. A province of the Ottoman Empire between 1516 and 1918, it was ruled immediately after the First World War by Faisal I (1885–1933), son of Hussein of Mecca. But it was also claimed by the French, who saw no reason why they should not repossess their pre-war imperial domains. By 1920, Faisal had been elected by a national congress to rule Syria (which then included Lebanon) from Damascus. French claims were disregarded. As far as the Arabs were concerned, Syria was independent.

In the summer of 1920 Arab and French differences were settled by a resort to arms, in which the French won an overwhelming victory. Faisal – driven out by the French – became King Faisal of Iraq (see below). The League of Nations gave France the mandate for Syria. Following the principle of divide and conquer, the French then split Syria into the states of Damascus, Lebanon, Aleppo, Jebel Druse and the area around the port of Alexandretta in the north (which Turkey claimed and in 1939 obtained from France). In

Lebanon, with the support of the Christian Maronite leaders, the French created a new state occupied by equal numbers of Christians and Muslims. Given a constitution in 1926 as the 'Greater Lebanon', the Lebanese nevertheless found that their national aspirations continued to be foiled by the French. Two decades of agitation took place before they gained their independence. By that time (1946), as a result of foreign intrusion, Lebanon had become so divided between Christians and Muslims that nothing could save it from the dreadful civil conflict that lay ahead.

In the early 1920s the French continued to stifle Syria's claims to independence. French action in shelling Damascus for two days in 1925, during which 1400 people were killed, was censured by the League of Nations. Only in 1936, after over a decade of conflict, did France promise that Syria would be granted independence within three years and become a member of the League of Nations. Before two years had passed, however, France was on the brink of war with Germany. By the end of 1938, Syria's existing constitution had been suspended. In June 1941 – by which time the French in Syria had opted for the Vichy government – British and Free French forces occupied the country. Independence seemed further away than ever, and many more Syrians were to die at French hands before independence was gained in 1944. French troops remained in the country until 1946.

Of Britain's three mandates in the Middle East – Iraq, Palestine and Trans-Jordan – Iraq was the first to be given a semblance of independence, in 1932. Ten thousand Iraqis had lost their lives in resisting the imposition of British rule in 1920.[14] The British seem to have been content to exercise their influence through Faisal, who, having been unseated in Syria, was installed by them as King of Iraq in 1921. Thus they repaid their debt to his father, Hussein of Mecca, who had led the Arab revolt in 1916 against his Turkish overlords. So successful was this relationship between the Iraqis and the British that in 1922 the British changed the mandate into an alliance. Yet Britain did not sacrifice its vital interests. It obtained Iraq's agreement to the construction of three airfields, which it promptly occupied. It also retained control of foreign affairs, defence and finance. By obtaining oil-rich Mosul in the north from the Turks in 1926, it further strengthened its oil interests in the Middle East. Iraq was admitted to the League of Nations in 1932. Oil pipelines from Mosul reached Tripoli and Haifa on the Mediterranean coast in 1935. As a result, British supplies of oil, as well as Iraq's revenues, were greatly increased.

In 1933 Faisal died and was succeeded by his son Ghazi, who ruled until his death at the end of the decade. During his reign German and Italian influence grew in Iraq: German trade increased rapidly, and the Italians came to predominate in the shipping of the Persian Gulf. Meanwhile, anti-British voices were heard more and more – particularly as passions had been aroused over the 'Jewish question' in Palestine, where Iraq's influence was cast in favour of the Palestinian Arabs against the Jews. As a protest, in 1936 the Grand Mufti of Jerusalem fled from British-controlled Palestine to Baghdad. British conduct in Palestine partly explains why, on the death of King Ghazi on 4 April 1939, the mob turned against the British and stoned Britain's consul to death. Faced by the needs of the Second World War, Britain forced its way back into the country in 1941.

From the moment the British assumed responsibility in Palestine in 1920, they found themselves involved in a never-ending dispute between Jews and Arabs. The Jews based their claim to Palestine on the historical and religious associations of their people with the area; in returning to Palestine they were returning to their spiritual home. The Balfour Declaration (1917) had promised the establishment of a Jewish national home there. At that time, Palestine was about 90 per cent Arab.[15] Woodrow Wilson (whose influence was crucial to the post-war arrangement whereby Britain was given a League of Nations mandate over Palestine), Lloyd George and South Africa's Jan Christiaan Smuts – among others – had all hoped for a Jewish state. Since the Zionist movement had been founded in the late 1890s by the Austrian journalist Theodor Herzl (1860–1904),[16] who in 1896 had published a pamphlet, *Judenstaat* (*Jewish State*), growing numbers of Eastern and Central European Jews had become persuaded that a meaningful life could be lived only in Palestine, which they called Israel. Everywhere else, they would be threatened by spiritual and cultural annihilation. The US Quota Acts of the 1920s reduced the flood of Jewish immigrants to America to one-fifth of what it had been immediately after the First World War. With the American door almost closed to the Jews, Palestine became their only option.

The problem of creating a national home did not become acute until the Holocaust of European Jewry resulted in an unparalleled increase of Jewish refugees after the Second World War. Between 1920 and 1927 only about 77,000 Jewish immigrants entered Palestine; they comprised 17 per cent of the population. In 1930, out of a total population of one million, three-quarters were Muslim Arabs – some of whom had migrated from Syria and Lebanon – with the rest Christians and Jews. A decade later, out of a total population of 1.5 million, the Jews numbered about 500,000. The right of Jews to enter Palestine was being interpreted as the right to create a Jewish majority.

According to the Jews, it was pointless for the Arabs to argue that Zionist ambitions or European imperial interests had caused their misfortunes. The British had broken Ottoman power; Western geologists had recently discovered the mineral wealth of Arab lands; Western not Arab initiatives had permitted the Arabs to move towards national independence. The Palestinian Arabs' response was that they were being gradually deprived of a land that their forebears had cultivated for a thousand years. Palestine never was a separate province to be administered by the Western powers before gradually being taken over by the Jews. Palestine was an Arab holy land and an integral part of Syria. The Arabs had fought during the First World War with Britain against the Ottoman Turks to gain their independence. Instead, they had been tricked and deceived at every turn and had had to endure British rule. No room could be made for a second nation in Palestine except by dislodging the Arabs, who were already in possession. As the Jews called upon world Jewry for help, the Palestinians called upon the Arabs and Islam.

In trying to give the same piece of territory to two contesting parties, the British came to be distrusted by Jews and Arabs alike. To Arab charges of duplicity, the British argued that they had never intended that the Arabs should have unconditional independence. To Jewish charges of perfidy, they pleaded that to give the Jews the whole of Palestine could not have been further from their thoughts. What they had promised was that the Jews should have a national home in Palestine, not that Palestine should become the national home of the Jews. To the British, the idea that the Jews should predominate over the larger Arab community was untenable. Given the desperate circumstances in which the British found themselves in 1917, their fault lay not in obtaining help wherever they could, but in believing that it was possible to satisfy the totally incompatible demands of both Jews and Arabs.

In 1922 the British published a white paper in which they reiterated that it was not their intention that Jewish nationalism should be imposed on the inhabitants of Palestine. There followed in 1930 a report by Sir John Hope-Simpson that was conciliatory towards the Arabs, and which again stressed British obligations to the non-Jewish inhabitants of Palestine.

By the 1930s uprisings in Palestine were endemic. Following widespread violence in 1936, the British established a royal commission under William Robert Wellesley Peel, whose plan of partition, like all previous plans, was refused by the Arabs. As Europe moved closer to war, British attitudes underwent a subtle change. Increasingly, the British became more anxious about future Arab cooperation than about pacifying the Zionists. In 1939 a new white paper was issued in which the British proposed that all further Jewish immigration should cease except with Arab approval. It also recommended that Jewish land purchases should be restricted, and that, as the British intended to abrogate their mandate, Jews and Arabs should begin to work out a scheme whereby they could live together peacefully. With the outbreak of the Second World War, the Arab–Jewish problem entered a new phase.

The inter-war years were equally decisive in determining the present-day political reality of Saudi Arabia and Yemen. In June 1916 Hussein ibn Ali, Sherif of Mecca, head of the Hashemites, proclaimed the Arab revolt against the Ottoman Empire. Yet Hussein had always been a staunch supporter of the Ottomans. Moreover, Arab nationalism between 1906 and 1916 had not developed among the Hashemites at all, but among the more sophisticated, Western-educated Syrians. It was with Ottoman support that Hussein had been able to control his Arab rivals. Hussein's about-face can be explained only by the fact that the war had provided him with an opportunity that he had sought for some time. The decision having been made to side with Britain against the Turks, Hussein proclaimed himself 'King of the Arab Countries'; to the Europeans, as well as to the leaders of the other Arab states, he remained only King of Hejaz. With Arab help, British forces defeated the Turks in the Middle East; in September 1918 they entered Damascus.

The following year a bitter, disillusioned Hussein refused to ratify the Treaty of Versailles, with its proposed mandatory regimes for Syria, Palestine and Iraq. The real threat against him, however, came not from British duplicity but from his Arab rival, Abd al-Aziz ibn Saud of eastern Arabia. With the help of the British, ibn Saud had risen from a landless exile to become the successful ruler of the Nejd, with his capital at Riyadh. In 1924 – leading a puritanical sect, the Wahabi – he defeated Hussein. The Wahabi movement, founded in the eighteenth century, was meant to purify the preponderant and, by their lights, increasingly decadent Sunni sect of Islam. As the British felt they had less to fear from ibn Saud than from Hussein, they chose not to intervene. Hussein abdicated and was given asylum in Cyprus. In 1927 London recognized ibn Saud's conquests.

In 1932 the kingdoms of Hejaz and Nejd were renamed Saudi Arabia. By then, ibn Saud had come to terms with Britain, Turkey, Persia, Iraq, Trans-Jordan and Egypt. Because the British were not prepared to see Yemen's independence (also founded after a revolt against the Ottomans) extinguished as Hejaz's had been, ibn Saud's attempts to seize it were foiled by them. Having won the territory in battle, ibn Saud was compelled to settle for a slight rectification of frontiers. To protect itself further from Saudi attacks, Yemen also turned for help to Iraq, Japan and Russia – states that hitherto had had almost no influence in this region.

In 1933 ibn Saud's desperate need for money caused him to grant to Standard Oil of California the right to explore and develop his country's oil resources. Five years later oil was discovered in commercial quantities. With hindsight, the sum paid by Standard Oil was trifling.

Deprived of his kingdom, Hussein, ibn Saud's rival, continued to have influence in the Arab world. As we have seen, one of his sons, Faisal, had become King of Iraq; another son, Abdullah, while on his way in 1920 to attack the French in Syria, had been persuaded by the British to take over the government of the British-mandated territory of Trans-Jordan, which included part of Palestine west of the Jordan River. In 1923, under pressure from Abdullah, Trans-Jordan was expressly excluded from the Balfour Declaration and given a status of semi-autonomy. In 1928 (when Trans-Jordan obtained its formal independence from Britain), Abdullah's powers as emir were increased. Throughout the remaining inter-war years, the British continued to provide Abdullah with arms and money. They did so primarily because of Trans-Jordan's strategic position, which had caused the British to thwart the attempt made by ibn Saud in 1924 to seize the country. The Second World War brought fundamental change to the Middle East. In 1945, partly as a result of British efforts, the Arab League was formed.

14

The Second World War: 1939–45

In the early hours of 1 September 1939, Germany attacked Poland on land and from the air. Two days later, Britain and France declared war on Germany. The second great war of the twentieth century – the greatest single slaughter in history – had begun.

The Second World War must be seen as a continuation of the war of 1914–18. It was the direct outcome of the spiritual malaise, the economic chaos and the political barbarism engendered by the First World War. The catastrophe – and the false peace that had followed in 1919, in which Germany suffered ignominy and humiliation – had made a further clash between the nations of the West almost inevitable.[1] If there is one reason more than any other why the Germans supported the radical agitator Adolf Hitler, it was because he expressed better than anybody else the real or imagined grievances of the Germans towards the Versailles Treaty, which the Germans felt had violated both national pride and national honour. The treaty and the chaotic conditions of post-war Europe made a confrontation between the liberal Western democracies and the totalitarian states unavoidable.[2]

While communism was entrenching itself in Russia in the post-war years, a rival ideology of fascism was making its appearance in Italy. In 1922, with Italy facing the possibility of civil war, a former schoolteacher, Benito Mussolini (1883–1945),[3] the leader of Italy's anti-communist, anti-democratic and anti-revolutionary Black Shirts, was charged by King Victor Emmanuel III to form a government. In the election of 1924, as conditions deteriorated, fraud, violence and intimidation gave the fascists two-thirds of the total poll. Fascism became the official ideology of Italy. Thenceforth, class gave way to nation. The outcome was the establishment of an authoritarian, all-powerful corporate state, in which intellectualism became suspect and obedience paramount; the rationalism and liberalism of an earlier Europe were spurned; faith in the traditional parties was lost. All those who failed to cooperate with the fascists were removed from office. Mussolini's desire to create an empire led to his annexation of Ethiopia in 1936 (and the flight of Emperor Haile Selassie; 1892–1975) and his attack on Albania in 1939.

By the early 1920s, Germany, like Russia and Italy in the post-war period, was ripe for revolution. The country was in turmoil; financial collapse was widespread; armed insurrection and political slayings were common, nihilism flourished, morals deteriorated; liberty begot licence, licence begot anarchy. Since 1920, the parties most identified with the newly formed Weimar Republic – the Social Democrats and the Roman Catholic parties – had had severe setbacks at the polls. The nationalists and the People's Party, on the right, and the Independent Socialists, on the left, achieved considerable gains. Thenceforth, the demands of the radical Right and the radical Left for the overthrow of the Weimar Republic and its leaders became unrestrained.[4] In coalition after coalition the republic fought to stay alive. The Western democracies – far from going to its help – hastened its end. The French and Belgian occupation of the Ruhr in 1923 – following Germany's default in reparation payments – added to the republic's financial troubles and precipitated its collapse. America's demands upon the Allies at this time for the repayment of war loans, coupled with the volatility of US financial leadership, made matters worse.

By 1924, Germany was in the grip of hyperinflation. It cost between 800 million and 900 million marks to buy a three-pound loaf of bread. Million-mark notes were sold on the streets of London for a penny each. In 1923 1 dollar had been worth 1 million paper marks; by 1924, it was 4 billion. At the end of 1923, as leader of the National Socialist German Workers' Party, Hitler tried to seize power in Munich. Having failed, he went to jail, where he wrote his biography *Mein Kampf* (*My Struggle*), in which he expressed his belief in the purity of the Aryan race (hence his anti-Semitism), his extreme nationalism, his determination to colonize Slavic lands and his opposition to democracy in general and the Weimar Republic in particular. He claimed that corrupt democratic politicians had been at the root of Germany's undoing in 1918.

Never had any politician provided a better guide to what he intended to do. His subsequent rise might have been avoided if the Genoa Conference of 1922, which tried to reconstruct European finance and commerce (and at which thirty-four nations, but not the USA, were represented), had not failed. Hastening its downfall was the separate treaty concluded between Germany and the USSR at Rapallo, while the Genoa Conference was still in session. The Locarno Treaty, concluded in 1925 between Britain, France, Germany, Italy and Belgium, which guaranteed Germany's frontiers with Belgium and France, also broke down.

Forced to choose between what many of them saw as communist-inspired chaos on the one hand and the Nazi promise of law and order on the other, an increasing number of Germans supported Hitler. Not even a demagogue, it was thought, could make matters worse. (History says otherwise: since ancient Greece and Rome,[5] the demagogue has always been the strangler of civilization.) In Germany anarchy and fear had opened the door to despotism. In the election of 1930, as the nation became desperate and the vast army of unemployed grew, the National Socialists (Nazis), embracing the two dominant political ideologies of the age – nationalism and socialism – increased their seats in the Reichstag from 12 to 107.[6] Their communist opponents also made considerable gains. Nazis and communists fought openly in the streets. In 1932, with the deepening of the world depression,[7] the Nazis became the largest single party. On 30 January 1933, the frail Reichspresident, Paul von Hindenburg (1847–1934), believing he could curb the majority party leader's excesses, appointed Hitler Chancellor of Germany.

The new government ruled by terror and duress, especially against communists and Jews – who among other charges were accused of so-called over-representation in the professions, judiciary, commerce, finance and industry. In March 1933, using the Reichstag fire of the previous month as evidence of a communist plot to over-throw the state, Hitler was granted emergency powers for four years; the Reichstag was eliminated as a political force; the Communist Party was outlawed. With the death of Hindenburg in August 1934, the office of Reichspresident was abolished. Hitler became Führer of the German Reich and people; he was to be an absolute dictator until his suicide in 1945.

Hitler did not create the chaotic conditions or the enthusiasm that brought him to power. He was endowed with power by the electorate, industry and the army because he promised to solve the desperate economic and social conditions of the time. Having lost faith in the Weimar Republic's democratic solutions, with condi-tions worsening, the electorate bestowed upon Hitler a blind faith.[8] They thought that the crises that had shaken German society since 1918 would now end; that through Hitler national and social redemption would be achieved. All of these hopes proved to be disastrous illusions.

Once in power, Hitler substituted propaganda and terror for public support. The National Socialist German Workers' Party was declared the only political party. In two years, 1932–4, German unemployment was reduced from 6 million to 2 million (in 1937 the figure would be 500,000). The judicial and administrative systems of the country were concentrated in Nazi hands. The power of organized labour was broken. The abuses of profiteers and speculators, as well as the deca-dence of some of Germany's elite, were used to advance the Nazi cause. Political, racial and religious persecution became the order of the day. Everything was sacrificed to the welfare of the party and the security of the state. Racist laws, the 'Nuremberg Laws' (1935), were introduced, excluding Jews from government, the professions and many walks of business and cultural life. Jews, the Nazis said, were *Untermenschen*, outside the human family. Envy against them was deli-berately stirred. At a time when the parliamentary democracies of Europe were under attack, Hitler magnified their weaknesses. He became the spokesman of all the anti-democratic, anti-liberal, anti-socialist, anti-Christian, anti-communist, anti-Semitic and anti-Slavic movements of Europe.

In the great purge of 29–30 June 1934, in one fell swoop, Hitler assassinated seventy-seven political opponents for alleged conspiracy. The next month, Austria's Chancellor, Engelbert Dollfuss (b. 1892), was murdered by Austrian Nazis, who had attempted an unsuccessful coup. (Although forbidden by the Treaty of Versailles, efforts had already been made by both Austria and Germany to form a political union.) The following year Hitler denounced the Versailles Treaty (Germany had joined the League of Nations in 1926 and left it in October 1933) and began rearming. The League's attempts to bring about general disarmament had been abandoned in 1934. The foreign ministers of Britain, France and Italy met at Stresa to protest at Hitler's actions, but nothing came of it. In 1935 Germany recovered the Saar territory by plebiscite. A year later German troops reoccupied the Rhineland, where much of Germany's heavy industry was located.

Italy's invasion of Abyssinia (Ethiopia)[9] in 1935 and Hitler's repudiation of the military clauses of the Versailles Treaty (which had included the demilitarization of the Rhineland) probably marked the point beyond which another European war could not be avoided. In 1936 Hitler repudiated the Locarno Treaty of 1925, which had defined Europe's post-war frontiers. In October 1936 the Rome–Berlin Axis was formed; in November the Anti-Comintern Pact between Germany and Japan was concluded.[10]

The year 1936 also witnessed the outbreak of the Spanish Civil War. The war had been threatening since the flight of King Alfonso XIII (b. 1886; reigned 1886–1931 (his mother was regent until 1902); d. 1941) and the establishment of a socialist-inclined republic in 1931. It ended in 1939 with the victory of the insurgents under General Francisco Franco (1892–1975). The war provided Germany and Italy (who supported Franco) with a dress rehearsal for the world conflict that was to follow. It also dramatized the ideological differences between the democracies and the dictatorships.

In 1938, with no one prepared to use force against him (and with the Romanov and Habsburg empires no longer in existence to restrain him), Hitler seized both Austria and the German-speaking areas of Czechoslovakia.[11] The surrender of parts of Czechoslovakia to Germans, Poles and Hungarians – which followed the Munich meetings in 1938 and to which the Czechs and the Russians were not invited – was described by the British prime minister, Neville Chamberlain, as 'peace with honour'. In reality, it was, of course, appeasement.[12] It is anybody's guess what might have happened had Chamberlain stood firm in 1938. We do know that shortly before he met Hitler he had read a minute from a meeting of the British Joint Chiefs of Staff that urged him, 'no matter what the cost, war must be averted until the rearmament programme begins to bear substantial fruit'.[13] Unable to challenge Hitler, Britain allowed Germany to become the strongest power on the continent. In November 1938, following the assassination by a Jew of the first secretary in the German embassy in Paris, the Nazis used open violence against the German Jewish community (Kristallnacht). Jews were killed; synagogues and businesses were destroyed.

In March 1939 Hitler proceeded to annex the whole of Czechoslovakia and the Lithuanian port of Memel. Intent now on conquering Poland and regaining the territory given to Poland by the Treaty of Versailles, especially the Polish Corridor, which divided German West Prussia from East Prussia, he made the 'Pact of Steel' with Italy in May 1939. Although in 1934 Germany had signed a non-aggression pact with Poland, in August 1939 Hitler agreed with Stalin (who desperately needed time to prepare for the feared German onslaught) to divide Poland. Russia's share was to be eastern Poland. Bessarabia, the northern Baltic States and parts of Finland were later overrun.[14] Stalin, who shared Hitler's contempt for the Western democracies, pledged material support to the Germans.

On 1 September, despite being warned by Britain and France that an invasion of Poland would bring them into war against him, Hitler attacked Poland. Two days later, conscious now that they were in deadly peril themselves, Britain (joined at once by its dominions) and France declared war on the German Reich.[15]

On the same day, Roosevelt, although anti-isolationist, declared that America would stay neutral.[16] Throughout the 1920s and 1930s, because of the Great Depression, appropriations for the US army and navy had been sharply reduced. Roosevelt's subsequent covert actions in supplying Britain with arms, and naval protection in the Western Atlantic, brought great relief to a besieged Britain. The day after Japan's attack on the US Pacific Fleet at Pearl Harbor, on 7 December 1941, America declared war on Japan. Committed to Japan, Hitler declared war on the United States on the 10th.[17] By 1945, all the nations of Latin America had broken relations with the Axis powers; Brazil sent troops to Europe; Mexico gave air support in the Pacific.

While Hitler bears major responsibility for the Second World War, he could never have done what he did had he not been faced by weak, divided French and British leaders.[18] Not even a fanatic like Hitler could have gained total power if the Western leaders had stood firm. Their failure was not only one of judgement, but of will. Hitler knew they would yield under threat, and he exploited their moral weakness. Not one of them stood up to him. Only a few – such as Winston Churchill – were even prepared to think the worst of him. Only when it was too late did they see through his guise of talking peace while preparing for war.[19]

Whereas Hitler and Mussolini sought victory at any price, the democracies sought compromise. The decent, middle-class, 'shopkeeper' mentality, epitomized by Chamberlain (who was already overwhelmed by the seemingly intractable political and economic problems facing his country), was pitted against the bullying, militaristic mentality of the dictators. Chamberlain and the French political leaders wanted to reconcile conflicting interests as one would do in business; the dictators wanted, by one ruse or another, to triumph over their rivals. Hitler had set his heart on war and was ready to take on Chamberlain or Churchill. Knowing only national law and national interests, talk of the supremacy of international law was anathema to him. Outside of war, the democracies could not hope to win.

The best thing that can be said for the British and French is that, having experienced the horrors of the Great War, they could not believe that anyone would plunge the world into war again. The mood of the time, in the European democracies and the United States, was pacifist; world war was unjustifiable and unlikely. Until the democracies found themselves at bay, the masses continued to prefer appeasement to war. The next-best thing that can be said is that appeasement bought for Britain some vital time needed for rearmament (especially in the air), and the development of what became indispensable to Britain's defences: radar.

The democracies' belief that no one could be evil enough to begin a second world war proved false. War followed on an unprecedented scale. In one month (September 1939) Poland was conquered. With Poland occupied by Germany and Russia (the Soviets had invaded eastern Poland on 17 September and Finland on 30 November), Hitler turned west. Ignoring the Copenhagen Declaration of Neutrality of July 1938, by means of which the smaller European states (Belgium, the Netherlands, Denmark, Norway, Switzerland, Finland and the Baltic States)[20] had hoped to stay out of the upcoming war, in April 1940 he struck at Denmark and Norway. In May he overran Belgium, the Netherlands and France. In a blitzkrieg (lightning war) all these countries, except Switzerland, fell one after the other. In ten days the Germans were at Calais and Boulogne. On 15 May, Churchill, who had replaced Chamberlain five days earlier, wrote to Roosevelt: 'the weight may be more than we can bear'. Saved by a miracle, a defeated British army held out on the sands of Dunkirk (26 May-4 June) until they were evacuated.[21] The Netherlands and Belgium had surrendered, France was tottering.

In five weeks Germany had overrun Western Europe; Paris had fallen. With a reckless determination to win, Germany had defeated a larger Allied force. On 10 June 1940, turning a deaf ear to the appeals of Roosevelt,[22] 'that jackal' Mussolini attacked France. For Britain, the French capitulation on 22 June was the greatest loss. The USSR was busy occupying Poland and the Baltic States. On 15 July, Hitler offered peace terms to Britain, which were rejected: Britain was not prepared to accept his conquest of Poland. The USA openly abandoned neutrality by providing the British with fifty destroyers. German U-boats in the Atlantic were causing havoc to British shipping; in one week in October 1940 thirty-two British ships were sunk. Meanwhile, with the German army occupying 60 per cent of France, French resistance continued from London and Algiers under General Charles de Gaulle (1890–1970). Bearing the emotional scar of a divided land, the unoccupied part of France was governed from Vichy as a neutral state.

Determined to knock Britain out of the war, Hitler gave orders for its invasion in the summer of 1940. The Battle of Britain began in the air on 8 August. Although the most intense period was between August and October 1940, after which plans to invade were postponed, the bombing of London and other parts of Britain continued (much of Coventry was destroyed on 15 November) until well into 1941 and accounted for 42,000 civilian deaths. (Later Hamburg and Dresden would lose many more than that in single air raids.[23])

Defeated by the Royal Air Force, and unable to penetrate Britain's naval defences, Hitler abandoned plans for the invasion of Britain on 12 October 1940 and prepared to attack the Soviet Union. 'Never in the field of human conflict,' said Churchill on 20 August 1940 (in praising the RAF), 'was so much owed by so many, to so few.'[24]

With the invasion of the Soviet Union, the hoped-for colonization by Germans of Slavic lands, about which Hitler had written in *Mein Kampf*, began. Hitler's action – however rash it might appear now – was prompted by the fact that Germany had defeated Russia in the First World War. Despite its much larger population (roughly 181 million against Germany's 69 million), Russia was expected to fall as France and Poland had done. 'Kick in the door and the whole rotten edifice will come crashing down,' Hitler kept saying. Echoing ancient racial myths about Eastern Europe, the Slavs, he said, were *Untermenschen*, inferior to the Germanic race. Germany's military might, its productive capacity and its general strategy were vastly superior to those of the Soviet Union. As Hitler saw it, with Russia out of the war, oil and territory would become available to the German Reich; Britain would be isolated; and final victory for the Germans in the West would be assured; America would have to come to terms. The Soviet Union's blundering in its conquest of tiny Finland in 1940 confirmed Hitler's low opinion of the Russians.

Germany's invasion of Russia on an almost 2000–mile-long front on 22 June 1941 – code name 'Barbarossa'[25] – had been planned since December 1940. The original plan had called for an invasion in May, but this was delayed for a crucial six weeks because Hitler, in response to an anti-Axis coup in Belgrade in March 1941, had invaded Yugoslavia instead.[26] It was well into April before the German troops could extricate themselves. The Russian invasion was also postponed because of unusually heavy spring floods, which hindered movement across the Polish–Russian river areas.[27] Against the advice of his generals, Hitler also decided to go to the aid of Mussolini, who faced almost certain defeat in Albania, Greece and North Africa. Reluctantly, Britain sent troops to Greece from the Western Desert to assist the Greeks.

Hitler's decision to go to Mussolini's aid opened a chapter of disasters, which played no small part in Germany's ultimate defeat. Mussolini may have boasted 'eight million bayonets', but over the long haul, as an ally, he proved to be a burden. By reinforcing the imperilled Italian army in Albania and Greece,[28] the Germans became ensnared in a prolonged and difficult campaign.[29] Having finally rescued the Italians there, the Germans launched an unparalleled airborne attack on British-held Crete. Although the Germans were victorious, the backbone of the German airborne command was broken for good. From Crete, the Germans once more went to the aid of the Italians, who by now were being driven from Libya by the British, Australians and New Zealanders. Under the command of General Erwin Rommel (1891–1944), the German Afrika Korps was formed. Step by step, largely on Italy's account, Germany found itself committed to war in the Mediterranean and the Middle East. Without any overall, long-term strategy in the Mediterranean, the Germans began to overreach themselves.

When at last the main German army was unleashed against Russia in June 1941, it was already six vital weeks too late. Moscow was still in Russian hands when winter set in. Taking the view that it was the lesser of two evils to have part of Europe under Russian control (the Soviets had also invaded Poland, whose independence Britain and France had guaranteed) than the whole of it under German control, the British joined ranks with the Soviet Union.

In June 1941, taking advantage of Germany's assault upon the Soviet Union, Japan began its expansion in Southeast Asia. Having overrun French Indo-China, it attacked the Americans in Hawaii and in the Philippines, the British in Hong Kong, Malaya and Burma, the Dutch in Indonesia and the Australians in New Guinea. By May–June 1942, with lightning speed, Japan had reached the furthermost point of its expansion.

With Germany's invasion of Russia and Japan's attack on Pearl Harbor (about which the Germans were not consulted),[30] the war became global. The Japanese attack ensured that the Americans would enter the war with their enormous industrial and human potential (twelve million Americans would eventually be mobilized). Britain had openly received equipment and supplies from America since the passing of the US Lend-Lease Act in March 1941. Germany's declaration of war against the USA also ensured that American priorities would be settled in favour of the Atlantic rather than the Pacific. The attack on Russia committed Germany to a prolonged, limitless war – the largest military campaign there had ever been – which, with all its other military adventures, it could hardly hope to win. The odds against it in manpower, armour and aircraft were formidable; enormous supplies of weapons reached Russia from Britain and America. It was on the Eastern Front that Germany lost the war.[31]

Yet, at the outset, the Germans could not have done better. By November 1941, they had overrun the Baltic States and the Ukraine and were outside Leningrad and Moscow. Millions of Russian soldiers had been captured. (In the course of the Russian campaign more than five million officers and men surrendered to the Germans.) The initial reaction in Britain and the USA to the Nazi invasion was relief: the threatened German attack on the British Isles had been postponed. But this relief soon turned to fear as the German army swept all before it. The West became concerned that the Russians might be defeated, leaving Germany free to deal with Britain alone. Only the harsh winter and a Soviet counter-attack in December 1941 robbed the Germans of what seemed to be certain victory.

The failure to seize a quick victory on the Eastern Front was Germany's undoing. Yet, not even after the USA had entered the war in December 1941 were the Axis powers halted. In 1942 Germany's armies still besieged Moscow and Leningrad; Rommel's Afrika Korps had reached the western borders of Egypt and was poised to seize the Suez Canal (Britain's lifeline to the East), thus imperilling control of the Mediterranean and Britain's vital oil supplies. Only from the middle of that year, with the Allied victories at Stalingrad (now

Volgograd), El Alamein[32] and at Midway and the Solomons in the Pacific against Japan was the Axis tide turned.

By May 1943, the Allies had defeated the German army in Africa and had invaded Sicily and Italy. Mussolini, having suffered defeat in East and North Africa, fell from power. By June 1944, Rome had been taken by the Allies, and Italy had switched sides and declared war on Germany.[33] With the failure of the German offensive at Kursk-Orel in July 1943 (in which, in a matter of 50 days, Germany lost 75,000 men and 1500 tanks), the initiative on the Eastern Front was taken out of German hands. By 1944, the Soviets had repossessed the Ukraine, broken the German siege of Leningrad and once more moved into the Baltic States. German U-boats in the Atlantic were hunted down by long-range aircraft now equipped with radar.

In the summer of 1944, under the command of the American General Dwight D. Eisenhower (b. 1890; president 1953–61; d. 1969), Allied armies landed in France.[34] The French contingent was led by General de Gaulle. The long-awaited D-Day, agreed upon at the Allied conference at Tehran in 1943, had arrived. Overnight, the powerful resistance movements of German-occupied Europe came into the open. Germany was now besieged from all sides. More than 600,000 civilians died from Allied air bombardments. In manpower, productivity and armaments Germany was hopelessly outclassed. Paris was liberated by the French under de Gaulle at the end of August 1944. By March 1945, Allied armies had crossed the Rhine. Nor was Germany able to stem the invasion by the use of its newly developed guided missiles. Instead, death began to rain down on the whole country.

The German attempt to recover the initiative in the west – by striking through the Ardennes in the autumn of 1944 (the Battle of the Bulge) failed, as the spring offensive had failed in 1918. In the east, in January 1945, Warsaw fell to the Russians (an uprising in August 1944 against the Germans had been crushed); in April Soviet troops reached Berlin. Hungary, Romania (both allied with Germany in 1941) and Bulgaria (which left the Axis powers for the Soviet Union in 1944) had already been overrun. On 25 April 1945, the Allied and Russian forces met on the Elbe. On the 30th, in a bunker in Berlin, Hitler committed suicide. Mussolini had already been shot by Italian partisans; with his mistress, he was hung by the heels by a bloodthirsty mob in Milan. On 7 May, the Germans surrendered unconditionally. The war in Europe was over.

It remained to defeat the Japanese, who in a series of brilliant campaigns had overrun the British, French and Dutch empires in Southeast Asia and had reached India, New Guinea and Guadalcanal in the Solomons.[35] In February 1942 British forces in Singapore surrendered. Combined Allied naval forces in the Pacific were sunk off Java in a battle with the Japanese. Britain's battleships *Prince of Wales* and *Repulse* were sent east without air cover to save the situation and were sunk off Malaya. By the spring of 1942 the last US stronghold in the Philippines had fallen, and much of Southeast Asia and the Western Pacific was in Japanese hands.

The turning points in the Pacific campaign were the defeat of the Japanese at the naval battles of the Coral Sea (May 1942) and especially at Midway (June 1942). Before Midway, Japan had never lost an important battle; after Midway, it never won one. In August Allied forces under General Douglas MacArthur (1880–1964) attacked Japanese positions in Guadalcanal. In September Japanese ground forces were driven back by the Australians on the Kokoda Trail in New Guinea. In the spring of 1944 the Japanese were defeated by the British and the Indians at Imphal on the border of India. By October 1944, the Americans had island-hopped across the Pacific and had retaken the Philippines. Wherever they went, they proved themselves more than a match for the Japanese. With the Battle of Leyte Gulf, the greatest sea battle of its kind in history, the threat of the Japanese navy was ended. The subsequent capture of Iwo Jima and Okinawa in March–April 1945 provided a base from which Japan could easily be bombed. Until Japanese resistance collapsed in August, the skies above Japan were rarely free of land-based and carrier-based American aircraft. The country was bombed and burned from one end to the other. US submarines also blockaded Japan.

With the American physicist J. Robert Oppenheimer (1904–67) in charge, on 16 July 1945 the USA detonated its first atomic bomb at Los Alamos in New Mexico. On 6 August an atomic bomb was dropped on Hiroshima, and on 9 August on Nagasaki. In Hiroshima more than 100,000 people died instantly; a similar number died later from the effects of radiation. One of the most powerful considerations in dropping the bomb was to avoid the immense casualties that invasion would have incurred;[36] another consideration was to end the war before the Soviets could stake a claim for the joint occupation of Japan. Had not President Harry S Truman (b. 1884; president 1945–53; d. 1972) and General MacArthur resisted Soviet proposals, Japan, like Germany, would probably have become a divided state. On 8 August, ignoring its non-aggression pact with Japan, the Soviet Union attacked Japanese positions in Manchuria.[37] Japanese resistance collapsed.

With Japan's acceptance of the Allied terms of capitulation on 14 August, the war in Asia was over. In allowing their ambitions to run wild, the Japanese had become committed to undertakings far greater than their strength could support. The consequences, which included a new constitutional structure imposed by the Allies, were incalculable.

Thus ended a cataclysm without parallel. War-related deaths were about fifty-five million worldwide, most of them in Eastern Europe.[38] Unprecedented mass exterminations had also taken place against minority groups and political opponents.[39] The number of European Jews, by flight and genocide, had been reduced by two-thirds. The Jews now speak of this as their Holocaust, an event of such unspeakable barbarity as to surpass understanding.[40] It was an event that would change both Jewish and world history. It led to the establishment of the state of Israel in 1948, and to the present discord between Arab and Jew in the Middle East; which in turn has affected US relations with the rest of the world. The war uprooted and dispersed millions of other people (including fourteen million Germans). The use of saturation bombing, which – official rhetoric aside – was meant to terrorize the civilian population, greatly increased the number of casualties. The Second World War was the first war in history in which the civilian losses outnumbered those of the military. It was a turning point in the history of warfare.

Germany and Japan emerged from the war at the mercy of the

Allies. An Allied garrison of 70,000 troops was left behind in Germany; 40,000 in Japan. East Germany was brutally ravaged and despoiled by Soviet soldiers; to strike back in revenge, to show no pity, was demanded of them by their generals. Japan was at least spared the horrors of Soviet occupation, but was stripped of the Pacific islands it had acquired before 1941, and of all possessions seized since 1941. The Soviet Union annexed the Kurile Islands north of Hokkaido, the USA took Okinawa (the Ryukyu Islands) and obtained a trusteeship of the Pacific islands formerly mandated to Japan – the Mariana, Caroline, Palau and Marshall islands.

The trial of Japanese and German war criminals followed. The Axis powers had been warned by Churchill and Roosevelt that they would be held responsible, and they were.[41] In bringing the Axis leaders to justice, the trials assembled the damning evidence of a uniquely barbaric age. Other than shooting the accused out of hand, which was the traditional way of dealing with the vanquished, it is difficult to see what else could have been done. Yet it was a victors' justice, with no guarantee that the victors were necessarily the more just. Without neutral judges, it assumed that truth and justice were on the victors' side. US Chief Justice Stone called the Nuremberg trials 'Jackson's lynching expedition' (Robert H. Jackson was US associate justice of the Supreme Court[42]). The defendants (22 at Nuremberg; 28 in Tokyo) were not allowed to cite Allied crimes – the Soviets' Katyn Forest massacre of 4500 prisoners of war in Poland in 1939[43] (thousands of other Polish prisoners disappeared without trace[44]), Britain's war in Norway in 1940 and the terror bombing by the Allies of Germany and Japan – as justification for their own acts. As the Japanese were tried with a complete disregard for Japanese values and traditions, in particular with neglect for bushido, the Tokyo trial has come to be viewed by some Japanese as little more than a farce.[45]

The novelty of the Nuremberg trials was to fix responsibility for those who directed the state; it was an advance in international justice, particularly where judgement was rendered for crimes against humanity. The chief legal criticism was that the laws applied were created retroactively. Men were sentenced for deeds which were not considered crimes when the acts were committed. The General

Treaty for the Renunciation of War (the Kellogg–Briand Pact of 1928, of which Germany and Japan were signatories) had not made war as such illegal. It had censured aggressive war, but that was a matter of legal interpretation.

Although Nuremberg gave new life to the concept of natural law, and raised questions about the legitimate authority of the state in war, the trials may have enlarged rather than limited war. Having established that guilt in war will be personal and that military necessity or the receipt of orders from a superior will not be admitted in defence,[46] those who are engaged in war will now either emerge victorious (whatever the cost) or will run the risk of being hanged.

Unfortunately for humanity, the Nuremberg trials have not banished barbarity.[47] Crimes against humanity have continued. Even genocide persists,[48] as the Biafrans, Kurds, Bosnians, Indonesians, Albanians, Cambodians, Laotians, Hutus, Tutsis, Darfurs and countless others could testify. As long as there is no international tribunal empowered to effectively uphold international law by force, as long as we are unable to reconcile universal laws with the wishes of national sovereignty, crimes against humanity will continue.

Power abhorring a vacuum, in 1945 the USA and the USSR emerged as the two greatest world powers. Unmatched in weaponry and industrial production, its country unscathed by invasion or bombing, and unequalled in economic strength, the USA was by far the stronger. Although three of the five great powers – the USA, the USSR, Britain, France and China[49] – were European, the Eurocentric world system, which had prevailed since the sixteenth century, was at an end. A bipolar world replaced the multipolar world of nineteenth-century geopolitics. The concessions made to Stalin at conferences in Tehran (1943), Yalta and Potsdam (both 1945), which gave Russia parts of Germany and Poland, gave Poland parts of Germany[50] and divided Germany itself, had greatly enlarged Russian tutelage in Eastern and Central Europe (see Map XV).[51] Despite what Hitler intended, for the first time in their history Central and Eastern Europe were at the mercy of the Russians. By 1948, except for Greece,[52] Turkey and Yugoslavia, Eastern Europe had come under

Soviet control; communist power had been established in Poland, East Germany, the Baltic States (except Finland), Romania, Yugoslavia, Hungary, Bulgaria and Albania. Except in Albania, Soviet power was never extended without military pressure. Also in 1948, in order to keep its outer defences intact, the Soviet Union seized power in Czechoslovakia.

One of the astonishing outcomes of the war was the way communist Russia was able to seize control of so much of Europe. In 1939 Britain and France had gone to war because Hitler had invaded Poland, whose independence they had guaranteed. Russia's invasions, which began with the conquest of eastern Poland and ended with the seizure of Czechoslovakia, raised no such furore in the West. Similarly, the atrocities committed by the Soviets in their rapid expansion in Europe have been glossed over.[53] The West seems to have adopted a curious double standard: one by which to judge the diabolical actions of Hitler; the other by which to judge the conduct of 'Uncle Joe' (Stalin). Hitler's invasion of Poland meant war; Stalin's invasion of Poland meant that he became an ally of the West. Yet Stalin altered the European map more than Hitler did. All of which seems to confirm the age-old dictum: *'Inter arma silent leges'* (In times of war the law is silent). Political expediency prevailed.

Russia's wary attitude towards the West at the end of the Second World War may partly be explained by Russia's incredible losses. The 'marriage of convenience' of the war years between capitalism and communism had ended. More importantly, from 1939 to 1948, nobody had the will or the power to halt Soviet transgressions. Regardless of America's superlative economic and military power, it had no desire to challenge Stalin's policy of brutally imposing the communist system as far as the Red Army could reach. It was out of the question for war-shattered Britain and France to intervene. Britain not only lacked the physical resources; after six years of war, it lacked the necessary fighting spirit to continue an endless war.

In 1945 there was no peace conference (such as Versailles) to settle the problems of the post-war world. Reparations took the form of Allied occupation of Germany and Japan, and the seizing of German industrial plant and equipment. France and the Soviet Union obtained the greatest share. Stalin continued to strip the East

Territory annexed by the USSR from
1. Finland (e.Karelia, Salia and Petsamo)
2. Germany (n.East Prussia)
3. Poland
4. Czechoslovakia (Ruthenia)
5. Romania (Bessarabia & n.Bukovina)

Territory annexed by Poland from Germany (Pommerania, Silesia, Danzig, s.East Prussia)

Territory annexed by Yugoslavia from Italy

Territory annexed by Romania from Hungary

△ Greece annexed Dodecanese Islands from Italy

"Iron Curtain" in 1948

* Member of the Warsaw Pact in 1955

Oder-Neisse line was recognized by German Federal Republic in 1970

Petsamo

Salia

Finland

1

Norway

Sweden

Estonia

USSR

Latvia

Lithuania

Denmark

2

Soviet Union *

East Germany *

Poland *

West Germany

Northern Bukovina

Czechoslovakia *

Bessarabia

5

4

Austria

Hungary *

Transylvania

France

Romania *

Istria

Yugoslavia

Italy

Bulgaria *

Spain

Albania *

Greece

Dodecanese Islands

Map XV Eastern Europe after the Second World War

German zone after reparations had ended in 1952. In atonement and reparation the Luxembourg Agreement of 1952 authorized the payment by Germany of the equivalent of $1.53 billion to Holocaust survivors for losses caused to Jews during the Nazi regime. Total German reparations amount to more than DM100 billion ($104 billion in current value), with some 40 per cent of this going to the state of Israel or recipients there. About $624 million is still paid out annually in compensation pensions.[54] In addition, Germany has granted low-interest loans and scientific and military aid to Israel. In 1947 the Allies made peace treaties with Italy, Hungary, Romania, Bulgaria and Finland; in 1951 with Japan; in 1955 with Austria; but not until 1990 with Germany.

In the summer of 1945 the line between the Western democracies and the Soviet Union had still to be drawn. At that time people's hopes were pinned on the United Nations Organization, which under American auspices had just been established to guarantee world peace. Such an organization had been Roosevelt's possessing ambition. Unlike in 1919, the USA now embraced the idea of collective security. President Truman's words at the inauguration of the United Nations – 'Oh, what a great day this can be in history' – echoed the hopes of mankind; a global conscience would be formed. But the dream of world peace soon gave way to the Cold War. At Fulton, Missouri, on 5 March 1946, Winston Churchill warned 'From Stettin on the Baltic, to Trieste in the Adriatic, an Iron Curtain has descended across the continent' (see Map XV). Thenceforth, it took a balance of terror to keep a third world war at bay.

15

The Balance of Terror

In 1945 the USA and the USSR emerged from the Second World War as supposedly close allies; the hope of a peaceful, stable world was born. Roosevelt had been prepared to go to any length to keep the alliance between his country and the Soviet Union intact:[1] nothing was allowed to divert him from that end. At Yalta, in February 1945, he had willingly agreed to Stalin's proposals for territorial expansion and hegemony in Eastern Europe. It is difficult to see how he could have done otherwise, outside of a declaration of war. To obtain Russia's willingness to enter the war against Japan, concessions were made to the Soviets in Sakhalin, the Kurile Islands, Korea and Manchuria.[2]

Roosevelt was much less suspicious of Soviet motives than he was of British and French post-war imperial ambitions. Churchill, with more historical insight, tried to get the president to see things differently: Churchill suspected that Stalin was primarily concerned with the post-war security of the Soviet Union and its sphere of influence, rather than with a world organization that would ensure world peace. When one allows for the ordeal through which Russia had just passed, this is not surprising. War to the Russian leaders was a continuum; they wanted to be prepared for every future threat.

In April 1945, with Roosevelt's death, a titan left the world stage. By the time President Truman attended the inconclusive Potsdam Conference of July–August 1945, the lines between Eastern and

Western Europe had already been drawn. The all-encompassing duel between the liberal democracy of the Western powers and the authoritarian socialism of the Soviet Union – the Cold War – had begun.[3]

Russia's marriage of convenience with the West broke down once the Germans were defeated. The cultural and ideological divide between the USA and the USSR was too deep for the marriage to continue. Serious differences had surfaced earlier at the Allied meetings at Tehran in 1943 and Yalta in February 1945, but these had been patched over. Each side naturally blamed the other for the deterioration of relations. Russia felt the West had reneged on Russia's need to have friendly governments in Eastern Europe; the West accused Russia of going back on its promises about the future status of Poland and the other governments of Eastern Europe, as well as about the future of Germany. Although neither the USA nor the Soviet Union was about to make a bid for world domination (in 1946 the USA removed most of its forces from Europe, and Russia's military budget fell sharply), relations between them became increasingly rigid and suspicious. As seen from Moscow in 1945, the capitalist West, with the atomic bomb at its disposal, was a far greater menace to Russian communism and its world ambitions than it had been in 1918. America's nuclear superiority certainly deterred the Soviet Union from using its ample conventional weapons in the immediate post-war years.

Churchill's premonition that the realities of power would invalidate Roosevelt's optimistic view of Stalin was soon confirmed. By the end of the war, the Soviet Union was already in occupation of the territories needed for its future defence. Despite its theoretical commitment to the destruction of worldwide capitalism, the Soviet Union's first priority after 1945 was to safeguard its own national interests. ('Russia', Churchill had said in 1939, 'is a riddle wrapped in a mystery inside an enigma. But perhaps there is a key. That key is Russian national interest.') Before the American-inspired United Nations had been able to devise a common and effective strategy, Stalin had consolidated his hold on East Germany, the Baltic States, Romania, Bulgaria, Hungary and Poland. The 'free and unfettered elections' Poland had been promised at Yalta were rejected by the Russian-imposed communist regime. Whereas Hitler had been condemned for invading Poland, Stalin (who invaded it in 1939 and 1945) acted with impunity. The Allies formally protested at the Russian occupation, but did little else. Yet in 1939 the German occupation of Poland had been the reason why the Allies had gone to war. Reluctantly, the Western powers accepted the political and military realities of Eastern Europe. Only the Socialist Federal Republic of Yugoslavia, led by Josip Broz Tito (1892–1980), which in June 1948 was expelled from the Moscow-controlled Cominform,[4] and Albania, which was already acting independently of the Kremlin, tried to foil Russian ambitions in the Balkans.

Emboldened by its successful territorial expansion, and convinced by now that America would not use its atom bomb against it, Moscow further tested the Allies' resolve in Greece (where in 1947–8 it went to help Greek communists in their attempt to overthrow the state) and East Germany (where in 1948–9 it tried to incorporate Berlin into its sphere of influence). In 1949 (having obtained critical data through espionage in the United Kingdom and the USA[5]) Russia exploded its first atom bomb; in 1952 it exploded its first hydrogen bomb.

Faced by the financial inability of Britain and France to protect Greece, Iran and Turkey, which were all coming under growing Soviet pressure, a resolute Truman announced his policy of containment.[6] America would not disregard its world responsibilities as it had done after 1919. A Cold War was declared against a world socialist order. Aimed originally at limiting Soviet expansion, the policy of containment eventually became concerned with the destruction of the Soviet system. What had been Roosevelt's belief in the possibility of lasting US–Soviet cooperation was exchanged for political, military and economic confrontation. In the late 1940s the danger that parts of Western Europe – especially France and Italy – would become communist was taken seriously in Washington. The USA openly threw its weight behind the non-communist parties. In the immediate post-war years communists were deliberately excluded from the cabinets of both countries.

On the economic front, an effort was begun in 1947, under the US Marshall Plan,[7] to bolster the European economies (to 'enslave them', the Russians said). The Soviet Union's response (in 1949) was Comecon, an organization that coordinated the economic policies of Soviet Bloc countries in Eastern Europe, as well as Mongolia and later Cuba (and, after 1978, Vietnam). On the military front, in 1948 the United States and its allies met the Soviet Union's attempt to cut off Berlin from the West with the Berlin airlift (June 1948–May 1949).[8] In 1949 the USA was instrumental in establishing the anti-Soviet front known as the North Atlantic Treaty Organization (NATO).[9] This was not strictly a North Atlantic alliance (Italy was a member); nor was it an unequivocal defender of democracy (Portugal's dictatorship made that claim invalid[10]); nor was it a treaty among equals (the USA had no intention of sharing control of its atom and hydrogen bombs). When, in 1955, West Germany joined NATO, the Soviets responded with the Warsaw Pact,[11] which thenceforth formed the basis for mutual defence cooperation within the Soviet Bloc. On the political front, the USA, Britain and France had ended the state of war with Germany in 1951. The Soviet Union did so in 1955, and in that year the Federal Republic of Germany was recognized by the Allies as a sovereign state. Russia responded by creating the German Democratic Republic in eastern Germany.

By the 1950s the Cold War between the USA and the Soviet Union had become worldwide. On 25 June 1950, North Korean troops had crossed the 38th Parallel and invaded South Korea. Assuming that the Soviets had decided to put the Truman Doctrine of containment of communism to the test, the Americans called for a special meeting of the United Nations Security Council the same day. The Council's demand for a ceasefire having been ignored, it at once called upon all member states to render assistance to the Republic of South Korea in repelling the invaders. As the Russians were boycotting the Council at the time, they were unable to use their veto to halt American action, so US troops, with token forces of other nations sympathetic to American aims, entered the war on the side of the South Koreans.

After initial North Korean successes, which carried their army deep into South Korea, the Americans under General Douglas MacArthur counter-attacked behind the North Koreans at Inchon and took up positions close to the Chinese frontier on the Yalu River. Vainly, the North Koreans tried to retreat. Convinced that the USA was about to invade their country, in November 1950 the Chinese directly intervened, driving the Americans back into South Korea. The Americans could have ended Chinese intervention with the use of the atom bomb, but they hesitated to use it. The war dragged on with neither side winning a decisive victory. Not until April 1951 did the UN forces regain the 38th Parallel. After three years of bitter fighting, and endless negotiations, Korea was partitioned (as it had been originally in 1945) between communist and non-communist forces at the 38th Parallel, where it still is.

The Korean War stimulated American efforts to complete its encircling military alliances and bases around the communist world. In 1951, while the war was being fought, the USA signed a peace treaty and a mutual security pact with Japan. In the same year it concluded a mutual security pact with Australia and New Zealand (ANZUS). In April 1952 Japan's sovereignty was restored. Between 1945 and 1952 the USA had granted $1.7 billion of aid to Japan, which, together with America's purchases of military equipment, boosted Japan's recovery. Gradually, Japan and Okinawa became American bastions in the East.[12]

Conscious by now that it was committed to a life-and-death struggle against communism, in 1953 the United States signed a ten-year military and economic agreement with its old enemy, fascist Spain, led by Franco. (The death of Franco in 1975 and the accession of Prince Juan Carlos (b. 1938), grandson of Alfonso XIII, to the Spanish throne further cemented US–Spanish relations.) In 1954, to deter possible future Chinese aggression, the Southeast Asia Treaty Organization (SEATO[13]) was formed; a US–Taiwan defence treaty was also signed (rescinded in favour of mainland China in 1980). In 1959 the Central Treaty Organization (CENTO)[14] replaced the Baghdad Pact of 1955. By the 1960s the USA had military bases in thirty-one countries. It also had a far larger nuclear stockpile than the USSR, and had supremacy at sea.[15]

Stalin died in 1953 (see Chapter 17). With Nikita Khrushchev's (b. 1894; first secretary 1953–64; d. 1971) accession to power in the 1950s, Stalin's body was removed from Lenin's tomb. In 1959, in a spirit of competitive coexistence, Khrushchev visited the United States. His friendly behaviour on that occasion contrasted sharply with the ruthlessness he had shown in putting down the revolts in East Berlin (1953), Poland and Hungary (both 1956). Nor did his proposed coexistence with the West discourage him from strengthening the Cominform and the Warsaw Pact. In 1960 he displayed his anger at President Eisenhower over the U-2 spy plane incident; in 1961 he built the Berlin Wall and continued to offset US aid to Israel by assisting the Arabs.

Khrushchev is especially responsible for changing Soviet relations with East Asia. Under his leadership, Soviet influence in Korea, India and Vietnam grew; in China it declined. (Russia had given assistance to China during the late 1940s and early 1950s.) Irked by personal taunts made against him by the Chinese for his adventurism in placing missiles in Cuba, and for his cowardice in later removing them, Khrushchev cut off all aid to China and strengthened Russian defences along the Chinese border. Until his removal from office in 1964, relations between the Soviet Union and China worsened.

It was during Khrushchev's regime that the USA and the USSR came closest to a nuclear confrontation. Following the failure in 1961 of a US-backed seaborne attempt to overthrow the Cuban government of Fidel Castro (the 'Bay of Pigs' landing), the Soviet Union placed medium-range ballistic missiles in Cuba in 1962. Overnight, America's superiority in intercontinental ballistic missiles was neutralized; Russian missiles were now off the coast of Florida. President John F. Kennedy (b. 1917; president 1961–3) responded by ordering a sea blockade of Cuba. Only by bringing the world to the brink of a nuclear war were the Russians compelled to remove their missiles the following year. The American government undertook not to invade Cuba again and to remove its missiles aimed at the Soviet Union from Turkey.

The Cuban Missile Crisis not only caused the Russians to challenge the Monroe Doctrine (under which the USA had held a protectorate over the Western Hemisphere for 150 years); it prompted the Soviets to begin a naval building programme which by the 1970s had ended American supremacy at sea. For the first time since 1945 the Soviet Union became a superpower not only on land and in the air, but at sea as well. The crisis also caused a shift in emphasis for the Russians from medium-range to intercontinental ballistic missiles.

In 1964, partly because of his loss of credibility over Cuba and the Sino-Soviet split, Khrushchev was forced to relinquish power to the collective leadership of Leonid Brezhnev (1906–82), Aleksei Kosygin (1904–81) and Nikolay Podgorny (1903–83). No sooner had Khrushchev been removed from office than his denunciations of Stalin came under attack. Stalin had been crucial to Soviet survival, Khrushchev's opponents argued; had Stalin not collectivized agriculture and expanded industrialization, had he not purged the higher ranks of the armed forces before war, Russia would have been defeated. Partially, at least, Stalin's image as the saviour of Russia was restored. It says a great deal for the changes going on in Russia at the time that Khrushchev's successor, Brezhnev, allowed him to live out his life in peace. Within two years, Brezhnev was effectively in full control of the USSR (although Podgorny and Kosygin remained in their posts). In 1968 he enforced the Soviet Union's right to 'intervene if socialism was threatened elsewhere' by invading and imposing his will on Czechoslovakia.

Even more important than Cuba in helping to shape the post-war outlook of the American people was the war the USA fought and lost in Vietnam (1964–73). Until Vietnam, all US wars had been moral, righteous and victorious. The Vietnam War proved to be an unmitigated disaster: it caused the deaths of 58,000 Americans, millions of Vietnamese and cost $250 billion directly. While the threat presented by North Vietnam was never direct or vital to American interests, the war came close to splitting the nation. To some, the war was morally justified and winnable; to others, it was totally reprehensible and a lost cause from the start. The divisive conflict would haunt the USA until its victory in 1991 in the first Gulf War. The US withdrawal from Southeast Asia in 1975 – precipitated by its defeat in Vietnam two years earlier – ended the Truman Doctrine of containing communism begun in 1947. Following the Vietnam War, a new and friendlier chapter in US–Soviet relations opened, known as détente.

*   *   *

Meanwhile new centres of power had appeared in Germany, Japan, communist China and (collectively) in the Third World. The bipolarism of 1945 gave way to the multipolarism of the 1970s and 1980s. Not only did new centres of power appear in the West and the East, the balance of terror, existing since 1945, was greatly affected by the proliferation of nuclear, chemical and biological weapons. Following upon American and Russian developments, Britain exploded an atom bomb in 1952; France in 1960; China in 1964; India in 1974; Pakistan in 1998. India, Israel and Pakistan are non-signatories of the Nuclear Non-Proliferation Treaty (NPT).[16] Israel is said to be a powerfully armed nuclear country. In 1989 US government sources confirmed that South Africa, aided by Israel, had successfully launched a ballistic missile. (Later, South Africa would abandon its nuclear programme.) Other countries have nuclear weapons (North Korea) or are working to obtain them (Iran). The proliferation of weapons of mass destruction is affecting every region of the world. Increasingly, the danger of war lies in the actions of minor powers or groups of fanatics armed with technologically advanced weapons.

US hegemony after the Second World War did not go unchallenged in the West. Canada declined US nuclear weapons, developed friendly relations with communist Cuba and China and ignored America's trade boycott of the communist world. In the 1970s it refused to support the USA in the Vietnam War. Evidence of Europe's growing sense of neutrality towards the United States was its lukewarm support of US Middle East policy in 1973, at the time of the Arab–Israeli War, when, for the second time, the USA and the USSR reached the brink of nuclear conflict. The United Nations (once a forum for praising the USA) became a tribunal before which America was often criticized or condemned.

The Arab oil embargo of 1973, which was the Arabs' response to America's support of Israel, challenged US power openly. For the first time in modern history the initiative in world economic affairs was wrenched (however temporarily) out of Western hands. There also was the extraordinary economic challenge presented by the resurgence of Germany and Japan. Economically, Germany became the strongest power in Europe; Japan became the leading creditor nation of the world. After the 1950s, these two countries began to challenge America's industrial monopoly.

By 1987, primarily because of fiscal profligacy, which began with President Lyndon B. Johnson's (b. 1908; president 1963–9; d. 1973) refusal to finance the Vietnam War through additional taxes, the USA had become the world's largest debtor nation. (By 2005 it had an unprecedented national debt of nearly $8 trillion.) The US budget and trade situation were also in disarray. In the short space of twenty years the nation had passed from the point where it felt it could dominate the world economy to being increasingly concerned about the effect of the rest of the world upon itself.

The post-war period also witnessed a decline of Soviet power. The Soviet Union experienced political setbacks in Egypt, Algeria, Somalia, Guinea, the Congo, Iraq, Yugoslavia, Romania and Berlin. The challenge presented by China to the USSR also grew. Decisions made during the 1980s by the Americans, the British and the French to sell arms to China, coupled with the visits made by Chinese leaders to Europe and the United States, added to the Soviet Union's paranoia about its security. Except for its invasion of Afghanistan (1979–89) – in support of a communist regime – the USSR undertook few direct foreign adventures. In Korea, Vietnam, Angola and the Middle East it let its communist allies do the fighting.

Between 1949 and 1973 the Cold War fought between the superpowers dominated world history. The threatened political fragmentation stemming from Europe's collapse after 1945 was deferred by the increase of American and Soviet power. For forty years the Cold War ensured a communist grip on Eastern Europe. Major landmarks were the Truman Doctrine of Containment, the Marshall Plan and the Greek (1947), Hungarian (1956) and Czechoslovakian (1968) crises. The two superpowers came close to war in Berlin (1949), Cuba (1962) and over Israel (1973). Landmarks in Asia were the conflicts in China, Korea, Vietnam and the Middle East. Besides the continuing struggle between the USA and the USSR, there have been other conflicts in Southeast Asia (China and India, Vietnam and Cambodia, China and Vietnam), in Southwest Asia (Iran and Iraq), in Africa (Algeria, Kenya, Angola, Namibia, Uganda, Mozambique, the Sudan, Libya, Rwanda and Congo) and in the Americas (Cuba, Chile, Panama, El Salvador, Grenada and Nicaragua).

Some saw the Cold War as having been inevitable, a price one had to pay to rid Europe of communism. That is why throughout the Cold War the majority of Western Europeans were pro-American. Others saw the Cold War as a war that need never have been waged. The surprising thing is that the Soviets, Americans and Europeans managed to get on with their lives despite the constant threat of nuclear annihilation. The blessing about the great-power rivalry was that it did not escalate into a third world war. It also ensured a degree of cooperation between the Western powers that might never have been achieved without the Russian threat. The curse of the Cold War (in addition to the deaths in Korea and Vietnam) was that it led to enormous and largely unnecessary military expenditures – particularly in nuclear weaponry – that bankrupted the Soviet Union, left the USA in unparalleled debt and placed the welfare of the entire planet in jeopardy.

The conclusion of a Four Power Agreement on Berlin in 1971, the Anti-Ballistic Missile (ABM) Treaty in 1972, which limited anti-ballistic systems, the US withdrawal from Vietnam in 1973 and the Helsinki Agreements of 1975, which in recognizing existing boundaries confirmed the Soviet sphere of influence in Eastern Europe, coupled with improved relations between East and West Germany, foreshadowed the end of the Cold War. While new setbacks to détente between the USA and the USSR occurred in the late 1970s and early 1980s, when the USA renewed the arms race, and President Ronald Reagan (b. 1911; president 1980–8; d. 2004) called the Soviet Union an 'evil empire', the accession to power of Mikhail Gorbachev (b. 1931; general secretary 1985–91) and the subsequent unravelling of communism in the whole of Eastern Europe carried the Cold War to its conclusion. In 1990 the Soviet Union was dissolved. The liberal, democratic view of the Western powers had triumphed.

Who won the Cold War is a difficult question to answer. The Soviet Union certainly lost it. The inner contradictions of communism, and the inability to match US defence spending, sealed its fate. Two clear winners were Japan (led by Eisaku Sato; 1901–75) and Germany (led by Konrad Adenauer; 1876–1967), who, forbidden to rearm, spent their money on rebuilding their infrastructures and industrial potentials to become world powers again.

The Decolonization of Africa

The declaration of principles by Churchill and Roosevelt in the Atlantic Charter in 1941, with its promise of self-determination and self-government for all, heralded the end of European colonialism in Africa.[1] As the Second World War progressed, a new generation of black leaders intent on obtaining self-rule emerged out of the native resistance movements. Among them were Kwame Nkrumah (1909–72) of the Gold Coast (who assumed power from a prison cell), Léopold Sédar Senghor (1906–2001) of Senegal, Jomo Kenyatta (1891–1978) and Tom Mboya (1930–69) of Kenya, Ahmed Sékou Touré (1922–84) of Guinea, Patrice Lumumba (1925–61) of the Belgian Congo (Zaire), Kenneth Kaunda (b. 1924) of Northern Rhodesia (Zambia) and Julius Nyerere (1922–99) of Tanganyika. Britain's granting of independence to India in 1947, coupled with Dutch and French defeats in Asia and the unprecedented threefold increase of Africa's population[2] after 1950, further ensured the success of the movements for African independence.

The decolonization of Africa began in the 1940s when the Italians were driven out of Ethiopia and Libya by the British (see Map XVI).[3] Until it was overrun by the Italians in 1936, Ethiopia had been the only African country of any consequence free of Western control. Regaining its independence in 1941, Ethiopia has remained self-governing. A Marxist-inspired revolution in 1974 was overthrown in 1991 with the collapse of the Soviet Union. After the

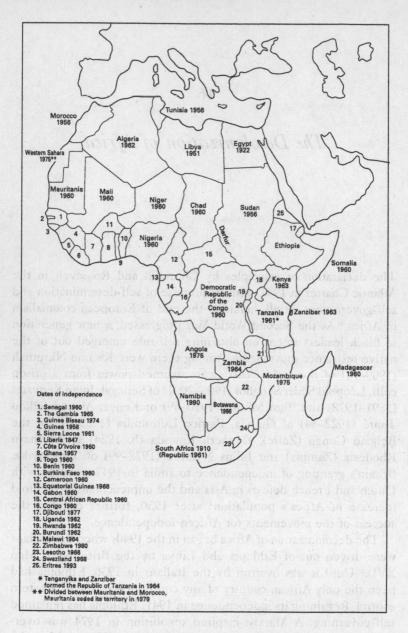

Morocco 1956

Western Sahara 1975**

Algeria 1962

Tunisia 1956

Libya 1951

Egypt 1922

Mauritania 1960

Mali 1960

Niger 1960

Chad 1960

Sudan 1956

25

17

Ethiopia

2   1
3
4
5   7   8
6
11
10
Nigeria 1960
9
Darfur
15
Somalia 1960

12

13
14
16
Democratic Republic of the Congo 1960

18   Kenya 1963

19

20

Tanzania 1961*

Zanzibar 1963

Angola 1975

21

Zambia 1964

Mozambique 1975

Madagascar 1960

22

Namibia 1990

Botswana 1966

24

23

South Africa 1910 (Republic 1961)

Dates of Independence

1. Senegal 1960
2. The Gambia 1965
3. Guinea Bissau 1974
4. Guinea 1958
5. Sierra Leone 1961
6. Liberia 1847
7. Côte D'Ivoire 1960
8. Ghana 1957
9. Togo 1960
10. Benin 1960
11. Burkina Faso 1960
12. Cameroon 1960
13. Equatorial Guinea 1968
14. Gabon 1960
15. Central African Republic 1960
16. Congo 1960
17. Djibouti 1977
18. Uganda 1962
19. Rwanda 1962
20. Burundi 1962
21. Malawi 1964
22. Zimbabwe 1980
23. Lesotho 1966
24. Swaziland 1968
25. Eritrea 1993

* Tanganyika and Zanzibar formed the Republic of Tanzania in 1964
** Divided between Mauritania and Morocco, Mauritania ceded its territory in 1979

Map XVI Decolonization of Africa, 1922–90

Second World War, Italy's one-time colony Libya was ruled by the British and the French. On 2 January 1952 it became an independent constitutional monarchy. In 1969 a military group, led by Colonel Muammar al-Qadhafi (b. 1942), seized power. In 1960 Italy's former colony of Somalia also became independent.

Unable or unwilling to repress the call for liberation, in 1956 France grudgingly granted independence to the protectorates of Tunisia and Morocco. Spain followed suit, peacefully surrendering its Moroccan territory the following year; the French finally recognized Mohammed V (1910–61) as the first king of Morocco. In Algeria, however, the French, who thought in terms of common citizenship for the Algerians (30 per cent of whom were Berbers) rather than independence, refused to yield control. Algeria, which had originally been colonized to compensate psychologically for French humiliation in the Napoleonic Wars, witnessed a seventeen-year struggle (1945–62) for independence. A million Algerians perished and more than three-quarters of the European population had to flee the country before independence was won. In 1992 a general election, won by an Islamist party, was revoked. The bitter fight that ensued between the Muslims and the military government claimed the lives of more than 150,000 people. An amnesty in 1999 reduced the violence, but a state of emergency still exists.

The example set by French Guinea in 1958 to disavow French rule was followed by all the former colonies of French West and French Equatorial Africa. Serious violence occurred only in the Cameroons. The last African colonial territory to be granted independence by a European power was French Djibouti in 1977.

Independence in British colonies followed a similar course. The decline of imperialist sentiment in Britain, and the ongoing decolonization of British possessions in Asia, made it imperative. Egypt had been a British protectorate from 1914 to 1922, when Britain established a constitutional monarchy under Sultan Ahmad Fuad (1868–1936). Britain continued to influence Egyptian affairs until the relations of the two countries were formalized in 1936. In 1951 Egypt finally gained its independence by abrogating that treaty. As a result of a military uprising led by Mohammed Neguib (1901–84) and Gamal Abd al-Nasser (1918–70) in July 1952, King Faruk (1920–65) was deposed and exiled. After the overthrow of Neguib in 1954, Nasser began a programme of Arab socialism, which included land reforms and economic and social development; Arab national pride was renewed. He challenged European control of Egypt's oil resources and nationalized the Suez Canal. This led to an abortive invasion of Egypt in 1956 by British, French and Israeli troops, which ensured his election to the presidency. In that year Egypt renounced claims on the Sudan, which became a republic. Nasser's success gave great stimulus to all African independence movements.

The humiliating language in which Britain was ordered out of Egypt by the UN (dominated by the USA and the USSR) in 1956 marked the end of Britain's great-power status. It subsequently curtailed its presence east of Suez. After Nasser's death, Pan-Arabism was taken up by Libyan President Qadhafi who advocated a policy of Islamic socialism. Qadhafi was of sufficient importance for the Western powers (particularly the USA) to make several attempts to assassinate him. In 2003, after prolonged negotiations with the UN and the USA, he abandoned his weapons of mass destruction programme, renounced terrorism and accepted financial responsibility for past terrorist attacks.

The Gold Coast was granted independence in 1957; renamed Ghana, this was the first British African colony south of the Sahara to achieve its freedom. British Nigeria, Cameroon and Togoland followed in 1960;[4] Sierra Leone in 1961. Also breaking away from Britain were the East African colonies of Somalia (1960), Tanganyika (1961),[5] Uganda (1962), Kenya (1963), Nyasaland and Northern Rhodesia (1964) and Gambia (1965). In Southern Rhodesia, a guerrilla uprising and UN sanctions preceded free elections in 1979.[6] In 1980, with Robert Mugabe (b. 1924) as its first president, the state of Zimbabwe was created. Defying historical trends, in 1990 it declared itself a Marxist–Leninist state. In Kenya, in 1956, Jomo Kenyatta led the Mau Mau insurrection against the British. In 1978 he was succeeded as president by Daniel arap Moi (b. 1924). On 30 December 2002 Moi was succeeded by Mwai Kibaki (b. 1931), who now fights an upward battle against corruption, tribal hatred, widespread sickness, a crumbling economy and the ever-present threat of violence.

Unable to resist the groundswell for independence – what in 1960 British Prime Minister Harold Macmillan (1894–1986) called 'the wind of change' (he might have said the desire to shake off foreign rule) – the Belgians followed the trend set by the other Europeans. Belgian rule ended in 1960 when major riots broke out in Léopoldville, and the Belgian colonial administration was bloodily replaced by the Democratic Republic of the Congo. (From 1971 until 1997 the Congo was called Zaire.) Since independence, Congo's history has been marred by unrelenting slaughter and looting.

Spain and Portugal were the last colonial powers to yield to native rule. Following a left-wing military coup in Lisbon in 1974, which led to democratic reforms, Mozambique and Angola obtained their independence from Portugal the next year. Spain's rule in the Spanish Sahara was terminated in 1976; its Saharan territory was divided between Morocco and Mauritania. Cold War-inspired conflict in Angola between black liberation groups resulted in a 1977 victory for the Marxists (with the help of Cuban troops, Soviet aid and illicit trade in diamonds and ivory). Throughout the 1980s, the USA and South Africa backed the National Union for the Total Independence of Angola (UNITA), the non-Marxist rebel movement, led by Jonas Savimbi (1934–2002). Angola's sixteen-year civil war officially ended in May 1991, when the warring factions signed a peace treaty. The elections in 1992 returned a Marxist government, which the USA recognized only in May 1993. Oil (Angola is a major producer and is rich with other natural resources) and the end of the Cold War caused the USA to switch sides from Savimbi to the leftist government. Britain followed America's example. In 1994 still another peace accord was signed, and UN peacekeepers were provided. However, increased fighting followed, and the UN peacekeepers were forced to withdraw. In August 1997 the UN Security Council, still trying to obtain an Angolan government of national unity, voted to impose sanctions on UNITA to force it to comply with the ineffective 1994 peace agreement. Paradoxically, although in 2000 the Marxist government had the support of most of the people, Savimbi's UNITA forces controlled most of the country. But in February 2002 Savimbi was killed in a gunfight. Two months later the government forces and the UNITA rebels ended their twenty-seven-year conflict, which had cost 1.2 million lives, by signing a ceasefire. Exhaustion and famine had at long last ended the war.

Because Southwest Africa had been conquered by South African troops during the First World War, South Africa was given a mandate over the territory by the League of Nations in 1920. (In 1967 its name was changed to Namibia.) After twenty-five years of guerrilla warfare between the South West Africa People's Organization (SWAPO; formed in 1959) and the South Africa-backed Democratic Turnhalle Alliance Party (DTA), UN-supervised elections in 1989 settled the course of Namibian independence by giving SWAPO a majority and ending South Africa's control. In March 1990 Namibia celebrated its independence after seventy-four years of South African rule. With a population of 1.6 million, Namibia has a minority of whites, who farm the best land and control most of the business sector, and a majority of native Namibians engaged in subsistence farming. However, it also possesses the richest diamond fields in the world, and the world's largest uranium mine. In the late 1990s secessionist troubles in the Caprivi Strip in eastern Namibia caused thousands to flee to neighbouring Botswana.

By and large, the European nations were as glad to surrender political power as the native leaders were to assume it. When one compares the struggles for independence in Asia, African independence – with the exception of Algeria – was won quietly and with relatively little bloodshed; in some instances it was thrust upon those who sought it. By the 1950s, the Europeans did not have the will or the resources to finance imperialism any longer; it had become too costly, and fell into disfavour. While vast private fortunes were made in Africa,[7] it was the European states that had to meet the ever-growing costs of defending and administering the acquired territories. Nor did the states get much out of it. Colonial trade – despite the exaggerated accounts of it – invariably represented the smallest fraction of a country's total trade; for Germany and Belgium on the eve of the First World War, the figure was 1 per cent. The exploitation of Asia by the West seems to have been a much better business proposition for Western governments than the exploitation of Africa. Perhaps that is why Western colonialism in Africa was so late and so short-lived.

Until 1994, only the Republic of South Africa remained as an example of white minority rule. The struggle in South Africa,[8] in so far as it was between black and white Africans, differed from that which had taken place in the rest of colonial Africa. Until the coming to power in 1989 of the more conciliatory, if less visionary, President F. W. de Klerk (b. 1936), the Afrikaner elite (firmly convinced that the black and white races should be culturally independent, separate and distinct, and concerned with its own survival as a group) ruled a predominantly black country.[9]

The principle of apartheid,[10] or separate development of the races – first defined and proclaimed by the Boer leader Daniel F. Malan (1874–1959) in 1948 (following the post-war victory of the Boer National Party at the polls) – was to plague South Africa until apartheid came to an end in 1994. It was one of the reasons why the Afrikaner Nationalist Party declared the independence of South Africa in 1958, and why (following a referendum) it withdrew from the British Commonwealth and became a republic in 1961. It was the cause of growing divestment by Western countries in South Africa in the 1980s, and the United Nations' arms embargo imposed in 1986.[11] In that year a state of emergency was proclaimed and thousands of dissidents were imprisoned. The forced resettlement of hundreds of thousands of black people by the South African government was denounced by the International Court of Justice.

The turning point in the history of apartheid was de Klerk's announcement in February 1991 to end all apartheid laws. His attitude towards the socialist African National Congress (ANC; formed in 1912), led by Nelson Mandela (b. 1918),[12] was much more flexible and sympathetic than that of P. W. Botha (b. 1916), who had preceded him. For the ANC, the collapse of the Soviet Union in 1991 (and the end of Soviet support) increased their willingness to negotiate. The time was ripe for a settlement from both sides.

With the overwhelming victory of the ANC at the polls in April 1994 (they received 62.7 per cent of the vote), and de Klerk's surrender of power to Mandela, white supremacy and apartheid came to an end. For the blacks, faith in their country's future was reborn. Thankfully, partly because of Mandela's vision and statesmanship, the end of apartheid did not result in civil war, but in reconciliation. In the spring of 2004 Mandela's successor, President Thabo Mbeki (b. 1942), was returned to power for a second term.

The Republic of South Africa is the greatest single industrial and military power on the continent, possessing one of the largest mineral lodes in the world. Its huge coal[13] and uranium reserves render it independent of outside energy supplies. The oil lifeline between the Western industrial nations and the Persian Gulf passes by the Cape route – one of the busiest shipping lanes in the world. At least twelve black nations are dependent upon South Africa for trade, access to the oceans and employment.

Since 1945, the whole of Africa has rid itself of colonial rule. In freeing themselves, sub-Saharan Africans have changed worldwide attitudes to race relations, especially in the United States. Between the 1960s and the 1980s, there were improvements in life expectancy, health services, education, housing, electricity and running water.[14] From the 1980s onwards, because of violence, famine, economic disruption and rapid population increases, achievements gave way to decline. Although some new leaders, such as Nelson Mandela, have put the state before the tribe or personal aggrandizement, economic progress has fallen short of expectations, and far short of what is needed. By 2004, many health, education and social welfare programmes were failing. In sub-Saharan Africa tuberculosis, cholera, yellow fever, malaria and sleeping sickness are on the rise. In West Africa yaws, which supposedly had been 'banished' in the 1950s, was growing in the 1980s. HIV-AIDS has become a scourge throughout the continent. In sub-Saharan Africa 25 million people are infected. The figure for Botswana and Swaziland is more than 35 per cent of the population. Africa is also suffering from a political malaise that few would have imagined earlier. The hope that it would evolve democratic, multi-party politics on the Western model has been dashed by regional and tribal rivalry.

When one considers African traditions, and the desperate economic condition of so many Africans, it was perhaps foolish to have expected Africa to adopt Western ways. With a tradition of hierarchical tribalism, Africa has never been disposed to democratic politics. While the number of democracies in the world is on the rise, Africa was not much closer to democratic rule in 2005 than it was in 1950. What the West understands as freedom of the individual under the law has still to be achieved. Where the rule of law has gained a foothold, it has often been broken by autocratic leaders. It provided no protection in Uganda against Idi Amin (1925–2003), who, having seized power in 1971, conducted a reign of terror until he was ousted in 1979. Civil war went on there until December 2004. When, in March 2000, Robert Mugabe approved an invasion of white-owned farms in Zimbabwe, the law failed to protect the farmers' basic human rights. Little wonder that the GDP of Zimbabwe in 2004 was only two-thirds of what it had been five years earlier. Respect for law has been replaced by anarchy. On 31 March 2005 Mugabe won an election, which his opponents say was rigged. In many African countries free elections and a free press (as the West would define them) are not tolerated; nor is an independent judiciary. All of these are considered destabilizing. One-party states and military rule are the norms. In 2004 the military was the dynamic element. Half of black African nations are military dictatorships.[15] The Western idea of freely held, multi-party elections is not widespread. Too many governments do not have a 'loyal opposition'; they have political enemies. Elections are means of conserving power, not introducing democracy. In a continent where power is personalized, few presidents have ever accepted defeat in an election. Concentrated, rather than shared, power is the African way. Countries that have nominally become democratic are still run by the military, who supposedly were deposed to make way for civil democracy.[16] The overthrow of civilian rule by the military is a constant threat. Having removed the colonial yoke, Africans now bear a yolk of their own making.

Many Africans trace their failures since independence to the political and economic distortion caused by the European colonial system. Africans are not only prisoners of a Western economic system, but of European languages.[17] Under Western tutelage, countries were forced to be part of the Western political and economic organization. The boundaries which the West arbitrarily imposed had very little to do with economic and ethnic realities. In consequence, ethnic differences have brought war to many parts of the continent. Scores of leaders have been assassinated in ever-recurring tribal purges and coups.

Since 1962, Ethiopia has fought Somalia over the Ogaden territory, to which the Somalis make ethnic claims. In the winter of 1992, in an effort to halt the slaughter and combat widespread famine arising out of tribal clashes, a UN force (including US soldiers) occupied parts of Somalia. Little was achieved. In December 2000 a peace deal was struck between Ethiopia and Eritrea to end a border war that had gone on for thirteen years and cost seventy thousand lives. Regrettably, in 2005 Ethiopia and Eritrea began to squabble about borders again.

Ethnic differences have been the cause of much bloodshed in the Sudan. Independent from Egypt in 1956, and a military dictatorship since 1958, the strongly Islamic, Arabic-speaking government of the Sudan has been at war with the non-Muslim African population of the southern Sudan since 1962. Exacerbating this is the problem of the division of income from oil exploitation. In 1972 the Sudanese government agreed to grant autonomy to the ethnically different South. Notwithstanding this action, however, the Sudan People's Liberation Army (SPLA), based in the Christian South, continued to fight a widespread war against the government. A ceasefire was eventually declared in 2002. Peace talks between the government and the southern rebels were held in 2003 but the next year the black Africans of the Darfur region in west Sudan were attacked and massacred by Arab groups supported by the government. Many thousands fled into Chad. Russia's opposition in September 2004 weakened the UN Security Council's threat to impose sanctions on Sudan. On 9 January 2005, after two million had died in Africa's longest civil war (1955–2005) and millions more had fled their homes, a peace agreement between the Khartoum government and the southern rebels was finally signed. Despite UN protests, the Khartoum government has continued to bomb the Darfur area with impunity. Although it was cleared of having committed genocide by a UN commission, Khartoum's 'heinous crimes' against refugees continue.[18] Sudan is an oil-rich nation, which explains the support of some of the great powers. Chinese, Malay and Indian companies are already engaged in oil exploration and the building of new pipelines. If peace emerges, there will be an invasion of oil companies from around the world.

The ongoing inter-tribal warfare in the Congo, which has claimed millions of lives, has impoverished the country and destabilized the whole of Central Africa. After a coup in 1963 the country adopted a Marxist posture. In 1965 Mobutu Sese Seko (b. 1930) declared himself president. Until his flight and death in 1997 – despite Western backing – he and his cohorts plundered Congo's wealth; under their rule, the country was brought to the point of disintegration. His successor, Laurent Kabila (1939–2001), who had driven Mobutu out of the country only to prove himself another petty tyrant, was assassinated. His eldest son, Joseph Kabila, assumed power. Since April 2000 there has been an uneasy ceasefire between the spoils-seeking five nations who have intervened (Angola, Zimbabwe and Namibia, who fought for Kabila, and Uganda and Rwanda, who opposed him). In July 2002 Congo and Rwanda agreed to end the fighting in eastern Congo. The next year a power-sharing accord was signed by the contesting parties. In 2005 the war-wrecked Congo remained in a state of dangerous uncertainty. Its nine neighbours fear that the war will be renewed and spread. They have no more confidence in the ceasefire of 2003 than in those that preceded it. Congo has too many enemies and too much gold and precious stones for peace to last. The country is too large, too difficult to traverse and too politically complicated for the UN and its peacekeeping force (established there in 1999) to have much influence on future developments. In March 2005 UN troops used force for the first time against rebel troops. The UN troops themselves are accused of major abuses. Because of the ongoing penetration of its northeast frontier with Rwanda, a state of emergency exists in that area. Dozens of local, smaller conflicts continue to blaze.

In Rwanda in April 1994, a renewal of ethnic strife between the Hutu majority and the Tutsi minority resulted in the slaughter of 800,000 Tutsis. Two million Tutsis fled to the Congo. Earlier in 1959 a similar number had fled to Burundi.

West Africa has also seen ethnic turmoil. The Ibo secession in Nigeria in 1967 cost one million lives and ended in 1970. In 1999, after nearly a decade of civil war, UN peacekeepers were provided for Sierra Leone, whose troubles spilled over into Equatorial Guinea. Liberia has endured a civil war since the rebel leader Charles Taylor outsed the dictator Samuel Doe in 1997. Having wrecked his own country, Taylor sponsored revolts in Sierra Leone, Guinea and Côte d'Ivoire, where after two and a half years of civil war a ceasefire was signed between rebel troops and the government in April 2005. Togo has forty distinct ethnic groups, which resent domination by the Ewe and Mina tribes in the south and the Kabye in the north.

A dangerous uncertainty also exists in the countries of North Africa, where a rising tide of Islamic fundamentalism has threatened the security of whole societies. Several years of brutal conflict between Algerian Islamists and the military-backed regime – which refused to recognize the Islamic Party's success at the ballot box – have cost more than fifty thousand lives.

Muslim fundamentalists were responsible for the assassination on 6 October 1981 of Egypt's president, Anwar el-Sadat (b. 1918). Throughout the 1990s, several attempts were made on the life of his successor, Mohamed Hosny Mubarak (b. 1928), who governs with a firm hand. Full democracy in Egypt would produce a regime hostile to both Mubarak and Israel.

Independence from colonial powers has not only brought widespread violence; it has led to a deterioration of Africa's economic lot. It is the world's poorest, most indebted continent; the debt repayments of some countries exceed the amount being spent on health and education. Between 1970 and 1976 Africa's public debt quadrupled. In the 1990s its foreign debt exceeded its annual GNP, amounting to twice that of any other region. Since 1970, it has increased more than twentyfold. More than thirty of the world's fifty least developed nations are African. The continent has a quarter of the world's refugees.[19] Millions of people have been displaced within their own countries. Many others are poorer than they were twenty years ago, and, relative to other continents, much of Africa has always been poor. But there are exceptions to the general rule of decline: Botswana, for example, possesses diamonds and is developing tourism; it has one of the highest economic growth rates in Africa.

Talk of improvement in Africa's economic performance by the World Bank[20] and the International Monetary Fund (IMF)[21] – particularly regarding the increase in direct investment – is heartening, but unconvincing. Despite half a century of foreign aid, Africa is worse off than it was. Too often the structural reforms recommended have left countries with worse living conditions than before. The problems surrounding the giving of financial help to Africa are legion. It is the only continent to which massive foreign aid has been transferred often without any visible results. Throughout the 1990s, Tanzania, a country of about 30 million people, received $1 billion per year in aid, with little to show for it. Critics argue that only a third of aid is used effectively, the rest being wasted or plundered by corrupt leaders. In the age of colonialism the West plundered Africa (here and there it still does); now Africa plunders itself. There is no example of an African country that has been developed with foreign aid. Nor does Africa appear to be able to help itself by increasing foreign trade. Despite the Lomé Conventions, in effect from 1975 to 2000, between the European Economic Community and a number of African countries, which promised reciprocal trade preferences, the foreign trade of many African states remains either stagnant or sluggish. Africa's share of world trade continues to decline. It is particularly vulnerable to volatile commodity prices and unfavourable changes in the terms of trade, which make Africa's primary produce cheap relative to Western industrial products. Prices for most of its exports – competing with European and American subsidized agriculture – have generally declined over the past half century.

In 2005, the general economic outlook for Africa remained bleak. The modest success in agriculture and new plantation enterprises, such as those developed by Swaziland's sugar industries in the 1950s and 1960s, coupled with the successful exploitation of mineral resources in Niger, Mauritania, Guinea, Liberia, Togo, Gabon, Congo, Angola, Cameroon, Nigeria and Botswana, seemed to promise future growth. However, since the 1970s, Africa's modest successes have turned to failure. Investment capital was diverted to provide a booming population with essential services. Oil prices, which had increased sixfold during the 1970s, fell sharply in the 1980s. Prices of copper and other minerals followed suit. Competing cheaper supplies reduced tropical Africa's share of world trade to its lowest level anyone can remember. Algeria and Nigeria, at one time considered classic examples of indigenous economic progress, have become economically crippled.[22] One cannot imagine how oil-rich Nigeria became the chaotic country it is. The proportion of people living in severe poverty has increased despite decades of profitable oil production. Its experience confirms the dictum that in poor countries oil money never reaches the poor; it is looted before that happens. Angola, Congo and Sudan, all potentially rich states, are bankrupt (see Appendix 2).

More disturbing is the fact that independence has been followed by a steady decrease in per capita food production. In 1957 nine-tenths of Africa fed itself; now, while there are some agricultural successes (Ghana and Mauritania have increased their grain production considerably), the Republic of South Africa is one of the few states self-sufficient in food. Most major Western-induced agribusiness experiments in Africa – designed to serve Western rather than African interests – have failed. Food production per capita between 1961 and 1995 fell by 12 per cent. The stress placed by the World Bank and the IMF on monocropping and the export of raw materials – the post-1945 cash-crop boom – has denied many countries the broad-based economic growth they so badly need.

Part of the dramatic change in Africa's food production must also be ascribed to widespread and devastating drought, which has affected the continent for more than a decade. Some of its economic troubles can be put down to unwise state interference and the fact that, for Africa, there has been no 'green revolution'. Increases in human and animal pestilence, locust plagues, general mismanagement and the loss of arable land have also reduced the food supply. Added to which, Africa suffers from the growing blights of malaria and HIV-AIDS. Combating these health problems with drugs and other treatment has been beyond its means (although in 2004 there were signs that relief from malaria might come from new developments).

Equally disturbing is the manner in which the infrastructure of Africa's roads, railways, cities and towns (generally built under European rule) has deteriorated.[23] For want of maintenance, industrial plant built or financed by Westerners has also been allowed to fall into disrepair: steel mills are rusting; dams yield no power. Where small, labour-intensive projects were needed, Western-inspired and

-financed technological 'white elephants' multiplied. One wonders how so many ruinous investments ever came to be made. The trouble with debt relief being contemplated by the Western powers is that it might increase the amount spent on arms.

In some respects Africa reflects the negative aspects of Western colonialism. In the post-1945 era it was thought to be an unquestionably good thing to help the underdeveloped world to develop along Western lines. It was a period when ignorance of Africa and Africa's past on the part of the Western banking community was bliss. Ignored were the difficulties of trying to lop off the technology and values of one culture and social history and fasten it on to another.

In all but a handful of African countries, tribal loyalties still persist, especially in rural areas where nationalist sentiment never penetrated. The greater unity sought by the Organization of African Unity (OAU) at its inception in 1963 at Addis Ababa, still has to be achieved.[24] The OAU's successor, the African Union (AU), was formed in 2000, with its lofty ideals of an African army and an EU-type union.

Those African countries that place the blame for their troubles on Western shoulders have supporters around the world. The present political despotism and economic malaise is at least to some degree the result of Western modernity. The disruption of traditional culture – not least the destruction of spiritual and social values associated with tribal life – is partly the result of Western intrusion. Western impact undermined the self-confidence of many Africans. Nor has independence and the end of the Cold War freed Africa from the threat of outside meddling. Witness the interference in Angola and Mozambique, Somalia, Ethiopia, Congo[25] and now the Sudan.

By holding the West responsible for the continent's extreme poverty, internal wars, tribalism, fatalism and irrationalism, autocracy, disregard of the future, stifling of individual initiative, military vandalism, staggering corruption, mismanagement and sheer incompetence, Africans are indulging in an act of self-deception. Ethiopia and Liberia were never colonized, the native people were not dispossessed of their land as elsewhere in Africa, but they remain as poor (or poorer) than other countries. A similar colonial background has not prevented certain Asian countries from achieving rapid economic development. Africa cannot hope to escape from its present economic and political dilemmas by placing the blame on others. If the borders defined by the colonial powers were divorced from reality, why then have the African nations not put them right? An independent Somalia has had no government for the past twelve years. What Africa needs – next to good government – is an increase in domestic and African-directed foreign trade. Outside investment is also needed, but is deterred by the turmoil that plagues the continent.[26] The crucial issue is not intervention or exploitation from outside – indeed, in recent years the West has shown a wilful neglect of Africa – but Africa's inability to cope with problems largely of its own making: a poor economic record, a lamentable failure of leadership and a heightened struggle for power between competing tribes.

The future of Africa is certainly not all doom and gloom. If the continent can break out of the pattern of setbacks that has plagued it since 1945, there is hope. The number of Africans engaged in civil wars in 2005 is far less than in the 1990s; many long-term conflicts have been resolved. South Africa stands as a worldwide example of racial reconciliation. There is much criticism of leadership in Africa today, but out of Africa came an incomparable Nelson Mandela. In May 2005 Ethiopia held its freest elections in thousands of years.

If Africa is to play a necessary and constructive role in the world community, it must first rediscover itself. Only Africans really know where they have been and where they might hope to go. They do not have to have Western values and Western goals to become economically viable; their cultural values are too deeply planted for that to happen. Western values and goals may be entirely inappropriate for them. Nor does their performance have to be judged by Western standards. Ultimately, African intrinsic values and goals must prevail. African ideas, confidence and resolve, rather than foreign leadership and foreign aid – much though it is needed – will eventually determine Africa's future. The continent's human qualities and its rich natural resources offer great hope.

17

Communism and its Collapse in the USSR and Eastern Europe

In 1945 the Russians emerged victorious from the greatest war they had ever fought. Building on an older Russian tradition of expansion, buffer states were made of eastern Poland, Bessarabia, northern Bukovina, eastern Karelia, Ruthenia and northern East Prussia. For the next forty years, Eastern Europe remained in the grip of the Soviet Union (see Map XV).

Having completed his defences against the capitalist West, Stalin proceeded to put the communist house in order. In 1948 he imposed his will on the Czech government, expelled the Yugoslavian Communist Party from the Cominform on the grounds of deviation from Marxism–Leninism, and, defying the Americans, laid siege to Berlin. In 1949 he purged other recalcitrant communist leaders, including the general secretary of the Polish Communist Party, Wladyslaw Gomulka (1905–82). In 1950, to counter American encirclement, the Soviets concluded a mutual defence treaty with China. They also gave support to national liberation movements in British Malaya and French Indo-China, as well as to North Korea in its invasion of South Korea.

On 5 March 1953, with the fate of South Korea still undetermined, Stalin died. He had defeated German attempts to enslave his country and post-war American attempts to encircle it. His first two five-year plans (1927–37) had made the USSR the world's third most powerful industrial state.

Stalin was replaced by the triumvirate of Georgi Malenkov (1902–88), Nikolai Bulganin (1895–75) and Nikita Khrushchev.[1] The formerly all-powerful Lavrenti Beria (1899–1953) was summarily executed as an 'imperialist spy'. In 1955 Khrushchev became first secretary of the Communist Party and later chairman of the Council of Ministers. Under pressure from him, Malenkov resigned as premier. At the Twentieth Communist Party Congress in February 1956 Khrushchev shocked the communist world by denouncing Stalin's brutality and narrow interpretation of Marxist doctrine. Far from having saved the USSR, he contended that Stalin had brought the country to the brink of defeat. Khrushchev's criticism brought him much support from the younger members of the Communist Party. In 1958, with Bulganin's resignation, he assumed sole power. In 1961, at the Twenty-second Party Congress, having survived an attempt to overthrow him, he delivered a second tirade against Stalin.

During the 1950s Khrushchev released most of Stalin's political prisoners, and adopted a policy of peaceful coexistence with the West. He expanded the Soviet space programme, launching the first satellite, *Sputnik*, in 1957. (The Soviet Union maintained a lead in manned space flights until 1969, when the US spacecraft *Apollo 11* landed on the moon.) However, his attempt to reduce Russia's dependence on the West for grain by ploughing the virgin steppes of Kazakhstan was an ecological disaster. In 1959 he became the first Soviet ruler to visit America. He also furthered Soviet influence in India, Korea, Vietnam and Cuba.

In October 1964 Khrushchev was ousted by Brezhnev, Kosygin and Podgorny. The reasons given for his dismissal were advanced age and poor health. Subsequent Russian explanations of his fall included recklessness, the Cuban Missile Crisis, his ideological feud with Mao Zedong and his ineffective economic performance. Under his watch, Romania and Albania had reasserted their full or partial independence; Soviet security in Eastern Europe was threatened. Although Khrushchev had not hesitated to put down the Hungarian revolt in 1956, his policy of détente with the Western powers had antagonized many of the Russian elite, especially Stalinist loyalists. He was also criticized for reducing the all-powerful Red Army.

Although instrumental in removing Khrushchev, Brezhnev continued his predecessor's policy of coexistence with the West. Despite America's intervention in Vietnam, war between the superpowers was avoided. In April 1971 Brezhnev openly supported détente and accepted the concept of strategic arms parity. Under SALT I (1971) he agreed to limit the production and deployment of nuclear weapons, and was eager to see SALT II concluded and approved by the US Senate. Trade with the USA was also encouraged.

Conciliatory as Brezhnev appeared to be (especially when compared with Khrushchev's earlier occasional threats and bluster), he protected the Soviet Union's interests. With his coming to power, Soviet strength on land and sea was increased rapidly; its sea power in the Pacific and Indian oceans was enlarged. In 1968 he halted the erosion of Soviet control in Eastern Europe by invading Czechoslovakia with Warsaw Pact forces; Alexander Dubcek's (1921–92) liberation movement was crushed. In December 1979 Brezhnev began Russia's invasion of Afghanistan. On the home front, he refused to yield to American demands over human rights, prosecuting Russian dissidents more assiduously than ever. Regardless of Russia's dependence on the West for grain, animal feed and highly sophisticated technology, he rejected Western attempts to interfere in Russia's internal affairs. The massive military aid he gave in the late sixties and early seventies to North Vietnam helped to ensure its victory over the South.

After his death in 1982, Brezhnev was replaced by Yuri Andropov (1914–84). Andropov was in turn replaced in 1984 by Konstantin Chernenko (1911–85), who died soon afterwards. In 1985 Mikhail Gorbachev (b. 1931)[2] became general secretary of the Communist Party of the Soviet Union (CPSU). A protégé of Andropov, he had risen to power quickly. Until his accession, there had been no real will to move beyond the elaborately centralized socialism prescribed by Marx as the precursor to the true communist era. Gorbachev's book *Perestroika* (economic and social restructuring),[3] published in 1987, although critical of the economic stagnation in the Soviet Union and its satellites, did not suggest the abandonment of communist ideology in geopolitics; communism was still preferable to Western capitalism. The growing gap between the living standards of the communist countries and the democratic West left him with little other choice. Yet his acceptance of the profit motive, free enterprise and a market economy, as well as private property and the freedom of religion, all flew in the face of Bolshevik doctrine. Like Luther and the Christian Church, his purpose was to reform communism, not destroy it. Like Luther, he was accused of heresy.

Gorbachev's actions led to a whirlwind of events, which he was unable to control. Seemingly overnight, the whole communist edifice began to crumble. In 1989 the Berlin Wall fell, symbolizing the collapse of communism. One after another, the satellite states of the Soviet Union began to break away from Moscow. In 1990 the constituent republics of the Soviet Union sought greater independence; freedom of religious worship was confirmed. In November 1990 the Cold War was formally ended; forty-five years of division in Europe had come to a close. In August 1991 CPSU activities were suspended; in the same month the Warsaw Pact was dissolved; in November the CPSU and the Russian Communist Party were banned; in December the USSR broke up into fifteen separate states. On 25 December, Gorbachev resigned as general secretary of the CPSU (which he had not reformed but destroyed). He also resigned as the first president of the USSR, a position he had helped to create, and which was now redundant. When he left the Kremlin, the red flag was replaced by the white, blue and red flag of the Russian Federation. Born in 1917 in the tumult and suffering of a terrible civil war, the USSR disappeared almost without a murmur. Gorbachev was as stunned by the turn of events as anyone else.

The communist system was deeply flawed long before Gorbachev appeared on the scene; ideas of independence and democracy were in the air before he assumed power. The ruinous arms race which led to the impoverishment of both superpowers was not his doing; hence his willingness to reduce conventional and nuclear armaments in 1987. In 1988 he negotiated the Intermediate-Range Nuclear Forces (INF) Treaty with the USA to reduce nuclear forces in Europe. Nor was he responsible for the invasion of Afghanistan – a war which he could not win, and which he could only end in 1989, after eight futile years, by damaging himself and the morale of the Red Army. Similarly, the

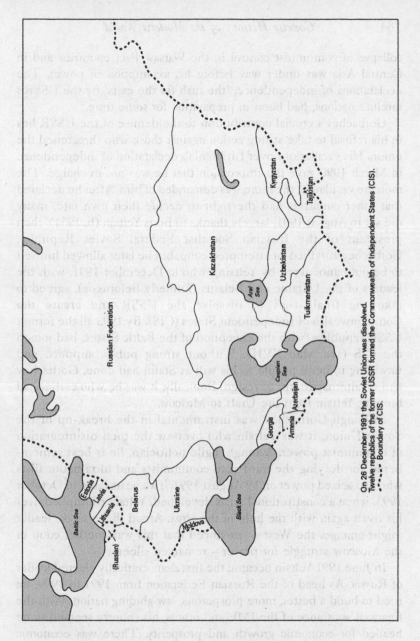

Kyrgyzstan

Tajikistan

Kazakhstan

Uzbekistan

Aral
Sea

Turkmenistan

Russian Federation

Caspian
Sea

Azerbaijan

Armenia

Georgia

On 26 December 1991 the Soviet Union was dissolved.
Twelve republics of the former USSR formed the Commonwealth of Independent States (CIS).
- - - - Boundary of CIS.

Estonia

Latvia

Lithuania

Baltic
Sea

Belarus

(Russian)

Ukraine

Moldova

Black Sea

Map XVII The Break-up of the Soviet Union in 1991

collapse of communist control in the Warsaw Pact countries and in Central Asia was under way before his assumption of power. The declarations of independence, 'the rush for the exits' by the USSR's satellite nations, had been in preparation for some time.[4]

Gorbachev's crucial contribution to the demise of the USSR lies in his refusal to take strong action against those who threatened the union. His vacillations over Lithuania's declaration of independence in March 1990 gave the impression that he was not in charge. The more he vacillated, the more was demanded of him. After he declared that other countries had the right to decide their own fate, many did so. In August 1991, largely thanks to Boris Yeltsin (b. 1931), then president of the Russian Socialist Federal Soviet Republic, Gorbachev survived an attempted coup, but he later allowed himself to be outmanoeuvred by Yeltsin,[5] who in December 1991, with the leaders of the Ukraine and Belarus (formerly Belorussia), agreed to take the final steps to dissolve the USSR and create the Commonwealth of Independent States (CIS). By 1993 all the former USSR republics, with the exception of the Baltic States, had joined the CIS (see Map XVII). Without strong public support, and unwilling to bend people to his will as Stalin had done, Gorbachev had no alternative but to resign. Ironically, it was he who earlier had brought Yeltsin from the Urals to Moscow.

Although Gorbachev was instrumental in the break-up of the Soviet Union, it was Yeltsin who oversaw the total disintegration of communist power. A tough, agile politician, he is best remembered for defying the hard-core communists and ultra-nationalists who had seized power on 19 August 1991. Two years later, in October 1993, when a constitutional crisis developed, Yeltsin triumphed over his rivals again with the help of the army. Afraid that a worse leader might emerge, the West – convinced that this was another coup in the Moscow struggle for power – remained silent.

In June 1991 Yeltsin became the first democratically elected leader of Russia. As head of the Russian Federation from 1991 to 1999, he tried to build a better, more prosperous, law-abiding nation. With the financial assistance of the IMF and others, his country seemed to be headed for economic growth and prosperity. There was economic restructuring and massive privatization of state-owned enterprises.

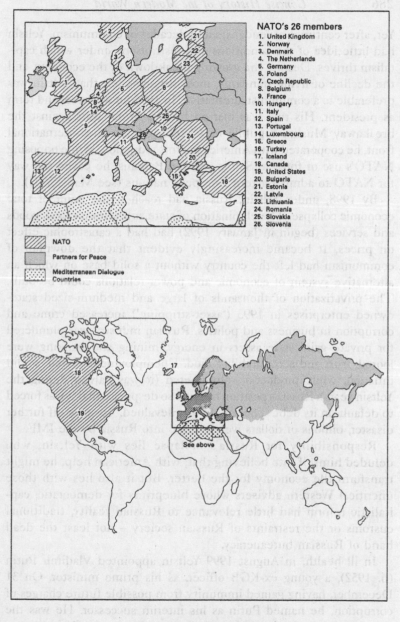

Map XVIII   NATO in 2004

Yet, after centuries of feudalism and decades of communism, Yeltsin had little idea of the conditions and institutions under which capitalism thrives. Despite the growing breakdown of the economy, and the decline of living standards, most Russians felt that Yeltsin was preferable to a communist alternative. In 1996 he won a second term as president. His rule was marred by two brutal wars against the breakaway Muslim republic of Chechnya.[6] On the international front, he cooperated with America in arms reduction. While opposing NATO's use of force in Serbia and the Balkans, he paved the way for NATO to admit Eastern European nations (see Map XVIII).

By 1998, under Yeltsin, Russia had reached the point of total economic collapse. The elimination of state subsidies on food, goods and services (begun in January 1992) had had a catastrophic effect on prices. It became increasingly evident that the downfall of communism had left the country without a solid base on which an alternative system of economic and power relations could be built. The privatization of thousands of large and medium-sized state-owned enterprises in 1993 ('asset-stripping') increased crime and corruption in business and politics. Russian industry was plundered for private gain; state assets in energy, mining and banking were looted; trust and accountability died. Unemployment soared, as did inflation, while production plummeted (it was halved during the Yeltsin years). Russia's position became so desperate that it was forced to default on its debt. The rouble was devalued. To stave off further disaster, billions of dollars were poured into Russia by the IMF.

Responsibility for Russia's collapse lies with Yeltsin, who deluded himself into believing that, with American help, he might transform the economy for the better. But it also lies with those uncritical Western advisers whose blueprints for democratic, capitalistic reform had little relevance to Russian reality, traditional customs or the restraints of Russian society – not least the dead hand of Russian bureaucracy.

In ill health, in August 1999 Yeltsin appointed Vladimir Putin (b. 1952), a young ex-KGB officer, as his prime minister. On 31 December, having gained immunity from possible future charges of corruption, he named Putin as his interim successor. He was the first Russian leader in modern times to cede power voluntarily.

In March 2000 Putin became president of the Russian Federation. He brought with him the asset which Russia most needed: stability. His toughness in handling the war in Chechnya – he scorned negotiations with the rebels – found general approval, but led to further terrorism. To the relief of the West, he affirmed his belief in a democratically controlled free market system. In words at least he left no doubt about his allegiance to free speech and the rights of private property. Thus far, he has been remarkably discreet about NATO's eastward drive and the EU's absorption of several ex-communist countries – which many Russians see as a dangerous intrusion into their sphere of influence. He has also been conciliatory to the other great powers and has accepted the independence of the Baltic States. In April 2000 he ratified two nuclear weapons treaties: the START II[7] arms reduction accord and the Comprehensive Nuclear Test-Ban Treaty. On the home front he declared war on terrorism, and introduced much-needed tax reform. From the start he has been engaged in a power struggle with regional chieftains, business tycoons and organized crime. In the Russian tradition he has placed stress on communal rather than individual benefits. His greatest strength has been to seek Russian solutions to Russian problems. Helped by high oil prices (after Saudi Arabia, Russia is the world's second-largest oil exporter), a very cheap currency, increased foreign investment, a trade surplus[8] and an improved growth rate (economic growth in 2004 was a record 8.3 per cent), the Russian economy has markedly improved under his stewardship.

By trying to consolidate his influence in the Ukraine, Belarus, Moldova, Armenia, Georgia and Azerbaijan, his critics say he has been trying to rebuild the old Soviet Union. The Ukraine has been persuaded to align its policies on military cooperation, weapons production and arms sales with Russia. There is cooperation between Russia and the Ukraine in European and other international organizations. In November 2004 Putin tried to influence Ukraine's presidential elections on the side of Viktor Yanukovych, who is pro-Russian. In December the victory went to Viktor Yushchenko, who is more Western inclined. In March 2005, following a popular uprising in Kyrgyzstan, Russian-leaning Askar Akaev was ousted from the presidency and fled to Moscow. Georgia, Ukraine and Kyrgyzstan have all broken free of Russian influence. It is feasible that parts of the old Central Asian Russian empire – Kazakhstan, Uzbekistan and Turkmenistan might follow suit. A popular uprising in Uzbekistan in May 2005 was crushed brutally.

While making friendly gestures to the Western powers, Putin, his critics argue, is in fact a ruthless calculator of Russia's national interests. Responding to the Beslan massacre of schoolchildren, he was quick to blame outsiders plotting to undermine the Russian state. He has sanctioned a 27 per cent increase in defence spending (almost $20 billion in 2005), conscription has been tightened; military training has been introduced in schools. And while talking about free speech, he has gagged the media. Whatever Putin's drawbacks, the relations between Russia and the West are better than they were under the much more eccentric Yeltsin. There are also growing improvements in everyday life. In its struggle to improve the common good, there are many things in Russia's favour: an indomitable spirit, vast material resources and an army of talented, skilled labour. Moreover, unlike the situation before 1991, there has been an extension of freedom: an elected parliament makes laws; private property has been established as a foundation of personal liberty; criminal and civil codes of justice have been enacted; and people can live, move about and change their jobs as they were never able to do in the pre-Gorbachev USSR. It may be another decade or more in the making, but Russia's strength as a great power is rising.

The breakdown of communist control in Russia in the late 1980s – 1989 was the crucial year – was accompanied (in some cases preceded) by threats to communist authority in other parts of Eastern Europe. As economic conditions worsened – they had fallen behind those of the West from the 1950s onwards – the governments of East Germany, Poland, Hungary, Czechoslovakia, Romania and Bulgaria were all induced to yield to the demand for political change. Freedom from communist control spread across Eastern Europe swiftly. Despotism was replaced by fairly free democratic elections (see Map XIX).

The overwhelming victory in June 1989 of Solidarity,[9] an anti-communist labour movement led by Lech Walesa (b. 1943), in

Map XIX Central and Eastern Europe in 2004

*Yugoslavia in 2000 consisted of
Serbia and Montenegro.
Prior to 1992 it included Croatia,
Slovenia, Bosnia-Herzegovina
and Macedonia.

EU Member States   ● NATO Member

Joined EU in 2004   ● Joined NATO in 1999

Applicant EU countries   ○ Joined NATO in 2004

Poland resulted in the establishment in August 1989 of a non-communist government, the first in forty years. Walesa became president on 22 December 1990. (Nine years earlier martial law had been imposed; labour leaders like Walesa had been imprisoned; the Solidarity movement had been crushed.) In 1993, however, Solidarity lost control to the ex-communists and their allies. The ex-communists won again in 1997; non-communists simply did not have the administrative skills or experience to replace them successfully. Although in 1995 Walesa was replaced by a former communist, Aleksander Kwasniewski (b. 1954, who was re-elected in October 2000), Solidarity's victory in June 1989 had been the spark that ignited the unravelling of communist power in Poland and elsewhere. In 1999 Poland joined NATO. It became a member of the EU in 2004.

In October 1989, Hungary peacefully declared itself a non-communist republic. In the free elections in March 1990 communism was repudiated at the polls; the introduction of democracy and a free market economy based on the Western model were subsequently acclaimed. In June 1991, forty-seven years of Soviet occupation ended. In 1997 Hungary formalized relations with the Catholic Church. Like Poland, in April 1999 it became a member of NATO, and in 2004 joined the EU.

Also in October 1989, large anti-government riots took place in Bulgaria. By December the Communist Party leader and head of state Todor Zhivkov (1911–98), who had held power for thirty-five years, had been unseated. In January 1990, he was convicted of corruption and abuse of power and jailed. The dominant role of the Communist Party was revoked, whereupon the Bulgarian communists renamed themselves the Bulgarian Socialist Party, and managed to retain control. Not until April 1997 did the Union of Democratic Forces, an anti-communist group, win parliamentary elections. In 1999, under NATO command, Bulgaria blocked Russian supplies to Yugoslavia during the Kosovo crisis.

Following widespread demonstrations, in November 1989 the communist government of Czechoslovakia also collapsed. In December, the first government in forty-one years without a communist majority took power. The writer Vaclav Havel (b. 1936) became its new president. He was defeated in 1992. A strong Slovak nationalist movement having emerged, on 1 January 1993 the country was divided into the Czech Republic and Slovakia. In March 1999 the Czech Republic joined NATO. Both it and Slovakia joined the EU in 2004.

In Romania on 16 December 1989, following the killing of hundreds of anti-government demonstrators at Timisoara, riots took place in the capital, Bucharest. On 25 December, the president, Nicolae Ceauşescu (b. 1918) and his wife were summarily tried and executed by the newly formed anti-communist Salvation Front. Not until a multi-party system took effect in December 1991 did the communists lose control and a transition to a free market economy began. Communists were swept from power in the elections of November 1996. In December 2000, Ion Iliescu, an ex-communist ex-president, regained the presidency.

By December 1989 the leaders of the East German Communist Party had resigned. In 1990 non-communists won the election. On 3 October 1990 German reunification – which until Gorbachev all Soviet governments had opposed – was achieved. After forty years, Germany was one country again.

The revolutionary yet almost bloodless upheaval that swept through Eastern Europe in 1989 was also felt in communist Albania, which Enver Hoxha (1908–85) had ruled from 1945 until his death as first secretary of the Albanian Communist Party. In 1961 Albania freed itself from Russian intervention. From then until 1978 it was allied with communist China, but in that year, because of Albania's criticisms of Chinese policy, China ended its alliance and cut off all aid to Albania. Yet it was not until March 1991 that the anti-communist forces succeeded in obtaining 'free' elections, which were declared a communist victory. After more demonstrations and a general strike, another election was held in March 1992, in which the communists were routed, and the first non-communist president since the Second World War, Sali Berisha (b. 1944), was appointed. The anti-communist forces won again in 1996. Since then government in Albania has bordered on anarchy. During 1996–7, in an attempt to restore order, a seven-thousand-strong UN security force occupied the country. During NATO's air war against

Yugoslavia, in March–June 1999, almost half a million ethnic Albanians from Kosovo found refuge in Albania. Since then, driven by hunger and fear, many Albanians have fled to Italy and the rest of the EU.

The coming of political change in Yugoslavia followed a different and a much more tragic course.[10] In January 1946, the six republics that had emerged from the Second World War – Bosnia-Herzegovina, Slovenia, Croatia, Serbia, Montenegro and Macedonia[11] – became the Socialist Federal Republic of Yugoslavia with Josip Broz Tito at its head. Under Tito's strong rule any attempt on the part of these republics to secede – there had been rumblings of separatism since 1946, especially in Croatia – was crushed. A Croat himself, Tito curbed Serbia's aspirations for a Greater Serbia by creating two autonomous provinces within Serbia: the republics of Voivodina in the north, which had a large Hungarian minority, and the largely Albanian-populated Kosovo in the south. A test of will between Tito and Stalin in 1948 resulted in Yugoslavia's expulsion from the Cominform. As a result, Yugoslavia drew closer to the West.

The federal republic that Tito had crafted remained united until his death in May 1980. Thenceforth, until the late 1980s, Yugoslavia's government was a rotating system of succession representing each republic. Because each republic had its own agenda, it was a system that pleased few. Discord and squabbling, which Tito would have stifled at birth, grew.

Caught up in the reform movement sweeping through Eastern Europe in the late 1980s, in January 1990 a Yugoslav Communist Party conference renounced the constitutionally guaranteed right of communism to have the leading role in government. There was also a call for a more democratic order, an independent judiciary and a mixed (command and private) economy. In the multi-party elections in Slovenia, Croatia, Bosnia-Herzegovina and Macedonia in April–May 1990, the non-communist parties which had triumphed at the polls proposed a new federal structure, favouring separatism. But, as everyone knew, this threatened the ethnic identity and religion of the minorities within a state's boundaries. After endless negotiations between the six republics had failed to find a solution,

Slovenia (where there were few Serbs and conflict was short-lived) and Croatia (where there were large Serbian-populated areas) declared their independence in June 1991. Bosnia-Herzegovina followed in March 1992. All of them feared Serb hegemony.

Bitter fighting between the different ethnic and religious groups in the three republics broke out almost at once. The pent-up fury and age-old animosity between Christians and Muslims, as well as between Slovenes, Croats and Serbs (especially in Croatia) exploded. The subsequent intervention of the Yugoslav army (increasingly a Serb army) resulted in the most devastating European war in half a century. To some, such as Slobodan Milosevic (b. 1941),[12] it was a war against secession; for him the unity of Yugoslavia was at stake. Others saw the war between Serbia and Croatia as a land grab on Milosevic's part. Accompanied by massacre (the Hague Court ruled that the massacre at Srebrenica was genocide[13]) and torture, the bitter hatreds of internecine warfare in that area during the Second World War were revived. For three years, 1991–4, a horrified world looked on. Macedonia – territory freed from the Ottoman Empire in 1913 – was the only republic to secede from Yugoslavia without bloodshed.

The recognition of the independence of Slovenia, Croatia and Bosnia-Herzegovina by many states in 1992 did not stop the Serbs from extending their rule in Bosnia to 70 per cent of its territory. The idea of a Greater Serbia was revived. Both Croatia and Serbia would gladly have divided Bosnia – and had agreed to do so before war began. The conquest of Bosnia-Herzegovina by the Serbs appeared certain until the USA and its NATO allies – disregarding their UN obligations – finally intervened with air strikes in May and August 1995. The siege of Sarajevo was lifted in September. At a conference at Dayton, Ohio, in December 1995 it was agreed to create two autonomous ethnic regions – one Serb the other Muslim–Croat – each region occupying about half of the country; American and European troops were provided for peacekeeping.

As a result of the Dayton Accord, the Federal Republic of Yugoslavia was divided into five independent sovereign republics – Slovenia, Croatia, Bosnia-Herzegovina, Serbia and Macedonia. With Croat and Serb entities still opposed to the independence of Bosnia-Herzegovina, the survival of that state is uncertain.[14]

Meanwhile, the long-standing struggle between Serbs and ethnic Albanians in the Yugoslavian province of Kosovo had worsened. Yugoslavia's response (under its socialist president Slobodan Milosevic) in 1990 to the ethnic Albanian proclamation of an independent Republic of Kosovo had been to revoke Kosovo's autonomy and rule its province by force. To the Serbs, there could be no question of allowing the Muslims to rule an area to which they had a deep historical claim. There followed endless negotiations and bitter fighting between the two sides. In 1997–8, among terrible atrocities and retribution, hundreds of thousands of Kosovars were forced to flee to Albania and Macedonia. Diplomacy having failed, in 1999 the USA and its NATO allies intervened militarily on the side of the ethnic Albanians. From March to June an air war was waged against the Serbs in Kosovo and Serbia proper. Its main object was to stop the 'ethnic cleansing' of Albanians.

In June 1999, Serbia was forced to surrender. It was compelled to remove its troops from Kosovo and a multinational peacekeeping force (from France, Italy, Britain, Germany and the USA) took control. With NATO's help, by September 1999, most Kosovan refugees had returned home. Fearing revenge, seventy thousand Serb civilians fled the impoverished region.

Defeated in presidential elections in September 2000, followed by an uprising in Serbia in October, Milosevic was replaced by another Serb nationalist, Vojislav Kostunica (b. 1944). By November, Yugoslavia, after being excluded for eight years, was readmitted to the UN. In the December election, Milosevic's ex-communists were thoroughly defeated at the polls. In April 2001, Milosevic was arrested by the Yugoslav government on charges of war crimes and handed over to the Hague Court for trial. In 2003 Yugoslavia was renamed Serbia and Montenegro.

In 2004 tension was rising in Kosovo again. The ethnic Albanians refuse to return to the autonomy they knew before Milosevic withdrew it in 1990. They demand complete independence, which no Yugoslav government could grant. The Albanians now terrorize the remaining Serbs as the Serbs had terrorized them. As in other parts of the war-torn Balkans, growing fears are being expressed about the possible withdrawal of Western peacekeeping troops. Their removal could cause a flare-up in the Balkans again. Unless another round of ethnic cleansing is to take place, peacekeeping is in for the long haul. In 2004 an EU-led peacekeeping force (EUFOR) took over from NATO in Bosnia-Herzegovina.

In 2005, a surprising development in the work of the war crimes tribunal in The Hague took place, when the prime minister of Kosovo, Ramush Haradinaj, surrendered to the court. Until then, genocide and gross human rights violations were thought to be uniquely Serbian. Thus far, Croatia has refused to hand over its fugitives.

A fragile peace reigns in the Balkans; ancient animosities remain and fester. The hope is that people of different ethnic groups, national and religious, having lived together peacefully before, might do so again. The present peace satisfies no one, but it is preferable to war. Even if the Western peace effort succeeds, it will be a long time before the wounds inflicted during the present and past wars heal. A tolerant multi-ethnic, multi-religious society seems as far away as ever. In the absence of strong control, there never has been a lack of excuses for making war in the Balkans (see Map XX).

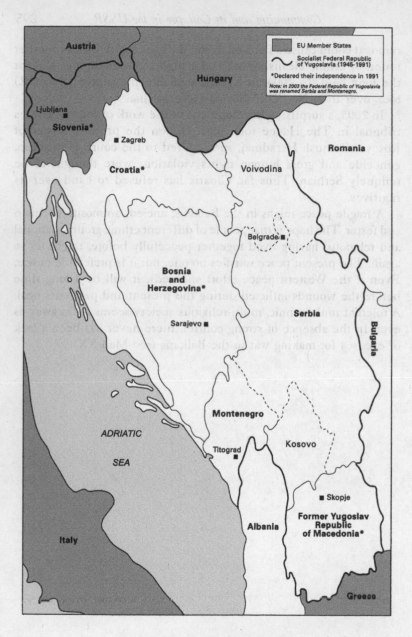

Map XX The Balkans, 1991-2004

18

Latin America and the United States in the Twentieth Century

There can be few areas of the world as complex or as rich in paradox as Latin America. Although most of the sovereign republics are strongly Iberian in culture and language, it is the enormous ethnic variation, the startling contrast, not the common pattern, that prevails. For most of the twentieth century, the countries varied from repressive military, authoritarian regimes – typified by the *caudillo* (Paraguay until 1989) – to liberal and democratic governments. Argentina, Mexico and southern Brazil are industrially developed economies. Ecuador and Paraguay, among others, are essentially agricultural economies. Brazil and the Caribbean nations share a distinct plantation tradition.

After the end of the nineteenth century, while Europe's influence on Latin American affairs declined, that of the United States grew. Even before the twentieth century began, in 1895, the US secretary of state, Richard Olney (when dealing with Britain's boundary dispute between British Guiana and Venezuela), declared his country's supremacy throughout the region. 'The United States', he said, 'is practically sovereign on this continent, and its fiat is law upon the subjects to which it confines its interposition.' It was a conclusion the British did not contest; nor did Latin America. In 1901, in the Hay–Pauncefote Treaty, Britain gave the USA a free hand in the Caribbean. (Britain at that time was more concerned with the Germans in the North Atlantic, the Russians in Manchuria, the Dutch in South Africa and the French on the Nile.)

Also in 1901, as a result of a vacuum of power created by the Spanish–American War of 1898, the USA extended its rule to the Spanish colonies of Cuba and Puerto Rico. Under the Platt Amendment to the new Cuban Constitution (1901), the USA assumed the right to intervene in Cuba and to set up a naval base at Guantánamo Bay, which it still occupies. In 1903, by which time Britain had definitely conceded primacy in Latin American affairs to the USA, President Theodore Roosevelt, who advised his countrymen to 'speak softly but carry a big stick', supported a revolution in Colombia's northern province, which eventually became the state of Panama. In 1904 the new nation authorized the USA to build the 51-mile-long Panama Canal joining the Gulf of Mexico and the Pacific. 'I took the Canal Zone,' Roosevelt declared forthrightly, 'and . . . while the debate goes on the Canal does also.'[1] Begun in 1904, the canal was completed in 1914. It gave the US naval forces easy access to both the Atlantic and the Pacific.

Under a corollary (announced by Roosevelt in 1904) to the Monroe Doctrine,[2] the USA reserved the right of unilateral intervention in the Western Hemisphere to rectify 'chronic cases of wrong doing' or an 'impotence which results in the general loosening of the ties of civilized society'. Subsequently, under the presidencies of Taft, who became known for his 'Dollar Diplomacy', Wilson, who seemed determined to recreate Latin America in the image of the United States, Warren G. Harding (b. 1865; president 1921–3) and Calvin Coolidge (b. 1872; president 1923–9; d. 1933), the USA assumed the right not only to police Latin America, but to judge it.

Nor did the USA fail to match words with deeds. Altogether, between 1898 and 1924, citing threats to the lives and property of its citizens, it intervened directly thirty-one times in the internal affairs of Latin America. In 1904, 1912, 1916–24 and 1965, the US army intervened in the Dominican Republic. Similar interventions were made in Honduras (1912–19, 1924–5), Nicaragua (1909–10, 1912–25 and 1926–33, and covertly in the 1980s during the Contra scandal) and Haiti (1915–34, 1994, 2004). There were also military incursions into Panama (1964 and 1989), Jamaica (1980) and Grenada (1983). In 1914, during Mexico's revolution (begun in 1911 by the Indian sharecropper Emiliano Zapata (1879–1919)), the US navy bombarded and seized the port of Vera Cruz. From 1914 to 1917 – when Mexico adopted a new constitution – the USA continued its military and naval intervention there.

By the end of the nineteenth century, the admiration of the Latin American countries for the USA had given way to growing distrust. Conscious of the need for common action – despite their own deep-rooted divisions[3] – they sought to improve relations with each other. Anxious to increase its own commercial, political and diplomatic influence throughout the hemisphere, the USA encouraged the movement. To that end, it hosted the First International Conference of American States in Washington, DC, in 1889. From this meeting sprang the Washington-based International Union of American Republics, which in 1910 became the Pan American Union.

With the outbreak of the First World War in 1914, Latin Americans showed a reluctance to follow Washington, which favoured the Allied cause. The USA had to use considerable pressure before eight of the twenty republics (seven of them tiny Caribbean and Central American nations under the financial control of either Britain or the USA) declared their nominal support for the Allies. Cuba and Brazil, most dependent upon US markets and money, were offered military aid; suitably persuaded, five others broke relations with the Central Powers; seven, including Argentina, Chile, Colombia and Mexico (which openly sympathized with Germany[4]), remained neutral. The supplies of primary produce from Latin America were indispensable to the Allied cause. Ironically, although President Wilson at the Paris Peace Conference in 1919 argued for national self-determination for European people, Cuba, the Dominican Republic, Haiti, Nicaragua and Panama remained under US military occupation.

Whereas US political pressure and direct intervention in the period 1900–18 was felt primarily in the lands around the Caribbean, US economic activity was much more widespread. In the closing decades of the nineteenth century (as the world demand for the region's food and raw materials grew) it shared in the growing prosperity of the whole area. By 1914, the USA had become Latin America's largest trading partner. Four years later, it was providing about one-third of the imports and took a little more than one-third of the region's exports. In 1929, the figures were about 40 per cent of the region's total imports and one-third of its exports. In the countries of the Caribbean and Central America, US influence was overwhelming. Like colonial trade elsewhere, the area's raw materials and tropical foods were exchanged for northern manufactures and investment capital.

With little intra-regional trade, and with Europe's share of total trade dwindling, by the 1920s foreign trade with North America had become crucial for many Latin American countries. Their economic destiny relied upon changes in North America and Europe to which they were peripheral and over which they had little influence. The wartime policy of import substitution adopted by Argentina, Brazil, Mexico, Chile, Uruguay and others, which led to the region's first industrialization (especially in Brazil), did little to change this.

Latin America's growing reliance upon its northern neighbour for trade was accompanied by a growing dependence upon US money. Although the USA remained the world's leading debtor nation until the First World War, it had been lending money to its southern neighbours since the 1890s. By 1914, US funds invested in Latin America stood at $1.7 billion, with Mexico and Cuba accounting for 30–40 per cent. By then US investors had acquired 50 per cent of Mexico's oil industry and 40 per cent of its land. Yet US holdings (many of them invested in commerce, public utilities, mines, railways, shipping and agriculture) were small compared with Europe's $7 billion.[5] Until the First World War, Europe and North America between them provided much-needed development capital. The exodus of migrants from Europe before 1914 helped to provide Latin American countries with the necessary skilled labour. Millions of Italians and Spaniards were drawn to Argentina. By 1914 the majority of people in Buenos Aires were foreign born. The populations in the major cities (Buenos Aires, Rio de Janeiro, São Paulo, Mexico City) boomed.

The First World War gave the North Americans a tremendous

opportunity to increase their financial stake in Latin America. US investments in the war years increased by 50 per cent. War-torn Europe had little money to spare; Germany and France suffered considerable losses in their Latin American holdings. Growing sums of US direct business investments were used to develop electrical utilities, railways and mining.[6] In 1920 Latin America was receiving almost half of US direct investments placed abroad. To safeguard its investments, the USA proceeded to impose control on the fiscal and monetary policies of Nicaragua (1911–24), the Dominican Republic (1905–41), Cuba (1920–3) and Haiti (1915–41). In Brazil, Venezuela and Chile, the USA also acted to extend its financial and political control whenever it felt its investments threatened.

Latin America emerged from the First World War with a new spirit of independence and a new sense of world responsibility. A number of the republics joined the League of Nations (the US Congress had declined membership) not only to play a greater role on the world stage, but also to provide a counterweight to what they thought were the growing colonizing ambitions of the USA. The German challenge in the Atlantic had died at the Versailles Peace Conference of 1919; the possible threats from Britain and Japan were removed by the Washington Naval Conference of 1921–2. This left the USA almost invulnerable. Brazil was large enough to lead opposition to US hegemony in Latin America, but its dependence on the coffee market of the USA ruled out any such action. Argentina was antagonistic to the USA but could not obtain support from its neighbours. Except for rare intervention by the League of Nations,[7] there was no counterbalance to US power in the Western Hemisphere.

Fearing no one either inside or outside the region, from 1918 onwards the USA intruded in Latin American affairs whenever it thought fit. In January 1926, it landed troops in Nicaragua to overthrow Emiliano Chamorro's government, which it had refused to recognize. Latin American countries denounced the invasion at the Inter-American Conference at Havana in January 1928, but nothing was done.

Relations between North and South took a turn for the better with the election of President Hoover in 1929. Early on in his presidency he embarked on a goodwill tour of eleven Latin American countries. In 1930, he renounced the Roosevelt corollary to the Monroe Doctrine (which had given the USA the right to intervene in the Western Hemisphere). In March 1933, in his first inauguration address, President Franklin D. Roosevelt declared his 'good neighbour' policy. In December that year, at the Seventh Conference of American States at Montevideo, Uruguay, the USA conceded that no state in the Pan American Union 'had the right to intervene in the internal or external affairs of another'. In 1934, the Platt Amendment of 1901, which had limited Cuban sovereignty, was abrogated by the US Senate. The surrender of treaty rights to intervene in the Caribbean basin followed. US troops were withdrawn from Nicaragua (1933) and Haiti (1934); the financial control that it had exercised in Nicaragua, Haiti and the Dominican Republic was relinquished. Gradually a sense of growing equality and mutual respect replaced the earlier domineering attitude of the USA.

On the economic front, by the mid-1920s, the countries of Latin America – all export dependent – had been hurt by the rapid decline of world trade. Overall, between 1929 and 1932, as the Great Depression worsened, the value of Latin American exports fell by two-thirds – a perilous situation for a region so heavily dependent for its livelihood and its government revenue upon overseas markets.[8] Supplies of foreign capital dried up. In the late 1920s and early 1930s, the price of food and raw materials fluctuated widely. Brazilian coffee, which sold at 22.5 cents a pound in 1929, sold at 8 cents a pound in 1931. The abandoning of the sterling bill of exchange – the most reliable means of financing foreign trade – and the breakdown of the international gold standard compounded the problems. With every country trying to save itself, there was a marked resurgence of economic self-sufficiency. So bad did things become that several of the republics were forced to resort to bilateral barter arrangements with European countries.

Efforts to halt these trends were unsuccessful. Having agreed at the Geneva Conference on Trade in 1927 that 'the time had come to put an end to the increase in tariffs', the USA then enacted the Smoot–Hawley Act of 1930, which did the exact opposite. Nor did the subsequent bilateral scaling down of its tariff levels (under the Reciprocal Trade Agreement Act of 1934) give much relief. By 1934 four-fifths of US financial holdings in South America and the Caribbean were in default. 'The bulk of the foreign loans in these years [1926–8] to public authorities in debtor countries', wrote one authority in 1932, 'would better not have been made.'⁹ (It took a second world war, with its demand for food and raw materials, especially oil, to make good Latin America's inter-war losses in both trade and investment.)

Helping to change the US outlook towards Latin America in the 1930s was the fear of communism. Different kinds of socialism had affected Chile, Brazil, Argentina and Mexico since the depression of the late 1920s. A growing sense of class conflict had developed. Unless Latin America found a way to end its dependency for markets and money on the developed countries of the world, so the socialists argued, the exploitation of Latin America would continue. The rich countries of the Northern Hemisphere, such as the USA, would get richer; the poor countries of the Southern Hemisphere would get poorer. In Brazil in the 1920s and 1930s, and in Argentina in the 1930s, there were armed uprisings of communists, which caused several governments to outlaw the communist parties in their countries. In 1938, under the presidency of Lázaro Cárdenas (b. 1895; president 1934–40; d. 1970), Mexico nationalized its foreign-owned oil resources. Yet the only major communist attempt to seize power by force was the unsuccessful 1935 insurrection led by Luís Carlos Prestes in Brazil.

By then, the menace of communism had been superseded by the much greater menace of world war. So great was the threat of war perceived to be that in December 1936, at the Buenos Aires Conference, Roosevelt warned Europeans that they would 'find a hemisphere wholly prepared to consult together for our mutual safety and our mutual good'. It was rare for an American president to speak of the Western Hemisphere as a whole. The Eighth Pan American Conference held at Lima in December 1938 – by which time both Europe and Asia were on the brink of war – not only reiterated a willingness to guarantee the territorial integrity of member states but expressed a determination jointly to resist foreign intervention in the Americas. In spite of opposition from Argentina, which preferred to seek hemispheric security through the League of Nations rather than through a collective defence pact based in Washington, the North American outlook prevailed.

When war came in September 1939, the foreign ministers of the Pan American states quickly convened at Panama City to devise a neutrality zone for the whole Western Hemisphere. The collapse of the Low Countries and France during the German invasion of May 1940 brought matters to a head. At a meeting in Havana later that year representatives of Latin America and the USA undertook to oppose the transfer of Dutch and French possessions in the Caribbean and the northeast coast of South America to the victorious Germans. It was further agreed that any foreign attack on any country of the Western Hemisphere should be considered as an attack upon them all. While some countries with close relations to Germany, such as Argentina, Chile and Uruguay, still feared the North Americans more than the Germans and the Japanese, the majority were persuaded to follow the US lead. In time all the countries joined the Allies; although Chile, Argentina and Uruguay delayed doing so until 1945. As in the First World War, the unprecedented quantities of Latin American food and raw materials proved vital to Allied success.

The war over, the southern republics met with the USA in Chapultepec in Mexico to work out a common position towards postwar development. Unwilling to sacrifice their independence of action to the United Nations, which was then dominated by European and US interests, the Latin Americans insisted upon a regional organization within the global network. This was a reversal of their attitude in 1919, when, unlike the USA, which had repudiated the League of Nations, they had insisted upon a global rather than a regional organization.

President Truman was persuaded to insert Article 51 into the United Nations Charter, which sanctioned the right of member states to establish regional organizations with powers of enforcement outside of UN authority. The outcome was the Treaty of Reciprocal

Assistance (a defence alliance giving safeguards from aggression from outside and inside the hemisphere) signed by the USA and twenty-one Latin American republics at Rio de Janeiro in September 1947.

As a sequel to the Mexico and Rio meetings, the Ninth International Conference of American States held at Bogotá, Colombia, in 1948 adopted the US-sponsored Charter of the Organization of American States (OAS).[10] The aims were to establish peace and justice throughout the hemisphere, to ensure collective security, safeguard the territorial integrity and independence of the republics and to facilitate their economic, social and political cooperation.

While the United States' primary concern in helping to found the OAS was hemispheric security, the main concern of the republics was to safeguard their sovereign rights. With the onset of the Cold War in 1948, the USA began to look upon the OAS as a military alliance in its fight against communism. In 1952 there had been an uprising among the wretchedly poor of Bolivia, which the USA dubbed 'communist'. The tin mines were nationalized, the Indians were enfranchised and agrarian reform was imposed. Alas, because of the growing poverty of the state, Bolivia's movement for social reform died. When the USA called upon the republics – at meetings in Caracas, Venezuela, in March 1954 – to condemn the domination of any member state by 'the international communist movement', its opinion was accepted only under the threat of economic reprisals.

The reluctance of the Latin Americans to support the USA in the Cold War against the Soviet Union meant that Washington had to act alone. The fall of the agrarian reformist, left-wing government of President Jacobo Arbenz of Guatemala in June 1954 (Arbenz and his communist supporters had antagonized foreign landowners, investors and the military) was widely attributed to covert US actions using armed Guatemalan exiles. Arbenz was followed by Carlos Castillo Armas, who revoked the land reforms, suppressed left-wing political parties and concluded a mutual defence pact with the USA. The Guatemalan affair fanned the smouldering fires of resentment against the United States. When, in 1958, Vice-President Nixon made a goodwill tour of eight of the republics, he met with extreme hostility in Guatemala, especially from the strong native Indian element. Violent crime (organized gangs and drug traffickers) has continued to mar the history of Guatemala; military coups took place in 1982, 1983 and 1993. A thirty-six-year civil war finally ended in 1996, with hundreds of thousands dead or missing. In 2004 Guatemala's besieged democracy still hung in the balance.

The USA took similar direct action against Fidel Castro (b. 1927) and his Marxist–Leninist, state-controlled regime in Cuba (the first communist state in the Western Hemisphere). Having overthrown the US-backed dictatorship of General Fulgencio Batistá (1901–73) in 1959, in June 1960 Castro expropriated the landholdings and refineries of the US sugar companies. In October that year he went on to nationalize US-owned financial, commercial and industrial undertakings on the island. The USA responded by reducing its Cuban sugar quota by 95 per cent, by imposing a trade embargo (still in effect forty years later), by breaking off diplomatic relations (in January 1961) and by making many unsuccessful efforts to assassinate Castro.

In April 1961 President Kennedy launched the disastrous Bay of Pigs invasion by Cuban exiles, who had been mobilized and trained in Guatemala and the USA. In February 1962, at a meeting of the OAS at Punta del Este, Uruguay, the USA succeeded in excluding Cuba from the Organization. Castro's request to the Kremlin for military protection led directly to the missile crisis of October 1962. By siting missiles in Cuba, the USSR challenged US hegemony in its own hemisphere. It also challenged a policy that had been in place since the Monroe Doctrine.

The dual threats of nuclear war and a possible communist take-over in other Latin American countries changed the more tolerant attitude of many Latin Americans towards Castro. In 1964, when Cuba was accused of providing arms to guerrilla movements in the region, the OAS broke off relations. With the exception of Mexico (which went on trading with communist Cuba and China), economic sanctions were upheld by the Organization until 1975. Castro hoped that Cuba would become the centre of Latin American revolution; he was convinced that Bolivia, Paraguay, Haiti, Venezuela, Colombia and the Central American states being exploited by foreign capital were ripe for revolt. But his hopes died with the expedition in 1967 of the Argentinian guerrilla leader Ernesto 'Che' Guevara (1928–67) to Bolivia (where the cry was 'land to the Indians, the mines to the state') and his death there. From then until the collapse of the Soviet Union in 1991 and the termination of Soviet aid, Castro was little more than a pawn in superpower rivalry. In 2004 the US government tried to deny Cuba the all-important remittances from Cubans living abroad. The porcupine relationship between Cuba and the US would be transformed if the present search for oil in the deep waters off Cuba proves to be successful. While Cuba's relations with the USA deteriorate, those with the rest of the world improve.

In November 2004 the Chinese President Hu Jintao and a large number of Chinese businessmen made their way across South America.[11] It was President Hu's first visit to Latin America, taking him to Brazil, Argentina, Chile and Cuba. On his agenda was an unfinished nickel mine in Cuba. In a letter of intent, the Chinese agreed to invest $500 million in Cuba's nickel industry. China also watches Cuba's search for oil with interest.

While Kennedy's handling of the Cuban Missile Crisis undoubtedly raised US prestige in Latin America, his death in November 1963 led to a worsening of hemispheric relations. In 1964 the Johnson administration used strong-arm tactics against rioters in Panama. In 1965, claiming 'to save the lives of our citizens and all people', as well as 'to prevent another communist state in this hemisphere', Johnson – in violation of the OAS Charter – mounted a unilateral military intervention against the Dominican Republic.

Johnson's counter-insurgency policy was continued by Richard M. Nixon (b. 1913; president 1969–74; d. 1994), who abandoned the social and humanistic Kennedy goals. In 1973 Nixon helped to topple Chile's government led by Salvador Allende (1908–73), the first democratically elected Marxist president in the hemisphere. While rampant inflation, government deficits and social tension were important in sealing Allende's fate, his support of the ongoing nationalization of copper and other foreign corporate assets was his undoing. The repressive military junta that succeeded Allende, led by General Augusto Pinochet (b. 1915) and supported by the USA, at once initiated a process of privatization. During the Pinochet years, thousands of dissidents protesting at his dictatorship were killed by the military or 'disappeared'. In 1990 Chile returned to its long democratic tradition. In late 2004, after many attempts to indict him, Chile's highest court ruled that Pinochet should be stripped of his immunity and stand trial.

Under President James Earl ('Jimmy') Carter (b. 1924; president 1977–81), the USA terminated military assistance to several right-wing dictatorships for violation of human rights – a policy he found difficult to apply. In 1977 Carter endeared himself to the Latin American republics by pledging to give up US control of the Panama Canal.[12] In 1980 he opened the door to more than 100,000 refugees (the Mariel Boatlift) from Cuba. But he failed to end the brutal civil war in El Salvador.

With Ronald Reagan's election in 1980, US policy in Latin America once more returned to unilateral military intervention. Reagan lifted the Carter restrictions on military assistance to governments that had been in violation of human rights. The USA intervened militarily in Jamaica in 1980, and in Grenada in 1983 (supposedly to prevent the establishment of a Cuban-dominated regime). The USA also invaded Panama in the autumn of 1989 to capture a former ally, General Manuel Noriega, the head of state, who was suspected of drug trafficking. More relevantly, of late he had opposed American policies. Noriega was tried under US law and jailed. All of these incursions were clear violations of the Charter of the OAS.

Fearful of the establishment of a communist state in impoverished Nicaragua in the 1980s,[13] the USA gave covert financial and military aid to thousands of armed exiles – the Contras – operating from bases in Honduras. In 1986 it was revealed that the Reagan administration – in the hope of releasing Western hostages held in Lebanon – had secretly diverted money to the Contras from illegal arms sales to Iran (the Iran–Contra Affair). In the elections of 1990, weary of war, Nicaraguan support turned from the Marxist guerrilla commander Daniel Ortega to US-sponsored President Violeta Barrios de Chamorro (b. 1929). The US Congress voted Chamorro's government a $300 million loan.

In El Salvador, where more than 75,000 people died in a bloody, twelve-year civil war, the USA also provided military aid to right-wing governments. The civil war finally ended in September 1989.

In 1982, during the Malvinas (Falkland Islands) War, the US unilaterally assisted its NATO ally, Britain. In doing so, it was accused by Latin Americans of practising a double standard; to the traditional charges of subversion and intervention was added the charge of betrayal. Political reality, despite the OAS Charter and its regional structure, was that the USA continued to intervene wherever it felt its interests were threatened.

The United States' apparent disregard for the OAS stems from the disunity and instability existing within the Latin republics themselves. Since the 1930s well over a hundred heads of state have been replaced by other than constitutional means. Bolivia, South America's poorest country, has experienced about two hundred coups since its independence in 1825. A long-standing dispute of the indigenous opposition movement against the exploitation of the country's natural gas by foreign-owned energy companies prompted President Carlos Mesa to submit his resignation in March 2005. Even Brazil, which was spared the worst abuses of *caudillism* (and which in 1989 returned once more from a military junta to popularly elected civilian rule), experienced Getúlio Vargas's (1883–1954) seizing of dictatorial power in 1937. His overthrow in the bloodless revolution of October 1945, and the military coup that once more ousted him from office in 1954, led to his suicide. With US assistance, João Goulart was likewise ousted by the military in 1964. Not until 1985 did the country return to civilian rule.

Since the Second World War Argentina has also been prone to military control. Juan Perón (1895–1974) came to power there in 1946 with the support of organized labour, but also with military support. Despite his populism he was overthrown by the military in 1955, before being reinstated by them in 1973. His death in 1974 was followed by a period of military dictatorship in which twenty thousand Argentinians lost their lives. Following Argentina's defeat by Britain in the Falkland Islands in 1982, a peaceful transfer of power was made from military to civilian rule.

Paraguay experienced thirty-five years of dictatorship under Alfredo Stroessner (b. 1912) until 1989. In 1973 Uruguay became a military dictatorship. In Peru President Alberto Fujimori (b. 1938) came to power in 1990, and set about suspending parts of the constitution and dismissing the congress. With the mineral-based (copper, zinc, gold, oil) economy booming and guerrilla warfare curtailed, he was re-elected in 1995. In July 2000, amid violent disturbances, he was elected again to an unprecedented third term. With the help of the military, he ruled above the law. However, amid many scandals, including accusations of a rigged election, he resigned as president and fled the country. Congress refused his resignation, dismissing him as 'morally unfit'. In July 2001, Alejandro Toledo took over the presidency. He pledged to fight a war on poverty, but in 2005 the poor of Peru were as poor as ever.

Authoritarian governments ruled Venezuela for much of the nineteenth and twentieth centuries. The benevolent despots Cipriano Castro (1858–1924) and Juan Vicente Gómez (1857–1935) ruled from 1899 to 1935. In 1959 the country returned to democratically elected government. Attempted military coups in February and November 1992 failed. The leader of the 1992 coup was a former paratrooper, Hugo Chávez. As a populist, he was elected president with a large majority in December 1998. One of his first acts was to stop the privatization of the oil industry (oil provides 80 per cent of Venezuela's income). In August 1999 he made an undisguised bid to seize absolute power. After being forced by the military to resign, in 2002, with the backing of the masses, he was swept to victory again. A crippling general strike organized by his opponents – who accused him of turning Venezuela into a communist state – resulted in further political violence. Following an attempt to suspend democratic institutions, he was restored to power. In 2003–4 his opponents tried to recall him by referendum but failed. In the spring of 2005 a new penal code was being drafted. This, his opponents charge, will be used to muzzle any opposition. Like Castro in Cuba, Chávez fosters relations with communist China.

Haiti is the poorest country in the Americas. Between 1957 and 1986 it was dominated by the brutal dictatorship of the Duvallier family, who believed in voodoo. With rare interludes of peace, military coups, strikes and violence marred their reign. In December 1990 Jean Bertrand Aristide, a dissident Catholic priest, became the first democratically elected president. In September 1991 he was arrested and expelled by the military, whose power was threatened. In response, in June 1993 the UN imposed a crippling embargo, and in 1994 authorized an invasion by a multinational force. The invasion was averted by the stepping down of the military and the re-appointment of Aristide to office. Without the army (which Aristide had disbanded in 1994), looting, murder and mayhem prevailed. Between 1994 and 1997 US and UN troops tried to restore order. Aristide resigned in 1996, but was re-elected under bizarre conditions in June 2000. In February 2004, with the outbreak of civil war, he was forced to resign again. US and French troops took over the following month. UN forces, including Chinese, arrived in June. In 2005 there still was no sign of a political reconciliation between pro- and anti-Aristide forces. Haiti remains in dire straits.

Wherever one looks in South and Central America (Ecuador, Colombia, Haiti, Nicaragua, Guatemala and Paraguay), legal and illegal armies threaten the democratic process. Latin America is changing, but its democratic roots are flimsy.

After the Second World War, Latin America continued to be precariously dependent on the outside world; especially those countries that rely on one or two major exports, such as Bolivia (tin and coca), Chile (nitrates and copper), Mexico (oil and cotton), Peru (cotton and oil), Uruguay (wool and hides), Venezuela (oil), Colombia (coffee and cocaine), Guatemala (coffee), central Brazil (coffee), Cuba (sugar and tobacco), Central America (bananas) and Argentina (wheat and beef). To add to Latin America's difficulties, the fluctuating price of primary produce has been tilted, since the 1880s, in favour of the manufacturing countries of the Northern Hemisphere. The price of Latin American imports has therefore exceeded the price of exports. However, the oil price rises in the 1970s brought temporary prosperity to oil-producing countries such as Venezuela and Mexico and caused an increase in domestic manufactures. With the discovery of oil in Ecuador in the 1960s an upturn of the whole economy took place. But, by 2000, partly from the fall of oil prices, as well as from inflation and unmanageable debt, Ecuador was in a deep recession. It remains to be seen whether the increase in the price of oil in the twenty-first century will reverse this trend.[14] Overall, from the 1950s onwards, the great population growth in Latin America, which far outstripped economic development, worsened the region's prospects.

Since the 1960s Latin America's disadvantages in world trade and investment were always about to be reversed by political and economic reform. The first and greatest outside effort to promote these changes was President Kennedy's Alliance for Progress,[15] launched in 1961. Though progress was made in some quarters, the Alliance, like all the efforts at integration before and since, proved to be disappointing. The necessary political, social and economic changes, agrarian reform and more equitable tax structures were never made. Gradually, Kennedy's optimistic view about America's role in the world gave way to a more realistic outlook. 'We must face the fact', he said, 'that the US is neither omnipotent nor omniscient . . . that we cannot right every wrong or reverse each adversity – and therefore there cannot be an American solution to every world problem.' With his assassination expectations receded still further, and the momentum of reform in Latin America was lost.

The collapse of the Alliance not only caused growing dissatisfaction with US policy; it encouraged the leaders of Latin America to cultivate inter-regional trade and their economic relations with countries outside the hemisphere. Since the 1970s Germany, Canada and Japan, and more recently China, have all grown in importance. In 2004 Chile, Brazil, Argentina and Cuba were all actively promoting their relations with China. There has also been an increase in the flow of money from Europe, Canada and Asia. Yet the USA still retains the leading position in private and public investments.[16] Chile signed a free-trade agreement with the USA in 2004.

Whatever economic reform there has been, primarily in Mexico, Argentina, Chile, Uruguay and Brazil, has not provided economic stability or independence. On the contrary, in very recent years, Mexico, Brazil and Argentina have all experienced severe setbacks. In too many states the dynamic element for economic change remains not the independent profit-seeking, risk-taking entrepreneur, but what it has always been: the state. While industrialization is under way in several countries, especially in Brazil, Mexico and Venezuela, the Southern Hemisphere cannot yet match the performance of the more industrialized areas of North America, Europe and Asia.

Like all developing countries, the countries of Latin America are plagued by debt. Stimulated by the inundation of Arab petro-dollars during the 1970s, Latin America's foreign debt ballooned. This would not have mattered if the money had been used to create sufficient funds to service the debt and improve economic development. Instead, much of it was used to re-equip and enlarge the military, conceal budget deficits, increase imports, offset flight capital and assuage political allies. Some of the money borrowed from international agencies such as the Inter-American Development Bank, the IMF and the World Bank was used to finance barren projects.

The end of the borrowing spree came with the second oil price shock of 1979. Because of steeply rising interest rates, between 1978 and 1981 Brazil's net interest payments on its foreign debt more than tripled (from $2.7 billion to $9.2 billion). During the 1970s and 1980s debt service payments as a percentage of exports rose sharply. Countries such as Brazil, Argentina, Peru, Ecuador and even oil-exporting countries such as Venezuela and Mexico were by 1984 paying almost half their foreign earnings in servicing their debt.[17] Relief was sought by trying to control the drastic price fluctuations in some of the region's principal exports: oil, copper, bauxite, tin, fruit, coffee, cocoa, iron ore, phosphates and mercury. Attempts were also made to seek relief through the Latin American Free Trade Association (LAFTA),[18] founded in 1960; the Central American Common Market (CACM),[19] 1960; the Andean Group,[20] 1969; the Caribbean Community (CARICOM),[21] including the Caribbean Common Market, 1973; and MERCOSUR, a free-trade agreement between Argentina, Brazil, Paraguay and Uruguay, 1991. Trade under MERCOSUR developed fast from about $40 billion in 1993 to more than double that figure in 2003. The US-proposed Free Trade Area of the Americas (FTAA) might threaten MERCOSUR's own attempts at integration. In December 2004, twelve South American countries signed an agreement to create the South American Community of Nations,

Latin American Republics with dates of independent statehood

1. Antigua and Barbuda[o] 1981
2. Argentina 1816
3. Bahamas[*o] 1973
4. Barbados[o] 1966
5. Belize[o] 1981
6. Bolivia[***] 1825
7. Brazil 1822
8. Chile[***] 1818
9. Colombia[***] 1866
10. Costa Rica[△] 1821
11. Cuba 1898
12. Dominica[o] 1978
13. Dominican Republic[△] 1844
14. Ecuador[***] 1830
15. El Salvador[△] 1841
16. Grenada[o] 1974
17. Guatemala[△] 1839
18. Guyana[o] 1966
19. Haiti[o] 1804
20. Honduras[△] 1838
21. Jamaica[o] 1962
22. Mexico 1821
23. Nicaragua[△] 1838
24. Panama 1903
25. Paraguay 1811
26. Peru[***] 1824
27. Saint Kitts and Nevis[o] 1983
28. Saint Lucia[o] 1979
29. Saint Vincent and the Grenadines[o] 1979
30. Suriname[o] 1975
31. Trinidad and Tobago[o] 1962
32. Uruguay 1825
33. Venezuela[***] 1830

34. Anguilla[oo](UK)
35. Bermuda[oo](UK)
36. British Virgin Islands[oo] (UK)
37. Cayman Islands[o] (UK)
38. French Guiana
39. Montserrat[o] (UK)
40. Puerto Rico (US)
41. Turks and Caicos[oo] (UK)

[o] Member of CARICOM

[oo] Associate member of CARICOM

[*] The Bahamas is a member of the Community but not the Common Market.

[***] Associate member of MERCOSUR

[△] Countries that joined the USA in 2005 to sign the Central American Free Trade Agreement (CAFTA)

Malvinas (Falkland Islands)

Economic groupings in 2004

MCCA (Central American Common Market – CACM)

SAI (Andean Integration System or Andean Community)

CARICOM (Caribbean Community and Common Market)

ALADI (Latin American Integration Association or LAIA, formerly LAFTA) +Cuba joined in 1998

MERCOSUR (Southern Common Market)

Map XXI Latin America in 2004

modelled on the EU. If Cuba becomes an associate member of MERCOSUR it will complicate negotiations over the FTAA (see Map XXI).

One should not allow the seeming intractability of Latin America's political and economic problems – and its acute vulnerability to outside forces – to obscure the richness and potential of the region. Nor should one overlook the region's resilience; it has survived repeated economic storms, made the necessary adjustments, resolved its debt crises and achieved recovery. The region as a whole has also successfully grappled with the problem of hyperinflation. In 2004 inflation in most countries was at a record low. Until the sharp fall in the world demand for raw materials in the 1980s, many countries, including Mexico and Brazil (which together account for half of Latin America's population and 60 per cent of its GDP) and Venezuela, had experienced remarkable rates of growth and development. State control, protectionism and inflation were gradually giving way to privatization (except for oil), liberalization of trade and balanced budgets. The economic reforms occurring in Brazil demonstrate this. In August 2000 it was Brazil, not the USA, which convened the first summit meeting of South American heads of state. Under the left-wing presidency of the popular Luiz Inácio Lula da Silva (b. 1945) it has been bold enough to make plain its aversion to Washington's grandiose plans for free trade throughout the hemisphere. Instead, a new strategic trade relationship is developing between Brazil, China, Russia and India. The visit of China's president to Brazil in 2004 strengthened the ties of trade and investment.

Mexico is also showing new strength. Helped by a North American Free Trade Agreement (NAFTA) with the USA and Canada, which came into effect in January 1994, together with rising oil prices (almost one-third of government revenue comes from oil), Mexico's economic growth began to exceed population growth. This has not affected the enormous illegal immigration to the USA. The forced return of Mexicans who try to cross the US border is a constant strain on diplomatic relations. In July 2000, as a result of corruption and mismanagement, the Institutional Revolutionary Party, which had been in power for more than seventy years, was defeated. In that year Mexico's growth rate, 7 per cent, was at its highest level since 1981.

Perhaps the greatest drawback about Latin America is its volatility. No matter how bright present prospects seem to be, collapse is an ever-present threat. Indeed, the economic and political gains of the early 1990s throughout the region were lost in the second half of that decade. In December 1994 Mexico's hailed 'economic miracle' was undone almost overnight by a precipitous recession. A badly handled devaluation caused money to pour out of the country. For the second time in twelve years Mexico was threatened by default. Only an austerity plan and pledges of US loans amounting to $20 billion saved the currency from collapsing. In 2001 Argentina's boom ended in complete collapse. There were record debt defaults and currency devaluation. It was not until 2003 that the Argentine economy improved, and only then with the help of the IMF. In 2005, Argentina was still fighting debt.

Helping to fuel the region's chronic instability and discontent are the problems of mass urbanization, high levels of population growth, poverty, unemployment, labour unrest,[22] hyperinflation,[23] globalization and corruption. Corruption exists throughout the world, but in Latin America it is endemic. In 1992, the entire cabinet of Brazilian president Fernando Collor de Mello was dismissed on the grounds of alleged corruption. In April of that year Alberto Fujimori sought help from the Peruvian military because the police, the judiciary and the Congress of Peru, so he claimed, were all corrupt. Respect for Peru's legal system was almost zero; a large part of the country was under the sway of the Shining Path guerrillas. In 1996 Mexico accused its ex-president Carlos Salinas de Gortari (b. 1948) of having siphoned tens of millions of dollars out of the treasury. In 1996, President Ernesto Samper Pizano (b. 1950) was accused by Washington of being in collusion with Colombia's drug barons. In 1997 the extraordinary economic achievements of President Fernando Henrique Cardoso (b. 1931) of Brazil were tainted with charges of corruption. In May 2001, new allegations of corruption were being made against Argentina's former president, Carlos Saúl Menem (b. 1930). Arnoldo Alemán Lacayo (b. 1946), who won the presidential election in Nicaragua in 1996, was accused in 2004 of having stolen $96 million during his presidency. A popular uprising against the president of Ecuador, Lucio Gutiérrez (b. 1957), in April 2005 caused him to flee to Brazil. Ousting unpopular presidents has become an accepted procedure in Ecuador during the past decade.

What emerges from Latin America's experience in recent decades is the difficulty of trying to help the region from the outside. As in Africa and the other poorer parts of the world, the economic development of Latin America – even allowing for the large differences between the individual countries – appears to have been much too volatile and complex, and much too paradoxical, for the outside world to be able to introduce fundamental and lasting change. Changes proposed by the IMF and the World Bank, which are seen as US-dominated institutions, have often resulted in greater austerity, insecurity and social unrest. (There is growing scepticism about US pledges to the area.) The gap between rich and poor is wider in Latin America than in almost any other part of the world, despite growing industrialization. Real per capita income in 2004 was lower than it was in the 1980s. In Brazil, Venezuela, Peru and Argentina, it was less than it was in 1970. The harder the Latin American worker works, the less he is paid. Too often, the internationally controlled industrial, commercial and financial sectors of an economy prosper, while the urban and rural poor grow poorer. The outcome is violence, cynicism, discontent and revolt.[24] Anyone who tries to improve the workers' lot pays a heavy price. Latin America is considered to be the world's most dangerous place for trade unionists. In Colombia more than 1300 unionists have been murdered since 1991.

In 2005, the landowning, commercial, financial and industrial oligarchies – in allegiance with the hierarchies of the Church and the military – continue to resist change. Most countries of the region are still committed to the past. Indeed, one might say that most violence has been exercised not to change the status quo – the colonial legacy – but to uphold it. Some believe that the Church might provide a solution. While it has always resisted change, in Brazil, Chile and El Salvador church elements have become progressive; in Chile the Church initiated agrarian reform; in El Salvador it has championed human rights. A theology of liberation, although discouraged by the Vatican,[25] flourishes in this continent; the *communidades de base* (Church-sponsored grass-roots groups) are important, dynamic elements. Efforts to improve conditions are also being made by the growing number of US Protestant missionaries in the area.

Whatever happens in the southern half of the American continent will affect the north and vice versa. Neither region can isolate itself from the other. Increasingly they are joined in trade, industry, business, finance, defence, people and cultural influence. Mexico is now the second-largest trading partner of the USA after Canada; the USA takes more of Mexico's exports (much of them coming from American-owned businesses in Mexico) than any other country. Legal and illegal Hispanic immigrants have given the USA the fourth-largest Spanish-speaking population in the Western Hemisphere. Latin Americans are now the USA's largest minority. Latin American illegal immigrants[26], debt and narcotics threaten the stability of the United States. Washington's financial and military support of Colombia's president Álvaro Uribe Vélez (b. 1952), who came to power in 2002, in his ongoing fight against left-wing FARC[27] and ELN[28] guerrillas, and right-wing paramilitary groups like the AUC,[29] might draw the USA into a quagmire of a war. Since 2000, the United States has given $2–3 billion to Colombia in military and economic aid in an effort to stem the flow of illegal drugs. Colombia is the source of most of the world's cocaine and heroin. No matter what has been done during the past decades to end the illegal drug trade, imports into the US (coming chiefly from Mexico, Colombia, Ecuador, Peru and Bolivia) have grown rather than declined.

'Latin America', said President Bush in 2000, 'often remains an afterthought of American foreign policy.' It still is. In November 2004, with his historic visit to several countries, China's president spent more time in Latin America in three weeks than President Bush spent there in his first four years in office. One attempt in 2005 to redress the USA's neglect of Latin America was the Central American Free Trade Agreement (CAFTA). Politically motivated, the agreement was narrowly approved by Congress. With a population of 550 million[30], Latin America can no longer be an 'afterthought' of the USA. For the first time in the past five hundred years, Asia's growing economic strength is beginning to cast a shadow in this hemisphere.

19

Western Europe and North America: 1945–2004

Out of the ashes of the Second World War – against all the dire predictions – emerged a new and powerful, democratic Western Europe. Nothing expressed its extraordinary recovery more than its growing unity.[1] The free movement of people, goods, capital and services, and the introduction of a common commercial policy, begun in 1948 with the Benelux customs union between Belgium, the Netherlands and Luxembourg, has exceeded all earlier expectations. In the same year France, Great Britain and the Benelux countries signed a defensive alliance at Brussels. Political integration began with the establishment of the European Parliament Assembly in 1949.[2] In 1951, as a result of the initiative of the French statesmen Robert Schumann (1886–1963) and Jean Monnet (1888–1979), there emerged the European Coal and Steel Community.[3] Britain, with its traditional mistrust of continental proposals, refused to join. In 1957, under the Treaty of Rome, the European Economic Community (EEC) and the Common Market were established. Again, Britain declined membership. In 1959, Britain set up an alternative organization by joining with Austria, Denmark, Norway, Portugal, Sweden, Switzerland, Liechtenstein, Finland and Iceland to form the European Free Trade Association (EFTA). In 1973, however, Britain, Ireland and Denmark joined the EEC. In 1987 Greece, Portugal and Spain followed suit.

Assisted by the quickening of the world economy from the 1950s onwards, European union ushered in a period of unparalleled economic growth and prosperity. By 1980, with a population of 250 million, with a productive capacity second to none, with slightly more than half the world's trade, with monetary resources in excess of those of the USA and with the largest merchant fleet, the EEC constituted one of the greatest economic blocs. In 1992 the Treaty of the European Union was signed at Maastricht; the foundation was laid for a single currency and a common foreign policy. In 1994 the European Community (EC) became the European Union (EU). In 1997, at Amsterdam, a greater integration of judicial and financial matters was achieved. In January 1999, Germany and ten other EU countries adopted a common currency, the euro. The Economic and Monetary Union (EMU) was implemented in 2002.[4] Consisting of fifteen countries with a population in 2004 of almost 400 million, the EU was expanded in May of that year by the addition of ten new members, eight of them from Central and Eastern Europe that not too long before were in the grip of communism.[5] The EU now stretches from Ireland to Poland (see Map XXII). Its economic strength is unmatched.

While Europeans do not yet think, still less act, as one, there has been far more consultation and cooperation between them in foreign affairs than ever before. Although common action among them over the war in Bosnia was slow in coming, it was eventually effective. In Brussels, in November 2000, the EU countries began to discuss the idea of establishing a 'rapid reaction force' separate from NATO. This force – still modest in size – took over from NATO troops in Macedonia in March 2003 and Bosnia in November 2004.

In 2005 the European Union was divided between those – Germany in particular – who want closer and stronger integration, and those – led by France and Britain – who do not. The former hope to found a Euro federation with more power and legitimacy given to the institutions of the Union; they seek a new constitution, a common foreign and defence policy and a stronger European Parliament. The anti-federalists want to limit the powers of the multinational body, while strengthening the sovereign powers of the nation states; they do not wish to devolve their sovereignty in foreign policy or defence to a superstate; the nation must remain the linchpin of the whole organization. The minor states, fearing that they might be suppressed by

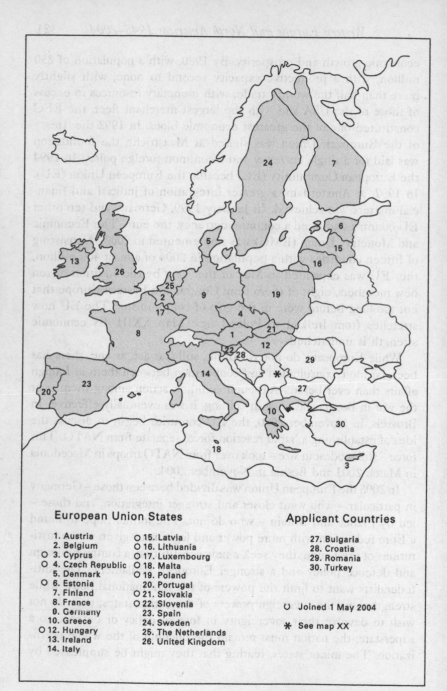

European Union States

1. Austria
2. Belgium
O 3. Cyprus
O 4. Czech Republic
5. Denmark
O 6. Estonia
7. Finland
8. France
0. Germany
10. Greece
O 12. Hungary
13. Ireland
14. Italy

O 15. Latvia
O 16. Lithuania
17. Luxembourg
O 18. Malta
19. Poland
20. Portugal
O 21. Slovakia
O 22. Slovenia
23. Spain
24. Sweden
25. The Netherlands
26. United Kingdom

Applicant Countries

27. Bulgaria
28. Croatia
29. Romania
30. Turkey

O Joined 1 May 2004

* See map XX

Map XXII The European Union 2004

the bigger ones, are also opposed to a supranational federation. With the EU's enlarged membership (from fifteen to twenty-five), the problems surrounding its budget, constitution and control can no longer be deferred. A new constitution was signed on 29 October 2004 in Rome. It is likely to be debated and ratified (or not) in 2005.[6] Endorsed or rejected (as France and the Netherlands did in 2005), it is a landmark in the history of Europe. The test is not only to provide a more stable Union but to see whether the new constitution brings the EU closer to those it represents.

In the post-war period the much poorer countries of Eastern Europe – such as Latvia and Lithuania – have not shared the economic stimulus experienced by the West; hence their eagerness – following the fall of communism in 1990 – to join the EU, with its financial benefits. Expressed in figures, the ten new EU countries have living standards far below those of the richer members. To avoid the Western states being flooded by job-seekers, the EU Commission allowed the richer countries to impose temporary barriers on the flow of labour from Eastern Europe. France, Spain, Italy, Greece and Portugal are concerned that some of the agricultural subsidies they are presently receiving will be paid, as they must be under EU rules, to the incoming poorer countries, whose budgetary demands must exceed anything they are likely to contribute.

The process of European unification still requires the inclusion of several Southeast European countries – Bulgaria, Romania, the former Yugoslav republics (except Slovenia), Albania and Turkey. Bulgaria and Romania have been given 2007 as a possible date for inclusion. No one knows when the rest will be admitted. The most contested candidate is Turkey, which is due to start entry talks to the EU in October 2005.

Long before the inclusion into the EU of the poorer ex-communist states, growing numbers of Eastern and Southern Europeans had already migrated to the West. Before the building of the Berlin Wall in 1961, three million East Germans had fled westward. Between the 1960s and the 1990s a large number of migrants from Italy, Portugal, Spain, Greece, Yugoslavia and Turkey also moved to the Federal Republic of Germany, France, Belgium,

Switzerland, the Netherlands and Denmark. Migrants entered Britain from its ex-colonies and empire, especially from India, Pakistan and the Caribbean.

By the late 1960s, in contrast to Europe's earlier trans-oceanic exodus, intra-European migration had taken precedence over emigration of Europeans overseas. Encouraged by the relatively prosperous economic conditions in Western Europe in the post-war years, more migrants were entering the continent than leaving it. Swelling the inward flow were the large numbers of European nationals being repatriated from their former empires. By the 1970s an unprecedented four million non-Europeans – chiefly Asians, North Africans and West Indians – were living in Northern and Western Europe. Long before the 'war on terrorism', anti-immigration political parties opposed to mass immigration (especially of Muslims) had already appeared in the Netherlands, Belgium, France, Austria, Britain, Italy, Spain, Portugal and Denmark. By 2001, the total of registered non-EU citizens in the EU was about eleven million. By 2004, it was in the region of 16 million; the total of foreign-born residents was over 7 million in Germany, over 4 million in France (with Europe's largest Islamic community) and approximately 2.5 million in the UK. The Netherlands, Belgium and Italy had more than a million each. All of these numbers are expected to increase as a result of the enlargement of the EU. The number of illegal migrants is unknown. Because of tighter controls, the number of legal immigrants has decreased while the smuggling and trafficking of illegal migrants has grown. Most migrants to France, Spain and Italy come from Morocco, Algeria, Tunisia and Egypt. Turkish nationals (chiefly Kurds) and Yugoslavs form significant minorities in Germany.

With the outbreak of the 'war on terrorism', following the bombing of the Twin Towers in New York on 11 September 2001, European countries have become extremely apprehensive about the Muslim minorities in their midst. In 2002 the anti-immigration Dutch populist Pim Fortuyn was assassinated by an Islamic fundamentalist. The terrorist bombs in Madrid (March 2004) and London (July 2005) were also the work of animal rights activists. Since the 1960s the problem of immigration and Islamic assimilation has grown to crisis proportions. In 2004, France outlawed the wearing of the Muslim headscarf in state schools.

Germany has played a leading role in the post-war development of Europe.[7] Divided into zones of occupation in 1945, West Germany became a Federal Republic (GFR) in 1949; East Germany became the German Democratic Republic (GDR). By 1955 – because of the Cold War – both had become fully independent sovereign states. The GFR became a member of NATO; the GDR became a member of the Warsaw Pact. In 1959 the Western powers supported the GFR to resist Russian efforts to isolate Berlin.

Helped by the Marshall Plan, West Germany's economic recovery under its finance minister Ludwig Erhard (1897–1977) was spectacular. The years 1949–63 were called a *Wirtschaftswunder* (economic miracle). By the 1950s, West Germany's GNP exceeded that of pre-war Germany. In 1957 it became a founding member of the EEC. In 1961 it helped to found the Organization for Economic Cooperation and Development (OECD). By the mid-1960s, it was the only country in Western Europe to have achieved full employment. To maintain economic expansion, hundreds of thousands of 'guest workers' were recruited from Italy, Spain, Greece, Turkey and Yugoslavia. German prosperity also attracted refugees from around the world. In those days of full employment anti-immigrant rhetoric was muted.[8]

Vital to Germany's recovery was its political stability. Konrad Adenauer (1876–1967) became West Germany's first chancellor in 1949. Under his leadership, a democratic system of government was reinstalled. He cooperated with the USA and sought reconciliation with France. With Charles De Gaulle (1890–1970), he promoted European union. In 1955 Adenauer made a goodwill visit to the Soviet Union. By then, American nuclear weapons had been deployed in the GFR; by 1957, the West Germans had developed their own. One of Adenauer's purposes in going to Moscow was the release of German prisoners of war. Of the 3.3 million German prisoners of war in 1945, the Russians released just 10,000 in 1955.

Willy Brandt (1913–92), who became chancellor in 1969, promoted *Ostpolitik*;[9] he did more than any other German statesman to improve the GFR's relations with Eastern Europe. In 1971 he negotiated an agreement with the Soviet Union on the frontiers of Eastern Europe and the status of Berlin. In 1972, he concluded an accord with the USSR and Poland, accepting the Oder–Neisse boundary, and signed an agreement with the GDR recognizing its existence. For his efforts he received the Nobel Prize for Peace.[10] In 1973 the GFR joined the UN. Helmut Schmidt (b. 1918), who served as chancellor from 1974 to 1982, continued *Ostpolitik* – even after German and Russian relations became soured over the Soviet Union's invasion of Afghanistan. The work of Schmidt's successor, Helmut Kohl (b. 1930), was helped by the general prosperity of the 1980s. Kohl furthered German relations with both the East and the West. Unification with East Germany (1990) and further integration with Europe were his two major achievements. In 1991 Berlin became Germany's capital once again. In the first ten years the eastern *Länder* received $750 billion in subsidies to raise productivity and wages. The final withdrawal of Russian troops took place in August 1994. A few days later, American, British and French troops were also withdrawn from Berlin. Foreign troops in Germany are now under the command of NATO.[11] Following the authorization of Germany's highest court (1994), in 1996 German troops supported the US-brokered Dayton Peace Accord in the Balkans. In 1999, under its new chancellor, Gerhard Schröder (b. 1944), Germany was beginning to play a greater role in European and world affairs. Despite American pressure, Schröder refused to support the US invasion of Iraq in 2003.

With the end of the Second World War, the political weakness and disunity that had crippled France[12] in the inter-war years recurred. Although a victor in the war, France had suffered in status as a dominant nation state. By 1946, a hastily established provisional government had collapsed. The newly created Fourth Republic that followed was also unable to set France on an even keel. Aggravating an already difficult situation were its disastrous colonial wars in Indo-China, Egypt and Algeria. Only with De Gaulle's recall from retirement and the formation of the Fifth Republic in 1958 did the situation improve. In 1962 he ended the turmoil in French North Africa by granting Algeria independence.

He also continued the French policy of decolonization elsewhere in Africa.

Convinced that France had as much to fear from American hegemony in Europe as from the communist powers – an attitude contrary to that held by the Germans and the British – in 1966 De Gaulle removed French forces from NATO control; he also requested the withdrawal of NATO and American bases from France. NATO, he held, was causing France to follow US military objectives. A nuclear power since 1958, France tested the hydrogen bomb, refused to have anything to do with the US-sponsored Test Ban Treaty and diminished the dollar's role in Europe by buying gold. In 1963, De Gaulle first blocked Britain's entry to the Common Market on the grounds that the UK was too weak economically, and that it might become America's Trojan horse. Eight days earlier France and Germany had signed the Elysée Treaty of Friendship. De Gaulle's reconciliation and cooperation with Germany was central to the integration of continental Europe. Regarded by American and British leaders as a slightly eccentric figure, De Gaulle strengthened France's relations with the Soviet Union, China and the Third World. In 1968–9 he became a victim of the storm of discontent sweeping through France. Denied the necessary power to cope with the deteriorating situation, he resigned his presidency. A year later he died.

His successor, Georges Pompidou (1911–74), rescinded France's veto on British membership of the EEC. As a result, French relations with Britain (and America) improved. (Britain agreed to be physically linked to the continent by the Channel Tunnel, which opened in 1994.) French relations with the USA became strained again with the coming to power of Valéry Giscard d'Estaing (b. 1926; president 1974–81). The Arab oil embargo of 1973 was only one of the points over which the USA and France differed. With its much greater need of Arab oil, France could not afford to upset the Islamic world by giving unqualified support to Israel as America did; nor could it afford to follow America's policy on the non-proliferation of nuclear energy. Quite apart from its own energy requirements, it needed to sell nuclear power, as well as nuclear arms, to balance its books.

In 1981 Giscard d'Estaing was defeated at the polls by the socialist François Mitterrand (1916–96). By then – after thirty years of extraordinary post-war growth – France had become the world's fourth-largest industrial power (after the USA, Japan and Germany), and the fourth-largest exporter. Mitterrand continued to support an independent French nuclear force and a strong foreign policy vis-à-vis the Soviet Union and the USA. In the EC he clashed with Britain's prime minister, Margaret Thatcher (b. 1925). The one thing Mitterrand shared with Thatcher was fear of a united Germany.

In 1993 France, like most other Western countries, was compelled to introduce tighter control of immigrants and refugees. In June 1994 it sent peacekeeping troops to Rwanda. In 1995–7 it was plagued with terrorist bombings, allegedly the work of Islamic extremists who were opposed to France's support of Algeria's military government. In September 1995, France's resumption of nuclear tests in the South Pacific aroused the criticism of the world community. In May 1995, former conservative prime minister Jacques Chirac (b. 1932) became president. In June 1997 the legislative election went in favour of the leftist party: under a conservative president, the socialist Lionel Jospin (b. 1937) was appointed prime minister. Regardless of the parties in power, French fear of American domination continued. Though the French fought alongside the Americans in the Balkans, they did not participate in the 2003 invasion of Iraq.

Only after 1945 – by which time two world wars and the loss of its empire had undermined its strength – did Britain's changed status as a great power become manifest.[13] As the centre for much of the world's trade, it was affected by every international crisis. Not even with the assistance of the USA and the IMF was it able to achieve a stable peacetime economic footing; several times it was forced to devalue its currency. By 1950, the welfare state introduced in 1945 by Labour prime minister Clement Attlee (1883–1967) was in peril. Britain's entry that year into the Korean War added to its financial burdens. In 1952 it exploded its first atomic bomb. In 1956, under the premiership of Anthony Eden (1897–1977), Britain joined Israel and France in a failed attempt to topple President Nasser of Egypt. By 1957, it possessed the hydrogen bomb.

By the time Harold Macmillan became prime minister in 1957, Britain's and Europe's situations had improved. His election slogan –

'Our people have never had it so good' – was generally believed. While inspiring new hope, Macmillan was unable to have any real effect upon Britain's seemingly insoluble balance-of-payment problems and its growing numbers of unemployed. In trying to control the large influx of immigrants from the British West Indies, India and Pakistan (the latter chiefly Muslims), the Commonwealth Immigration Act was passed in 1962. By 2004, a more racially conscious Britain required an oath of allegiance from immigrants seeking citizenship. Between 1964 and 1979 Conservative and Labour governments alternated in power without making any real difference. In 1976, with its financial reserves exhausted, and its economy torn by industrial and racial unrest, Britain came close to bankruptcy.

In foreign affairs, Macmillan supported President Kennedy during the Cuban Missile Crisis; he also reached an agreement with America for British submarines to be armed with US missiles. His 'wind of change' speech given in South Africa in February 1960 was a landmark in the West's acceptance of decolonization. In 1961 he helped to form the OECD. In 1963, he played a leading role in negotiating a nuclear test-ban treaty between Britain, the USA and the USSR which banned the testing of nuclear weapons in the atmosphere, in outer space and under water. With Edward Heath (1916–2005), who became prime minister in 1970, he worked to make Britain a member of the EC.

With the ascendancy to power of Margaret Thatcher in 1979,[14] Britain regained some of its wartime confidence and sense of superiority: 'I know I can save this country and that no one else can,' she said on becoming prime minister. The North Sea oil surpluses after 1980 alleviated some of the deep-seated structural problems that had bedevilled British politics for thirty years. In domestic and foreign affairs she brought great intensity of purpose and conviction to her task. She wanted Britain to be first among equals; she had a keen sense of power and sought a better financial deal for her country from the EU. Fearing a loss of sovereignty, Thatcher was critical of any further European integration. Her government's victory over Argentina in the Falklands War (1982) helped to restore Britain's national pride. By 1990, however, plagued by high unemployment, declining GDP and growing urban unrest, the 'Iron Lady' faced more opposition than ever before. After three election victories, she was unseated by a revolt from within her own party.

She was succeeded by John Major (b. 1943), who led the Conservatives to a narrow victory at the polls in April 1992. In foreign affairs he drew closer to the USA, but showed a 'corrosive ambivalence' to the EU. Although Parliament ratified the Maastricht Treaty of July 1992, debate over Britain's role in the Union, especially over plans to introduce a single European currency, led to division in the Conservative Party. Overshadowing all else was the deep recession in the early years of Major's tenure: inflation soared; unemployment reached record post-war levels. In September 1992 his government raised interest rates from 10 to 15 per cent in one day. Meanwhile, he continued Thatcher's policy of privatizing state-run industries. Recovery in Britain's troubled economy finally came in the mid-1990s, but it was too late to save Major. In 1997 he was unseated by a landslide victory of the New Labour Party led by Tony Blair (b. 1953).

Once in power, Blair introduced his promised separate parliaments for Scotland and Wales, and his proposed reform of the House of Lords. Abandoning the old Labour tenet of faith – the public ownership of industry – he stressed the importance of free enterprise, privatization and economic well-being. On this he did not differ from Thatcher's Conservative policies. Where he differed from his political opponents was in the emphasis he placed on social justice, on group well-being as well as that of the individual. By all measures a strong Atlanticist, he worked hard to maintain the 'special relationship' that Churchill, Macmillan and Thatcher had cultivated with the USA. He supported the US attack on the Serbs in the Balkans in 1999. Britain's relations with the EU have also been strengthened. A referendum is pending in Britain on monetary union with Europe and the acceptance of the EU's new constitution. Despite its nuclear arsenal and what remains of its North Sea oil reserves, Britain is no longer able to play its historic role of preventing any single power from dominating the continent.

In relentlessly pursuing war against Saddam Hussein, Blair became George W. Bush's closest ally. Realizing that Britain's best interests would be served by keeping the US–UK alliance strong, he forged ahead with preparations for the Iraq War, even though the majority of his people were against it. Attempts to unseat him in the Commons over this issue were unsuccessful. In May 2005 he was reelected for the third time, though with a reduced majority. His support of the Iraq War undermined the electorate's trust.

Despite Blair's efforts to bring peace between Catholics and Protestants in Northern Ireland, hostilities have continued. In March 1972 the British suspended the Northern Ireland parliament and imposed direct rule. An IRA bombing in London in February 1996 ended an eighteen-month ceasefire. Following the Good Friday Agreement of 10 April 1998 prospects for peace improved. Unfortunately, while both sides agreed to share power in the newly established Northern Ireland Assembly, there followed one impasse after another. Ancient misunderstandings, bickering, recriminations and hostility resurfaced. After a bombing in August 1998 in the town of Omagh killed twenty-eight people, deadlock ensued. Only a last-minute concession by the IRA on 23 October 2001 kept the Northern Ireland Assembly alive. Although the IRA's willingness to decommission weapons in 2004 offered new hope of a compromise between Sinn Féin and the Ulster Unionists, the possibility of more bloody confrontation remained. For more than five hundred years the animosity between the Catholic Irish and the Protestant British in Northern Ireland has refused to die. Peace efforts continued to be made. In September 2005, after being granted immunity from arrest, the IRA decommissioned its arms.

Italy's disastrous alliance with Nazi Germany ended in 1943, but it was not until 1947 that it signed a peace treaty with the Allies, and foreign troops were removed from the peninsula. In that year, massive aid was given to Italy under the Marshall Plan. In the mid-1950s, Italy was admitted to NATO and the UN. Nuclear weapons were deployed there by the USA in 1957. Thenceforth, its relations with the Western world improved. On the formation of the EEC in 1958, it was accepted as a member. With a population in excess of France's and half its trade being conducted with Europe, this was hardly surprising.

By the 1960s, in the post-war boom that affected the whole of Western Europe, Italy achieved one of the highest rates of economic growth. The roads and infrastructure linking northern and southern Italy were improved. An extraordinary migration of Italians then took place from the south to the more prosperous north, as well as to countries of Northwestern Europe. In Italy itself, the industrial and service sectors grew while agriculture declined. By 1970, Italy's industrial production stood at twice its 1939 level. But then came the OPEC oil embargo and the recession of 1973. By 1978, Italy's economy was in disarray: it had the highest youth unemployment rate in Europe; inflation rose to unacceptable levels; unemployment and the imbalance in the country's trade figures continued to grow. Signs of political instability, disintegration, anarchy and ideologically motivated terrorism became common. After the assassination of the former prime minister Aldo Moro (1916–78) by Italy's ultra-left Red Brigade, the Italian democratic process seemed to grind to a halt.

Whether Italy's troubles were symptomatic of the unsatisfied rising expectations of the post-1945 years across the whole of Western Europe, its future is inseparable from that of the Western world. With a population of nearly sixty million, it is an indispensable member of the EU and the OECD. Similarly, its political fortunes affect its fellow members in NATO. There can be no significant change in the power structure in the Adriatic or the Mediterranean without repercussions being felt in Italy. This is especially true of developments in the Balkans, as it is in Muslim Africa and the Arab world, upon which Italy relies for most of its oil. Like the other Western powers, it has been beset with would-be immigrants and refugees.[15] In 1991, forty thousand illegal Albanian immigrants were forcibly returned to their homeland. In 2004, despite clamping down on Albanian, North African and Turkish immigration, the number of illegal immigrants into Italy was still a major problem.

In the 1990s Italy was shaken by corruption scandals that implicated some of its most prominent politicians, including the media and business tycoon Silvio Berlusconi (b. 1936), who in May 2001 was re-elected to the premiership (he had been prime minister briefly in 1994). Italy's efforts in recent years to root out corruption, revise the constitution, improve government and eliminate the stranglehold of the conservative Popular Party have always ended in failure. One weak government invariably followed another; by 2005 post-war Italy had had scores of cabinets. Despite the defeat of his party, Berlusconi obtained a vote of confidence in Italy's lower house of parliament and returned to his post as prime minister.

The political shift to the left in Europe that began in 1945 resulted in rightist Spain being ostracized by all except the Portuguese. The USA under President Eisenhower was the first Western power to seek closer relations with the Franco regime. In 1953, the USA signed a ten-year military and economic agreement with Spain under which, in return for $1 billion in grants and loans, America obtained military bases. Between 1967 and 1974 the USA backed the Spanish dictatorship. Spain became a member of the UN in 1955, of NATO in 1982, of the EC in 1986 and of the OECD and the euro zone later. Aid from the EU has boosted Spain's development and raised its standard of living. It is now closely linked with the rest of Europe (roughly 70 per cent of its trade is done there).

With the death of Franco in 1975, Prince Juan Carlos became king and head of state. With the new monarch in place, Spain underwent a profound economic, cultural and political transformation. Under the direction of Adolfo Suárez (prime minister 1977–81) universal suffrage was introduced and political parties were legalized (including the Spanish Communist Party). Elections were held. Though torn by the clerical–liberal divide of its history, Franco's Concordat with the Vatican was retained.

After decades of dictatorship, Spain has emerged as a defender of democracy and the rule of law. In 1977, in the first free election since 1936, moderates and democratic socialists emerged as the largest parties. A new constitution was adopted in October 1978. In 1978 and 1981 attempted coups by right-wing military officers were foiled. In 1982 a socialist government led by Felipe González Márquez was elected. The socialists won the next four general elections (1982–93).

Although Catalonia and the Basque country were granted autonomy in 1980, Basque extremists – who carry out terrorist attacks and assassinations – continue to demand total independence. In 1996, although lacking an outright majority in parliament, the conservatives under José Maria Aznar defeated the socialists. Under Aznar there was a shift to the American camp. Spain provided troops for the Balkan wars in Bosnia and Kosovo.

Like other EU countries, Spain is plagued by the problem of illegal immigrants, many of whom come from Morocco. After a Madrid railway bombing by terrorists in 2004 (most of whom proved to be Moroccan), Aznar was defeated by the socialist José Luis Rodríguez Zapatero (b. 1961), who is more likely to follow a European line. One of his first moves was to repatriate Spanish soldiers fighting in Iraq.

Spain was rocked by a widespread Basque bombing campaign at the beginning of December 2004.

Portugal – neutral in the Second World War – became a member of NATO in 1949, the UN in 1955, the OECD in 1961 and the EC in 1986 (from which it received large sums in grants and loans). At that time its living standards were about half the EC average; by 2000, they were almost three-quarters. Between 1932 and 1968 Portugal was dominated by the dictator António de Oliveira Salazar (1889–1970), who refused to yield to demands for the decolonization of Portugal's overseas possessions. He also discouraged foreign investors in Portugal. He was succeeded by Marcello José De Neves Alves Caetano (1904–81), who was toppled in 1974 by General António de Spinola in a bloodless coup. In March 1975, Spinola fled to Spain. By then, Portugal was edging towards chaos. In November 1975, there was still another coup – led by General António Eanes (b. 1935). In that year, after endless bitter fighting, Angola and Mozambique gained their independence. A degree of normalcy returned with the election of 1976 – the first free democratic election in forty years – in which Mario Soares became prime minister. Portugal's African territory of Guinea-Bissau became independent in the same year.

The weakened condition of the economy had undermined efforts to keep the country out of the hands of extremists. In the 1960s one million people – an eighth of the population – migrated to seek work elsewhere. Twice, in 1977 and 1983, the IMF saved Portugal from financial collapse. Despite these efforts, Portugal is still one of the poorest countries in Western Europe. Without its traditional avenues of employment in its ex-colonies,[16] and with the earlier flood of Portuguese 'guest workers' to the rest of Europe stemmed, Portugal is plagued with political and economic instability. Its foreign possessions today comprise the Azores and Madeira (it returned Macao to China in 1999). To add to its troubles, it has become a country of immigration. In the 1970s and 1980s, a million Portuguese returned from its ex-colonies. However, Portugal still retains its strong links with Portuguese communities in Brazil, France, Canada and South Africa. As in fellow-Catholic Ireland and Spain, its fertility rates have fallen dramatically in recent years – from the highest in Western Europe to the lowest. In January 2001 Jorge Sampaio (b. 1939), a socialist, was comfortably re-elected president. In 2005 the socialists won an absolute majority in parliament.

Unlike Portugal, Greece was an occupied country in the Second World War. In 1940 the Italians invaded Greece and were defeated. The Germans came to the aid of the Italians, British troops were sent from North Africa to support the Greeks; many were subsequently taken prisoner. The Greek monarch fled in 1941. The country remained under Axis control (Germans, Italians and Bulgarians) for the rest of the war.

In November 1944, after the withdrawal of the Axis troops from Greece, a communist-led resistance movement tried to seize power; civil war ensued. The attempt was thwarted by Greek and British troops; the monarchy was restored. A second communist-led revolt during 1946–9 was similarly defeated by the British and the French. American help was also given under the Truman Doctrine. Despite US efforts to obtain stability, military coups occurred in 1960 (when US nuclear weapons were deployed in Greece), 1967 (when the monarch fled to Italy) and in 1973 (when the dictator Georgios Papadopoulos (1919–99) was ousted).

In 1974, a Greek junta encouraged the Greeks in Cyprus to seize power over the Turkish minority and link the island with Greece. Whereupon Turkey invaded Cyprus to protect its nationals. Having failed in Cyprus, the Greek junta was replaced by a civilian government. In 1975 the monarchy was abolished and democratic rule restored. The Greek–Turkish hostility over Cyprus has impaired the roles of these nations in NATO and other international organizations.[17] From 1981 until 1989 the Greek socialists continued to hold power. Defeated in the elections of 1989, they returned to power in 1993, 1996 and 2000.

Having survived war, foreign occupation and dictatorship, Greece in 2005 was a strong democracy. Appropriately, in 2004 it hosted the Olympic Games.

Norway and Sweden have played important roles in international affairs since the Second World War. In April 1940 Germany attacked neutral Norway and occupied it until May 1945. In the post-war years Sweden – which had been neutral – provided much aid to war-ravaged Europe. Although small in population, it assisted UN peace-keeping missions in Egypt, Cyprus, the Congo and Namibia. Earlier, in 1956, in the Nordic Council, Sweden and Norway formed an economic link with Finland, which also has a long tradition of neutrality. Sweden joined the EU in January 1995, but rejected adoption of the euro currency. (Norway, in a referendum in 1994, had rejected EU membership.) Sweden has a strong tradition of social-democratic-led coalition governments, the most recent of which was elected in September 2002.

Since 1945, Switzerland has continued its traditional policy of neutrality. It did not join the UN until September 2002, and then only reluctantly. It has maintained an armed neutrality since 1815. The last war it fought was in 1515. It is the location of many UN and other international agencies and has long been a world banking centre. Difficult to explain is the recent rise of the Swiss People's Party – a far-right organization. After all, Switzerland claims to be the world's oldest democracy.

In 1945, the USA emerged from the war relatively unscathed with a productive capacity that dwarfed all others. Of world GDP it accounted for almost half. By the late 1940s, it possessed two-thirds of the world's gold reserves, half the world's shipping and half the world's income; it had a high savings rate and was the major source of investment capital; the dollar became the reserve currency for the Western world. Its exports, especially in manufactures, boomed; its trade surpluses were unparalleled. The period 1950–73, the golden age of American capitalism, can be compared only with the business boom experienced a hundred years earlier by the northern states following the American Civil War.

By the 1960s, the USA had become the greatest agrarian, industrial and financial power of the world. (Unlike its present immense public debt, it was the leading creditor nation.) Generalizing from its own unique passage of history, a new and totally unwarranted stress came to be placed upon America's supposed ability to promote the economic growth and development of the non-communist world. Overshadowing the gospels of Christianity and democracy was the promise of a better material existence. In the development decade of the 1960s, America also provided much foreign aid aimed at modernizing the poorer parts of the world along Western lines. Alas, not much modernization took place.

Far from turning its back on the world as it had done after the First World War, after 1945 the USA assumed its new post-war responsibilities. For the first time in its history, it became a major peacetime military power. Under President Truman it took up the leadership of the United Nations and built up a world of alliances. In 1947 a policy was devised to contain Soviet expansionism in Iran, Greece and Turkey. Under the Marshall Plan it provided Western European countries with $13 billion of aid (more than $100 billion in today's terms). Foreign aid, given or withdrawn, became a diplomatic tool. American money was used in Europe's and Japan's defence. In 1948, with the help of the World Bank and the IMF, the USA worked to free world trade and finance; the General Agreement on Tariffs and Trade (GATT) was founded in 1947 to liberalize commerce. In 1948 America supported the creation of Israel.

In 1953 General Eisenhower was elected president with the largest popular vote in US history. He had promised to end the Korean War, which he did. US nuclear weapons were placed in several countries of Western Europe to guard against the Soviet threat.[18] In 1955 and 1958, by threatening the use of nuclear weapons, the USA protected the Taiwanese islands of Quemoi and

Matsu from Chinese attack. In his second term Eisenhower, against the more aggressive stance of his secretary of state, John Foster Dulles (1888–1959), sought to achieve détente with the USSR, but the shooting down on 1 May 1960 of a US U-2 reconnaissance plane over Russia ended the thaw in US–USSR relations.

By the time the youthful John Fitzgerald Kennedy (1917–1963) assumed the presidency in 1961, Americans had begun to feel that their power was limitless. 'Let every nation know,' said Kennedy in his inaugural address, 'whether it wishes us well or ill, we shall pay any price, bear any burden, meet any hardship, support any friend, or oppose any foe to ensure the survival and the success of liberty.' Most of Kennedy's time in office was taken up with confronting the communist powers in Berlin, Laos, Cuba and Vietnam. On balance, he was a cautious leader, chosing a naval blockade instead of reinforcing invading troops in Cuba.

At the outset, Kennedy was less conciliatory to the Russians than Eisenhower had been. After meeting Khrushchev in Vienna in 1961 (during which the Soviet premier thought Kennedy weak), the following year he forced Khrushchev to remove missiles from Cuba in return for removing American missiles from Turkey. In 1963 he successfully negotiated the first Partial Test Ban Treaty with the USSR. He created the US Peace Corps to aid developing countries, supported racial integration in the USA and accelerated the US space programme, which in 1969 resulted in the first man landing on the moon. On 22 November 1963, Kennedy was assassinated in Dallas, Texas. Five years later, on 3 June 1968, his brother Robert was assassinated in Los Angeles. Many blame JFK for America's involvement in Vietnam, but, while it is true that he was the first president to send military advisers and troops in combat readiness to Vietnam, it was left to others to commence hostilities and involve the country in the war.

Vietnam became the nemesis of Kennedy's successor, Lyndon Johnson (1908–73). His decision to persuade Congress to go to war divided the nation, and subsequently overshadowed everything he did. The longer the war continued, the more Americans saw it as neither politically nor morally defensible. While American troops were dying in Vietnam, no sacrifices were asked of Americans on the home front. By widening and financing the war out of borrowed money (as would later be done in the second Iraq War) rather than taxes, Johnson hastened the transition of America from the world's leading creditor to the world's leading debtor nations. No matter what he did, the tension in the USA over Vietnam grew. There were also serious race riots in the 1960s, as well as the assassinations of the black leaders Martin Luther King and Malcolm X. Fears of a communist takeover closer to home caused Johnson to intervene militarily in the Dominican Republic in 1965. He is remembered positively for his contribution to civil rights, his anti-poverty programme for the aged and the deprived, and for the improvements in education and health-care (Medicare). In 1968 he signed the Nuclear Non-Proliferation Treaty with Britain and the Soviet Union, which was subsequently endorsed by 188 other states.

It was left to Richard Nixon (b. 1913; president 1969–74; d. 1994) and his secretary of state Henry Kissinger (b. 1923) to end the Vietnam War. Ironically, Nixon began by secretly extending the war to Cambodia (1970) and Laos (1971). In 1972 he ordered the bombing of Hanoi and the mining of Haiphong Harbour. But also in that year, by visiting Beijing, he dramatically changed relations between China and the USA. Since 1949, the only China officially recognized by the USA had been Taiwan. With American support, the People's Republic of China now replaced Taiwan at the UN and on the Security Council. Nixon also made the first visit of an American president to the Soviet Union, with whom in 1972 he had signed the first Strategic Arms Limitation Treaty (SALT I). In the Arab–Israeli War of 1973, he gave crucial military aid to Israel. The Arabs responded with the OPEC oil embargo in October 1973, which caused the average price of crude oil to double. For the first time America became acutely aware of its dependence on foreign oil. The embargo marked the end of a period of rising expectations (1960–73), and the beginning for some Americans of growing disillusionment. Nixon resigned in August 1974 as a result of the Watergate scandal.

President Gerald Ford's (b. 1913) period of office (1974–7) was chiefly concerned with economic problems, including inflation and growing unemployment. In 1975 he supported the Helsinki Conference on basic human rights. He was responsible for the evacuation of a quarter of a million US military and civilian refugees from South Vietnam following its annexation by North Vietnam. Towards the Soviet Union and China, he continued Nixon's policy of détente.

In 1977 James Earl ('Jimmy') Carter (b. 1924) became president. Since Woodrow Wilson, no one had come to office with a higher moral intent. Alas, his presidency was dogged by ill fortune. On 4 November 1979, with relations between the USA and Iran's theocratic government worsening by the day, fifty-two US citizens were taken hostage in Tehran. They were then held for 444 days. The hostage crisis dominated Carter's presidency as Vietnam had dominated Johnson's. His attempts in April 1980 to free the hostages by military action ended in disaster. Carter's much-hailed Camp David Accord of September 1978 between Menachem Begin (1913–92) of Israel and Anwar el-Sadat of Egypt failed to bring peace to the Middle East. The accord was concluded only by promising large sums of financial aid to both Egypt and Israel, which have continued to the present day. With the exception of Egypt (which regained the Sinai) the accord was rejected by the Arab world. Egypt was expelled from the Arab League, and President Sadat was assassinated as a direct result of his dealings with Israel and the USA.

Carter's efforts in 1979 to conclude a second SALT treaty were not ratified by the US Senate. His energy policy, aimed at reducing America's need for imported oil, was similarly rejected. A much weakened US economy was not helped by his refusal to trade with or aid countries violating human rights. Russia's invasion of Afghanistan in December 1979, coupled with the beginning of the Iran hostage crisis, halted his work for peace. In January 1980 he declared what came to be known as the Carter Doctrine: 'The US', he said, 'would use military force to resist an attempt by any "outside force" to gain control of the Persian Gulf Region.' In his retirement, Carter has defused several threats of war and dislocation in the world, for which he was awarded the Nobel Prize for Peace in 2002.

Ronald Reagan (b. 1911; president 1981–9; d. 2004), who

replaced Carter, said less about morality and more about success; less about peace and more about strengthening the military; less about the welfare state and more about free enterprise and cutting taxes. On his inauguration day in 1981, Iran released the hostages. Under his leadership, relations with the Soviet Union improved; following on Carter's efforts, in 1982 negotiations on strategic nuclear weapons resumed. After prolonged discussions in Geneva (1985), Reykjavik (1986) and Washington (1987), a treaty to eliminate intermediate-range nuclear weapons was achieved. With the extraordinary co-operation of Mikhail Gorbachev, who believed that the fewer nuclear weapons the better, in June 1988 Reagan signed the Intermediate-Range Nuclear Forces Treaty in Moscow. Relations with China also improved; trade between the two countries blossomed.

Reagan took decisive action in Beirut (1982), when Israel invaded Lebanon to drive out the Palestine Liberation Organization; Grenada (1983), allegedly to prevent a Cuban plot to take over the island; Nicaragua (throughout the 1980s), where his government secretly led an army of Contras against the legitimate government; Panama (1989–90), which US forces invaded to remove General Manuel Noriega (b. 1938) on drug-trafficking charges; and Libya, against which the USA made several bombing raids in an effort to oust Muammar al-Qadhafi. Reagan was roundly criticized for his tendency to resort to military solutions rather than diplomacy. During his presidency there was an enormous increase in federal spending (from $631 billion in 1981 to more than $1 trillion in 1986), much of which financed the largest peacetime military build-up in US history. The national debt doubled in the same period, while budget deficits multiplied threefold. The difference between US income and US spending was made up by further domestic and foreign borrowing. Almost without comment, ever-growing private and public debt became America's greatest danger; it still is. Reagan is also remembered for his support after 1983 of the Strategic Defence Initiative (SDI or 'Star Wars') and for financing the Contras in Nicaragua covertly from the profits of illegal arms sales to Iran. In spite of this, the 'Great Communicator' remained popular throughout his presidency.

The collapse of the Soviet Union in 1991 presented George

Herbert Walker Bush (b. 1924; president 1989–93) with world problems he had not expected. As Reagan's vice-president, he had supported Gorbachev's attempts to reduce international tensions. He refrained from criticizing China's repression of pro-democracy demonstrators in Tiananmen Square in 1989, but did condemn Iraq's invasion of Kuwait in August 1990. Oil and the security of Saudi Arabia and Israel were at stake. In January–February 1991 a US-led Allied force (operation Desert Storm), including Arab and NATO contingents, defeated the Iraqi army and drove it from Kuwait. The US victory went a long way to dispelling America's introspection over Vietnam. In 1993, on behalf of the UN, Bush made a hapless, if well-intentioned, intervention in Somalia. Despite his strong leadership in the Gulf War, his success was undermined by prolonged recession on the home front. He was defeated by Bill Clinton (b. 1946) in the 1992 election.

Although he remained popular with the electorate, Clinton's two terms as president (1993–2000) were rarely free from allegations of wrongdoing. In 1998 he was acquitted by the Senate of impeachment charges made by the House of Representatives on the grounds of perjury and obstruction of justice. Clinton oversaw America's longest peacetime boom. He reduced the budget deficit, and in 1993 obtained congressional approval of the North American Free Trade Agreement (NAFTA). In foreign relations, he cooperated with the UN in the war in Bosnia, but ignored UN resolutions for a peaceful settlement of the crisis in Kosovo. In 1999 he was primarily responsible (through NATO) for the aerial bombardment of Serbia, a war fought without international consensus or clear legal authority. Although the terrorizing and ethnic cleansing of Albanian Kosovars was halted, US relations with the UN deteriorated. By 2001 most Serbs had fled Kosovo. The relations between Muslim Albanians and Christian Serbs, instead of healing, have continued to fester. The fate of the Gypsies, who were driven out of Kosovo by the Kosovo Albanians, is ignored.

While Clinton improved US relations with both China and Russia, the accidental bombing of the Chinese embassy in Belgrade in May 1999 undid much of his work. His unceasing efforts to bring peace to the Middle East were similarly dogged by misfortune. By the time he left office, Arab and Israeli relations were much worse than when he began his presidency. His Comprehensive Nuclear Test Ban Treaty of 1996 was not ratified by the Senate.

His successor in the White House, George W. Bush (son of President George H. W. Bush) narrowly won the election in 2000. On 11 September 2001 Arab terrorists connected to al Qaeda hijacked planes and flew them into the Twin Towers of the World Trade Center in New York and the Pentagon in Washington (with the loss of more than 3000 lives). Bush's response was to declare a worldwide 'war on terrorism', which led to the bombing of Afghanistan and the invasion of Iraq.

The 9/11 attacks were the worst in a list of terrorist acts against the USA that stretched back over a decade. In December 1988 a US passenger plane was blown up over Lockerbie in Scotland. In February 1993 the World Trade Center was bombed. In April 1995 a bomb exploded in Oklahoma City. In June 1996, American soldiers were killed at a base in Saudi Arabia. In August 1998, explosions decimated the American embassies in Kenya and Tanzania. On 12 October 2000 the US destroyer *Cole* was attacked in the port of Aden.

Believing that Iraq had weapons of mass destruction (WMDs) and that it was about to attack America, Bush ordered the invasion of Iraq on 20 March 2003. When it was proved that Iraq had no WMDs, was not about to make war on the USA, and was not directly connected with al Qaeda, the overthrowing of Saddam Hussein became the justification for war. Although there was a quick military victory, US and coalition forces now face growing guerrilla resistance; the danger of civil war grows. On 30 January 2005 elections were held in Iraq, but they have done little to halt the ongoing disintegration of the country. Yet Saddam Hussein has been overthrown and a new constitution was promised for 2005.

All of which left a lot of people dissatisfied. America's 'shock and awe' war in Iraq has alienated both the UN and (with the exception of Britain) America's major allies. The USA is criticized for fighting an unnecessary and illegal war, for the lack of preparation to deal with Iraq after the invasion, for the deaths of almost 2000 young Americans and untold numbers of Iraqi civilians. The calls in America for an 'exit strategy' are growing – which runs contrary to the Bush administration's long-term intention to impose its will on Iraq and the rest of the Middle East.

While America's overwhelming supremacy had come to an end long before the two Gulf Wars, the present neo-conservative US government believes that, through the spread of 'freedom and democracy', it has a moral duty to save the world, an aim embedded in the great liberating traditions of the country. This outlook is difficult to distinguish from the 'white man's burden' or the civilizing mission of nineteenth-century European imperialists. They too were messianic, willing to fight long and limitless wars to achieve their goals.

The political reality for the USA is that it is living in a world where its options are becoming narrower; and where its ends – military and economic – have exceeded its means. Projected military spending in 2005 is \$466 billion,[19] which exceeds the total for the rest of the world – about \$360 billion. With a public debt of nearly \$8 trillion, there is a danger that the dollar might lose its role as the world's reserve currency. Also threatened is America's manufacturing industry, which is vital to any would-be great power and is presently being outsourced to Asia and Latin America.

What is not appreciated is that the proliferation of ballistic missiles and nuclear, chemical and biological weapons in non-American hands has diminished America's relative might. A score of countries now possess short- and medium-range missiles. At home and abroad, the USA is much more vulnerable to terrorism; the more it intrudes in other countries' affairs, the more vulnerable it becomes. It cannot hope to act as the world's policeman; nor can it hope, against the UN and the great powers, unilaterally to dominate the world. The shift in world realities these past sixty years (even allowing for good intentions, unmatched military power and global reach[20]) is that the USA has no choice but to cooperate with its mutually dependent allies through NATO and the United Nations. 'Going it alone' for the USA belongs to another phase of history.[21] At least it did until the arrival of the Clinton administration, which, in its war over Kosovo, disregarded the UN and its accepted rules of warfare. In June 2000 Amnesty International accused NATO (specifically the USA and Britain) of breaking the rules of war during its bombing campaign against Yugoslavia in the previous year.

The Balkan, Afghanistan and Iraq wars have caused US relations with the UN to deteriorate sharply.[22] In the spring of 2001, it lost its seats on the UN Human Rights Commission and the International Narcotics Control Board. The USA refused to ratify the Convention on the Rights of the Child, the Convention on the Rights of Women and the treaty banning anti-personnel landmines. The Bush administration has announced its intention unilaterally to abandon the Anti-Ballistic Missile Treaty, which has been a linchpin of strategic arms control since 1972. At the risk of starting a new arms race, Bush proposed to resurrect Reagan's 'Star Wars' programme. 'America needs to project power in, from and through space,' said Donald Rumsfeld, Bush's secretary of defense. The USA has also rejected the Kyoto Protocol on climate change and – with Israel – has declared its unwillingness to ratify the Rome Statute of the international criminal court. In July 2002 America modified its position on the Hague Court, telling the UN Security Council that it no longer demanded permanent immunity for its soldiers serving as peacekeepers, but it still wants to prevent any prosecution of them for a year, subject to renewal. Negotiations continue.

It would be disastrous for everyone if the USA were to leave the UN. Yet it cannot continue to act unilaterally without serious consequences to world peace. The USA certainly cannot isolate itself from a world upon which a quarter of its economy depends, and from which (in the military sphere) its shield of distance has vanished. While no one should minimise America's power, the world has become more interdependent and more dangerous than it ever was.

With the Second World War over and the Cold War begun, Canada found itself between the two contending superpowers.[23] To avoid siding with the USA against the USSR, in the 1950s it refused to accept American nuclear weapons. In foreign trade it ignored America's trade boycott of the communist world, developing friendly relations with communist Cuba and China. It fought in Korea, but refused to join America in Vietnam. Its rejection in 1957 of a proposed British–Canadian free trade area brought home Canada's self-assertion to Britain and the USA. In 1982, while remaining a member of the Commonwealth, with Elizabeth II nominally its queen, Canada severed its last legislative link with Britain by obtaining the right to amend its own constitution. Yet it did join with the USA and Britain in calling for the control of atomic energy; it also cooperated with the USA in the establishment of a distant early-warning system of radar stations from Alaska to Baffin Island against any threatened invasion of North America from the USSR – a system now obsolete. Since 1945, it has sent troops on many UN peacekeeping missions.

From the late 1950s onwards, partly through the long premiership (1968–79) of Pierre Elliot Trudeau (1919–2000), the ties between the Canadian and US economies have grown. In 1988, Prime Minister Brian Mulroney (b. 1939) was re-elected on the issue of closer relations with the USA in trade and industry. In June 1993, Canada became the first nation to ratify the North American Free Trade Agreement. By this time – although since 1973 Canada has controlled investment by foreigners – some of its major industries (particularly the exploitation of its rich mineral and timber resources) were controlled by Americans. Its exports to the USA between 1989 and 1998 grew rapidly. In 2004 there was about $400 billion of annual cross-border trade. Although the number of emigrants from Canada to the USA has declined in recent years, the flow of highly skilled professional workers and managers has grown.

Recently, Canada's national autonomy has been threatened by the growing cleavage between the cultural descendants of France and Britain. On a visit to Quebec in 1967, President De Gaulle stirred separatist passions with his call 'Vive le Québec libre'. Calling for a separate French-speaking state is the Parti Québecois, founded by René Levesque in 1968. In May 1980 a referendum on Quebec's independence resulted in a defeat for the separatists. They were defeated again (by the narrowest of margins) in another referendum in October 1995. All other attempts since then to make Quebec a 'distinct' society have failed. The third victory of the anti-separatist (and anti-American) Prime Minister Jean Chrétien (b. 1934) at the polls in December 2000 and the resignation in January 2001 of Lucien Bouchard (premier of Quebec and head of the separatist Parti Québecois) lessened the chance of secession. In 2003 one of Paúl Martin's (b. 1938) first jobs as prime minister was to quash charges made against his predecessor Chrétien, who was accused of using corrupt methods to prevent Quebec seceding in 1995. Martin survived a vote of no confidence in May 2005.

Through a liberal immigration policy, Canada is rapidly becoming a multiracial society. By the 1990s a strong link had been developed between its west coast and China, Vietnam, the Philippines and other Asian countries. Vancouver has an Asian population of about 500,000. In the USA the myth or the reality of the 'melting pot' still prevails; in Canada multiculturalism is honoured. Since 1972, multiculturalism has had its own ministry.

In November 2004 President Bush made his first official visit to Canada. It was hurriedly planned and hurriedly executed, and little seems to have been achieved. Over the years, Canada and the USA have taken each other for granted. Paradoxically, while the commercial ties binding the two countries grow, the cultural gap widens. Unlike its action in the first Gulf War, Canada refused to join the USA in the Iraq War in 2003. In 2005 it also refused to join it in the development of a ballistic missile defence system (BMD); instead it is increasing its own armed forces.

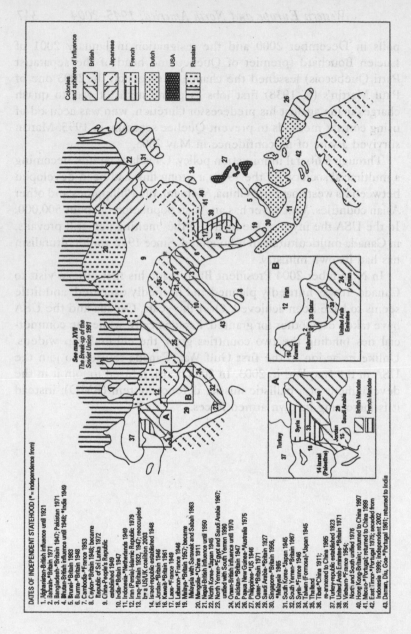

DATES OF INDEPENDENT STATEHOOD (* = independence from)

Colonies and spheres of influence: British | Japanese | French | Dutch | USA | Russian

1. Afghanistan-British influence until 1921
2. Bahrain-*Britain 1971
3. Bangladesh-*Britain 1947; Pakistan 1971
4. Bhutan-British influence until 1948; *India 1949
5. Brunei-*Britain 1983
6. Burma-*Britain 1948
7. Cambodia-*France 1953
8. Ceylon-*Britain 1948; became Republic of Sri Lanka 1972
9. China-People's Republic established 1949
10. India-*Britain 1947
11. Indonesia-*Netherlands 1949
12. Iran (Persia)-Islamic Republic 1979
13. Iraq-*Britain 1932, 1947; reoccupied br a US/UK coalition 2003
14. Israel-republic established 1948
15. Jordan-*Britain 1946
16. Kuwait-*Britain 1961
17. Laos-*France 1949
18. Lebanon-*France 1946
19. Malaya-*Britain 1957; became Malaysia with Sarawak and Sabah 1963
20. Mongolia-*China 1911
21. Nepal-British influence until 1950
22. North Korea-*Japan 1945
23. North Yemen-*Egypt and Saudi Arabia 1967; unified with South 1990
24. Oman-British influence until 1970
25. Pakistan-*Britain 1947
26. Papua New Guinea-*Australia 1975
27. Philippines-*US 1946
28. Qatar-*Britain 1971
29. Saudi Arabia-*Britain 1927
30. Singapore-*Britain 1956, *Malaysia 1965
31. South Korea-*Japan 1945
32. South Yemen-*Britain 1967
33. Syria-*France 1946
34. Taiwan (Formosa)-*Japan 1945
35. Thailand
36. Tibet-*China 1911; re-annexed to China 1965
37. Turkey-republic established 1923
38. United Arab Emirates-*Britain 1971
39. Vietnam-*France 1954; North and South unified 1976
40. Hong Kong-*Britain; returned to China 1997
41. Macao-*Portugal; returned to China 1999
42. East Timor-*Portugal 1975; seized from Indonesia 1999; independence 2002
43. Daman, Diu, Goa-*Portugal 1961; returned to India

See map XVII
The Break-up of the
Soviet Union 1991

A
Turkey | Syria | Iraq | Israel (Palestine) | Jordan | Saudi Arabia
British Mandate
French Mandate

B
Iran | Kuwait | Bahrain | Qatar | United Arab Emirates | Oman

Map XXIII Decolonization of Asia in the Twentieth Century

The Resurgence of Asia

The West's grip on its majestic Eastern empires was broken by Japan in the Second World War. In 1945, unable to realize that the age of European dominance had ended, the Europeans hastened to reoccupy their Asian empires (see Map XXIII).

The first European colonial territory to gain its independence in the post-war period was India. When the Japanese began their conquest of Southeast Asia in 1941, the century-old struggle for the independence of India from Britain was still under way. By 1942, the growth of civil disturbance had led to the imprisonment of its nationalist leaders. Faced by growing insurrection, in 1944 the British Labour Party – which had adopted a policy of anti-imperialism – promised independence for India if it gained power. The Labour Party having won the election of 1945, in 1947 India duly became independent. Although a republic, it opted to retain dominion status in the Commonwealth. Separate states headed by princes were also assimilated into the new India. In contrast to what had happened to the Dutch in Indonesia or the French in Indo-China, the British gave up their power in India in an atmosphere of good will.

Unable to obtain agreement between the Indian Congress Party, led by Jawaharlal Nehru (1889–1964)[1] and the Muslim League (founded 1907), led by Mohammad Ali Jinnah (1876–1948),[2] the British viceroy, Lord Louis Mountbatten (1900–79) was forced to agree to the tragic division of India between Hindu and Muslim. Against Gandhi's warnings, the Muslim areas of the Punjab in the northwest were joined with the eastern sector of Bengal to form Pakistan. Fifteen million people were uprooted. In the subsequent massive exchange of populations, more than 200,000 Hindus, Muslims and Sikhs died. Out of partition arose the dispute over Indian-held, predominantly Muslim, Kashmir which has bedevilled Indo-Pakistani relations ever since. Partition also strengthened the Sikh demand for autonomy in the Punjab, and exacerbated the discord between Sinhalese and Tamils in Sri Lanka (Ceylon).

After Gandhi's assassination in 1948, Nehru became the dominant figure in India politics. He had given thirty-one of his fifty-seven years to the struggle for independence, many of them spent in British jails. His aim was to transform India into a social-democratic, secular, industrial state, with economic self-sufficiency as its goal. In January 1950, India became a democratic republic. Realizing that population increase would swallow up whatever gains were made by industrialization, in 1951, a year of famine, Nehru introduced India's first family-planning programme. Refusing to take sides in the Cold War, in 1955 Nehru was instrumental in convening a meeting of Third World African, Asian and Latin American 'neutral' states at Bandung in Indonesia.[3] By the 1970s, these states had become the most politically powerful group at the United Nations. Communist China's brutal reconquest of Tibet in the 1950s, as well as its invasion of India's northern territory in 1962, undermined Nehru's work for peace. To meet China's attack on northern India, he was forced to turn to the USA for military aid. Earlier, in 1960, he had rid India of its last Portuguese colony, Goa. In 1965 Pakistani and Indian forces clashed in Kashmir; on and off, they have continued to do so, despite several ceasefire agreements. As US sympathies were with India, Pakistan turned to China for military help.

In 1966 Nehru's daughter Indira Gandhi (1917–84)[4] succeeded him as prime minister. She is credited with the 'Green Revolution', which provided India with desperately needed food;[5] for the first time, widespread famine was avoided. While adhering to her father's policy of neutrality, in practice she favoured the socialist Russians more than the capitalist Americans – state capitalism rather than private enterprise. Under her leadership, in 1969–70 India won its second war with a much weaker Pakistan. In 1971, India signed a twenty-year treaty of peace, friendship and cooperation with the Soviet Union, which consistently supported India against Pakistan, and against China in its separate border conflict. Its swift defeat of East Pakistan (Bangladesh) in 1971 gave notice that India had become a major power in Asia. In 1975 Gandhi invoked emergency powers; two years later, she was defeated in the general election. Having returned to power in 1979, she was assassinated by two of her Sikh bodyguards in retaliation for her government's attack in June 1984 on the Golden Temple in Punjab, the Sikhs' holiest shrine. In vengeance, thousands of Sikhs were slaughtered, and clashes between Hindus and Sikhs have continued. Indira Gandhi's son Rajiv (1944–91) became prime minister in 1984. He was also assassinated (allegedly by a Tamil) during an election campaign to regain power. In October 1999, India's leader Atal Bihari Vajpayee (b. 1924), leader of the National Party, was re-elected. In May 2004 the Nationalists' chief opponent at the polls, the Congress Party, unexpectedly won the general election, but Sonia Gandhi, the widow of Rajiv, declined to become prime minister; Manmohan Singh (b. 1932) was appointed instead.

With a population of over one billion, India is now second in numbers only to China, and its population is increasing at a faster rate. It has at its disposal both the atomic bomb (1974) and intermediate-range ballistic missiles (1989). Only India and Japan can seriously affect the moves of China and Russia in Asia, and India has the scale and the military power which Japan, as a pacifist country, lacks. With the end of the Cold War in 1991, and the breakup of the Soviet Empire, relations between India and the USA have improved. The extraordinary rise of China makes that inevitable. With the opening up of foreign investment and freer markets, Nehru's state socialism was exchanged for privatization and participation in the world economy.

After 1991, when India chose the market economy over the planned state, the number of people living below the poverty line fell from half the population in 1978 to a quarter in 2000; GDP and growth rates have risen; India has achieved self-sufficiency in food; its people are living longer; the rigidity of caste has been lessened; its middle class has grown; and the fundamentals of its economy and finances in 2005 were sound. It speaks volumes that India should have divested itself of foreign aid. The wonder about India is that, having enfranchised the masses, it has managed to retain the open, democratic form of government introduced in 1950.

Be that as it may, if the living standards of those countless millions who scratch a living in the traditional village economy are to be raised, India will have to improve its economy still more. Its growth rate and national income per head in 2005 were about half those of China. The race is between growing numbers and economic performance.

The political outlook in India is more disturbing than the economic. The country is in danger of succumbing to religious, communal, linguistic and regional political rivalries. Demands for autonomy are made by the Sikhs, the Kashmiris and the Tamils. The Muslim minority feels threatened by the Hindu majority. In the 1980s there were several violent clashes between Sikhs and Hindus. In May 1987 the decision to bring the state of Punjab under the control of the central government led to more bloodshed. In December 1992, following the destruction by Hindus of a sixteenth-century mosque, there were nationwide riots, and bombings in Bombay and Calcutta. Relations between Muslims and Hindus are always close to boiling point in Kashmir. After more than half a century, the region's desire for independence remains unfulfilled. In 2005, it was still garrisoned by half a million Indian soldiers. There are other threats from neighbouring Nepal, where a Maoist victory might stir up India's communist movement. In 2005 India had hopes of obtaining a permanent seat on a reformed UN Security Council, for which it will need China's vote.

India's independence in 1947 was accompanied by the birth of Pakistan, described in its constitution of 1956 as 'an Islamic Republic under the governance of Allah'. Inspired by the poet Muhammad Iqbal (1873–1938), founder of the Muslim League, Pakistan was a new nation based on religious conviction rather than historical tradition. Consisting in 1947 of two halves, located on opposite sides of India, and with entirely different linguistic and cultural traits, the new nation was governed from Karachi in the west.

Pakistan has been governed for half its life by the military. Despite all the face-saving rhetoric, it is probably the world's largest military dictatorship. In 1958, appalled at the disunity and disintegration of the state, Field Marshal Muhammad Ayub Khan (1907–74) seized power. The constitution was dissolved and 'basic democracy', a euphemism for military government, was installed. Unable to do any better than the civilian government that had preceded him, Ayub Khan was replaced in 1969 by General Agha Muhammad Yahya Khan (1917–80). Thenceforth, military rule alternated with sporadic attempts to introduce democracy. In 1971, the growing conflict of interests between East and West Pakistan resulted in war. The eastern half, assisted by India, became Bangladesh. In 1972, following Britain's recognition of Bangladesh, Pakistan withdrew from the Commonwealth. The loss of East Pakistan resulted in Pakistan's return to civilian government under the Western-educated Zulfikar Ali Bhutto (1928–79), who introduced constitutional, social and economic reforms. By nationalizing industries, he undercut the predominant Indian role in the industrial and commercial sectors of the economy. In 1979, Bhutto was ousted and executed by yet another military government under General Mohammad Zia ul-Haq (1924–88), who promised to introduce a state truly conforming to Islamic principles.

Following Russia's invasion of Afghanistan in 1979, more than three million Afghan refugees flooded into Pakistan (more than a million have remained there). Aided by the USA and enforced by martial law, Zia began a massive military build-up. In this period Pakistan's support for the Afghan Islamic mujaheddin (who frustrated Soviet aims) grew. Russia's response was to draw closer to India, Pakistan's major enemy. The covert use of Pakistan by the USA to strike at the Russian-sponsored regime in Afghanistan caused a deterioration in Indo US relations.

The appointment of Zulfikar Bhutto's daughter Benazir (b. 1953) in 1988 as prime minister of Pakistan made her the first woman to lead a Muslim nation. She was ousted by the military in 1990 for alleged corruption, but returned to power in 1993. In November 1996, she was ousted again, largely for the same reason. Nawaz Sharif (b. 1949), who replaced her, began his second term as prime minister in February 1997. Under Sharif, as under his predecessors, the military, religious and political turbulence that has dogged Pakistan since its inception has denied it the necessary stability for social and economic advance.

In May 1997 Nawaz Sharif met with the Indian prime minister, Inder Kumar Gujral (b. 1919), to declare a 'new era of friendship'. Unfortunately, in April 1999, the nuclear arms race between the two countries escalated. Pakistan became the only nuclear-armed Muslim state. In October 1999, following the repulse of Pakistani guerrilla troops from India's side of the disputed Kashmir state, Nawaz Sharif was ousted by a military coup led by General Pervez Musharraf (b. 1943). In January 2000, Sharif was tried on criminal charges and jailed, but in December he was freed and went into exile in Saudi Arabia.

US–Pakistani relations have had a mixed record. In 2003, Pakistan was accused by the USA of harbouring Islamic extremists, and (through the Pakistani nuclear specialist Abdul Qadeer Khan) diffusing nuclear bomb technology to Libya, Iran and North Korea. Though Musharraf pleaded ignorance of Pakistan's role in the spread of nuclear technology, it is unlikely that Qadeer Khan acted independently. Since coming to power, Musharraf has also been accused of sponsoring armed insurgency and cross-border infiltration into Kashmir.

Paradoxically, by 2004 Pakistan had become an American ally in its fight against terrorism. Since late 2001, its air space and logistical support have been used by the USA for its war against the Taliban in Afghanistan. Pakistani soldiers (in an about-face) have helped to capture Taliban and other terrorist leaders, while pursuing Osama bin Laden and his followers.

The new relationship between the USA and Pakistan confirms the dictum that the art of politics is the art of the possible. On 25 February 2004, the US State Department in its annual Human Rights Report cited Pakistan as a government dominated by the army with a poor record on human rights. However, the very next day Colin Powell appeared before Congress to justify a $5.7 billion bill for countries that had joined the USA in the war against terrorism; heading the list was Pakistan with $700 million. In 2005, in spite of India's protests, the US was selling F16 fighter planes to Pakistan.

* * *

During the Second World War, Nepal was virtually closed to the rest of the world. The traditional control of the government by the Ranas family ended in 1950 with a coup and the restoration of the monarchy. The caste system, polygamy and child marriage were not abolished until 1963. Absolute monarchy gave way to a constitutional monarchy in 1990. Over the next decade Maoist insurgency and guerrilla warfare in the countryside (aimed at overthrowing the monarchy) claimed more than ten thousand lives. There have also been thousands of unexplained abductions. Following violent demonstrations against the king, pro-republican parties won the election in 1994. In June 2001 the king and eight members of his family were murdered by the crown prince, who then committed suicide. Since 2002, King Gyanendra, a Hindu (b. 1947), the political parties and the Maoists (who want a democratically established republic) have continued the struggle for power. Although the king controls the army, the Maoists control much of the countryside. In January 2005, in an attempt to seize sole power, the king dismissed the government and installed a cabinet more responsive to his wishes. If all order breaks down, either India (which arms and trains the Nepalese army) or China will likely intervene. In May 2005 India resumed its military aid.

Sri Lanka obtained its independence under the Ceylon Independence Act of 1947, whereupon it became a dominion within the Commonwealth. Sinhalese replaced English as the official language; British military bases were closed. In May 1970, a socialist government came to power. The fact that the minority Tamils held power in this administration was openly resented by the majority Sinhalese; relations deteriorated into full-scale civil war. Thenceforth, the government's purpose was to ensure Sinhalese ascendancy and deny the Tamils the rights of secession. India intervened in 1987, only to withdraw its troops in 1989, when fighting between the two sides broke out again. On 26 December 2004 a tsunami caused the loss of tens of thousands of lives. In 2005 a new understanding was reached between the government and the rebels.

Tibet broke away from China in 1911 but was forcefully re-conquered in 1951. A systematic destruction of Tibetan culture by the Chinese followed. A communist government was installed in 1953. Since the revolt of 1959, when the Dalai Lama and one hundred thousand Tibetans fled to India, any aspirations for Tibetan independence have been suppressed by China.

Following the liberation of India in 1945, the British – who had tried to subjugate Burma in three wars between 1824 and 1884 – yielded to Burmese demands for home rule. The Union of Burma[6] came formally into existence on 4 January 1948. The first to recognize Mao Zedong's victory in 1949, in 1960 the Burmese signed a treaty of friendship and non-aggression with China. From the post-war struggle between communists and non-communists there emerged – as a result of an army coup in 1962 – the communist military ruler Ne Win (1911–2002). As constitutional president, he abolished the parliamentary system and proclaimed the Socialist Republic of the Union of Burma in 1974. In establishing a one-party state, he was greatly influenced by his visits to China. All land, industry and commerce became state owned and directed. By expelling three hundred thousand foreigners, he ended Chinese and Indian control of Burmese business and administration. Resentment against foreign control had been going on for five hundred years.[7]

Ne Win's harsh rule led to the impoverishment of his country. On his resignation in July 1988, following anti-government riots, power was seized by General Saw Maung, who promised a return to democracy. The next year Burma was renamed Myanmar (the traditional name). Although democratic forces easily triumphed in the free election of May 1990 (the first in thirty years), the military refused to relinquish power. Opponents, including Nobel laureate Aung San Suu Kyi (whose father Aung San, leader of the democratic movement, had been murdered in 1947), were placed under house arrest; the USA and the UN responded with sanctions. Burma is an example of a rich country (once the richest in Southeast Asia) impoverishing itself through disunity and bad government. In May 1997 (with Indonesia's support and in spite of America's opposition), Myanmar became a member of the Association of Southeast Asian Nations (ASEAN).[8] It is also a member of the World Trade Organization (WTO). In May 2004 a new constitution was drafted, but the military junta remained in power. In an attempt to improve relations with India, in October 2004 the latest military dictator, Than Shwe (b. 1933), visited Delhi.

With the end of the Japanese occupation of Malaya in 1945,[9] a bitter struggle took place between the British and communist-led rebels. Not until Malaya became independent in 1957 within the Commonwealth was a peaceful, integrated, multi-ethnic, multi-religious society attained. In that year, it was admitted to the UN. In 1963 Malaya, with Singapore, Sabah and Sarawak, became the Federation of Malaysia. Thenceforth, until President Sukarno's fall from power in 1965, Indonesia waged an undeclared war against Malaysia. (The Philippines claimed Sabah until 1978.) Because of the growing tensions between ethnic Chinese (who dominated the economic structure) and ethnic Malays (who dominated politics), Singapore peacefully seceded from Malaysia and became a separate state in 1965. With the exception of the short-lived Asian recession of 1998, it has since thrived. In 1967, Malaysia became one of the founding members of ASEAN. Under the strong leadership of Dr Mahathir bin Mohamad (b. 1925) – who imposed strict currency controls – it declined help from the international community to recover independently from the business collapse of the late 1980s. In October 2003, Mahathir retired after twenty-two years in power. In 2004 Malaysia's economy was well integrated into the WTO and it is one of the few Islamic countries that claims to be a democracy. It remains to be seen whether the racial tolerance between Malays, Chinese and Indians will continue undisturbed.

The post-war struggle for independence in French Indo-China followed a violent course. By the time the French returned in 1945, Laos, Cambodia and Vietnam had all developed powerful communist movements demanding independence.[10] As a result of a revolution that broke out in August 1945, North Vietnam became communist. Although the French granted autonomy to the monarchies of Laos and Cambodia (both neutral until the 1960s), they withheld it from Vietnam. Instead, the latter was divided into a communist north (Democratic Republic of Vietnam) and a French–US-supported non-communist south (eventually to be known as the Republic of Vietnam). Widespread insurrection against the French followed.

Supported by considerable US military aid, the French began a seemingly endless struggle against the communist Vietminh.

Despite American money and military advisers, French power in Vietnam was finally overturned with the decisive defeat of French troops by the North Vietnamese at Dien Bien Phu in 1954. At a conference at Geneva in the same year, Vietnam was divided once more at the 17th Parallel into two zones: the communist northern half led by the guerrilla leader Ho Chi Minh (1890–1969) and the non-communist south (which became an independent republic in 1955) led by US-supported Ngo Dinh Diem (1901–63). In 1956, Diem reneged on his promise to hold the national elections called for by the Geneva Accord. As a result, northern-armed Vietcong guerrillas began their revolt against his unpopular rule in the south; they were backed by northern troops (armed by the Soviets and China), who began to infiltrate South Vietnam. Determined to contain the communist challenge, in 1963 the Americans began what would prove to be a disastrous intervention. Vietnam became a pawn in the much wider power struggle of the Cold War.

On 2 November 1963, with the political situation in South Vietnam becoming desperate, the Americans connived with the Saigon military in the overthrow of President Diem. On 7 August 1964, the US Congress authorized the use of force in Vietnam after two US destroyers had supposedly been attacked in the Gulf of Tonkin. (The claim has never been substantiated.) In February 1965, with the whole of Southeast Asia supposedly threatened by 'communist tyranny' – the 'domino effect' – President Johnson made the fatal decision to send more troops and planes to South Vietnam. The heavy fighting between communist and non-communist (supported by the USA) troops, coupled with massive bombing by the USA of North Vietnam as well as Vietcong positions in the south, caused the deaths of about four million Vietnamese (one in ten of the total population). More than two million Vietnamese fled, about one million of them to the USA. Thousands of Vietnamese became refugee 'boat people'. Thirty years of conflict between Vietnam, France and the USA finally came to an end in 1973, when the last US troops left. At a cost of 58,000 troops, and having been unwilling to wage a nuclear war for fear of drawing China into the conflict, the Americans had fought and lost their longest war. For the first time, a Third World country had defeated the army of the most powerful Western industrial society. With the Americans gone, in 1975 the communist North Vietnam conquered South Vietnam. In June 1976, the country was officially reunited. Vietnam's expansion into Cambodia and Laos in the late 1970s and early 1980s resulted in a brief but intense border war with China.

In February 1994, partly as a result of the deterioration of its relations with China, and partly because of Vietnamese moves towards capitalism, the USA reversed its hostile attitude to Vietnam and ended its nineteen-year embargo on trade. In July 1995 it extended full diplomatic recognition to the communist government – a move that China considered encirclement and Russia did not applaud. In that year Vietnam was admitted to the UN. In 1999, China and Vietnam settled their dispute over borders and territorial waters in the Gulf of Tonkin. In an attempt to cement relations, in November 2000 President Clinton visited Vietnam; he was the first US president to do so. In 2005 power in Vietnam still lay in communist hands.

The US had first intervened militarily in Cambodia in May 1966, and had secretly bombed North Vietnamese forces on Cambodian soil in 1969. Cambodia itself had been fighting North Vietnamese communist troops, as well as Khmer Rouge communist guerrillas led by Pol Pot (1925–98). Following the Khmer Rouge capture of Phnom Penh in April 1975, and the overthrow of the US-backed government of Lon Nol, about 1.5 million Cambodians were executed or worked or starved to death.[11] Cambodia became the Democratic Republic of Kampuchea, with Pol Pot as the premier. The USA continued to support him because of his anti-Soviet stance in the Cold War. Civil war persisted, with heavy loss of life. Border fighting in 1978 between Cambodia and Vietnam led to the latter's invasion of both Laos and Cambodia. A massive flight of Cambodians to Thailand took place. Prince Norodom Sihanouk (b. 1922), who was recognized by many Cambodians as their leader, fled to Beijing.

In 1993, UN-sponsored elections were boycotted by the remnants of the Khmer Rouge. A new constitution restored Sihanouk to the monarchy. In August 1996 negotiations began between a breakaway faction of the Khmer Rouge and the

Cambodian government. The next year, tensions between the different political factions made stable government in Phnom Penh almost impossible. Corruption was and still is rampant. Pol Pot was ousted from power by the Khmer Rouge in 1997 and died the following year. Cambodia joined ASEAN on 30 April 1999 and the WTO in September 2003. Earlier, in January 2003, a serious riot had broken out against Thais resident in Cambodia. In 2004 Cambodia held its third election. In October, Prince Sihanouk retired and his son ascended the throne.

Although a Conference at Geneva in 1962 had guaranteed the neutrality and independence of Laos, a chaotic political situation ensued out of which – despite US air support and military aid to the non-communists – the Laotian communists and their Vietnamese allies emerged triumphant. In trying to destroy the so-called Ho Chi Minh Trail, American planes made 580,000 bombing runs and dropped about 2 million tons of explosives over Laos. In 1973 a ceasefire finally ended this bombing.

The Lao People's Democratic Republic was proclaimed on 3 December 1975, with the monarchy being abolished. In 1977, Laos signed a twenty-five-year treaty of friendship with Vietnam. With that country's help, the Democratic Republic remained in power for the next fifteen years. The Vietnamese army did not withdraw from Laos and Cambodia until 1989. The massive flight of refugees from Vietnam, Cambodia and Laos, which had begun in the 1940s, ended about the same time.

In the early 1990s, Laos nominally abandoned communism for capitalism. It also sought to make friends with such former enemies as China, Thailand and the USA. Laos joined ASEAN in July 1997. In 2004, a long-forgotten insurgency was reappearing; bombs exploded in the capital, Vientiane. The Chinese of both Laos and Cambodia, having fled the area earlier, were filtering back in spite of the fact that it would be difficult to imagine an economy that is in worse shape than that of Laos.

Thailand was never colonized by the Western powers.[12] In 1932 a bloodless coup established a parliament under a constitutional monarchy. Invaded by Japan in 1941, the next year it declared war against its traditional British, French and American allies. In retaliation, US air raids were made on Bangkok. With the defeat of the Japanese in 1945 Thailand became pro-Western again. In 1946 it joined the UN. In 1948 a military coup ousted the communists from government. In 1954, with Pakistan and the Philippines, Thailand became a member of SEATO. In 1967 it became one of the founding members of ASEAN. In the 1960s and 1970s, with the Vietnamese occupying Laos and Cambodia, and the border threatened by thousands of refugees and Vietnamese troops, Thailand could no longer remain neutral. It provided air bases from which the USA bombed North Vietnam, and sent thousands of Thai troops to support South Vietnam.

After the abolition of absolute monarchy in 1932, military coups and growing corruption have become endemic in Thailand. Since the coup in 1976 by General Kriangsak Chomanan (1917–2003), other military coups have alternated with democratic elections. From the 1980s onwards, a large export-oriented manufacturing sector has been developed almost entirely by groups of Thai-Chinese (about 10 per cent of the population). Border relations with Myanmar have worsened. A predominantly Buddhist country, Thailand's sixty-two million people have been relatively free of the violence caused by separatist militias elsewhere. Communist-led insurgencies have flared up periodically since the 1950s, but have never been strong enough to threaten the government. A deal struck between Thailand and China in 1979 ended Chinese support for Thai communists. In July 1997 a deep recession in the Thai economy caused a crisis in Asian financial markets. Thailand recovered only with major financial support from abroad. Following elections, in 2001 Thaksin Shinawatra (b. 1949) became prime minister, and two years later he launched a war on drugs, which claimed the lives of several thousand people. Thailand's tourist regions were seriously affected by the 2004 tsunami.

The fierce struggle for independence that followed the surrender of Japanese forces in Vietnam in 1945 had its parallel in Indonesia, where nationalists were determined to rid themselves of Dutch rule. The Indonesian leader Achmed Sukarno (1902–70)[13] had cooperated with the Japanese throughout the war as the head of a puppet government. In 1945 he declared Indonesia independent. The arms which he subsequently used in his struggle against the returning Dutch had been provided by the Japanese. It was not until December 1949 – after much bloodshed – that Dutch forces finally conceded defeat and returned to the Netherlands. An Indonesian republic was established in August 1950 with Sukarno as president 'for life'. The Celebes, the Moluccas (in 2001 the scene of growing violence between Christians and Muslims) and parts of Borneo were annexed after the war. The western part of New Guinea remained under Dutch control until 1963, when it was annexed by Indonesia as Irian Jaya (the name was changed to West Papua in 1999). Sukarno's claims in the 1960s to Sarawak and Sabah were resisted by Malaysia. In 1967 Indonesia became a member of ASEAN.

Following an abortive coup, in 1968 Sukarno was replaced by the more US-inclined head of the army, General Suharto (b. 1921), who repressed the communists (estimates vary from 300,000 to 1 million deaths), Islamic fundamentalists and many Chinese businessmen who had controlled much of Indonesia's economy. He also ended hostilities against Malaysia, re-established close ties with the USA and rejoined the UN. In December 1976, with the collapse of Portuguese rule, Suharto annexed the largely Roman Catholic province of East Timor – an act condemned by the international community. He was re-elected for a sixth five-year term in 1993. By now, the Chinese had reasserted their control of commerce, as they had done down the centuries.

While the Suharto family enriched itself, the conditions of the majority of Indonesians worsened. Suharto's policy of moving landless people to other parts of the archipelago only increased ethnic violence. In May 1998, with anti-Chinese riots breaking out across the country, Suharto stepped down. Power was assumed by Vice-President B. J. Habibie (b. 1936). By curbing the power of Chinese-controlled companies, he exacerbated the problems of the economy. In October 1999, after thirty-two years of dictatorship, Abdurrahman Wahid (b. 1940) became Indonesia's first democratically appointed leader. Reform-minded, his leadership lasted just two years.

Since then, Indonesia has been plagued by violent uprisings, including those in Aceh, West Papua and East Timor. After twenty-three years of occupation, East Timor gained its independence in 1999 when UN and Australian forces intervened. Amid the general turmoil, in July 2001 ex-president Suharto was placed under house arrest. President Wahid was replaced by Megawati Sukarnoputri (b. 1947), the daughter of Sukarno. In July 2002, she was re-elected in the first direct presidential election but she was perpetually burdened with the demands of several provinces to secede, a lacklustre economy, continuing corruption and Islamic militants, some of whom were responsible for the Bali bombings of 2002. In 2004 Megawati was defeated by former general Susilo Bambang Yudhoyono (b. 1949). The election was remarkably peaceful but promised little change. Indonesia's embattled Aceh province was devastated by the 2004 tsunami. In August 2005 the Indonesian government signed a peace agreement with the Free Aceh Movement.

In contrast to Burma and Indonesia, the Japanese invasion of the Philippines in December 1941 was fiercely resisted by the Americans and the Filipinos.[14] Equally fierce fighting against the Japanese accompanied the return of the Americans in 1944. Fulfilling a promise made by the USA in 1934, the Republic of the Philippines came into existence on 4 July 1946. Since then, the Philippines has been plagued by economic and ethnic troubles; communist insurgency has become widespread; Muslim separatists (the Moro National Liberation Front) in the southern islands have grown in influence and numbers. Conflict has ravaged the islands for decades, with no end in sight. In December 1972, with the political situation deteriorating, President Ferdinand Marcos (1917–89) introduced martial law; opposition parties were suppressed. Martial law was not lifted until 1981, and thereafter the insurgents re-emerged. In danger of his life, Marcos fled the country in February 1986. After becoming president that year, with the aid of the American military, Maria Corazón Aquino (b. 1933) survived several attempted coups. Until the USA vacated the Subic Bay Naval Station in 1992, the Philippines was under US protection. A democratic form of government of sorts prevailed and Aquino was successful in negotiating with some of the Muslim secessionists, but she failed to overcome the communist insurgency. In February 1992, General Fidel Valdez Ramos (b. 1928) replaced her. He was followed by Joseph Estrada (b. 1937), who in November 2000 was impeached for corruption, but his trial before the Senate was postponed indefinitely. By January 2001, mass protests in Manila had forced him to flee. With the help of the military, his vice-president, Gloria Macapagal-Arroyo (b. 1947), assumed power. Although still hard pressed by communist and Muslim secessionist forces, she was successful in the presidential elections of May 2004.

South and Southeast Asia's location at one of the world's main cross-roads, its population density, its significance as a centre of the Islamic religion and its importance as a source of food all ensure that it will play a major role in world affairs. It was to offset great-power intervention in their domestic affairs that the Association of Southeast Asian Nations (ASEAN) was formed in 1967. This association largely replaced the earlier (1954), American-inspired SEATO agreement. It differs from SEATO in so far as it places stress not on military security, nor on containing communism, but on modernization and regional economic integration. Its chief successes have been in commercial and diplomatic collaboration.

In East Asia the Japanese invasion of China in 1937 set the stage for the civil war between communists and nationalists that followed the Japanese surrender in 1945. Despite America's willingness to back Chiang Kai-shek (as Stalin did at the outset), the communists under the leadership of Mao Zedong extended their control to northern China and overran much of Manchuria. Far from ignoring the peasantry (as Marx had done) or repressing them (as Stalin had done), Mao looked upon them as the core of the revolution. In January 1949 the communists entered Tientsin and Beijing; Nanking, the nationalists' capital, fell in April. In the summer of 1949, with the help of the US Seventh Fleet, about two million non-communist refugees fled mainland China for Taiwan. For the next three decades, the USA regarded the nationalists on Taiwan as the legitimate government of China.

In September 1949 the People's Republic of China was officially proclaimed, with Mao and Chou En-lai at its head. The new regime was immediately recognized by the Soviet Union and its allies. In 1950,

China made a thirty-year treaty of friendship, alliance and mutual assistance with the USSR. In November of that year, it intervened against the USA in the Korean War.

By 1955, about one million Chinese so-called 'traitors, counter-revolutionaries and bourgeois capitalists' had been put to death by the communists; whole social classes were wiped out. Mao, who systematically destroyed his enemies, is said to have killed more of his own people than any other leader in history. The number maimed by him for life is beyond counting. No remorse was shown to the victims. The system of public accusation adopted by the communists, whereby the accused was forced to indulge in self-criticism, followed Chinese traditions, as did the brainwashing and thought-control tactics. Many of those who responded to Mao's call (1956) to 'let a hundred flowers bloom, let a hundred schools of thought contend' were subsequently killed or jailed as 'poisonous weeds'. In 1958, following the Russian and Indian examples of forced industrialization, Mao launched his Great Leap Forward. China would and could industrialize independently of the West. Chinese agriculture was simultaneously forcibly collectivized. The outcome on both counts was disastrous: millions died of famine; the economic development of China was retarded.

No sooner had the reverberations of the Great Leap Forward subsided than the Great Proletarian Cultural Revolution (1966–70) began.[15] By encouraging students, organized into units of Red Guards, to attack anyone who stood in the way of a continuing cultural revolution (Mao's 'little red book', *Quotations from Chairman Mao Zedong*, became the basis of communist indoctrination), Mao's aim was to rid himself of his critics and entrenched party veterans who, he was convinced, were planning to betray the socialist cause. But the Cultural Revolution reduced some provinces of China to a state of anarchy, and in 1969 Mao was compelled to use the army to restore order. Under its command, the exercise in cultural purification was terminated. In condemning his critics – in his mindless terror – Mao set back China twenty years. The positive aspect of his rule was that he ended the West's exploitation of China, and made it a great power with a permanent seat on the UN Security Council.

With the Cultural Revolution halted, many senior party members, army leaders and bureaucrats proceeded to reverse its effects. A start was made in 1971 with the purging of Marshal Lin Piao (defence minister and vice-chairman of the republic), who had headed the purification movement. Lin died in mysterious circumstances while trying to defect to Russia later the same year. Nine months after Mao's death in 1976, his widow Chiang Ching (b. 1914) was also called to account for her actions during the Cultural Revolution. In October 1977, she and the rest of the Gang of Four were arrested.[16] Two years later Chiang Ching was sentenced to death, which was later commuted to life imprisonment. (She committed suicide in jail in 1991.) In 1978–9, political outcasts purged under Mao were rehabilitated.

Under the leadership of Hua Guofeng, the party's new chairman, and Deng Xiaoping (1904–97),[17] vice-chairman, there followed a shift in emphasis from class struggle and continuing revolution to modernization. Deng had been a 'capitalist roader' all along: prosperity first, ideology last. In place of central planning, the market system was partly restored. Many techniques of capitalist production, such as wage incentives and the appointment of professional managers to factories and farms, were introduced. Economic management was decentralized and agricultural production was stimulated by partial privatization. The effect on economic and political power was deep and widespread. By the 1990s China's productive capacity had surpassed that of India. Between 1978 and 2004 the improvement in the standard of living of some Chinese was unprecedented; a new middle class appeared; many of the poor have improved their lot. In the past twenty-five years GDP has increased on average by 9 per cent each year. Beijing claims that 160 million people have been lifted out of poverty. Even allowing for the dislocation (some say chaos) caused by rapid growth, widespread unemployment, pollution and deterioration of health-care, it is a remarkable achievement, although often exaggerated. In 2005 the economy was still roaring ahead; China had replaced Japan as the world's third-greatest trader.

Deng's successor, Jiang Zemin (b. 1926), the power behind the throne for many years, declared himself in favour of Deng's policy of privatization. At the fiftieth anniversary of communist rule in October 2000, Jiang's giant portrait was placed alongside those of

Mao and Deng. He had become a revered figure in the Chinese hierarchy.

The changes in China's foreign relations since the Second World War have been as dramatic as its domestic upheavals. Immediately following Mao's triumph, China reasserted itself in Manchuria, Inner Mongolia and Chinese Turkistan. In 1950 the People's Liberation Army reclaimed Tibet (which had broken away during China's 1911 revolution). The Chinese also assisted the post-war revolutionary movements against the British in Malaya and the French in Indo-China. When, in 1950, American-led UN forces in Korea approached the Chinese Yalu River, a quarter of a million Chinese were launched against them. The Chinese also became strong supporters of the North Vietnamese in their war against the South Vietnamese and their French and US supporters. In the Suez Crisis of 1956, China openly supported Nasser.

Dominating all else in East Asia in the post-war period were communist China's relations with the Soviet Union. In 1950 Stalin rescinded the 1945 treaty with Chiang Kai-shek's nationalists in favour of one with the communists. This treaty decisively changed the balance of power in Asia. The first publicly expressed rift between the Chinese and the Russians came in 1960 at the Moscow International Conference of Communist Parties. Three years later, the Chinese condemned Khrushchev's policy of peaceful co-existence with the West. Paradoxically, despite centuries of rivalry and tension, in 2005 Russia (along with the USA) was by far the biggest source of conventional weapons to China.

The Americans have had a similar love–hate relationship with the Chinese.[18] After Mao's victory in 1949 they sought to isolate communist China from the rest of the world. In 1954 President Eisenhower's government undertook to defend Taiwan from armed incursions from the mainland. Nuclear war was even threatened. China did not possess its own hydrogen bomb until 1967. In 1971, with a changed outlook on the part of the USA, the Chinese People's Republic became a member of the United Nations in place of Taiwan. Following President Nixon's visit to Beijing in 1972, US liaison offices were established there. As a result of Nixon's second journey to China in 1977, Sino-American relations improved still more. In December 1978, after thirty years of estranged relations, the two countries established normal diplomatic ties. All the preconditions demanded by China were met: the USA terminated its formal diplomatic relations with Taiwan, abrogated the 1954 defence treaty that committed the USA to defend the island, and removed its troops.

By the late 1980s, China had become one of the world's largest economies. US businessmen hastened to China in the hope of exploiting its limitless market – just as they had done in the late nineteenth century. They eagerly competed with each other in trying to satisfy China's needs. Only with the massacre of pro-democracy demonstrators in Tiananmen Square, Beijing, in June 1989 did Sino-US relations experience a setback.[19] They remained on a downward course until friendly overtures were made by the Bush (Senior) and Clinton administrations. China could no longer be sidelined.

After two centuries of weakness and humiliation, China seeks the status and prestige it feels it deserves. In Asia, Africa and Latin America, it is expanding its economic and diplomatic presence. Its foreign trade has grown at an extraordinarily rapid rate since 1978. US–Chinese relations worsened again after America's bombing of the Chinese embassy in Belgrade in 1999, and its accusation that China had been spying on America's nuclear-weapons programme. While offering assistance, China has consistently resisted US proposals to pressure North Korea to abandon its nuclear programme.

A major challenge to Western political as well as economic interests in East Asia and the Pacific must ultimately come from China. A country that until recently claimed historical right to the entire South China Sea, including the Paracel and Spratly Islands (which have untapped oil and natural gas reserves), that challenges other countries' claims to the oil and gas of Central Asia, that is rearming at an unusually fast rate (its projected defence budget for 2005 is $50–60 billion) and that is preparing for conflict with Taiwan has to be taken seriously. Yet there are grounds for hope. The economies of the USA and China are greatly interdependent. Roughly half of China's exports go to the USA. Also, while the Chinese Communist Party's rule is still absolute, there is more political participation and elections are more competitive. These days individuals are arrested, not whole classes. In late 2003, while steadfastly opposed to sharing sovereignty with any other state, China signed a treaty of amity and cooperation with ASEAN.[20] China has also participated in UN operations in Cambodia, East Timor, Congo and Liberia.

In June 2004 President Hu Jintao met the presidents of Russia, Kazakhstan, Kyrgyzstan, Tajikistan and Uzbekistan in Tashkent to form a security alliance, the Shanghai Cooperation Organization (SCO). For Russia and China it was a matter of countering the growing US military presence in Central Asia; there was talk of US encirclement. In 2005 trade between China and Central Asian countries was many times greater than it had been in 1992. China has made investments in the oil industry of Kazakhstan and Iran[21] (see Map XXIV).

Because of its history, China is sensitive to outsiders meddling in its affairs, especially over Taiwan. A civilization that is more than four thousand years old does not like to be told what to do by the Americans. In 2005 it particularly resented the USA advising the EU to leave the arms embargo against China in place. Until November 1999 the USA had been reluctant to support China's entry into the WTO. In 2003 it complained that China was using a fixed exchange rate to undercut US manufactures; these complaints were supported by the IMF and the G8. In 2005 there was growing criticism by the US Congress of China's trade practices. However, a country that has a huge trade surplus with the USA, and (together with Japan) is financing America's debt ('Asia lends, America spends') is not likely to give Americans serious trouble at this point. The hope is that China and the USA will move cautiously and think in the long term. The stronger China becomes, the greater the rivalry there will be between it and the USA in Southeast Asia and the Pacific.

With the exceptions of Japan and Korea, overseas Chinese affect the economics of every country on the Asian side of the Pacific rim. The wealth and influence of the Chinese living in Malaysia, Thailand, Indonesia and Vietnam far exceed their numbers.[22] The GNP of Chinese living abroad in 2001 was larger than that of mainland China. Their investments in mainland China exceed those of the Americans and the Japanese. They have provided much of the capital and business talent fuelling China's present drive to modernization.[23]

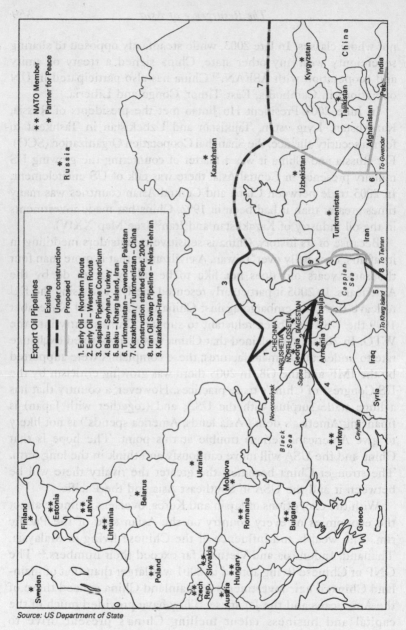

Source: US Department of State

Map XXIV Central Asia in 2004

China's success has been so great that it seems churlish to mention its drawbacks. Yet many of China's people are still desperately poor; many rural Chinese are even poorer than they were; income inequality is growing. Simply keeping 1.3 billion people alive often drains the country of much of what it has achieved. The Chinese bureaucracy and its eccentric commercial environment hamper business with outsiders; so does its lack of respect for property rights and business law. Much has been done to improve property rights; much still remains to be done. Corruption is a major problem. The primary fear about the economy in 2005 was that it was overheated and might implode. The country is also threatened by ethnic, religious, social and political challenges. In 2001 the religious sect Falun Gong was seen as a threat to social stability; members of the sect protested at government persecution by setting themselves ablaze in Tiananmen Square. The major long-term problem for China is the growing tension between the rigid, static, political system of a police state and the dynamic development of the economic sector. Sooner or later one will have to yield to the other. Outside the walls, the problems of Taiwan and North Korea weighed heavily in Beijing.

The British Crown Colony of Hong Kong surrendered to the Japanese on 25 December 1941. Thousands of British and Canadian troops were taken prisoner. Reoccupied by the British in 1945, the colony experienced an influx of refugees from China following Mao's victory in 1949. The Korean War in the 1950s provided Hong Kong with an opportunity to develop its industry and manufactures; by the 1980s it had become one of the world's leading centres of trade and finance with a per capita GDP among the highest in the world. In 1984 Britain agreed to hand back the colony to China. China agreed not to alter the existing economic and social structure for fifty years. When Hong Kong reverted to China in 1997, Beijing appointed Tung Chee-hwah its chief controller. Growing tensions between the autocratic mainland and the would-be democratic territory, coupled with the effects of a depressed economy, came to a head in July 2003 when five hundred thousand demonstrators in Hong Kong denounced China's plans for the territory.

The outcome was that the proposed legislation was withdrawn. In March 2005 Hong Kong's chief controller was replaced by Donald Tsang. The stand-off between Beijing and Hong Kong continues.

Since 1949, Taiwan has remained economically and militarily strong. It has a powerful economy and abundant world trade. It trades and invests heavily in mainland China. The election in 1978 of Chiang Kai-shek's eldest son, Chiang Ching-kuo (following his father's death in 1975), stiffened Taiwan's resistance to communist China's demands for reunification. In 1987 martial law was lifted after thirty-eight years; in 1991 forty-three years of emergency rule ended. Taiwan now has a US-supported democratic form of government, but tensions between Taiwan and the mainland are growing; the need for reunification is supported by a growing majority of the Chinese people. Taiwan has its own ethnic and political problems; corruption is widespread.

Despite growing threats being made by Beijing, Taiwan's twenty-three million people continue to hang on to their independence. In April 2001 President G. W. Bush stated that America has a duty to defend Taiwan in the event of an attack by China in spite of the fact that in the Shanghai Communiqué of 1972 the USA declared that there is only one China. Most observers believe that as long as Taiwan refrains from declaring its independence from the mainland, and shuns nuclear weapons, the problem of reunification might drag on.

In March 2004 Chen Shui-bian was re-elected as Taiwan's president by a narrow margin. As expected, his election was protested against by Beijing, which accused him of 'playing with fire'. His falling popularity at the polls in December 2004 was a relief to both China and the USA, neither of whom wishes to pick a bone with each other about Taiwan. In March 2005 China increased the tension by approving a counter-secession law to deter the island from asserting its independence. Regardless of US views, Taiwan is the one subject over which China will not compromise. China's present strategy is to woo Taiwan's opposition leaders.

The defeat and occupation of Japan in 1945 by the USA gave the Americans an opportunity to express their innate messianism.[24] A new constitution of parliamentary rule was drafted by them. Contrary to Japanese tradition, which recognized a separation of executive, legislative and judicial power, the American-inspired constitution was based on the principle of judicial supremacy. The system of law, which hitherto had drawn its inspiration from the Germans and the French, was forced into an Anglo-American mould. Shinto ceased to be the state religion; the emperor was divested of his divinity and of any responsibility for a war waged in his name; the army and navy were disbanded; women were given the vote and equal legal status with men; compulsory education was extended to nine years; many existing school textbooks of history and geography were destroyed; the number of universities was increased; 40 per cent of the land under cultivation was confiscated and redistributed. The settled pattern of family and succession laws also underwent radical change. Under the new constitution of 1947 Japan formally renounced war

Since the 1950s Japan has been the industrial giant of the East – particularly in cars and electronics. Reluctant to take Western advice, it reintroduced a pre-war model of economic development of its own making. In the 1970s and 1980s a great deal of real estate and industry in America passed to Japanese ownership and control.[25] At the same time Japan – by buying more US Treasury Bonds than anyone else – played a vital role in the financing of the US government. By the 1990s, its total productivity was second only to that of the USA; its branch factories had invaded the manufacturing centres of the Western world; its trade surpluses were unparalleled. By 2004 it was the world's second-largest economy.

Harsh US criticism of Japanese trade policy in the 1990s resulted in Japan seeking closer ties with China and the other countries of East Asia. This process had begun earlier, with the Treaty of Peace and Friendship ratified with China in October 1978, which ended a state of war that had existed between the two nations since 1931. Since then Japan has given billion of dollars in aid to China. In an eight-year trade agreement, also signed in 1978 and extended since then, Japan had become one of China's largest trading partners. In August 1993 the Japanese government made a long-awaited apology to China for its atrocious conduct towards the Chinese in the 1930s and 1940s. In 2001 Japan's sales to Asia were greater than those to the USA; they were much more than those to the EU. In 2004 China became Japan's biggest trading partner, accounting for a 20 per cent share, compared with 18 per cent with the United States. In the 1990s there was also a shift in the share of Japan's foreign direct investments from the USA and parts of Europe to East and Southeast Asia. Japan was the largest outside investor in Russian Siberia. Until the shift in policy, about 50 per cent of Japanese direct foreign invest-ment had been made in North America. In making available to China and Russia its economic and technological resources, Japan is helping to alter the balance of power in East Asia.

The stronger Japan has become, the greater has been the emphasis placed upon its achievements since the war. Changes in politics and education introduced by the Americans during their six years and eight months of occupation are being reassessed. Despite its pacifist constitution – it is defended by the USA – the martial values of traditional Japan are returning; rearmament is growing. Projected military spending in 2005 ($40–50 billion) is the sharpest rise since 1997. Some of the war criminals executed in Tokyo after the Second World War are being rehabilitated as heroes. Protests against US troops garrisoned on Japanese soil might be stifled by the Pentagon's announcement in 2004 that it is reviewing its deploy-ment of troops in Asia. Japan is seeking a permanent seat on the United Nations Security Council. For that to happen it must have China's support.

Given Japan's limitations in material resources, area and popu-lation, its tremendous burst of energy since the 1960s may have run its course. From 1992 to 1996 it had almost zero economic growth, but the effects of this were concealed by massive trade surpluses and domestic savings. Its world-beating industries are moving offshore. Certainly the giant gains made by the Japanese in the world economy from the Korean War to the 1990s cannot be dissociated from a perilous vulnerability to world forces. No major country is more dependent upon the world economy than Japan. Demographically, it is ageing; the traditional Japanese work and savings ethics are being eroded by demands for a higher standard of living. Added to Japan's trials were the Kobe earthquake and the poison gas attacks by the Aum Shin Rikyo cult in the Tokyo underground in 1995. In April 2001 Junichiro Koizumi became Japan's prime minister; he was re-elected in 2004, and again in 2005, after calling a surprise election.

Communist North Korea emerged as a result of the Cold War in 1948. Little was known about it in the West. The dictator of North Korea, Marshal Kim Il-sung (1912–94), the 'Great Leader', who had ruled for more than forty years, died in July 1994. He was succeeded by his son, Kim Jong-il (b. 1942), who was named secretary of the Communist Party in 1997.

Following the Korean War (for which there is still no peace settlement), Korea was divided between the largely Russian-equipped and -trained North and the American-supported South. The North accused the South of being an instrument of American imperialism. In 1968 North Korea seized the US intelligence ship *Pueblo*, and imprisoned its crew for eleven months. In 1969 it shot down a US reconnaissance plane. Talks aimed at the peaceful reunification of North and South Korea began in 1972, and were given fresh impetus in the mid-1980s and 2000 (when South Korea's president Kim Dae-jung (b. 1925) visited the North).

Since 1994 negotiations have taken place between the USA and North Korea on nuclear issues. The firing of a missile over Japan in 1998 galvanized the debate about North Korea's nuclear potential. In June 2002 a dispute over territorial waters in the Yellow Sea resulted in the death of a number of North Korean sailors. In January 2003 North Korea caused a stir by withdrawing from the Nuclear Non-Proliferation Treaty.

In the hope of making North Korea more amenable to discussing nuclear arms limitation and human rights, since 1995, when North Korea admitted its 'temporary' inability to feed its people, South Korea, the USA, Europe and Japan have all provided aid. But US hopes that the food crisis would make the North Koreans more compliant have not been realized. In 2004 a six-party commission (China, USA, Japan, South Korea, North Korea and Russia) was established in an effort to resolve North Korea's continuing stand-off on nuclear proliferation. Negotiations for disarmament continue.

All the great powers have a stake in keeping North Korea stable. Whether they will succeed in overcoming the emotional and ideological barriers separating North Korea from the rest of the world is something else. Reality is that North Korea is spending an infinitesimal amount on defence compared with the USA's almost half a trillion dollars. In February 2005 North Korea confirmed that it possessed nuclear weapons.

Until his assassination by a member of his government in October 1979, South Korea was governed by General Park Chung Hee (b. 1917), who had seized power in a military coup in 1961. Widespread student unrest in 1987 resulted in a new and more democratic constitution being proclaimed. Kim Young-sam (b. 1927), elected in 1993, was the first civilian president since 1961. South Korea has become one of the world's major economies. More of the country's investment flows into China than anywhere else. Bilateral trade between the two in 1992 (when they established diplomatic ties) was $6.2 billion; in 2004 it was estimated to be $60 billion. Roh Moo-hyan (b. 1946), a liberal reformer, won the election in 2002 and survived an impeachment attempt in 2004.

In 1991 both Koreas joined the UN. In the summer of 2004 America announced its intention – after fifty years – to withdraw some of its troops from the South.

In order to obtain some of the benefits that would accompany an Allied victory, in February 1945 Turkey declared war on Germany. With the end of hostilities, Turkey was pressured by Russia to place the Turkish Straits – Russia's gateway from the Black to the Mediterranean Sea – under Soviet control. Only Allied intervention at Potsdam in 1945 saved Turkey from having to yield to these demands.

Until 1948, Turkey relied on a much-weakened Britain to protect it from renewed Russian claims. In 1948 the USA (under the Truman Doctrine of containing communism) took upon itself the obligation of keeping both Turkey and Greece out of the Russian camp. By 1952, Turkey had abandoned Kemal Atatürk's neutrality and had become an important bastion of NATO's defences. It continued to honour its NATO obligations until the age-old feud between the Greek majority and the Turkish minority on the island of Cyprus came to a head in the summer of 1974. Yielding to Greek influence, in 1975 the US Congress ceased to supply arms to Turkey, which responded by closing its NATO bases. In the summer of 1978 the US arms embargo was lifted, and NATO's second-biggest land army was back within the Western fold.

In the 1990s it was not world affairs but increasingly bitter internal struggles among Turkey's ever-warring factions and sects that threatened the life of the critically weak Second Republic (formed in 1961). Although some stability was restored with the return of civilian power in 1983 (martial law imposed in 1978 ended in 1984; the state of emergency ended in 1988), brutal fighting between Turks, Kurds and Armenians caused thousands of deaths. Following the Gulf War in 1991, Turkey was besieged by thousands of Kurds fleeing Iraq. Subsequent clashes between Turks and Kurds led to heavy casualties. Many Turks have avoided their country's economic woes, and its religious and ethnic tensions, by migrating to Germany.

In June 1996 – although denounced by the Arab world – a military accord was signed between Israel and Turkey. In 1997 Prime Minister Necmettin Erbakan, the first Muslim elected to lead secular Turkey, resigned under pressure from the military. (Since 1960 the military has removed the prime minister from office three times.) Two major earthquakes in northwest Turkey in 1999, followed by an earthquake in Greece, have paradoxically improved Turkish–Greek relations.

In 1999, following its rejection in 1997, Turkey was invited to apply for membership of the EU. Although Turkey has fought alongside Americans since the Korean War, it was almost totally opposed to President George W. Bush's Iraq War, and denied America the use of Turkish bases. The Turks' biggest problem with the US invasion of Iraq is that it might result in the establishment of an autonomous Kurdish state, including oil-rich Kirkuk, which would in turn reignite its own Kurdish problems. Turkey remains the most populous Islamic country in the Middle East.

Anticipating the French promise of freedom (1936), in 1944 Syria unilaterally declared itself an independent republic.[26] A struggle followed which resulted in the French bombardment of Damascus and the loss of hundreds of lives. Only by the intervention of the United Nations in 1946 was Syria able to free itself of French control.

On 14 May 1948, the same day that the Jewish state of Israel was created, Syria (with Jordan, Egypt and the Palestinian Arabs) declared war upon the new Zionist state. Jewish arms having triumphed, in February 1949 Egypt was forced to sign a general armistice agreement with Israel; Jordan and Syria followed suit. In 1958 Syria joined Egypt in a United Arab Republic. Because of irreconcilable differences, however, the union was dissolved in 1961. In the Arab–Israeli War of 1967 Syria lost the Golan Heights. Rearmed by the Soviet Union, in 1973, in the fourth Arab–Israeli War, Syria joined Egypt again in an attack on Israel. Following America's intervention on Israel's side, Syria was defeated again. By then, the cooperation that the Arab world had shown America prior to the creation of Israel had evaporated. In July–August 1973 an army plot to kill President Hafez al-Assad (1930–2000) was suppressed. In 1974 Syria and Israel signed an agreement in Geneva that ended the fighting. Israel pulled back to the 1967 ceasefire line; a buffer zone was established and patrolled by UN troops. In 1976 Syria sent forces into Lebanon in an attempt to end that country's civil war. In February 1982 an uprising of Islamic fundamentalists took place at Hamah in Syria. It was led by the Muslim Brotherhood, a radical religious and political organization founded in 1928 in Egypt. The uprising was crushed and thousands of the insurgents were killed. Like Iran and Iraq, Syria has a large Kurdish minority.

On 6 June 1982, in response to terrorist attacks, Israel invaded Lebanon. Syrian troops were pushed back, and the fighting ended with a ceasefire. Syria's Golan Heights were seized by Israel, which proceeded to establish Jewish settlements there. In 1991 Syria joined the Allies in the first Gulf War. Since then, interminable and inconclusive negotiations have gone on concerning a peace settlement in the Middle East. Faced with Israel's refusal to evacuate occupied territory, President al-Assad remained inflexible.

In June 2000 Hafez al-Assad died and was replaced by his son Bashar (b. 1965). Although Syria fought on the side of the Americans against Iraq in 1991, it was totally opposed to the war against Iraq in 2003. With only Iran to turn to (a two-hundred-year alliance exists between Syria and Iran), Syria walks a fine line between war and peace. The Syrian government has been accused by the USA of sponsoring international terrorism and aiding insurgents within Iraq. Fortunately for Syria, though, its oil reserves are relatively small, and America's attention is focused elsewhere. In January 2005, in an unexpected move, Russia cancelled Syria's debt.

Lebanon also gained its independence from the French in 1946. This was the first time in history that Lebanon had been separated from Syria. Since the 1950s Lebanon has undergone sixteen years of invasion, civil war, violence and terrorism. In July–October 1958, at the request of the Lebanese president, US troops intervened to prevent the escalation of a civil war. In another civil war in the mid-1970s – in which Arab Muslims (70 per cent of the population) fought Arab Christians for power – sixty thousand people were killed. In the end, it was Syrian intervention that brought the fighting to a halt. Raids upon Israel by Palestinians operating from inside Lebanon caused Israel to invade in 1978 and 1980. In June 1982, in an attempt to crush the Palestine Liberation Organization (PLO; founded in 1964), Israel invaded Lebanon once more. Syria entered the battle on Lebanon's side on 9 June but was defeated. At the cost of thousands of lives (including the Sabrah and Shatila massacres of Palestinian refugees by Israel's Christian allies), Beirut was captured and the PLO driven from Lebanon – after which Israeli forces withdrew to a 'security zone' on the Israeli border, where they had to contend with the hostility of the two main Islamic parties, Hamas and Jihad al-Islami, as well as the Hezbollah Shi'ite militia. In September 1982 Lebanon's President Bashir Jemayel was assassinated.

With the breakdown of all order during Lebanon's civil war in the 1980s, terrorist bombing and hostage-taking became common. In October 1983 the deaths of hundreds of US and French peacekeepers in Beirut caused both countries to withdraw their troops, but that did not deter Israel from bombing Lebanon and its infrastructure. However, because of growing casualties and unceasing pressure from Hezbollah guerrillas, Israel withdrew its ground troops from Lebanon. In September 2004 the UN Security Council requested Syria to remove the troops it had kept in Lebanon for the past twenty-eight years. Following the assassination in March 2005 of Rafik Hariri (Lebanon's ex-prime minister) and the anti-Syrian demonstrations it stirred, Syria withdrew its armed forces.

War and discord also marked the administration of the British mandate in the Middle East, which included Palestine. Despite British efforts to resist free immigration of Jews into Palestine, by 1945 the Jewish proportion of the population of Palestine had increased sharply. On 14 May 1948, the British, unable to find a peaceful solution to the Arab–Jewish problem, relinquished their mandate to the United Nations. The Arabs having refused a UN proposal to partition Palestine into Jewish and Arab states, the state of Israel was created; the USA was the first to recognize it. The Soviet Union's help in arming Israel in 1948 was intended to diminish British power (later, the Soviets would arm the Arabs against Israel). The outcome of the war that followed was the expansion of Israel's frontiers and the dispersal of more than a million Palestinian Arabs to Jordan, the West Bank, Gaza, Syria and Lebanon. In Lebanon and Jordan the arrival of so many Palestinian refugees seriously upset the political balance of existing groups (see Map XXV).

In October 1956 Britain, France and Israel briefly invaded Egypt, but they were ordered to withdraw by the Security Council, backed by the USA and the Soviet Union. In May 1967 Egypt closed the Gulf of Aqaba to Israeli shipping, blockading the Israeli port of Elat. Believing itself to be in imminent danger, Israel struck pre-emptively against Egypt, Syria, Iraq and Jordan. In a six-day war (5–10 June 1967), it occupied the Sinai peninsula, crossed the Suez Canal, penetrated Egypt as far as Luxor and encircled the Egyptian army. It also seized east Jerusalem, the Golan Heights, the Gaza Strip and the West Bank. Many Arabs fled to Jordan, Lebanon and Syria. UN Resolution 242, calling upon Israel to withdraw from occupied territory, was disregarded. Following the 1967 war, and ignoring the Fourth Geneva Convention,[27] which forbids victors in war colonizing land seized in battle, Israel began building settlements on Arab territory. In October 1973 Egypt and Syria made a pre-emptive strike against Israel but they were defeated.

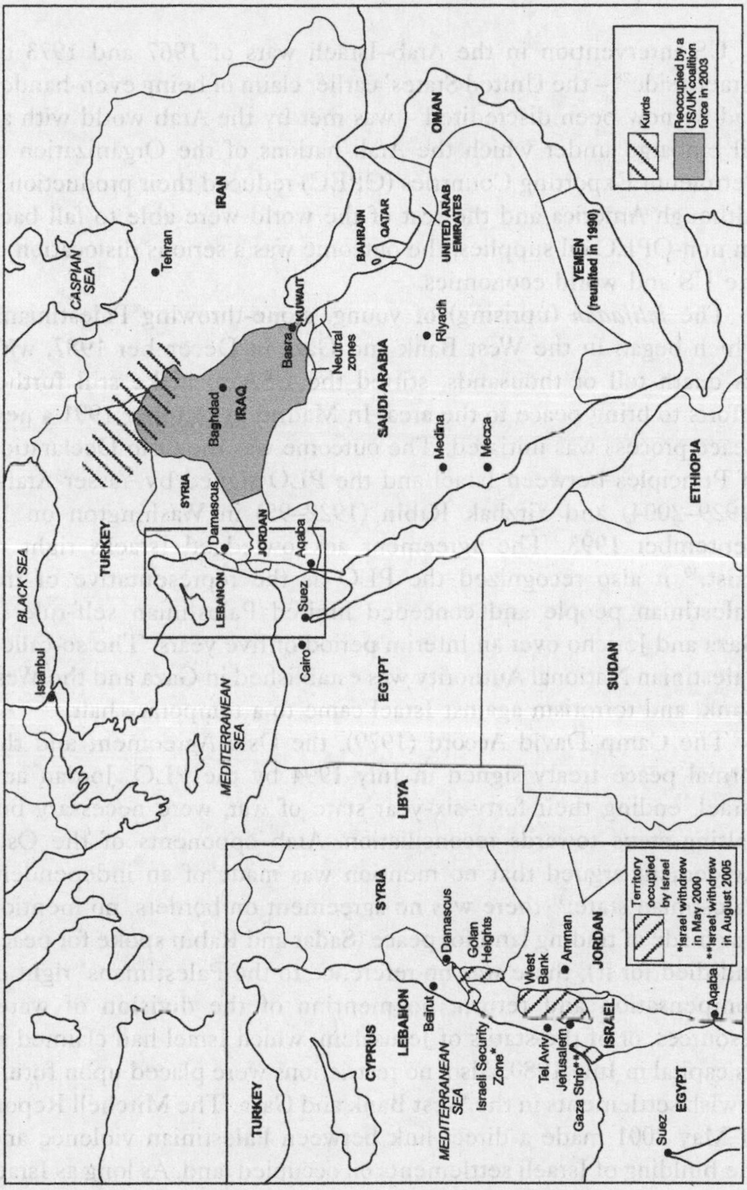
BLACK SEA
TURKEY
CASPIAN SEA
Tehran
IRAN
Istanbul
SYRIA
Damascus
LEBANON
JORDAN
Baghdad
IRAQ
Basra
KUWAIT
Neutral zones
SAUDI ARABIA
Riyadh
Medina
Mecca
BAHRAIN
QATAR
UNITED ARAB EMIRATES
OMAN
YEMEN (reunited in 1990)
Kurds
Reoccupied by a US/UK coalition force in 2003
MEDITERRANEAN SEA
Cairo
Suez
Aqaba
EGYPT
SUDAN
ETHIOPIA
LIBYA
TURKEY
CYPRUS
LEBANON
SYRIA
MEDITERRANEAN SEA
Beirut
Damascus
Golan Heights
Israeli Security Zone*
Tel Aviv
Jerusalem
Gaza Strip**
West Bank
Amman
JORDAN
ISRAEL
EGYPT
Suez
Aqaba
Territory occupied by Israel
*Israel withdrew in May 2000
**Israel withdrew in August 2005

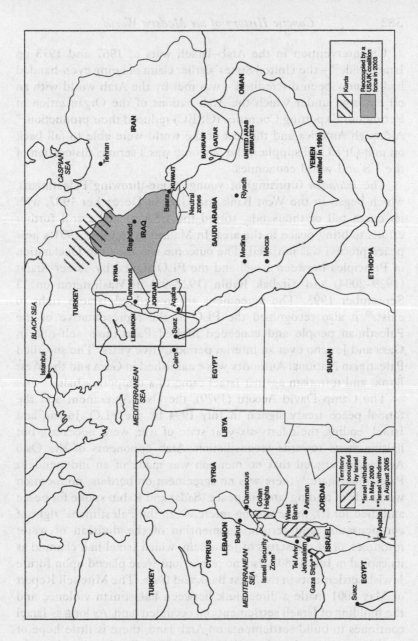

Map XXV The Middle East, 2000-4

US intervention in the Arab–Israeli wars of 1967 and 1973 on Israel's side[28] – the United States' earlier claim of being even-handed had by now been discredited – was met by the Arab world with an oil embargo under which the Arab nations of the Organization of Petroleum Exporting Countries (OPEC) reduced their production.[29] Although America and the rest of the world were able to fall back on non-OPEC oil supplies, the outcome was a serious dislocation of the US and world economies.

The *intifadah* (uprising) of young, stone-throwing Palestinians, which began in the West Bank and Gaza in December 1987, with its death toll of thousands, stirred the USA to make still further efforts to bring peace to the area. In Madrid in October 1991 a new peace process was initiated. The outcome was the Oslo Declaration of Principles between Israel and the PLO signed by Yasser Arafat (1929–2004) and Yitzhak Rabin (1922–95) in Washington on 13 September 1993. The agreement acknowledged Israel's right to exist;[30] it also recognized the PLO as the representative of the Palestinian people and conceded limited Palestinian self-rule in Gaza and Jericho over an interim period of five years. The so-called Palestinian National Authority was established in Gaza and the West Bank, and terrorism against Israel came to a temporary halt.

The Camp David Accord (1979), the Oslo Agreement and the formal peace treaty signed in July 1994 by the PLO, Jordan and Israel, ending their forty-six-year state of war, were necessary but halting steps towards reconciliation. Arab opponents of the Oslo Agreement argued that no mention was made of an independent Palestinian state;[31] there was no agreement on borders; no mention was made of trading land for peace (Sadat and Rabin spoke for peace and died for it); there was no reference to the Palestinians' right of compensation and return; no mention of the division of water resources, or of the status of Jerusalem, which Israel had claimed as its capital in July 1980. Also, no restrictions were placed upon future Jewish settlements in the West Bank and Gaza. The Mitchell Report of May 2001 made a direct link between Palestinian violence and the building of Israeli settlements on occupied land. As long as Israel continues to build settlements on Arab land, there is little hope of reaching a comprehensive solution. In 1995 talk of trading land for peace cost Yitzhak Rabin his life, and brought to power the ultra-conservative Binyamin Netanyahu, who in 1999 was replaced by Ehud Barak. The latter's peace efforts having failed at Camp David in 2000 and at Taba in Egypt in 2001,[32] he was replaced in January 2001 by Ariel Sharon, a member of the right-wing Likud Party. Sharon's visit to the al-Aqsa Mosque in Jerusalem (Islam's third holiest shrine) precipitated a new cycle of violence and a second *intifadah*, more deadly than the first.

There has been too much suffering over more than half a century for the Middle East to become peaceful any time soon. Rage, desperation, fear, hatred – especially hatred – and the desire for revenge defy the efforts of the peacemakers. There is no tolerance, no compassion and little tradition of compromise. Only wildly divergent views prevail. Except for Arafat's death in 2004 and Sharon's decision to remove Jewish settlements from the Gaza Strip, the two warring parties are back to where they were before the Oslo accords. If the Israelis have their way, the Palestinians will be divested of their identity and human rights. If the Palestinians have their way, Israel's very existence will be threatened. If Israel gives the Palestinians the right to return, it might mean the submerging of its own identity. Israel is few in number – 6.6 million in 2004 (more than a million of whom are non-Jews) – compared with the Arabs surrounding it (200 million). The Arab–Israeli dilemma also has worldwide implications: it has played a large part in the rise of Islamic militancy, and the growth of anti-Americanism.

The dilemma is that each side demands what the other cannot give. Whatever else, there is something terribly wrong in the relations between Israel and Palestine that so many innocent people on both sides should continue to die a violent death. For many Palestinians suicide bombing is all that is left. There is something equally wrong in the military confinement of the Palestinians to security zones in the West Bank and the Gaza Strip. The Palestinian refugee camps have been in use for more than fifty years. Ultimately, both sides will have to settle for less. A solution will never be achieved through violence. Israel has triumphed in battle after battle, but has never known peace. As both sides claim the right to the same piece of land, a negotiated settlement establishing two states is the only settlement there will ever be.

Israel, with US military and financial aid,[33] was clearly in the ascendancy in 2005,[34] but it cannot hope to impose its will on the Palestinians for ever. There is always the possibility that America's attention might be diverted elsewhere. The greatest threat to Israel is not Palestinian militancy, but demography and time.

The election on 9 January 2005 of Mahmoud Abbas (b. 1935) as Palestinian prime minister (as successor to Arafat) has stirred the two sides to try once more to reach a peaceful settlement. In February 2005 the Israeli and Palestinian leaders met in Egypt in an attempt to agree to a ceasefire.

Sooner or later, when both sides are exhausted, the guns will fall silent and the men of peace will try again, and succeed. The history of countries like Ireland, Greece and Poland, among others, provides hope that the statesmanship and the will for a peaceful solution shall emerge.

One country whose survival since the Second World War has disproved all prophecy is Jordan. Britain's mandate having ended in 1946, it changed its name from Trans-Jordan to the Hashemite Kingdom of Jordan. It emerged from the war with Israel in 1948 with a considerable part of Palestine, including Hebron, Bethlehem, Ramallah and Nablus, as well as some of the old city of Jerusalem. On 20 July 1951, King Abdullah ibn Hussein (b. 1882), the founder of the Hashemite Kingdom, was assassinated in Jerusalem by a Palestinian Arab. In 1953 his grandson, Hussein ibn Talal (b. 1935), replaced his father, Talal, who had reigned ineffectively for one year before being exiled. Under Hussein, Britain's influence in Jordan was reduced.

In 1967 Hussein reluctantly joined Egypt and Syria in making war on Israel again. As a result, Jordan lost territory to Israel; it also added to its already large number of Palestinian refugees. In 1970 it was forced to fight a civil war to bring Palestinian émigrés and guerrillas under control. In the Arab–Israeli War of 1973 Jordan sent a token force to fight on the Syrian front. The first Gulf War, which Jordan opposed, brought another flood of Palestinian refugees, expelled from Kuwait and Saudi Arabia; it also saw the loss of Jordan's principal market and major source of oil – Iraq. But, refusing to be identified with either the conservative or the more radical Arab leaders, Hussein survived the pressures of Syria and Iraq, the threat of Israel and the revolts of Palestinian refugees. He died in February 1999, whereupon his son, King Abdullah II (b. 1962), assumed power. In 2005 half of Jordan's 5.5 million people were Palestinians. Had Jordan been a richer kingdom, it would long since have been swallowed up in the power struggle going on around it.

Remnants of Ottoman and British rule, the two Yemens – the Yemen Arab Republic (1962) and the Marxist People's Democratic Republic of Yemen (1967) – were formally united in May 1990. The new republic became a member of the UN and participated on the side of the Allies in the first Gulf War. Full-scale war between Yemen's clan-based rivals was renewed in May 1994, when secessionists in the south declared their independence. North Yemen troops prevailed, capturing Aden in July. More recently, Yemen has become better known as a centre of anti-US sentiment.

Iraq gained its independence from Britain in 1932. In 1958, in a leftist military coup, King Faisal was killed and the monarchy abolished. The country was then ruled by a twenty-one-member Revolutionary Command Council, whose leaders also led the Ba'th Arab Socialist Party. In the 1950s and 1960s relations between Iraq and the monarchies of Iran and Saudi Arabia worsened. Because of the ongoing Arab–Israeli dispute, Iraq's relations also became strained with the USA. In 1967 it broke off its relations with Washington as a protest against US support of Israel. The next year the Ba'th Party, made up primarily of Sunni Muslims, who distrusted the majority Shi'ites, took over the government. In 1972 Iraq signed a friendship treaty with the Soviet Union. The next year it fought Israel for the third time, and nationalized its Western-owned oil companies. (Iraq has large oil reserves.) In 1975 it inflicted a major defeat on its Kurdish minority.

Until the spring of 1978, Iraq was governed by the Revolutionary Command Council headed by General Ahmed Hassan al-Bakr (1914–82). This was effectively a coalition between the Ba'th Arab

Socialist Party and the Iraqi Communist Party. But in that year Iraq curtailed its cooperation with the communist bloc and suppressed its own Soviet-oriented Communist Party. In July 1979 Saddam Hussein (b. 1937) came to power, forcing Bakr out. A plot to topple Saddam at the beginning of the Iran–Iraq War (1980–8) – fought over the Shatt al-Arab waterway – resulted in a bloody purge of the Ba'th Party, in which opponents of Saddam were ruthlessly eliminated. In June 1981 Israel made a surprise attack against Iraq's nuclear facilities near Baghdad. Throughout the 1980s the Western powers covertly supported Iraq against Iran. In 1988 Saddam launched the Anfal Campaign against the rebellious Kurdish minority, depopulating large areas of Kurdistan; more than five thoussand people died from poison gas in the town of Halabja.

A dispute in 1990 between Iraq and Kuwait resulted in Iraq's occupation of Kuwait and the consequent Gulf War of January 1991, in which Iraq was defeated by a UN-supported, US-led coalition. Iraq was compelled to withdraw from Kuwait, after which came renewed Kurdish demands for autonomy in the north and Shi'ite unrest in the south. In 1991 UN sanctions were imposed on Iraq, which until the autumn of 1996 precluded its sale of oil. The intermittent bombing by the USA and the UK of its military installations continued throughout the 1990s. The second Gulf War of 2003 toppled Saddam Hussein, whose trial before an Iraqi court is due to begin in October 2005. In January 2005, amid the worst violence in two years, Iraq held its first democratic election. The threat of civil war between Shi'ite, Sunni and Kurd, with its possible repercussions throughout the Middle East, still persists.

During the Second World War, Iran was occupied by the USSR and the USA. Until 1951, when anti-Shah and anti-foreign extremists led by Premier Mohammed Mossadegh (1880–1967) tried to nationalize British oil interests, Iran's impact on world politics was slight. Even when the Iranian oil industry was brought to a standstill, the West was able to meet its needs elsewhere. In 1953 (with US and British support) the ousted Mohammed Reza Shah Pahlavi (1918–80) was returned to power and Mossadegh was imprisoned.[35] A democratic leader was thereby toppled in favour of a dictatorial Shah who was responsive to Western needs. In 1955 Iran became a member of the Baghdad Pact, the chief aim of which was to contain Soviet expansion. With Britain's withdrawal from the Persian Gulf in 1968, Iran sought to become the dominant military power in the area.

Uprisings in Tehran and other Iranian cities in January 1979 culminated in the Shah's abdication. Instrumental in bringing his reign to an end was the Shi'ite spiritual leader Ayatollah (Mark of God) Khomeini (1900–89),[36] who had been repeatedly jailed and exiled since he began his attacks on the monarchy in 1941. No matter what concessions the Shah offered, Khomeini would settle for nothing less than the end of the monarchy and the establishment of an Islamic republic. Everything upon which the Shah had depended – his unquestioned authority, his race to modernization, his staggering purchases of arms, his lavishing of oil wealth on the armed forces and his ever-closer relations with the USA and Israel – proved to be his undoing. His pro-Western stance and his suspected contempt for Islam perhaps weighed most; he badly misjudged the Islamic threat. Under the Islamic revolution initiated by Khomeini, Iran was transformed; the mosque became the symbol of Iranian resistance to Westernization. The Shah's fall and the subsequent taking of American hostages in Tehran (November 1979–January 1981) brought the USA and Iran close to war.

Possessing crude-oil reserves of almost a hundred billion barrels, and vast reserves of natural gas, Iran is destined to play a major role in the region. Although its leaders still speak of the West as the source of all evil – and Israel as its chief enemy – the May 1997 election of the more tolerant cleric Mohammed Khatami to the presidency offered a compromise between Islam and democracy. He was overwhelmingly re-elected in June 2001, but without the support of the ruling clerics there was little enthusiasm for Khatami's reforms.

On 15 December 2004 Iran began talks with Britain, France, Germany and the EU concerning its nuclear ambitions. The most pressing question in 2005 was whether Iran – a signatory of the Non-Proliferation Treaty – was about to develop nuclear weapons. The International Atomic Energy Agency (IAEA) is suspicious of its claim that it intends only the peaceful use of nuclear power. It is known that Iran – helped by the Pakistani nuclear scientist Abdul

Qadeer Khan – possesses enriched uranium. In June 2005, with the election of the non-clerical but ultra-conservative Mahmoud Ahmadinejad (b. 1956) to the presidency, uranium processing was resumed.

Although neighbouring Afghanistan (an almost totally Islamic country) had joined the Allies during the Second World War, and later participated in the British-inspired Colombo Plan (formed in 1951 to improve the living standards of twenty-one developing nations in South and Southeast Asia), it was not until the overthrow of the monarchy of Zahir Shah (b. 1914) in 1973 that it began to claim world attention. The 1978 coup by the pro-Moscow Khalq, or People's Democratic Party, led by the new head of state, Noor Mohammed Taraki (1917-79), heralded a marked change in Afghanistan's foreign relations.

The overthrow of the Moscow-oriented Taraki by Prime Minister Hafizullah Amin (1929–79) in September 1979 (when the Russians invaded Afghanistan), and Amin's subsequent overthrow and execution in December 1979 by Babrak Karmal (1929–96), resulted in a long and bitter war between the Soviets and Afghan Muslim rebels. Ten years later the Soviets, having given up all hope of subjugating Afghanistan, withdrew their last troops. Since 1979 more than two million Afghans had been killed; six million fled as refugees. On the USSR's withdrawal, fierce fighting broke out between the Taliban Islamic rebel forces and government troops. In February 1992 the communist President, Mohammad Najibullah (b. 1947), resigned. In September 1996 the Taliban entered Kabul and executed Najibullah. In August 1998 the Taliban took Mazar-i-Sharif and gained control of 90 per cent of the country. In that month US missiles struck southeast of Kabul, at what the USA said were al Qaeda terrorist training camps. In November 1999, prompted by Russia and the USA, UN sanctions were imposed on Afghanistan. In the summer of 2001 the Taliban were still trying to defeat enemy forces in the north. With most of the country under their control, they began to impose harsh, fundamentalist Islamic rule.

In September 2001, after the bombing of the World Trade Center in New York, the US government declared a new policy of pre-emptive strikes against terrorists and the countries that harbour them. It also demanded that the Taliban hand over Osama bin Laden. In October 2001 terrorist strongholds in Afghanistan were bombed by the USA and the UK. Supported by the USA, the anti-Taliban Northern Alliance defeated the Taliban and took Kabul on 13 November. In early December an interim government, headed by Hamid Karzai (b. 1957), a Pashtun tribal leader, was established. On 20 December a multinational security force was authorized by the UN. At the beginning of 2002, after decades of civil war and the worst drought in thirty years, Afghanistan's twenty-six million people had become desperate. On 13 June 2002, at a meeting of a traditional council in Kabul, Karzai became the head of the new transitional government. In spite of the hard conditions, in 2002–3 a flood of Afghan refugees returned home. Although the USA felt confident enough to declare the end of major hostilities in May 2003, lawlessness and guerrilla resistance, except for Kabul, have continued. On 10 August 2003, because of attacks on its staff, the UN suspended its operations in Afghanistan. The next day NATO assumed control of the peacekeeping forces.

At the beginning of 2004 delegates from across the country approved a new constitution for Afghanistan. Karzai was elected president in December 2004, and parliamentary elections are planned for September 2005. Opium production has increased twentyfold since the fall of the Taliban. At the beginning of 2005 Afghanistan was still in a critical condition. Hindered by a lack of foreign aid, water, electricity, schooling and health are worse than in 1978. Karzai is faced with the almost impossible task of improving conditions for his people, pacifying the warlords and making his government representative. The government is still dominated by tribesmen from the former Northern Alliance; there has been no peace settlement with the defeated Taliban; the country needs to be cleared of landmines; three-quarters of the livestock is dead; and there is no economy, no banking system and little trade except in precious stones and opium.

Because of the links formed in the inter-war years between Saudi Arabia and the USA, the kingdom of Saudi Arabia assisted the Allied cause in the Second World War. In return, Standard Oil and the US

government tided over Saudi Arabia financially until oil development was resumed in 1946 – as were the pilgrimages to Mecca and
Medina. Ten years later Saudi Arabia's undreamed-of wealth from
oil – it possesses the world's largest oil reserves – had enabled it to
occupy a commanding position among the Arab countries of the
Middle East. Having subsidized Egypt, Jordan and Syria, as well as
the Palestinians, Saudi Arabia saw itself as the centre of pan-Arabism
and resurgent Islam. In 1945, with Egypt, Jordan, Iraq, Syria,
Lebanon and Yemen, it helped form the Arab League. From its
strict Wahabi fundamentalism comes its authority and identity as
the protector of the Arab soul.

More than any other country in the Middle East, it is conservative, almost feudalistic Saudi Arabia that feels menaced by
change.[37] On a per capita basis, in its seemingly endless quest for
security, its spending on defence has exceeded that of any other
nation. Ringed by enemies – it has been threatened by socialist
governments in Iraq, Syria, Sudan and Yemen – it has good reason
to feel nervous. Most feared, though, is Israel, against whom it
fought in 1948 and 1973. The military coup in Yemen in 1962,
which was supported by Egypt, presented another major threat.
An end to Egypt's meddling in the region came with its defeat
by Israel in 1967. The Arab–Israeli War of 1973 forced Saudi Arabia
to play a pivotal role in Arab councils. It also brought it into open
confrontation with the USA and Israel. Since its display of power
in the oil embargo of 1973, which taught the world that it was
dependent on a global economy, the old patron–client relationship between the USA and Saudi Arabia has given way to an interdependence of equals. The fall of the Shah of Iran in 1979, which
destroyed the strategic balance in the Gulf, brought new perils,
as did civil war in Lebanon, Israel's invasion of Lebanon and
Russia's invasion of Afghanistan.

Since al Qaeda's attack on the USA on 11 September 2001, Saudi-
American relations have become strained. With so many Saudis among
the attackers (fifteen out of the nineteen), Saudi Arabia is being
blamed for allowing America's enemies to flourish in its country.

As an absolute monarchy, bound only by Islamic law, Saudi Arabia
is particularly vulnerable to the problem of succession. Until recently,

democracy played no part. In a land in which one king (Saud, 1964) has been deposed and another (Faisal, 1975) assassinated, and two attempts have been made to topple the regime, the possibility of a coup is ever present. In July 2005 King Fahd died and was succeeded by Crown Prince Abdullah (b. 1924).

Iran has long challenged Saudi Arabia as the world's leader of Islam. In November 1979 several hundred Iranian zealots, calling for the overthrow of the Saudi government, seized the sacred mosque at Mecca. In 1987, in a clash between Saudi and Iranian pilgrims, hundreds were killed. While, to some extent, America can protect Saudi Arabia from the threat of Islamic militancy from abroad (in 1990 it led an international force to protect Saudi Arabia from Iraq), it cannot protect it from internal disintegration. Since the 1990s there have been several Islamic terrorist attacks against both Saudi and US troops in Saudi Arabia. In May 2003 there were several suicide bombings against Western targets in Riyadh. US forces were withdrawn in September (thereby fulfilling one of Osama bin Laden's key demands).

In 2005, there is no area in the world that is absorbing more weapons than the Middle East.

The resurgence of Asia since the Second World War has had particular significance for the European communities of Australia and New Zealand. Worsened economic conditions in the inter-war years almost put an end to British emigration to Australasia. Only after the Second World War (during which Australia turned for its very survival to the United States) did white immigration to Australia and New Zealand recover. By then, though, it was continental Europeans – Latins, Dutch, Germans, Poles, Greeks and Balts – most of them fleeing the post-war chaos, who predominated. With the cry of 'Populate or Perish', Australia absorbed approximately four million migrants between 1945 and 1990, the majority of them European.

Despite having an area larger than India and thirty-two times the size of the United Kingdom, Australia is one of the most urbanized countries in the world. Asians and other non-whites are no longer excluded on grounds of race. In 2000 almost half of Australia's immigrants were Asian, compared with about a third from Europe. It is also beset by illegal migrants from Vietnam, Indonesia and China. The Aboriginal population, which it was thought might disappear altogether, has made a remarkable recovery in numbers (now totalling 390,000) and political influence since the 1970s. Australia's total population in 2004 was 19.2 million.

The Asian presence in Australasia is even more apparent in trade and investment than it is in migration. Before 1945 Australia's and New Zealand's commercial ties had been almost exclusively with Britain and the USA. By the 1990s, its trade was virtually dependent on Asia. Since the 1970s Japan has become Australia's leading trader, and East Asia its largest market. In economic orientation Australians are becoming white Asians; relative to Asia, the traditional European and North American markets are now minor. After the USA and Europe, Japan has become the leading investor. In 1976 a treaty of cooperation and friendship was signed between Australia and Japan. Japan is also Australia's biggest buyer of minerals, which are Australia's leading export and its greatest natural resource. In the 1990s Australia was the world's largest supplier of coal; it possessed almost one-third of the Western world's uranium reserves; and it had enormous reserves of natural gas. The rest of the world also draws upon it for bauxite, iron and zinc.

Until the recent growth of Taiwan's influence in New Zealand, the country's economy had not been affected so much by Asian as by European developments. Britain's entry into the European Common Market in 1973 ended the protected market in Britain for New Zealand's all-important dairy and meat products. New Zealand has since then strengthened its trade links with Australia and Asia.

In the 1950s and 1960s New Zealand (like Australia) sent troops to the Korean and Vietnam wars. In 1972 it withdrew from SEATO and brought its troops home from Vietnam (Australia had withdrawn its troops the previous year). Because of its concern over nuclear weapons, in 1986 it excluded nuclear shipping from its ports and withdrew from the ANZUS Treaty,[38] which nevertheless remains the formal framework of mutual security for Australia, New Zealand and the USA in the Pacific. Diplomatic links between the USA and New Zealand were restored in March 1990.

Like few other countries in the world, both Australia and New

Zealand are only too keenly aware of Asia's resurgence and their growing dependence upon it. Both countries are also troubled by a crisis of identity. Countries that at one time were intensely British are becoming multicultural. As long as the West dominated the East, Australia's and New Zealand's lot as Caucasians was relatively secure. The new, volatile order in the Pacific region, in which Asia must undoubtedly play an increasing role, has not yet been decided. Whatever the outcome, it will demand major adjustments by both countries. While treating Asia as a top priority, Australia is hedging its bets by strengthening its military ties with the USA. In 2001, after years of neglect, Australia began to invest in its defence forces. In 2004, at the summit meeting of ASEAN in Laos, Australia and New Zealand (who are non-members) declined to sign ASEAN's Treaty of Amity and Cooperation.

Gathering storms in the South Pacific (in Indonesia, Fiji[39] and the Solomons) have brought new worries to what had been called the 'lucky country'. Relations between Australia and Indonesia have hardened since East Timor won its independence in May 2002 with Australia's help. In October 2002 a bombing of nightclubs in Bali resulted in many Australian deaths.

Whether as a result of wise government or luck, or a bit of both, the Australian economy has prospered since 1990, with GDP growing on average by 4 per cent each year. Between 1992 and 2004 unemployment fell from 11 to 6 per cent; inflation remained low (2.4 per cent), and Asian markets, which take more than half of Australia's exports, have increased dramatically. There is also hope of exploiting an oil field that lies between East Timor and Australia. If there are any weaknesses in the Australian economy, they are to be found in its low rate of domestic savings, its excessive speculation and its growing indebtedness.

Asia has grown in world significance since 1945 because of the revival of Islam, the world's fastest-growing religion. Islam has about 1.3 billion adherents, of whom Sunnis make up 88 per cent. It is the key to the survival of Islamic communities, the basis of their resistance to the inroads made in their societies by the West and a denial of Western superiority. It is becoming clear to the Muslim world that its future does not necessarily have to be linked with the abandonment of Islam (as happened earlier to so many of the faithful in Turkey, Egypt and Iran) in favour of Western modernity. The dilemma of Islamic countries is that they want the benefits of Western technology without the cultural baggage that has always accompanied it.

Islam now occupies centre-stage in world politics. In the countries of North Africa and the Middle East, as well as in the Sudan, Nigeria, Indonesia and elsewhere, Islamic fundamentalists are intent not only on justice but on obtaining political power. Religion for the Islamic fundamentalist is the be-all and end-all of life; it involves a rigid ethic able to distinguish between right and wrong, good and bad; it is concerned with absolute truth rather than peace, with faith rather than reason. Life for the fundamentalist is to know the truth and live it, and be prepared to die for it. Attempts to suppress Islam only make it more extreme.

To some countries, political Islam has brought with it a direct threat to secular government. It is regarded as such by Egypt's President Mubarak, who refuses to tolerate its ambitions. The leaders of Russia, Algeria and other countries are equally intolerant. Islamic militancy is especially strong in the countries of Russia's former empire in Central Asia.

While not minimizing the importance of Islam's resurgence, one should not ascribe to it a strength which, divided as it is by national, tribal and sectarian differences, it does not possess. Nor should Islam be blamed for uprisings that spring more from corrupt, autocratic government than from religion. There are many different currents of political thought in Islam, some authoritarian, others democratic. The religious fanaticism of Algerian rebels, or the Taliban in Afghanistan, cannot be compared to Islamic states elsewhere. Present dire conditions in Pakistan and Indonesia cannot be blamed on Islam. A shared religion did not save Iran and Iraq from fighting a costly eight-year war in the 1980s; in 1990 it similarly failed to prevent Iraq from invading Kuwait. Islam has had a degree of religious unity since the eighth century; political unity, especially among the Arabs, has always eluded it.

* * *

As the twenty-first century unfolds, belief in an imminent Asian future gains sway. Asia is, after all, the largest and most populous continent. It accounts for three-fifths of the world's people. Having suffered a temporary eclipse at Western hands during the past half-millennium, it is returning to prominence. Since 1970 more than eight million immigrants came to the USA from Asia.[40] In 2004 American trade with Asia and the Pacific (which in 1960 was about half that done with Europe) exceeded Europe's share. The world's fastest-growing economies are Asian; in geopolitics Asia is becoming pivotal once more.

It is tempting to conclude this chapter by ascribing to Asia a power it does not yet possess. It is easy to speak about Asia when no homogeneous Asia exists; it is equally easy to exaggerate the threat to the West of the combined strength of the rapidly growing group-oriented economies of East Asia. While there has been a remarkable increase in trade among China and the Pacific Rim economies, the truth is that they remain highly dependent on the world economy, and especially on the US market. In trade and economy these countries are still closely linked with the West. Nor does it follow that Asia's increased economic power will necessarily translate into political or cultural power.

Whatever reservations one has, it cannot be denied that there has been a shift in the centre of gravity of world power towards Asia and the Pacific. In 2005 the economies of East and Southeast Asia that had seemed stricken in the 1990s were robust again. An arms race is under way in China, India and Pakistan. Japan is in the process of abandoning the pacifist doctrine imposed by the USA after the Second World War. If the shift of economic and political power from the West to the East continues, it must have far-reaching implications for the Western world, especially the USA.

21

The Threat of World Anarchy

Five hundred years ago the centre of world power lay in Asia. Four centuries later Europe had gained dominion over the earth. Inspired by the messianism and dynamism of Christianity, by the rationalism and sense of curiosity and progress which emerged from the Renaissance and the Enlightenment, as well as by the new stress placed upon individualism by the Protestant Reformation, the Europeans laid claim not only to the lands but to the seas and oceans of the world. Paramount in their success were their will to power and their sense of racial superiority. It was an era in which the Western few dominated the world's many.

By 1914, almost the whole world had become an appendage to the West. Only Japan in Asia and Liberia and Ethiopia in Africa had remained free of European control. Western resolution, Western confidence, Western modes of thought (which envisaged an inherently orderly world), Western economics, Western values and laws, Western systems of transport and communications on land and sea, Western science and technology, Western industries and finance, Western trade, Western diseases and medicines, and especially Western armaments had combined to change the world. Under Western sway the drama of life shifted from a tribal to a national, and from a national to a world, stage. The planet shrank; wealth grew; famine was reduced; the scourge of many sicknesses was lessened. Its superiority matched only by its moral outlook, the West felt that in organizing, governing and developing the world, it was fulfilling its destiny.

But then came the First World War, dwarfing in horror all the wars that had preceded it. The past ages of faith and hope gave way to an age of fear and uncertainty. The Europeans, having created wealth on an unprecedented scale, proceeded to use it to destroy each other. Never before had Europe inflicted so much suffering upon itself. At Verdun and Passchendaele, on the Somme and at Ypres – in a tragedy that might have been avoided – Europe's hopes were buried. Because Europe was the fulcrum of world political and economic power, the war eventually became worldwide. The economic stability upon which the Eurocentric world economy had been built was undermined. Out of the post-war chaos emerged Lenin and communism, Mussolini and fascism, Hitler and Nazism. Marxism and Leninism first took hold in Russia and then around the world.

In 1939 – demonstrating the height of human folly – a second and even greater war broke out. Nothing has had greater influence in shaping the world in which we live than the two world wars. They are landmarks in a peculiarly barbaric and revolutionary century. Faced by the dictators' use of brute force, the Western democracies had no choice but to fight. After six years of savagery, by 1945 much of Europe lay in ruins.

Out of the ashes of the Second World War arose two superpowers, the USA and the Soviet Union. Britain and France, which had held the line against the dictators at an earlier stage of the war, were now too weak to lead. With the collapse of Germany in Central Europe, the two new superpowers, for the first time in their histories, found themselves facing each other. They deceived themselves into believing that, although together they made up only 12 per cent of world population, they could impose their will everywhere. Only gradually did they realize that there were parts of the world that were beyond the control of either Washington or Moscow. By the 1950s, an anti-Western front of non-aligned nations had been formed in Asia, Africa, Latin America and the Middle East. In the Third World a new pride was born, a new hope was expressed for material improvement. When in 1949 Mao said, 'Our nation will never again be an insulted nation, we have stood up,' he was expressing the hope of many of the poorer people of the world to be able to break the economic and political ties with the West, which had kept them subservient for so long.

Since the late 1940s the disparity of wealth between nations, as well as between people within a nation, which at one time would have been taken for granted, has become a central issue in world politics. The idea of egalitarianism in a democracy which Europe first put abroad, magnified by the twentieth-century information revolution, revealed to the poor of the world the very different levels on which life is lived. There is now an exceedingly rich, sophisticated, visible and vulnerable capitalist global economy, whose glass temples soar like minarets above the cities of the world, and national economies whose people are beginning to look upon the global dimension as a mixed blessing. Globalization, say its critics, has become a system of redistributing wealth to the rich. Fierce opposition to globalization was expressed at the World Trade Organization's meetings at Seattle in 1999, at Okinawa in 2000, at Milan in 2001 and at Cancún in 2003.[1] There can be no denying that the increased wealth across the world in recent decades has not reached those at the bottom of the wealth scale (see Appendix 1).[2] Worldwide – even in the USA[3] – absolute poverty is growing.[4] Between 1945 and 1965, a period of unparalleled increase of wealth, the gap between the developed and the least developed countries – between the First World and the Third – widened until one-sixth of the world's population was obtaining 70 per cent of the world's real income. In 2004 just 1 per cent of the world's population owned as much as the poorest 57 per cent. The richest 20 per cent account for 86 per cent of all the world's private consumption expenditures. The poorest countries' share of world trade is equally disturbing. Faced by the declining trend in world prices for the primary commodities of the Third World, conditions have further deteriorated.[5]

Other than that the world is better informed, there is nothing essentially new about the disparity in wealth between the rich and the poor. 'Single Tax' Henry George (1839–97) wrote on the issue more than a hundred years ago:

This association of poverty with progress is the great enigma of our time . . . it is the riddle which the Sphinx of Fate puts to our civilization, and which not to answer is to be destroyed. So long as all the increased wealth which modern progress brings goes but to build up great fortunes, to increase luxury and make sharper the contrast between the House of Have and the House of Want, progress is not real and cannot be permanent.[6]

Extreme poverty and extreme affluence cannot live in peace together. It matters greatly to the rich as well as to the poor of the world that an effort should be made to lessen the widening gap. It will never be closed, but it can and must be lessened. The alternative is to ensure social upheaval.[7]

The outcome of the growing disparity of wealth between nations has been a vast increase in the migration – legal and illegal – of people looking for a better life. In 2003 seventeen million refugees, asylum-seekers and others were on the move in the world.[8] Approximately half a million illegals enter Europe annually; about a million enter the USA. Nothing, it seems, can stem the flood. Economically, it might be a good thing for the rich world to benefit from cheap labour; politically and socially, however, it is increasingly seen by the receiving countries as a threat to their own welfare.

The relationship between the poorer and richer nations has reached a paradox. The disparity of wealth between the rich and the poor has led to the phenomenal indebtedness of the Third World to the First. While the repayment of loans by the poorer nations is impoverishing them still more, the richer parts of the world continue to absorb the capital of both the developed and the underdeveloped world. As much of the money loaned to the Third World is subsequently channelled back to the USA and Europe as debt service and flight capital, the developing world is receiving little financial assistance. Even where massive transfers of capital have taken place, money alone seems to have done little good in underdeveloped countries.

Perhaps one reason why the poor are poorer than they need be is because of the inordinate capacity of the world's defence industries to consume an ever-greater proportion of the world's wealth.

In 2004 military expenditure in the world had reached $1 trillion; the USA accounted for about half, Russia, the UK, France, Germany and Israel for most of the rest. Military spending, except for a short period after the Second World War, has always followed an upward course, but the curve has never been as steep, or as alarming, as it is now. Defence spending, like crime, has become one of the indispensable pillars of the international economy. In 2005 the USA allocated $466 billion for defence and $70.5 billion for education.[9] In many nations military expenditures exceed public outlays for education and health combined. By 1990, the military–industrial complex against which President Eisenhower had warned in his 1961 Farewell Address had become a reality: 'This conjunction of an immense military establishment and a large arms industry is new in the American experience. We must guard against the acquisition of unwarranted influence, whether sought or unsought by the military–industrial complex. The potential for the disastrous rise of misplaced power exists and will persist.'[10] The escalation of defence spending between the late 1940s and the formation of the Russian Commonwealth in 1991 was no better in the Soviet Union. By 2005, Russia had rapidly increased its world sales of conventional weapons.

No less a threat to the world community has been the growth of violent religious extremism, particularly in the Middle East. Even though Israel, Syria, Iraq, Jordan and the PLO, all major players in the Middle East drama, are secular-oriented, the militant versions of Judaism and Islam have become increasingly volatile.[11] Irrational forces based on faith and passion rather than reason are growing.[12] The Semites (both Arabs and Jews) now influence world affairs, since the creation of Israel in 1948, and especially since the OPEC oil embargo of 1973, as they have not done for centuries. Religion, the secular West is rediscovering, is a factor of great political importance. We are faced again with the religious fanaticism – with its overwhelming self-assurance and courage – that preceded the Age of Enlightenment.

If Islam reserves its sharpest criticism for the USA, it is because America's influence has grown at a time when the other colonial powers have been in retreat. It is seen as the last of the Western colonial powers, the successor to the Iberians, the Dutch, the British and the French. Many Iraqis see the US invasion of their country as a re-emergence of Western imperialism. Regardless of the insistence of many Americans that all they want to do in the world is 'good', the Amerindians, Mexicans, Filipinos, the Iraqis and many others do not see it that way.[13] Too many Napoleons and Lenins have set out to bring liberty and freedom to the world, only to create a hell on earth.

The more the US intrudes in the affairs of the Islamic world, the more it is resisted with terrorist acts, which is the terrorists' only way to counter America's military strength. Paramount in arousing the hostility of Muslims is the unqualified US support of Israel. Regardless of America's victories in the Gulf Wars of 1991 and 2003, the underlying friction between the Islamic world and the USA remains. In fact, every victory of the USA in the Middle East has only added to the enmity shown towards the West.

With the resurgence of Judaism and Islam, and the new vigour Pope John Paul II (1978–2005) gave to Christianity, as well as the growing numbers of US Protestant missionaries abroad, especially in Latin America and Africa, theism is on the rise. A sense of the sacred is returning. The world is witnessing a new search for meaning, for consolation, for refuge, for a total perspective, which cannot be found in the materialism of communism, nationalism or Western modernism. The power of the spiritual word, whether voiced by Jerusalem, Mecca or Rome (and now perhaps Washington and Moscow), is once more in the ascendancy. The secular, rationalist humanism that has informed the Western world, with its power of reason and its promise of progress, is being overtaken by transcendence (see Map XXVI). Could anyone have dreamed that religious worship would be freed in Russia, or that the state would once more support the Russian Orthodox Church?[14]

Another intangible force at work in the world today that threatens world peace – or for that matter the global economy – is revolutionary nationalism. The idea of nationalism, which first became powerful in the West two hundred years ago, has now been taken up across the globe. Nationalism provides an identity and

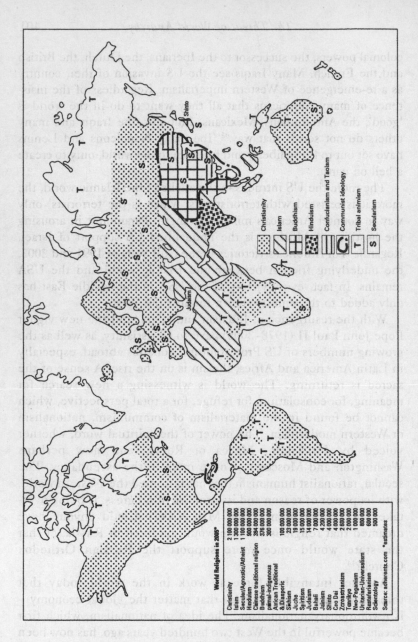

Map XXVI World Religions in 2005

a sense of belonging; it has also demonstrated its worth in government. While it is true that there are more sovereign nation states at the UN than there have ever been – in 2005 there were 191 – it is equally true that there are more groups than ever seeking nationhood. National aspirations (as well as religious fanaticism) account for the ongoing war since 1948 between the Israelis and the Palestinians. In Sri Lanka a civil war drags on, with the Tamils no closer to forming an independent state. Twenty-five million Kurds, living in Turkey, Iran, Iraq, Syria, Armenia and Azerbaijan, are seeking nationhood. Until now their lack of support by any great power, their own disunity and the absence of a common language have contributed to their inability to secure self-determination. Other minority groups seeking independence include the Maronites of Lebanon, the Berbers of Morocco and Algeria, the Copts of Egypt and the Christians of the southern Sudan. Of all the minority groups in the Middle East, only the Israelis have achieved sovereignty, and that through a combination of Jewish resolve and US and UK support. Age-old national aspirations lie at the heart of the discord between the British and the Catholic Irish in Northern Ireland, between Flemings and Walloons in Belgium, and between English- and French-speaking Canadians. Although Catalonia and the Basque country gained limited autonomy in 1977, Spain is still troubled by separatist violence. Ethnic groups seeking nationhood played principal roles in the outbreaks of brutality in Kosovo, East Timor and Rwanda. Some national conflicts were resolved by the break-up of the Soviet Union in 1991, when it was replaced by the Russian Federation and the independent states of Ukraine, Kazakhstan, Azerbaijan, Tajikistan, Kyrgyzstan, Uzbekistan, Belarus, Georgia and Turkmenistan. Other conflicts remain, such as that between Chechnya and Russia (renewed in September 1999 and still very much alive in 2005).

Similar problems face the Balkans in the dispute between Serbs, Croats and Muslims. In 1999 a war was fought between US-led NATO forces and Serbia over Kosovo. Hungary and Romania still dispute the territory of Transylvania. Following the Yalta Settlement in 1945, German Pomerania, Silesia and part of East

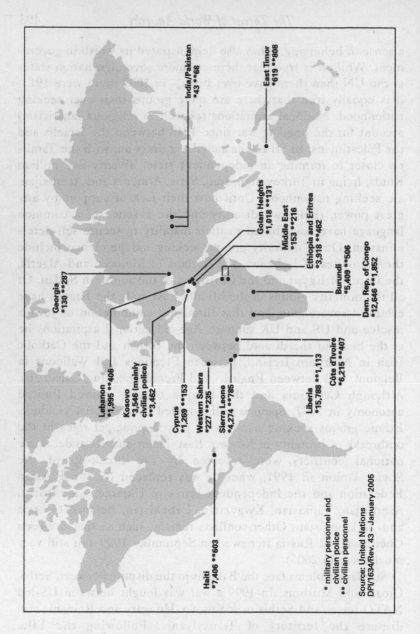

Map XXVII United Nations Peacekeeping Missions in 2004

Prussia were transferred to Poland, thereby perhaps sowing the seeds of future disputes. Since 1974 an armed truce has existed between Turkey and Greece in Cyprus. Afghanistan has its dissenting Baluchis and Pathans. India is plagued with the national aspirations of the Sikhs, the Hindu Bengalis, the Kashmiris and the Tamils. Indonesia is resisting demands for independence from the province of Aceh and West Papua (formerly Irian Jaya). China is faced with growing demands for autonomy from Tibetans and its Islamic minority living mostly in Xingiang Province. The Ibos' failure to form an independent state of Biafra in 1966–70 and enrich themselves with the oil resources beneath their feet was perhaps the first of many unsuccessful attempts made since 1945 by groups of Africans to achieve self-determination. In 2004–5 fighting between Christians and Muslims in Nigeria, as well as between Arabs and Africans in the Darfur region of the Sudan, brought with it threats of general disorder. Elsewhere the threat to world peace of militant, exaggerated nationalism grows, rather than lessens. UN forces are spread across the world trying to maintain peace (see Map XXVII). Since 2000 the UN has made new commitments in Ethiopia and Eritrea, East Timor, Liberia, Côte d'Ivoire, Haiti and Burundi.

Ethnic hatred and envy have also been poured upon highly successful business minorities within a country. Over the last century, the 'tyranny of the majority' has claimed the lives of millions of people from ethnic minorities. Such has been the fate of the Chinese in the countries of Southeast Asia, the Jews in Europe and the Middle East, the Indians in East Africa, the Lebanese in West Africa, the Croatians in the former Yugoslavia and the Tutsis in Rwanda.[15]

The threat to world peace – whether it springs from an economic, spiritual or political source – is as strong today as it was in 1500. While there is no world war, there are more civil wars being waged within states than ever before. In 2005 there were somewhere in the region of forty civil conflicts under way. Crude power, strategy and interest remain the language of international relations. Moral criteria, love, voluntary cooperation and international law have not determined the outcome of world affairs these past five hundred

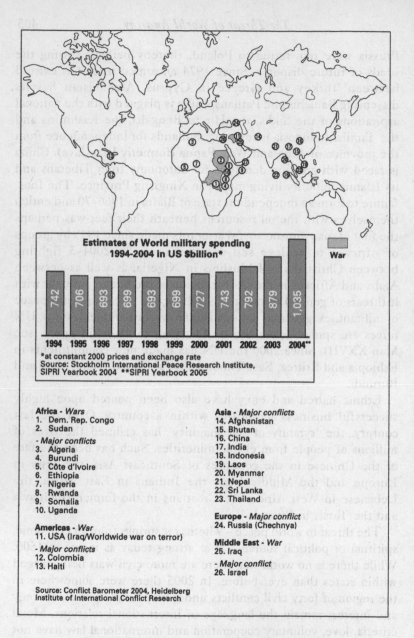

Estimates of World military spending 1994-2004 in US $billion*

1994	1995	1996	1997	1998	1999	2000	2001	2002	2003	2004**
742	706	693	699	693	699	727	743	792	879	1,035

*at constant 2000 prices and exchange rate
Source: Stockholm International Peace Research Institute,
SIPRI Yearbook 2004 **SIPRI Yearbook 2005

War

Africa - Wars
1. Dem. Rep. Congo
2. Sudan

- Major conflicts
3. Algeria
4. Burundi
5. Côte d'Ivoire
6. Ethiopia
7. Nigeria
8. Rwanda
9. Somalia
10. Uganda

Americas - War
11. USA (Iraq/Worldwide war on terror)

- Major conflicts
12. Colombia
13. Haiti

Source: Conflict Barometer 2004, Heidelberg
Institute of International Conflict Research

Asia - Major conflicts
14. Afghanistan
15. Bhutan
16. China
17. India
18. Indonesia
19. Laos
20. Myanmar
21. Nepal
22. Sri Lanka
23. Thailand

Europe - Major conflict
24. Russia (Chechnya)

Middle East - War
25. Iraq

- Major conflict
26. Israel

Map XXVIII Wars and Major Conflicts in 2004

years; nor have the supposed death throes of capitalism and communism. Regrettably, conflicting interests and ever-changing levels of force have been the deciding factors (see Map XXVIII).

The destructive power of thermonuclear weapons has increased exponentially since the atomic bomb dropped on Hiroshima. In addition, a battery of biological and chemical weapons is in the hands of the great powers, and perhaps terrorists too. With missiles, national frontiers no longer count. The world has been at bay since 1945 not because (as in 1939) a group of evil men sought world domination, but because of the almost incomprehensible damage that man can now inflict upon the earth. If there is any correlation between the number of existing nuclear weapons (equivalent to tons of TNT for every human being on the planet) and the security of the human race, one must reluctantly conclude that the world is a very dangerous place.[16] Plans for a new US anti-missile system – banned by the Anti-Ballistic Missile Treaty of 1972 – might promote a new arms race. Somewhere down the road, perhaps because of the ongoing proliferation of weapons, perhaps out of desperation, impulse, weariness, madness or terrorism, some individual, group or state will use nuclear, biological or chemical weapons.[17] As long as countries strive for power and influence, as long as they nurse historical grievances, as long as they have incompatible cultures, religions and political, economic and territorial ambitions, as long as hatred exists, there will be conflict. On the evidence of the past, if it's war we prepare for, it's war we will get.

Alas, the threat of world war is only one of the threats that face mankind. In economics, health-care, politics, widespread drought, climate change, the wasting of the world's non-renewable resources and especially in the growth and migration of the world's population,[18] mankind is also at risk. Ecology and the pollution of the biosphere present us with particular problems. The real loser of the new millennium might be the planet itself.[19] The need is for a greater symbiotic relationship between nature and humanity.

But this is surely too gloomy a view. An optimist might argue that in terms of war and peace the world is more stable than it has been since the beginning of the twentieth century. World war has passed from being unthinkable to being unacceptable. The retreat of communism in Eastern Europe, coupled with the efforts made by Russian, American and Chinese leaders to improve their relations, has helped to strengthen the belief that the threat of world war has been banished. The threat of nuclear conflict between the leading powers has certainly receded. The spectre of a Russian invasion, which haunted Europe from the 1940s until the 1980s, has vanished. On 19 November 1990, in Paris, the twenty-two nations making up the North Atlantic Treaty Organization and the Warsaw Pact signed an arms control treaty that provided for a massive reduction of conventional weapons.[20] Also in November 1990, in the Charter of Paris, thirty-four European and North American states proclaimed the end of the 'era of confrontation and division'. Free elections and democracy were recognized as the criteria for statehood. In January 1995 the Organization for Security and Cooperation in Europe was formed to further East–West relations through a commitment to non-aggression and human rights, as well as cooperation in other fields. A more coherent European order was taking shape.

The optimist might also point out that since 1945, among the leading powers, problems have never been allowed to get completely out of hand. Civil and regional wars have never been allowed to become worldwide. In Berlin, Korea, Vietnam, Afghanistan, Angola, Israel, Syria, Egypt and Iraq, the great powers have had a dozen excuses for going to war, but have always drawn back. The first Gulf War was confined to the Gulf. Thus far the Iraq War has been confined to Iraq. Except for skirmishes along the border between China and the USSR, and China and India, words were always substituted for blows. Time and again, the balance of terror saved the world from utter destruction or total anarchy. Even allowing for the diffusion of power that has taken place since the 1950s – allowing, that is, for the resurgence of Beijing, Tokyo and Berlin, and the rise of Riyadh and Rio – it is evident that none of the major actors in the world power struggle seeks war.

On the evidence of the past sixty years, there are further grounds for hope for an alternative to warfare in the growing voluntary economic and political cooperation between nations. With the receding of bipolarism, future emphasis would seem to lie not in worldwide military alliances but in coalitions of nations based upon regional, religious, cultural, economic and political ties and interests. The EEC/EU has brought more peace to Europe over a longer period than crude force ever did. Likewise the OECD, established in 1960.[21] Other examples are the Asia-Pacific Economic Cooperation (APEC),[22] the Arab League,[23] the Association of Southeast Asian Nations (ASEAN), the Commonwealth (formerly the British Commonwealth)[24] the European Free Trade Association (EFTA)[25] the Group of Eight (G8),[26] the Organization of the Islamic Conference (OIC),[27] the Organization of American States (OAS) and the African Union (AU). The multinational European Union, of 450 million people, founded with the object of gradually integrating the European economies and obtaining political union, has become, in Churchill's words, the 'United States of Europe'. A greater stability might also come from the ever-growing number of international corporations, as well as from internationally recognized financial organizations, such as the World Bank and the IMF, which operate freely across national borders. In the World Trade Organization (created in 1995 as a successor to the General Agreement on Tariffs and Trade, 1947) the nation state has to abide by a set of global rules. All of which depends on order prevailing in the global system – anarchy is always ready to take its place. It is also not beyond the realm of possibility for globalization to be replaced by national autarchy.

Not only is the form of international organization changing, so is the theory behind economics. We are beginning to realize how inadequate some of our earlier economic assumptions really were.[28] The universal theories put forward by the West to stimulate the economic growth of the developing world have had little relevance to the actual situation. The wealth being calculated today on a world scale ignores the degradation of the environment and the exploitation of people and non-renewable resources. A new global economic order far from Adam Smith's stress on the nation is emerging, in which emphasis is placed on the weal (well-being) as well as the wealth of nations.[29] The world power struggle must surely take account of productive economic forces – the most easily measured attributes – but it must also allow for what people feel, think and do. The limits to the possible have been set in the past more by human imagination than by material resources. How else can we explain the astonishing recoveries of Japan and Germany from their post-Second World War chaos? It is here that the intangible forces, including spiritual, religious, ethnic and cultural forces, play important roles.

A study of the world during the past half-millennium suggests, however, that an optimistic view of world security needs to be guarded. Not least because a blind trust in reason as a sovereign standard of truth, applicable at every level of human activity, is recent in history and very fragile. In human affairs there is always the element of the incalculable and the unexpected. The West is not only the heir of ancient Greece, the Renaissance and the Enlightenment, but of palaeolithic man. Passion and emotion rather than reason have always had a fatal attraction for the human race. How else could we have fought two devastating world wars? The leaders of the French Revolution of 1789 took pure reason as the basis of their formidable work of destruction. The Russian Revolution of 1917, in its search for social justice and reason, created one of the greatest tragedies in history: 'Corruptio optimi pessima' (The greatest evil is the good corrupted). The West errs in assuming that its exceptional 'Age of Reason' (that spawned the American Constitution) is normal and universal – especially at a time when there is a flight from reason occurring in the West itself. 'If everything on earth were rational, nothing would happen,' said Dostoevsky. Reason, we are discovering, is not a universal attribute. On the contrary, it is a tiny island threatened by a sea of primeval emotions, passions, prejudices and vitality. In this unreasonable world talk of 'lasting peace' and 'global village' is premature.

One also questions whether Western forms of democracy should be thought of as universal. Democracy and individualism are essential to the Western way of life, but they are not universal. Great as the contribution of Western man has been, it is wrong to think of democracy as superior to all other forms of government. Democracy is not something that can be imposed from the outside by wishful thinking. If it is not to end in violence, it must be preceded by education and economic, legal and social change. It is not the vote that matters as much as the institutions that precede it, such as the rule of law, a stable infrastructure, social stability and security. The ballot box alone might end up with the rule of the mob led by a demagogue. 'Democracy', wrote Karl Marx, 'is the road to socialism.' Some Western ideas will be accepted in the world, others will be rejected. There is simply no one pattern of government entirely suitable for every country. China is autocratic and flourishes; some democracies live a hand-to-mouth existence. Although there are more democratic governments than there ever were, in 2005 there are remarkably few examples of a working democracy in either Africa or the Middle East. In the Islamic world God, not man, is the final arbiter. The new democratic states that have appeared in the past twenty years in Eastern Europe and Latin America should not lead us to believe that a new age of reason and democracy has arrived. Meanwhile President Clinton's hope that 'the world's greatest democracy will lead a whole world of democracies', like President Bush's desire (in his Inaugural Address in January 2005) to 'liberate the world', is delusory. There is a strange disjunction here between rhetoric and action.

Far from another general conflagration being unlikely, some problems seem to invite conflict. War still threatens in Kashmir; the Arab–Jewish conflict could spread throughout the Middle East; civil wars still menace the Balkans. Several agreements between Russia and the secessionist republic of Chechnya have been reached, only to be broken. Twenty-five years after Turkey invaded Cyprus, a settlement of conflicting claims is as elusive as ever. A wrong move by North Korea or Taiwan could have frightening results. The USA and China would be drawn in. No less a threat to world peace is the tension that exists on the border between Russia and China.[30] In the 1850s Russia seized about half a million square miles of Chinese territory, which it still possesses. India also has frontier problems with China, which still occupies the territory it took from India in 1962. The most we can hope for at this point is not to banish war, but to limit it.[31]

In the search for a more civilized, peaceful, rational, human way of life we cannot be satisfied with the moral poverty of present-day

Machiavellism, which postulates that the world of international relations is regulated ultimately by the exercise of political and economic
power. Indeed, what must strike anyone who studies world history
since 1500 is the relativism in ethics. Sometimes the difference
between one country's outlook and that of another strikes one as
hypocritical. The very countries that pointed the finger at Saddam
Hussein's Iraq are those with the greatest stocks of chemical and
biological weapons of mass destruction. More than a score of countries are making such weapons. It seems possible for the greatest
powers (democratic or totalitarian) to uphold the sanctity of law and
moral obligation on the one hand while espousing lawlessness on
the other. Violation of human rights in one country is deplored while
equal or worse violations elsewhere, despite the Helsinki Final Act
of 1975, are ignored or subject to political expediency.[32] Mistreatment
of prisoners in Afghanistan, Cuba and Iraq by US soldiers violates
the very basis of our modern Western civilization – the rule of law.
There can be no true justice in world affairs as long as hypocrisy
and double standards prevail.

Nor is there a solution to be found as yet in international law.
Supra-national institutions with authority over national jurisdiction
are treated with suspicion by many countries, including the USA.[33]
International courts and tribunals might decide what is legally and
morally right or wrong, but they have always had difficulty enforcing
their decisions. Until the founding of the UN in 1945, only a nation
state could do that.[34] Against the backcloth of the past half-
millennium, the nation state too often did so not because of legal
or moral principle but because of national interest and expediency.
Perhaps George Orwell said it all: 'Political language is designed to
make lies sound truthful and murder respectable.'

Unless we can effectively ensure international law and order – and
that means meeting acts of aggression with superior force (as is hoped
for in Darfur in 2005) – we run the risk of world anarchy. While a
body of international law exists and is generally accepted, its details
are still very much disputed.[35] Law by itself, national or international,
without moral foundation or the will to abide by it and enforce it, is
not going to take us very far. To ensure international law and order
we must first formulate an international moral imperative.[36] China's

world view, for instance, is not that of the USA. International law and order does, in fact, entail the formulation of new moral criteria.[37] The Hague Court is a beginning,[38] but it cannot possibly deal with the number of people who should be tried. Nor is it easy to exclude revenge and political expediency in war crimes trials. This is evident at the UN's tribunal established at Arusha in Tanzania to try those responsible for the murder of eight hundred thousand people in Rwanda in 1994.

In 1945 the world looked towards the United Nations to maintain world peace; collective security was the hope of the world. The UN was charged with authorizing the use of force under international law. Over half a century later, the UN's role has become ambiguous.[39] War was made in the Balkans and Iraq contrary to UN resolutions. Although the world has changed, the UN still reflects the Western power structure that existed after the Second World War.[40] India, with a population of one billion, still does not have a permanent seat on the Security Council; nor does Japan, Nigeria, Germany or Brazil. In March 2005 Kofi Annan, Secretary General of the UN, submitted an overall reform plan which, among other recommendations, seeks to make the Security Council more representative. The concept of national sovereignty under international law, these past sixty years, has become blurred and needs to be redefined. Since the beginning of the twentieth century the Peace of Westphalia (1648) has been repeatedly disregarded; frontiers are no longer an absolute defence of sovereignty.

Politically, the UN has scored successes in peacekeeping in Palestine (1947), Kashmir (1948), Indonesia (1962), Cyprus (1964), the Middle East (1956, 1967 and 1973), the Congo (1960–4) and in Central Africa and the Balkans. The Korean War (1950–3) and the first Gulf War (1991) were fought in its name. It played a role in ending the war between Iran and Iraq in 1988, and Ethiopia and Eritrea in 2000 and helped to withdraw combatants from Afghanistan, Cambodia, Mozambique and Namibia. The UN was less successful in Hungary (1956), Czechoslovakia (1968), Rhodesia (1965–80) and South Africa. It failed to prevent the Falklands War (1982), and its intervention in Somalia in 1992 was calamitous. Its policy in the more recent outbreaks of violence in Rwanda, Congo, Sierra Leone, Timor, the Southern Sudan and Darfur has been too little, too late. That situation will continue as long as its authority is undermined and it is denied the financial means to do what the Security Council asks of it. Thus far, the road leading to the acceptance of world responsibilities and collective security has been difficult to follow. Despite all the efforts made, we are still in the foothills of an undertaking that might one day lead to the acceptance of a world outlook.

Whatever the basis of future rivalry or accord between human beings in the building of a better, safer world, we shall have to live and let live. Peace means successful adjustment to the endless conflicts and differences inherent in humankind. There will be no peace among us as long as we refuse to accept the fact that truth is shared; that no nation, no continent, no race has a monopoly of truth; that all societies, all human institutions, have relative strengths and weaknesses that cannot be judged universally. It is wrong and dangerous for any nation to claim to know what everybody in all parts of the world ought to do. That is to assume that life on this planet is simple and predictable, whereas it could hardly be more complex and uncertain. There are no universal, final answers known only to the chosen few. The world is going to have to tolerate different concepts of God, nature, morality, economics, government and society. It is going to have to reconcile national interests with those of the earth as a whole. Our need is not to control life, which will always elude us, but to come to terms with the unpredictable, the perpetual and the incalculable elements in life. Unless our efforts are directed to enhancing the value and significance of human life, life itself will have been in vain. The choice is ours to make.

For myself, I turn from this study of the past five hundred years strengthened in the belief that the human spirit will prevail.

Appendix 1

Population and gross national income per capita

Country	Population (millions)	GNI* per capita
Albania	3	$1,450
Algeria	31	$1,720
Argentina	36	$4,220
Armenia	3	$790
Australia	20	$19,530
Austria	8	$23,860
Azerbaijan	8	$710
Bangladesh	136	$380
Belarus	10	$1,360
Belgium	10	$22,940
Benin	7	$380
Bolivia	9	$900
Bosnia-Herzegovina	4	$1,310
Botswana	2	$3,010
Brazil	174	$2,830
Bulgaria	8	$1,770
Burkina Faso	12	$250
Burundi	7	$100
Cambodia	12	$300

Cameroon	16	$550
Canada	31	$22,390
Central African Republic	4	$250
Chad	8	$210
Chile	16	$4,250
China	1,280	$960
Colombia	44	$1,820
Congo (Democratic Republic)	52	$100
Congo (Republic)	4	$610
Costa Rica	4	$4,070
Côte d'Ivoire	17	$620
Croatia	4	$4,540
Czech Republic	10	$5,480
Denmark	5	$30,260
Ecuador	13	$1,490
Egypt	66	$1,470
El Salvador	6	$2,110
Eritrea	4	$190
Estonia	1	$4,190
Ethiopia	67	$100
Finland	5	$23,890
France	59	$22,240
Gabon	1	$3,060
Gambia	1	$270
Georgia	5	$650
Germany	82	$22,740
Ghana	20	$270
Greece	11	$11,660
Guatemala	12	$1,760
Guinea	8	$410
Guinea-Bissau	1	$130
Haiti	8	$440
Honduras	7	$930
Hong Kong	7	$24,690
Hungary	10	$5,290
India	1,049	$470

Indonesia	212	$710
Iran	66	$1,720
Ireland	4	$23,030
Israel	7	$16,020
Italy	58	$19,080
Jamaica	3	$2,690
Japan	127	$34,010
Jordan	5	$1,760
Kazakhstan	15	$1,520
Kenya	31	$360
Kuwait	2	$16,340
Kyrgyzstan	5	$290
Laos	6	$310
Latvia	2	$3,480
Lebanon	4	$3,990
Lesotho	2	$550
Liberia	3	$140
Lithuania	3	$3,670
Macedonia	2	$1,710
Madagascar	16	$230
Malawi	11	$160
Malaysia	24	$3,540
Mali	11	$240
Mauritania	3	$280
Mauritius	1	$3,860
Mexico	101	$5,920
Moldova	4	$460
Mongolia	2	$430
Morocco	30	$1,170
Mozambique	18	$200
Namibia	2	$1,790
Nepal	24	$230
Netherlands	16	$23,390
New Zealand	4	$13,260
Nicaragua	5	$710
Niger	11	$180
Nigeria	133	$300

Norway	5	$38,730
Oman	3	$7,830
Pakistan	145	$420
Panama	3	$4,020
Papua New Guinea	5	$530
Paraguay	6	$1,170
Peru	27	$2,020
Philippines	80	$1,030
Poland	39	$4,570
Portugal	10	$10,720
Romania	22	$1,870
Russian Federation	144	$2,130
Rwanda	8	$230
Saudi Arabia	22	$8,530
Senegal	10	$470
Serbia and Montenegro	8	$1,400
Sierra Leone	5	$140
Singapore	4	$20,690
Slovak Republic	5	$3,970
Slovenia	2	$10,370
South Africa	45	$2,500
South Korea	48	$9,930
Spain	41	$14,580
Sri Lanka	19	$850
Sudan	33	$370
Swaziland	1	$1,240
Sweden	9	$25,970
Switzerland	7	$36,170
Syria	17	$1,130
Tajikistan	6	$180
Tanzania	35	$290
Thailand	62	$2,000
Togo	5	$270
Trinidad and Tobago	1	$6,750
Tunisia	10	$1,990
Turkey	70	$2,490
Uganda	25	$240

Ukraine	49	$780
United Kingdom	59	$25,510
United States	288	$35,400
Uruguay	3	$4,340
Uzbekistan	25	$310
Venezuela	25	$4,080
Vietnam	80	$430
West Bank and Gaza	3	$1,110
Yemen	19	$490
Zambia	10	$340

Not ranked

Afghanistan	28	$735 or less
Angola	11	Undefined
Cuba	11	$736–$2,935
Dominican Republic	9	$736–$2,935
Iraq	24	$736–$2,935
Libya	5	$2,936–$9,075
Myanmar	49	$735 or less
North Korea	22	$735 or less
Puerto Rico	4	$9,076 or more
Somalia	9	$735 or less
Turkmenistan	5	$736–$2,935
United Arab Emirates	3	$9,076 or more
Zimbabwe	13	$735 or less

Source: World Bank's Development Indicators 2004, April 2004, in respect of 2002.
*GNI per capita (formerly GNP per capita) is the gross national income, converted to US dollars using the World Bank Atlas method, divided by the mid-year population.

Appendix 2

Top World Oil Consumers, 2003[*]
(million barrels per day)

Country	Total Consumption
United States	20.0
China	5.6
Japan	5.4
Germany	2.6
Russia	2.6
India	2.2
South Korea	2.2
Canada	2.2
Brazil	2.1
France	2.1
Mexico	2.1

[*]Table includes all countries that consumed more than 2 million bbl/d in 2002.

Top World Oil Net Importers, 2003[*]
(million barrels per day)

Country	Net Imports
United States	11.1
Japan	5.3
Germany	2.5
South Korea	2.2
China	2.0
France	2.0
Italy	1.7
Spain	1.5
India	1.4

Table includes all countries that imported more than 1 million bbl/d in 2002.

Top World Oil Producers, 2003[*]
(million barrels per day)

Country	Total Production[**]
Saudi Arabia	9.95
United States	8.84
Russia	8.44
Iran	3.87
Mexico	3.79
China	3.54
Norway	3.27
Canada	3.11
United Arab Emirates	2.66
Venezuela	2.58
United Kingdom	2.39
Kuwait	2.32
Nigeria	2.25

*Table includes all countries whose total oil production exceeded 2 million barrels per day in 2002.

** includes crude oil, natural gas liquids, condensate, refinery gain and other liquids
(OPEC members in italics)

Top World Oil Net Exporters, 2003[*]
(million barrels per day)

Country	Net Exports
Saudi Arabia	8.38
Russia	5.81
Norway	3.02
Iran	2.48
United Arab Emirates	2.29
Venezuela	2.23
Kuwait	2.00
Nigeria	1.93
Mexico	1.74
Algeria	1.64
Libya	1.25

[*]Table includes all countries with net exports exceeding 1 million barrels per day in 2002.

(OPEC members in italics)

Source: Energy Information Administration, US Government

Bibliography

Abu-Lughod, J., *Before European Hegemony*, New York, 1989.

Acheson, D., *Present at the Creation*, New York, 1969.

Adamthwaite, A. P., *The Lost Peace: International Relations in Europe 1918–1939*, London, 1980.

Addington, L. H., *The Patterns of War since the Eighteenth Century*, Bloomington, Ind., 1984.

Adenauer, K., *Memoires, 1945–1953*, trans. B. Ruhm von Oppen, Chicago, Ill., 1966.

Ahmad, F., *The Making of Modern Turkey*, London and New York, 1993.

Ahmed, A. S., *Jinnah, Pakistan and Islamic Identity: The Search for Saladin*, London and New York, 1997.

Aikman, D., *Pacific Rim*, New York, 1986.

Ajami, F., *The Arab Predicament*, New York, 2003.

Albertini, R. von, *Decolonization*, New York, 1985.

Allison, G. T., *Nuclear Terrorism: The Ultimate Preventable Catastrophe*, New York, 2004.

Ambrose, S., *Rise to Globalism: American Foreign Policy since 1938*, 4th edn, New York, 1985.

Anderson, M. S., *Peter the Great*, London, 1978.

——, *The Ascendancy of Europe, 1815–1914*, 2nd edn, London, 1985.

Andrews, K. R., *Trade, Plunder and Settlement*, Cambridge, 1983.

Antolic, M., *ASEAN and the Diplomacy of Accommodation*, New York, 1990.

Apter, D. E. and C. G. Rosberg, *Political Development and the New Realism in Sub-Saharan Africa*, Charlottesville, Va., 1994.

Armstrong, K., *Islam: A Short History*, New York and London, 2000.

——, *The Battle for God: Fundamentalism in Judaism, Christianity and Islam*, New York, 2001.

Arney, G., *Afghanistan*, New York, 1990.

Aroian, L. and R. P. Mitchell, *The Modern Middle East and North Africa*, London, 1984.

Aron, L., *Yeltsin: A Revolutionary Life*, New York, 2000.

Ash, T. G., *The Polish Revolution: Solidarity*, New York, 1984.

Ashton, T. S., *The Industrial Revolution*, Oxford, 1948.

Aslan, R., *No god but God: The Origins, Evolution, and Future of Islam*, New York, 2005.

Bailyn, B., *To Begin the World Anew*, New York, 2003.

Bainton, R., *Erasmus of Christendom*, New York, 1969.

——, *Here I Stand: A Life of Martin Luther*, New York, 1950.

Baker, P. and S. Glasser, *Kremlin Rising: Vladimir Putin's Russia and the End of Revolution*, New York, 2005.

Baldwin, W. H., *Battles Lost and Won*, New York, 1966.

Balfour, M. L. G., *The Kaiser and his Times*, Boston, Mass., 1964.

——, *West Germany: A Contemporary History*, London, 1983.

Bamford, J., *A Pretext for War: 9/11, Iraq, and the Abuse of America's Intelligence Agencies*, New York, 2004.

Barakhat, H., *The Arab World*, Berkeley, Cal., 1993.

Barnett, A. D., *China's Economy in Global Perspective*, Washington, DC, 1981.

Barnett, C., *Napoleon*, London, 1978.

Barnett, T. P. M., *The Pentagon's New Map: War and Peace in the Twenty-first Century*, New York, 2004.

Barraclough, G., *An Introduction to Contemporary History*, London, 1967.

——, (ed.), *The Times Atlas of World History*, 4th edn, Maplewood, NJ, 1993.

Bartlett, C. J., *The Global Conflict, 1880–1970: The International Rivalry of the Great Powers*, London, 1984.

Barzun, J., *From Dawn to Decadence*, New York, 2000.

Bass, G. J., *Stay the Hand of Vengeance: The Politics of War Crimes Tribunals*, New York, 2000.

Bat Ye'or, *Eurabia: the Euro-Arab Axis*, Madison, NJ, 2005.

Bateson, C., *The War with Japan*, East Lansing, Mich., 1968.

Baumgart, W., *Imperialism: The Idea and Reality of British and French Colonial Expansion, 1880–1914*, Oxford, 1982.

Baumont, M., *The Origins of the Second World War*, New Haven, Conn., 1978.

Baxter, C., *Bangladesh: A New Nation in an Old Setting*, Boulder, Col., 1984.

Bayart, J.-F., *The State in Africa: The Politics of the Belly*, London, 1993.

Beale, H. K., *Theodore Roosevelt and the Rise of America to World Power*, New York, 1962.

Beasley, W. G., *The Meiji Restoration*, Stanford, Cal., 1972.

——, *Japanese Imperialism, 1894–1945*, Oxford and New York, 1987.

Beilin, Y., *The Road to Geneva*, New York, 2004.

Beinart, W., *Twentieth-Century South Africa*, 2nd edn, Oxford and New York, 2001.

Belitho, H., *Jinnah*, London, 1954.

Bell, P. M. H., *The Origins of the Second World War in Europe*, 2nd edn, London and New York, 1997.

——, *France and Britain 1940–1994: The Long Separation*, New York, 1997.

Bennigson, A. and M. Broxup, *The Islamic Threat to the Soviet State*, London, 1983.

Bennis, P., *Calling the Shots: How Washington Dominates Today's UN*, New York, 2001.

Ben-Zvi, A., *The United States and Israel: The Limits of the Special Relationship*, New York, 1993.

——, *Decade of Transition: Eisenhower, Kennedy, and the Origins of the American–Israeli Alliance*, New York, 1998.

Berghahn, V. R., *Germany and the Approach of War in 1914*, London, 1973.

Berman, H. A. O., *Luther*, New York, 1992.

Berman, P., *Terror and Liberalism*, New York, 2003.

Best, G. F. A., *War and Society in Revolutionary Europe, 1770–1870*, London, 1982.

——, *War and Law since 1945*, Oxford and New York, 1994.

Bethell, N., *The Last Secret: The Delivery to Stalin of Over Two*

Million Russians by Britain and the United States, New York, 1974.

Bevan, D. L., P. Collier and J. W. Gunning, *Nigeria and Indonesia: The Political Economy of Poverty, Equity and Growth*, Oxford, 1999.

Bhagwati, J., *In Defense of Globalisation*, New York, 2004.

Bhatia, K., *Indira: A Biography*, New York, 1974.

Bianco, L., *Origins of the Chinese Revolution, 1915–1949*, Stanford, Cal., 1971.

Bill, J. A., *The Eagle and the Lion: The Tragedy of American–Iranian Relations*, New Haven, Conn., 1988.

Billington, J. H., *Fire in the Minds of Man: Origins of Revolutionary Faith*, New Brunswick, NJ, 1999.

Birmingham, D., *A Concise History of Portugal*, Cambridge, 1993.

Black, C., *F.D.R.: Champion of Freedom*, London, 2003.

Black, J., *War and the World: Military Power and the Fate of Continents, 1450–2000*, New Haven, Conn., 1998.

Blackburn, G., *The West and the World since 1945*, New York, 1985.

Blix, H., *Disarming Iraq: The Search for Weapons of Mass Destruction*, London and New York, 2004.

Blunt, W. S., *Gordon at Khartoum: Being a Personal Narrative of Events in Continuation of 'A Secret History of the English Occupation of Egypt'*, London, 1912.

Blumenberg, H., *The Genesis of the Copernican World*, trans. R. Wallace, Cambridge, Mass., 1987.

Bobbitt, P., *The Shield of Achilles: War, Peace, and the Course of History*, New York, 2002.

Bodin, J., *Six Books of the Commonwealth*, abridged and trans. M. J. Tooley, New York, 1967.

Boorstin, D. J., *The Discoverers*, New York, 1983.

Borden, W. S., *The Pacific Alliance*, Madison, Wis., 1984.

Bosworth, J. R. B., *Italy and the Approach of the First World War*, London, 1983.

Bothwell, R., T. Drummond and J. English, *Canada since 1945*, Toronto, 1981.

Bottome, E. M., *The Balance of Terror: A Guide to the Arms Race*, rev. edn, Boston, Mass., 1986.

Boussard, J., *The Civilization of Charlemagne*, trans. F. Partridge, New York, 1968.

Bouwsma, W. J., *John Calvin*, New York, 1988.

Boxer, C. R., *The Christian Century in Japan, 1549–1650*, Berkeley, Cal., 1951.

——, *The Portuguese Seaborne Empire*, New York, 1969.

Bracken, P., *The Command and Control of Nuclear Weapons*, New Haven, Conn., 1983.

Bradley, J., *Allied Intervention in Russia 1917–1920*, New York, 1968.

Bradsher, H. S., *Afghanistan and the Soviet Union*, Durham, NC, 1983.

Brass, P. R., *The Politics of India since Independence*, 2nd edn, Cambridge and New York, 1994.

Braudel, F., *The Mediterranean and the Mediterranean World in the Age of Philip II*. 2 vols, New York, 1972.

Braybon, G., *Women Workers in the First World War*, London, 1981.

Brice, W. C. (ed.), *An Historical Atlas of Islam*, Leiden, 1981.

Brierly, J. L., *The Law of Nations: An Introduction to the International Law of Peace*, Oxford, 1955.

Brinkley, D., *Dean Acheson: The Cold War Years, 1953–1971*, New Haven, Conn., 1992.

Brogan, P., *World Conflicts*, 3rd edn, Lanham, MD., 1998.

Bronk, R., *Progress and the Invisible Hand: The Philosophy and Economics of Human Advance*, London, and New York, 2000.

Brooke, R., *The Complete Poems*, New York, 1977.

Brown, A., *The Gorbachev Factor*, Oxford and New York, 1996.

Brown, J. M., *Gandhi: Prisoner of Hope*, New Haven, Conn., 1989.

——, *Modern India: Origins of an Asian Democracy*, 2nd rev. edn, Oxford, 1994.

——, *Nehru – A Political Life*, New Haven, Conn., 2003.

Brumberg, D., *Reinventing Khomeini: The Struggle for Reform in Iran*, Chicago, Ill., 2001.

Buchanan, R., *The Power of the Machine: The Impact of Technology from 1700 to the Present Day*, New York, 1992.

Bull, H., *The Anarchical Society: A Study of Order in World Politics*, New York, 1977.

Bullen, R. and F. R. Bridge, *The Great Powers and the European State System, 1815–1914*, London, 1980.

Bullock, A., *Hitler: A Study in Tyranny*, New York, 1958

——, *Hitler and Stalin: Parallel Lives*, London, 1991.

Burckhardt, J., *The Civilization of the Renaissance in Italy* (1860), trans. S. G. C. Middlemore, London, 1944.

Burleigh, M., *The Third Reich: A New History*, New York, 2001.

Buruma, I., *Inventing Japan, 1853–1964*, London, 2003.

——, and M. Avishai, *Occidentalism: The West in the Eyes of its Enemies*, New York, 2004.

Bury, J. B., *The Idea of Progress*, New York, 1955.

Bushnell, D. and N. Macaulay, *The Emergence of Latin America in the Nineteenth Century*, New York, 1988.

Butow, R. J., *Tojo and the Coming of War*, Princeton, NJ, 1961.

Butterfield, H., *The Origins of Modern Science*, New York, 1962.

Buzo, A., *The Guerilla Dynasty: Politics and Leadership in North Korea*, New York, 1999.

Cameron, E., *The European Reformation*, New York, 1991.

Cameron, R., *A Concise Economic History of the World from Paleolithic Times to the Present*, New York, 1989.

Camilleri, J. A., *China's Foreign Policy: The Maoist Era and Its Aftermath*, Seattle, Wash., 1980.

Carpenter, T. G. (ed.), *NATO's Empty Victory*, Chicago, Ill., 2000.

Carr, E. H., *The Russian Revolution from Lenin to Stalin (1917–1929)*, London, 1979.

Carr, R., *Spain 1808–1975*, 2nd, edn, Oxford, 1982.

Carsten, F. L., *The Origins of Prussia*, Oxford, 1954.

Cassese, A., *International Law in a Divided World*, Oxford and New York, 1986.

Catherwood, C., *Churchill's Folly: How Winston Churchill Created Modern Iraq*, New York, 2004.

Chabal, P., *Power in Africa: An Essay in Political Interpretation*, New York, 1994.

Chafe, W., *The Unfinished Journey: America since World War II*, New York, 1991.

Challiand, G. and J. P. Rageau, *Strategic Atlas: A Comparative Geopolitics of the World's Powers*, New York, 1985.

Chan, S., *East Asian Dynamism: Growth, Order, and Security in the Pacific Region*, Boulder, Col., 1990.

Chandler, D. P., *The Tragedy of Cambodian History: Power, War and Revolution since 1945*, New York, 1992.

Chang, J, and J. Halliday, *Mao: The Unknown Story*, New York, 2005.

Chanock, M., *Law, Custom, and Social Order: The Colonial Experience in Malawi and Zambia*, Portsmouth, NH, 1998.

Charmley, J., *Churchill, the End of Glory: A Political Biography*, London, 1993.

Chase, J., *The Consequences of the Peace: The New Internationalism and American Foreign Policy*, Oxford, 1992.

Chaudhuri, K. N., *Trade and Civilization in the Indian Ocean*, Cambridge, 1985.

Chomsky, N., *A New Generation Draws the Line: Kosovo, East Timor and the Standards of the West*, New York, 2001.

——, *Hegemony or Survival: America's Quest for Global Dominance*, New York, 2003.

——, *Middle East Illusions*, New York, 2003.

Chua, A., *World on Fire: How Exporting Free Market Democracy Breeds Ethnic Hatred and Global Instability*, New York, 2003.

Churchill, W., *The Second World War*, vols 1–6, London and Boston, Mass., 1948–53.

——, *A History of the English-Speaking Peoples*, London, 1956–8.

Cipolla, C. M., *The Economic History of World Population*, Baltimore, Virg., 1962.

——, *Guns, Sails, and Empire 1400–1700*, New York, 1965.

Clapham, J. H., *The Economic Development of France and Germany 1815–1914*, Cambridge, 1948.

Clark, A., *Barbarossa, the Russo-German Conflict, 1941–1945*, London, 1965.

Clark, G. N., *Early Modern Europe from about 1450 to about 1750*, London, 1957.

Clark, R. W., *Lenin*, New York, 1988.

Clark, W. K., *Winning Modern Wars: Iraq, Terrorism, and the American Empire*, New York, 2004.

Clarke, P. F., *Hope and Glory: Britain, 1900–1990*, 2nd ed, London and New York, 2004.

Clausewitz, C. von, *On War*, London, 1908.

Clements, D. S., *Yalta*, Oxford, 1970.

Cleveland, W. L., *A History of the Modern Middle East*, 3rd edn, Boulder, Col., 2004.

Clodfelter, M., *Warfare and Armed Conflicts: A Statistical Reference to Casualty and Other Figures, 1500–2000*, Jefferson, NC, 2001.

Clogg, R., *A Concise History of Greece*, Cambridge, 1992.

Cohen, M. R., *The Meaning of Human History*, New York, 1947.

Cohen, R. (ed.), *The Cambridge Survey of World Migration*, Cambridge, 1995.

Cohen, S. F., *Failed Crusade: America and the Tragedy of Post-Communist Russia*, New York, 2000.

Coll, S., *Ghost Wars: The Secret History of the CIA, Afghanistan, and Bin Laden, from the Soviet Invasion to September 10, 2001*, New York, 2005.

Commager, H. S. and E. Giordanetti, *Was America a Mistake? An Eighteenth Century Controversy*, New York, 1967.

Connelly, O., *The French Revolution and the Napoleonic Era*, 2nd edn, Fort Worth, Tex., 1991.

Conquest, R., *The Great Terror: Stalin's Purges of the Thirties*, rev. edn, New York, 1973.

——, *The Harvest of Sorrow: Soviet Collectivization and the Terror-Famine*, Oxford, 1986.

——, *The Dragons of Expectation: Reality and Delusion in the Course of History*, New York, 2005.

Cordesman, A. H., *Jordanian Arms and the Middle East Balance*, New York, 1983.

Cosio Villegas, D., *American Extremes*, Austin, Tex., 1964.

Costigliola, F., *France and the US: The Cold Alliance since World War II*, New York, 1992.

Craig, G. A., *Germany, 1866–1965*, Oxford, 1978.

Crankshaw, E., *Bismarck*, New York, 1981.

Creighton, D. G., *Canada's First Century, 1867–1967*, Toronto, 1970.

Crosby, A. W., *The Columbia Exchange: Biological and Cultural Consequences of 1492*, Westport, Conn., 1972.

——, *Ecological Imperialism: The Biological Expansion of Europe, 900–1900*, Cambridge, 1986.

——, *America's Forgotten Pandemic: The Influenza of 1918*, Cambridge, 1989.

Crossette, B., *So Close to Heaven: The Vanishing Buddhist Kingdoms of the Himalayas*, New York, 1995.

Crowe, S. E., *The Berlin West African Conference*, Westport, Conn., 1970.

Crozier, A. J., *Appeasement and Germany's Last Bid for Colonies*, London, 1988.

Cummings, B., *The Origins of the Korean War*, Princeton, NJ, 1981.

Cunliffe, B., *Facing the Ocean: The Atlantic and Its Peoples*, London and New York, 2000.

Curtin, P., *The Atlantic Slave Trade*, Madison, Wis., 1969.

——, *Death by Migration*, New York, 1989.

Dahms, H. G., *Die Geschichte des zweiten Weltkrieges*, Munich, 1983.

Dalrymple, T., *Our Culture, What's Left of It: The Mandarins and the Masses*, Chicago, 2005.

Daniels, R. V., *Russia, the Roots of Confrontation*, Cambridge, Mass. 1985.

Davenport, T. R. H., *South Africa: A Modern History*, 2nd edn, Toronto, 1978.

Davidson, B., *Modern Africa*, London, 1989.

Davies, L. E. and R. A. Huttenback, *Mammon and the Pursuit of Empire*, Cambridge, 1988.

Davis, D. B., *Slavery and Human Progress*, New York, 1984.

Dawson, C., *The Dynamics of World History*, New York, 1956.

De Bellaigue, C., *In the Rose Garden of the Martyrs: A Memoir of Iran*, New York, 2005.

De Klerk, F. W., *The Last Trek – A New Beginning: An Autobiography*, New York, 1999.

Deane, P., *The First Industrial Revolution*, Cambridge, 1965.

Dehio, L., *The Precarious Balance*, New York, 1963.

Deighton, A., *The Impossible Peace: Britain, the Division of Germany and the Origins of the Cold War*, Oxford and New York, 1990.

Deng, Y. and F. Wang (eds), *In the Eyes of the Dragon, China Views the World*, New York, 2000.

DePorte, A. W., *Europe between the Superpowers: The Enduring Balance*, 2nd edn, New Haven, Conn., 1986.

Díaz del Castillo, B., *The True History of the Conquest of New Spain*, trans. A. P. Maudslay, London, 1908–16.

Dickens, A. G., *The Counter Reformation*, New York, 1969.

Diebold, J., *The Innovators: The Discoveries, Inventions, and Breakthroughs of Our Time*, New York, 1990.

Dommen, A. J., *Laos*, New York, 1985.

Dower, J. W., *Embracing Defeat: Japan in the Wake of World War II*, New York, 1999.

Downing, B., *The Military Revolution and Political Change*, Princeton, NJ, 1991.

Doyle, M. W., *Empires*, New York, 1986.

——, *Ways of War and Peace: Realism, Liberalism, and Socialism*, New York, 1997.

Doyle, W., *Origins of the French Revolution*, 2nd edn, New York, 1988.

Dudden, A., *The American Pacific: From the Old China Trade to the Present*, New York, 1992.

Dunn, R. S., *The Age of Religious Wars 1559–1715*, 2nd edn, New York, 1979.

Duus, Peter, *The Abacus and the Sword: The Japanese Penetration of Korea, 1895–1910*, Berkeley, Cal., 1995.

Edwardes, M., *The West in Asia, 1815–1914*, New York, 1967.

Eisenberg, C., *Drawing the Line: The American Decision to Divide Germany, 1944–1949*, Cambridge, 1996.

Eisenhower, D. D., *Crusade in Europe*, New York, 1948.

Elkins, C., *Imperial Reckoning: The Untold Story of the End of Empire in Kenya*, New York, 2005.

Elliot, J. H., *Imperial Spain, 1469–1716*, Harmondsworth, 1970.

——, *The Old World and the New*, New York, 1992.

Ellis, J., *The Russian Orthodox Church: Triumphalism and Defensiveness*, Oxford, 1996.

Elm, M., *Oil, Power, and Principle: Iran's Oil Nationalization and Its Aftermath*, Syracuse, NY, 1992.

Evans, R., *Deng Xiaoping and the Making of Modern China*, rev. edn, New York, 1997.

Evans, R. J., *The Coming of the Third Reich*, New York, 2004.

Evans, R. J. W., *The Making of the Habsburg Monarchy, 1550–1700*, Oxford, 1984.

Facaros, D. and M. Pauls, *Turkey*, New York, 1987.

Fairbank, J. K. (ed.), *The Chinese World Order*, Cambridge, Mass., 1968.

Fairbank, J. K., E. O. Reischauer and A. Craig, *East Asia*, rev. edn, Boston, Mass., 1989.

Farah, D., *Blood from Stones: The Secret Financial Network of Terror*, New York, 2004.

Fearon, P., *The Origins and Nature of the Great Slump, 1929–1932*, London and New York, 1979.

Feis, H., *Churchill, Roosevelt, Stalin*, Princeton, NJ, 1966.

Fenby, J., *Generalissimo: Chiang Kai-shek and the China He Lost*, New York, 2004.

Fenno, R., *The Yalta Conference*, Boston, Mass., 1955.

Ferguson, N., *The Pity of War*, New York, 1999.

——, *The Cash Nexus. Money and Power in the Modern World, 1700–2000*, New York, 2001.

——, *Empire: The Rise and Demise of the British World Order and the Lessons for Global Power*, New York, 2003.

——, *Colossus: The Price of America's Empire*, New York, 2004.

Ferguson, W. K., *The Renaissance in Historical Thought: Five Centuries of Interpretation*, New York, 1948.

Fernández-Armesto, F., *Millennium: A History of the Last Thousand Years*, New York, 1995.

——, *The Americas: The History of a Hemisphere*, London, 2003.

Feroz, A., *The Making of Modern Turkey*, London, 1993.

Ferrell, R. H., *Woodrow Wilson and World War I, 1917–1921*, New York, 1985.

Ferro, M., *Colonization: A Global History*, trans. K. D. Prithipaul, Quebec, 1997.

Fest, J. C., *Hitler*, trans. R. Winston and C. Winston, New York, 1974.

Field, D., *The End of Serfdom: Nobility and Bureaucracy in Russia 1855–1861*, Cambridge, 1976.

Fieldhouse, D. K., *The Colonial Empires: A Comparative Study from the Eighteenth Century*, London, 1966.

——, *Black Africa*, London, 1986.

Figes, O., *A People's Tragedy: The Russian Revolution, 1891–1924*, New York, 1998.

Fischer, F., *Germany's Aims in the First World War*, New York, 1967.

Fitzpatrick, S., *The Russian Revolution*, New York, 1982.

Ford, F. L., *Europe, 1780–1830*, 2nd edn, London and New York, 1989.

Fraser, D., *Frederick the Great, King of Prussia*, London and New York, 2000.

Freedman, L., *Kennedy's Wars: Berlin, Cuba, Laos and Vietnam*, London and New York, 2001.

Freud, S., *Civilization and Its Discontents*, Garden City, NY, 1958.

Frieden, J. A., *Banking on the World: The Politics of International Finance*, New York, 1987.

Friedrich, J., *Der Brand (The Fire: Germany under Bombardment 1940–45)*, Berlin, 2002.

Friend, T., *Indonesian Destinies*, Cambridge, Mass., 2003.

Fromkin, D. A., *Peace to End All Peace: Creating the Modern Middle East, 1914–1922*, London, 1989.

Fukuyama, F., *The Great Disruption: Human Nature and the Reconstitution of Social Order*, New York, 1999.

Fulbright, J. W., *The Arrogance of Power*, New York, 1966.

Fulbrook, M., *The Divided Nation: A History of Germany, 1918–1990*, Oxford, 1991.

Fusi, J. P., *Franco: A Biography*, New York, 1987.

Gaddis, J. L., *We Now Know: Rethinking Cold War History*, New York, 1997.

Galbraith, J. K., *The Great Crash*, 3rd edn, Boston, Mass., 1972.

Gandhi, M. K., *An Autobiography*, Boston, Mass., 1957.

Gann, L. H. and P. Duignan, *Africa and the World*, San Francisco, Cal., 1972.

Gansler, J. S., *The Defense Industry*, Cambridge, Mass., 1980.

Gardner, L. C., *Spheres of Influence*, Chicago, Ill., 1993.

Garthoff, R. L., *The Great Transition: American–Soviet Relations and the End of the Cold War*, Washington, DC, 1994.

Garton Ash, T., *The Polish Revolution: Solidarity, 1980–82*, London, 1983.

——, *In Europe's Name: Germany and the Divided Continent*, New York, 1993.

——, *History of the Present: Essays, Sketches, and Dispatches from Europe in the 1990s*, New York, 1999.

Gentili, A., *De Jure Belli Libri Tres*, Oxford, 1933.

George, H., *Progress and Poverty: An Inquiry into the Cause of Industrial Depressions and of Increase of Want with Increase of Wealth: The Remedy*, 1879, reprinted New York, 1954.

Gibney, F., *The Pacific Century: America and Asia in a Changing World*, New York, 1992.

Gilbert, M., *Churchill: A Life*, New York, 1991.

——, *History of the Twentieth Century*, New York, 2001.

Gildea, R., *Barricades and Borders, Europe 1800–1914*, Oxford, 1987.

Giliomee, H. B., *The Afrikaners: Biography of a People*, Charlottesville, Va., 2003.

Gillard, D., *The Struggle for Asia 1828–1961*, London, 1977.

Gilley, B., *China's Democratic Future*, New York, 2004.

Gilpin, R., *War and Change in World Politics*, Cambridge and New York, 1981.

——, *The Challenge of Global Capitalism: The World Economy in the 21st Century*, Princeton, NJ, 2000.

Gingerich, O., *The Book Nobody Read: Chasing the Revolutions of Nicolaus Copernicus*, New York, 2004.

Ginsborg, P., *A History of Contemporary Italy, 1943–1988*, London, 1990.

Glenny, M., *The Rebirth of History: Eastern Europe in the Age of Democracy*, New York, 1992.

——, *The Balkans, 1804–1999*, New York, 1999.

Golan, G., *Soviet Policies in the Middle East: From World War II to Gorbachev*, New York, 1990.

Goldschmidt, A., *Modern Egypt*, Boulder, Col., 1988.

——, *A Concise History of the Middle East*, Boulder, Col., 1991.

Goldsmith, J. L. and E. A. Posner, *The Limits of International Law*, Oxford and New York, 2005.

Goodwin, J., *Lords of the Horizons: A History of the Ottoman Empire*, New York, 1999.

Gorbachev, M. S., *Perestroika*, New York, 1987.

——, *Memoirs*, New York, 1995.

——, *On My Country and the World*, New York, 1999.

Grabbe, H. and K. Hughes, *Enlarging the EU Eastwards*, London, 1998.

Graebner, N. A., *America as a World Power*, Wilmington, Del., 1984.

Graham, E. M., and P. R. Krugman, *Foreign Direct Investment in the United States*, 3rd edn, Washington, DC, 1995.

Grayling, A. C., *What is Good?: The Search for the Best Way to Live*, London, 2003.

Greider, W., *One World, Ready Or Not: The Manic Logic of Global Capitalism*, New York, 1997.

Griffith, W. E., *The Ostpolitik of the Federal Republic of Germany*, Cambridge, Mass., 1978.

Grigg, J., *Lloyd George: The Last Best Hope of the British Empire*, Caernarfon, 1999.

Grotius, H., *De Juri Belli ac Pacis*, ed. and trans. W. Whewell, London, 1853.

Guéhenno, J.-M., *The End of the Nation-State*, trans. V. Elliott., Minnesota, 1995.

Guillen, M., *Five Equations that Changed the World*, New York, 1995.

Hahn, E., *Chiang Kai-shek: An Unauthorized Biography*, New York, 1955.

Halperin Donghi, T., *The Contemporary History of Latin America*, trans. J. C. Chasteen, Durham, NC, 1993.

Hamnett, B. R., *A Concise History of Mexico*, New York, 2000.

Hancock, G., *Lords of Poverty: The Power, Prestige and Corruption of the International Aid Business*, New York, 1989.

Hardach, K., *The Political Economy of Germany in the 20th Century*, Berkeley, Cal., 1980.

Harding, H., *A Fragile Relationship: The US and China since 1972*, Washington, DC, 1992.

Hargreaves, J. D., *The Decolonization of Africa*, London, 1988.

Hart, A., *Arafat, a Political Biography*, Bloomington, Ind., 1989.

Harvey, R., *Liberators: Latin America's Struggle for Independence*, New York, 2000.

Hayes, P., *Fascism*, London, 1973.

Headrick, D., *The Invisible Weapon, Telecommunications and International Politics, 1851–1945*, Oxford, 1991.

Heilbroner, R. L., *Marxism: For and Against*, New York, 1980.

Henig, R., *The Origins of the First World War*, London, 1989.

Herman, A., *To Rule the Waves: How the British Navy Shaped the Modern World*, New York, 2004.

Herring, G., *America's Longest War: The United States and Vietnam, 1950–1975*, New York, 1979.

Hiden, J., *Germany and Europe, 1919–1939*, London, 1977.

Higham, R., *Air Power: A Concise History*, Manhattan, Kan., 1984.

Hillerbrand, H. J., *The World of the Reformation*, New York, 1973.

Hinsley, F. H., *Power and the Pursuit of Peace*, Cambridge, 1963.

Hitchcock, W. L., *The Struggle for Europe: The Turbulent History of a Divided Continent, 1945–2002*, New York, 2002.

Hobsbawm, E. J., *The Age of Revolution 1789–1848*, London, 1962.

——, *Age of Extremes: The Short Twentieth Century, 1914–1991*, London, 1994.

Hochschild, H., *Bury the Chains*, Boston, 2005.

Höffe, O., *Kant, Leben, Werk, Wirkung*, 5th edn, Munich, 2000.

——, *Wirtschaftsbürger, Staatsbürger, Weltbürger: politische Ethik im Zeitalter der Globalisierung*, Munich, 2004.

Hogan, M., *The Marshall Plan*, Cambridge, Mass., 1987.

Holland, J., *Hope against History: The Course of Conflict in Northern Ireland*, New York, 1999.

Hoskings, G., *A History of the Soviet Union*, London, 1985.

Hough, R., *The Great War at Sea*, Oxford, 1983.

Hourani, A. H., *Syria and Lebanon*, New York, 1977.

——, *A History of the Arab Peoples*, New York, 1992.

Howard, M. E., *The Invention of Peace: Reflections on War and International Order*, New Haven, Conn., 2000.

——, *War in European History*, Oxford, 2001.

——, *The First World War*, Oxford, 2002.

Hsü, I., *The Rise of Modern China*, New York, 1975.

Huizinga, J., *In the Shadow of Tomorrow*, New York, 1936.

Huneidi, S., *A Broken Trust: Herbert Samuel, Zionism and the Palestinians 1920–1925*, London, 2001.

Hunter, J., *The Emergence of Modern Japan*, London, 1989.

Huntington, S., *The Clash of Civilizations and the Remaking of World Order*, New York, 1996.

——, *Who Are We: The Challenges to America's National Identity*, New York, 2004.

Hyam, R., *Britain's Imperial Century, 1815–1914*, London, 1975.

Iklé, F. C., *Every War Must End*, 2nd rev. edn, New York, 2005.

Iliffe, J., *Africans: The History of a Continent*, Cambridge and New York, 1995.

Israel, J. I., *Dutch Primacy in World Trade, 1585–1740*, Oxford, 1989.

James, H., *Europe Reborn: A History, 1914–2000*, New York, 2003.

James, L., *The Rise and Fall of the British Empire*, London, 1994.

Jansen, M. B., *Japan and Its World*, Princeton, NJ, 1980.

Jarausch, K. H., *The Rush to German Unity*, New York, 1994.

Jaspers, K., *Origin and Goal of History*, London, 1953.

Jansen, D. L., *Reformation Europe*, 2nd edn, Lexington, Mass., 1990.

Johnson, C., *Blowback. The Costs and Consequences of America's Empire*, New York, 2000.

Johnson, D. H., *The Root Causes of Sudan's Civil Wars*, Bloomington, Ind., 2003.

Joll, J., *The Origins of the First World War*, London, 1984.

Jones, C., *The Great Nation: France from Louis XV to Napoleon 1715–99*, London, 2002.

Jones, E. L., *The European Miracle*, Cambridge, 1981.

Jones, F. C., *Japan's New Order in East Asia: Its Rise and Fall, 1937–1945*, London, 1954.

Judah, T., *Kosovo: War and Revenge*, New Haven, Conn., 2000.

Juergensmeyer, M., *Terror in the Mind of God: The Global Rise of Religious Violence*, Berkeley, Cal., 2000.

Jung, C. A., *Modern Man in Search of a Soul*, London, 1933.

Kagan, R., *Of Paradise and Power: America and Europe in the New World Order*, New York, 2003.

Kaiser, D., *Economic Diplomacy and the Origins of the Second World War*, Princeton, NJ, 1980.

——, *Politics and War: European Conflict from Philip II to Hitler*, New York, 1990.

Kamen, H. A. F., *Empire: How Spain Became a World Power, 1492–1763*, New York, 2003.

Kann, R. A., *A History of the Habsburg Empire, 1526–1918*, Berkeley, Cal., 1974.

Kaplan, R. D., *The Coming Anarchy: Shattering the Dreams of the Post Cold War*, New York, 2000.

Karlen, A., *Man and Microbes*, New York, 1995.

Karnow, S., *Mao and China: Inside China's Cultural Revolution*, New York, 1972.

——, *Vietnam*, New York, 1984.

——, *In Our Image: America's Empire in the Philippines*, New York, 1989.

Kaufman, J., *A Hole in the Heart of the World: Being Jewish in Eastern Europe*, New York, 1997.

Kazemzadeh, F., *Russia and Britain in Persia, 1864–1914, a Study in Imperialism*, New Haven, Conn., 1968.

Keay, J., *India: A History*, New York, 2000.

Kedourie, E., *England and the Middle East*, London, 1956.

——, *Democracy and Arab Political Culture*, London, 1994.

Keegan, J., *The Second World War*, London, 1989.

——, *A History of Warfare*, New York, 1993.

——, *Churchill*, London, 2002.

Keen, B. and M. Wasserman, *A Short History of Latin America*, 3rd edn, Boston, Mass., 1988.

Keep, J. L. H., *Last of the Empires: A History of the Soviet Union, 1945–1991*, Oxford, 1995.

Keiger, J. F., *France and the Origins of the First World War*, New York, 1984.

Kemp, P. K., *Key to Victory*, Boston, Mass., 1958.

Kennan, G. F., *Russia and the West under Lenin and Stalin*, Boston, Mass., 1961.

——, *Memoirs*, New York, 1983.

Kennedy, P., *The Rise and Fall of the Great Powers*, New York, 1985.

Kepel, G., *Jihad: The Trail of Political Islam*, trans. A. F. Roberts, Cambridge, Mass., 2002.

——, *Muslim Extremism in Egypt: The Prophet and Pharaoh*, trans. J. Rothschild, Berkeley, Cal., 2003.

——, *The War for Muslim Minds: Islam and the West*, trans. P. Ghazaleh. Cambridge, Mass., 2004.

Kersaudy, F., *Churchill and De Gaulle*, London, 1981.

Kershaw, I., *Hitler, 1936–1945: Nemesis*, London, 2000.

Keylor, W. R., *The Twentieth Century World: An International History*, Oxford, 1984.

Keynes, J. M., *The Economic Consequences of the Peace*, New York, 1920.

Khadduri, M., *The Gulf War*, New York, 1988.

Khalidi, R., *Resurrecting Empire: Western Footprints and America's Perilous Path in the Middle East*, Boston, Mass., 2004.

Khilnani, S., *The Idea of India*, New York, 1997.

Khouri, F. J., *The Arab–Israeli Dilemma*, Syracuse, NY, 1968.

Khrushchev, N., *Khrushchev Remembers*, trans. S. Talbot, Boston, Mass., 1970.

Kindleberger, C. P., *The World in Depression, 1929–1939*, rev. edn, Berkeley, Cal., 1986.

Kinross, P. B., *Atatürk: A Biography of Mustafa Kemal, Father of Modern Turkey*, New York, 1992.

Kinzer, S., *All the Shah's Men: An American Coup and the Roots of Middle East Terror*, Hoboken, NJ, 2003.

Kissinger, H., *The White House Years*, Boston, Mass., 1979.

——, *Diplomacy*, New York, 1994.

Klare, M.T., *Blood and Oil: The Dangers and Consequences of America's Growing Petroleum Dependency*, New York, 2004.

Knorr, K. E., *The Power of Nations*, New York, 1975.

Kolater, G., *Flu*, New York, 2000.

Kolodziej, E., *French International Policy under De Gaulle and Pompidou: The Politics of Grandeur*, Ithaca, NY, 1974.

Kramer, J., *Unsettling Europe*, New York, 1992.

Krugman, P. R., *The Great Unraveling: Losing Our Way in the New Century*, New York, 2003.

Khrushchev, N., *Khrushchev Remembers*, trans. Strobe Talbot, Boston, Mass., 1970.

Küng, H., *Global Responsibilities: In Search of a New World Ethic*, New York, 1990.

Kyle, K., *Suez*, New York, 1991.

Lach, D. F., *Asia in the Making of Europe*, Chicago, Ill., 1965.

Lamb, D., *The Arabs: Journeys beyond the Mirage*, New York, 1987.

Landes, D. S., *The Unbound Prometheus: Technological Change and Industrial Development in Western Europe from 1750 to the Present*, Cambridge, 1969.

——, *Wealth and Poverty of Nations*, New York, 2000.

Langer, W. L., *European Alliances and Alignments*, 2nd edn, New York, 1966.

——, *An Encyclopedia of World History*, Boston, Mass., 1972.

Laqueur, W., *Europe in Our Time*, New York, 1992.

Laue, T. H. von, *The World Revolution of Westernization*, New York, 1987.

Laughland, J., *Tainted Source: The Undemocratic Origins of the European Idea*, London, 1998.

LeBor, A., *Milosevic: A Biography*, New Haven, Conn., 2004.

Legge, J., *Sukarno*, New York, 1972.

Lenin, V. I., *Imperialism, the Highest Stage of Capitalism*, New York, 1933.

Lettow, P. V., *Ronald Reagan and His Quest to Abolish Nuclear Weapons*, New York, 2005.

Levering, R. V., *The Cold War*, Arlington Heights, Ill., 1982.

Levin, N., *The Holocaust: The Destruction of European Jewry, 1933–1945*, New York, 1968.

Levy, J., *War in the Modern Great Power System*, Lexington, Ky., 1983.

Lewis, B., *The Arabs in History*, 6th edn, Oxford and New York, 1993.

——, *The Emergence of Modern Turkey*, 3rd edn, New York, 2002.

—— (ed.), *A Middle East Mosaic: Fragments of Life, Letters, and History*, New York, 1999.

Lieven, A., *America Right or Wrong: An Anatomy of American Nationalism*, New York, 2004.

Lieven, D. C. B., *Russia and the Origins of the First World War*, New York, 1984.

——, *The Russian Empire and Its Rivals*, London, 2000.

Limm, P., *The Thirty Years War*, London and New York, 1984.

Lind, M., *Vietnam: The Necessary War*, New York, 2000.

Linder, S. B., *The Pacific Century*, Stanford, Cal., 1986.

Liska, G., *The Ways of Power: Patterns and Meaning in World Politics*, Cambridge, 1990.

Little, D., *American Orientalism: The United States and the Middle East since 1945*, Chapel Hill, NC, 2002.

Lukacs, J., *The Hitler of History*, New York, 1998.

——, *Democracy and Populism: Fear and Hatred*, New Haven, 2005.

Macaulay, N., *The Sandino Affair*, Durham, NC, 1985.

Mac Smith, D., *Mussolini: A Biography*, New York, 1982.

MacCulloch, D., *The Reformation*, New York, 2004.

Machiavelli, N., *The Prince*, trans. C. E. Detmold, New York, 1963.

MacKenzie, D. and M. W. Curran, *A History of Russia and the Soviet Union*, Homewood, Ill., 1977.

Maddison, A., *The World Economy: A Millennial Perspective*, Paris, 2001.

——, *The West and the Rest in the World Economy: Growth and the Interaction in the Past Millennium*, Washington, DC, 2004.

Mahon, A. T., *The Influence of Sea Power upon History, 1660–1783*, London, 1965.

Mahoney, D. J., *De Gaulle: Statesmanship, Grandeur, and Modern Democracy*, Westport, Conn., 1996.

Maier, C. S., *The Unmasterable Past: History, Holocaust and German Identity*, Cambridge, Mass., 1989

Maier, K., *This House Has Fallen: Midnight in Nigeria*, London, 2000.

Mallaby, S., *The World's Banker: A Story of Failed States, Financial Crises and the Wealth and Poverty of Nations*, New Haven, Conn., 2004.

Malcolm, N., *Bosnia: A Short History*, New York, 1994.

Mandelbaum, M., *The Ideas that Conquered the World: Peace, Democracy, and Free Markets in the Twenty-first Century*, New York, 2003.

Mango, A., *Atatürk*, London 1999.

Manning, P., *Slavery and African Life*, New York, 1990.

Mansfield, P., *A History of the Middle East*, 2nd edn, New York, 2004.

Maren, M., *The Road to Hell: The Ravaging Effects of Foreign Aid and International Charity*, New York, 1997.

Marks, S., *The Illusion of Peace: 1918–1933*, New York, 1976.

Marks, S. G., *Road to Power: The Trans-Siberian Railroad and the Colonization of Asian Russia, 1850–1917*, Ithaca, NY, 1991.

Marr, P., *The Modern History of Iraq*, London, 1985.

Martelli, G., *Leopold to Lumumba: A History of the Belgian Congo 1877–1960*, London, 1963.

Massie, R. K., *Castles of Steel: Britain, Germany, and the Winning of the Great War at Sea*, New York, 2004.

Mathias, P., *The First Industrial Nation, an Economic History of Britain, 1700–1914*, 2nd edn, New York, 1983.

Matlock, J. F., *Autopsy on an Empire, the American Ambassador's Account of the Collapse of the Soviet Union*, New York, 1995.

Mayer, A. J., *Why Did the Heavens Not Darken? The Final Solution in History*, New York, 1989.

McAuley, M., *Soviet Politics, 1917–1991*, New York, 1992.

McCullough, D. G., *Truman*, New York, 1992.

——, *1776*, New York, 2005.

McEvedy, C. and R. Jones, *Atlas of World Population History*, Harmondsworth, 1978.

McKinnon, M., *Independence and Foreign Policy: New Zealand in the World since 1935*, Auckland, 1993.

McLellan, D., *Karl Marx: His Life and Thought*, New York, 1974.

McNeil, R. H., *Stalin: Man and Ruler*, New York, 1988.

McNeill, W. H., *Rise of the West: A History of the Human Community*, Englewood Cliffs, NJ, 1970.

——, *Plagues and People*, New York, 1976

——, *The Pursuit of Power*, Chicago, Ill., 1982.

Meacham, J., *Franklin and Winston: An Intimate Portrait of an Epic Friendship*, New York, 2003.

Mead, R. O., *Atlantic Legacy*, New York, 1969.

Menzies, G., *1421: The Year China Discovered the World*, London, 2002.

Michael, F. and C. Chung-li, *The Taiping Rebellion*, 3 vols, Seattle, 1966–71.

Miles, J. A. R., *The Legacy of Tiananmen Square, China in Disarray*, Ann Arbor, Mich., 1996.

Minear, R. H., *Victor's Justice: The Tokyo War Crimes Trial*, Princeton, NJ, 1971.

Morgenthau, H. J., *Politics among Nations*, New York, 1948.

Morison, S. E., *The Oxford History of the American People*, New York, 1965.

——, *The European Discoveries of America*, New York, 1974.

Morris, B., *Righteous Victims: A History of the Zionist–Arab Conflict 1881–1999*, New York, 1999.

Mortimer, E., *The World that FDR Built: Vision and Reality*, New York, 1988.

Mortimer, R. A., *The Third World Coalition in International Politics*, New York, 1980.

Mosse, G., *Fallen Soldiers: Reshaping the Memory of the World Wars*, New York, 1990.

Mottahedeh, R. P., *The Mantle of the Prophet: Religion and Politics in Iran*, New York, 1986.

Moynihan, D. P., *On the Law of Nations*, Cambridge, Mass., 1990.

Murphy, C., *Passion for Islam: Shaping the Modern Middle East: The Egyptian Experience*, New York, 2002.

Myrdal, G., *The Challenge of World Poverty*, New York, 1970.

Naimark, N. M., *The Russians in Germany: A History of the Soviet Zone of Occupation, 1945–1949*, Cambridge, Mass., 1995.

Needham, J., *Science and Civilization in China*, vols. 1–5, Cambridge, 1954–62.

Nehru, J., *The Autobiography of Jawaharlal Nehru*, New York, 1941.

New, J. F., *The Renaissance and the Reformation: A Short History*, New York, 1969.

Nietzsche, F. W., *The Will to Power, an Attempted Transvaluation of all Values*, New York, 1924.

Nish, I., *The Origins of the Russo-Japanese War*, London, 1985.

Nogueira, A. F., *The Third World*, London, 1967.

Norman, P., *The Accidental Constitution: The Story of the European Convention*, London and New York, 2003.

North, D. and R. P. Thomas, *Rise of the Western World*, Cambridge, 1973.

Nussbaum, A., *A Concise History of the Law of Nations*, New York, 1947.

Nye, J. S., *The Paradox of American Power: Why the World's Only Superpower Can't Go It Alone*, Oxford, 2002.

O'Rourke, K. and J. Williamson, *Globalization and History: The Evolution of a Nineteenth-Century Atlantic Economy*, Boston, Mass., 1999.

Oberdorfer, D., *The Two Koreas*, Reading, Mass., 1997.

Ogata, S. N., *The Turbulent Decade: Confronting the Refugee Crises of the 1990s*, New York, 2005.

Oliver, R. and A. Atmore, *Africa since 1800*, London, 1969.

——, *The African Experience*, New York, 1992.

Otsuka, Hisao, *The Spirit of Capitalism, the Max Weber Thesis in an Economic Historical Perspective*, trans. Masaomi Kondo, Tokyo, 1982.

Owen, D., *Balkan Odyssey*, San Diego, Cal., 1995.

Owen, R., *The Middle East in the World Economy, 1800–1914*, London and New York, 1987.

Pakenham, T., *The Boer War*, London, 1979.

——, *The Scramble for Africa, 1876–1912*, New York, 1991.

Panikkar, K. M., *Asia and Western Dominance*, London, 1959.

Parish, P. J., *The American Civil War*, New York, 1975.

Parker, G., *The Military Revolution: Military Innovation and the Rise of the West, 1500–1800*, Cambridge, 1988.

Parker, R. A. C., *The Second World War: A Short History*, rev. edn, Oxford and New York, 2001.

Parker, W., *Europe, America, and the Wider World*, vol. I: *Europe and the World Economy*, New York, 1984; vol. II: *America and the Wider World*, New York, 1991.

Parry, J. H., *The Age of Reconnaissance*, London, 1963.

Parsons, A., *From Cold War to Hot Peace: UN Interventions 1946–1994*, London, 1995.

Paul, K., *Whitewashing Britain: Race and Citizenship in the Postwar Era*, Ithaca, NY, 1997.

Paxton, R. O., *The Anatomy of Fascism*, New York, 2004.

Pemsel, H., *Atlas of Naval Warfare*, London, 1977.

Perrin, N., *Giving Up the Gun: Japan's Reversion to the Sword, 1543–1879*, Boston, Mass., 1979.

Petran, T., *The Struggle over Lebanon*, New York, 1987.

Pinder, J., *The Building of the European Union*, 3rd edn, Oxford and New York, 1998.

Pipes, R., *Russia under the Bolshevik Regime*, New York, 1993.

Poitras, G., *The Ordeal of Hegemony: The United States and Latin America*, Boulder, Col., 1990.

Pollack, K. M., *The Threatening Storm: The Case for Invading Iraq*, New York, 2002.

Pope, N., and Pope H., *Turkey Unveiled: A History of Modern Turkey*, Woodstock, NY, 1998.

——, *The Persian Puzzle: The Conflict between Iran and America*, New York, 2004.

Porter, B., *The Lion's Share: A Short History of British Imperialism, 1850–1983*, 2nd edn, London and New York, 1984.

Powell, J., *Wilson's War: How Woodrow Wilson's Great Blunder Led to Hitler, Lenin, Stalin, and World War II*, New York, 2005.

Power, J., *Like Water on Stone: The Story of Amnesty International*, London, 2001.

Power, S., *A Problem from Hell: America and the Age of Genocide*, New York, 2002.

Preston, P., *Juan Carlos: Steering Spain from Dictatorship to Democracy*, New York, 2004.

Prestowitz, C. V., *Rogue Nation: American Unilateralism and the Failure of Good Intentions*, New York, 2003.

Price, A. G., *The Western Invasions of the Pacific and Its Continents*, Oxford, 1963.

——, *Island Continent, Aspects of the Historical Geography of Australia and Its Territories*, Sydney, 1972.

Priest, D., *The Mission: Waging War and Keeping Peace with America's Military*, New York, 2003.

Pyle, K. B., *The Making of Modern Japan*, 2nd edn, Lexington, Mass., 1996.

Quandt, W. B., *Saudi Arabia in the 1980s*, New York, 1981.

Qutb, S., *Milestones*, trans. B. Hasan, Karachi, 1981.

Radzinski, E., *Stalin*, New York, 1996.

Ramet, S., *Nationalism and Federalism in Yugoslavia*, Bloomington, Ind., 1992.

Randal, J. C., *Osama: The Making of a Terrorist*, New York, 2004.

Randle, R. F., *The Origins of Peace. A Study of Peacemaking and the Structure of Peace Settlements*, New York, 1973.

Rashid, A., *Taliban*, New York, 2000.

Read, A. and D. Fisher, *The Deadly Embrace: Hitler, Stalin, and the Nazi–Soviet Pact 1939–1941*, London, 1988.

Rees, D., *A Short History of Modern Korea*, New York, 1988.

Rees, M. J., *Our Final Hour: A Scientist's Warning: How Terror, Error, and Environmental Disaster Threaten Humankind's Future in This Century on Earth and Beyond*, New York, 2004.

Reich, B., *Israel: Land of Tradition and Conflict*, Boulder, Col., 1985.

Reid, A., *Southeast Asia in the Age of Commerce, 1450–1680*, New Haven, Conn., 1989.

Reid, T. R., *The United States of Europe: The New Superpower and the End of American Supremacy*, New York, 2004.

Reischauer, E. O., *Japan: The Story of a Nation*, New York, 1974.

Remnick, D., *Lenin's Tomb: The Last Days of the Soviet Empire*, New York, 1994.

Riddell, P., *The Thatcher Decade*, Oxford, 1989.

Riley, P. F., *et al.* (eds), *The Global Experience, Readings in World History since 1500*, Englewood Cliffs, NJ, 1987.

Roberts, J. M., *A History of Europe*, London and New York, 1996.

——, *Twentieth Century: A History of the World from 1901 to the Present*, London and New York, 1999.

Roberts, M., *Gustavus Adolphus*, 2nd edn, London and New York, 1992.

Robinson, R., J. Gallagher and A. Denny, *Africa and the Victorians: The Official Mind of Imperialism*, 2nd edn, London, 1982.

Rodgers, P., *Herzl's Nightmare: One Land, Two Peoples*, New York, 2005.

Rostow, W. W., *The World Economy*, Austin, Tex., 1978.

Rubin, B., *Iran since the Revolution*, Boulder, Col., 1985.

Rusinov, D., *The Yugoslav Experiment, 1948–1974*, London, 1977.

Russel, P., *Prince Henry the Navigator: A Life*, New Haven, Conn., 2000.

Rywkin, M., *Moscow's Muslim Challenge*, New York, 1982.

Sachar, H. M., *The Emergence of the Middle East*, New York, 1969.

——, *A History of the Jews in the Modern World*, New York, 2005.

Safran, N., *Saudi Arabia: The Ceaseless Quest for Security*, Cambridge, Mass., 1985.

Sagan, S. D. and K. N. Waltz, *The Spread of Nuclear Weapons: A Debate Renewed*, 2nd edn, New York, 2003.

Said, E. W., *Orientalism*, New York, 1979.

——, *The Politics of Dispossession: The Struggle for Palestinian Self-determination, 1969–1994*, New York, 1994.

Sampson, A., *The Changing Anatomy of Britain*, New York, 1982.

——, *Mandela: The Authorized Biography*, New York, 1999.

Sands, P., *Lawless World: America and the Making and Breaking of Global Rules*, New York, 2005.

Savory, R. M., *Iran under the Safavids*, Cambridge, 1980.

Schaller, M., *The American Occupation of Japan*, New York, 1985.

——, *The US and China in the Twentieth Century*, New York, 1990.

Schell, J., *The Fate of the Earth*, New York, 1982.

Schiffrin, H. Z., *Sun Yat-sen and the Origins of the Chinese Revolution*, New Haven, Conn., 1968.

Schirokauer, C., *A Brief History of Chinese and Japanese Civilizations*, 2nd edn, San Diego, Cal., 1989.

Schlesinger, S. C., *Act of Creation: The Founding of the United Nations: A Story of Superpowers, Secret Agents, Wartime Allies and Enemies, and Their Quest for a Peaceful World*, Boulder, Cal., 2003.

Schoenfeld, G., *The Return of Anti-Semitism*, San Francisco, 2004.

Schram, S., *Mao Tse-Tung*, New York, 1966

Sciolino, E., *Persian Mirrors: The Illusive Face of Iran*, New York, 2000.

Seagrave, S., *Lords of the Rim, the Invisible Empire of the Overseas Chinese*, New York, 1995.

Seale, P., *The Struggle for Syria: A Study of Post-war Arab Politics, 1945–1958*, New Haven, Conn., 1987.

——, with M. McConville, *Asad of Syria: The Struggle for the Middle East*, London, 1988.

Sen, A., *Development as Freedom*, Oxford, 1999.

Service, R., *A History of Twentieth-Century Russia*, Cambridge, Mass., 1998.

——, *Lenin, a Biography*, Cambridge, Mass., 2000.

——, *Stalin, a Biography*, London, 2004.

Shaw, S. J., *History of the Ottoman Empire and Modern Turkey*, New York, 1976–7.

Sheldrake, R., *A New Science of Life*, London, 1981.

——, *The Presence of the Past*, New York, 1988.

Shennan, A., *De Gaulle*, London and New York, 1993.

Sherwig, J. M., *Guineas and Gunpowder: British Foreign Aid in the Wars with France, 1793–1815*, Cambridge, Mass., 1969.

Shevtsova, L. F., *Yeltsin's Russia: Myths and Reality*, Washington, DC, 1999.

Shillington, K., *History of Africa*, New York, 1989.

Shlaim, A., *The Iron Wall: Israel and the Arab World since 1948*, New York, 1999.

Shoenbaum, D., *The US and the State of Israel*, New York, 1993.

Short, P., *Mao: A Life*, New York, 2000.

——, *Pol Pot: Anatomy of a Nightmare*, New York, 2005.

Sick, G., *All Fall Down: America's Tragic Encounter with Iran*, New York, 1985.

Silverstein, J., *Burmese Politics: The Dilemma of National Unity*, New Brunswick, NJ, 1980.

Simes, D. K., *After the Collapse: Russia Seeks Its Place as a Great Power*, New York, 1999.

Singleton, F. B., *A Short History of the Yugoslav Peoples*, Cambridge and New York, 1985.

Skeet, I., *OPEC: Twenty-five Years of Prices and Politics*, New York, 1991.

Skidelsky, R. J. A., *The World after Communism: A Polemic for Our Times*, London, 1995.

Smith, A. G. R., *Science and Society in the Sixteenth and Seventeenth Centuries*, London, 1972.

Smith, B. G., *Changing Lives: Women in European History since 1700*, Lexington, Mass., 1989.

Smith, D. M., *Victor Emmanuel, Cavour and the Risorgimento*, London, 1971.

——, *Mussolini: A Biography*, New York, 1982.

Smith, T., *America's Mission: The United States and the Worldwide Struggle for Democracy in the Twentieth Century*, Princeton, NJ, 1994.

Snow, P., *The Fall of Hong Kong: Britain, China, and the Japanese Occupation*, New Haven, Conn., 2003.

Sobel, D., *Longitude: The True Story of a Lone Genius Who Solved the Greatest Scientific Problem of His Time*, New York, 1998.

Soderberg, N. E., *The Superpower Myth: The Use and Misuse of American Might*, Hoboken, NJ, 2005.

Solomon, L., *Multinational Corporations and the Emerging World Order*, New York, 1978.

Sombart, W., *Der Moderne Kapitalismus*, Leipzig, 1902–28.

Sontag, R. J., *A Broken World, 1919–1939*, New York, 1971.

Soros, G., *The Bubble of American Supremacy*, New York, 2003.

Soto, H. de, *The Mystery of Capital: Why Capitalism Triumphs in the West and Fails Everywhere Else*, New York, 2000.

Spence, J. D., *The Search for Modern China*, 2nd edn, New York, 1999.

Ssu-yu Teng and J. K. Fairbank (eds), *China's Response to the West*, New York, 1970.

Stares, P., *The New Germany and the New Europe*, Washington, DC, 1992.

Stavrianos, L. S., *The Balkans, 1815–1914*, New York, 1963.

——, *The Promise of the Coming Dark Age*, New York, 1976.

——, *Global Rift: The Third World Comes of Age*, New York, 1981.

Steinberg, D. J., *The Philippines*, Boulder, Col., 1971.

Steiner, Z. S., *Britain and the Origins of the First World War*, New York, 1977.

Sterling, C., *Thieves' World: The Threat of the New Global Network of Organized Crime*, New York, 1994.

Stern, J., *Terror in the Name of God: Why Religious Militants Kill*, New York, 2003.

Stokes, G., *The Walls Came Tumbling Down: The Collapse of Communism in Eastern Europe*, New York, 1993.

Storry, R., *A History of Modern Japan*, Harmondsworth, 1982.

Strachan, H., *The First World War*, vol. I, New York and London, 2001.

Stueck, W. W., *The Korean War: An International History*, Princeton, NJ, 1995.

Swisher, C. E., *The Truth about Camp David: The Untold Story about the Collapse of the Middle East Peace Process*, New York, 2004.

Taubman, W., *Khrushchev: The Man and His Era*, New York, 2003.

Tawney, R. H., *Religion and the Rise of Capitalism*, London, 1936.

Taylor, A. J. P., *The Origins of the Second World War*, London, 1961.

Taylor, R., *The Sino-Japanese Axis*, New York, 1985.

Taylor, T., *The Anatomy of the Nuremberg Trials: A Personal Memoir*, New York, 1992.

Telhami, S., *The Stakes: America and the Middle East: The Consequences of Power and the Choice for Peace*, Boulder, Col., 2002.

Thapa, M., *Forget Kathmandu: An Elegy for Democracy*, New Delhi, 2005.

Thernstrom, S., *A History of the American People*, 2nd edn, San Diego, Cal., 1989.

Thomas, H., *World History*, London and New York, 1996.

Thornton, J., *Africa and Africans in the Making of the Atlantic World, 1400–1680*, New York, 1992.

Thornton, R., *An American Indian Holocaust and Survival: A Population History since 1492*, Norman, Okla., 1987.

Tilly, C., *European Revolutions, 1492–1992*, Oxford and Cambridge, Mass., 1993.

Tismaneanu, V., *Reinventing Politics: Eastern Europe from Stalin to Havel*, New York, 1992.

Tocqueville, A. de, *Democracy in America and Two Essays on America*, trans. G. E. Bevan, London, 2003.

Toland, J., *The Rising Sun: The Decline and Fall of the Japanese Empire*, New York, 1970.

——, *Infamy, Pearl Harbor and Its Aftermath*, New York, 1982.

Tompson, W. J., *Khrushchev – A Political Life*, New York, 1995.

Toynbee, A. J., *Mankind and Mother Earth: A Narrative History of the World*, New York, 1976.

Trachtenberg, M., *Reparations in World Politics*, New York, 1980.

Treadgold, D. W., *The Great Siberian Migration*, Princeton, NJ, 1957.

Treasure, G., *The Making of Modern Europe, 1648–1780*, London, 1985.

Treblicock, C., *The Industrialization of the Continental Powers, 1780–1914*, London, 1981.

Trevor-Roper, H. R., *The Rise of Christian Europe*, New York, 1965.

Troeltsch, E., *Protestantism and Progress*, Boston, Mass., 1958.

Trollope, J., *Britannia's Daughters*, London, 1983.

Trotsky, L., *A History of the Russian Revolution*, vols 1–3, New York, 1932.

Tuck, R., *Natural Rights Theories: Their Origin and Development*, Cambridge and New York, 1979.

Turner, H. A., *Germany from Partition to Reunification*, New Haven, Conn., 1992.

Tusa, A. and J. Tusa *The Nuremberg Trial*, New York, 1984.

——, *The Berlin Blockade*, London, 1988.

Ullman, R. H. (ed.), *The World and Yugoslavia's Wars*, New York, 1996.

Van Alstyne, R. W., *The Rising American Empire*, New York, 1960.

Van Creveld, M. L., *The Transformation of War*, New York, 1991.

Van Leeuwen, A. T., *Christianity in World History*, London, 1964.

Vargas Llosa, M., *Liberty for Latin America: How to Undo Five Hundred Years of State Oppression*, New York, 2005.

Vital, D., *The Origins of Zionism*, Oxford, 1975.

Vogel, E. F., *The Four Little Dragons*, Cambridge, Mass., 1991.

Von Vorys, K., *Democracy without Consensus: Communalism and Political Stability in Malaysia*, Princeton, NJ, 1975.

Wakeman, F., *The Fall of Imperial China*, New York, 1975.

Wallis, J., *God's Politics: Why the Right Gets it Wrong and the Left Doesn't Get It*, San Francisco, 2005.

Walters, F. P., *A History of the League of Nations*, London and New York, 1952.

Watson, A., *The Evolution of International Society: A Comparative Historical Analysis*, London and New York, 1992.

Webb, W. P., *The Great Frontier*, Boston, Mass., 1952.

Weber, M., *The Protestant Ethic and the Spirit of Capitalism*, London, 1930.

Weimer, A., *Making Sense of War: The Second World War and the Fate of the Bolshevik Revolution*, London and New York, 2001.

Weinberg, G., *A World at Arms: A Global History of World War II*, Cambridge, 1994.

Whaley, A., *The Opium War through Chinese Eyes*, London, 1958.

Wheen, F., *Karl Marx: A Life*, London and New York, 2000.

White, S., *Gorbachev and After*, Cambridge, 1991.

Whitrow, G., *Time in History*, New York, 1988.

Wiener, M. J., *English Culture and the Decline of the Industrial Spirit, 1850–1980*, Cambridge and New York, 1981.

Wight, M., *Power Politics*, London, 1978.

Wilhelm, D., *Emerging Indonesia*, London, 1980.

Williams, P. and M. Harrison, *Politics and Society in De Gaulle's Republic*, New York, 1991.

Williamson, E., *The Penguin History of Latin America*, London, 1992.

Wilson, C. H., *The Transformation of Europe 1558–1648*, London, 1976.

Wilson, M., *George Kennan and the Making of American Foreign Policy, 1947–1950*, Princeton, NJ, 1992.

Wolf, M., *Why Globalization Works*, New Haven, Conn., 2003.

Wolpert, S. A., *Jinnah of Pakistan*, New York, 1984.

——, *New History of India*, rev. edn, Oxford, 1989.

Woodruff, W., *Emergence of an International Economy*, London, 1971.

——, *America's Impact on the World, a Study of the Role of the United States in the World Economy, 1750–1970*, London, 1975.

——, *The Struggle for World Power, 1500–1980*, London, 1981.

——, *Impact of Western Man, a Study of Europe's Role in the World Economy 1750–1960*, rev. edn, Washington, DC, 1982.

Wrigley, E. A., *Continuity, Chance, and Change: The Character of the Industrial Revolution*, New York, 1988.

Wyatt, D. K., *Thailand, a Short History*, New Haven, Conn., 1982.

Yapp, M. E., *The Near East since the First World War*, London, 1991.

Yergin, D., *The Prize: The Epic Quest for Oil, Money, and Power*, New York, 1991.

Zakaria, F., *The Future of Freedom: Illiberal Democracy at Home and Abroad*, New York, 2003.

Zamoyski, A., *1812: Napoleon's Fatal March on Moscow*, New York, 2004.

Zeldin, T., *An Intimate History of Humanity*, New York, 1995.

Zimmermann, W., *First Great Triumph: How Five Americans Made Their Country a World Power*, New York, 2002.

Notes

PREFACE

1. The historian-philosophers Ernst Troeltsch (1865–1923), Benedetto Croce (1866–1952) and R. G. Collingwood (1889–1943) considered the comprehension of the present as the final goal of all historical study. Understanding the present is not the only legitimate goal of history, but it is a very important one.

1. INTRODUCTION

1. Published in Leipzig in nine volumes, 1883–8.
2. 'Nationalism' is difficult to define in terms of race or language. The word gained importance in the nineteenth century because of the urge of different ethnic groups to break away from the existing European empires. The idea of nationalism was a major cause of the First World War.
3. The International Court of Justice (ICJ), with its seat in The Hague, is the principal judicial organ of the United Nations; it was founded in 1946.
4. See Niall Ferguson, *Cash Nexus*, New York, 2004, p. 270.
5. See Douglas Farah, *Blood from Stones: The Secret Financial Network of Terror*, New York, 2004.
6. See C. Sterling, *Thieves' World: The Threat of the New Global Network of Organized Crime*, New York, 1994. Also P. Eigen, Transparency International, *Das Netz der Korruption: Wie eine weltweite Bewegung gegen Bestechung kämpft* (*The Web of Corruption: How a Global Movement Fights Graft*), Frankfurt-am-Main, 2003. (There is now a Corruption Perceptions Index compiled by Transparency International.)

7. See M. K. Gandhi, *An Autobiography*, Boston, Mass., 1957; also J. M. Brown, *Gandhi: Prisoner of Hope*, New Haven, Conn., 1989.
8. A point emphasized by the philosopher Karl Jaspers (1883–1969): 'All the crucial problems are world problems.' See his *The Origin and Goal of History*, London, 1953, the first part of which deals with 'World History'. See also J. Huizinga (1872–1945), *In the Shadow of Tomorrow*, New York, 1936.
9. In November 2001 the Legal Committee of the UN General Assembly suggested that acts of terrorism were 'criminal acts intended or calculated to provoke a state of terror', and were under any circumstances unjustifiable.
10. According to a report of 11 May 2005 of the International Labour Office (ILO) in Geneva, there are about 12.3 million people being exploited as forced labour in the world, many of them women and children.
11. The line that had been drawn along arbitrarily chosen meridians of longitude was moved 270 leagues (about 810 miles) to the west in 1494. The new line brought Brazil within the Portuguese half of the world.
12. Prior to the mid-nineteenth century, the term 'Christian nations' was used regularly in Western diplomatic exchanges. After Muslim Turkey was invited to join the Concert of Europe in the mid-nineteenth century, the term 'civilized nations' replaced it.

2. ORIGIN OF OUR TIMES: AN ASIAN-DOMINATED WORLD

1. The Islamic religion began with Mohammed's flight from Mecca to Medina on 16 July AD 622 (the *hajira*). The basic statement of Muslim belief is contained in the *shahada*, which holds that 'There is no God but Allah, and Mohammed is His prophet.' The whole of Mohammed's revelation is written down in the Koran. Islam claims to be the most perfect revelation of God's will. Islam has a definite set of laws – the *sharia*, or straight path – which provides guidance in every aspect of a Muslim's life. The god of Islam, unlike the Christian god of love, is a god of power, who tempers His justice with mercy. In their monotheism, Islam and Christianity are the two branches of the Judaic tree.
2. The feud between the Sunni sect and that of the Shi'a (the party of Ali, son-in-law of Mohammed), the chief minority sect, dates from Mohammed's death in AD 632. The Shi'a differ from the orthodox Sunni sect in their belief that succession to the Prophet should have remained in Mohammed's family. The Sunnis believe that they have a direct relationship with God (the principal role of the Sunni imams

is to lead the prayers of the congregation); the Shi'ites accord great importance to their religious leaders, who are responsible for interpreting Islam. Following the example set by the martyred Hussein, they also stress martyrdom, which is a reward, not a penalty. When Mohammed died, Ali, his son-in-law, was initially denied his right to become Islam's leader. But he persisted in his claim and in AD 656 was installed as the rightful successor (caliph) to Mohammed. Five years later he was assassinated by religious rivals. His son Hussein, who now fought to establish his own claim as Islam's leader, was subsequently tortured and killed at Karbala in Iraq. 'Karbala' was used by the Shi'ite Iranians as a rallying cry in their war against Iraq.

3. Persian for Mongol. Babar was a descendant of Timur and Genghis Khan.

4. Its population in the fifteenth century, between 100 and 130 million, is thought to have been twice that of the whole of Europe.

5. However primitive the Mongols may have appeared, adopting military and administrative techniques from the Chinese, they founded the largest contiguous empire there has ever been. The Venetian Marco Polo, carrying a Mongol 'passport' in the form of a seal, made an unhindered journey from the Mediterranean to the Yellow Sea in the late thirteenth century. Only the Egyptians in the West (in 1260 at Ain Jalut, Syria) and the Japanese in the East (in 1274 and 1281) were able to withstand the Mongol tide.

6. Confucius, known originally as K'ung Ch'iu (551–479 BC) was a public administrator and teacher who profoundly influenced Chinese philosophy and ethos. Confucianism used to be blamed for Chinese underdevelopment; more recently, it has been given credit for an 'Asian miracle'.

7. See Philip F. Riley *et al.* (eds), 'Cheng Ho: Ming Maritime Expeditions', in *The Global Experience, Readings in World History since 1500*, Englewood Cliffs, NJ, 1987, Vol. II, pp. 3–5. See also Gavin Menzies, *1421: The Year China Discovered the World*, New York and London, 2002, who suggests that the Chinese may have circumnavigated the world in 1421.

8. Members of the Society of Jesus played a leading role in all early East–West relations. The Treaty of Nerchinsk (1689), the first treaty concluded between China and the West, was their doing.

9. See P. F. Riley *et al.* (1987), pp. 26–7. 'If the Chinese were warlike they could conquer the world,' wrote Marco Polo in the thirteenth century, 'thank goodness they're not.'

10. Certain Jesuits remained in Beijing to care for the dynastic calendar. Two centuries later, in 1939, the pope decreed that ancestor worship and Confucian rites were not incompatible with the dogma of the Church.

11. Japan had a population of about 25 million at the beginning of the seventeenth century (against approximately 16 million in France, 7 million in Spain and 4.5 million in England.
12. See P. F. Riley *et al.* (1987), pp. 31–2. See also C. R. Boxer, *The Christian Century in Japan, 1549–1650*, Berkeley, Cal., 1951.

3. THE RISE OF THE WEST

1. The Renaissance shed the 'fantastic bonds of the Middle Ages'. See Jakob Burckhardt, *The Civilization of the Renaissance in Italy* (1860); trans. S. G. C. Middlemore, London, 1944. Burckhardt provided the first rounded synthesis of Italy's contribution. On the contributions of Arab Spain, Byzantium and northern Germany, see Wallace K. Ferguson, *The Renaissance in Historical Thought: Five Centuries of Interpretation*, New York, 1948. Despite all the work that has been done on character, causes, geographical and chronological limits, the Renaissance remains one of the most intractable problems of historiography.
2. Copernicus studied at Padua and Bologna. In 1503 he obtained his doctorate of canon law at Ferrara. Galileo was professor of mathematics at Padua. See Owen Gingerich, *The Book Nobody Read: Chasing the Revolutions of Nicolaus Copernicus*, New York, 2004.
3. See J. B. Bury, *The Idea of Progress*, New York, 1955.
4. Lao-tzu, its founder, was born *c.* 600 BC.
5. See C. M. Cipolla, *Guns, Sails, and Empire 1400–1700*, New York, 1965.
6. See Geoffrey Parker, *The Military Revolution*, New York, 1989.
7. In 2540 years of recorded Chinese history the Yellow River has flooded 1590 times.
8. See E. L. Jones, *The European Miracle*, Cambridge, 1981, and W. H. McNeill, *Rise of the West: A History of the Human Community*, Englewood Cliffs, NJ, 1970.

4. EUROPE: 1500–1914

1. The name given to the Christian territory ruled by German kings between AD 962 (when Otto I was crowned Holy Roman Emperor) and 1806 (when it was dissolved by Napleon). Earlier, Pope Leo III had conferred the title of Roman Emperor on Charlemagne (742–814). The Holy Roman Empire was partly a revival of Charlemagne's empire, established more than a century before.
2. In 1498 the Venetian mariner John Cabot (1450–98), in the service of England, had 'explored for lands unknown to Christians'; in 1764

the English mariner John Byron (1723–86) sought lands 'unvisited by any European power'.

3. The dominant political system of Europe from the ninth to the fifteenth century was based on the relation of lord and land to serf and homage.

4. See R. Bainton, *Erasmus of Christendom*, New York, 1969.

5. See R. Bainton, *Here I Stand: A Life of Martin Luther*, New York, 1950.

6. The sale of indulgences had been increased greatly by Pope Leo X (reigned 1513–22) to raise funds to complete St Peter's Basilica in Rome on a scale worthy of a universal faith.

7. Henry VII, Henry VIII, Edward VI, Mary Tudor and Elizabeth I.

8. See W. J. Bouwsma, *John Calvin*, New York, 1988.

9. In 1567 Mary was forced to yield the throne to her Protestant son, James. Her last and greatest blunder was to seek refuge with her Protestant cousin, Queen Elizabeth I. Although considered the rightful heir to the English throne, Mary was executed by Elizabeth twenty years later.

10. Charles V came to power through the matrimonial statecraft and bribery of the Habsburgs and the financial power of the Fugger family of Augsburg.

11. See A. G. Dickens, *The Counter Reformation*, New York, 1969.

12. Nothing failed like success for the Jesuits. By the mid-eighteenth century Western rulers had turned against them. The Jesuits' defence of the native peoples of Spain's empire in the New World had created enemies in high places, and in 1773 Pope Clement XIV (reigned 1769–75) was persuaded to disband the society. In Protestant Prussia and Silesia, though, the Jesuits continued their work undisturbed. Their presence was also tolerated by Catherine II, the Great (b. 1729; reigned 1762–96), of Russia, as well as by Catholic Poland. In 1814, times having changed, the order was re-established by Pope Pius VII (reigned 1800–23).

13. See R. S. Dunn, *The Age of Religious Wars 1559–1715*, 2nd edn, New York, 1979. The vital port of Antwerp was sacked in 1576.

14. Contrast this with the English novelist Tobias George Smollett (1721–71), who wrote at a time when England's respect for money and commerce grew by the hour: 'Without money, there is no respect, honour, or convenience to be acquired in life.'

15. Werner Sombart (*Der Moderne Kapitalismus*, 3 vols, Leipzig, 1902–28) ascribes Spain's penury to the persecution of the Jews. The Inquisition, Sombart argues, drove from Spain the best Jewish financial talent. Max Weber (*The Protestant Ethic and the Spirit of Capitalism*, London, 1930) and R. H. Tawney (*Religion and the Rise of Capitalism*, London, 1936) place greater stress on the Protestant spirit, which enabled both Britain and Holland to outstrip Spain.

16. Even though a Spanish state did not yet exist in 1492. The Reconquista was chiefly the work of Castile.

17. See J. I. Israel, *Dutch Primacy in World Trade, 1585–1740*, Oxford, 1989.

18. *Anti-Machiavel oder Versuch einer Kritik über Nic. Machiavels Regierungskunst eines Fürsten*, Berlin and Leipzig, 1745.

19. See G. Parker, *The Military Revolution*, New York, 1988.

20. See R. Bullen and F. R. Bridge, *The Great Powers and the European State System, 1815–1914*, London, 1980.

21. See C. Jones, *The Great Nation: France from Louis XV to Napoleon, 1715–99*, London, 2002.

22. Netherlands (1795–1806), northern Italy (1797–1805), Switzerland (1798–1803), Genoa (1797–1805), southern Italy (1799).

23. See J. M. Sherwig, *Guineas and Gunpowder: British Foreign Aid in the Wars with France, 1793–1815*, Cambridge, Mass., 1969.

24. See C. Barnett, *Napoleon*, London, 1978.

25. France's boundaries were settled along those existing in 1792, which included areas that the French had not possessed in 1789. Britain gave back all that it had taken from the French except the islands of Tobago, St Lucia, Mauritius and Malta. It also undertook to return any Dutch territory seized during the war, but not Ceylon or the Cape of Good Hope. No indemnity was demanded.

26. In 1621 Gustavus Adolphus II had carried his country into the Thirty Years War. He consolidated Swedish hegemony over the Baltic and, by acquiring Polish Livonia, reduced the threat posed by Catholic Poland to Swedish Protestantism. His spectacular sweep through German territory ended with his death in battle on 16 November 1632 at Lutzen.

27. Sweden's constitutional monarchy is descended from a Napoleonic general, Jean Baptiste Bernadotte, who became Crown Prince in 1810.

28. France had to give up its frontier fortresses and was to be garrisoned by an allied force for three to five years, pay an indemnity of 200 million francs and have its boundaries reduced from those of 1792 to those of 1790. None of this amounted to humiliation.

29. See R. Gildea, *Barricades and Borders, Europe 1800–1914*, Oxford, 1987.

30. The Quadruple Alliance or Holy Alliance was formed in 1816 as a counter-revolutionary measure against the French. Its aim was to uphold the status quo in Europe – especially the conservative monarchies – for twenty years.

31. See D. M. Smith, *Victor Emmanuel, Cavour and the Risorgimento*, London, 1971.

32. See E. Crankshaw, *Bismarck*, New York, 1981.

5. THE EXPANSION OF THE RUSSIAN EMPIRE

1. 'Tatar' was used to describe Mongols and Turks in old Russian and Chinese texts.
2. See J. V. Stalin, *Works*, Vol. XIII, 1915.
3. The 1908 poem 'On the Field of Kulikovo' by the Russian poet Alexander Blok is a brilliant distillation of the Russian view of war and the nature of power.
4. See M. S. Anderson, *Peter the Great*, London, 1978.
5. Russia's population was about 17.5 million; France 19 million; Britain 9 million; the Habsburg Empire 8 million; Spain 6 million; Prussia 2 million.
6. In one day in October 1698 he had 250 suspected dissidents put to 'a direful death' (they were roasted alive). He also had his own son tortured to death.
7. Russian historians stress the brilliant strategy of the Russian commanders, the tsar's courage and persistence and the heroism and patriotism of the Russian people. French historians stress the immensity of the task Napoleon undertook, as well as the impossible logistics and climate.
8. In 1849 Russia had helped put down a rebellion against the Austrian throne. In 1866, when Prussia fought Austria, Russia left Austria to her fate.
9. See S. G. Marks, *Road to Power: The Trans-Siberian Railroad and the Colonization of Asian Russia, 1850–1917*, Ithaca, NY, 1991.
10. See D. Field, *The End of Serfdom: Nobility and Bureaucracy in Russia 1855–1861*, Cambridge, 1976.

6. AFRICA: 1500–1914

1. Propelled by the reconquest of Spain in 1492, the Iberians attacked the North African Muslim cities of Morocco, Algiers, Tunis, Jerba and Tripoli.
2. See H. Hochschild, *Bury the Chains: Prophets and Rebels in the Fight to Free an Empire's Slaves*, Boston, 2005.
3. As the nineteenth century progressed, some of these outposts changed hands: the Iberians, Danes, Dutch and Swedes retired or ceased to extend their hold on the continent; the British, French, Germans and Lebanese gradually expanded their influence from the coast to the interior.
4. Mungo Park (1771–1806) and Hugh Clapperton (1788–1827) the Niger; David Livingstone (1813–73) the Zambezi; Richard Burton (1821–90) and John Speke (1827–64) the Nile; and Henry Stanley (1841–1904) the Congo.

5. See T. Pakenham, *The Scramble for Africa, 1876–1912*, New York, 1991.
6. See S. E. Crowe, *The Berlin West African Conference*, Westport, Conn., 1970.
7. See W. S. Blunt, *Gordon at Khartoum: Being a Personal Narrative of Events in Continuation of 'A Secret History of the English Occupation of Egypt'*, London, 1912.
8. See T. Pakenham, *The Boer War*, London, 1979. Britain's Colonial Secretary, Joseph Chamberlain, who held the office from 1895 to 1903, played a leading role in bringing this war about.
9. In 1795, during the French wars, Britain had seized the Cape from the Dutch. It handed it back after the Peace of Amiens in 1803, and re-occupied it in 1806. It was ceded to the British by the Convention of London in 1814.

7. THE EXPANSION OF THE AMERICAN EMPIRES

1. Columbus's four voyages (1492, 1493, 1498 and 1502) did nothing to dissuade him. See S. E. Morison, *The European Discoveries of America*, New York, 1974.
2. At the time of the arrival of the Spaniards, overall population density was not very different from that of Europe, Persia, India and China. See R. Thornton, *An American Indian Holocaust and Survival: A Population History since 1492*, Norman, Okla., 1987.
3. See Bernal Díaz del Castillo, *The True History of the Conquest of New Spain* (1632); trans. A. P. Maudslay, 5 vols, London, 1908–16.
4. See A. W. Crosby, *The Columbia Exchange*, Westport, Conn., 1972.
5. Imports of gold at Seville between 1503 and 1560 totalled 185,000 kilograms; imports of silver were 16 million kilograms. Silver production of the Spanish Indies in 1570 was about five times Europe's and Africa's combined production thirty years earlier.
6. The native population of North America at this time numbered about one million.
7. It is estimated that 21 million Amerindians died.
8. See A. W. Crosby, op. cit. (1972).
9. Friedrich von Gentz, 'On the Influence of the Discovery of America on the Prosperity and Culture of the Human Race', trans. and quoted in H. S. Commager and Elmo Giordanetti, *Was America a Mistake? An Eighteenth Century Controversy*, New York, 1967, p. 219.
10. Britain regained naval supremacy with the defeat of Admiral de Grasse in the Battle of the Saints in the Caribbean in 1782.
11. 'And God . . . said . . . replenish the earth and subdue it; and have

dominion over... every living thing that moveth upon the earth', Genesis: I, 28.

12. See Daniel Cosio Villegas, *American Extremes*, Austin, Tex., 1964, pp. 37–8, who speaks of Mexico as a miracle of survival. In contrast, he describes the USA as a miracle of fecundity.

13. Lincoln's Emancipation Proclamation was made in 1863. In theory it abolished slavery; in practice it freed few slaves.

14. See W. W. Howard, 'The Rush to Oklahoma', *Harpers*, 18 May 1889, pp. 391–2.

15. See P. J. Parish, *The American Civil War*, New York, 1975.

16. Then, as now, the countries most attracted by a gold standard were those that stood to gain from it. Because of its access through its ally Portugal to Brazilian – and later Australian and South African – gold deposits, Britain led the way.

17. Comparative figures, per capita, were: Britain $244; Germany $184; France $153; Italy $108; Austria-Hungary $57; Russia $41; Japan $36. Similarly, its national income of $37 billion far exceeded that of Germany ($12 billion), Britain ($11 billion), Russia ($7 billion), France ($6 billion), Italy ($4 billion), Austria-Hungary ($3 billion) and Japan ($2 billion).

18. See S. Karnow, *In Our Image: America's Empire and the Philippines*, New York, 1989.

19. See H. K. Beale, *Theodore Roosevelt and the Rise of America to World Power*, New York, 1962.

20. The number of American missionaries to China rose from 436 in 1874 to 5462 in 1914.

8. THE WEST IN THE WORLD

1. See T. Severin, *The Brendan Voyage*, New York, 1978. Also A. W. Crosby, *Ecological Imperialism*, Cambridge, 1986, chapter 3, 'The Norse and the Crusaders'. Artefacts found off the coast of Brazil suggest that the Romans may have discovered the New World before the birth of Christ. Also G. Menzies, op. cit.

2. So much so that in 1707 England and Scotland began to call themselves the United Kingdom of Great Britain.

3. Coupled with British victories at Wandewash (1760), Pondicherry (1761) and Buxar (1764).

4. Abandoned in 1973.

5. See Heinrich von Treitschke, *Politics*, trans. Blanche Dougdale and Torbende Bille, 2 vols, London, 1916, Vol. I, pp. 115–16.

6. 'The term civilization refers literally to a city-state . . . [I]n its more general usage it implies a system of living where law and order are maintained with justice and equality, human conflicts both inside and outside the group are resolved with a minimum of violence, and there is a moral code which people keep, more because they believe in it than because they are afraid of the consequences of breaking it.' In this light Africa has a long tradition of civilization. See Colin M. Turnbull, *The Peoples of Africa*, Leicester, 1963, pp. 29–30.

7. George Martelli, *Leopold to Lumumba: A History of the Belgian Congo 1877–1960*, London, 1963, p. 19.

8. Some of the reasons given for the increase in numbers are: the retreat of the plague (which last appeared in England in the seventeenth century and in France in the eighteenth), New World crops, including potatoes, a marked fall in infant-mortality rates, better transport and improved sanitation and medicine. See T. McKeown, *The Modern Rise of Population*, London, 1976.

9. Including measles, smallpox, typhus, influenza, tuberculosis, diphtheria, chicken pox, whooping cough, typhoid fever and scarlet fever from Europe, and trachoma, yellow fever, dengue fever, amoebic dysentery and malaria from Africa. See Alfred W. Crosby (1986), chapter 9, 'Ills'. Also W. H. McNeill, *Plagues and People*, New York, 1976, and Arno Karlen, *Man and Microbes*, New York, 1995.

10. Until the 1870s the foreign investments made by the British and the French were roughly the same. With Germany's defeat of France in 1871, Britain became the leading banker in the world. In 1914 it accounted for almost half of total European foreign investments.

11. In the Ottoman Empire all railways were operated by European companies; in China most of the railways belonged to Europeans by 1911. The same was true of Africa and South America.

12. Its introduction to Africa is said to have altered the course of African history. According to some writers, maize helped to offset the loss of lives caused by the slave trade. Statistically, very little is certain.

13. The term 'mercantile system' (whereby a seventeenth-century state – by exchanging trade goods for bullion – could obtain the money to fight its many wars) was coined by Adam Smith, whose free trade policy was set out in *The Wealth of Nations*, 1776. The adoption of free trade, he argued, would enrich Britain and the world. He was proved right.

14. Karl Jaspers, in his *Origin and Goal of History*, London, 1953, p. 76, quotes the German philosopher Hegel: 'The Europeans have sailed around the world and for them it is a sphere. Whatever has not yet fallen under their sway is either not worth the trouble, or it is destined to fall under it.'

9. EUROPE'S SCIENTIFIC AND INDUSTRIAL
REVOLUTIONS

1. The root of 'science' is the Latin *scientia*, which means 'knowledge'. See H. Butterfield, *The Origins of Modern Science*, New York, 1962.

2. Made possible by Johannes Gutenberg's (*c.* 1400–1468) invention of moveable type.

3. Gerardus Mercator (1512–94), a Flemish cartographer, was the first to draw a map of the globe based on his scientific 'Mercator' projection.

4. Protagoras (480–415 BC) had said that 'man is the measure of all things'.

5. The Greek astronomer Aristarch had put forward a sun-centred theory in the third century BC, but the time was not ripe and his ideas were rejected. See Hans Blumenberg, trans. Robert Wallace, *The Genesis of the Copernican World*, Cambridge, Mass., 1987.

6. In November 1992 the Roman Catholic Church finally conceded that it was wrong to have condemned Galileo for asserting that the earth orbits the sun.

7. Until quite modern times 'knowledge' also meant 'magic'. The Sanskrit word *Vidya* has this double meaning. Copernicus, Galileo, Kepler and Newton all dabbled in occult science.

8. Bacon's work was preceded by that of William Gilbert (1544–1603), who was one of the first to stress the importance of experimentation.

9. John Harrison's (1693–1776) developments of the marine chronometer made it possible to determine longitude at sea. See Dava Sobel, *Longitude: The True Story of a Lone Genius who Solved the Greatest Scientific Problem of His Time*, New York, 1998.

10. Alexander Pope (1688–1744).

11. In some aspects of his work on relativity, Einstein was preceded by James Clerk Maxwell (1831–79), Hendrik Antoon Lorentz (1853–1928), Henri Poincaré (1854–1912) and Arthur Stanley Eddington (1882–1944).

12. Anyone who has studied Isaac Newton's law of gravity, Daniel Bernoullis's (1700–82) law of hydrodynamic pressure, Michael Faraday's law of electromagnetic induction, Rudolf Clausius's (1822–88) law of entropy (the second law of thermodynamics) or Albert Einstein's law of mass-energy equivalence cannot doubt that these 'attempts to make infinite realities comprehensible to finite beings' are examples of objective truth. See Michael Guillen, *Five Equations that Changed the World*, New York, 1995.

13. Important contributions were made by Antoine Henri Becquerel (1852–1908), the Curie family (Pierre (1859–1906), Marie (1867–1934) and Irène (1897–1956)), Frédéric Joliot (1900–58), James Chadwick

(1891–1974), Otto Hahn (1879–1968), Fritz Strassmann (1902–80), Joseph John Thomson (1856–1940), Ernest Rutherford (1871–1937), who in 1919 split the atom, and Niels Bohr (1885–1962).

14. Technology is derived from the Greek word *techne*, meaning art or skill.

15. Arnold Toynbee, who popularized the term, dates the Industrial Revolution to the reign of George III (1760–1820). See P. Mathias, *The First Industrial Nation: An Economic History of Britain, 1700–1914*, 2nd edn, New York, 1983; also E. A. Wrigley, *Continuity, Chance, and Change: The Character of the Industrial Revolution*, New York, 1988.

16. See C. Treblicock, *The Industrialization of the Continental Powers, 1780–1914*, London, 1981.

17. Between 1815 and 1840 the output of coal quadrupled; the production of iron grew from 17,000 tons in the 1740s to 3 million tons in the 1850s.

18. Other contributing factors helping to explain Britain's predominance were the abundant harvests England enjoyed between 1720 and 1750, the introduction of new crops and agricultural practices and the more profitable use of land (the enclosure movement). Even in Britain, where the agricultural sector shrank in comparison with the expansion of the manufacturing and service industries, agriculture remained one of the pillars of the economy.

19. In 1781 Britain imported about five million tons of raw cotton; the figure for 1789 was six times greater.

20. Watt made Newcomen's engine more economical in fuel. He also developed (in 1782) the rotary motion to drive other kinds of machinery. The first known Newcomen engine was built in 1712. In 1821 Aaron Manby (1776–1815), a British engineer, patented his design for an oscillating steam engine suitable for marine propulsion.

21. Though it is not until 1957 that world trade in manufactured goods exceeded the trade in primary produce.

22. The first successful internal combustion engine was invented in 1859 by Etienne Lenoir of France. German contributions were made by N. A. Otto (1876), Gottlieb Daimler and Wilhelm Maybach (1886), Rudolf Diesel (1892) and Karl Benz (1894).

23. In 1909 Louis Blériot (1872–1936) made the first flight across the English Channel. In 1919 the Britains John Alcock (1892–1919) and Arthur Whitten Brown (1886–1948) flew nonstop across the Atlantic Ocean in just over sixteen hours. In 1927 Charles Lindbergh (1902–74) made the first solo flight across the Atlantic. In 1930 Amy Johnson (1903–41) flew from Australia to London. In 1933 Wiley Post (1898–1935) flew solo around the world. In 1976 supersonic jet airliners were introduced on transatlantic flights.

24. Penicillin was discovered by Alexander Fleming (1881–1955) in 1928. Howard Walter Florey (1898–1968) and Ernst Boris Chain (1906–79) shared the Noble Prize in 1945 for this discovery. The biochemist Norman George Heatley (1911–2004), a member of Florey's team at Oxford, is the unacknowledged contributor to the antibiotic era.

25. The first to travel into space was the Russian Yuri Gagarin in 1961; the first to set foot on the moon were the Americans Neil Armstrong and Edward Aldrin in 1969.

26. See Rupert Sheldrake, *A New Science of Life*, London, 1981, and *The Presence of the Past*, New York, 1988. See also John Maddox, 'A Book for Burning', *Nature*, Vol. 293, pp. 245–6, 1981.

10. 'WHITE PERIL' IN THE EAST

1. See A. Whaley, *The Opium War through Chinese Eyes*, London, 1958.

2. In 1836 British sales of opium in China totalled $18 million; Chinese sales of tea and silk to the British amounted to $17 million.

3. Four new ports – in addition to Canton (Ghangzhou) – were opened up for Western trade; tariffs on imported British goods were limited; under the principle of extra-territoriality, British subjects in China could be tried only by British laws; a substantial indemnity – $21 million – was demanded. The opium trade was never mentioned.

4. The famine of 1877–9 in northern China left ten million dead.

5. See F. Michael and C. Chung-li, *The Taiping Rebellion*, 3 vols, Seattle, 1966–71.

6. It is to the credit of the US government that its share of the indemnity was used to enhance Chinese education.

7. See H. Z. Schiffren, *Sun Yat-sen and the Origins of the Chinese Revolution*, New Haven, Conn., 1968.

8. See F. Wakeman, *The Fall of Imperial China*, New York, 1975.

9. The manufacture of guns was restricted as a safeguard against insurrection under the long peace of the Tokugawas; more importantly, in comparison with the sword, a gun was culturally unacceptable. See Noel Perrin, *Giving up the Gun*, Boston, Mass., 1979.

10. See W. G. Beasley, *The Meiji Restoration*, Stanford, Cal., 1972.

11. See I. Nish, *The Origins of the Russo-Japanese War*, London, 1985.

12. See D. Rees, *A Short History of Modern Korea*, New York, 1988.

13. Mutinies had also occurred in 1764, 1829 and following Britain's defeat in Afghanistan in 1844.

14. See F. Kazemzadeh, *Russia and Britain in Persia, 1864–1914*, New Haven, Conn., 1968.

15. See A. Reid, *Southeast Asia in the Age of Commerce, 1450–1680*, New Haven, Conn., 1989.

16. The sultanate of Brunei was a powerful state in the sixteenth century, with authority over the islands of Borneo, part of the Sulu Islands and the Philippines.

11. THE GREAT WAR: 1914–18

1. See D. C. B. Lieven, *Russia and the Origins of the First World War*, New York, 1984.

2. Helmuth von Moltke, chief of the German General Staff at the outbreak of war, is thought to have exaggerated the importance of railways in general mobilization. Nevertheless, strategy (even by 1870) depended less on soldiers' legs and more on railway wheels. The German General Staff had planned to move 3 million men and 600,000 horses in 11,000 trains in 312 hours.

3. See F. Fischer, *Germany's Aims in the First World War*, New York, 1967; also J. Joll, *The Origins of the First World War*, London, 1984; and R. Henig, *The Origins of the First World War*, London, 1989.

4. Greece had won its independence from the Ottoman Empire in 1830; Romania in 1856; Serbia and Bulgaria in 1878; Albania, Macedonia and Montenegro in 1912.

5. See L. S. Stavrianos, *The Balkans, 1815–1914*, New York, 1963.

6. See J. R. B. Bosworth, *Italy and the Approach of the First World War*, London, 1983.

7. The United Kingdom's share of world manufacturing output declined from 22.9 per cent in 1880 to 13.6 per cent in 1913. A similar downward trend occurred in Britain's share of world trade, which fell from 23.2 per cent in 1880 to 14.1 per cent in 1911–13.

8. See Z. S. Steiner, *Britain and the Origins of the First World War*, New York, 1977.

9. See Michael Balfour, *The Kaiser and his Times*, Boston, Mass., 1964, p. 425.

10. 'Were Germany united,' said David Hume in 1748, 'it would be the greatest power that ever was in the world.'

11. See V. R. Berghahn, *Germany and the Approach of War in 1914*, London, 1973; also G. Barraclough, *Factors in German History*, Oxford, 1946.

12. See J. F. Keiger, *France and the Origins of the First World War*, New York, 1984.

13. In 1913 France's GNP, its share of world manufacturing production and its national income were all about half those of Germany. On the eve of war it planned to mobilize 80 divisions, the Germans 100.

14. See R. W. Clark, *Lenin*, New York, 1988; also Robert Service, *Lenin: A Biography*, Cambridge, Mass., 2000.

15. Wars take place for all kinds of reasons. The inner dilemma of capitalism might explain Britain's onslaught on China in the nineteenth century, but it does not explain the struggles going on in Italy and Greece, where independence was at stake. Britain's war against China in 1839–42, Japan's wars with China in 1894–5 and Russia in 1904–5, as well as the US clash with Spanish forces in 1898, were wars of conquest, but this was not true of Austria's war against France in 1859 or France's war against Prussia in 1870. Apprehension, impatience, exasperation and downright stupidity were at work there. The militarists may have played a leading role in causing the war between France and Prussia in 1870, but this can hardly have been true of the Crimean War or the Spanish–American War. In the latter two conflicts, the militarists and the ruling elites would have gladly preserved the peace but for the popular will. The Crimean War began over a religious dispute.

16. See Richard Hough, *The Great War at Sea*, Oxford, 1983. Hough maintains that the unrelenting pressure of the Royal Navy was the prime factor which led to the defeat of the Central Powers on land in 1918.

17. There is some controversy about the value of the Dreyse breech-loading rifle. It had been available since the 1840s and had been rejected by Austria and other countries. Comment of the time leaves no doubt that the Dreyse rifle helped Prussia to prevail.

18. At that time France was conscripting 89 per cent of its eligible young males; Germany 53 per cent. Germany's army budget grew from $204 million in 1910 to $442 million in 1914. Similar figures for France were $188 million and $197 million.

19. Inspired by eighteenth-century Enlightenment ideas, the First International of the International Workingmen's Association was established in London in 1864. Karl Marx drafted its constitution. The Second International was formed in London in 1889. Since 1919 there have been two separate international organizations of labour: the Third Communist International in Moscow, based on revolutionary principles, and the non-revolutionary Labour and Socialist International in Zurich. When war came, despite all rhetoric, the labour movement shed its internationalism. To reassure his wartime allies, who were providing massive aid to Russia and had promised to open a second front in the west in 1944, Stalin abolished the Communist International (established by Lenin in 1919).

20. Between 1864 and 1949 four conventions were held at Geneva dealing

with war casualties on land and sea, the treatment of prisoners of war and the protection of civilians during times of war.

21. Rupert Brooke, 'Peace', in *The Complete Poems*, New York, 1977, p. 146.
22. Before the war ended the 4 per cent (on average) of the national incomes being spent by the combatants before 1914 on armaments had risen to 25–30 per cent. In 1914 Russia was spending 35 per cent of total government expenditures on the military – much more than the advanced industrial nations were doing.
23. Rupert Brooke, 'The Dead', in Brooke (1977), p. 148.
24.

First World War Deaths

Austro-Hungarian Empire	1,050,000
Belgium	41,000
British Empire	1,000,000
Bulgaria	49,000*
France	1,500,000
Germany	1,950,000
Greece	5000*
Italy	533,000
Japan	2000*
Montenegro	3000*
Portugal	7222
Romania	158,000*
Serbia	322,000*
USA	116,000
Russia	1,700,000*
Ottoman Empire	325,000*

Note: *estimates

Source: Geoffrey Barraclough (ed.), *The Times Atlas of World History*, London, 1978

25. There was even controversy on how dead German airship crew should be buried in England – as soldiers (with military honours) or as pirates.
26. In 1925 under the Geneva Protocol, the Western nations again banned the use of toxic gas.
27. The decision meant *'finis Germaniae'*, said the German Chancellor Bethmann-Hollweg, who had resolutely opposed the move.

28. The sinking of the SS *Lusitania* with the loss of 1198 lives, including 128 Americans, helped to turn US public opinion against Germany. For the sharp divergence between official and non-official accounts of this tragedy, see Colin Simpson, *The Truth about the Lusitania*, Boston, Mass., 1972.

29. Germany's secret proposal of an alliance with Mexico against the USA, the Zimmerman Note of January 1917, harmed the isolationist cause in the United States.

30. Under which Russia surrendered the Baltic Provinces, Poland, Ukraine, West Byelorussia, Finland and parts of Transcaucasia. Russia lost one million square miles of territory and sixty million people.

31. Wilson's Fourteen Points included commitments to open rather than secret diplomacy, disarmament, adjudication, self-determination and international cooperation. They became the basis of the Paris Peace Conference and the League of Nations.

32. See J. M. Keynes, *The Economic Consequences of the Peace*, New York, 1920, which did much to create the legend of the 'Carthaginian Peace' imposed on the Germans at Versailles. See also M. Trachtenberg, *Reparations in World Politics*, New York, 1980.

33. Wilson's Covenant of the League of Nations was written into the four subsequent European treaties: St Germain (September 1919 with Austria); Neuilly (November 1919 with Bulgaria); Trianon (June 1920 with Hungary) and Lausanne (July 1923 with Turkey).

34. The signatories to the Covenant pledged themselves to work for disarmament, provide mutual protection, guarantee national independence and territorial integrity, submit to arbitration in case of conflict and agree to apply economic sanctions on dissident members. Positive contributions were made by the League in labour legislation and in the control of international health and disease.

35. Hitler, the son of an Austrian customs official, was a decorated veteran of the First World War. He was probably the most disturbing figure in world affairs since Napoleon. At thirty, with the war over, he returned to the life of a drifter, obtaining a precarious living as a painter. His astonishing political career began in 1919 when he joined the anti-communist German Workers' Party, which in 1921 became the Nationalsozialistische Deutsche Arbeiterpartei (Nazi – National Socialist German Workers' Party). See Alan Bullock, *Hitler: A Study in Tyranny*, New York, 1952, and *Hitler and Stalin: Parallel Lives*, London, 1991; also John Lukacs, *The Hitler of History*; New York, 1998.

36. Wilfred Owen, 'Dulce et Decorum Est', in *The Complete Poems and Fragments*, Vol. I: *The Poems*, New York, London, 1984, p. 140.

37. Poland had been divided in 1772, 1793, 1795 and 1815 because Britain

and France would not risk war. It regained its freedom in 1919, not because of President Wilson, but because Austria-Hungary, Russia and Germany were convulsed and defeated.

38. The Kingdom of Serbs, Croats and Slavs, founded after the First World War, was formed from the former provinces of Croatia, Dalmatia, Bosnia, Herzegovina, Slovenia, Voyvodina and the independent state of Montenegro, and renamed Yugoslavia in 1929.

39. The Irish Republic was first proclaimed with the uprising in Dublin in April 1916. Under the leadership of Eamon De Valera (1882–1975), Ireland (except Northern Ireland) eventually obtained full independence (partial independence had been gained by the Anglo-Irish Treaty of December 1921) under the Republic of Ireland Act in April 1949.

40. During 1915 and 1916, Sir Henry McMahon, British High Commissioner in Egypt, exchanged ten letters with Hussein ibn Ali, Sherif of Mecca. The purpose: to enlist Arab support against the Turks. The promise behind the correspondence, however ambiguously worded, was Arab independence. See *British Parliamentary Papers*, 1939, Misc. No. 3, Cmd. 5957.

41. The Balfour Declaration was contained in a letter dated 2 November 1917, addressed to Lord Rothschild, a European Zionist leader (who had, along with President Wilson's legal aide Louis Brandeis, an American Zionist, already helped in its drafting). It was signed by Britain's foreign secretary, Arthur James Balfour (1848–1930), and appeared in the London *Times*, 9 November 1917.

42. The Dawes and Young plans were terminated by the Lausanne Conference in 1932. After this date reparation payments ceased.

43. See C. P. Kindleberger, *The World in Depression, 1929–1939*, rev. edn, Berkeley, Cal., 1986.

44. See R. J. Sontag, *A Broken World, 1919–1939*, New York, 1971.

45. See Alfred Crosby, *America's Forgotten Pandemic: The Influenza of 1918*, Cambridge, 1989. See also Gina Kolater, *Flu*, New York, 2000.

46. New Zealand (1893), Finland (1906) and Norway (1913) had led the way. Women's suffrage was not granted in Italy, Spain, France and Switzerland until after the Second World War. Only then did feminism become a popular movement, especially in the USA.

47. In February 2001 Turkey protested at the decision of France's president to sign into law (as the Greeks had already alone) a bill describing the massacre of Armenians in 1915 as 'genocide'.

48. See P. B. Kinross, *Atatürk: A Biography of Mustafa Kemal, Father of Modern Turkey*, New York, 1992.

12. 1917: COMMUNISM – A NEW WORLD RELIGION

1. The revolution of 1905 had forced Nicholas II (who had come to the throne in 1894) to accept an elected Duma (parliament). But its power was limited and it was in constant conflict with the tsar.

2. He had left the affairs of state in the hands of the Tsarina Alexandra. Ominous rumours of her incompetence, and that of the corrupt courtiers who surrounded her (including the *stannik* (holy man) Rasputin, who was assassinated in 1916), circulated in Petrograd.

3. In 1903 the Russian Socialist Democratic Party had split into two groups: the Bolsheviks, extremists who wanted party leadership to be restricted to a select number of revolutionaries, and the Mensheviks, moderates who wanted a wider membership and a more democratic leadership.

4. See Leon Trotsky, *A History of the Russian Revolution*, vols 1–3, New York, 1932. Earlier, Trotsky had been a Menshevik who denounced the Bolsheviks.

5. See R. H. McNeil, *Stalin: Man and Ruler*, New York, 1988.

6. The Provisional Government's warrant for the arrest of the Bolshevik leaders, issued on 6 July, did not include Stalin.

7. By the old Julian Calendar then used in Russia; 7 November by the Gregorian Calendar.

8. The election returns, released in November 1918, showed the Bolsheviks with 225 out of the 707 delegates.

9. Which in 1922 became the GPU, and in 1923 the United Government Political Organization – OGPU.

10. See J. Bradley, *Allied Intervention in Russia 1917–1920*, New York, 1968.

11. See D. McLellan, *Karl Marx*, New York, 1974. Also Francis Wheen, *Karl Marx: A Life*, London and New York, 2000.

12. Volumes II and III were published posthumously, 1885–94.

13. Contrary to the commonly held opinion that pre-revolutionary Russia was a country of economic stagnation, Russia's growth rate between 1908 and 1914 was 8.8 per cent. Production of pig iron – in those days one of the yardsticks of economic development – rose faster in Russia than it did in Germany.

14. One hundred years after Pope Leo XIII issued 'Rerum Novarum', the historic encyclical on economic issues, Pope John Paul II released his encyclical on economics, 'Centessimus Anno', in which he endorsed the market economy enjoined with powerful changes. John Paul II uses the term 'free economy', not capitalism.

15. The socialist theoretician Eduard Bernstein (1850–1932) said that

Marxism is Calvinism without God. Marxism has the comfort of faith and religion without believing in a supreme being.

16. See Max Weber, *The Protestant Work Ethic and the Spirit of Capitalism*, London, 1930.

17. Lenin wrote *Imperialism: The Highest Stage of Capitalism*, 1917, and *The State and Revolution*, 1918.

18. J. V. Stalin, *Works*, vol. 5, Moscow, 1953, p. 270.

19. See Robert Conquest, *The Harvest of Sorrow*, Oxford, 1986.

13. ASIA IN THE INTER-WAR YEARS

1. During the First World War Japan had made demands upon China that threatened China's independence. In 1915 it established its rule in Shantung, Manchuria and Inner Mongolia.

2. In 1921 Outer Mongolia declared its independence. In 1924 it became the Mongolian People's Republic and was recognized as such by China in 1946; its independence was guaranteed by China and the Soviet Union in February 1950.

3. Sun Yat-sen founded the Republic of South China in 1911. See H. Z. Schiffrin, *Sun Yat-sen and the Origins of the 1911 Revolution*, Berkeley, Cal., 1969.

4. See E. Hahn, *Chiang Kai-shek: An Unauthorized Biography*, New York, 1955.

5. For a first-hand view, see the autobiography of Han Suyin, Book 3, *Birdless Summer*, London, 1968.

6. See Stuart Schram, *Mao Tse-Tung*, New York, 1966; also Peter Short, *Mao: A Life*, New York, 2000.

7. Participants were the USA, Britain, China, Japan, France, Italy, Belgium, the Netherlands and Portugal. China's independence and territorial integrity were guaranteed; Japan undertook to return Shantung Province to China; a ten-year moratorium on capital ship construction was agreed.

8. The Chinese Exclusion Act of 1882 had made the Chinese the first nationality specifically banned from immigration into the USA. US concern about Japan grew after the latter's victory over Russia in 1904–5. In the Second World War all Japanese Americans were interned.

9. See R. J. Butow, *Tojo and the Coming of War*, Princeton, NJ, 1961.

10. On 10 December 1941, they sank Britain's only two battleships in eastern waters, the *Repulse* and the *Prince of Wales*.

11. The trend towards Indian nationalism and representative government

was stimulated by the British. In 1885 Allan Hume, a retired British civil servant, helped to found the Indian National Congress, the first all-India political organization.

12. Leader of the Muslim League and later the founder of Pakistan.

13. Ho Chi Minh became a communist early in life. He fought with the Allies in France in the First World War. In 1918 he helped to found the French Communist Party. In 1930, after socialist activities in Russia and southern China, he returned secretly to Vietnam, where he established the Communist Party of Indo-China and the Vietminh movement. Forever fleeing his political enemies, he was jailed in Hong Kong by the British and in China by the nationalists. In September 1945, when the Democratic Republic of Vietnam was proclaimed, Ho Chi Minh was in Hanoi, ready to seize power.

14. See C. Catherwood, *Churchill's Folly: How Winston Churchill Created Modern Iraq*, New York, 2004.

15. A 1893–4 census by the Ottoman Empire, which controlled Palestine until the end of the First World War, showed a total of 9817 Jews in Palestine and 371,969 Arabs. The figures for 1914 were 60,000 Jews and 500,000 Arabs.

16. See D. Vital, *The Origins of Zionism*, Oxford, 1975.

14. THE SECOND WORLD WAR: 1939–45

1. See David Kaiser, *Economic Diplomacy and the Origins of the Second World War*, Princeton, NJ, 1980.

2. See S. Marks, *The Illusion of Peace: 1918–1933*, New York, 1976.

3. Benito Mussolini was born in north-central Italy, the son of a blacksmith. In 1911 he became the editor of the socialist paper *Avanti!*. Abandoning his socialist and pacifist principles, in 1915 he joined the Italian army on the Northern Front. The war over, he helped to form the Fasci d'Italiani di Combattimento (Black Shirts), which quickly attracted the support of anti-communist groups throughout Italy. Following the murder of his political opponent Giacomo Matteotti in 1924, all opposition to fascism was silenced. See D. M. Smith, *Mussolini: A Biography*, New York, 1982.

4. The Weimar Republic, which replaced the Second Reich, provided a democratic and more centralized constitution. It was adopted at Weimar in 1919.

5. Tacitus tells us that the Roman Republic succumbed to the Caesars because people became weary of disorder.

6. Most historians attribute the ninefold increase in Nazi votes to the

deepening of the economic crisis. Yet the communal elections of 1929 – a relatively prosperous year – show that the appeal of the Nazis had already begun to grow.

7. The onset of the Great Depression began with commercial collapse in the USA in 1929. By 1932, Germany's output and trade had fallen to about half their 1928 figures.

8. See 'Great Men in History', in Morris R. Cohen, *The Meaning of Human History*, New York, 1947.

9. The League's failure to halt Mussolini in Abyssinia convinced Hitler that the democracies lacked the will to uphold the Covenant of the League.

10. Joining the Anti-Comintern Pact were: Italy (1937), Hungary and Spain (1939), Slovakia and Bulgaria (1940) and Romania (1941).

11. Czechoslovakia was one of a number of nation states (others were Austria, Hungary, Poland, Yugoslavia, Finland, Estonia, Latvia and Lithuania) which came into existence as a result of the First World War. Finland, Estonia, Latvia and Lithuania gained their independence as a result of the breakdown of Russian rule in 1917–18. Except for Finland, they were repossessed by the Soviet Union under the secret protocol of the Soviet-German frontier treaty of August 1939.

12. Before 1938 the term was commonly understood to mean a necessary and desirable relation between nations. See Andrew J. Crozier, *Appeasement and Germany's Last Bid for Colonies*, London, 1988.

13. See Lieutenant Commander P. K. Kemp, *Key to Victory*, Boston, Mass., 1958, p. 26.

14. See Anthony Read and David Fisher, *The Deadly Embrace: Hitler, Stalin, and the Nazi–Soviet Pact 1939–1941*, London, 1988. In 1940 the USSR forcibly annexed Estonia, Latvia and Lithuania. Finland, attacked in the winter of 1939, offered heroic resistance, but by March 1940 was forced to accept Russia's terms. Because it had violated the Covenant, the USSR was expelled from the League of Nations on 14 December 1939.

15. In the First World War the Germans had invaded Belgium not knowing what the British would do. This time they knew that an attack upon Poland would bring Britain (and France) into the war. On 31 March 1939 Chamberlain had announced in Parliament that if Poland were attacked, 'His Majesty's Government would feel themselves bound at once to lend the Polish Government all support in their power.' Having declared war, Britain and France found themselves virtually unable to help Poland.

16. Influential in helping to form American policy was J. P. Kennedy (US ambassador in London). Like many other ardent American isolation-

ists, he supported the powerful America First movement led by the famous aviator Charles Lindbergh. This movement, which at one time appeared to represent the majority opinion in the USA, died within hours of Japan's attack on Pearl Harbor in December 1941.

17. Well might Winston Churchill write: 'I slept that night with the peace of one who knows he has been saved.'

18. Including Edouard Daladier, Georges Bonnet, Pierre Laval, Stanley Baldwin, Samuel Hoare, Ramsay MacDonald, John Simon, Edward Halifax and Neville Chamberlain.

19. In 1938 Germany devoted 17 per cent of its GNP to war preparation, an amount exceeding that of Britain, France and the USA combined.

20. Only Portugal, Spain, Switzerland, Sweden, Eire and Turkey succeeded in remaining neutral.

21. At this point the United States' naval protection against German warships was advanced to the mid-Atlantic; economic and military aid was given to Britain.

22. 'The hand that held the dagger', said President Roosevelt in a speech made at the University of Virginia on the same day, 'has struck it into the back of its neighbour.'

23. German civilian casualties from Allied bombing were 635,000. See J. Friedrich, *Der Brand* (*The Fire: Germany under Bombardment 1940–45*), Berlin, 2002.

24. The British lost 449 fighter pilots and 900 aircraft.

25. See A. Clark, *Barbarossa, The Russo-German Conflict, 1941–1945*, London, 1965.

26. In the terrible blood-letting in Yugoslavia in the Second World War between communist-led partisans, Serbian royalist Chetniks and the forces of Nazi-supported Croatians, 1.7 million died.

27. See W. H. Baldwin, *Battles Lost and Won*, New York, 1966, pp. 112–13.

28. Emulating Hitler's annexation of Czechoslovakia in 1939, Mussolini annexed Albania. He went on to attack Greece in October 1940, but was defeated by the Greek military leader Ioannis Metaxas (1871–1941).

29. These efforts were frustrated by communist resistance led by Marshal Tito (Josip Broz; 1892–1980), who later became head of the Socialist Federal Republic of Yugoslavia.

30. Japan sank or put out of action all 8 US battleships, 3 of its 7 cruisers and 3 destroyers. See John Toland, *Infamy, Pearl Harbor and its Aftermath*, New York, 1982. Toland argues that Roosevelt and his top advisers knew about the planned attack but remained silent in order to draw the USA into the war. Major damage was done to US aircraft and battleships, but the fleet's aircraft carriers were out of

harbour. More recent writers have suggested that code-breaking was involved: Washington wished to conceal the fact that it had already broken the Japanese codes.

31. For three years, from June 1941 until June 1944, the Red Army inflicted over 90 per cent of German army battle losses.

32. At the outset of the battle, in October 1942, the British had overwhelming superiority in the air, three times the number of soldiers and six times as many tanks as the Germans and the Italians combined.

33. Being an ally rather than an enemy was to make a great difference to Italy once the war was over.

34. The Allies had an almost inexhaustible supply of troops, a 20:1 advantage in armour and a 25:1 advantage in aircraft. In addition they had complete command of the English Channel.

35. Although none of the Japanese victories had a crippling effect on overall Allied strategy. See C. Bateson, *The War with Japan*, East Lansing, Mich., 1968.

36. Truman was advised that the use of the bomb would save half a million Allied lives.

37. The Japanese had 600,000 troops in the area.

38.

Second World War Deaths[*]

	Military	Civilian	Jewish[a]
Austria	380,000	145,000	(60,000)
Belgium	9,600	75,000	(25,000)
Britain	271,300	60,000[b]	—
British			
Commonwealth	133,000	—	—
Bulgaria	18,500	n.a.	14,000
China	1,324,500	10,000,000[c]	—
Czechoslovakia	6700	310,000	(250,000)
Denmark	4300	n.a.	—
Estonia	—	140,000	[d]
Finland	79,000	n.a.	—
France	205,700	173,300	(65,000)
Germany[b]	4,000,000	3,100,000	188,000
Greece	16,400	155,300	(60,000)
Hungary	147,400	280,000	(200,000)

Italy	262,400	93,000	(8000)
Japan	1,140,400[c]	953,000	—
Latvia	—	120,000	d
Lithuania	—	170,000	d
Netherlands	13,700	236,300	(104,000)
Norway	4800	5400	900
Poland	320,000	6,028,000	(3,200,000)
Romania	519,800	465,000	(425,000)
USA	292,100	—	—
USSR	13,600,000	7,720,000	(1,252,000)
Yugoslavia	305,000	1,355,000	(55,000)
Total	23,054,600	31,584,300	5,906,900

Notes:

*Estimates for some countries vary greatly.

[a]Figures in parentheses are also included as civilian casualties. [b]Figures taken from H. G. Dahms, *Die Geschichte des Zweiten Weltkrieges*, Munich, 1983, p. 616. [c]Estimate. [d]Baltic States (228,000). [e]In the 1990s the Japanese updated their military casualties to two million.

Source: Robert Goralski (ed.), *World War II Almanac*, New York, 1981.

See also M. Clodfelter, *Warfare and Armed Conflicts: A Statistical Reference to Casualty and Other Figures, 1500–2000*, Jefferson, NC, 2001.

39. During the war toxic gases (despite being outlawed by the Geneva Protocol of 1925, which had been signed by thirty-eight countries) were used to kill imprisoned minorities in Manchuria and Eastern Europe, but were not used on the battlefield (despite the discovery in the 1930s of far deadlier substances, such as the nerve gas Tabun).

40. See Arno J. Mayer, *Why Did the Heavens Not Darken? The Final Solution in History*, New York, 1989. Also Charles S. Maier, *The Unmasterable Past: History, Holocaust and German Identity*, Cambridge, Mass., 1989, and Gabriel Schoenfeld, *The Return of Anti-Semitism*, San Francisco, 2004.

41. Not Italy, which avoided indictments by changing sides in 1944.

42. Said Jackson: 'The wrongs which we seek to condemn and punish have been so calculated, so malignant and so devastating, that civilization cannot tolerate their being ignored because it cannot survive their being repeated' (Robert H. Jackson, 'Opening Address', in *Trial of German War Criminals*, Senate Doc. no. 129, 79th Cong., 1st sess., Washington DC, Government Printing Office, 1946, p. 1). Twelve of the accused at Nuremberg, and seven in Japan, were sentenced to death by hanging.

43. The Geneva Convention of 1897 and the Hague Convention of 1899, concerning the treatment of civilians and prisoners of war, were violated to a greater or lesser extent by all the warring powers.

44. In 1990 the Russians acknowledged that the Soviet secret police had murdered fifteen thousand Polish officers.

45. See Dahms (1983), p. 618.

46. Those on trial at Nuremberg and Tokyo used the same defence as Shakespeare's soldiers accused of crime in *Henry V*: 'We know enough if we know we are the king's men. Our obedience to the king wipes the crime of it out of us.'

47. See Ann Tusa and John Tusa, *The Nuremberg Trial*, New York, 1984; also, R. H. Minear, *Victor's Justice: The Tokyo War Crimes Trial*, Princeton, NJ, 1971. The Japanese leader for most of the war, Hideki Tojo (1885–1948), was executed. See G. J. Bass, *Stay the Hand of Vengeance: The Politics of War Crimes Tribunals*, New York, 2000.

48. The evidence since 1945, despite the United Nations General Assembly's approval of the Convention of the Prevention and Punishment of the Crime of Genocide in 1948, and the Geneva Conventions in 1949, which grew out of the Nuremberg trials, suggests that the Nuremberg and Tokyo trials have had limited effect.

49. At the Cairo Conference in 1945 Roosevelt had insisted on treating China as the fifth power. Churchill had demurred.

50. In invading Poland, Russia was reoccupying the land it had lost to Poland in 1919–20. Poland was compensated for its losses to Russia with German territory. About one-third of present-day Poland, comprising Silesia, Pomerania, West Prussia and part of East Prussia, was German territory. Germans were banished from areas they had occupied for more than half a millennium. The Yalta settlement not only laid the groundwork for future discord between Poland and Germany but made Poland a hostage to Russia.

51. Because the Russians were now feared more than the Germans, and the weakening of Germany would have meant the strengthening of Soviet communism, some Americans and Britons (particularly Churchill) prevented Secretary of the Treasury Henry Morgenthau from reducing Germany to a pastoral state. The Russians were the strongest supporters of the Morgenthau Plan.

52. A communist-led attempt to seize power in Greece in 1944 was thwarted by British intervention. Further communist attempts to seize power (1946–9) were foiled by the USA.

53. See N. Naimark, *The Russians in Germany: A History of the Soviet Zone of Occupation, 1945–1949*, Cambridge, Mass., 1995.

54. According to the German embassy, Washington, DC, in 2001 former slave labourers also received compensation from Germany.

15. THE BALANCE OF TERROR

1. Roosevelt's ideas reflected the same grand design for world peace put forward by Metternich, the Austrian foreign secretary, in the Holy Alliance of 1815. It is chiefly due to Roosevelt that the idea of the United Nations came to fruition.

2. Also to the shame of those involved, the British and the Americans agreed to Russian demands to return those displaced Russians who had either fought for Germany or fled to the West, even though it was realized at the time that many of these former prisoners of war would be executed. See Nicholas Bethell, *The Last Secret: The Delivery to Stalin of over Two Million Russians by Britain and the United States*, New York, 1974.

3. Truman's reserve with the Russians (after they received news at Potsdam that America possessed the atomic bomb), and his inexperience, helped the Cold War to get under way.

4. In October 1947 the Communist Information Bureau (Cominform, successor to the Comintern – the Third Communist International – which had been dissolved by Stalin in 1943) was established to coordinate communist action throughout the world. As a gesture of renewed friendship with Yugoslavia, the Cominform was dissolved in 1956.

5. In 2005 Russian archives revealed that hundreds of communist sympathizers in the West had been passing critical information to Russia.

6. The authors of America's policy of containment were Paul H. Nitze (1907–2004) and the US ambassador to the USSR, George F. Kennan. See the latter's article, signed 'X', in *Foreign Affairs*, July 1947. Also M. Wilson, *George Kennan and the Making of American Foreign Policy, 1947–1950*, Princeton, NJ, 1992.

7. Proposed in 1947 by US Secretary of State General George Marshall (1880–1959), it provided Western European countries, which soon included Germany, with $13.5 billion of economic and financial assistance. (Aid was rejected by Moscow; Poland was ordered by the Kremlin to withdraw its application for assistance.) Introduced in 1948, Marshall Aid was discontinued in 1952. See A. Milward, *The Reconstruction of Western Europe, 1945–1951*, Berkeley, Cal., 1984, and M. J. Hogan, *The Marshall Plan*, Cambridge, 1987. On balance, the importance of the Marshall Plan to the recovery of Western Europe has been exaggerated.

8. See Ann Tusa and John Tusa, *The Berlin Blockade*, London, 1988. The blockade lasted for almost a year. Hundreds of thousands of flights to

Berlin were made by British and US aircraft carrying food and other essential supplies.

9. Member states were: Belgium, Canada, Denmark, France (nominal membership since 1966), United Kingdom, Iceland, Italy, Luxembourg, Netherlands, Norway, Portugal and the USA. Greece and Turkey joined in 1952; the Federal Republic of Germany in 1955; Spain in 1982; the Czech Republic, Hungary and Poland in 1999; Bulgaria, Estonia, Latvia, Lithuania, Romania, Slovakia and Slovenia in 2004.

10. Portugal was a dictatorship under António de Oliveira Salazar, whose retirement in 1968 prompted a struggle between militarists and communists.

11. Including Czechoslovakia, East Germany, Poland, Hungary, Romania, Bulgaria, Albania and the Soviet Union.

12. Hostilities between the Soviet Union and Japan were officially terminated in 1956. With Russian opposition withdrawn, Japan took its place as a member of the United Nations. In June 1968, the USA returned to Japan control of certain Pacific islands, including Iwo Jima and the Marcus Islands. In May 1972 Okinawa was returned, although the USA retained its military bases there. By 2004 there was still no peace treaty between Russia and Japan.

13. It included Australia, France, New Zealand, Pakistan, the Philippines, Thailand, the UK and the USA.

14. This was meant to guard against possible Russian aggression. It included Iran, Iraq, Pakistan, Turkey and the United Kingdom. Although the USA had sponsored the defence agreement, it refused to become a full member.

15. See E. M. Bottome, *The Balance of Terror: A Guide to the Arms Race*, rev. edn, Boston, Mass., 1986.

16. The NPT came into effect in 1970 with the goal of reducing the spread of nuclear weapons, while facilitating the use of peaceful applications of nuclear energy. On 20 May 1989 India became the first Third World nation to admit developing an intermediate-range ballistic missile. In May 2005 the Review Conference of the treaty was concerned with the rise of potential nuclear terrorism through a nuclear black market, clandestine nuclear weapons programmes and the failure by the nuclear states to reduce their nuclear arms stockpiles.

16. THE DECOLONIZATION OF AFRICA

1. The National Congress of British West Africa, formed in 1919, set the stage for future developments.

2. Due to dramatic falls in child mortality rates, increased fertility, fewer wars and famines and improved medicine.

3. See J. D. Hargreaves, *The Decolonization of Africa*, London, 1988.

4. Following the Berlin Conference of 1884, Germany took possession of Togoland and Cameroon. It also obtained a block of coastal land that became German Southwest Africa. Germany lost these territories to Britain in 1919.

5. Tanganyika had been proclaimed the protectorate of German East Africa in 1890. In return for a German promise to keep out of Uganda, the British gave up German Heligoland, which they had obtained from Denmark in 1815. German East Africa, together with all other German possessions in Africa, was seized by the British during the First World War.

6. In 1966, to combat anti-black racial laws, the UN Security Council imposed sanctions on Southern Rhodesia (Zimbabwe since 1980); these were followed by a trade embargo in 1968.

7. See L. E. Davies and R. A. Huttenback, *Mammon and the Pursuit of Empire*, Cambridge, 1988.

8. See T. R. H. Davenport, *South Africa: A Modern History*, 2nd edn, Toronto, 1978; also F. W. de Klerk, *The Last Trek – A New Beginning: An Autobiography*, New York, 1999; and Anthony Sampson, *Mandela: The Authorized Biography*, New York, 1999.

9. Ethnic groups in 2004 were: black 75.2 per cent; white 13.6 per cent; coloured 8.6 per cent; Indian 2.6 per cent.

10. Apartheid had been rigorously applied by the Prime Minister, Hendrik F. Verwoerd (1901–66). See H. B. Giliomee, *The Afrikaners: Biography of a People*, Charlottesville, Va., 2003. Giliomee contends that the racial practices of the Afrikaners did not deviate greatly from those of other European colonies.

11. In the 1980s the United Nations tried to strengthen its hand against white-controlled South Africa by imposing sanctions.

12. Mandela was banned from South Africa in the 1950s for his opposition to apartheid. He was given a life sentence in the 1960s, and released in 1990 after twenty-seven years.

13. South Africa is the only country in the world presently producing significant quantities of oil from coal.

14. On African accomplishments see 'Whose Dream Was It Anyway? Twenty-Five Years Of African Independence', Michael Crowder, *African Affairs*, January 1987.

15. Until the 1990s, only four nations – Botswana, Gambia, Mauritius and Senegal – had allowed their people to express their political wishes freely. More recently Mozambique (1990), Benin (1991 and 1996),

Zambia (1991), Ghana (1992), Tanzania (1992), Malawi (1994), Ethiopia (1995), Sierra Leone (1996), Uganda (1996) and Nigeria (1999) have obtained elective governments. The coup against the government of Sierra Leone in 1997 – the culmination of years of anarchic fighting – was condemned throughout the continent.

16. On 7 March 2004 Guinea announced that it had foiled a plot to overthrow its government.

17. The African Union adopted the rule that 'The working languages of the Assembly shall be, if possible, African languages, Arabic, English, French, Portuguese, and Spanish.' In 2004 Swahili was recognized as an official language.

18. In April 2005, a UN commission recommended the referral of the crimes committed in Darfur to the International Criminal Court. Of the eleven members of the commission, four (including the USA) abstained.

19. *The World Refugee Survey* (2003), published by the US Committee for Refugees, lists 13 million refugees and asylum-seekers and 22 million internally displaced people worldwide

Estimates of African Refugees at the End of 2003

Algeria	10,000
Angola	410,000
Burundi	400,000
Central African Republic	15,000
Congo (Democratic Republic of)	410,000
Congo (Republic of)	25,000
Côte d'Ivoire	25,000
Eritrea	290,000
Ethiopia	20,000
Ghana	10,000
Guinea-Bissau	5000
Liberia	280,000
Mauritania	45,000
Nigeria	30,000
Rwanda	50,000
Sierra Leone	130,000
Somalia	300,000

Sudan	475,000
Uganda	25,000
Western Sahara	110,000

Source: US Committee for Refugees

20. The World Bank was organized in 1945 as the International Bank for Reconstruction and Development (an agency of the UN) with headquarters in Washington, DC.

21. Established in 1945 as an agency of the United Nations. Its headquarters are in Washington, DC.

22. See Karl Maier, *This House Has Fallen: Midnight in Nigeria*, London, 2000.

23. When the Belgian Congo gained its independence in 1960, it had an efficient transport system. Years of corruption and civil war led to the neglect of road repair, disrupted air and rail links and even blocked river transport.

24. The OAU's aims were the furtherance of African unity, the co-ordination of political, economic, cultural, health, scientific and defence policies, the elimination of colonialism, the retention of existing frontiers and neutrality in the Cold War. All fifty-three African nations are members of the AU.

25. Belgium and the USA were long supportive of the Congo despot Mobutu and his predecessor Moïse K. Tshombe (1919–69). Fearing a Soviet-led takeover, in 1961 both countries played a role in the removal of his socialist rival Patrice Lumumba.

26. Sub-Saharan Africa receives very little of the private direct investment in the developing world. East Asia and the Pacific region receive most.

17. COMMUNISM AND ITS COLLAPSE IN THE USSR AND EASTERN EUROPE

1. See Nikita Khrushchev, *Khrushchev Remembers*, trans. Strobe Talbot, Boston, Mass., 1970.

2. See S. White, *Gorbachev and After*, Cambridge, 1991.

3. M. S. Gorbachev, *Perestroika*, New York, 1987; also *On My Country and the World*, New York, 1999.

4. Estonia, Latvia and Lithuania declared their independence in the spring of 1990, Kazakhstan in October 1990, Georgia, Ukraine, Belorussia, Moldova, Azerbaijan, Uzbekistan, Kyrgyzstan, Armenia, Tajikistan and Turkmenistan in 1991.

5. Yeltsin became a member of the Politbureau in 1986, and president of the Russian Socialist Federal Soviet Republic in 1991, which after the

dissolution of the USSR became the Russian Federation. See L. Aron, *Yeltsin: A Revolutionary Life*, New York, 2000.

6. Although the war between the Russian Federation and Chechnya formally ended with truces in 1996 and 2001, the future status of Chechnya has still to be resolved. Its history has been one long story of suffering ever since Russia colonized it from the eighteenth century. During the Second World War Stalin exiled the Chechens to Central Asia. They were not repatriated until the 1950s. Since 1991 – when the republic tried to break away from Russia – Chechnya has fought two wars to escape the Russian Federation. Thousands of Chechens and Russians have been killed or injured. Hundreds of thousands of Chechens have lost their homes. Overwhelmed by Russia's military, the Chechens have resorted to guerrilla war and acts of terrorism. At the beginning of 2005 there was little hope of a lasting truce between Russia and Chechnya.

7. Treaty between the USA and the Soviet Union on the Reduction and Limitation of Strategic Offensive Arms, 31 July 1991.

8. Trade with the USA is minuscule: 1 per cent of America's total. Five per cent of Russia's trade is with the EU. In September 2003 the Commonwealth of Independent States met to enlarge trade between themselves.

9. See T. G. Ash, *The Polish Revolution: Solidarity*, New York, 1984.

10. See S. Ramet, *Nationalism and Federalism in Yugoslavia*, Bloomington, Ind., 1992.

11. Macedonia was the southern area of Serbia. In 1946 Tito created it to weaken the Serbs, to help Yugoslavia make a claim to Greek Macedonia and to neutralize Bulgaria's ambitions in the area.

12. See A. LeBor, *Milosevic: A Biography*, New Haven, Conn., 2004.

13. The 1949 Geneva Convention defines genocide as acts committed with the intent to destroy, in whole or in part, a national, ethnic, racial or religious group.

14. Yugoslavia fought four wars in the 1990s: Slovenia 1991, Croatia 1991–2, Bosnia 1992–5 and Kosovo 1999. On the war fought in 1999 by NATO against Serbia over Kosovo, see *NATO's Empty Victory*, ed. Ted Galen Carpenter, Chicago, Ill., 2000.

18. LATIN AMERICA AND THE UNITED STATES IN THE TWENTIETH CENTURY

1. In 1921, after seven years of dispute, the USA paid Colombia $25 million for the loss of its Panamanian territory.

2. Proclaimed by President James Monroe on 2 December 1823, it forbade further colonization of the Western Hemisphere by Europeans. Until well into the twentieth century, it was the British not the American navy that guarded the Latin American republics from outside political interference and military intimidation.

3. In the nineteenth century national rivalries and boundary disputes caused the republics to fight at least five wars among themselves. Between 1825 and 1828 Brazil fought Argentina. Between 1842 and 1852 Argentina fought Uruguay and then Brazil. Between 1864 and 1870 Paraguay fought Brazil, Uruguay and Argentina. Between 1836 and 1839, and 1879 and 1883, Chile fought Peru and Bolivia. Bolivia lost access to the Pacific coast. In the twentieth century, in 1940 and 1941, Ecuador fought Peru over an area between Ecuador and western Brazil. Peru defeated Ecuador and annexed most of the territory.

4. On 19 January 1917 the German foreign secretary, Alfred Zimmermann, sent a coded message to von Eckhardt, German minister in Mexico, trying to enlist Mexico's support in the event the USA entered the war. The Germans undertook to restore Mexico's lost territories in New Mexico, Texas and Arizona. The message was intercepted by the British and released to the US press on 1 March 1917.

5. Britain's total investment between 1900 and 1914 grew from $2.5 billion to $3.7 billion, with Argentina and Brazil receiving 60 per cent of the total, and Chile, Peru, Mexico and Uruguay taking most of the remainder. In 1914 British investments in the Western Hemisphere were almost equally divided: 20 per cent of the total was in Latin America, 20 per cent in the USA. French investments, a major source since the 1860s, had grown threefold by 1914 to $1.2 billion. German investments in 1914, principally in Argentina, Brazil, Chile and Mexico, were about $900 million. Like those of Britain, German funds were equally divided between the northern and southern halves of the continent.

6. By 1918, 92 per cent of Chilean copper, 50 per cent of Venezuelan, Peruvian and Colombian oil, 50 per cent of Venezuelan iron and two-thirds of Cuban sugar were in the hands of US investors. By then banana monopolies had been established with US money in Guatemala, Nicaragua, Honduras and Panama (hence the term the Banana Republics).

7. During the 1930s the League intervened to halt warfare between Bolivia and Paraguay (1928–38) and Peru and Colombia (1932–5).

8. The value of a country's exports varied from 20 to 40 per cent of its GNP.

9. Arthur Salter, quoted in *The Problem of International Investment* (1937), reprinted edn, New York, 1965, p. 11.

10. All thirty-five countries of the Americas belong to the Organization, but

Cuba has been excluded from participation since 1962. The OAS was effective in settling regional conflicts between Nicaragua and Costa Rica in the 1940s and 1950s, a boundary dispute between Nicaragua and Honduras in 1957 and the war between El Salvador and Honduras in 1969.

11. China's appetite for the natural resources of Latin America seems insatiable. Imports to China (soya products and minerals) have nearly trebled since 2002.

12. Carter reaffirmed the United States' commitment to 'honour national sovereignty and the principle of non-intervention'. Under the treaty, ratified in 1978, the Panama Canal passed into complete Panamanian control on 31 December 1999. Plans have been afoot for at least a decade to enlarge the canal in order to accommodate the larger ships being launched worldwide.

13. Rebel leader Augusto Sandino was assassinated in 1934 by the Nicaraguan National Guard and became a national hero. Led by Daniel Ortega, in 1979 the Sandinistas were successful in ending the forty-year, US-backed dictatorial regime of Anastasio Somoza Debayle. See Neill Macaulay, *The Sandino Affair*, Durham, NC, 1985.

14. Oil prices quadrupled from $2.70 per barrel in 1972 to $9.76 in 1976. The second round of oil price increases in 1979 raised the price per barrel to $33.47 in 1982. In 2005 oil sold at $70 a barrel.

15. Formalized at the Inter-American Economic and Social Conference at Punta del Este, Uruguay, in August 1961.

16. In 1989 Japan supplanted the USA as the largest donor of foreign aid.

17. In 1982 the fall of oil prices caused Mexico to default on its international debt. Brazil's external debt repayment in 1989 (on a principal of $115 billion) was 4.5 per cent of its GNP, which in 1989 increased by 0.5 per cent. To make matters worse, the world dollar price for its primary produce continued to decline.

18. LAFTA was established under the Treaty of Montevideo, Uruguay, in June 1960. Members were Argentina, Brazil, Chile, Mexico, Paraguay, Peru and Uruguay. Colombia and Ecuador joined in 1961, Venezuela and Bolivia in 1966 and 1967, respectively. It was replaced in 1980 by the Latin American Integration Association (LAIA or ALADI).

19. The groundwork was laid in December 1960 by the Treaty of Central American Economic Integration; it included El Salvador, Guatemala, Honduras (withdrew in 1969) and Nicaragua; Costa Rica joined in 1962. It was also called the Organization of Central American States or ODECA (Organización de Estados Centroamericanos).

20. Members are Bolivia, Colombia, Ecuador, Peru and Venezuela (Chile withdrew in 1976).

21. Members were Barbados, Guyana, Jamaica, Trinidad and Tobago. They were joined in 1974 by Antigua and Barbuda, Belize, Dominica, Grenada, St Lucia, St Vincent and the Grenadines, Montserrat and St Kitts and Nevis. Suriname joined in 1995; Haiti in 1997. The Bahamas is a member of the Community but not the Common Market. It was also called CARIFTA (Caribbean Free Trade Association), founded early in 1968.

22. In protest against the austerity programmes imposed by the World Bank and the IMF, in March 1989 Brazil experienced the largest general strike in its history.

23. Peru's inflation rate in 1988 was 1720 per cent; in 1989, it was 2775 per cent. In early 1990 Argentina had an inflation rate of about 3000 per cent. In 2004 the problem of hyperinflation had lessened.

24. Demonstrations by students in Tlatelolcho Square in Mexico City on 2 October 1968 were crushed by President Luis Echeverría Álvarez at the cost of hundreds of lives. Riots in Caracas in 1989 and 2002 were accompanied by widespread bloodshed.

25. Pope John Paul II largely put an end to official support for liberation theology by his statement in January 1979 that 'this conception of Christ as a political figure . . . does not tally with the Church's teachings'.

26. It is estimated that one million illegals enter the USA annually. In 2003, 12 per cent of the US population was foreign born.

27. Fuerzas Armadas Revolucionarias de Colombia (Revolutionary Armed Forces of Colombia), based in the south, was founded by peasants with a Marxist ideology.

28. Ejercito de Liberación Nacional (National Liberation Army) was founded in 1964; it was inspired by the Cuban Revolution.

29. Autodefensas Unidas de Colombia (United Self-Defence Forces of Colombia).

30. Mid-2004 estimates of population were: South America 365 million; Central America 146 million; and the Caribbean 39 million.

19. WESTERN EUROPE AND NORTH AMERICA: 1945–2004

1. Fittingly, the idea of unity stretches back to ancient Rome. In unifying Europe, Napoleon had the same goal: cooperation and peace. See J. Boussard, *The Civilization of Charlemagne*, New York, 1968. Also J. Laughland, *The Tainted Source: The Undemocratic Origins of the European Idea*, London, 1998.

2. The European Parliamentary Assembly dates back to the signing of the Statute of the Council of Europe in May 1949. Founding members were

Belgium, Denmark, France, the Irish Republic, Italy, Luxembourg, the Netherlands, Norway, Sweden and the United Kingdom.

3. Members were Belgium, Luxembourg, Netherlands, West Germany, France and Italy.

4. In September 2000 the Danes rejected membership of the euro currency zone.

5. European Union member states in 2004 were Austria, Belgium, Cyprus, Czech Republic, Denmark, Estonia, Finland, France, Germany, Greece, Hungary, Ireland, Italy, Latvia, Lithuania, Luxembourg, Malta, Poland, Portugal, Slovakia, Slovenia, Spain, Sweden, the Netherlands and the United Kingdom. Applicant countries were Bulgaria, Croatia, Romania and Turkey.

6. By July 2005, Austria, Cyprus, Greece, Hungary, Italy, Latvia, Lithuania, Luxembourg, Malta, Slovakia, Slovenia and Spain had ratified the draft constitution.

7. See M. L. G. Balfour, *West Germany: A Contemporary History*, London, 1983.

8. Estimated population of Germany in July 2004 was 82,424,609: German 91.5 per cent, Turkish 2.4 per cent, other 6.1 per cent (made up largely of Greek, Italian, Polish, Russian, Serbo-Croatian and Spanish).

9. See W. E. Griffith, *The Ostpolitik of the Federal Republic of Germany*, Cambridge, Mass., 1978.

10. He resigned in 1974 over a spy scandal involving a close aide.

11. Although the collapse of the Soviet Union in 1990 made NATO's original purpose redundant, in 2005 NATO's Partnership for Peace programme was extended to Russia and other countries of the former USSR. Its new mission to assist in planning, training and equipping national defence forces to cooperate within a larger NATO framework. Cooperation with NATO was also established with Mediterranean Dialogue Countries: Algeria, Egypt, Israel, Jordan, Mauritania, Morocco and Tunisia.

12. See P. Williams and M. Harrison, *Politics and Society in De Gaulle's Republic*, New York, 1991.

13. See A. Sampson, *The Changing Anatomy of Britain*, New York, 1982.

14. See P. Riddell, *The Thatcher Decade*, Oxford, 1989.

15. For Italy, there is nothing new about intra-European migration. In the 1890s more Italians migrated to France and Germany than to America.

16. Guinea-Bissau, Cape Verde Islands, Angola, Mozambique, São Tomé and Principe.

17. In April 2004, the Greek Cypriots rejected a UN plan for a peace settlement. The Greek Cypriots – who refused to compromise – entered the

EU. The Turkish Cypriots – who were amenable to the UN plan for the island – were left out.

18. Britain 1954, West Germany 1955, Iceland 1956, Italy 1957, France and Spain 1958, Turkey 1959, the Netherlands and Greece 1960, Belgium 1963.

19. Source: US House Budget Committee, 2005.

20. The US Defense Department's annual 'Base Structure Report' for fiscal year 2003 lists 702 US overseas bases in about 130 countries. The report does not include bases in Afghanistan, Uzbekistan, Kyrgyzstan, Kuwait, Kosovo and Iraq.

21. See J. S. Nye, *The Paradox of American Power: Why the World's Only Superpower Can't Go It Alone*, Oxford, 2002.

22. See P. Bennis, *Calling the Shots: How Washington Dominates Today's UN*, New York, 2001.

23. See R. Bothwell, T. Drummond and J. English, *Canada since 1945*, Toronto, 1981.

20. THE RESURGENCE OF ASIA

1. He was the first prime minister of independent India (1947–64) and was four times President of the Indian National Congress Party (1929–30, 1936–7, 1946 and 1951–4. See *The Autobiography of Jawaharlal Nehru*, New York, 1941; also J. M. Brown, *Nehru – A Political Life*, New Haven, Conn., 2003.

2. See H. Belitho, *Jinnah*, London, 1954.

3. A second conference of the non-aligned nations took place at Belgrade in 1961.

4. See K. Bhatia, *Indira: A Biography*, New York, 1974.

5. The 'green revolution' was an international effort in the 1960s, led by the US agricultural scientist Norman E. Borlaug (b. 1914), to increase crop production in Third World countries by introducing hybrid, high-yielding, disease-resistant grains, along with irrigation, fertilizers, pesticides and mechanization. In Mexico, India, Pakistan and elsewhere the so-called 'revolution' increased yields – especially in wheat. In Africa these changes had only limited effect. Because these techniques are best suited to large-scale, commercial farming, which can lead to loss of biodiversity, pollution and soil degradation, the green revolution has come under growing criticism.

6. See J. Silverstein, *Burmese Politics: The Dilemma of National Unity*, New Brunswick, NJ, 1980.

7. See Amy Chua, *World on Fire*, New York, 2003.

8. Formed in August 1967; members in 2004 included Brunei Darussalam, Cambodia, Indonesia, Laos, Malaysia, Myanmar, Philippines, Singapore, Thailand and Vietnam.
9. See K. von Vorys, *Democracy without Consensus*, Princeton, NJ, 1975.
10. See S. Karnow, *Vietnam*, New York, 1983.
11. See P. Short, *Pol Pot: The History of a Nightmare*, London, 2004.
12. See D. Wyatt, *Thailand*, New Haven, Conn., 1982.
13. Sukarno helped to found the Indonesian National Party in 1928. In 1955, with Nehru, he hosted the Bandung Conference of non-aligned African and Asian nations. In 1959, he assumed dictatorial powers. See J. Legge, *Sukarno*, New York, 1972.
14. See D. J. Steinberg, *The Philippines*, Boulder, Col., 1971.
15. See S. Karnow, *Mao and China: Inside China's Cultural Revolution*, New York, 1972; also P. Short, *Mao – A Life*, New York, 2000.
16. Chiang Ching, Zhang Chungqiao (then deputy prime minister), Wang Hongwen (the vice-chairman of the party) and Yao Wenyuan (the polemicist).
17. See R. Evans, *Deng Xiaoping and the Making of Modern China*, New York, 1994.
18. See H. Harding, *A Fragile Relationship: The US and China since 1972*, Washington, DC, 1992.
19. Massacres of students and civilians have been common in recent Asian history: in 1976, the Thai army killed hundreds of students at Thammasat University, Bangkok; in 1980 the South Korean army killed thousands of civilians in Kwangju; the rules of Chiang Kai-shek in Taiwan and Suharto in Indonesia were established only after the massacre of thousands; Mao's killing of his countrymen is legendary.
20. See B. Gilley, *China's Democratic Future*, New York, 2004.
21. See M. T. Klare, *Blood and Oil: The Dangers and Consequences of America's Growing Petroleum Dependency*, New York, 2004.
22. See E. F. Vogel, *The Four Little Dragons*, Cambridge, Mass., 1991.
23. China's outflow of foreign direct investment in 2003 was almost $3 billion; the inflow was $50 billion.
24. See M. Schaller, *The American Occupation of Japan*, New York, 1985; also J. W. Dower, *Embracing Defeat*, New York, 1999.
25. See M. Tolchin and S. Tolchin, *Buying into America*, New York, 1988. For a more sanguine view see E. M. Graham and P. R. Krugman, *Foreign Direct Investment in the United States*, Washington, DC, 1990.
26. Greater Syria existed from biblical times to 1920, when it became a French mandate under the UN. At one time it included Palestine, Trans-Jordan, Lebanon and parts of Iraq and Turkey.

27. The Fourth Geneva Convention was adopted on 12 August 1949.

28. In the United Nations the USA has regularly used its veto on Israel's behalf.

29. OPEC was founded in 1960. Members in 2004 were Algeria, Indonesia, Iran, Iraq, Kuwait, Libya, Nigeria, Qatar, Saudi Arabia, United Arab Emirates and Venezuela. Saudi Arabia, Iran and Iraq have the greatest oil reserves.

30. Until 1993 Israel had refused to negotiate with the PLO because it had denied Israel's right to exist. In 1985, King Hussein of Jordan and Yasser Arafat of the PLO declared their willingness to make peace with Israel provided Israel withdrew from the territories occupied in 1967. Arafat undertook to accept United Nations Resolution 242 guaranteeing Israel's right to exist if the USA explicitly endorsed the right of Palestinians to self-determination. On 13 November 1988 the PLO accepted UN Resolution 242.

31 See Edward W. Said, *The Politics of Dispossession*, New York, 1995; also Benny Morris, *Righteous Victims: A History of the Zionist–Arab Conflict 1881–1999*, New York, 1999; and Avi Shlaim, *The Iron Wall: Israel and the Arab World since 1948*, New York, 1999.

32. See C. E. Swisher, *The Truth about Camp David: The Untold Story about the Collapse of the Middle East Peace Process*, New York, 2004.

33. No other country has received as much American aid; in 2004 Israel was still the largest recipient. Between 1949 and 2003 direct US aid totalled $90 billion, about half in military aid. 'Israel is not economically self-sufficient, and relies on foreign assistance and borrowing to maintain its economy' (Congressional Research Service, Library of Congress, IB85066).

34. In 2004 President Bush – against a UN ruling – decided unilaterally that Israel need not make a 'full and complete' withdrawal from occupied territory.

35. See Stephen Kinzer, *All the Shah's Men: An American Coup and the Roots of Middle East Terror*, Hoboken, NJ, 2003.

36. Iran's population of seventy million is overwhelmingly Shi'ite.

37. See Nadav Safran, *Saudi Arabia: The Ceaseless Quest for Security*, Cambridge, Mass., 1985.

38. Australia, New Zealand, United States Treaty, 1951.

39. In May 2000 Fiji's first Indian-led government was overthrown by indigenous Fijians. In November 2000 Fiji's High Court ruled that the deposed government of Mahendra Chaudhry should be reinstated.

40. See table opposite.

US Immigration 1820–2003, and Selected Years after 1971

	1820–2003	1971–80	1981–90	1991–2000	2000	2001	2002	2003
Europe	38,919,125	800,368	761,550	1,359,737	133,362	177,833	177,652	102,843
Asia	9,715,328	1,588,178	2,738,157	2,795,672	255,860	337,566	326,871	236,039
Americas	18,813,275	1,982,735	3,615,225	4,486,806	397,201	473,351	478,777	306,793
Africa	841,068	80,779	176,893	354,939	40,969	50,209	56,135	45,640
Oceania	279,358	41,242	45,205	55,845	5962	7253	6536	5102
Total	68,923,308	4,493,314	7,338,062	9,095,417	849,807	1,064,318	1,063,732	705,827

Source: US Citizenship and Immigration Services, *Fiscal Year 2003 Yearbook of Immigration Statistics*

21. THE THREAT OF WORLD ANARCHY

1. Interestingly, there was an earlier dramatic period of globalization in the late nineteenth century. It was undone because countries were eventually forced to safeguard their own interests. See Kevin O'Rourke and Jeffrey Williamson, *Globalization and History, The Evolution of a Nineteenth-Century Atlantic Economy*. Boston, Mass., 1999.

2. See World Bank, *Globalization, Growth and Poverty: Building an Inclusive World Economy*, Oxford, 2002; also G. Soros, *On Globalization*, New York, 2002; and M. Wolf, *Why Globalization Works*, New Haven, Conn., 2003.

3. There are forty million people without health insurance in the USA.

4. On the USA see Economic Policy Institute, *The State of Working America 2004–05*, Washington, DC.

5. See United Nations Conference on Trade and Development, *Report 1989*, Part II: *The Least Developed Countries*, New York, 1990.

6. From *Progress and Poverty: An Inquiry into the Cause of Industrial Depressions and of Increase of Want with Increase of Wealth: The Remedy* (1879), reprinted New York, 1954.

7. The disparity of wealth and the resultant migration of the poor was predicted by Willy Brandt in his report for the UN: 'North–South: A Program for Survival, 1980'. A later report of the Brandt Commission in 1983, '*Common Crisis: North-South Cooperation for World Recovery*', foresaw 'conflict and catastrophe' unless the problem of the disparity of wealth in the world was addressed. In 2005 the General Assembly of the UN is to review the progress towards the Millennium Development Goals agreed upon in 2000.

8.

Asylum-seekers, Refugees and Others of Concern

Asia	6,187,800
Africa	4,285,100
Europe	4,268,000
Latin America and Caribbean	1,316,400
North America	962,000
Oceania	74,100
Total	17,093,400

Source: UNHCR: 1 January 2004.

9. In comparison, it would take an investment of only an additional $7 to $17 billion annually to achieve universal primary education, according to the UN Millennium Development Goal for 2015.

10. Public Papers of the Presidents, Dwight D. Eisenhower, 1960, p. 1035–40.

11. The Middle East is not the only part of the world where religious wars are under way. Tension remains between Protestants and Catholics in Northern Ireland; between Hindus, Muslims and Sikhs in India; between Buddhists and Hindus in Sri Lanka; and between Christians and Muslims in Indonesia, Bosnia, Kosovo and the Sudan.

12. See K. Armstrong, *A History of God*, New York, 1993; *The Battle for God*, New York, 2000; and *Islam: A Short History*, New York, 2000.

13. 'Do not attempt to do us any more good. Your good has done us too much harm already,' said Sheikh Muhammed Abduh, an Egyptian, in London in 1884.

14. See J. Ellis, *The Russian Orthodox Church: Triumphalism and Defensiveness*, Oxford, 1996.

15. See Chua (2003).

16. Negotiations to control nuclear weapons reach from the Limited Test Ban Treaty between the US, USSR and Britain on 5 August 1963 to the US withdrawal from the ABM Treaty, and Russia's withrawal from START II in June 2002.

Approximate Known Nuclear Arsenals in 2005

Country	Strategic warheads	Tactical warheads	Stockpiled (strategic and tactical)
Britain	200		
China	300	120	
France	350		
India	45–95		
Israel	200*		
North Korea**			
Pakistan	30–50		
Russia	4,978	3,500	11,000
United States	5,968	1,000	3,000

Source: Arms Control Association, Nuclear Threat Initiative

* Not confirmed by government

** In February 2005 North Korea confirmed that it has nuclear weapons.

17. In 1972, a Biological and Toxin Weapons Convention was signed by more than a hundred nations.

18. In the nineteenth century the world's population was thought to have expanded more rapidly than in any other period of history. Twentieth-century population has grown approximately four times faster, from two billion in 1930 to more than six billion today. Fortunately, there are signs that the growth is stabilizing. Bedevilling the problem of food production is not so much the lack of good land as the lack of good government. Birth control or more food is the only immediate answer to our rapid growth in numbers. Plant technology is promising.

19. See M. J. Rees, *Our Final Hour: A Scientist's Warning: How Terror, Error, and Environmental Disaster Threaten Humankind's Future in This Century on Earth and Beyond*, New York, 2004.

20. Under the Treaty on Conventional Armed Forces in Europe (which was in effect between 1992 and 1995) a great deal of military equipment was destroyed; there followed a temporary reduction in military expenditures.

21. Founded to promote the liberalization of international trade and finance, together with the coordination of economic aid to developing countries, its member states in 2005 were Australia, Austria, Belgium, Canada, Czech Republic, Denmark, Finland, France, Germany, Greece, Hungary, Iceland, Ireland, Italy, Japan, Luxembourg, Mexico, the Netherlands, New Zealand, Norway, Poland, Portugal, Slovak Republic, South Korea, Spain, Sweden, Switzerland, Turkey, UK and USA.

22. Formed in 1989 to further cooperation among the nations of the region. In 2005 its twenty-one members were Australia, Brunei Darussalam, Canada, Chile, China, Hong Kong Indonesia, Japan, Malaysia, Mexico, New Zealand, Papua New Guinea, Peru, Philippines, Russia, Singapore, South Korea, Taiwan, Thailand, USA and Vietnam.

23. Inspired by Jamal ad-Din al-Afghani (1838–97) and the Arab awakening of the nineteenth century, and in response to increased Jewish immigration into Palestine, the Arab League was formed in Cairo, Egypt, in 1945. Original members were Egypt, Iraq, Saudi Arabia, Syria, Lebanon, Jordan and Yemen. Membership in 2005 included Algeria, Bahrain, Comoros, Djibouti, Kuwait, Libya, Mauritania, Morocco, Oman, the Palestine Liberation Organization, Qatar, Somalia, Sudan, Tunisia, the United Arab Emirates and Yemen.

24. In 2005 it consisted of fifty-three self-governing, independent nations, sixteen of which recognized the British monarch. Its purpose is consultation and cooperation on economic, scientific, educational, financial, legal and military matters.

25. Created in May 1960 to promote expansion of trade. In 1992 the EFTA and the FU concluded an agreement to create a single market of the two organizations. In 2005 members were Iceland, Lichtenstein, Norway and Switzerland.

26. Established in September 1975 as the Group of Six (G6), it included the major industrial economies: France, Germany, Italy, Japan, the UK and the USA. It became the G7 when Canada joined in 1976, and the G8 when Russia joined in 1998. The EU is represented as one member.

27. Formed in 1969 in Morocco, its members now include fifty-six Islamic countries, plus the Palestine Liberation Organization.

28. Under GNP the earnings of a multinational corporation are counted in the country where the corporation is owned. Under GDP the earnings are counted in the country where the factory is located, but where the profit will not stay.

29. Adam Smith placed his theories in a firm moral framework. See R. Bronk, *Progress and the Invisible Hand: The Philosophy and Economics of Human Advance*, London and New York, 2000.

30. From the Chinese point of view, three things prevented the normalization of relations with Russia: Soviet support for Vietnam in Cambodia; Russia's intervention in Afghanistan; and the Sino-Soviet frontier dispute. The frontier dispute remains.

31. The Kellogg–Briand Pact of 1928 foolishly outlawed war while taking no steps to prevent it.

32. In April 1993 ASEAN countries meeting in Bangkok condemned the West's attempt to use human rights as a condition for development aid. So used, human rights become an obstacle in the improvement of international relations. They also questioned the right of the rich world to set standards, arguing that human rights should be considered against a background of geography, culture and religion.

33. See J. L. Goldsmith and E. A. Posner, *The Limits of International Law*, Oxford and New York, 2005.

34. In a 1986 ruling of the International Court of Justice concerning the illegal mining by the USA of Nicaragua's harbours, the USA was found in violation of international law. Before the ruling the USA had already withdrawn from the compulsory jurisdiction of the court. Since then it has again accepted the court's jurisdiction.

35. See D. P. Moynihan, *On the Law of Nations*, Cambridge, Mass., 1990.

36. See H. Küng, *Global Responsibilities: In Search of a New World Ethic*, New York, 1990.

37. The eighteenth-century philosopher Immanuel Kant argued that war

would cease only when there was nothing left to fight about, or when new moral insights were obtained. See O. Höffe, *Wirtschaftsbürger, Staatsbürger, Weltbürger: politische Ethik im Zeitalter der Globalisierung,* Munich, 2004.

38. The Lockerbie trial in the Netherlands, which on 3 February 2001 found one of the two Libyan suspects guilty of destroying the American plane and its passengers, offers hope for the effective of a permanent international criminal court of justice.

39. In March 2005 (following the publication of the report of the Independent Inquiry Committee into the Iraq Oil-for-Food Programme, chaired by Paul Volcker) the UN and its Secretary General came under harsh criticism.

40. The victors of the Second World War have a 'permanent' status on the Security Council and the power to veto. Although since 1965 there have been fifteen members on the council, they do not reflect the demographic and political realities of a truly democratic world community. The UN declaration on reform in September 2005 left many delegates dissatisfied. At least some of the difficulties must be ascribed to the fact that the 'spirit of 1945' – when the establishment of the organization was pre-eminent – is no longer present.

Index